COGNITIVE SCIENCE

Second edition

Cognitive Science combines the interdisciplinary streams of cognitive science into a unified narrative in an all-encompassing introduction to the field. This text presents cognitive science as a discipline in its own right, and teaches students to apply the techniques and theories of the cognitive scientist's "toolkit" – the vast range of methods and tools that cognitive scientists use to study the mind. Thematically organized, rather than by separate disciplines, *Cognitive Science* underscores the problems and solutions of cognitive science, rather than those of the subjects that contribute to it – psychology, neuroscience, linguistics, etc. The generous use of examples, illustrations, and applications demonstrates how theory is applied to unlock the mysteries of the human mind. Drawing upon cutting-edge research, the text has been updated and enhanced to incorporate new studies and key experiments since the first edition. A new chapter on consciousness has been added.

JOSÉ LUIS BERMÚDEZ is Dean of the College of Liberal Arts and Professor of Philosophy at Texas A&M University. He has been involved in teaching and research in cognitive science for over twenty years, and is very much involved in bringing an interdisciplinary focus to cognitive science through involvement with conference organization and journals. His 100+ publications include the textbook *Philosophy of Psychology: A Contemporary Introduction* (2005) and a companion collection of readings, *Philosophy of Psychology: Contemporary Readings* (2007). He has authored the monographs *The Paradox of Self-Consciousness* (1998), *Thinking without Words* (2003), and *Decision Theory and Rationality* (2009) in addition to editing a number of collections including *The Body and the Self* (1995), *Reason and Nature* (2002), and *Thought, Reference, and Experience* (2005).

COGNITIVE SCIENCE

An Introduction to the Science of the Mind

Second Edition

José Luis Bermúdez

CAMBRIDGE
UNIVERSITY PRESS

CAMBRIDGE
UNIVERSITY PRESS

University Printing House, Cambridge CB2 8BS, United Kingdom

Cambridge University Press is part of the University of Cambridge.

It furthers the University's mission by disseminating knowledge in the pursuit of education, learning and research at the highest international levels of excellence.

www.cambridge.org
Information on this title: www.cambridge.org/9781107653351

© José Luis Bermúdez 2014

First published 2010
Second edition 2014
6th printing 2018

Printed in the United Kingdom by Clays, St Ives plc.

A catalogue record for this publication is available from the British Library

Library of Congress Cataloguing in Publication data
Bermúdez, José Luis.
Cognitive science : an introduction to the science of the mind / José Luis Bermúdez. – Second edition.
    pages cm
ISBN 978-1-107-05162-1 (Hardback) – ISBN 978-1-107-65335-1 (Paperback)   1. Cognition.
2. Cognitive science.   I. Title.
BF311.B458 2014
153–dc23   2013047706

ISBN 978-1-107-05162-1 Hardback
ISBN 978-1-107-65335-1 Paperback

Additional resources for this publication at www.cambridge.org/bermudez2

CONTENTS

CONTENTS

BOXES

FIGURES

TABLES

About this book

There are few things more fascinating to study than the human mind. And few things that are more difficult to understand. Cognitive science is the enterprise of trying to make sense of this most complex and baffling natural phenomenon.

The very things that make cognitive science so fascinating make it very difficult to study and to teach. Many different disciplines study the mind. Neuroscientists study the mind's biological machinery. Psychologists directly study mental processes such as perception and decision-making. Computer scientists explore how those processes can be simulated and modeled in computers. Evolutionary biologists and anthropologists speculate about how the mind evolved. In fact, there are very few academic areas that are not relevant to the study of the mind in some way. The job of cognitive science is to provide a framework for bringing all these different perspectives together.

This enormous range of information out there about the mind can be overwhelming, both for students and for instructors. I had direct experience of how challenging this can be when I was Director of the Philosophy-Neuroscience-Psychology program at Washington University in St. Louis. My challenge was to give students a broad enough base while at the same time bringing home that cognitive science is a field in its own right, separate and distinct from the disciplines on which it draws. I set out to write this book because my colleagues and I were unable to find a book that really succeeds in doing this.

Different textbooks have approached this challenge in different ways. Some have concentrated on being as comprehensive as possible, with a chapter covering key ideas in each of the relevant disciplines - a chapter on psychology, a chapter on neuroscience, and so on. These books are often written by committee - with each chapter written by an expert in the relevant field. These books can be very valuable, but they really give an introduction to the cognitive sciences (in the plural), rather than to cognitive science as an interdisciplinary enterprise.

Other textbook writers take a much more selective approach, introducing cognitive science from the perspective of the disciplines that they know best - from the perspective of philosophy, for example, or of computer science. Again, I have learnt much from these books and they can be very helpful. But I often have the feeling that students need something more general.

This book aims for a balance between these two extremes. Cognitive science has its own problems and its own theories. The book is organized around these. They are all ways of working out the fundamental idea at the heart of cognitive science - which is that the mind is an information processor. What makes cognitive science so rich is that this single basic idea can be (and has been) worked out in many different ways. In presenting these different models of the mind as an information processor I have tried to select as wide a range of examples as possible, in order to give students a sense of cognitive science's breadth and range.

Cognitive science has only been with us for forty or so years. But in that time it has changed a lot. At one time cognitive science was associated with the idea that we can understand the mind without worrying about its biological machinery – we can understand the software without understanding the hardware, to use a popular image. But this is now really a minority view. Neuroscience is now an absolutely fundamental part of cognitive science. Unfortunately this has not really been reflected in textbooks on cognitive science. This book presents a more accurate picture of how central neuroscience is to cognitive science.

How the book is organized

This book is organized into five parts.

Part I: Historical overview

Cognitive science has evolved considerably in its short life. Priorities have changed as new methods have emerged – and some fundamental theoretical assumptions have changed with them. The three chapters in Part I introduce students to some of the highlights in the history of cognitive science. Each chapter is organized around key discoveries and/or theoretical advances.

Part II: The integration challenge

The two chapters in Part II bring out what is distinctive about cognitive science. They do this in terms of what I call the integration challenge. This is the challenge of developing a unified framework that makes explicit the relations between the different disciplines on which cognitive science draws and the different levels of organization that it studies. In Chapter 4 we look at two examples of *local integration*. The first example explores how evolutionary psychology has been used to explain puzzling data from human decision-making, while the second focuses on what exactly it is that is being studied by techniques of neuro-imaging such as functional magnetic resonance imaging (fMRI).

In Chapter 5 I propose that one way of answering the integration challenge is through developing models of mental architecture. A model of mental architecture includes

1   an account of how the mind is organized into different cognitive systems, and
2   an account of how information is processed in individual cognitive systems.

This approach to mental architecture sets the agenda for the rest of the book.

Part III: Information-processing models of the mind

The four chapters in Part III explore the two dominant models of information processing in contemporary cognitive science. The first model is associated with the physical symbol system hypothesis originally developed by the computer scientists Allen Newell and Herbert Simon. According to the physical symbol system hypothesis, all information processing involves the manipulation of physical structures that function as symbols. The theoretical case for the physical symbol system hypothesis is discussed in Chapter 6, while Chapter 7 gives three very different examples of research within that paradigm – from data mining, artificial vision, and robotics.

The second model of information processing derives from models of artificial neurons in computational neuroscience and connectionist artificial intelligence. Chapter 8 explores the motivation for this approach and introduces some of the key concepts, while Chapter 9 shows how it can be used to model aspects of language learning and object perception.

Part IV: How is the mind organized?

A mental architecture includes a model both of information processing and of how the mind is organized. The three chapters in Part IV look at different ways of tackling this second problem. Chapter 10 examines the idea that some forms of information processing are carried out by dedicated cognitive modules. It looks also at the radical claim, proposed by evolutionary psychologists, that the mind is simply a collection of specialized modules. In Chapter 11 we look at how techniques such as functional neuroimaging can be used to study the organization of the mind. Chapter 12 shows how the theoretical and methodological issues come together by working through an issue that has received much attention in contemporary cognitive science – the issue of whether there is a dedicated cognitive system response for our understanding of other people (the so-called mindreading system).

Part V: New horizons

As emerges very clearly in the first four parts of the book, cognitive science is built around some very basic theoretical assumptions – and in particular around the assumption that the mind is an information-processing system. In Chapter 13 we look at two ways in which cognitive scientists have proposed extending and moving beyond this basic assumption. One of these research programs is associated with the dynamical systems hypothesis in cognitive science. The second is opened up by the situated/ embodied cognition movement. Chapter 14 explores recent developments in the cognitive science of consciousness – a fast-moving and exciting area that raises fundamental questions about possible limits to what can be understood through the tools and techniques of cognitive science.

Using this book in courses

This book has been designed to serve as a self-contained text for a single semester (12–15 weeks) introductory course on cognitive science. Students taking this course may have taken introductory courses in psychology and/or philosophy, but no particular prerequisites are assumed. All the necessary background is provided for a course at the freshman or sophomore level (first or second year). The book could also be used for a more advanced introductory course at the junior or senior level (third or fourth year). In this case the instructor would most likely want to supplement the book with additional readings. There are suggestions on the instructor website (see below).

Text features

I have tried to make this book as user-friendly as possible. Key text features include:

■ **Part-openers and chapter overviews**   The book is divided into five parts, as described above. Each part begins with a short introduction to give the reader a broad picture of what lies ahead. Each chapter begins with an overview to orient the reader.

CHAPTER SIX

Physical symbol systems and the language of thought

OVERVIEW 141
6.1 The physical symbol system hypothesis 142
Symbols and symbol systems 144
Solving problems by transforming symbol structures 144
Intelligent action and the physical symbol system 150
6.2 From physical symbol systems to the language of thought 151
Intentional realism and causation by content 153

The computer model of the mind and the relation between syntax and semantics 155
Putting the pieces together: Syntax and the language of thought 157
6.3 The Chinese room argument 160
The Chinese room and the Turing test 162
Responding to the Chinese room argument 163
The symbol-grounding problem 165

Overview

This chapter focuses on one of the most powerful ideas in cognitive science. This is the analogy between minds and digital computers. In the early days of cognitive science this analogy was one of cognitive science's defining ideas. As emerged in the historical overview in Part I, cognitive science has evolved in a number of important ways and what is often called the computational theory of mind is no longer "the only game in town." Yet the computational theory, and the model of information processing on which it is built, still commands widespread support among cognitive scientists. In this chapter we see why.

For a very general expression of the analogy between minds and computers we can turn to the physical symbol system hypothesis, proposed in 1975 by the computer scientists Herbert Simon and Allen Newell. According to this hypothesis, all intelligent behavior essentially involves transforming physical symbols according to rules. Section 6.1 spells out how this very general idea is to be understood. Newell and Simon proposed the physical symbol system hypothesis in a

141

■ **Exercises**   These have been inserted at various points within each chapter. They are placed in the flow of the text to encourage the reader to take a break from reading and engage with the material. They are typically straightforward, but for a few I have placed suggested solutions on the instructor website (see below).

■ **Boxes and optional material**   Boxes have been included to provide further information about the theories and research discussed in the text. Some of the more technical material has been placed in boxes that are marked optional. Readers are encouraged to work through these, but the material is not essential to the flow of the text.

■ **Summaries, checklists, and further reading**   These can be found at the end of each chapter. The summary shows how the chapter relates to the other chapters in the book. The checklist allows students to review the key points of the chapter, and also serves as a reference point for instructors. Suggestions of additional books and articles are provided to guide students' further reading on the topics covered in the chapter.

168   Physical symbol systems

Summary

Chapter 5 introduced the concept of a mental architecture, which combines a model of how information is stored and processed with a model of the overall organization of the mind. This chapter has looked at one of the two principal models of information storage and processing – the physical symbol system hypothesis, originally proposed by Newell and Simon. After introducing the physical symbol system hypothesis we saw a particular application of it in the language of thought hypothesis developed by Jerry Fodor in order to solve problems associated with the psychological explanation of behavior. The chapter also discussed two objections to the physical symbol system hypothesis – the Chinese room argument and the symbol-grounding problem.

Checklist

The physical symbol system hypothesis states that a physical symbol system has necessary and sufficient means for general intelligent action. In more detail:

(1) These symbols are physical patterns.
(2) Physical symbols can be combined to form complex symbol structures.
(3) Physical symbol systems contain processes for manipulating complex symbol structures.
(4) The processes for manipulating complex symbol structures can be represented by symbols and structures within the system.
(5) Problems are solved by generating and modifying symbol structures until a solution structure is reached.

The physical symbol system hypothesis is very programmatic. Fodor's language of thought hypothesis is one way of turning the physical symbol system hypothesis into a concrete proposal about mental architecture.

(1) The language of thought hypothesis is grounded in realism about the propositional attitudes. Propositional attitudes such as belief and desire are real physical entities. These entities are sentences in the language of thought.
(2) It offers a way of explaining causation by content (i.e. how physical representations can have causal effects in the world as a function of how they represent the world).
(3) Fodor suggests that we understand the relation between sentences in the language of thought and their contents on the model of the relation between syntax and semantics in a formal system.
(4) The syntax of the language of thought tracks its semantics because the language of thought is a formal language with analogs of the formal properties of soundness and completeness.

The Chinese room argument is a thought experiment directed against the idea that the rule-governed manipulation of symbols is sufficient to produce intelligent behavior.

(1) The person in the Chinese room is manipulating symbols according to their formal/syntactic properties without any understanding of Chinese.

Further reading   169

(2) According to the systems reply, the Chinese room argument misses the point, because the real question is whether the system as a whole understands Chinese, not whether the person in the room understands Chinese.
(3) According to the robot reply, the Chinese room does not understand Chinese. But this is not because of any uncrossable gap between syntax and semantics. Rather, it is because the Chinese room has no opportunity to interact with the environment and other people.
(4) The Chinese room argument can be viewed as an instance of the more general symbol-grounding problem.

Further reading

The paper by Newell and Simon discussed in section 6.1 is reprinted in a number of places, including Boden 1990b and Bermúdez 2006. A good introduction to the general ideas behind the physical symbol system hypothesis in the context of artificial intelligence is Haugeland 1985, particularly ch. 2, and Haugeland 1997, ch. 4. See also chs 1–3 of Johnson-Laird 1988, chs 4 and 5 of Copeland 1993, ch. 2 of Dawson 1998, and the *Encyclopedia of Cognitive Science* entry on Symbol Systems (Nadel 2005). Russell and Norvig 2009 is the new edition of a popular AI textbook. Also see Poole and Mackworth 2010, Warwick 2012, and Proudfoot and Copeland's chapter on artificial intelligence in *The Oxford Handbook of Philosophy of Cognitive Science* (Margolis, Samuels, and Stich 2012).

Fodor 1975 and 1987 are classic expositions of the language of thought approach from a philosophical perspective. For Fodor's most recent views see Fodor 2008. For a psychologist's perspective see Pylyshyn's book *Computation and Cognition* (Pylyshyn 1984) and his earlier target article in *Behavioral and Brain Sciences* (Pylyshyn 1980). More recent philosophical discussions of the language of thought can be found in Schneider 2011 and Schneider and Katz 2012. The *Encyclopedia of Cognitive Science* has an entry on the topic, as does the *Stanford Encyclopedia of Philosophy*. For a general, philosophical discussion of the computational picture of the mind Crane 2003 and Sterelny 1990 are recommended. Block 1995 explores the metaphor of the mind as the software of the brain. Fodor's argument for the language of thought hypothesis is closely tied to important research in mathematical logic and the theory of computation. Rogers 1971 is an accessible overview. For general introductions to philosophical debates about mental causation and the more general mind-body problem, see Heil 2004 and Searle 2004.

Searle presents the Chinese room argument in his "Minds, brains, and programs" (1980). This was originally published in the journal *Behavioral and Brain Sciences* with extensive commentary from many cognitive scientists. Margaret Boden's article "Escaping from the Chinese room" (Boden 1990a), reprinted in Heil 2004, is a good place to start in thinking about the Chinese room. The entry on the Chinese room argument in the online *Stanford Encyclopedia of Philosophy* is comprehensive and has a very full bibliography. The *Encyclopedia of Cognitive Science* has an entry as well. The symbol-grounding problem is introduced and discussed in Harnad 1990 (available in the online resources).

Course website

There is a course website accompanying the book. It can be found at www.cambridge.org/bermudez2. This website contains:

- links to useful learning resources, videos, and experimental demonstrations
- links to online versions of relevant papers and online discussions for each chapter
- study questions for each chapter that students can use to structure their reading and that instructors can use for class discussion topics

Instructors can access a password-protected section of the website. This contains:

- sample syllabi for courses of different lengths and different level
- PowerPoint slides for each chapter, organized by section
- electronic versions of figures from the text
- test bank of questions
- suggested solutions for the more challenging exercises and problems

The website is a work in progress. Students and instructors are welcome to contact me with suggestions, revisions, and comments. Contact details are on the website.

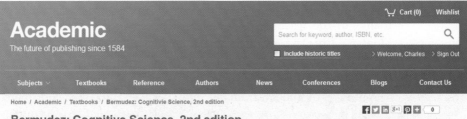

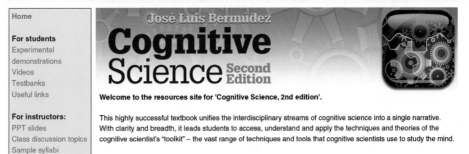

ACKNOWLEDGMENTS FOR THE FIRST EDITION

Many friends and colleagues associated with the Philosophy-Neuroscience-Psychology program at Washington University in St. Louis have commented on sections of this book. I would particularly like to thank Maurizio Corbetta, Frederick Eberhardt, David Kaplan, Clare Palmer, Gualtiero Piccinnini, Marc Raichle, Philip Robbins, David Van Essen, and Jeff Zacks. Josef Perner kindly read a draft of Chapter 12.

I have benefited from the comments of many referees while working on this project. Most remain anonymous, but some have revealed their identity. My thanks to Kirsten Andrews, Gary Bradshaw, Rob Goldstone, Paul Humphreys, and Michael Spivey.

Drafts of this textbook have been used four times to teach PNP 200 Introduction to Cognitive Science here at Washington University in St. Louis - twice by me and once each by David Kaplan and Jake Beck. Feedback from students both inside and outside the classroom was extremely useful. I hope that other instructors who use this text have equally motivated and enthusiastic classes. I would like to record my thanks to the teaching assistants who have worked with me on this course: Juan Montaña, Tim Oakberg, Adam Shriver, and Isaac Wiegman. And also to Kimberly Mount, the PNP administrative assistant, whose help with the figures and preparing the manuscript is greatly appreciated.

A number of students from my Spring 2009 PNP 200 class contributed to the glossary. It was a pleasure to work with Olivia Frosch, Katie Lewis, Juan Manfredi, Eric Potter, and Katie Sadow.

Work on this book has been made much easier by the efforts of the Psychology textbook team at Cambridge University Press - Raihanah Begum, Catherine Flack, Hetty Reid, Sarah Wightman, and Rachel Willsher (as well as to Andy Peart, who signed this book up but has sinced moved on). They have been very patient and very helpful. My thanks also to Anna Oxbury for her editing and to Liz Davey for coordinating the production process.

ACKNOWLEDGMENTS FOR THE SECOND EDITION

I am very grateful to my colleagues in the Office of the Dean at Texas A&M University, particularly my administrative assistant Connie Davenport, for helping me to carve out time to work on the second edition of the textbook. T. J. Kasperbauer has been an excellent research assistant, providing numerous improvements to the text and supporting resources and helping me greatly with his deep knowledge of cognitive science. It has been a pleasure to work once again with Hetty Marx and Carrie Parkinson at Cambridge University Press. I particularly appreciate their work gathering feedback on the first edition. Thanks again to Anna Oxbury for her copyediting skills.

PART I

HISTORICAL LANDMARKS

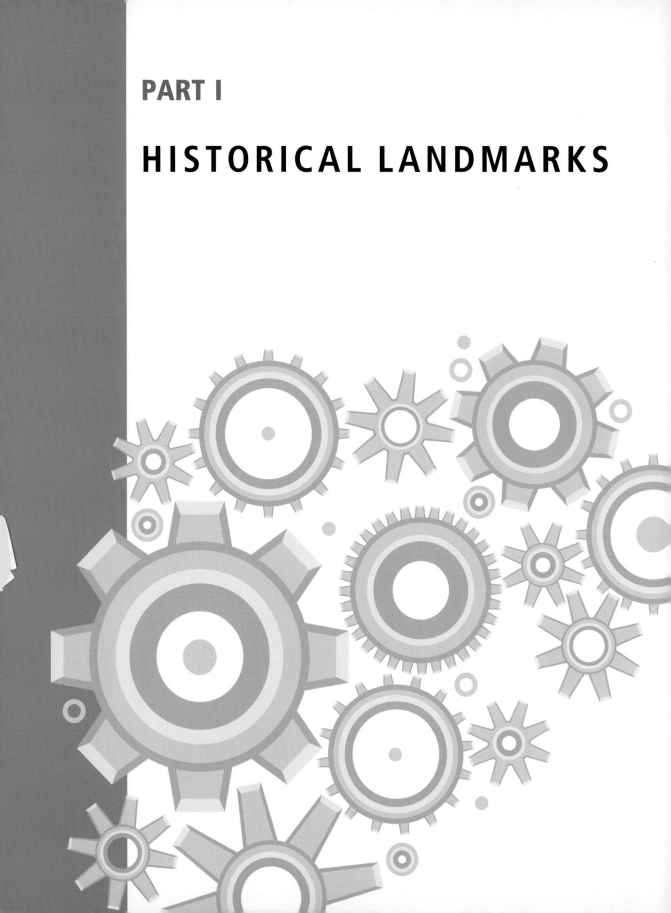

INTRODUCTION

Here is a short, but accurate, definition of cognitive science: Cognitive science is the science of the mind. Much of this book is devoted to explaining what this means. As with any area of science, cognitive scientists have a set of problems that they are trying to solve and a set of phenomena that they are trying to model and explain. These problems and phenomena are part of what makes cognitive science a distinctive discipline. Equally important, cognitive scientists share a number of basic assumptions about how to go about tackling those problems. They share a very general conception of what the mind is and how it works. The most fundamental driving assumption of cognitive science is that minds are information processors. As we will see, this basic idea can be developed in many different ways, since there are many different ways of thinking about what information is and how it might be processed by the mind.

The chapters in this first section of the book introduce the picture of the mind as an information processor by sketching out some of the key moments in the history of cognitive science. Each chapter is organized around a selection of influential books and articles that illustrate some of the important concepts, tools, and models that we will be looking at in more detail later on in the book. We will see how the basic idea that the mind is an information processor emerged and look at some of the very different ways in which it has been developed.

We begin in Chapter 1 by surveying some of the basic ideas and currents of thought that we can, in retrospect, see as feeding into what subsequently emerged as cognitive science. These ideas and currents of thought emerged during the 1930s, 1940s, and 1950s in very different and seemingly unrelated areas. The examples we will look at range from experiments on problem-solving in rats to fundamental breakthroughs in mathematical logic, and from studies of the grammatical structure of language to information-processing models of how input from the senses is processed by the mind.

The early flourishing of cognitive science in the 1960s and 1970s was marked by a series of powerful and influential studies of particular aspects of mental functioning. In Chapter 2 we survey three examples, each of which has been taken by many to be a paradigm of cognitive science in action. These include the studies of mental imagery carried out by Roger Shepherd and various collaborators; Terry Winograd's computer program SHRDLU; and David Marr's tri-level model of the early visual system.

The latter decades of the twentieth century saw challenges to some of the basic assumptions of the "founding fathers" of cognitive science. This was cognitive science's "turn to the brain." A crucial factor here was the development of new techniques for studying the brain. These include the possibility of studying the responses of individual neurons, as well as of mapping changing patterns of activation in different brain areas. In Chapter 3 we look at two pioneering sets of experiments. The first is Ungerleider and Mishkin's initial development of the hypothesis that there are two different pathways along which visual information travels through the brain. The second is the elegant use of positron emission tomography (PET) technology by Steve Petersen and collaborators to map how information about individual words is processed in the human brain. Another important factor was the emergence of a new type of model for thinking about cognition, variously known as connectionism or parallel distributed processing. This is also introduced in Chapter 3.

CHAPTER ONE

The prehistory of cognitive science

Overview

In the late 1970s cognitive science became an established part of the intellectual landscape. At that time an academic field crystallized around a basic set of problems, techniques, and theoretical assumptions. These problems, techniques, and theoretical assumptions came from many different disciplines and areas. Many of them had been around for a fairly long time. What was new was the idea of putting them together as a way of studying the mind.

Cognitive science is at heart an interdisciplinary endeavor. In interdisciplinary research great innovations come about simply because people see how to combine things that are already out there but have never been put together before. One of the best ways to understand cognitive science is to try to think your way back until you can see how things might have looked to its early pioneers. They were exploring a landscape in which certain regions were well mapped and well understood, but where there were no standard ways of getting from one region to another. An important part of what they did was to show how these different regions could be connected in order to create an interdisciplinary science of the mind.

In this chapter we go back to the 1930s, 1940s, and 1950s – to explore the *prehistory* of cognitive science. We will be looking at some of the basic ideas and currents of thought that, in retrospect, we can see as feeding into what came to be known as cognitive science. As we shall see in more detail later on in this book, *the guiding idea of cognitive science is that mental operations involve processing information*, and hence that we can study how the mind works by studying how information is processed. This basic idea of the mind as an information processor has a number of very specific roots, in areas that seem on the face of it to have little in common. The prehistory of cognitive science involves parallel, and largely independent, developments in psychology, linguistics, and mathematical logic. We will be looking at four of these developments:

- The reaction against behaviorism in psychology (section 1.1)
- The idea of algorithmic computation in mathematical logic (section 1.2)
- The emergence of linguistics as the formal analysis of language (section 1.3)
- The emergence of information-processing models in psychology (section 1.4)

In concentrating on these four developments we will be passing over other important influences, such as neuroscience and neuropsychology. This is because until quite recently the direct study of the brain had a relatively minor role to play in cognitive science. Almost all cognitive scientists are convinced that in some fundamental sense the mind just is the brain, so that everything that happens in the mind is happening in the brain. Few, if any, cognitive scientists are *dualists*, who think that the mind and the brain are two separate and distinct things. But for a long time in the history of cognitive science it was widely held that we are better off studying the mind by abstracting away from the details of what is going on in the brain. This changed only with the emergence in the 1970s and 1980s of new technologies for studying neural activity and of new ways of modeling cognitive abilities. Until then many cognitive scientists believed that the mind could be studied without studying the brain.

1.1 The reaction against behaviorism in psychology

Behaviorism was (and in some quarters still is) an influential movement in psychology. It takes many different forms, but they all share the basic assumption that psychologists should confine themselves to studying observable phenomena and measurable behavior. They should avoid speculating about unobservable mental states, and should instead rely on non-psychological mechanisms linking particular stimuli with particular responses. These mechanisms are the product of conditioning. For examples of conditioning, think of Pavlov's dogs being conditioned to salivate at the sound of the bell, or the rewards/punishments that animal trainers use to encourage/discourage certain types of behavior.

According to behaviorists, psychology is really the science of behavior. This way of thinking about psychology leaves little room for cognitive science as the scientific study of cognition and the mind. Cognitive science could not even get started until behaviorism ceased to be the dominant approach within psychology. Psychology's move from behaviorism was a lengthy and drawn-out process (and some would say that it has not yet been completed). We can appreciate some of the ideas that proved important for the later development of cognitive science by looking at three landmark papers. Each was an important statement of the idea that various types of behavior could not be explained in terms of stimulus–response mechanisms. Instead, psychologists need to think about organisms as storing and processing information about their environment, rather than as responding mechanically to reinforcers and stimuli. This idea of organisms as information processors is the single most fundamental idea of cognitive science.

Learning without reinforcement: Tolman and Honzik, "'Insight' in rats" (1930)

Edward Tolman (1886–1959) was a behaviorist psychologist studying problem-solving and learning in rats (among other things). As with most psychologists of the time, he started off with two standard behaviorist assumptions about learning. The first assumption is that all learning is the result of *conditioning*. The second assumption is that conditioning depends upon processes of *association* and *reinforcement*.

We can understand these two assumptions by thinking about a rat in what is known as a Skinner box, after the celebrated behaviorist B. F. Skinner. A typical Skinner box is illustrated in Figure 1.1. The rat receives a reward for behaving in a particular way (pressing a lever, for example, or pushing a button). Each time the rat performs the relevant behavior it receives the reward. The reward *reinforces* the behavior. This means that the association between the behavior and the reward is strengthened and the rat's performing the behavior again becomes more likely. The rat becomes *conditioned* to perform the behavior.

The basic idea of behaviorism is that all learning is either reinforcement learning of this general type, or the even simpler form of associative learning often called classical conditioning.

In classical conditioning what is strengthened is the association between a *conditioned stimulus* (such as the typically neutral sound of a bell ringing) and an *unconditioned stimulus* (such as the presentation of food). The unconditioned stimulus is *not* neutral for the organism and typically provokes a behavioral response, such as salivation. What happens during classical conditioning is that the strengthening of the association between conditioned stimulus and unconditioned stimulus eventually

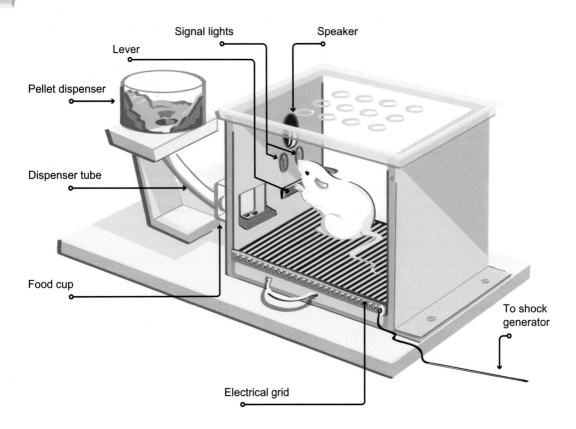

Lever

Signal lights

Speaker

Pellet dispenser

Dispenser tube

Food cup

To shock
generator

Electrical grid

Figure 1.1 A rat in a Skinner box. The rat has a response lever controlling the delivery of food, as well as devices allowing different types of stimuli to be produced. (Adapted from Spivey 2007)

leads the organism to produce the unconditioned response to the conditioned stimulus alone, without the presence of the unconditioned stimulus. The most famous example of classical conditioning is Pavlov's dogs, who were conditioned to salivate to the sound of a bell by the simple technique of using the bell to signal the arrival of food.

So, it is a basic principle of behaviorism that all learning, whether by rats or by human beings, takes place through processes of reinforcement and conditioning. What the studies reported by Tolman and Honzik in 1930 seemed to show, however, is that this is not true even for rats.

Tolman and Honzik were interested in how rats learnt to navigate mazes. They ran three groups of rats through a maze of the type illustrated in Figure 1.2. The first group received a reward each time they successfully ran the maze. The second group never received a reward. The third group was unrewarded for the first ten days and then began to be rewarded. As behaviorism would predict, the rewarded rats quickly learnt to run the maze, while both groups of unrewarded rats simply wandered

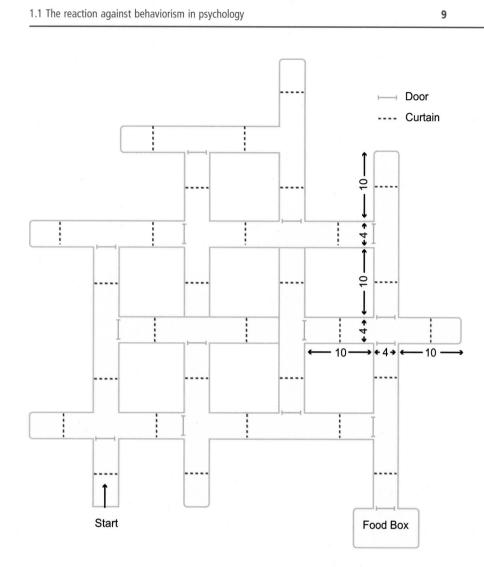

Figure 1.2 A 14-unit T-Alley maze (measurements in inches). Note the blocked passages and dead ends. (Adapted from Elliott 1928)

around aimlessly. The striking fact, however, was that when the third group of rats started to receive rewards they learnt to run the maze far more quickly than the first group had.

Tolman and Honzik argued that the rats must have been learning about the layout of the maze during the period when they were not being rewarded. This type of *latent learning* seemed to show that reinforcement was not necessary for learning, and that the rats must have been picking up and storing information about the layout of the maze when they were wandering around it, even though there was no reward and hence no reinforcement. They were later able to use this information to navigate the maze.

Exercise 1.1 Explain in your own words why latent learning seems to be incompatible with the two basic assumptions of behaviorism.

Suppose, then, that organisms are capable of latent learning – that they can store information for later use without any process of reinforcement. One important follow-up question is: What sort of information is being stored? In particular, are the rats storing information about the spatial layout of the maze? Or are they simply "remembering" the sequences of movements (responses) that they made while wandering around the maze? And so, when the rats in the latent-learning experiments start running the maze successfully, are they simply repeating their earlier sequences of movements, or are they using their "knowledge" of how the different parts of the maze fit together?

Tolman and his students and collaborators designed many experiments during the 1930s and 1940s to try to decide between *place learning* and *response learning* accounts of how rats learn to run a maze. Some of these experiments were reported in a famous article in 1946.

Cognitive maps in rats? Tolman, Ritchie, and Kalish, "Studies in spatial learning" (1946)

One experiment used a cross-maze with four end-points (North, South, East, West), like that illustrated in Figure 1.3. Rats were started at North and South on alternate trials. One group of rats was rewarded by food that was located at the same end-point, say East. The relevant feature of the map for this group was that the same turning response would not invariably return them to the reward. To get from North to East the rat needed to make a left-hand turn, whereas a right-hand turn was required to get from South to East. For the second group the location of the food reward was shifted between East and West so that, whether they started at North or South, the same turning response was required to obtain the reward. A rat in the second group starting from North would find the reward at East, while the same rat starting from South would find the reward at West. Whether it started at North or South a left turn would always take it to the reward.

This simple experiment shows very clearly the distinction between place learning and response learning. Consider the first group of rats (those for which the food was always in the same place, although their starting-points differed). In order to learn to run the maze and obtain the reward they had to represent the reward as being at a particular place and control their movements accordingly. If they merely repeated the same response they would only succeed in reaching the food reward on half of the trials. For the second group, though, repeating the same turning response would invariably bring them to the reward, irrespective of the starting-point.

Tolman found that the first group of rats learnt to run the maze much more quickly than the second group. From this he drew conclusions about the nature of

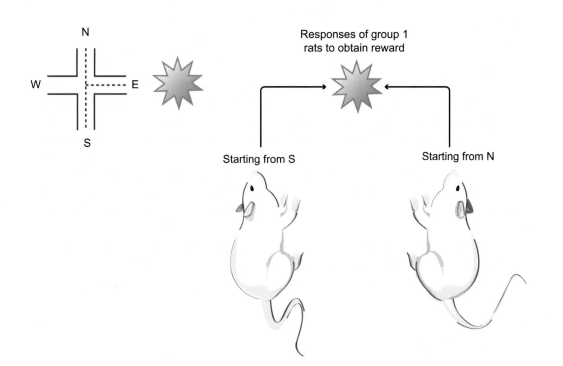

Figure 1.3 A cross-maze, as used in Tolman, Ritchie, and Kalish (1946). The left-hand part of the figure illustrates the maze, with a star indicating the location of the food reward. The right-hand side illustrates how the group 1 rats had to make different sequences of movements in order to reach the reward, depending on where they started.

animal learning in general – namely, that it was easier for animals to code spatial information in terms of places rather than in terms of particular sequences of movements.

Exercise 1.2 Explain in your own words why the experimental results seem to show that rats engage in place learning rather than response learning.

Tolman took his place-learning experiments as evidence that animals form high-level representations of how their environment is laid out – what he called *cognitive maps*. Tolman's cognitive maps were one of the first proposals for explaining behavior in terms of *representations* (stored information about the environment). Representations are one of the fundamental explanatory tools of cognitive science. Cognitive scientists regularly explain particular cognitive achievements (such as the navigational achievements of rats in mazes) by modeling how the organism is using representations of the environment. Throughout this book we will be looking at different ways of thinking about how representations code information about the environment, and about how those representations are manipulated and transformed as the organism negotiates and engages with its environment.

Plans and complex behaviors: Lashley, "The problem of serial order in behavior" (1951)

At the same time as Tolman was casting doubt on standard behaviorist models of spatial navigation, the psychologist and physiologist Karl Lashley was thinking more generally about the problem of explaining complex behavior.

Much of human and animal behavior has a very complex structure. It involves highly organized sequences of movements. Stimulus–response behaviorists have limited resources for thinking about these complex behaviors. They have to view them as linked sequences of responses – as a sort of chain with each link determined by the link immediately preceding it. This is the basic idea behind response-learning models of how rats run mazes. The standard behaviorist view is that rats learn to chain together a series of movements that leads to the reward. Tolman showed that this is not the right way to think about what happens when rats learn to run mazes. Lashley made the far more general point that this seems to be completely the wrong way to think about many complex behaviors.

Think of the complicated set of movements involved in uttering a sentence of English, for example. Or playing a game of tennis. In neither of these cases is what happens at a particular moment solely determined by what has just happened – or prompted by what is going on in the environment and influencing the organism. What happens at any given point in the sequence is often a function of what will happen later in the sequence, as well as of the overall goal of the behavior. According to Lashley, we should think about many of these complex behaviors as products of prior planning and organization. The behaviors are organized hierarchically (rather than linearly). An overall plan (say, walking over to the table to pick up the glass) is implemented by simpler plans (the walking plan and the reaching plan), each of which can be broken down into simpler plans, and so on. Very little (if any) of this planning takes place at the conscious level.

Exercise 1.3 Give your own example of a hierarchically organized behavior.

Lashley's essay contains the seeds of two ideas that have proved very important for cognitive science. The first is the idea that much of what we do is under the control of planning and information-processing mechanisms that operate below the threshold of awareness. This is the *hypothesis of subconscious information processing*. Even though we are often conscious of our high-level plans and goals (of what goes on at the top of the hierarchy), we tend not to be aware of the information processing that translates those plans and goals into actions. So, for example, you might consciously form an intention to pick up a glass of water. But carrying out the intention requires calculating very precisely the trajectory that your arm must take, as well as ensuring that your hand is open to the right degree to take hold of the glass. These calculations are carried out by information-processing systems operating far below the threshold of conscious awareness.

The second important idea is the *hypothesis of task analysis*. This is the idea that we can understand a complex task (and the cognitive system performing it) by breaking it down into a hierarchy of more basic sub-tasks (and associated sub-systems). The hypothesis has proved a powerful tool for understanding many different aspects of mind and cognition. We can think about a particular cognitive system (say, the memory system) as carrying out a particular task – the task of allowing an organism to exploit previously acquired information. We can think about that task as involving a number of simpler, sub-tasks – say, the sub-task of storing information and the sub-task of retrieving information. Each of these sub-tasks can be carried out by even more simple sub-sub-tasks. We might distinguish the sub-sub-task of storing information for the long term from the sub-sub-task of storing information for the short term. And so on down the hierarchy.

1.2 The theory of computation and the idea of an algorithm

At the same time as Tolman and Lashley were putting pressure on some of the basic principles of behaviorism, the theoretical foundations for one highly influential approach to cognitive science (and indeed for our present-day world of omnipresent computers and constant flows of digital information) were laid in the 1930s, in what was at the time a rather obscure and little-visited corner of mathematics.

In 1936–7 Alan Turing published an article in the *Proceedings of the London Mathematical Society* that introduced some of the basic ideas in the theory of computation. Computation is what computers do and, according to many cognitive scientists, it is what minds do. What Turing gave us was a theoretical model that many have thought to capture the essence of computation. Turing's model (the so-called Turing machine) is one of the most important and influential ideas in cognitive science, even though it initially seems to have little to do with the human mind.

Algorithms and Turing machines: Turing, "On computable numbers, with an application to the Decision Problem" (1936–7)

Turing, together with a number of mathematicians working in the foundations of mathematics, was grappling with the problem (known as the Halting Problem) of determining whether there is a purely mechanical procedure for working out whether certain basic mathematical problems have a solution.

Here is a way of thinking about the Halting Problem. We can think about it in terms of computer programs. Many computer programs are not defined for every possible input. They will give a solution for some inputs, the ones for which they are defined. But for other inputs, the ones for which they are not defined, they will just endlessly loop, looking for a solution that isn't there. From the point of view of a computer programmer, it is really important to be able to tell whether or not the computer program is defined for a given input – in order to be able to tell whether the program is simply taking a very long time to get to the solution, or whether it is in an endless loop. This is what a solution to the Halting Problem would give – a way of telling, for a given computer program and a given input, whether the program is defined for that input. The solution has to work both ways. It has to give the answer "Yes" when the program is defined, and "No" when the program is not defined.

It is important to stress that Turing was looking for a purely mechanical solution to the Halting Problem. He was looking for something with the same basic features as the "recipes" that we all learn in high school for multiplying two numbers, or performing long division. These recipes are mechanical because they do not involve any insight. The recipes can be clearly stated in a finite set of instructions and following the instructions correctly always gives the right answer, even if you don't understand how or why.

Since the notion of a purely mechanical procedure is not itself a mathematical notion, the first step was to make it more precise. Turing did this by using the notion of an *algorithm*. An algorithm is a finite set of rules that are unambiguous and that can be applied systematically to an object or set of objects to transform it or them in definite and circumscribed ways. The instructions for programming a DVD recorder, for example, are intended to function algorithmically so that they can be followed blindly in a way that will transform the DVD recorder from being unprogrammed to being programmed to switch itself on and switch itself off at appropriate times. Of course, the instructions are not genuinely algorithmic since, as we all know, they are not idiot-proof.

Exercise 1.4 Think of an example of a genuine algorithm, perhaps from elementary arithmetic or perhaps from everyday life.

One of Turing's great contributions was a bold hypothesis about how to define the notion of an algorithm within mathematics. Turing devised an incredibly simple kind of computing mechanism (what we now call, in his honor, a *Turing machine*). This is an idealized machine, not a real one. What makes a Turing machine idealized is that it consists of an infinitely long piece of tape divided into cells. The point of the tape being infinitely long is so that the machine will not have any storage limitations. A Turing machine is like a computer with an infinitely large hard disk. Turing did not think that a Turing machine would ever have to deal with infinitely long strings of symbols. He just wanted it to be able to deal with arbitrarily long, but still finite, strings of symbols.

Each of the cells of the Turing tape can be either blank or contain a single symbol. The Turing machine contains a machine head. The tape runs through the machine head, with a single cell under the head at a given moment. This allows the head to read the

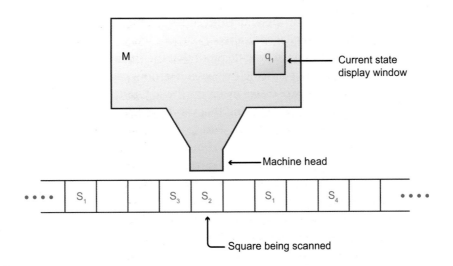

Figure 1.4 Schematic representation of a Turing machine. (Adapted from Cutland 1980)

symbol the cell contains. The machine head can also carry out a limited number of operations on the cell that it is currently scanning. It can:

- delete the symbol in the cell
- write a new symbol in the cell
- move the tape one cell to the left
- move the tape one cell to the right

Any individual Turing machine has a set of instructions (its *machine table*). The machine can be in any one of a (finite) number of different states. The machine table determines what the Turing machine will do when it encounters a particular symbol in a particular cell, depending upon which internal state it is in. Figure 1.4 is a schematic representation of a Turing machine.

The beauty of a Turing machine is that its behavior is entirely determined by the machine table, its current state, and the symbol in the cell it is currently scanning. There is no ambiguity and no room for the machine to exercise "intuition" or "judgment." It is, in fact, purely mechanical in exactly the way required for an algorithm.

Turing did not actually build a Turing machine. (It is difficult to build a machine with an infinitely long piece of tape!) But he showed how Turing machines could be specified mathematically. The machine table of a Turing machine can be represented as a sequence of numbers. This allowed him to prove mathematical results about Turing machines. In particular, it allowed him to prove that there is a special kind of Turing machine, a *Universal Turing machine,* that can run any specialized Turing machine. The Universal Turing machine can take as input a program specifying any given specialized

Turing program. It is the theoretical precursor (with unlimited storage) of the modern-day general-purpose digital computer.

Turing's paper contained a subtle proof that the Halting Problem cannot be solved. It was also significant for articulating what we now call the *Church–Turing thesis* (in recognition of the contribution made by the logician Alonzo Church). According to the Church–Turing thesis, anything that can be done in mathematics by an algorithm can be done by a Turing machine. Turing machines are computers that can compute anything that can be algorithmically computed.

What Turing contributed to the early development of cognitive science (although at the time his work was little known and even less appreciated) was a model of computation that looked as if it might be a clue to how information could be processed by the mind. As theorists moved closer to the idea that cognition involves processing information it was an easy step to think about information processing as an algorithmic process along the lines analyzed by Turing - a step that became even easier in the light of the huge advances that were made in designing and building digital computers (which, if the Church–Turing thesis is true, are essentially large and fast Turing machines) during and after the Second World War.

Exercise 1.5 Explain in your own words why the Church–Turing thesis entails that any computer running a program is simply a large and fast Turing machine.

1.3 Linguistics and the formal analysis of language

The study of language played a fundamental role in the prehistory of cognitive science. On the one hand, language use is a paradigm of the sort of hierarchically organized complex behavior that Lashley was talking about. On the other hand, the emergence of transformational linguistics and the formal analysis of *syntax* (those aspects of language use that have to do with how words can be legitimately put together to form sentences) provided a very clear example of how to analyze, *in algorithmic terms*, the bodies of information that might underlie certain very basic cognitive abilities (such as the ability to speak and understand a language). In retrospect we can identify one crucial landmark as the publication in 1957 of *Syntactic Structures* by Noam Chomsky, unquestionably the father of modern linguistics and a hugely important figure in the development of cognitive science. The transformational grammar proposed by Chomsky (and subsequently much modified by Chomsky and others) reflects some of the basic ideas that we have discussed earlier in this chapter.

The structure of language: Chomsky's *Syntactic Structures* (1957)

Chomsky's book is widely held to be the first example of a linguist proposing an explanatory theory of *why* languages work the way they do (as opposed to simply describing and classifying *how* they work). Chomsky was interested not in mapping the differences between different languages and in describing their structure, but rather in providing a theoretical account of why they have the structure that they do. Crucial to his approach is the distinction between the *deep structure* of a sentence (as given by what Chomsky calls a *phrase structure grammar*) and its *surface structure* (the actual organization of words in a sentence, derived from the deep structure according to the principles of transformational grammar).

The deep structure, or phrase structure, of a sentence is simply how it is built up from basic constituents (syntactic categories) according to basic rules (phrase structure rules). We only need a small number of basic categories to specify the phrase structure of a sentence. These are the familiar parts of speech that we all learn about in high school – nouns, verbs, adjectives, and so on. Any grammatical sentence (including those that nobody is ever likely to utter) is made up of these basic parts of speech combined according to basic phrase structure rules (such as the rule that every sentence is composed of a verb phrase and a noun phrase).

In Figure 1.5 we see how these basic categories can be used to give a phrase structure tree of the sentence "John has hit the ball." The phrase structure tree is easy to read, with a bit of practice. Basically, you start at the top with the most general characterization. As you work your way down the tree the structure of the sentence becomes more finely articulated, so that we see which words or combinations of words are doing which job.

Analyzing sentences in terms of their phrase structure is a powerful explanatory tool. There are pairs of sentences that have very different phrase structures, but are clearly very similar in meaning. Think of "John has hit the ball" and "The ball has been hit by John." In most contexts these sentences are equivalent and interchangeable, despite having very different phrase structures. Conversely, there are sentences with superficially similar phrase structures that are plainly unrelated. Think of "Susan is easy to please" and "Susan is eager to please."

Exercise 1.6 Explain in your own words the difference between these two sentences. Why are their phrase structures different?

The basic aim of transformational grammar is to explain the connection between sentences of the first type and to explain the differences between sentences of the second type. This is done by giving principles that state the acceptable ways of transforming deep structures. This allows linguists to identify the transformational structure of a sentence in terms of its transformational history.

The transformational principles of transformational grammar are examples of *algorithms*. They specify a set of procedures that operate upon a string of symbols to convert it into a different string of symbols. So, for example, our simple phrase structure grammar might be extended to include an active–passive transformation rule that takes the following form (look at the key in Figure 1.5 for the translation of the symbols):

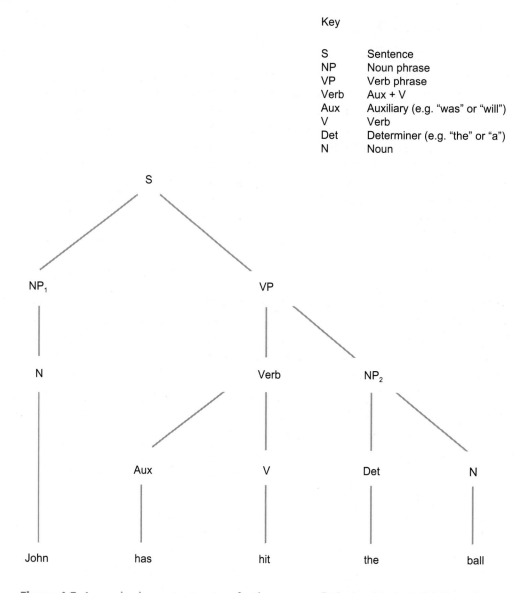

Key

S	Sentence
NP	Noun phrase
VP	Verb phrase
Verb	Aux + V
Aux	Auxiliary (e.g. "was" or "will")
V	Verb
Det	Determiner (e.g. "the" or "a")
N	Noun

Figure 1.5 A sample phrase structure tree for the sentence "John has hit the ball." The abbreviations in the diagram are explained in the key.

$$NP_1 + Aux + V + NP_2$$
$$\Rightarrow$$
$$NP_2 + Aux + been + V + by + NP_1$$

This transforms the string "John + has + hit + the + ball" into the string "the + ball + has + been + hit + by + John." And it does so in a purely mechanical and algorithmic way.

Exercise 1.7 Write out an algorithm that carries out the active–passive transformation rule. Make sure that your algorithm instructs the person/machine following it what to do at each step.

What's more, when we look at the structure of the passive sentence "The ball has been hit by John" we can see it as illustrating precisely the sort of hierarchical structure to which Lashley drew our attention. This is a characteristic of languages in general. They are hierarchically organized. In thinking about how they work, transformational grammar brings together two very fundamental ideas. The first idea is that a sophisticated, hierarchically organized, cognitive ability, such as speaking and understanding a language, involves stored bodies of information (information about phrase structures and transformation rules). The second idea is that these bodies of information can be manipulated algorithmically.

1.4 Information-processing models in psychology

In the late 1950s the idea that the mind works by processing information began to take hold within psychology. This new development reflected a number of different influences. One of these was the emergence of information theory in applied mathematics. Rather unusually in the history of science, the emergence of information theory can be pinned down to a single event – the publication of an article entitled "A mathematical theory of communication" by Claude E. Shannon in 1948. Shannon's paper showed how information can be measured, and he provided precise mathematical tools for studying the transmission of information.

These tools (including the idea of a *bit* as a measure of information) proved very influential in psychology, and for cognitive science more generally. We can illustrate how information-processing models became established in psychology through two very famous publications from the 1950s.

The first, George Miller's article "The magical number seven, plus or minus two: Some limits on our capacity for processing information," used the basic concepts of information theory to identify crucial features of how the mind works. The second, Donald Broadbent's 1954 paper "The role of auditory localization in attention and memory span," presented two influential experiments that were crucial in Broadbent's later putting forward, in his 1958 book *Perception and Communication*, one of the first information-processing models in psychology. The type of flowchart model that Broadbent proposed (as illustrated in Figure 1.6) has become a standard way for cognitive scientists to describe and explain different aspects of cognition.

How much information can we handle? George Miller's "The magical number seven, plus or minus two" (1956)

The tools of information theory can be applied to the study of the mind. One of the basic concepts of information theory is the concept of an information channel. In

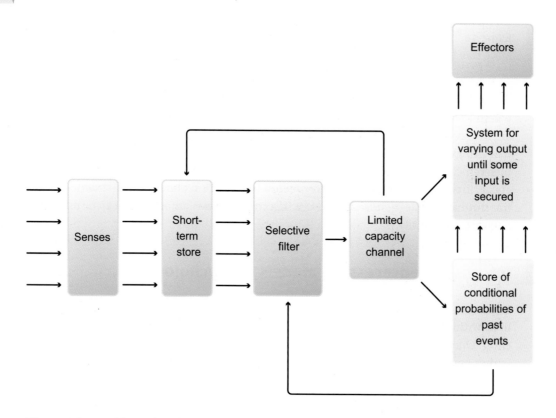

Figure 1.6 Donald Broadbent's 1958 model of selective attention.

abstract terms, an information channel is a *medium* that transmits information from a *sender* to a *receiver*. A telephone cable is an information channel. So is the radio frequency on which a television station broadcasts. We can think of perceptual systems as information channels. Vision, for example, is a medium through which information is transmitted from the environment to the perceiver. So are audition (hearing) and olfaction (smell). Thinking about perceptual systems in this way gave Miller and other psychologists a new set of tools for thinking about experiments on human perception.

Miller's article drew attention to a wide range of evidence suggesting that human subjects are really rather limited in the *absolute judgments* that they can make. An example of an absolute judgment is naming a color, or identifying the pitch of a particular tone - as opposed to relative judgments, such as identifying which of two colors is the darker, or which of two tones is higher in pitch.

In one experiment reported by Miller, subjects are asked to assign numbers to the pitches of particular tones and then presented with sequences of tones and asked to identify them in terms of the assigned numbers. So, for example, if you assigned "1" to middle C, "2" to the first E above middle C, and "3" to the first F# and then heard the sequence E-C-C-F#-E, the correct response would be 2-1-1-3-2.

When the sequence is only one or two tones long, subjects never make mistakes. But performance falls off drastically when the sequence is six or more tones long. A similar phenonemon occurs when we switch from audition to vision and ask subjects to judge the size of squares or the length of a line. Here too there seems to be an upper bound on the number of distinct items that can be processed simultaneously.

Putting these (and many other) experimental results into the context of information theory led Miller to propose that our sensory systems are all information channels with roughly the same *channel capacity* (where the channel capacity of an information channel is given by the amount of information it can reliably transmit). In these cases the perceiver's capacity to make absolute judgments is an index of the channel capacity of the information channel that she is using.

What Miller essentially did was propose an *information-processing bottleneck*. The human perceptual systems, he suggested, are information channels with built-in limits. These information channels can only process around seven items at the same time (or, to put it in the language of information theory, their channel capacity is around 3 bits; since each bit allows the system to discriminate 2 pieces of information, n bits of information allow the system to discriminate 2^n pieces of information and 7 is just under 2^3).

At the same time as identifying these limits, Miller identified ways of working round them. One way of increasing the channel capacity is to *chunk* information. We can relabel sequences of numbers with single numbers. A good example (discussed by Miller) comes when we use decimal notation to relabel numbers in binary notation. We can pick out the same number in two different ways – with the binary expression 1100100, for example, or with the decimal expression 100. If we use binary notation then we are at the limits of our visual channel capacity. If we use decimal notation then we are well within those limits. As Miller pointed out, to return to a theme that has emerged several times already, natural language is the ultimate chunking tool.

Exercise 1.8 Think of an informal experiment that you can do to illustrate the significance of chunking information.

The flow of information: Donald Broadbent's "The role of auditory localization in attention and memory span" (1954) and *Perception and Communication* (1958)

Miller's work drew attention to some very general features of how information is processed in the mind, but it had little to say about the details of how that information processing takes place. The experiments reported and analyzed by Miller made plausible the idea that the senses are information channels with limited capacity. The obvious next step was to think about how those information channels actually work. One of the first models of how sensory information is processed was developed by the British psychologist Donald Broadbent in his 1958 book *Perception and Communication*. As with Miller, the impetus came from experiments in the branch of psychology known as *psychophysics*. This is the branch of psychology that studies how subjects perceive and discriminate physical stimuli.

We can appreciate what is going on by thinking about the so-called *cocktail party phenomenon*. When at a cocktail party, or any other social gathering, we can often hear many ongoing and unrelated conversations. Somehow we manage to focus only on the one we want to listen to. How do we manage this? How do we screen out all the unwanted sentences that we hear? It is plain that we only *attend* to some of what we hear. Auditory attention is selective. There is nothing peculiar to audition here, of course. The phenomenon of *selective attention* occurs in every sense modality.

Broadbent studied auditory attention by using *dichotic listening experiments*, in which subjects are presented with different information in each ear. The experiments reported in his paper "The role of auditory localization in attention and memory span" involved presenting subjects with a string of three different stimuli (letters or digits) in one ear, while simultaneously presenting them with a different string in the other ear. The subjects were asked to report the stimuli in any order. Broadbent found that they performed best when they reported the stimuli ear by ear – that is, by reporting all three presented to the left ear first, followed by the three presented to the right ear. This, and other findings, were explained by the model that he subsequently developed.

The basic features of the model can be read off Figure 1.6. Information comes through the senses and passes through a short-term store before passing through a selective filter. The selective filter screens out a large portion of the incoming information, selecting some of it for further processing. This is what allows us selectively to attend to only a portion of what is going on around us in the cocktail party. Only information that makes it through the selective filter is semantically interpreted, for example. Although people at cocktail parties can hear many different conversations at the same time, many experiments have shown that they have little idea of what is said in the conversations that they are not attending to. They hear the words, but do not extract their meaning.

Broadbent interpreted the dichotic listening experiments as showing that we can only attend to a single information channel at a time (assuming that each ear is a separate information channel) – and that the selection between information channels is based purely on physical characteristics of the signal. The selection might be based on the physical location of the sound (whether it comes from the left ear or the right ear, for example), or on whether it is a man's voice or a woman's voice.

The selective filter does not work by magic. As the diagram shows, the selective filter is "programmed" by another system that stores information about the relative likelihoods of different events. We are assuming that the system is pursuing a goal. What is programming the selective filter is information about the sorts of things that have led to that goal being satisfied in the past. Information that makes it through the selective filter goes into what Broadbent calls the limited capacity channel. Information that is filtered out is assumed to decay quickly. From the limited capacity channel information can go either into the long-term store, or on to further processing and eventually into action, or it can be recycled back into the short-term store (to preserve it if it is in danger of being lost).

We can see how Broadbent's model characterizes what is going on in the cocktail party phenomenon. The stream of different conversations arrives at the selective filter. If my goal, let us say, is to strike up a conversation with Dr X (who is female), then the selective filter might be attuned in the first instance to female voices. The sounds that make it through the selective filter are the sounds of which I am consciously aware. They can provide information that can be stored and perhaps eventually feed back into the selective filter. Suppose that I "tune into" a conversation that I think involves Dr X but where the female voice turns out to belong to Mrs Z, then the selective filter can be instructed to filter out Mrs Z's voice.

Exercise 1.9 Give an example in your own words of selective attention in action. Incorporate as many different aspects of Broadbent's model as possible.

1.5 Connections and points of contact

This chapter has surveyed some crucial episodes in the prehistory of cognitive science. You should by now have a sense of exciting innovations and discoveries taking place in very different areas of intellectual life – from experiments on rats in mazes to some of the most abstract areas of mathematics, and from thinking about how we navigate cocktail parties to analyzing the deep structure of natural language. As we have looked at some of the key publications in these very different areas, a number of fundamental ideas have kept recurring. In this final section I draw out some of the connections and points of contact that emerge.

The most basic concept that has run through the chapter is the concept of information. Tolman's latent learning experiments seemed to many to show that animals (including of course human animals) are capable of picking up information without any reinforcement taking place. The rats wandering unrewarded through the maze were picking up and storing information about how it was laid out – information that they could subsequently retrieve and put to work when there was food at stake. Chomsky's approach to linguistics exploits the concept of information in a very different way. His *Syntactic Structures* pointed linguists towards the idea that speaking and understanding natural languages depends upon information about sentence structure – about the basic rules that govern the surface structure of sentences and about the basic transformation principles that underlie the deep structure of sentences. In the work of the psychologists Miller and Broadbent we find the concept of information appearing in yet another form. Here the idea is that we can understand perceptual systems as information channels and use the concepts of information theory to explore their basic structure and limits.

Hand in hand with the concept of information goes the concept of representation. Information is everywhere, but in order to use it organisms need to represent it. Representations will turn out to be the basic currency of cognitive science, and we have seen a range of very different examples of how information is represented in this chapter. Tolman's place-learning experiments introduced the idea that organisms have cognitive maps representing the spatial layout of the environment. These maps are representations of the environment. Turing machines incorporate a very different type of representation. They represent the instructions for implementing particular algorithms in their machine table. In a similar vein, Chomsky suggested that important elements of linguistic understanding are represented as phrase structure rules and transformational rules. And Miller showed how representing information in different ways (in terms of different types of chunking, for example) can affect how much information we are able to store in memory.

Information is not a static commodity. Organisms pick up information. They adapt it, modify it, and use it. In short, organisms engage in *information processing*. The basic idea of information processing raises a number of questions. One might wonder, for example, about the *content* of the information that is being processed. What an organism does with information depends upon how that information is encoded. We saw some of the ramifications of this in Tolman's place-learning experiments. The difference between place learning and response learning is a difference in how information about location is encoded. In response learning, information about location is encoded in terms of the movements that an organism might make to reach that location. In place learning, in contrast, information about location is encoded in terms of the location's relation to other locations in the environment.

Even once we know how information is encoded, there remain questions about the mechanics of information processing. How does it actually work? We can see the germ of a possible answer in Turing's model of computation. Turing machines illustrate the idea of a purely mechanical way of solving problems and processing information. In one sense Turing machines are completely unintelligent. They blindly follow very simple instructions. And yet, if the Church–Turing thesis is warranted, they can compute anything that can be algorithmically computed. And so, in another sense, it would be difficult to be more intelligent than a Turing machine.

If the basic assumptions of transformational linguistics are correct, then we can see one sphere in which the notion of an algorithm can be applied. The basic principles that transform sentences (that take a sentence from its active to its passive form, for example, or that transform a statement into a question) can be thought of as mechanical procedures that can in principle be carried out by a suitably programmed Turing machine (once we have found a way of numerically coding the basic categories of transformational grammar).

A final theme that has emerged from the authors we have studied is the idea that information processing is done by dedicated and specialized systems. This idea comes across most clearly in Broadbent's model of selective attention. Here we see a complex information-processing task (the task of making sense of the vast amounts of information picked up by the hearing system) broken down into a number of simpler tasks (such as the task of selecting a single information channel, or the task of working out what sentences mean). Each of these information-processing tasks is performed by dedicated systems, such as the selective filter or the semantic processing system.

One powerful idea that emerges from Broadbent's model of selective attention is the idea that w*e can understand how a cognitive system as a whole works by understanding how information flows through the system*. What Broadbent offered was a flowchart showing the different stages that information goes through as it is processed by the system. Many psychologists and cognitive scientists subsequently took this type of information-processing flowchart to be a paradigm of how to explain cognitive abilities.

In the next chapter we will look at how some of these ideas were put together in some of the classic theories and models of early cognitive science.

Summary

This chapter has surveyed five of the most important precursors of what subsequently became known as cognitive science. Cognitive science emerged when experimentalists and theoreticians began to see connections between developments in disciplines as diverse as experimental psychology, theoretical linguistics, and mathematical logic. These connections converge on the idea that cognition is a form of information processing and hence that we can understand how the mind works and how organisms negotiate the world around them by understanding how information about the environment is represented, transformed, and exploited.

Checklist

Important developments leading up to the emergence of cognitive science
(1)   The reaction against behaviorism in psychology
(2)   Theoretical models of computation from mathematical logic
(3)   Systematic analysis of the structure of natural language in linguistics
(4)   The development of information-processing models in psychology

Central themes of the chapter
(1)   Even very basic types of behavior (such as the behavior of rats in mazes) seems to involve storing and processing information about the environment.

(2)   Information relevant to cognition can take many forms – from information about the environment to information about how sentences can be constructed and transformed.

(3)   Perceptual systems can be viewed as information channels and we can study both:
      (a)   the very general properties of those channels (e.g. their channel capacity)
      (b)   the way in which information flows through those channels

(4)   Mathematical logic and the theory of computation shows us how information processing can be mechanical and algorithmic.

(5)   Much of the information-processing that goes on in the mind takes place below the threshold of awareness.

Further reading

The story of how cognitive science emerged is told in Gardner's *The Mind's New Science* (1985). Flanagan's *The Science of the Mind* (1991) goes further back into the prehistory of cognitive science and psychology, as do the papers in Brook 2007. Margaret Boden's two-volume *Mind as Machine: A History of Cognitive Science* (2006) is detailed, but places most emphasis on computer science and artificial intelligence. Abrahamsen and Bechtel's chapter in Frankish and Ramsey 2012 provides a concise summary of the history of cognitive science.

The basic principles of classical and operant conditioning are covered in standard textbooks to psychology, such as Gazzaniga, Halpern, and Heatherton 2011, Plotnik and Kouyoumdjian 2010, and Kalat 2010. Watson's article "Psychology as the behaviorist views it" is a classic behaviorist manifesto (Watson 1913). It can be found in the online resources. Tolman's article "Cognitive maps in rats and men" (1948) gives an accessible introduction to many of his experiments and is also in the online resources. Gallistel 1990 is a very detailed and sophisticated presentation of a computational approach to animal learning.

Turing's paper on undecidable propositions (Turing 1936) will defeat all but graduate students in mathematical logic. His paper "Computing machinery and intelligence" (Turing 1950) is a much more accessible introduction to his thoughts about computers. There are several versions online, the best of which are included in the online resources. Martin Davis has written two popular books on the early history of computers, *Engines of Logic: Mathematicians and the Origin of the Computer* (Davis 2001) and *The Universal Computer: The Road from Leibniz to Turing* (Davis 2000). Copeland 1993 gives a more technical, but still accessible, account of Turing Machines and the Church–Turing thesis. A good article illustrating the algorithmic nature of information processing is Schyns, Gosselin, and Smith 2008.

At more or less the same time as Turing was working on the mathematical theory of computation, the neurophysiologist Warren McCulloch and logician Walter Pitts were collaborating on applying rather similar ideas about computation directly to the brain. Their paper "A logical calculus of the ideas immanent in nervous activity" (McCulloch and Pitts 1943) was influential at the time, particularly in the early development of digital computers, but is rarely read now. It is reprinted in Cummins and Cummins 2000. An accessible survey of their basic ideas can be found in Anderson 2003. See also ch. 2 of Arbib 1987 and Piccinini 2004, as well as Schlatter and Aizawa 2008.

Most people find Chomsky's *Syntactic Structures* pretty hard going. Linguistics tends to be technical, but Chomsky's article "Linguistics and Philosophy," reprinted in Cummins and Cummins 2000, contains a fairly informal introduction to the basic distinction between surface structure and deep structure. Ch. 2 of Newmeyer 1986 is a good and accessible introduction to the Chomskyan revolution. More details can be found in standard textbooks, such as Cook and Newson 2007, Isac and Reiss 2013, and O'Grady, Archibald, Aronoff, and Rees-Miller 2010. Chomsky's rather harsh review of B. F. Skinner's book *Verbal Behavior* (Chomsky 1959) is often described as instrumental in the demise of radical behaviorism – and hence in bringing about the so-called "cognitive revolution." The review is reprinted in many places and can be found in the online resources.

Miller's (1956) article is widely available and is included in the online resources. Broadbent's model of selective attention was the first in a long line of models. These are reviewed in standard textbooks. See, for example, ch. 5 of Gleitman, Fridlund, and Reisberg 2010. Christopher Mole's chapter on attention in Margolis, Samuels, and Stich 2012 summarizes Broadbent's influence as well as recent departures from Broadbent. The cocktail party phenomenon was first introduced in Cherry 1953. A concise summary of the cocktail party phenomenon can be found in McDermott 2009.

CHAPTER TWO

The discipline matures: Three milestones

Overview

Chapter 1 explored some of the very different theoretical developments that ultimately gave rise to what is now known as cognitive science. Already some of the basic principles of cognitive science have begun to emerge, such as the idea that cognition is to be understood as information processing and that information processing can be understood as an algorithmic process. Another prominent theme is the methodology of trying to understand how particular cognitive systems work by breaking down the cognitive tasks that they perform into more specific and determinate tasks. In this second chapter of our short and selective historical survey we will look closely at three milestones in the development of cognitive science. Each section explores a very different topic. In each of them, however, we start to see some of the theoretical ideas canvassed in the previous section being combined and applied to understanding specific cognitive systems and cognitive abilities.

In section 2.1 we look at a powerful and influential computer model of what it is to understand a natural language. Terry Winograd's computer model SHRDLU illustrates how grammatical rules might be represented in a cognitive system and integrated with other types of information about the environment. SHRDLU's programming is built around specific procedures that carry out fairly specialized information-processing tasks in an algorithmic (or at least quasi-algorithmic way).

The idea that the digital computer is the most promising model for understanding the mind was at the forefront of cognitive science in the 1960s and 1970s. But even in the 1970s it was under pressure. Section 2.2 looks at the debate on the nature of mental imagery provoked by some very influential experiments in cognitive psychology. These experiments seemed to many theorists to show that some types of cognitive information processing involve forms of representation very different from how information is represented in, and manipulated by, a digital computer. One of the results of the so-called imagery debate was that the question of how exactly to think about information and information processing came to the forefront in cognitive science.

The third section introduces what many cognitive scientists still consider to be cognitive science's greatest single achievement – the theory of early visual processing developed by David Marr. Marr's theory of vision was highly interdisciplinary, drawing on mathematics, cognitive psychology, neuroscience, and the clinical study of brain-damaged patients and it was built on a hierarchy of different levels for studying cognition that is often taken to define the method of cognitive science.

2.1   Language and micro-worlds

The human ability to speak and understand natural language is one of our most sophisticated cognitive achievements. We share many types of cognitive ability with non-linguistic animals. Many cognitive scientists assume, for example, that there are significant continuities between human perceptual systems and those of the higher primates (such as chimpanzees and macaque monkeys), which is why much of what we know about the neural structure of the human perceptual system is actually derived from experiments on monkeys. (See Chapter 11 for more details.) And there is powerful evidence that prelinguistic infants are capable of representing and reasoning about their physical and social environment in comparatively sophisticated ways. (See Chapter 9 for more details.)

Nonetheless, just as in human development (*ontogeny*) there is a cognitive explosion that runs more or less in parallel with the acquisition of language, much of what distinguishes humans from other animals is intimately bound up with our linguistic abilities. Language is far more than a tool for communication. It is a tool for thinking. Without language there would be no science and no mathematics. Language allows us to engage in incredibly sophisticated types of coordinated behavior. It underpins our political and social structures. In fact, it would not be much of an exaggeration to say that *Homo linguisticus* would be a better name than *Homo sapiens*.

Unsurprisingly, then, the study of natural language has always been at the center of cognitive science. If cognitive scientists want to understand the human mind then they have to confront the fundamental challenge posed by our understanding of natural language. As we saw in the last chapter, Chomsky's diagnosis of what he saw as the insuperable challenges facing a behaviorist account of language was very important in setting the stage for the cognitive revolution. So too was the discovery, also due to Chomsky, of ways of describing the underlying structures that lie beneath the patterns of surface grammar. But Chomsky's transformational linguistics had relatively little to say about the mechanics of how linguistic understanding actually takes place. It is one thing to describe the abstract structure of human language and quite another to explain how human beings can master that abstract structure. What Chomsky's work tells us (if it is indeed the correct way to think about the deep structure of language) is what we know when we understand a language. It tells us what we have to know. But it has nothing to say about how that knowledge is stored or how it is used.

Natural language processing: Winograd, *Understanding Natural Language* (1972)

The first study that we examine in this chapter confronts this challenge head on. One way of trying to model how we store and use linguistic knowledge is to build a machine that is capable of some form of linguistic understanding. The early days of *artificial intelligence* (AI) saw a number of attempts to write computer programs that could engage in some very elementary forms of conversational exchanges, but none of these programs was capable of anything that really resembled linguistic understanding.

The aim of programs such as ELIZA (written by Joseph Weizenbaum in 1966) was to simulate human conversation. The basic idea behind ELIZA (which, depending upon who one asks, was either based upon or intended to parody typical conversational exchanges between psychotherapists and their patients) was to create the illusion of conversation by rephrasing statements as questions and by programming the computer to give certain fixed responses where this is not possible. A sample "conversation" is given in Box 2.1.

Although ELIZA is said to have fooled a number of people into thinking that it was a human (including the unknowing participant in the conversation recorded in the box) nobody has ever suggested that it displays anything like a genuine understanding of language. For one thing, ELIZA does not in any sense analyze the syntactic structure or the meaning of the sentences that it encounters. It is simply programmed to respond to certain cues by making one of a small set of responses. Nor could ELIZA use the conversations in which it engaged to report on or navigate its environment. So-called *chatterbot* programs such as ELIZA are interesting for many reasons, but not as serious models of how we understand and use language.

Exercise 2.1 Explain in your own words what you think we can learn from programs such as ELIZA. Is it important that a person might be fooled by ELIZA into thinking that we were communicating with another human being?

Terry Winograd's program SHRDLU, initially presented in his 1970 doctoral dissertation at MIT, was one of the first attempts to write a program that was not just trying to simulate conversation, but that was capable of using language to report on its environment, to plan actions, and to reason about the implications of what is being said to it.

BOX 2.1   A conversation with ELIZA (ELIZA's responses are in upper case)

Men are all alike
IN WHAT WAY?

They are always bugging us about something or other
CAN YOU THINK OF A SPECIFIC EXAMPLE?

Well, my boyfriend made me come here
YOUR BOYFRIEND MADE YOU COME HERE

He says I'm depressed much of the time
I'M SORRY TO HEAR THAT YOU ARE DEPRESSED

It's true. I am unhappy
DO YOU THINK COMING HERE WILL HELP YOU NOT TO BE UNHAPPY?

I need some help. That much seems certain
WHAT WOULD IT MEAN TO YOU IF YOU GOT SOME HELP?

Perhaps I could learn to get along with my mother
TELL ME MORE ABOUT YOUR FAMILY

(From Boden 1977: 106–7)

One of the distinctive features of SHRDLU is that it is programmed to deal with a very limited *micro-world* (as opposed to being a general-purpose language program, which is what ELIZA and other chatterbot programs are, in their very limited ways). The SHRDLU micro-world is very simple. It consists simply of a number of colored blocks, colored pyramids, and a box, all located on a tabletop, as illustrated in Figure 2.1. (The micro-world is a virtual micro-world, it should be emphasized. Everything takes place on a computer screen.)

SHRDLU is capable of various actions in the micro-world, which it can carry out through a (virtual) robot arm. It can pick up the blocks and pyramids, move them around, and put them in the box. Corresponding to the simplicity of the micro-world, SHRDLU's language is relatively simple. It only has the tools to talk about what is going on in the micro-world.

There are three principal reasons why SHRDLU was very important in the development of cognitive science. The first is that it gave a powerful illustration of how abstract rules and principles such as those in the sort of grammar that we might find in theoretical linguistics could be practically implemented. If we assume that a speaker's understanding of language is best understood as a body of knowledge, then SHRDLU provided a model of how that knowledge could be *represented* by a cognitive system and how it could be *integrated* with other, more general, forms of knowledge about the environment.

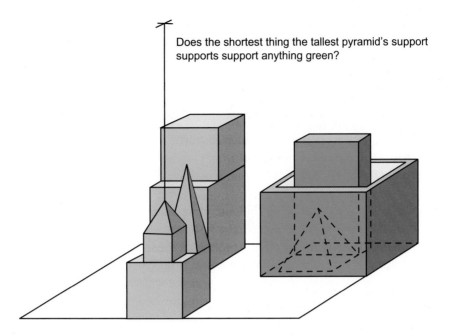

Figure 2.1 A question for SHRDLU about its virtual micro-world. (Adapted from Winograd 1972)

The second reason for highlighting SHRDLU is that it illustrated the general approach of trying to understand and model cognitive systems by breaking them down into distinct components, each of which carries out a specific information-processing task. One of the many interesting things about SHRDLU is that these distinct components are not completely self-contained. The separate processing systems collaborate in solving information-processing problems. There is *cross-talk* between them, because the programs for each processing system allow it to consult other processing systems at particular moments in the computation.

A final significant feature of the SHRDLU program is that it is based on the fundamental assumption that understanding language is an *algorithmic* process. In Winograd's own words, "All language use can be thought of as a way of activating procedures within the hearer" (1973: 104). As we will see, each component system is essentially made up of a vast number of procedures that work algorithmically to solve very specific problems. The system as a whole works because of how these procedures are linked up and embedded within each other.

SHRDLU in action

As is often the case in so-called *classical cognitive science*, the best way to understand what is going on in SHRDLU is to work from the top down – to start by looking at the general overall structure and then drill down into the details. Strictly speaking, SHRDLU consists of twelve different systems. Winograd himself divides these into three groups. Each group carries out a specific job. The particular jobs that Winograd identifies are not particularly surprising. They are exactly the jobs that one would expect any language-processing system to carry out.

1   *The job of syntactic analysis:* SHRDLU needs to be able to "decode" the grammatical structure of the sentences that it encounters. It needs to be able to identify which units in the sentence are performing which linguistic function. In order to *parse* any sentence, a language user needs to work out which linguistic units are functioning as nouns (i.e. are picking out objects) and which are functioning as verbs (i.e. characterizing events and processes).

2   *The job of semantic analysis:* Understanding a sentence involves much more than decoding its syntactic structure. The system also needs to assign meanings to the individual words in a way that reveals what the sentence is stating (if it is a statement), or requesting (if it is a request). This takes us from *syntax* to *semantics.*

3   *The job of integrating the information acquired with the information the system already possesses:* The system has to be able to explore the implications of what it has just learnt for the information it already has. Or to call upon information it already has in order to obey some command, fulfill a request, or answer a question. These all require ways of deducing and comparing the logical consequences of stored and newly acquired information.

We can identify distinct components for each of these jobs – the *syntactic system,* the *semantic system,* and the *cognitive-deductive system.* As mentioned earlier, Winograd does not see these as operating in strict sequence. It is not the case that the syntactic system does its job producing a syntactic analysis, and then hands that syntactic analysis over to the semantic system, which plugs meanings into the abstract syntactic structure, before passing the result on to the cognitive-deductive system. In SHRDLU all three systems operate concurrently and are able to call upon each other at specific points. What makes this possible is that, although all three systems store and deploy different forms of knowledge, these different forms of knowledge are all represented in a similar way. They are all represented in terms of *procedures.*

The best way to understand what procedures are is to look at some examples. Let us start with the syntactic system, since this drives the whole process of language under-standing. (We cannot even get started on thinking about what words might mean until we know what syntactic jobs those words are doing – even if we have to make some hypotheses about what words mean in order to complete the process of syntactic analysis.) One very fundamental "decision" that the syntactic system has to make is whether its input is a sentence or not. Let us assume that we are dealing with a very simple language that only contains words in the following syntactic categories: Noun (e.g. "block" or "table"), Intransitive Verb (e.g. "___ is standing up"), Transitive Verb (e.g. "___ is supporting ___"), Determiner (e.g. "the" or "a").

Figure 2.2 presents a simple procedure for answering this question. Basically, what the SENTENCE program does is exploit the fact that every grammatical sentence must

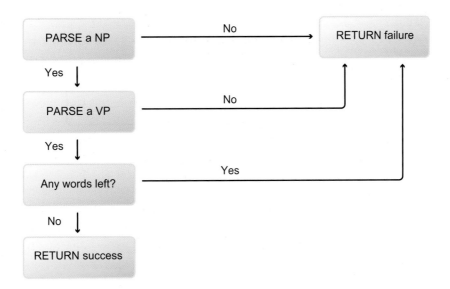

Figure 2.2 An algorithm for determining whether a given input is a sentence or not. (Adapted from Winograd 1972)

contain a noun phrase (NP) and a verb phrase (VP). It tests for the presence of a NP; tests for the presence of a VP; and then checks that there is no extra "junk" in the sentence.

Of course, in order to apply this procedure the syntactic system needs procedures for testing for the presence of noun phrases and verb phrases. This can be done in much the same way – by checking in an algorithmic manner whether the relevant syntactic units are present. Figure 2.3 gives two procedures that will work in our simple language.

Moving to the job of semantic analysis, SHRDLU represents the meanings of words by means of comparable procedures. Instead of procedures for picking out syntactic categories, these procedures involve information about the micro-world and actions that the system can perform in the micro-world. One of the words in SHRDLU's vocabulary is CLEARTOP. We can say that something (say, a block) is CLEARTOP when it does not have anything on it. CLEARTOP can also function as a command (as the command to remove anything resting on the block). CLEARTOP is represented in SHRDLU by the very simple procedure presented in Figure 2.4. This definition of CLEARTOP exploits other "concepts," such as SUPPORT and GET RID OF. Each of these other concepts has its own procedure, which may well call upon the CLEARTOP procedure.

In order to see how these procedures work to allow SHRDLU to follow instructions in the micro-world and answer questions about it we can look at the first few exchanges in a sample dialog described by Winograd in his 1973 paper. SHRDLU's contributions are in capital letters, while the sentences in italics were typed by a person. The commentary in normal type is by Winograd.

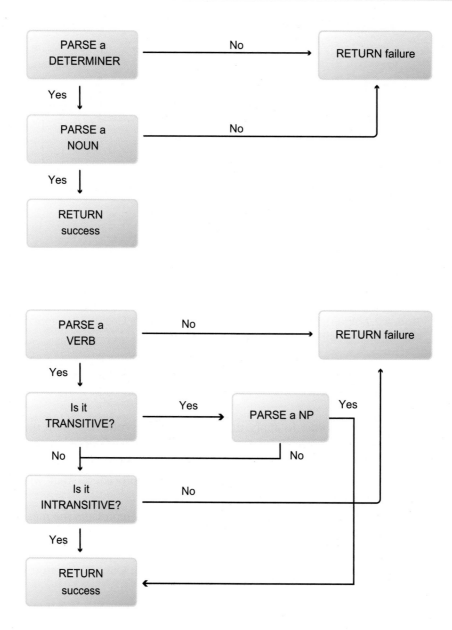

Figure 2.3 Algorithms for identifying noun phrases and verb phrases. (Adapted from Winograd 1973)

1. *Pick up a big, red block.*
OK

The system answers "OK" when it carries out a command. In order to pick up the red block, it had to clear it off by finding a space for the green one and moving it away. The result is shown in Figure 2.5.

To cleartop X

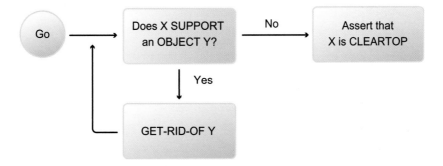

Figure 2.4 Procedure for applying the concept CLEARTOP. (Adapted from Winograd 1972)

2. *Grasp the pyramid.*
I DON'T UNDERSTAND WHICH PYRAMID YOU MEAN.

There are three pyramids in the scene and the program knows that phrases beginning with "the" are intended to refer to a specific object the speaker has in mind. So SHRDLU does nothing.

3. *Find a block which is taller than the one you are holding and put it in the box.*
The situation is depicted in Figure 2.5. The system has to figure out what is meant by "one" and "it," as well as use deduction to decide which block it is holding.
BY "IT" I ASSUME YOU MEAN THE BLOCK WHICH IS TALLER THAN THE ONE I AM HOLDING

There were two possible referents for "*it*": the one selected, and "*the one you are holding,*"
OK

The hand has to set down the red block to pick up the taller blue one. We are now at Figure 2.6.

4. *What does the box contain?*
THE BLUE PYRAMID AND THE BLUE BLOCK

5. *What is the pyramid supported by?*
THE BOX

Earlier the system responded to "*the pyramid*" by saying "I DON'T UNDERSTAND WHICH PYRAMID YOU MEAN." Now SHRDLU has identified the pyramid that was meant – the pyramid just mentioned in the response to the previous question.

Certainly, SHRDLU has its limitations. No one (certainly not Winograd) has ever claimed that it provides an accurate model of human language use – or even of a small segment of

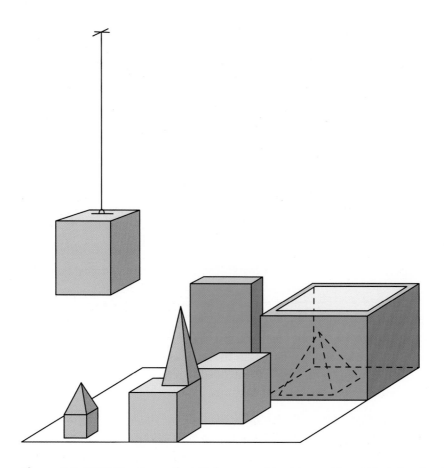

Figure 2.5 SHRDLU acting on the initial command to pick up a big red block. See the dialog in the text for what led up to this. (Adapted from Winograd 1972: 8)

human language use. As Winograd himself was quick to acknowledge, SHRDLU does not really do justice to how conversations actually work in real life. Conversations are social interactions, not simply sequences of unconnected questions and answers. They involve agents trying to make sense of the world and of each other simultaneously.

Every level of linguistic understanding involves assumptions and guesses about what the other partner in the conversation is trying to communicate. It also involves assumptions and guesses about what they are trying to achieve. These are not always the same. In making and assessing those assumptions and guesses we use all sorts of heuristics and principles. We tend to assume, for example, that people generally tell the truth; that they don't say things that are pointless and uninformative; and that what they say reflects what they are doing more generally. This is all part of what linguists call the *pragmatics* of conversation. But there is nothing in SHRDLU's programming that even attempts to do justice to pragmatics.

But to criticize SHRDLU for neglecting pragmatics, or for steering clear of complex linguistic constructions such as counterfactuals (statements about what *would* have

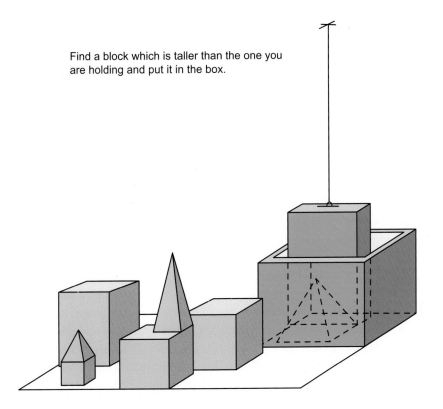

Find a block which is taller than the one you are holding and put it in the box.

Figure 2.6 Instruction 3 in the SHRDLU dialog: "Find a block which is taller than the one you are holding and put it in the box." (Adapted from Winograd 1972: fig. 3)

happened, had things been different) is to miss what is genuinely pathbreaking about it. SHRDLU illustrates a view of linguistic understanding as resulting from the interaction of many, independently specifiable cognitive processes. Each cognitive process does a particular job - the job of identifying noun phrases, for example. We make sense of the complex process of understanding a sentence by seeing how it is performed by the interaction of many simpler processes (or procedures). These cognitive processes are themselves understood algorithmically (although this is not something that Winograd himself stresses). They involve processing inputs according to rules. Winograd's procedures are sets of instructions that can be followed mechanically, just as in the classical model of computation (see section 1.2 above).

2.2 How do mental images represent?

One way to try to understand a complex cognitive ability is to try to build a machine that has that ability (or at least some primitive form of it). The program that the machine runs is a model of the ability. Often the ability being modeled is a very primitive and simplified form of the ability that we are trying to understand. This is the case with

SHRDLU, which was intended to model only a very basic form of linguistic understanding. But even in cases like that, we can still learn much about the basic principles of cognitive information processing by looking to see how well the model works. This is why the history of cognitive science has been closely bound up with the history of artificial intelligence.

We can think of artificial intelligence, or at least some parts of it, as a form of experimentation. Particular ideas about how the mind works are written into programs and then we "test" those ideas by seeing how well the programs work. But artificial intelligence is not the only way of developing and testing hypotheses open to cognitive scientists. Cognitive scientists have also learnt much from the much more direct forms of experiment carried out by cognitive psychologists. As we saw in the previous chapter, the emergence of cognitive psychology as a serious alternative to behaviorism in psychology was one of the key elements in the emergence of cognitive science. A good example of how cognitive psychology can serve both as an inspiration and as a tool for cognitive science came with what has come to be known as the imagery debate.

The imagery debate began in the early 1970s, inspired by a thought-provoking set of experiments on mental rotation carried out by the psychologist Roger Shepard in collaboration with Jacqueline Metzler, Lynn Cooper, and other scientists. This was one of the first occasions when cognitive scientists got seriously to grips with the nature and format of mental representation – a theme that has dominated cognitive science ever since. The initial experiments (and many of the follow-up experiments) are rightly recognized as classics of cognitive psychology. From the perspective of cognitive science, however, what is most interesting about them is the theorizing to which they gave rise about the format in which information is stored and the way in which it is processed.

Mental rotation: Shepard and Metzler, "Mental rotation of three-dimensional objects" (1971)

The original mental rotation experiments are easy to describe. Subjects were presented with drawings of pairs of three-dimensional figures. Figure 2.7 contains examples of these pairs.

Each figure is asymmetric and resembles its partner. In two cases the figures resemble each other because they are in fact the same figure at different degrees of rotation. In a third case the figures are different. The subjects were asked to identify as quickly as possible pairs of drawings where the second figure is the same as the first, but rotated to a different angle. (You can do this experiment for yourself. Several versions of the Shepard–Metzler paradigm can be carried out online. See the Further Reading for an example. Putting "mental rotation" into a search engine will find others.)

Exercise 2.2 Which pair is the odd one out? In the pair with two distinct figures, how are those figures related to each other?

Shepard and Metzler found that there is a direct, linear relationship between the length of time that subjects took to solve the problem and the degree of rotation

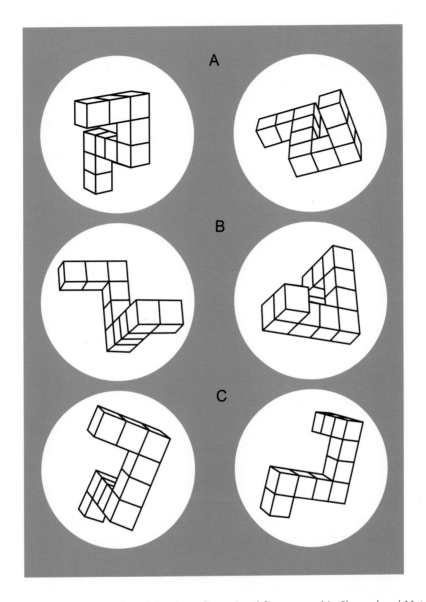

Figure 2.7 Examples of the three-dimensional figures used in Shepard and Metzler's 1971 studies of mental rotation. Subjects were asked to identify which pairs depicted the same figure at different degrees of rotation. (Adapted from Shepard and Metzler 1971)

between the two figures (see Figure 2.8). The larger the angle of rotation (i.e. the further the figures were from each other in rotational terms), the longer subjects took correctly to work out that the two drawings depicted the same figure. And the length of time increased in direct proportion to the degree of rotation. These findings have proved very robust. Comparable effects have been found in many follow-up experiments. Much more controversial is how to interpret what is going on.

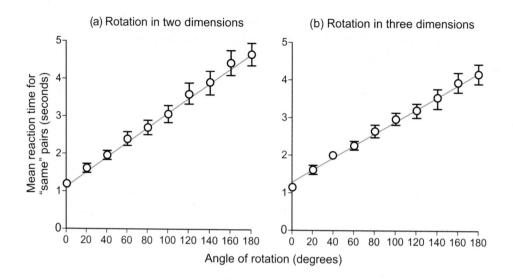

Figure 2.8 Results of Shepard and Metzler's 1971 studies of mental rotation. (a) depicts the mean reaction time for shape rotation in two dimensions. (b) depicts the mean reaction time for shape rotation in three dimensions.

The subjects in the original experiment were not asked to solve the problem in any particular way. They were simply asked to pull one lever if the two pictures represented the same figure, and another lever if the pictures represented different figures. The explanation that comes quickest to mind, though, is that the subjects solved the problem by mentally rotating one figure to see whether or not it could be mapped onto the other. This would certainly provide a neat explanation of the findings. And this is indeed how Shepard, Metzler, and many others did interpret them (not least because that is what many of the subjects described themselves as doing). This interpretation of the experiments raises some fundamental questions about the format in which information is encoded and manipulated in tasks of this type.

Exercise 2.3 Present in your own words Shepard and Metzler's conclusion. Explain their reasoning. What sort of assumptions does it rest on?

Suppose that we take the subject's report of what they are doing in the experiments at face value. Suppose, that is, that we think of the subjects as rotating mental images in their "mind's eye." It seems on the face of it that this is really just an application of a skill that we use all the time - the skill of transforming mental images in order to calculate, for example, whether one's car will fit into a tight parking space, or where a tennis ball will land. The question is not really whether we have such skills and abilities, but rather what makes them possible. And this is really a question about how the brain processes information.

The rotation in my "mind's eye" does not explain how I solve the problem. It is itself something that needs to be explained. What is the cognitive machinery that makes it possible for me to do what I might describe to someone else as rotating the mental image of a shape? Most cognitive scientists think that our conscious experience of rotating a mental image is the result of unconscious information processing. Information about the shape is derived from perception and then transformed in various ways that enable the subject to determine whether the two drawings are indeed drawings of the same shape. But the question is: How is that information represented and how is it transformed?

Information processing in mental imagery

The standard way of thinking about the mind as an information processor takes the digital computer as a model. (This was almost unchallenged in the early 1970s, and remains a popular view now, although we now have a much clearer sense of some alternative ways of thinking about information processing.) Digital computers store and manipulate information in a fixed format. Essentially, all forms of information in a digital computer are represented using the binary numerals 0 and 1. Each binary digit carries a single unit of information (a *bit*). Within the computer these units of information are grouped into words – a *byte*, for example, is an 8-bit word that can carry 256 units of information. This way of carrying information in discrete quantities is often called digital information storage. One feature of digitally encoded information is that the length of time it takes to process a piece of information is typically a function only of the quantity of information (the number of bits that are required to encode it). The particular information that is encoded ought not to matter. But what the mental rotation experiments have been taken by many to show is that there are information processing tasks that take varying amounts of time even though the quantity of information remains the same.

Exercise 2.4 Why does a byte carry 256 units of information?

In order to get an intuitive picture of what is going on here and why it might seem puzzling, look again at the experimental drawings in Figure 2.7 and think about how each of them might be digitally encoded. Suppose that we think of each drawing as divided into many small boxes (rather like pixels on a television screen or computer monitor). Since the drawings are in black and white we can convey a lot of information about the drawing by stating, for each pixel, whether it is black or white. But this will not give us a full characterization, since the figures are represented three-dimensionally. This means that our characterization of each pixel that represents part of a surface will have to include a value for the surface's degree of orientation, degree of brightness, and so on.

Now, suppose that this has been done and that we have a pixel-by-pixel description of each drawing. This will be a collection of pixel descriptions. Each pixel description is simply a set of numbers that specifies the values on the relevant dimensions at the particular pixel locations. The overall pixel-by-pixel description of each drawing puts all those individual descriptions into an ordering that will allow it to be mathematically manipulated. One way of doing this would be to assign a set of coordinates to each pixel. In any event, the point is that each drawing can be represented by a set of numbers.

The information-processing task that the experiment requires is essentially to compare two such numerical descriptions to see if one can be mapped onto the other. Solving this problem is a tricky piece of mathematics that we fortunately do not have to go into, but there is no obvious reason why it should take longer to solve the problem for pairs of figures that are at greater degrees of rotation from each other than for pairs that are at smaller degrees from each other – and certainly no reason why there should be a linear relationship between reaction time and degree of rotation.

For reasons such as these, then, it has been suggested that cognitive tasks like those investigated by the mental rotation experiments involve ways of encoding information very differently from how information is encoded in a digital computer. We will be looking in more detail at different ways of thinking about information in the chapters in Part III. For the moment we can present the distinction with relatively broad strokes of the brush. One distinctive feature of how information is represented in digital computers (what is often called digital representation) is that the connection between what we might think of as the unit of representation and what that unit represents is completely arbitrary.

There is no reason, for example, why we should use the symbol "0" to represent a black pixel and the symbol "1" to represent a white pixel, rather than the other way around. The symbol "0" represents a black pixel because that is how the computer has been set up. (As we'll see later, it's no easy matter to explain just how computers are set up to represent things, but we can gloss over this for the moment.)

Contrast this with how, for example, a map represents a geographical region. Here there is a large-scale resemblance between the principal geographical features of the region and the discernible features of the map – if there is no such resemblance then the map will not be much use. The weaving and winding of a river is matched by the weaving and winding of the line on the map that represents the river. The outlines of a region of forestry are matched by the edges of the green patch on the map. Undulations in the terrain can be mapped onto the contour lines. And so on. A map is an excellent example of what we might think of as an imagistic representation. The basic characteristic of an imagistic representation is that representation is secured through resemblance.

Exercise 2.5 Can you think of other differences between digital representation and imagistic representation?

One popular interpretation of the mental rotation experiments is as showing that at least some types of information are represented imagistically at the level of subconscious information processing. It is not just that we have the experience of consciously rotating figures in our mind's eye. The shapes are also represented imagistically in the subconscious information processing that makes possible these types of conscious experience. The point of this interpretation is that certain operations can be carried

Figure 2.9 Examples of vertically and horizontally oriented objects that subjects were asked to visualize in Kosslyn's 1973 scanning study. (Adapted from Kosslyn, Thompson, and Ganis 2006)

out on imagistically represented information that cannot be carried out on digitally represented information. So, for example, it is relatively straightforward to think of rotating an imagistic representation, but as we saw earlier, difficult to think of rotating a digital representation. This gives us one way of explaining what is going on in the mental rotation experiments.

The idea that the information processing in mental imagery involves operations on imagistic representations also makes sense of many of the other effects identified in the experimental literature provoked by the imagery debate. So, for example, in a famous experiment carried out by Stephen Kosslyn in 1973 subjects were asked to memorize a set of drawings like those illustrated in Figure 2.9.

Kosslyn then gave them the name of one of the objects (e.g. "aeroplane") and asked them to focus on one end of the memorized drawing. The experiment consisted of giving the subjects the names of possible parts of the object (e.g. "propeller") and asking them to examine their images to see whether the object drawn did indeed have the relevant part (which it did on 50 percent of the trials). The subjects pushed a button only if they did indeed see the named part in their image of the drawn object.

Kosslyn found an effect rather similar to that in the mental rotation studies - namely, that the length of time it took the subjects to answer varied according to the distance of the parts from the point of focus. If the subjects were asked to focus on the tail of the plane, it would take longer for them to confirm that the plane had a propeller than that there was not a pilot in the cockpit. Kosslyn's interpretation of his own experiment was that the type of information processing involved in answering the test questions involves scanning imagistic representations. Instead of searching for the answer within a digitally encoded database of information about the figures, the subjects scan an imagistically encoded mental image of the aeroplane.

Exercise 2.6 Can you think of a way of explaining the results of Kosslyn's experiments without the hypothesis of imagistically encoded information?

The lengthy theoretical and practical debate that began with the mental rotation and scanning experiments goes to the heart of one of the fundamental issues in cognitive science. Almost all cognitive scientists agree that cognition is information processing. But what emerged in a particularly clear form in the imagery debate is that there are competing models of how information is stored and how it is processed. The mental rotation experiments were the first in a long line of experiments that tried to decide between these competing models. One of the great benefits of this lengthy experimental literature has been much greater clarity about how each model thinks about information and information processing – and about what exactly it is that we are trying to explain. We will return to these issues in later chapters.

2.3   An interdisciplinary model of vision

The mind can be studied at many different levels. We can study the mind from the bottom up, beginning with individual neurons and populations of neurons, or perhaps even lower down, with molecular pathways whose activities generate action potentials in individual neurons, and then trying to build up from that by a process of *reverse engineering* to higher cognitive functions (reverse engineering being the process by which one takes an object and tries to work backwards from its structure and function to its basic design principles). Or we can begin from the top down, starting out with general theories about the nature of thought and the nature of cognition and working downwards to investigate how corresponding mechanisms might be instantiated in the brain. On either approach one will proceed via distinct levels of explanation that often have separate disciplines corresponding to them. One of the fundamental problems of cognitive science (see Chapters 4 and 5 below) is working out how to combine and integrate different levels of explanation.

Levels of explanation: Marr's *Vision* (1982)

The earliest systematic approach to tackling this problem is David Marr's model of the human visual system, as developed in his 1982 book *Vision: A Computational Investigation into the Human Representation and Processing of Visual Information*. Marr's conception of how different levels of explanation connect up with each other has been deeply influential, both among practicing scientists and among theorists interested in understanding the nature of explanation in cognitive science.

Marr distinguishes three different levels for analyzing cognitive systems. The highest is the *computational level*. Here cognitive scientists analyze in very general terms the particular type of task that the system performs. The tasks of an analysis at the computational level are:

1   to translate a general description of the cognitive system into a specific account of the particular information-processing problem that the system is configured to solve, and
2   to identify the constraints that hold upon any solution to that information-processing task.

The guiding assumption here is that cognition is ultimately to be understood in terms of information processing, so that the job of individual cognitive systems is to transform one kind of information (say, the information coming into a cognitive system through its sensory systems) into another type of information (say, information about what type of objects there might be in the organism's immediate environment). A computational analysis identifies the information with which the cognitive system has to begin (the *input* to that system) and the information with which it needs to end up (the *output* from that system).

Exercise 2.7 Think of a specific cognitive system and explain what it does in information-processing terms.

The next level down is what Marr calls the *algorithmic level*. The algorithmic level tells us how the cognitive system actually solves the specific information-processing task identified at the computational level. It tells us how the input information is transformed into the output information. It does this by giving algorithms that effect that transformation. An algorithmic level explanation takes the form of specifying detailed sets of information-processing instructions that will explain how, for example, information from the sensory systems about the distribution of light in the visual field is transformed into a representation of the three-dimensional environment around the perceiver.

In contrast, the principal task at the *implementational level* is to find a physical realization for the algorithm – that is to say, to identify physical structures that will realize the representational states over which the algorithm is defined and to find mechanisms at the neural level that can properly be described as computing the algorithm in question.

Exercise 2.8 Explain in your own words the difference between algorithmic and implementational explanations.

Figure 2.10 is a table from Marr's book that explains how he sees the different levels of explanation fitting together. Marr's approach is a classic example of what is called *top-down* analysis. He starts with high-level analysis of the specific information-processing

The three levels at which any machine carrying out an information-processing task must be understood

Computational theory	Representation and algorithm	Hardware implementation
What is the goal of the computation, why is it appropriate, and what is the logic of the strategy by which it can be carried out?	*How can this computational theory be implemented? In particular, what is the representation for the input and output, and what is the algorithm for the transformation?*	*How can the representation and algorithm be realized physically?*

Figure 2.10 A table illustrating the three different levels that Marr identified for explaining information-processing systems. Each level has its own characteristic questions and problems. (From Marr 1982)

problems that the visual system confronts, as well as the constraints under which the visual system operates. At each stage of the analysis these problems become more circumscribed and more determinate. The suggestions offered at the algorithmic and implementational levels are motivated by discussions of constraint and function at the computational level – that is, by considering which features of the environment the organism needs to model and the resources it has available to it.

Applying top-down analysis to the visual system

We can get a better sense of how this general model of top-down analysis works in practice by looking at how Marr applied it in thinking about human vision. The first point to note is that Marr's model is very interdisciplinary. His thinking at the computational level about what the visual system does was strongly influenced by research into brain-damaged patients carried out by clinical neuropsychologists. In his book he explicitly refers to Elizabeth Warrington's work on patients with damage to the left and right parietal cortex – areas of the brain that when damaged tend to produce problems in perceptual recognition.

Warrington noticed that the perceptual deficits of the two classes of patient are fundamentally different. Patients with right parietal lesions are able to recognize and verbally identify familiar objects *provided that they can see them from familiar or "conventional" perspectives*. From unconventional perspectives, however, these patients would not only fail to identify familiar objects but would also vehemently deny that the shapes

Figure 2.11 The image on the left is a familiar or conventional view of a bucket. The image on the right is an unfamiliar or unconventional view of a bucket. (From Warrington and Taylor 1973)

they perceived could possibly correspond to the objects that they in fact were. Figure 2.11 provides an example of conventional and unconventional perspectives.

Patients with left parietal lesions showed a diametrically opposed pattern of behavior. Although left parietal lesions are often accompanied by language problems, patients with such lesions tend to be capable of identifying the shape of objects. One index of this is that they are as successful as normal subjects on matching tasks. They have little difficulty, for example, in matching conventional and unconventional representations of the same object.

Marr drew two conclusions about how the visual system functions from Warrington's neuropsychological observations. He concluded, first, that information about the shape of an object must be processed separately from information about what the object is for and what it is called and, second, that the visual system can deliver a specification of the shape of an object even when that object is not in any sense recognized. Here is Marr describing how he used these neuropsychological data to work out the basic functional task that the visual system performs.

> Elizabeth Warrington had put her finger on what was somehow the quintessential fact about human vision – that it tells us about shape and space and spatial arrangement. Here lay a way to formulate its purpose – building a description of the shapes and positions of things from images. Of course, that is by no means all that vision can do; it also tells us about the illumination and about the reflectances of the surfaces that make the shapes – their brightnesses and colors and visual textures – and about their motion. But these things seemed secondary; they could

be hung off a theory in which the main job of vision was to derive a representation of shape. (Marr 1982: 7)

So, at the computational level, the basic task of the visual system is to derive a representation of the three-dimensional shape and spatial arrangement of an object in a form that will allow that object to be recognized. Since ease of recognition is correlated with the ability to extrapolate from the particular vantage point from which an object is viewed, Marr concluded that this representation of object shape should be on an object-centered rather than an egocentric frame of reference (where an egocentric frame of reference is one centered on the viewer). This, in essence, is the theory that emerges at the computational level.

Exercise 2.9 Explain in your own words why Marr drew the conclusions he did from Elizabeth Warrington's patients.

Moving to the algorithmic level, clinical neuropsychology drops out of the picture and the emphasis shifts to the very different discipline of psychophysics – the experimental study of perceptual systems. When we move to the algorithmic level of analysis we require a far more detailed account of how the general information-processing task identified at the computational level might be carried out. Task-analysis at the computational level has identified the type of inputs and outputs with which we are concerned, together with the constraints under which the system is operating. What we are looking for now is an algorithm that can take the system from inputs of the appropriate type to outputs of the appropriate type. This raises a range of new questions. How exactly is the input and output information encoded? What are the system's *representational primitives* (the basic "units" over which computations are defined)? What sort of operations is the system performing on those representational primitives to carry out the information-processing task?

A crucial part of the function of vision is to recover information about surfaces in the field of view – in particular, information about their orientation; how far they are from the perceiver; and how they reflect light. In Marr's theory this information is derived from a series of increasingly complex and sophisticated representations, which he terms the *primal sketch*, the *2.5D sketch*, and the *3D sketch*.

The primal sketch makes explicit some basic types of information implicitly present in the retinal image. These include distributions of light intensity across the retinal image – areas of relative brightness or darkness, for example. The primal sketch also aims to represent the basic geometry of the field of view. Figure 2.12 gives two illustrations. Note how the primal sketch reveals basic geometrical structure – an embedded triangle in the left figure and an embedded square in the right.

The next information-processing task is to extract from the primal sketch information about the depth and orientation of visible surfaces from the viewer's perspective. The result of this information processing is the 2.5D sketch. The 2.5D sketch represents certain basic information for every point in the field of view.

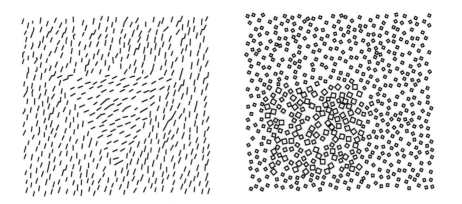

Figure 2.12 Two examples of Marr's primal sketch, the first computational stage in his analysis of the early visual system. The primal sketch contains basic elements of large-scale organization (the embedded triangle in the left-hand sketch, for example). (Adapted from Marr 1982)

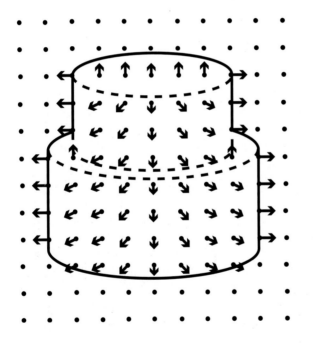

Figure 2.13 An example of part of the 2.5D sketch. The figure shows orientation information, but no depth information. (Adapted from Marr 1982)

It represents the point's distance from the observer. Figure 2.13 is an example from Marr's book.

The final information-processing stage produces the representation that Marr claims it is the job of the early visual system to produce. The 2.5D sketch is

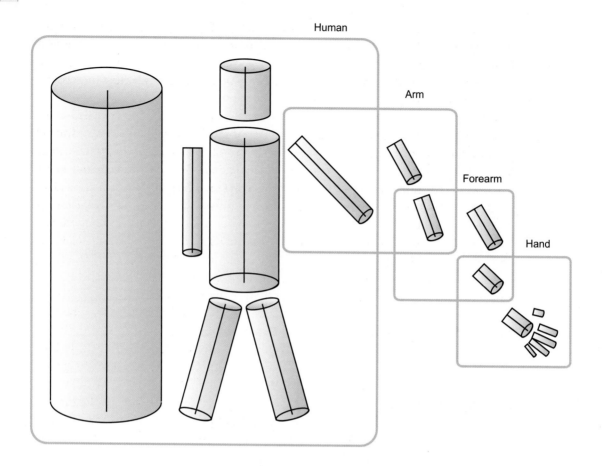

Figure 2.14 An illustration of Marr's 3D sketch, showing how the individual components are constructed. The 3D sketch gives an observer-independent representation of object shape and size. (Adapted from Marr 1982)

viewer-centered. It depends upon the viewer's particular vantage point. One of the crucial things that the visual system allows us to do, though, is to keep track of objects even though their visual appearance changes from the viewer's perspective (because either the object or the viewer is moving, for example). This requires a stable representation of object shape that is independent of the viewer's particular viewpoint. This viewer-independent representation is provided by the 3D sketch, as illustrated in Figure 2.14.

These are the three main stages of visual information processing, according to Marr. Analysis at the algorithmic level explains how this information processing takes place.

At the algorithmic level the job is to specify these different representations and how the visual system gets from one to the next, starting with the basic information arriving at the retina. Since the retina is composed of cells that are sensitive to light, this basic information is information about the intensity of the light reaching each of those cells. In thinking about how the visual system might work we need (according to Marr) to think about which properties of the retinal information might provide clues for recovering the information we want about surfaces.

What are the starting-points for the information processing that will yield as its output an accurate representation of the layout of surfaces in the distal environment? Marr's answer is that the visual system needs to start with discontinuities in light intensity, because these are a good guide to boundaries between objects and other physically relevant properties. Accordingly the representational primitives that he identifies are all closely correlated with changes in light intensity. These include *zero-crossings* (registers of sudden changes in light intensity), blobs, edges, segments, and boundaries. The algorithmic description of the visual system takes a representation formulated in terms of these representational primitives as the input, and endeavors to spell out a series of computational steps that will transform this input into the desired output, which is a representation of the three-dimensional perceived environment.

Moving down to the implementational level, a further set of disciplines come into play. In thinking about the cognitive architecture within which the various algorithms computed by the visual system are embedded we will obviously need to take into account the basic physiology of the visual system – and this in turn is something that we will need to think about at various different levels. Marr's own work on vision contains relatively little discussion of neural implementation. But the table from his book shown here as Figure 2.15 illustrates where the implementational level fits into the overall picture. Figure 2.16 is a more recent attempt at identifying the neural structures underlying the visual system.

Marr's analysis of the visual system, therefore, gives us a clear illustration not only of how a single cognitive phenomenon can be studied at different levels of explanation, but also of how the different levels of explanation can come together to provide a unified analysis. Marr's top-down approach clearly defines a hierarchy of explanation, both delineating the respective areas of competence of different disciplines and specifying ways in which those disciplines can speak to each other. It is not surprising that Marr's analysis of the visual system is frequently taken to be a paradigm of how cognitive science ought to proceed.

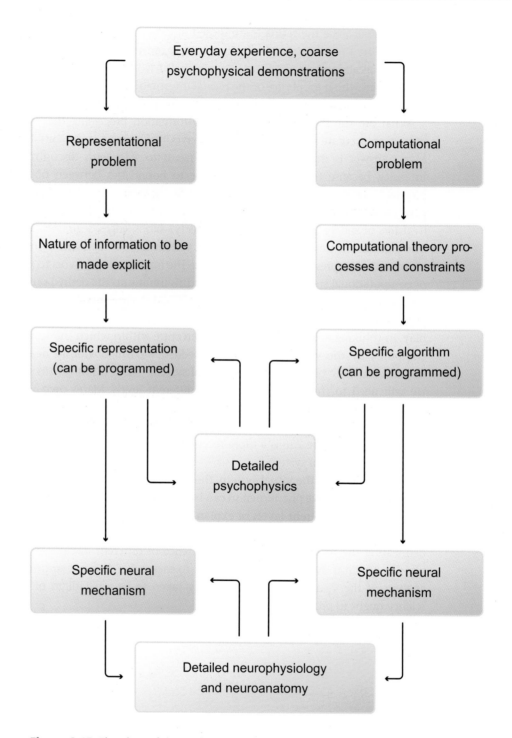

Figure 2.15 The place of the implementational level within Marr's overall theory. Note also the role he identifies for detailed experiments in psychophysics (the branch of psychology studying how perceptual systems react to different physical stimuli). (Adapted from Marr 1982)

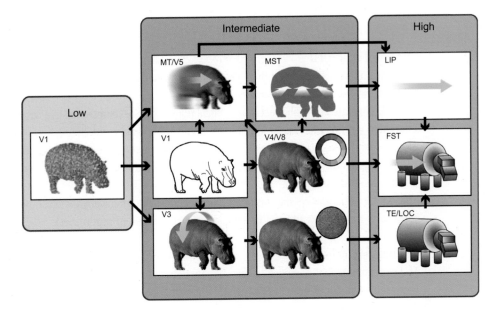

Key:

V1–V8:   areas of the visual cortex in the occipital lobe (the back of the head). V1 produces the color and edges of the hippo but no depth. V2 produces the boundaries of the hippo. V3 produces depth. V4/V8 produces color and texture.

MT: medial temporal area (often used interchangeably with V5). Responsible for representing motion.

MST: medial superior temporal area. Responsible for representing size of the hippo as it gets nearer in space.

LIP: lateral intraparietal area. Registers motion trajectories.

FST: fundus of the superior temporal sulcus. Discerns shape from motion.

TE: temporal area. Along with LOC, is responsible for shape recognition.

LOC: lateral occipital complex

Figure 2.16 An illustration of the hierarchical organization of the visual system, including which parts of the brain are likely responsible for processing different types of visual information. (From Prinz 2012)

Summary

This chapter has continued our historical overview of key steps in the emergence and evolution of cognitive science. We have reviewed three case studies: Terry Winograd's SHRDLU program for modeling natural language understanding; the explorations into the representational format of mental imagery inspired by the mental rotation experiments of Roger Shepard and others; and the multilevel analysis of the early visual system proposed by David Marr. Each of these represented a significant milestone in the emergence of cognitive science. In their very different ways they show how researchers brought together some of the basic tools discussed in Chapter 1 and applied them to try to understand specific cognitive capacities.

Checklist

Winograd's SHRDLU

(1) SHRDLU is more sophisticated than a conversation-simulating chatterbot because it uses language to report on the environment and to plan action.

(2) SHRDLU illustrated how abstract grammatical rules might be represented in a cognitive system and integrated with other types of information about the environment.

(3) The design of SHRDLU illustrates a common strategy in cognitive science, namely, analyzing a complex system by breaking it down into distinct components, each performing a circumscribed information-processing task.

(4) These information-processing tasks are implemented algorithmically (as illustrated by the flowcharts that Winograd used to explain SHRDLU's different procedures).

The imagery debate

(1) The experiments that gave rise to the imagery debate forced cognitive scientists to become much more reflective about how they understand information and information processing.

(2) The imagery debate is not a debate about conscious experiences of mental imagery. It is about the information processing underlying those conscious experiences.

(3) The mental rotation and scanning experiments were taken by many cognitive scientists to show that some information processing involves operations on geometrically encoded representations.

(4) The debate is about whether the different effects revealed by experiments on mental imagery can or cannot be explained in terms of digital information-processing models.

Marr's theory of vision

(1) Marr identified three different levels for analyzing cognitive systems.

(2) His analysis of vision is a classic example of the top-down analysis of a cognitive system. The analysis is driven by a general characterization at the computational level of the information-processing task that the system is carrying out.

(3) This general analysis at the computational level is worked out in detail at the algorithmic level, where Marr explains how the information-processing task can be algorithmically carried out.

(4) The bottom level of analysis explains how the algorithm is actually implemented. It is only at the implementational level that neurobiological considerations come directly into the picture.

Further reading

The general historical works mentioned at the end of the previous chapter also cover the material in this chapter and will provide further useful context-setting.

A web-based version of ELIZA can be found in the online resources. The principal resource for SHRDLU is Winograd's book *Understanding Natural Language* (1972). This is very detailed, however, and a more accessible treatment can be found in his article "A procedural model of language understanding" (1973), which is reprinted in Cummins and Cummins 2000. One of the important descendants of the micro-world strategy exploited in SHRDLU was research into expert systems. A helpful introduction is the entry on expert systems in the *Macmillan Encyclopedia of*

Cognitive Science (Medsker and Schulte 2003). The online *Encyclopedia of Cognitive Science* (Nadel 2005) also has an entry on SHRDLU.

Many of the most important original articles in the imagery debate are collected in Block 1981. The experiments described in the text were originally reported in Shepard and Metzler 1971, Kosslyn 1973, and Cooper and Shepard 1973. Demonstrations and further discussion of mental imagery can be found in the online resources. The imagery debate has received a good deal of attention from philosophers. Rollins 1989 and Tye 1991 are book-length studies. The *Stanford Encyclopedia of Philosophy* also has an entry on mental imagery at http://plato.stanford.edu/entries/mental-imagery/mental-rotation.html. Kosslyn, Thompson, and Ganis 2006 is a recent defense of geometric representation from one of the central figures in the debate. The best meta-analyses of mental imagery studies can be found in Voyer, Voyer, and Bryden 1995 and Zacks 2008.

Marr's book on vision (1982) has recently been reprinted (2010). Shimon Ullman's foreword in the new edition and Tomaso Poggio's afterword provide some background to Marr. Ullman discusses where the field has moved since Marr, while Poggio discusses Marr's contribution to computational neuroscience and how the field can benefit from looking back to Marr. The first chapter of Marr's book is reprinted in a number of places, including Bermúdez 2006 and Cummins and Cummins 2000. Marr's selected papers have also been published together (Vaina 1991). Dawson 1998 is a textbook on cognitive science that is structured entirely around Marr's tri-level hypothesis. Also see Tsotsos 2011. Chapter 2 of Prinz 2012 gives a general assessment of the accuracy of Marr's account, in light of current research on visual processing. Elizabeth Warrington's classic studies can be found in Warrington and Taylor 1973, 1978.

CHAPTER THREE

The turn to the brain

Overview

One of the most striking features of contemporary cognitive science, as compared with cognitive science in the 1970s for example, is the fundamental role now played by neuroscience and the study of the brain. This chapter reviews some landmarks in cognitive science's turn to the brain.

For both theoretical and practical reasons neuroscience was fairly peripheral to cognitive science until the 1980s. We begin in section 3.1 by looking at the theoretical reasons. The key idea here is the widely held view that cognitive systems are functional systems. Functional systems have to be analyzed in terms of their function – what they do and how they do it. Many cognitive scientists held (and some continue to hold) that this type of functional analysis should be carried out at a very abstract level, without going at all into the details of the physical machinery that actually performs that function.

This conception of cognitive systems goes hand in hand with a *top-down* approach to thinking about cognition. Marr's study of the visual system is a very clear example of this. For Marr, the key to understanding the early visual system is identifying the algorithms by which the visual system solves the basic information-processing task that it confronts – the task of specifying the distribution and basic characteristics of objects in the immediate environment. As we saw, these algorithms are specifiable in abstract information-processing terms that have nothing to do with the brain. The brain enters the picture only at the implementational level.

In section 3.2, in contrast, we will look at an influential study that approaches vision from a fundamentally different direction. The two visual systems hypothesis, originally proposed by the neuroscientists Leslie Ungerleider and Mortimer Mishkin, draws conclusions about the structure and organization of vision from data about the pathways in the brain that carry visual information. The direction of explanation is bottom-up, rather than top-down.

As in most branches of science, experiment and models are intimately linked in cognitive science. A very important factor in the turn towards the brain was the development of ways of modeling cognitive abilities that seem to reflect certain very general properties of brains. As sketched out in section 3.3, so-called connectionist networks, or artificial neural networks, involve large populations of neuron-like units. Although the individual units are not biologically plausible in any detailed sense, the network as a whole behaves in ways that reflect certain high-level properties of brain functioning.

Moreover, artificial neural networks behave in certain ways rather like real neural networks. Because they can be trained, they can be used to model how cognitive abilities are acquired. And, like human brains, they are not "all-or-nothing" – even when damaged they can continue to perform, albeit in a limited way (unlike digital computers, which function either optimally or not at all).

One reason for cognitive science's neglect of the brain is that until the 1980s techniques for studying human brains while cognitive tasks were actually being carried out were relatively unsophisticated and not widely known among cognitive scientists. This changed with the emergence of functional neuroimaging in the 1980s. Functional neuroimaging was seen by many as providing a powerful tool for studying what goes on in the brain when subjects are actually performing different types of cognitive task. In section 3.4 we look at an early and very influential application of positron emission tomography (PET) scanning technology to the study of visual word processing. This study shows how functional neuroimaging can be used to generate information-processing models of how cognitive tasks are carried out – information-processing models that are derived, not from abstract task analysis, but rather from detailed study of neural activity.

3.1   Cognitive systems as functional systems

Many cognitive scientists have argued that cognitive processes can be studied independently of their physical realization. Just as we can understand a piece of software without knowing anything about the machine on which it runs, so too (many people have thought) we can understand cognitive processes without knowing anything about the neural machinery that runs them. In fact, for many cognitive scientists the software/hardware analogy is more than an analogy. It is often taken literally and the mind is viewed as the software that runs on the hardware of the brain. What cognitive scientists are doing, on this view, is a form of *reverse engineering*. They are looking at the human organism; treating it as a highly complex piece of computing machinery; and trying to work out the software that the machine is running. Details of neurons, nerve fibers, and so on are no more relevant to this project than details of digital circuitry are relevant to the project of trying to reverse engineer a computer game.

In fact, for many cognitive scientists it is not just that cognitive processes *can* be studied independently of the neural machinery on which they run. They have to be studied that way. This is because they think of cognitive systems as *functional* systems. The important point is, as the word suggests, that functional systems are to be understood primarily in terms of their function – what they do and how they do it. And, these cognitive scientists emphasize, this type of analysis can be given without going into details about the particular physical structure implementing that function.

An analogy will help. Consider a heart. What makes something a heart? The most important thing is what it does. Hearts are organs that pump blood around the body – in particular, they collect deoxygenated blood and pump it towards the lungs where it becomes reoxygenated. The actual physical structure of the heart is not particularly important. An artificial heart will do the job just as well (although not perhaps for as long) and so still counts as a heart. Crocodiles and humans have hearts with four chambers, while most reptiles have hearts with three chambers. What matters is the job the heart does, not how it does it. A grey whale's heart is no less a heart than a hummingbird's heart just because the first beats 9 times per minute while the second beats 1,200 times per minute. One way of putting this is to say that functional systems are *multiply realizable*. The heart function can be realized by multiple different physical structures.

Exercise 3.1 Give another example of a multiply realizable system.

If cognitive systems are functional systems that are multiply realizable in the way that the heart is multiply realizable, then, the argument goes, it is a mistake to concentrate on the details of how the brain works. In fact, according to cognitive scientists opposed to looking at the brain, focusing on how the brain works is likely to lead to a misleading picture of how cognition works. It might lead us to take as essential to memory, say, things that are really just contingent properties of how our brains have evolved. We would be making the same mistake as if we were to conclude that hearts have to have four chambers because the human heart does, or if we decided that Microsoft Word has to run on a 2.33 GHz Intel Core 2 Duo processor just because that is the processor in my Apple Macintosh.

Exercise 3.2 How convincing do you find this analogy between studying the mind, on the one hand, and studying hearts and computer programs, on the other?

Some of the things that we know about brains actually support this way of thinking about the mind. One of the things neuroscientists have learnt from studying the brain is that it is highly flexible (or, as neuroscientists often say, *plastic*). Specific areas of the brain and neuronal circuits can change their function, perhaps as a way of dealing with traumatic damage to one part of the brain, or perhaps simply as a result of learning and other forms of natural *rewiring*. But this is just another way of saying that certain types of mental activity are multiply realizable – they can be carried out by different neural structures. Similarly, there are many differences between human brains and the brains of non-human animals. But there are also many cognitive abilities that we share with non-human animals – perceptual abilities, for example; certain types of memory; the capacity to feel pain; and the capacity to reason in certain very basic ways. These abilities are multiply realizable. They are not tied to particular types of brain structure.

The theoretical issues in this area have been much debated by philosophers and cognitive scientists. It is fair to say, though, that in the last twenty or so years this way of thinking about cognitive science has become less dominant and the pendulum has swung towards seeing the study of the brain as an integral part of cognitive science. There are many reasons for this change. Some of them have to do with the development of new techniques and machinery for studying the brain. Cognitive scientists have also been influenced by the development of powerful tools for modeling and simulating brain processes. In this chapter we will look at three major events in cognitive science's turn towards the brain.

3.2 The anatomy of the brain and the primary visual pathway

In order to understand the significance of the two visual systems hypothesis we need a little information about the large-scale anatomy of the brain. Sketching with very broad strokes of the brush, anatomists distinguish three different parts of the mammalian brain – the *forebrain*, the *midbrain*, and the *hindbrain*. This structure is illustrated for the human brain in Figure 3.1.

As the figure shows, the forebrain is the largest of the three regions. Most of the forebrain is taken up by the *cerebrum* (see Figure 3.2), which is the main portion of the brain and the most important for cognitive and motor processing. The cerebrum is divided into two hemispheres – left and right. The outer layer of each hemisphere comprises what is known as the cerebral cortex (popularly known as "grey matter"). Moving inwards from the outer, cortical layer we find the sub-cortex (the so-called "white matter"). In the human brain the cerebral cortex is about 2–4 mm thick.

Each cerebral hemisphere is divided into four main regions, called *lobes*. Each lobe is believed to be responsible for carrying out different cognitive tasks. Figure 3.3 illustrates the organization of the left hemisphere into four lobes, while Box 3.1 summarizes what each lobe is believed to be specialized for.

There is further organization within each lobe. In 1909 the German neurologist Korbinian Brodmann proposed a mapping of the cerebral cortex into fifty-two areas. These Brodmann areas are still in use today. An example particularly relevant to us now is Brodmann area 17, which is also known as the *primary visual cortex*, the *striate cortex*, or area V1. Brodmann area 17 is located in the *occipital lobe* and (as the name "primary visual cortex" suggests) it is the point of arrival in the cortex for information from the retina.

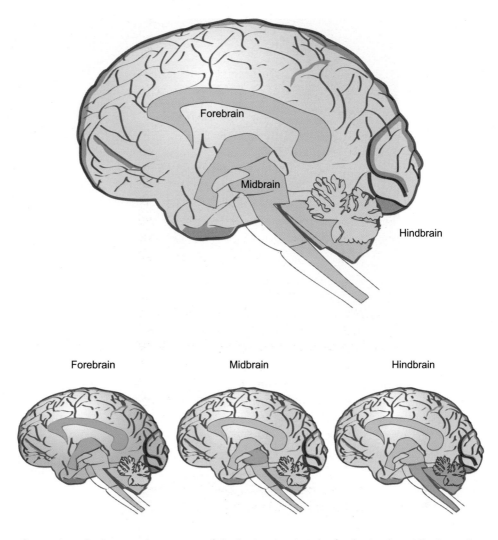

Figure 3.1 The large-scale anatomy of the brain, showing the forebrain, the midbrain, and the hindbrain.

The information pathway leading from the retina to the primary visual cortex is relatively well understood. It is clearly represented in Figure 3.4, which shows how visual information from each eye is transmitted by the optic nerve to the lateral geniculate nucleus (a sub-cortical area of the forebrain) and thence to the primary visual cortex. The diagram clearly shows the *contralateral* organization of the brain. Each hemisphere processes information deriving from the opposite side of space. So, visual information from the right half of the visual field is processed by the left hemisphere (irrespective of which eye it comes from).

Much more complicated than the question of how information from the retina gets to the primary visual cortex is the question of what happens to that information when it leaves the primary visual cortex. This is where we come to the two visual systems hypothesis and to the work of Ungerleider and Mishkin.

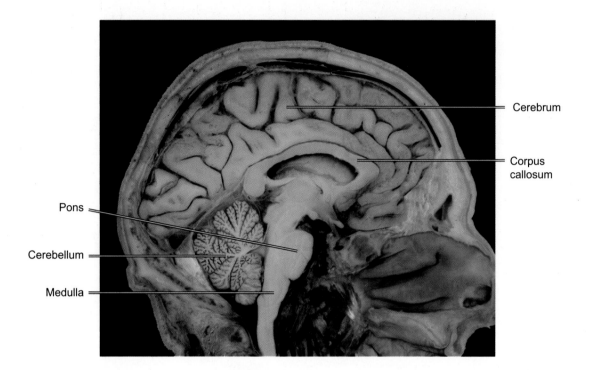

Cerebrum

Corpus callosum

Pons

Cerebellum

Medulla

Figure 3.2 A vertical slice of the human brain, showing the cerebrum.
© TISSUEPIX/SCIENCE PHOTO LIBRARY

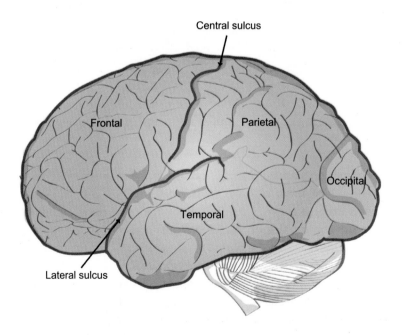

Central sulcus

Frontal

Parietal

Occipital

Temporal

Lateral sulcus

Figure 3.3 The division of the left cerebral hemisphere into lobes.

BOX 3.1   What does each lobe do?

- Frontal lobe – reasoning, planning, parts of speech, movement, emotions, and problem solving
- Parietal lobe – movement, orientation, recognition, perception of stimuli
- Occipital lobe – associated with visual processing
- Temporal lobe – associated with perception and recognition of auditory stimuli, memory, and speech

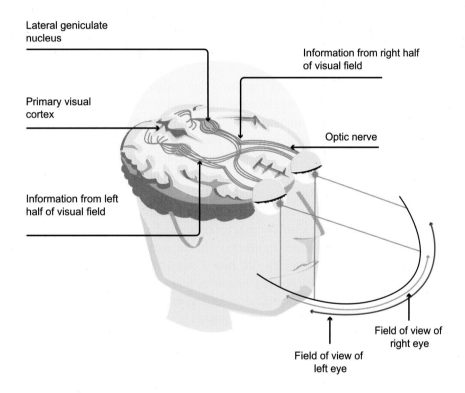

Figure 3.4 The primary visual pathway. Note the contralateral organization, with information from the right side of space processed by the left side of the brain.

The two visual systems hypothesis: Ungerleider and Mishkin, "Two cortical visual systems" (1982)

This section introduces the two visual systems hypothesis, first proposed by the neurologists Leslie Ungerleider and Mortimer Mishkin. The two visual systems hypothesis is important both because of the tools that were used to arrive at it (including the study of brain-damaged patients and experiments on monkeys) and because it illustrates a bottom-up, as opposed to top-down, way of studying the mind.

BOX 3.2 Brain vocabulary

Neuroscientists and neuroanatomists use an unusual vocabulary for talking about the layout of the brain:

Rostral = at the front
Caudal = at the back
Ventral = at the bottom
Dorsal = at the top
Ipsilateral = same side
Contralateral = opposite side

Ungerleider and Mishkin suggested that visual information does not take a single route from the primary visual cortex. Instead, the route the information takes depends upon the type of information it is. Information relevant to recognizing and identifying objects follows a *ventral route* (see Box 3.2) from the primary visual cortex to the temporal lobe, while information relevant to locating objects in space follows a *dorsal* route from the primary visual cortex to the posterior parietal lobe. The two routes are illustrated in Figure 3.5

The reasoning that led Ungerleider and Mishkin to this conclusion came both from the study of cognitive impairments due to brain damage and from neuroanatomical experiments on monkeys. The neuroanatomical experiments were their distinctive contribution. By the time Ungerleider and Mishkin were writing there was already considerable evidence from brain-damaged patients that damage to the temporal and parietal lobes produced very different types of cognitive problem. Damage to the temporal cortex is associated with problems in identifying and recognizing objects, while damage to the parietal cortex tends to result in problems locating objects.

Evidence of this type has always been very important in working out the function of the different lobes (see Box 3.1 for a standard "division of labor" between the lobes). But being able to localize specific functions in this way falls a long way short of telling us the full story about the path that information takes in the brain. For this Ungerleider and Mishkin turned to experiments on monkeys.

The particular type of experiments that they carried out are called *cross-lesion disconnection experiments*. This is a methodology explicitly designed to trace the connections between cortical areas and so to uncover the pathways along which information flows. It addresses a fundamental problem with making inferences about the function and specialization of particular brain areas from what happens when those areas are damaged. Simply finding specific cognitive problems associated with damage to a specific brain region gives us no way of telling whether the impaired cognitive abilities are normally carried out by the damaged brain region itself, or by some other brain region that

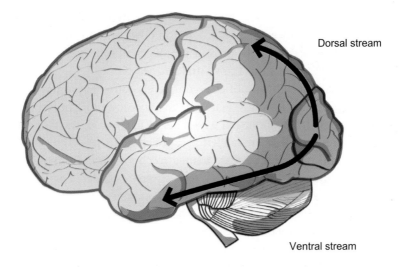

Dorsal stream

Ventral stream

Figure 3.5 Image showing ventral stream (purple) and dorsal stream (green) in the human brain visual system.

crucially depends upon input from the damaged brain region. Solving this problem cannot be done simply by observing the results of brain damage. Precise surgical intervention is required, in the form of targeted removal of specific brain areas to uncover the connections between them.

The cross-lesion disconnection experiments exploit the fact that the cerebrum is divided into two hemispheres, with duplication of the principal cortical areas. Suppose that investigators think that they have identified a cortical pathway that connects two cortical areas. They can remove the area assumed to be earlier in the pathway from one hemisphere and the area assumed to be later from the other hemisphere. Ungerleider and Mishkin, for example, working on the hypothesis that there is a pathway connecting the primary visual cortex and the inferior temporal area, performed surgery in monkeys to remove the primary visual cortex from one hemisphere in monkeys and the inferior temporal area from the other hemisphere. This destroyed the postulated pathway in each hemisphere. However, because the hemispheres can communicate through a large bundle of fibers known as the *corpus callosum* (illustrated in Figure 3.2), it turned out that there was little or no loss of function in the monkeys.

So, for example, it is well documented that monkeys who have had their inferior temporal cortex removed from both hemispheres are severely impaired on basic pattern discrimination tasks. But these pattern discrimination tasks were successfully performed by monkeys with primary visual cortex removed from one hemisphere and inferior temporal cortex from the other. Cutting the corpus callosum, however, reduced performance on those pattern discrimination tasks to chance and the monkeys were unable to relearn it. Using experiments such as these (in addition to other types of neurophysiological evidence), Ungerleider and Mishkin conjectured that information relevant to object identification and recognition flows from the primary visual cortex to the inferior temporal cortex via areas in the occipital lobe collectively known as the *prestriate cortex*. They called this the ventral pathway.

Ungerleider and Mishkin identified a completely different pathway (the *dorsal* pathway) leading from the primary visual cortex to the posterior parietal lobe. Once again they used cross-lesion disconnection experiments. In this case the task was the so-called landmark task, illustrated in the top left part of Figure 3.6

In the landmark task monkeys are trained to choose food from one of two covered foodwells, depending on its proximity to a striped cylinder. The striped cyclinder is moved at random and what the task tests is the monkey's ability to represent the spatial relation between the striped cylinder and the two foodwells.

The basic methodology of the experiments was the same as for the visual recognition pathway. The surgery proceeded in three stages. In the first stage (b in Figure 3.6) the posterior parietal cortex was removed from one side. The second stage (c) removed the primary visual cortex on the opposite side. The final stage (d) was a *transection* (severing) of the corpus callosum.

As indicated in Figure 3.6, the monkeys were tested on the landmark task both before and after each stage. However, the impairments on the landmark task were much more complicated than in the earlier experiments. The numbers in Figure 3.6 indicate the number of trials required to train the monkeys to a 90 percent success rate on the landmark task. So, for example, prior to the first stage of the surgery the average number of training trials required was 10. After lesion of the posterior parietal cortex the number of training trials went up to 130.

One interesting feature of these experiments is that the most severe impairment was caused by the second stage in the surgery, the removal of the primary visual cortex (in contrast to the other experiments on the visual recognition pathway, where severe impairments appeared only with the cutting of the corpus callosum). Ungerleider and Mishkin concluded from this that the posterior parietal cortex in a given hemisphere does not depend much upon information about the ipsilateral visual field (see Box 3.2) from the opposite hemisphere's primary visual cortex.

This raises the following intriguing possibility, since it is known that each hemisphere is specialized for the contralateral region of space. It may be that the posterior parietal cortex in each hemisphere is specialized for processing information about the opposite region of space. This would mean, for example, that the left posterior parietal cortex processes information about the layout of space on the perceiver's right-hand side. This could be particularly important for thinking about the neurological disorder of *unilateral spatial neglect*. Patients with this disorder typically "neglect" one half of the space around them, eating food from only one side of the plate and describing themselves as unaware of stimuli in the neglected half of space. Unilateral spatial neglect typically follows damage to the posterior parietal cortex in one hemisphere (most often the right) and the neglected region is contralateral to the damage (so that, most often, the left-hand side of space is neglected).

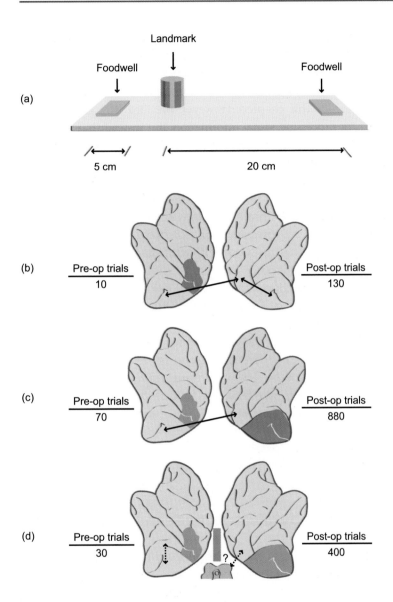

Figure 3.6 Design and results of Ungerleider and Mishkin's cross-lesion disconnection studies. (a) Landmark task. Monkeys were rewarded for choosing the covered foodwell located closer to a striped cylinder (the "landmark"), which was positioned on the left or the right randomly from trail to trail, but always 5 cm from one foodwell and 20 cm from the other. Training was given for 30 trials per day to a criterion of 90 correct responses in 100 consecutive trials. (b) Discrimination retention before and after first-stage lesion (unilateral posterior parietal; V = 3); 10 preoperative trials and 130 postoperative trials. (c) Discrimination retention before and after second-stage lesion (contralateral striate; y = 3); 70 preoperative and 880 postoperative trials. (d) Discrimination retention before and after third-stage lesion (corpus callosum; N = 3); 30 preoperative and 400 postoperative trials. At each stage the lesion is shown in dark brown and the lesions of prior stages in light brown. Arrows denote hypothetical connections left intact by lesions. (Adapted from Ungerleider and Mishkin 1982)

The visual systems hypothesis was a very important step in mapping out the *connectivity* of the brain. Ungerleider and Mishkin's basic distinction between the "what" system (served by the ventral pathway) and the "where" system (served by the dorsal pathway) has been refined and modified by many researchers (see the references in the further reading section of this chapter). However, the idea that there is no single pathway specialized for processing visual information, but instead that visual information takes different processing routes depending upon what type of information it is, has proved very enduring. From the perspective of cognitive science, the significance of the two visual systems hypothesis is that it exemplifies in a particularly clear way the bottom-up study of how information is processed in the mind.

There are recognizable affinities between what Ungerleider and Mishkin were doing, on the one hand, and the top-down approach of cognitive scientists such as Marr, on the other. So, for example, both are concerned with identifying distinct processing systems in terms of the functions that they perform. The real difference comes, however, with how they arrive at their functional analyses. For Marr, the primary driver is top-down thinking about the role of visual processing within the overall organization of cognition and the behavior of the organism. For Ungerleider and Mishkin, the primary driver is thinking that starts at what Marr would term the implementational level. Instead of abstracting away from details of the channels and pathways between neural systems along which information processing flows, Ungerleider and Mishkin started with those channels and pathways and worked upwards to identifying distinct cognitive systems carrying out distinct cognitive functions.

Exercise 3.3 Make as detailed a list as you can of similarities and differences between these two different approaches to studying the organization of the mind.

3.3 Extending computational modeling to the brain

Computational modeling is one of the principal tools that cognitive scientists have for studying the mind. One of the best ways to understand particular cognitive abilities and how they fit together is by constructing models that "fit" the data. The data can take many different forms. In the case of SHRDLU, the data are given simply by the human ability to use language as a tool for interacting with the world. In other models, such as the two visual systems hypothesis considered in the previous section, the data are experimentally derived. The two visual systems hypothesis is essentially a model of the visual system designed to fit a very complex set of neurological and neurophysiological data. Experiments on mental rotation and mental scanning provide the data for the model of mental imagery proposed by Kosslyn and others.

All of the models that we have looked at in our historical survey share certain very basic features. They all think of cognition in terms of information-processing mechanisms. Whereas Ungerleider and Mishkin were interested primarily in the neural pathways and channels along which information travels, the other models we have considered have focused primarily on the algorithms that govern information processing. Loosely speaking, these algorithms have all been driven by the computer model of the mind. They have all assumed that the processes by which information is transformed and transmitted in the brain share certain general characteristics with how information is transformed and transmitted in digital computers. And just as we can study computer algorithms without thinking about the hardware and circuitry on which they run, so too do most of these models abstract away from the details of neural machinery in thinking about the algorithms of cognition.

There are several reasons, however, why one might think that abstracting away from neural machinery in studying the algorithms of cognition may not be a good idea. One set of reasons derives from the temporal dimension of cognition. Cognitive activity needs to be coordinated with behavior and adjusted online in response to perceptual input. The control of action and responsiveness to the environment requires cognitive systems with an exquisite sense of timing. The right answer is no use if it comes at the wrong time. Suppose, for example, that we are thinking about how to model the way the visual system solves problems of predator detection. In specifying the information-processing task we need to think about the level of accuracy required. It is clear that we will be very concerned about false negatives (i.e. thinking that something is not a predator when it is), but how concerned should we be about false positives (i.e. thinking that something is a predator when it is not)?

Exercise 3.4 Can you think of a cognitive task for which it is more important to minimize false positives, rather than false negatives?

There is a difference between a model that is designed never to deliver either false positives or false negatives and one that is designed simply to avoid false negatives. But which model do we want? It is hard to see how we could decide without experimenting with different algorithms and seeing how they cope with the appropriate temporal constraints. The ideal would be a system that minimizes both false negatives and false positives, but we need to factor in the time taken by the whole operation. It may well be that the algorithm that would reliably track predators would take too long, so that we need to make do with an algorithm that merely minimizes false negatives. But how can we calculate whether it would take too long or not? We will not be able to do this without thinking about how the algorithm might be physically implemented, since the physical implementation will be the principal determiner of the overall speed of the computation.

Moreover, the mind is not a static phenomenon. Cognitive abilities and skills themselves evolve over time, developing out of more primitive abilities and giving rise to further cognitive abilities. Eventually they deteriorate and, for many of us, gradually fade out of existence. In some unfortunate cases they are drastically altered as a result of traumatic damage. This means that an account of the mind must be compatible with plausible accounts of how cognitive abilities emerge. It must be compatible with what we know about how cognitive abilities deteriorate. It must be compatible with what we know about the relation between damage to the brain and cognitive impairment.

All of these factors derive directly from the fact that minds are realized in brains. We know, for example, that cognitive abilities tend to *degrade gracefully*. Cognitive phenomena are not all-or-nothing phenomena. They exhibit gradual deterioration in performance over time. As we get older reaction times increase, motor responses slow down, and recall starts to become more problematic. But these abilities do not (except as a result of trauma or disease) disappear suddenly. The deterioration is gradual, incremental, and usually imperceptible within small time frames. This type of graceful degradation is a function of how brains are wired, and of the biochemistry of individual neurons. The same holds for how cognitive abilities emerge and develop. Brains learn the way they do because of how they are constructed – and in particular because of the patterns of connectivity existing at each level of neural organization (between neurons, populations of neurons, neural systems, neural columns, and so forth). It is plausible to expect our higher-level theories of cognitive abilities to be constrained by our understanding of the neural mechanisms of learning.

Exercise 3.5 Can you think of other reasons for thinking that we should not theorize about cognition without theorizing about the brain?

A new set of algorithms: Rumelhart, McClelland, and the PDP Research Group, *Parallel Distributed Processing: Explorations in the Microstructure of Cognition* (1986)

The very influential two-volume collection of papers published by Rumelhart, McClelland, and the PDP research group in 1986 proposed and pursued a new set of abstract mathematical tools for modeling cognitive processes. These models, sometimes called *connectionist* networks and sometimes *artificial neural networks*, abstract away from many biological details of neural functioning in the hope of capturing some of the crucial general principles governing the way the brain works. Most artificial neural networks are not biologically plausible in anything but the most general sense. What makes them so significant, however, is that they give cognitive scientists a bridge between algorithm and implementation.

We will be looking in much more detail at artificial neural networks in later chapters (particularly Chapters 8 and 9). For the moment we will simply give a brief sketch of some of the key features. The first is that they involve *parallel processing*. An artificial neural network contains a large number of units (which might be thought of as artificial neurons). Each unit has a varying level of activation, typically represented by a real number between -1 and 1. The units are organized into layers with the activation value of a given layer determined by the activation values of all the individual units. The simultaneous activation of these units, and the consequent spread of activation through the layers of the network, governs how information is processed within the network. The processing is parallel because the flow of information through the network is determined by what happens in all of the units in a given layer – but none of those units are connected to each other.

The second key feature is that each unit in a given layer has connections running to it from units in the previous layer (unless it is a unit in the input layer) and will have connections running forward to units in the next layer (unless it is a unit in the output layer). The pattern of connections running to and from a given unit is what identifies that unit within the network. The strength of the connections (the *weight* of the connection) between individual neurons varies and is modifiable through learning. This means that there can be several distinct neural networks each computing a different function, even though each is composed of the same number of units organized into the same set of layers and with the same connections holding between those units. What distinguishes one network from another is the pattern of weights holding between units.

The third key feature is that there are no intrinsic differences between one unit and another. The differences lie in the connections holding between that unit and other units. Finally, most artificial neural networks are trained, rather than programmed. They are generally constructed with broad, general-purpose learning algorithms that work by changing the connection weights between units in a way that eventually yields the desired outputs for the appropriate inputs. These algorithms work by changing the weights of the connections between pairs of neurons in adjacent layers in order to reduce the "mistakes" that the network makes.

Let us look at how an artificial neural network is set up in a little more detail. Figure 3.7 is a schematic diagram of a generic neural network with three layers of units. The basic architecture of the network is clearly illustrated within the diagram. The network is composed of a set of processing units organized into three different layers. The first layer is made up of input units, which receive inputs from sources outside the network. The third layer is made up of output units, which send signals outside the network. The middle layer is composed of what are called hidden units. Hidden units are

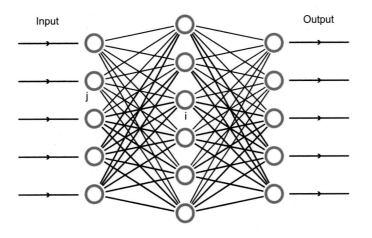

Figure 3.7 A generic three-layer connectionist network (also known as an artificial neural network). The network has one layer of hidden units. (Adapted from McLeod, Plunkett, and Rolls 1998)

distinctive by virtue of communicating only with units within the network. The hidden units are the key to the computational power of artificial neural networks. Networks without hidden units are only capable of carrying out a limited variety of computational tasks. The illustrated network only has one layer of hidden units, but in fact networks can be constructed with as many layers as required. (More details will come in Chapter 8.)

The process of training a network is somewhat lengthy. It is usual to begin with a random assignation of weights and then present the network with a training series of input patterns of activation, each of which is associated with a target output pattern of activation. The input patterns are presented. Differences between the actual output pattern and the target output pattern result in changes to the weights. (This is what the learning algorithm does – adjust the weights in order to reduce the difference between actual and desired output.)

This training process (known as the *backpropagation* of error) continues until errors have diminished almost to zero, resulting in a distinctive and stable pattern of weights across the network. The overall success of a network can be calculated by its ability to produce the correct response to inputs on which it has not been trained. In the next sub-section we will work through a relatively straightforward example to illustrate the sort of task that a network can be trained to do and how it proceeds.

Pattern recognition in neural networks: Gorman and Sejnowski's mine/rock detector

Artificial neural networks are particularly suited for pattern recognition tasks. One such pattern recognition task has become a classic of artificial neural network design. Consider the task of identifying whether a particular underwater sonar echo comes from a submerged mine, or from a rock. There are discriminable differences between the sonar echoes of mines and rocks, but there are equally discriminable differences between the sonar echoes from different parts of a single mine, or from different parts of a single rock. It is no easy matter to identify reliably whether a sonar echo comes from a mine or from a rock. Human sonar operators can do so reasonably well (after a considerable amount of practice and training), but it turns out that artificial neural networks can perform significantly better than humans.

The first problem in devising a network is finding a way to code the external stimulus as a pattern of activation values. The external stimuli are sonar echoes from similarly shaped and sized objects known to be either mines or rocks. In order to "transform" these sonar echoes into a representational format suitable for processing by the network the sonar echoes are run through a spectral analyzer that registers their energy levels at a range of different frequencies. This process gives each sonar echo a unique "fingerprint" to serve as input to the network. Each input unit is dedicated to a different frequency and its activation level for a given sonar echo is a function of the level of energy in the relevant sonar echo at that frequency. This allows the vector of activation values defined over the input units to reflect the unique fingerprint of each sonar echo.

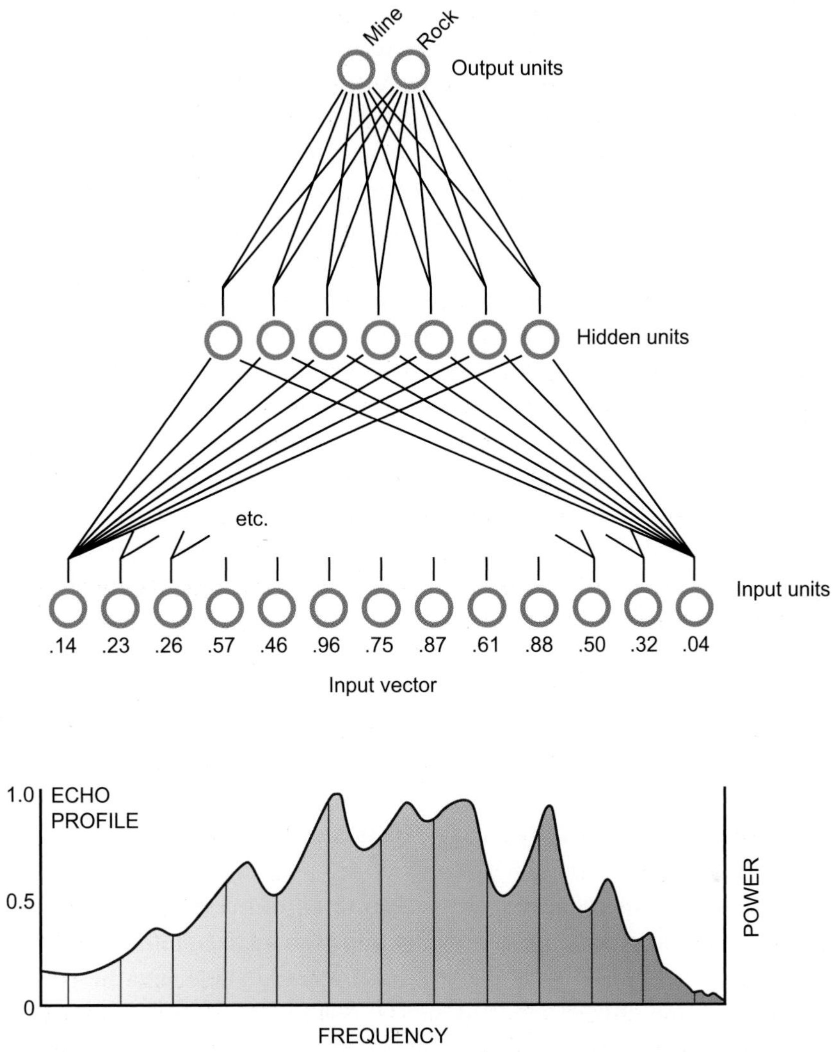

Figure 3.8 Gorman and Sejnowski's mine/rock detector network. (Adapted from Gorman and Sejnowski 1988)

The neural network developed by Paul Gorman and Terrence Sejnowski to solve this problem contains sixty input units, corresponding to the sixty different frequencies at which energy sampling was carried out, and one layer of hidden units. Since the job of the unit is to classify inputs into two groups, the network contains two output units – in effect, a rock unit and a mine unit. The aim of the network is to deliver an output activation vector of $\langle 1, 0 \rangle$ in response to the energy profile of a rock and $\langle 0, 1 \rangle$ in response to the energy profile of a mine. Figure 3.8 is a diagrammatic representation of Gorman and Sejnowski's mine/rock network.

The mine detector network is a standard feedforward network (which means that activation is only ever spread forward through the network) and is trained with the backpropagation learning algorithm. Although the network receives information during the training phase about the accuracy of its outputs, it has no memory of what happened in early sessions. Or rather, more accurately, the only traces of what happened in earlier training sessions exist in the particular patterns of weights holding across the network. Each time the network comes up with a wrong output (a pattern of $\langle 0.83, 0.2 \rangle$ rather than $\langle 1, 0 \rangle$, for example, in response to a rock profile), the error is propagated backwards through the network and the weights adjusted to reduce the error. Eventually the error at the output units diminishes to a point where the network can generalize to new activation patterns with a 90 percent level of accuracy.

The mine/rock detection task is a paradigm of the sort of task for which neural networks are best known and most frequently designed. The essence of a neural network is pattern recognition. But many different types of cognitive ability count as forms of pattern recognition and the tools provided by artificial neural networks have been used to model a range of cognitive processes – as well as many phenomena that are not cognitive at all (such as predicting patterns in the movements of prices on the stock markets, valuing bonds, and forecasting demand for commodities).

Exercise 3.6 Give examples of cognitive abilities that you think would lend themselves to being modeled by artificial neural networks.

3.4   Mapping the stages of lexical processing

It is standard for cognitive scientists to think of information processing in sequential terms. We can make sense of how the mind can solve an information-processing task by breaking that task down into a series of simpler sub-tasks, and then thinking about how each of those simpler sub-tasks can be performed. Those sub-tasks can themselves be analyzed in the same way, until eventually we "bottom out" in individual, computational steps that can be carried out by a non-cognitive mechanism. The strategy is one of conquering by simplifying. In the terms introduced by Marr in his theory of vision, we can think of this process of analysis and simplification as taking place at the algorithmic level. It is part and parcel of working out an algorithm that will carry out the task.

In the previous section we looked at a number of different types of constraint that there might be on this process of algorithmic analysis. We saw, for example, how when identifying particular algorithms cognitive scientists might need to take into account the time that each would take to run – and how algorithmic analyses of cognitive abilities need to be sensitive to the characteristic patterns by which those abilities are acquired and lost. The tools offered by connectionist neural networks are intended to give an overarching framework for thinking about computation that will allow particular algorithms to satisfy these general constraints. In this section we turn back from thinking about computational modeling in the abstract to thinking about how the direct study of the brain can help cognitive scientists to formulate and decide between different models. In the first section of this chapter we looked at how neurological experiments on monkeys have been used to identify the channels and pathways along which visual information flows. We turn now to a different set of techniques that have become an increasingly important part of the cognitive scientist's toolkit.

Functional neuroimaging

Functional neuroimaging is a tool that allows brain activity to be studied non-invasively. No surgery is required and subjects can be studied while they are actually performing experimental tasks. Our topic for this section is a very influential set of experiments on how information about individual words is processed. These experiments illustrate very vividly how the bottom-up study of the brain can contribute to the construction and refinement of information-processing models of cognitive abilities.

There are different types of functional neuroimaging. The experiments we are interested in use the technique known as *positron emission tomography* (better known under its acronym PET). We will be looking at other techniques (such as fMRI – functional magnetic resonance imaging) later on in the book.

The basic idea behind the PET technology (as with functional neuroimaging in general) is that we can study the function of different brain areas by measuring blood flow in the brain. We can work out which brain areas are involved in carrying out particular cognitive tasks by identifying the areas to which blood is flowing. The distinctiveness of the PET technology is that it provides a safe and precise way of measuring short-term blood flow in the brain. Subjects are given (typically by injection) a small quantity of water containing the positron-emitting radioactive isotope oxygen-15 (^{15}O). The radioactive water accumulates in the brain in direct proportion to the local blood flow, so that areas to which the most blood is flowing will show the greatest concentration of ^{15}O. The PET scanner is able to track the progress of the radioactive water through the brain (for about a minute, before the radioactive isotope decays to a non-radioactive atom). This provides an indirect, but highly reliable, measure of blood flow in the brain, and hence a way of telling which brain regions are active during the minute after administering the water. If subjects are carrying out particular experimental tasks during that time, then the PET technology gives scientists a tool for identifying which brain regions are actively involved in carrying out that task.

Admittedly, simply identifying which brain regions have blood flowing to them while a particular task is being performed is not enough to tell us which brain regions are actively involved in carrying out the task. There may be all sorts of activity going on in the brain that are not specific to the particular experiment that the subject is performing. The art in designing PET experiments is finding ways to filter out potentially irrelevant, background activity. The experiments we will be focusing on, carried out by Steve Petersen and a distinguished group of collaborators at Washington University in St. Louis, provide a very nice illustration of how this sort of filtering can be done – and of how careful experimental work can refine information-processing models.

⬛ Petersen *et al.*, "Positron emission tomographic studies of the cortical anatomy of single-word processing" (1988)

Petersen and his colleagues were interested in understanding how linguistic information is processed in the human brain. They started with individual words – the basic building-blocks of language. Many different types of information are relevant to the normal course of reading, writing, or conversing. There is visual information about the shape and layout of the word, as well as auditory information about how the word sounds and *semantic* information about what the word means. The interesting question is how these different types of information are connected together. Does silently reading a word to oneself involve processing information about how the word sounds? Does simply repeating a word involve recruiting information about what the word means?

The two leading information-processing models of single-word processing (often called *lexical access*) answer these two questions very differently. Within neurology the dominant model, derived primarily from observing brain-damaged patients, holds that the processing of individual words in normal subjects follows a single, largely invariant path. The information-processing channel begins in the sensory areas. Auditory information about how the word sounds is processed in a separate brain region from information about the word's visual appearance. According to the neurological model, however, visual information about the word's appearance needs to be phonologically recoded before it can undergo further processing. So, in order to access semantic information about what a written word means, the neurological model holds that the brain needs to work out what the word sounds like. Moreover, on this model, semantic processing is an essential preliminary to producing phonological motor output. So, for example, reading a word and then pronouncing it aloud involves recruiting information about what the word means.

Exercise 3.7 Draw a flowchart illustrating the distinct information-processing stages in single-word processing according to the neurological model.

The principal alternative to the neurological model is various different varieties of cognitive model (derived primarily from experiments on normal subjects, rather than from studies of brain-damaged patients). The neurological model is *serial*. It holds that information travels through a fixed series of information-processing "stations" in a fixed order. In contrast, the cognitive model holds that lexical information processing is *parallel*. The brain can carry out different types of lexical information processing at once, with several channels that can feed into semantic processing. Likewise, there is no single route into phonological output processing.

Petersen and his colleagues designed a complex experiment with a series of conditions to determine which model reflects more accurately the channels of lexical information processing in the brain. The basic idea was to organize the conditions hierarchically, so that each condition could tap into a more advanced level of information processing than its predecessor. The hierarchy of conditions mapped onto a hierarchy of information-processing tasks. Each level involved a new type of information-processing task. Successfully carrying out the new task required successfully carrying out the other tasks lower in the hierarchy. What this means is that by looking at which *new* brain areas are activated in each task we can identify the brain areas that are specifically involved in performing that task – and we can also see which brain areas are *not* involved.

The baseline condition was simply asking subjects to focus on a fixation point (a small cross-hair) in the middle of a television screen. The point of asking the subjects to do this was to identify what is going on in the brain when subjects are visually attending to something that is not a word. The second condition measured brain activity while subjects were passively presented with words flashed on the screen at a rate of forty words per minute. The subjects were not asked to make any response to the words. In a separate condition the same words were spoken to the subjects. Combining the results from these two different conditions allowed Petersen and his colleagues to work out which brain areas are involved in visual and auditory word perception. The key to doing this is to subtract the image gained from the first condition from the image derived from the second condition. The image of brain activity while fixating on the cross-hair acts as a control state. In principle (and we will look much more closely at some of the methodological difficulties in functional neuroimaging in Chapter 11), this allows us to filter out all the brain activation that is responsible for sensory processing in general, rather than word perception in particular.

The third and fourth levels of the experimental hierarchy measured brain activation during more complex tasks. The aim here was to trace the connections between initial sensory processing and the semantic and output processing that takes place further "downstream." In the third condition subjects were asked to say out loud the word appearing on the screen. Subtracting the resulting image from the word perception image allowed Petersen and his colleagues to calculate which brain areas are involved in speech production. Finally, the highest level of the experimental hierarchy involved a task that clearly requires semantic processing. Here the subjects were presented with nouns on the television monitor and asked to utter an associated verb. So, for example, a subject might say "turn" when presented with the word "handlebars." As before, Petersen and his colleagues argued that subtracting the image of brain activation during this semantic association task from the image obtained from the speech production task would identify the brain areas involved in semantic processing.

Exercise 3.8 Make a table to show the different levels in the hierarchy and the aspects of single-word processing that they are intended to track.

Statistical comparison of the brain images in the different stages of the experiment produced a number of striking results. As we see in Figure 3.9, each of the tasks activated very different sets of brain areas. (The areas with the maximum blood flow are colored white, followed in decreasing order by shades of red, yellow, green, blue, and purple.)

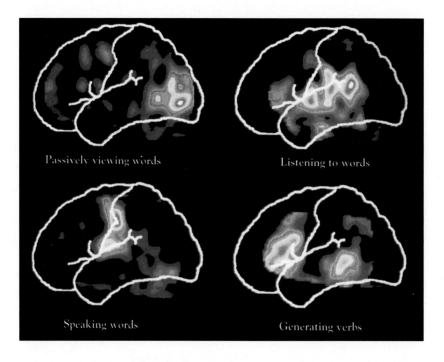

Figure 3.9 Images showing the different areas of activation (as measured by blood flow) during the four different stages in Petersen *et al.*'s lexical access studies. (From Posner and Raichle 1994)

Moreover, the patterns of activation seemed to provide clear evidence against the neurological model. In particular, when subjects were asked to repeat visually presented words, there was no activation of the regions associated with auditory processing. This suggested to Petersen and his colleagues that there is a direct information pathway from the areas in the visual cortex associated with visual word processing to the distributed network of areas responsible for articulatory coding and motor programming, coupled with a parallel and equally direct pathway from the areas associated with auditory word processing. Moreover, the areas associated with semantic processing (those identified in the condition at the top of the hierarchy) were not involved in any of the other tasks, suggesting that those direct pathways did not proceed via the semantic areas.

The situation can most easily be appreciated in an information-processing diagram. Figure 3.10 is drawn from a paper by Petersen and collaborators published in the journal *Nature* in 1988. Unlike many information-processing flowcharts, this one is distinctive in that it identifies the particular brain areas that are thought to carry out each distinct stage. This is not an accident. It reflects how the information-processing model was reached – on the basis of direct study of the brain through PET scan technology. This model, and the methodology that it represents, is a powerful illustration of how the bottom-up study of the brain can be used in developing higher-order models of cognition.

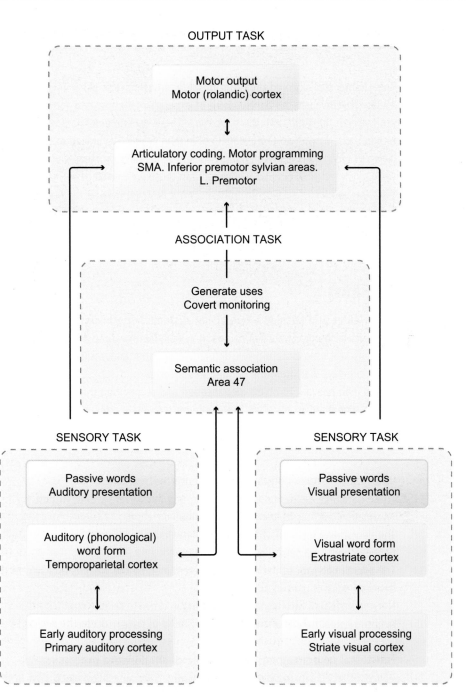

Figure 3.10 A flowchart relating some of the areas of activation in Petersen *et al.*'s study to the different levels of lexical processing. The dashed boxes outline the different subtraction. The solid boxes outline possible levels of coding and associated anatomical areas of activation. (From Petersen *et al.* 1988)

Summary

This chapter has explored the "turn to the brain" that took place in cognitive science during the 1980s. This involved the development of experimental paradigms for studying the information pathways in the brain from the bottom up. These experimental paradigms included lesion studies on monkeys, as well as neuroimaging of human brains. We looked at two examples of how these different techniques allowed cognitive scientists to develop models of cognitive capacities that were much less abstract and functional than those we looked at in Chapter 2. One example came from the two visual systems hypothesis developed primarily on the basis of monkey experiments, and another from a model of single-word processing developed from neuroimaging studies. Another important factor in the turn to the brain was the development of computational modeling techniques based on an idealized model of how neurons work.

Checklist

Ungerleider and Mishkin's two visual systems hypothesis
(1) The cross-lesion disconnection paradigm, coupled with various other anatomical and neurological methods, was used to identify two different information-processing pathways for visual information.
(2) Both pathways start from the primary visual cortex.
(3) Information relevant to object identification and recognition travels along the ventral pathway, from the primary visual cortex to the inferior temporal cortex via the prestriate cortex.
(4) Information relevant to locating objects flows from the primary visual cortex to the posterior parietal lobe.

Information processing in artificial neural networks
(1) These networks are designed to reflect certain high-level features of how the brain processes information, such as its parallel and distributed nature.
(2) The neuron-like units in artificial neural networks are organized into layers, with no connections between units in a single layer.
(3) The overall behavior of the network is determined by the weights attached to the connections between pairs of units in adjacent layers.
(4) Networks "learn" by adjusting the weights in order to reduce error.
(5) Artificial neural networks are particularly suited to pattern recognition tasks.

Functional neuroimaging: The example of single-word processing
(1) Allows brain activity to be studied non-invasively by measuring blood flow in the brain while subjects are performing particular cognitive tasks.
(2) The paired-subtraction paradigm aims to focus on the brain activity specific to the task by subtracting out the activity generated by carefully chosen control tasks.
(3) In studies of how single words are processed experimenters constructed a four-level hierarchy of tasks of increasing complexity.

(4)   The patterns of activation they identified across the different tasks supported a parallel rather than a serial model of single-word processing.

Further reading

Ungerleider and Mishkin's paper "Two cortical visual systems" is reprinted in Cummins and Cummins 2000. Mishkin, Ungerleider, and Macko 1983/2001 is a little more accessible. David Milner and Melvyn Goodale have developed a different version of the two visual systems hypothesis, placing much more emphasis on studies of brain-damaged patients. See, for example, their book *The Visual Brain in Action* (2006). A more recent summary can be found in Milner and Goodale 2008 (including discussion of Ungerleider and Mishkin). A different development in terms of vision for action versus vision for higher mental processes has been proposed by the cognitive neuroscientist Marc Jeannerod, as presented in *Ways of Seeing*, co-authored with the philosopher Pierre Jacob (Jacob and Jeannerod 2003). A recent critique of the two-system account (with commentary from Milner, Goodale, and others) can be found in Schenk and McIntosh 2010.

The Handbook of Brain Theory and Neural Networks (Arbib 2003) is the most comprehensive single-volume source for different types of computational neuroscience and neural computing, together with entries on neuroanatomy and many other "neural topics." It contains useful introductory material and "road maps." Dayan and Abbott 2005 and Trappenberg 2010 are other commonly used introductory textbooks. Scholarpedia.org is also a good source for introductory articles specifically on topics in computational neuroscience. McLeod, Plunkett, and Rolls 1998 is a good introduction to connectionism that comes with software allowing readers to get hands-on experience in connectionist modeling. Bechtel and Abrahamsen (2002) is also to be recommended. Useful article-length presentations are Rumelhart 1989 (in Posner 1989, reprinted in Haugeland 1997) and Churchland 1990b (in Cummins and Cummins 2000). A more recent discussion of connectionism can be found in McClelland *et al*. 2010, with commentary and target articles from others in the same issue. The mine/rock network described in the text was first presented in Gorman and Sejnowski 1988 and is discussed in Churchland 1990a.

A very readable book introducing PET and functional neuroimaging in general is Posner and Raichle (1994), written by two senior scientists participating in the lexical access experiments discussed in the text. These experiments are discussed in the article by Petersen *et al*. cited in the text and also (more accessibly) in Petersen and Fiez 2001. Rowe and Frackowiak 2003 is an article-length introduction to the basic principles of functional neuroimaging. Another good introduction to neuroimaging, including discussion of many of the experiments mentioned in this chapter (and with a lot of colorful illustrations), is Baars and Gage 2010.

PART II

THE INTEGRATION CHALLENGE

INTRODUCTION

The chapters in Part I highlighted some of the key landmarks in the development of cognitive science. We saw how the foundations for cognitive science were laid in psychology, linguistics, and mathematical logic. We looked at three key studies that helped to establish cognitive science as a field of study in the 1970s. These studies provided different perspectives on the idea that the mind could be modeled as a form of digital computer. In their different ways, they each reflected a single basic assumption. This is the assumption that, just as we can study computer software without studying the hardware that runs it, so too can we study the mind without directly studying the brain. As we saw in Chapter 3, however, cognitive science has moved away from this confidence that the brain is irrelevant. Cognitive scientists are increasingly coming to the view that cognitive science has to be bottom-up as well as top-down. Our theories of what the mind does have to *co-evolve* with our theories of how the brain works.

Two themes were particularly prominent in Part I. The first was the interdisciplinary nature of cognitive science. Cognitive science draws upon a range of different academic disciplines and seeks to combine many different tools and techniques for studying the mind. This interdisciplinarity reflects the different levels of organization at which the mind and the nervous system can be studied. The second theme was the idea that cognition is a form of information processing. As we saw, this is one of the guiding ideas in the prehistory of cognitive science and it remained a guiding assumption both for theorists who modeled the mind as a digital computer and for theorists who favored the direct study of the brain and neurally inspired models of computation. These two themes are the focus of Part II.

Chapter 4 shows how the interdisciplinary nature of cognitive science gives rise to what I call the *integration challenge*. Cognitive science is more than just the sum of its parts and the integration challenge is the challenge of developing a unified framework that makes explicit the relations between the different disciplines on which cognitive science draws and the different levels of organization that it studies. We will look at two examples of what I call *local integrations*. These are examples of fruitful "crosstalk" between different levels of organization and levels of explanation. The first example is relatively high-level. We will look at how evolutionary psychologists have proposed a particular type of explanation of experimental results in the psychology of reasoning. The second is much lower-level. It concerns the relation between systems-level cognitive activity, as measured by functional neuroimaging, and activity at the level of individual neurons, as measured by electrophysiology.

In Chapter 5 we look at two global models of integration in cognitive science. One model is derived from reflections on the unity of science in the philosophy of science. This model proposes to think about integration directly in terms of the relation between levels of explanation, by reducing cognitive science to a single, fundamental theory of the brain. A second model, very popular among cognitive scientists, is derived from Marr's study of the visual system (discussed in section 2.3). We see that neither model is really appropriate for solving the integration challenge. In section 5.3 I propose a more modest approach. The mental architecture approach proposes tackling the integration challenge by developing an account (1) of how the mind is organized into different cognitive systems, and (2) of how information is processed in individual cognitive systems.

CHAPTER FOUR

Cognitive science and the integration challenge

Overview

Cognitive science draws upon the tools and techniques of many different disciplines. It is a fundamentally *interdisciplinary activity*. As we saw in our tour of highlights from the history of cognitive science in Chapters 1 through 3, cognitive science draws on insights and methods from psychology, linguistics, computer science, neuroscience, mathematical logic . . . The list goes on. This basic fact raises some very important and fundamental questions. What do all these disciplines have in common? How can they all come together to form a distinctive area of inquiry? These are the questions that we will tackle in this chapter and the next.

The chapter begins in section 4.1 with a famous picture of how cognitive science is built up from six constituent disciplines. Whatever its merits as a picture of the state of the art of cognitive science in the 1970s, the Sloan hexagon is not very applicable to contemporary cognitive science. Our aim will be to work towards an alternative way of thinking about cognitive science as a unified field of investigation.

The starting-point for the chapter is that the different disciplines in cognitive science operate at different levels of analysis and explanation, with each exploring different levels of organization in the mind and the nervous system. The basic idea of different levels of explanation and organization is introduced in section 4.2. We will look at how the brain can be studied at many different levels, from the level of the molecule upwards. There are often specific disciplines or sub-disciplines corresponding to these different levels – disciplines with their own specific tools and technologies.

The basic challenge this poses is explaining how all these different levels of explanation fit together. This is what in section 4.3 I term the *integration challenge*. As we will see, the integration challenge arises because the field of cognitive science has three dimensions of variation. It varies according to the aspect of cognition being studied. It varies according to the level of organization at which that aspect is being studied. And it varies according to the degree of resolution of the techniques that are being used.

There are two different strategies for responding to the integration challenge. There are global strategies and local strategies. Global strategies look for overarching models that will explain how cognitive science as a whole fits together. Marr's tri-level model of explanation (discussed in section 2.3) is a good example. We will look at global strategies in Chapter 5. This chapter, in contrast, paves the way by looking at examples of *local* integrations across levels of organization and levels of explanation. These are cases where cognitive scientists have built bridges between different levels of explanation and different levels of organization.

Our first example of a local integration comes from disciplines that are relatively high-level. In section 4.4 we will look at the proposal from evolutionary biologists to integrate evolutionary biology with psychological studies of reasoning. The second local integration, covered in section 4.5, is located at the opposite end of the spectrum. It is the integration of studies of blood oxygen levels (as measured by functional neuroimaging technologies) with studies of the activity of populations of neurons.

4.1 Cognitive science: An interdisciplinary endeavor

The hexagonal diagram in Figure 4.1 is one of the most famous images in cognitive science. It comes from the 1978 report on the state of the art in cognitive science commissioned by the Sloan Foundation and written by a number of leading scholars, including George Miller (whom we encountered in Chapter 1). The diagram is intended to illustrate the interdisciplinary nature of cognitive science. The lines on the diagram indicate the academic disciplines that the authors saw as integral parts of cognitive science, together with the connections between disciplines particularly relevant to the study of mind and cognition.

Each of the six disciplines brings with it different techniques, tools, and frameworks for thinking about the mind. Each of them studies the mind from different perspectives and at different levels. Whereas linguists, for example, develop abstract models of linguistic *competence* (the abstract structure of language), psychologists of language are interested in the mechanisms that make possible the *performance* of language users.

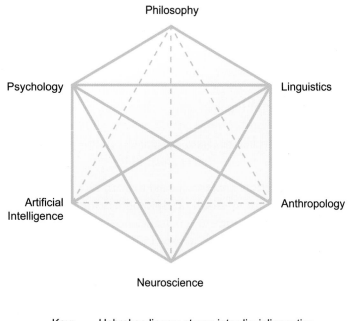

Key:　Unbroken lines = strong interdisciplinary ties
　　　　Broken lines = weak interdisciplinary ties

Figure 4.1 Connections among the cognitive sciences, as depicted in the Sloan Foundation's 1978 report. Unbroken lines indicate strong interdisciplinary links, while broken lines indicate weaker links. (Adapted from Gardner 1985)

Whereas neuroscientists study the details of how the brain works, computer scientists abstract away from those details to explore computer models and simulations of human cognitive abilities. Anthropologists are interested in the social dimensions of cognition, as well as how cognition varies across cultures. Philosophers, in contrast, are typically interested in very abstract models of how the mind is realized by the brain.

Faced with these obvious differences between the six disciplines occupying the individual nodes of the hexagon, it is natural to wonder whether there is anything bringing them together besides a shared interest in the study of the mind and cognition. The authors of the Sloan report certainly thought that there was. The diagram is intended to convey that there is far more to the collective and collaborative nature of cognitive science than simply an overlap of interest and subject matter. Cognitive science, according to the report, is built on partnerships and connections. Lines on the diagram indicate where the authors saw interdisciplinary connections.

Some of the connections identified in the diagram were judged stronger than others. These are marked with a solid line. The weaker connections are marked with a broken line. In a retrospective memoir published in 2003, Miller explained some of the connections represented in the figure:

> Thus, cybernetics used concepts developed by computer science to model brain functions elucidated in neuroscience. Similarly, computer science and linguistics were already linked through computational linguistics. Linguistics and psychology are linked by psycholinguistics, anthropology and neuroscience were linked by studies of the evolution of the brain, and so on. Today, I believe, all fifteen possible links could be instantiated with respectable research, and the eleven links we saw as existing in 1978 have been greatly strengthened. (Miller 2003: 143)

At least one of the connections that was judged weak in 1978 has now become a thriving sub-discipline of philosophy. A group of philosophers impressed by the potential for fruitful dialog between philosophy and neuroscience have taken to calling themselves neurophilosophers, after the title of a very influential book by Patricia Churchland (1986).

Exercise 4.1 Can you think of other illustrations of the lines that the Sloan report draws between different disciplines?

Miller's own account of how the Sloan report was written is both disarming and telling. "The committee met once, in Kansas City. It quickly became apparent that everyone knew his own field and had heard of two or three interesting findings in other fields. After hours of discussion, experts in discipline X grew unwilling to make any judgments about discipline Y, and so forth. In the end, they did what they were competent to do: each summarized his or her own field and the editors – Samuel Jay Keyser, Edward Walker and myself – patched together a report" (Miller 2003: 143). This may be how reports get written, but it is not a very good model for an interdisciplinary enterprise such as cognitive science.

In fact, the hexagon as a whole is not a very good model for cognitive science. Even if we take seriously the lines that mark connections between the disciplines of cognitive science, the hexagon gives no sense of a unified intellectual enterprise. It gives no sense, that is, of something that is more than a composite of "traditional" disciplines such as philosophy and psychology. There are many different schools of philosophy and many different specializations within psychology, but there are certain things that bind together philosophers as a group and psychologists as a group, irrespective of their school and specialization. For philosophers (particularly in the so-called *analytic* tradition, the tradition most relevant to cognitive science), the unity of their discipline comes from certain problems that are standardly accepted as philosophical, together with a commitment to rigorous argument and analysis. The unity of psychology comes, in contrast, from a shared set of experimental techniques and paradigms. Is there anything that can provide a similar unity for cognitive science?

This is the question we will tackle in the rest of this chapter and in Chapter 5.

4.2 Levels of explanation: The contrast between psychology and neuroscience

Neuroscience occupies one pole of the Sloan report's hexagonal figure and it was not viewed as very central to cognitive science by the authors of the report. The report was written, after all, before the "turn to the brain" described in Chapter 3, and its focus reflected the contemporary focus on computer science, psychology, and linguistics as the core disciplines of cognitive science. Moreover, the authors of the report treated neuroscience as a unitary discipline, on a par with anthropology, psychology, and other more traditional academic disciplines. The explosion of research into what became known as cognitive neuroscience has since corrected both of these assumptions. Most cognitive scientists place the study of the brain firmly at the heart of cognitive science. And it is becoming very clear that neuroscience is itself a massively interdisciplinary field.

How psychology is organized

One way of thinking about what distinguishes neuroscience from, say, psychology is through the idea of levels. I am talking here about what is sometimes called scientific psychology (psychology as it is taught and studied in university departments), as opposed, for example, to humanistic psychology, self-help psychology, and much of what is routinely classified as psychology in bookstores. But even narrowing it down like this, there are many different fields of psychology.

A quick look at the courses on offer in any reputable psychology department will find courses in cognitive psychology, social psychology, abnormal psychology, personality psychology, psychology of language, and so on. It is normal for research psychologists to specialize in at most one or two of these fields. Nonetheless, most psychologists think that psychology is a single academic discipline. This is partly because there is a continuity of methodology across the different specializations and sub-fields. Students in psychology are typically required to take a course in research methods. Such courses cover basic principles of experimental design, hypothesis formation and testing, and data analysis that are common to all branches of psychology.

Equally important, however, is the fact that many of these branches of psychology operate at the same level. The data from which they begin are data about cognitive performance and behavior at the level of the whole organism (I am talking about the whole organism to make clear that these ideas extend to non-human organisms, as studied in comparative psychology).

Within cognitive psychology, for example, what psychologists are trying to explain are the organism's capacities for perception, memory, attention, and so on. Controlled experiments and correlational studies are used to delimit and describe those capacities, so that psychologists know exactly what it is that needs to be explained. We saw an example of this in the experiments on mental rotation discussed in Chapter 2. These experiments identify certain features of how visual imagery works that any adequate theory of visual imagery is going to have to explain. Particular explanations are then tested by devising further experiments to test the predictions that they make. These predictions are typically predictions about how subjects will respond or behave in certain specially designed situations.

We will look in detail at many of these issues later on. For the moment the important point is that theories in psychology are ultimately accountable to the behavior (both verbal and nonverbal) of the whole organism. The basic *explananda* (the things that are to be explained) in psychology are people's psychological capacities, which includes both cognitive and emotional capacities. The organization of psychology into different sub-fields is a function of the fact that there are many different types of cognitive and emotional capacities. Social psychologists study the capacities involved in social under-standing and social interactions. They are interested, for example, in social influences on behavior, on how we respond to social cues, and on how our thoughts and feelings are influenced by the presence of others. Personality psychologists study the traits and pat-terns of behavior that go to make up what we think of as a person's character. And so on. If we were to map out some of the principal sub-fields in scientific psychology it would look something like Figure 4.2. The diagram is intended to show that the different sub-branches all study different aspects of mind and behavior at the level of the organism.

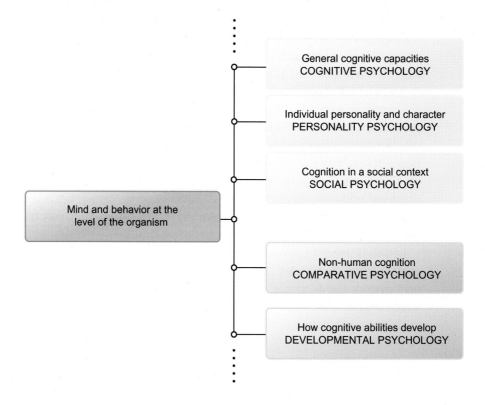

Figure 4.2 Some of the principal branches of scientific psychology.

Exercise 4.2 Can you extend the diagram to cover other branches of psychology that you have encountered elsewhere?

How neuroscience is organized

Things are very different in neuroscience. There are many branches of neuroscience, but they are not related in the same way. The organization of neuroscience into branches closely follows the different levels of organization in the brain and the central nervous system. These levels of organization are illustrated in Figure 4.3, drawn from Gordon Shepherd's textbook *Neurobiology* (1994).

The highest level of organization in the brain is in terms of neural systems and neural pathways. We have already looked at this level of organization when we considered the two visual systems hypothesis in section 3.2 and the different models of lexical access in section 3.4. In each case what is at stake is the route that a particular type of information takes through the brain. We can think about these routes in terms of the "stations" that they run between. These stations are neural systems as identified in terms of their location in the brain. The examples we have considered include the primary visual cortex and the inferior temporal lobe (two stations on the so-called ventral pathway), as well as the temporoparietal cortex (which is involved in the auditory processing of single words, on the model developed by Petersen and colleagues).

Activity at this level of organization is the result of activity at lower levels of organization. In Shepherd's diagram this takes us to levels C and E – the level of centers, local circuits, and microcircuits. In order to get a picture of what is going on here we can think further about the primary visual cortex.

Using methods and technologies such as those discussed in sections 3.2 and 3.4, neuroscientists have determined that the primary visual cortex processes the basic spatiotemporal dimensions of information coming from the retina. It is sensitive to orientation, motion, speed, direction, and so on. But how is this information computed within the primary visual cortex? Neurophysiologists using techniques of single-cell recording have been able to identify individual neurons that are sensitive to particular properties and objects. But neuroscientists generally believe that the basic information-processing units in the brain are populations of neurons rather than individual neurons.

Somehow the collective activity of populations of neurons codes certain types of information about objects in a way that organizes and coordinates the information carried by individual neurons. These populations of neurons are the local circuits in Shepherd's diagram. In many ways this is the most complex and least understood level of organization in the nervous system. Neuroscientists have tools and techniques such as functional neuroimaging for studying the large-scale behavior of neural systems. And they can use single-cell recording techniques to study the activity of individual neurons. But there are no comparable ways of directly studying the activity of populations of neurons. As we will explore in much more detail in Chapters 8 and 9, this is the level of

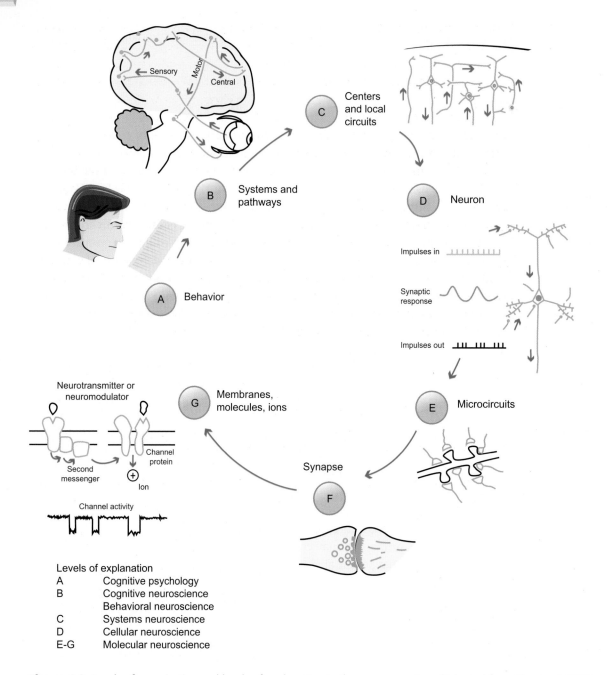

Figure 4.3 Levels of organization and levels of explanation in the nervous system. (Adapted from Shepherd 1994)

organization and analysis at which computational models (such as the connectionist networks discussed in section 3.3) become very important.

The activity of populations of neurons is certainly a function of the behavior of individual neurons. But neurons do not constitute the most basic level of organization in the nervous system. In order to understand how neurons work we need to understand how they communicate. This brings us to Shepherd's level F, because neurons communicate across synapses. Most synapses are chemical, but some are electrical. The chemical synapses work through the transmission of neurochemicals (*neurotransmitters*). These neurotransmitters are activated by the arrival of an electrical signal (the *action potential*). The propagation of neurotransmitters works the way it does because of the molecular properties of the synaptic membrane – properties that are ultimately genetically determined. With this we arrive at level G in Shepherd's diagram.

The point of this whistlestop tour through the levels of organization in the brain is that the sub-fields of neuroscience map very closely onto the different levels of organization in the brain. At the top level we have cognitive neuroscience and behavioral neuroscience, which study the large-scale organization of the brain circuits deployed in high-level cognitive activities. These operate at what in discussing the sub-fields of psychology I termed the level of the whole organism. Systems neuroscience, in contrast, investigates the functioning of neural systems, such as the visual system. The bridge between the activity of neural systems and the activity of individual neurons is one of the central topics in computational neuroscience, while cellular and molecular neuroscience deal with the fundamental biological properties of neurons.

Exercise 4.3 Make a table mapping the different sub-fields of neuroscience onto Shepherd's diagram of levels of organization in the brain.

It is not surprising that different branches of neuroscience (and cognitive science in general) employ tools appropriate to the level of organization at which they are studying the brain. These tools vary in what neuroscientists call their temporal and spatial resolution. The tools and techniques that neuroscientists use vary in the scale on which they give precise measurements (spatial resolution) and the time intervals to which they are sensitive (temporal resolution).

Some of the important variations are depicted in Figure 4.4. We will explore the differences between these different tools and technologies in much more detail in later chapters (particularly Chapter 11).

The next section explores these basic ideas of levels of organization, levels of resolution, and levels of explanation from a more abstract and theoretical perspective. As we shall see, the fact that cognition can be studied at many different levels is what gives rise to one of the fundamental challenges that define cognitive science as a genuine academic field of study. This is the *integration challenge*.

4.3 The integration challenge

The previous two sections explored two of the fundamental aspects of cognitive science. The first feature is that it is an essentially interdisciplinary activity. Cognitive science draws upon the contributions of several different disciplines. Six disciplines were highlighted in the Sloan report, but there is no reason to take that number as fixed.

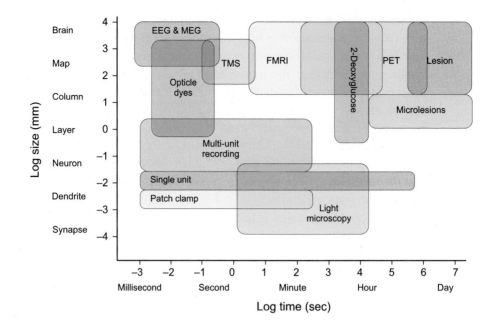

Figure 4.4 The spatial and temporal resolution of different tools and techniques in neuroscience. Time is on the *x*-axis and size on the *y*-axis. (Adapted from Baars and Gage 2010)

Cognitive scientists have profitably exploited many fields not mentioned in the Sloan report. Later on in this book we will be looking at the idea that cognitive processes should be modeled using the mathematical tools of dynamical systems theory. For cognitive scientists pursuing this approach, mathematics is their most obvious interdisciplinary partner. On the other hand, cognitive scientists who try to understand the relation between human cognitive abilities and the cognitive abilities of non-human animals will look most naturally to cognitive ethology (the study of animal cognition in the wild) and behavioral ecology (the study of the evolutionary and ecological basis of animal behavior). Some cognitive scientists have gone even further afield. Ed Hutchins's influential book *Cognition in the Wild* (1995) is based on a close study of ship navigation!

Exercise 4.4 Can you think of any academic disciplines not yet mentioned that might be relevant to cognitive science? Explain your answer.

How the fields and sub-fields vary

The interdisciplinary nature of cognitive science is very well known. Something that has received less attention, however, is the second feature we looked at. If we think of cognitive science as drawing upon a large number of potentially relevant fields and sub-fields, we can see those fields and sub-fields as differing from each other along three dimensions. One dimension of variation is illustrated by the sub-fields of neuroscience.

Neuroscience studies the brain at many different levels. These levels are organized into a hierarchy that corresponds to the different levels of organization in the nervous system.

A second dimension of variation comes with the different techniques and tools that cognitive scientists can employ. As illustrated in Figure 4.4, these tools vary both in spatial and in temporal resolution. Some tools, such as PET and fMRI, give accurate measurements at the level of individual brain areas. Others, such as microelectrode recording, give accurate measurements at the level of individual neurons (or small populations of neurons).

The third dimension of variation is exemplified by the different sub-fields of psychology. By and large, the different sub-fields of psychology study cognition at a relatively high level of organization. Most of psychology operates at Shepherd's level A (which is not to say that there may not be higher levels). What the different areas of psychology set out to explore, map, describe, and explain are the cognitive abilities that generate the myriad things that human beings do and say. The differences between different sub-fields of psychology map fairly closely onto differences between different aspects of human behavior. These are differences between what one might think of as different cognitive domains (the social domain, the linguistic domain, and so on).

The space of cognitive science

We can think of the different parts of cognitive science, therefore, as distributed across a three-dimensional space illustrated in Figure 4.5. The *x*-axis marks the different cognitive domains that are being studied, while the *y*-axis marks the different tools that might be employed (ordered roughly in terms of their degree of spatial resolution).

The *z*-axis marks the different levels of organization at which cognition is studied. This three-dimensional diagram is a much more accurate representation of where cognitive science stands in the early years of the twenty-first century than the two-dimensional hexagon proposed by the authors of the Sloan report (which is not to say, though, that the hexagon failed to capture how things stood at the end of the 1970s).

One way of thinking about the ultimate goal for cognitive science is that it sets out to provide a unified account of cognition that draws upon and integrates the whole space. This is what I call the *integration challenge*. The basic assumption behind the integration challenge is that cognitive science is more than just the sum of its parts. The aim of cognitive science as an intellectual enterprise is to provide a framework that makes explicit the common ground between all the different academic disciplines that study the mind and that shows how they are related to each other. There is an analogy to be made with physics. Just as many theoretical physicists think that the ultimate goal of physics is to provide a unified Theory of Everything, so too (on this way of thinking about cognitive science) is it the mission of cognitive science to provide a unified Theory of Cognition. And, as we shall see in due course, just as a number of physicists have expressed skepticism that there is any such unified Theory of Everything to be had, so too is there room for skepticism about the possibility of a unified Theory of Cognition.

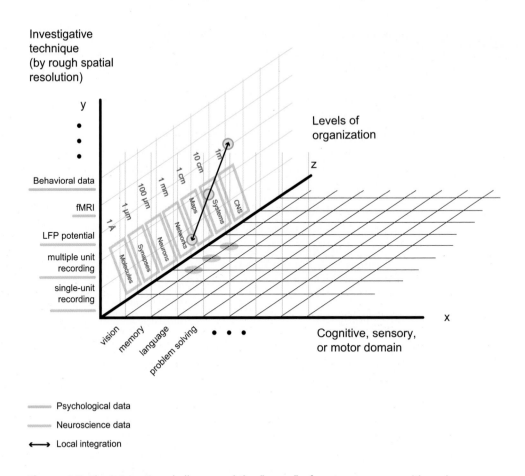

Figure 4.5 The integration challenge and the "space" of contemporary cognitive science.

In any event, whether the integration challenge is ultimately soluble or not, it is very clear that, as things stand, we are nowhere near solving it. Even the most ambitious theories and studies that have been carried out by cognitive scientists set out to cover only a tiny region of the space across which cognitive science ranges. Marr's theory of vision is one of the more ambitious undertakings of cognitive science, and Marr's tri-level hypothesis is often taken as a textbook example of how cognitive science can span different levels of explanation. But the target of Marr's theory is really just a very small part of vision. Marr's theory of vision is ultimately a theory of early visual processing. It has nothing to say about object recognition and object identification, nor about how vision is integrated with other sensory modalities or how visual information is stored in memory. So, Marr's theory of vision covers only a very small slice of what we might think of as the *y*-axis of cognitive science – alternatively, it occupies only a very small horizontal slice of cognitive science. Moving to the *x*-axis, Marr had relatively little to say about what he called the implementational level. And in fact, as we shall see in the next chapter (section 5.2), the very idea that there is a single implementational level is deeply flawed.

4.4 Local integration I: Evolutionary psychology and the psychology of reasoning

Cognitive psychologists have paid close attention to human problem-solving. We have already seen an example of this in the experiments on mental imagery and mental rotation. The issue there was how people solve problems that are framed in imagistic terms – problems involving the congruence of two figures, for example. Even more attention has been paid to problems that are linguistically framed, such as problems where subjects have to determine how likely it is that certain propositions are true, or whether one proposition follows from (is entailed by) another. These problems are all reasoning problems, and psychologists have studied them with the aim of uncovering the mechanics of reasoning.

A natural hypothesis in this area (particularly from those who have sat through courses on logic and probability theory) is that human reasoning is governed by the basic principles of logic and probability theory. People exploit the basic principles of logic when they are trying to solve problems that have a determinate "yes-or-no" answer fixed by logical relations between propositions, and they use the principles of probability theory when the problem is to work out how likely some event is to happen. This may seem too obvious to be worth stating. How could we use anything but logic to solve logic problems? And how could we use anything but probability theory to solve probability problems?

Actually, however, the hypothesis is far from obviously true. Logic and probability theory are branches of mathematics, not of psychology. They study abstract mathematical relations. Those abstract mathematical relations determine the correct solution to particular problems. But logic and probability theory have nothing to say about how we actually go about solving those problems. In order to work out the reasoning principles that we actually use, psychologists have devised experiments to work out the sorts of problems that we are good at (and the sorts of problems that we are bad at).

Before going on to look at some of those experiments we need to make explicit an important feature of both logic and probability theory. The basic laws of logic and principles of probability theory are universal. Logical relations hold between sentences irrespective of what those sentences actually say. We might, for example, make the following inference: "If that's the cathedral, then the library must be over there. But it's not. So, that can't be the cathedral." The logical rule here is known as *modus tollens*. This is the rule stating that a conditional (*If A then B*) and the negation of the consequent of that conditional (*not-B*) jointly entail the negation of the antecedent of that conditional (*not-A*).

In our example the sentence "that's the cathedral" takes the place of *A* (the antecedent of the conditional) and "the library must be over there" takes the place of *B* (the consequent of the conditional). What is distinctive about this sort of inference is that it makes no difference what sentences one puts in place of *A* and *B*. In the standard terminology, this inferential transition is *domain-general*. Whatever one puts in place of *A* and *B* the inference from *If A then B* and *not-B* to *not-A* will always be valid, simply because it is impossible for the two premises *If A then B* and *not-B* to be true and the conclusion *not-A* to be false. The subject matter of the inference is completely irrelevant.

Exercise 4.5 Can you explain why it is impossible for the premises to be true and the conclusion to be false?

The rules of the probability calculus share this feature. Once a numerical probability has been assigned to a particular proposition, the rules governing the calculations one can perform with that number are completely independent of what the proposition is. It does not matter whether one assigns a probability of 0.25 to the proposition that the next toss of two coins will result in two heads, or to the proposition that aliens will take over the world before the day is out, the probability calculus still dictates that one should assign a probability of 0.75 to the negation of that proposition (i.e. to the proposition that at least one coin will come up tails, or that the world will still be under the control of earthlings tomorrow).

Conditional reasoning

Some of the most influential and best-known experiments in the reasoning literature are on what is known as conditional reasoning, namely, reasoning that employs the "if … then …" construction. What has emerged from extensive research into conditional reasoning is that people are generally not very adept at mastering conditionals. Most of us are very bad at applying some basic rules of inference governing the conditional. We have particular difficulties with the rule of *modus tollens* outlined earlier. Moreover, we regularly commit fallacious inferences involving the conditional – fallacies such as the fallacy of affirming the consequent.

To affirm the consequent is to conclude *A* from a conditional *if A then B* and its consequent *B*. We can compare the two forms of inference side by side:

Valid	*Invalid*
If A then B	If A then B
Not B	B
___	___
Not-A	A

The two forms of inference are superficially very similar – but in the case of affirming the consequent, as is not the case with *modus tollens*, it is possible to have true premises and a false conclusion.

E C 4 5

Figure 4.6 A version of the Wason selection task. Subjects are asked which cards they would have to turn over in order to determine whether the following conditional is true or false: **If a card has a vowel on one side then it has an even number on the other**.

Exercise 4.6 Give an example that shows affirming the consequent to be fallacious.

The most developed studies of conditional reasoning are inspired by the so-called Wason selection task. Let us start with a typical version of the basic task that inspired the whole research program. Subjects were shown the four cards illustrated in Figure 4.6 and told that each card has a letter on one side and a number on the other. Half of each card was obscured and the subjects were asked which cards they would have to turn over to determine whether the following conditional is true or false: **If a card has a vowel on one side then it has an even number on the other**.

It is obvious that the *E* card will have to be turned over. Since the card has a vowel on one side, the conditional will certainly be false if it has an odd number on the other side. Most subjects get this correct. It is fairly clear that the second card does not need to be turned over, and relatively few subjects think that it does need to be turned over. The problems arise with the two numbered cards.

Reflection shows (or should show!) that the *4* card does not need to be turned over, because the conditional would not be disconfirmed by finding a consonant on the other side. The conditional is perfectly compatible with there being cards that have a consonant on one side and an even number on the other. The *5* card, however, does need to be turned over, because the conditional will have to be rejected if it has a vowel on the other side (this would be a situation in which we have a card with a vowel on one side, but no even number on the other). Unfortunately, very few people see that the *5* card needs to be turned over, while the vast majority of subjects think that the *4* card needs to be turned over. This result is pretty robust, as you will find out if you try it on friends and family.

So what is going wrong here? It could be that the experimental subjects, and indeed the rest of us more generally, are reasoning in perfectly domain-general ways, but simply employing the wrong domain-general inferential rules. On this interpretation, instead of applying the domain-general rule of *modus tollens* we all have an unfortunate tendency to apply the equally domain-general, but hopelessly unreliable, principle of affirming the consequent.

However, one of the most interesting aspects of the literature spawned by the Wason selection task is the powerful evidence it provides that this may well not be the right way to think about the psychology of reasoning. It turns out that performance on the selection task varies drastically according to how the task is formulated. There are "real-world" ways of framing the selection task on which the degree of error is drastically

| Beer | Coke | 25 | 16 |

Figure 4.7 Griggs and Cox's deontic version of the selection task. Subjects are asked to imagine that they are police officers checking for under-age drinkers and asked which cards they would need to turn over in order to assess the following conditional: **If a person is drinking beer, then that person must be over 19 years of age**.

diminished. One striking set of results emerged from a variant of the selection task carried out by Richard Griggs and Jerome Cox. They transformed the selection task from what many would describe as a formal test of conditional reasoning to a problem-solving task of a sort familiar to most of the experimental subjects.

Griggs and Cox preserved the abstract structure of the selection task, asking subjects which cards would have to be turned over in order to verify a conditional. But the conditional was a conditional about drinking age, rather than about vowels and even numbers. Subjects were asked to evaluate the conditional: **If a person is drinking beer, then that person must be over 19 years of age** (which was, apparently, the law at the time in Florida). They were presented with the cards shown in Figure 4.7 and told that the cards show the names of drinks on one side and ages on the other. Before making their choice, subjects were told to imagine that they were police officers checking whether any illegal drinking was going on in a bar.

The correct answers (as in the standard version of the selection task we have already considered) are that the *BEER* card and the *16* card need to be turned over. On this version of the selection task, subjects overwhelmingly came up with the correct answers, and relatively few suggested that the third card would need to be turned over. What is particularly interesting is the subsequent discovery that if the story about the police officers is omitted, performance reverts to a level comparable to that on the original selection task.

The finding that performance on the selection task can be improved by framing the task in such a way that what is being checked is a condition that has to do with permissions, entitlements, and/or prohibitions has proved very robust. The fact that we are good at reasoning with so-called *deontic* conditionals (conditionals that express rules, prohibitions, entitlements, and agreements) has suggested to many theorists that we have a *domain-specific* competence for reasoning involving deontic conditionals. This competence does not carry over to conditional reasoning in other domains (which explains why we are generally not very good at the abstract form of the selection task).

The reasoning behind cooperation and cheating: The prisoner's dilemma

Nonetheless, it is a little unsatisfying simply to state as a brute fact that we have a domain-specific competence for reasoning involving deontic conditionals. This does not give us much explanatory leverage. What we really need is an account of why we should have it. This brings us to the example of local integration that I want to highlight.

The evolutionary psychologists Leda Cosmides and John Tooby have suggested that the human mind (perhaps in common with the minds of other higher apes) has a dedicated cognitive system (a *module*) for the detection of cheaters. This module, the cheater detection module, is just one of a range of highly specialized and domain-specific modules that evolved to deal with specific problems, such as danger avoidance, finding a mate, and so on. The cheater detection module is supposed to explain the experimental data on the Wason selection task. When the selection task is framed in terms of permissions and entitlements it engages the cheater detection module. This is why performance suddenly improves.

But why should there be a cheater detection module? What was the pressing evolutionary need to which the cheater detection module was a response? Cosmides and Tooby's account of the emergence of the cheater detection module is very closely tied to a particular theory of the emergence of cooperative behavior.

Biologists, and evolutionary theorists more generally, have long been puzzled by the problem of how cooperative behavior might have emerged. Cooperative behavior presumably has a genetic basis. But how could the genes that code for cooperative behavior ever have become established, if (as seems highly plausible) an individual who takes advantage of cooperators without reciprocating will always do better than one who cooperates? Evolution seems to favor free riders and exploiters above high-minded altruists.

A popular way of thinking about the evolution of cooperation is through the model of the prisoner's dilemma. The prisoner's dilemma is explained in Box 4.1. Many interpersonal interactions (and indeed many interanimal interactions) involve a series of encounters each of which has the structure of a prisoner's dilemma, but where it is not known how many encounters there will be. Game theorists call these indefinitely iterated prisoner's dilemmas.

Social interactions of this form can be modeled through simple heuristic strategies in which one bases one's plays not on how one expects others to behave but rather on how they have behaved in the past. The best known of these heuristic strategies is TIT FOR TAT, which is composed of the following two rules:

1   Always cooperate in the first encounter
2   In any subsequent encounter do what your opponent did in the previous round

Theorists have found TIT FOR TAT a potentially powerful explanatory tool in explaining the evolutionary emergence of altruistic behavior for two reasons. The first is its simplicity. TIT FOR TAT does not involve complicated calculations. It merely involves an application of the general and familiar rule that "you should do unto others as they do unto you." The second is that it is what evolutionary game theorists call an *evolutionarily stable strategy* – that is to say, a population where there are sufficiently many "players" following the TIT FOR TAT strategy with a sufficiently high probability of encountering each other regularly will not be invaded by a sub-population playing

BOX 4.1 The prisoner's dilemma

A prisoner's dilemma is any strategic interaction where each player's adopting his or her dominant strategy leads inevitably to an outcome where each player is worse off than she could otherwise have been. A dominant strategy is one that promises greater advantage to that individual than the other available strategies, irrespective of what the other players do.

In the standard example from which the problem derives its name, the two players are prisoners being separately interrogated by a police chief who is convinced of their guilt, but lacks conclusive evidence. He proposes to each of them that they betray the other, and explains the possible consequences. If each prisoner betrays the other then they will both end up with a sentence of five years in prison. If neither betrays the other, then they will each be convicted of a lesser offence and both end up with a sentence of two years in prison. If either prisoner betrays the other without himself being betrayed, however, then he will go free while the other receives ten years in prison. We can see how this works by looking at the pay-off table.

		PLAYER B	
		Betray	Silence
PLAYER A	Betray	5, 5	0, 10
	Silence	10,0	2, 2

The table illustrates the pay-offs for the different possible outcomes of a one-shot prisoner's dilemma. Each entry represents the outcome of a different combination of strategies on the part of prisoners A and B. The bottom left-hand entry represents the outcome if prisoner A keeps silent at the same time as being betrayed by prisoner B. The outcomes are given in terms of the number of years in prison that will ensue for prisoners A and B respectively. So, the outcome in the bottom left-hand box is ten years in prison for prisoner A and none for prisoner B.

Imagine looking at the pay-off table from Prisoner A's point of view. You might reason as follows.

Prisoner B can do one of two things – betray me or keep quiet. Suppose he betrays me. Then I have a choice between five years in prison if I also betray him – or ten years if I keep quiet. So, my best strategy if he betrays me is to betray him. But what if he remains silent? Then I have got a choice between two years if I keep quiet as well – or going free if I betray him. So, my best strategy if he is silent is to betray him. Whatever he does, therefore, I'm better off betraying him.

Unfortunately, prisoner B is no less rational than you are and things look exactly the same from her point of view. In each case the *dominant strategy* is to betray. So, you and prisoner B will end up betraying each other and spending five years each in prison, even though you both would have been better off keeping silent and spending two years each in prison.

another strategy (such as the strategy of always defecting). TIT FOR TAT, therefore, combines simplicity with robustness.

Here, finally, we come to the cheater detection module. Simple though TIT FOR TAT is, it is not totally trivial to apply. It requires being able to identify instances of cooperation and defection. It involves being able to tell when an agent has taken a benefit without paying the corresponding price. Without this basic input the TIT FOR TAT strategy cannot be applied successfully. An agent who consistently misidentifies defectors and free riders as cooperators (or, for that matter, vice versa) will not flourish. And this, according to evolutionary psychologists such as Cosmides and Tooby, is where the selective pressure came from for the cheater detection module.

According to Cosmides and Tooby we evolved a specialized module in order to allow us to navigate social situations that depend crucially upon the ability to identify defectors and free riders. Since the detection of cheaters and free riders is essentially a matter of identifying when a conditional obligation has been breached, this explains why we are so much better at deontic versions of the selection task than ordinary versions – and why we are better, more generally, at conditional reasoning about rules, obligations, and entitlements than we are at abstract conditional reasoning.

This bridge between the cognitive psychology of reasoning and evolutionary psychology is an excellent example of a local integration. It illustrates how moving levels and disciplines gives cognitive scientists access to new explanatory tools and models. Certainly, the hypothesized cheater detection module is far from universally accepted. But the discussion it has provoked is a further illustration of the interdisciplinary nature of cognitive science. It has had ramifications for how cognitive scientists think about the organization of the mind (as we shall see in Chapter 10), and the theoretical issues it raises have generated a flourishing interdisciplinary research program in the study of reasoning.

4.5 Local integration II: Neural activity and the BOLD signal

Our second example of a local integration comes from a very different location within the overall "space" of cognitive science. Whereas the cheater detection module and the experimental results on the psychology of reasoning that it is trying to explain are very high-level, our next example takes us down to the interface between functional neuroimaging and the physiology of the brain.

As we saw in section 3.4, the development of functional neuroimaging technology was a very important factor in cognitive science's turn to the brain. Functional neuroimaging allows us to study the workings of the brain at the level of neural systems and large-scale neural circuits. In some sense, that is, it allows us to study the behavior of large populations of neurons. But when one is looking at brightly colored pictures communicating the results of PET or fMRI scans it is only too easy to forget that very little is known about the relation between what those scans measure and the cognitive activity that is going on while the measurements are being made. It is only in the very recent past that progress has been made on building a bridge between functional neuroimaging and neurophysiology. This is the topic of our second case study.

There are two principal technologies in functional neuroimaging. In section 3.4 we looked at the PET technology, which measures cerebral blood flow by tracking the movement of radioactive water in the brain. A newer, and by now dominant, technology is functional magnetic resonance imaging (fMRI). Whereas PET measures local blood flow, fMRI measures levels of blood oxygenation. Unlike PET, which can track a direct index of blood flow, fMRI works indirectly. The basic fact underlying fMRI is that deoxygenated hemoglobin (which is the oxygen-carrying substance in the red blood cells of humans and other vertebrates) disrupts magnetic fields, whereas oxygenated hemoglobin does not.

The standard background assumption in neuroimaging is that blood flow to a particular region of the brain increases when cellular activity in that region increases. This increase in blood flow produces an increase in oxygen. The degree of oxygen *consumption*, however, does not increase in proportion to the increase in blood supply (as opposed, for example, to the level of glucose consumption, which does increase in proportion to the increase in blood supply). So, the blood oxygen level increases in a brain region that is undergoing increased cellular activity – because the supply of oxygen exceeds the demand for it. The increase in blood oxygen level can be detected in the powerful magnetic field created by the MRI scanner, since oxygenated and deoxygenated blood have different magnetic properties. This difference is known as the BOLD (blood oxygen level dependent) contrast. It is what is measured by functional magnetic resonance imaging.

So, fMRI measures the BOLD contrast. But what does the BOLD contrast measure? In some sense the BOLD contrast has to be an index of cognitive activity – since it is known that cognitive activity involves increased activity in populations of neurons, which in turn results in increased oxygen levels and hence in a more pronounced BOLD contrast. But what exactly is the neuronal activity that generates the BOLD contrast? This problem here is a classic integration problem. We are trying to integrate information about blood flow with information about the behavior of populations of neurons. And we are trying to understand how individual neurons contribute to the behavior of neural populations. In doing this we are trying to integrate two different levels of explanation (two different parts of neuroscience), since functional neuroimaging is a very different enterprise from the study of individual neurons.

Neuroscientists study the behavior of individual neurons through single-cell recordings (to be discussed in more detail in Chapter 11). Microelectrodes can be inserted into the brains of animals (and also of humans undergoing surgery) and then used to record activity in individual cells while the animal performs various behavioral tasks. Figure 4.8 below illustrates a microelectrode recording in the vicinity of a single neuron. This type of single-cell recording has been used primarily to identify the response profiles of individual neurons (i.e. the types of stimuli to which they respond).

Response profiles are studied by looking for correlations between the neuron's firing rate and properties of the environment around the subject. Experimenters can identify

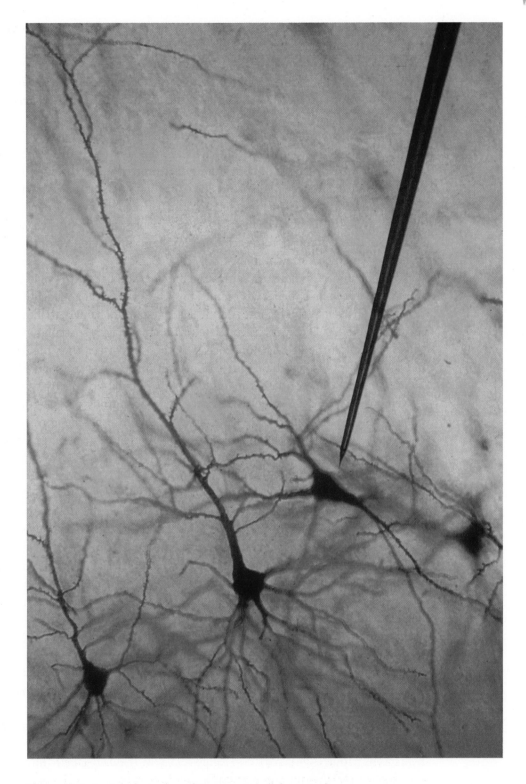

Figure 4.8 A microelectrode making an extracellular recording.

those properties by tracking the relation between the firing rates of individual neurons and where the animal's attention is directed. They are usually low-level properties, such as the reflectance properties of surfaces. But in some cases neurons seem to be sensitive to higher-level properties, firing in response to particular types of object and/or situations. The basic assumption is that individual neurons are "tuned" to particular environmental properties.

Since the salient property of individual neurons is their firing (or *spiking*) behavior, it is a natural assumption that the neural activity correlated with the BOLD contrast is a function of the firing rates of populations of neurons. In fact, this is exactly what was suggested by Geraint Rees, Karl Friston, and Christoph Koch in a paper published in 2000. They proposed that there is a linear relationship between the average neuronal firing rate and the strength of the BOLD signal – two variables are linearly related when they increase in direct proportion to each other, so that if one were to plot their relation on a graph it would be a straight line.

This conclusion was based on comparing human fMRI data with single-cell recordings from monkeys. In fact, their study seemed to show a very clear and identifiable relationship between average spiking rate and the BOLD response – namely, that each percentage increase in the BOLD contrast is correlated with an average per second increase of nine spikes per unit. If the Rees–Friston–Koch hypothesis is correct, then the BOLD response directly reflects the average firing rate of neurons in the relevant brain area, so that an increase in the BOLD contrast is an index of higher neural firing activity.

Neurons do more than simply fire, however. We can think of a neuron's firing as its *output*. When a neuron fires it sends a signal to the other neurons to which it is connected. This signal is the result of processing internal to the neuron. This processing does not always result in the neuron's firing. Neurons are selective. They fire only when the level of internal activity reaches a particular threshold. This means that there can be plenty of activity in a neuron even when that neuron does not fire. We might think of this as a function of the *input* to a neuron, rather than of its output. A natural question to ask, therefore, is how cognitively relevant this activity is. And, given that we are thinking about the relation between neural activity and the BOLD contrast, we have a very precise way of formulating this question. We can ask whether the BOLD signal is correlated with the input to neurons, or with their output (as Rees, Friston, and Koch had proposed).

This is exactly the question explored in a very influential experiment by Nikos Logothetis and collaborators. Logothetis compared the strength of the BOLD signal against different measures of neural activity in the monkey primary visual cortex (see section 3.2 for a refresher on where the primary visual cortex is and what it does). The team measured neural activity in an anaesthetized monkey when it was stimulated with a rotating checkerboard pattern while in a scanner. In addition to using fMRI to measure the BOLD contrast, researchers used microelectrodes to measure both input neural activity and output neural activity. At the output level they measured the firing rates both of single neurons and of small populations of neurons near the electrode tip ("near" here means within 0.2 mm or so). In Figure 4.9 below these are labeled SDF (spike density function) and MUA (multi-unit activity).

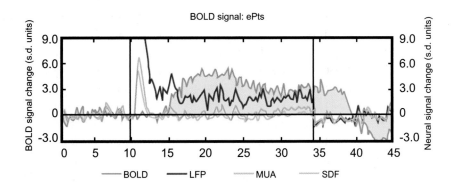

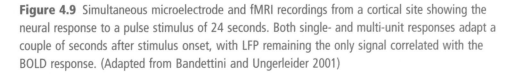

Figure 4.9 Simultaneous microelectrode and fMRI recordings from a cortical site showing the neural response to a pulse stimulus of 24 seconds. Both single- and multi-unit responses adapt a couple of seconds after stimulus onset, with LFP remaining the only signal correlated with the BOLD response. (Adapted from Bandettini and Ungerleider 2001)

The experimenters measured input neural activity through the *local field potential* (LFP). The LFP is an electrophysiological signal believed to be correlated with the sum of inputs to neurons in a particular area. It is also measured through a microelectrode, but the signal is passed through a *low-pass* filter that smooths out the quick fluctuations in the signal that are due to neurons firing and leaves only the low-frequency signal that represents the inputs into the area to which the electrode is sensitive (an area a few millimeters across).

The striking conclusion reached by Logothetis and his team is that the BOLD contrast is more highly correlated with the LFP than with the firing activity of neurons (either at the single-unit or multi-unit level). This is nicely illustrated in the graph in Figure 4.9. In many cases, the LFP will itself be correlated with the firing activity of neurons (which is why Logothetis's results are perfectly compatible with the results reached by Rees, Friston, and Koch). But, if Logothetis's data do indeed generalize, then they show that when spiking activity and LFP are *not* correlated, the LFP is the more relevant of the two to the BOLD contrast.

This is a very significant example of a local integration. The Logothetis experiments build a bridge between two different levels of organization in the nervous system. The large-scale cognitive activity that we see at the systems level (when we are thinking, for example, about the primary visual cortex as a cognitive system) is more closely tied to neural activity that does not necessarily involve the firing of neurons. They also build a bridge between two different levels of explanation and two different technologies for studying the brain – between studying blood flow as an index of cognitive activity through functional neuroimaging, on the one hand, and through studying the electrical behavior of individual neurons, on the other.

Exercise 4.7 Make a table of relevant similarities and differences between the two case studies, thinking particularly about how they each serve as local solutions to the integration challenge.

Summary

This chapter has begun the project of explaining what makes cognitive science a unified and focused field of study with its own distinctive problems and tools. The interdisciplinary study of the mind is a huge field spanning many different levels of explanation and analysis. This raises what I have termed the integration challenge. This is the challenge of providing a unified theoretical framework encompassing the whole "space" of the cognitive sciences. This chapter has introduced the integration challenge and illustrated two local integrations – two cases where cognitive scientists have built bridges across disciplines and across levels of explanation in order to gain a deeper theoretical understanding of a particular cognitive phenomenon. The first local integration brought the psychology of reasoning into contact with evolutionary biology and game theory. The second explores the connections between two different tools for studying activity in the brain – microelectrode recordings and functional neuroimaging.

Checklist

Integration across levels

(1) Cognitive science is an inherently interdisciplinary enterprise.

(2) The hexagonal figure from the Sloan report is not a good representation of the interdisciplinary nature of cognitive science.

(3) Disciplines and sub-fields across cognitive science differ across three dimensions – the type of cognitive activity that they are interested in, the level at which they study it, and the degree of resolution of the tools that they use.

(4) The different branches of psychology vary primarily across the first dimension, while those of neuroscience vary primarily across the second and third.

(5) The integration challenge for cognitive science is the challenge of providing a unified theoretical framework for studying cognition that brings together the different disciplines studying the mind.

Integrating the psychology of reasoning with evolutionary biology

(1) Experiments such as those with the Wason selection task have shown that abilities in conditional reasoning are highly context-sensitive.

(2) Subjects are much better at tasks involving permissions and entitlements than they are at abstract reasoning tasks.

(3) Evolutionary psychologists have explained this by hypothesizing that we have evolved a specific module dedicated to detecting cheaters and free riders.

(4) Part of the theoretical justification for this module comes from using heuristic strategies for solving iterated prisoner's dilemmas to model the evolution of cooperation and altruism.

Integrating the BOLD response with neural activity

(1) Functional magnetic resonance imaging (fMRI) provides a measure of blood flow in terms of levels of blood oxygenation (the BOLD signal). This gives an index of cognitive activity.

(2) This poses the integration question of how this cognitive activity is related to neural activity.

(3)   One possibility is that cognitive activity detected by fMRI is correlated with the outputs of populations of neurons (as manifested in their firing activity). Another possibility is that the correlation is with the input to populations of neurons (as measured by the local field potential).

(4)   The experiments of Logothetis and his collaborators seem to show that the correlation is with the input to neural areas, rather than with their output.

Further reading

Historical background on the Sloan report can be found in Gardner 1985 and Miller 2003 (available in the online resources). The report itself was never published. A very useful basic introduction to levels of organization and structure in the nervous system is ch. 2 of Churchland and Sejnowski 1993. For more detail, the classic neuroscience textbook is Kandel, Schwarz, and Jessell 2012. Stein and Stoodley 2006, and Purves, Augustine, Fitzpatrick, Hall, Anthony-Samuel, and White 2011 are alternatives. Craver 2007 discusses the interplay between different levels of explanation in the neuroscience of memory. Piccinini and Craver 2011 is a more general discussion. For opposing perspectives see Bickle 2006 and Sullivan 2009. For more details on general strategies for tackling the interface problem, see the suggestions for further reading in Chapter 5.

Evans and Over 2004 gives a good and succinct overview of the cognitive psychology of conditional reasoning. Also see Oberauer 2006, Byrne and Johnson-Laird 2009, and Oaksford, Chater, and Stewart's chapter in *The Cambridge Handbook of Cognitive Science* (Frankish and Ramsey 2012). For the deontic version of the selection task see Griggs and Cox 1982, and Pollard and Evans 1987. Cosmides and Tooby 1992 is a clear statement of the reasoning that led them to postulate the cheater detection module. For experimental support for the cheater detection module see Cosmides 1989. More recent summaries of Cosmides and Tooby's research can be found in Cosmides, Barrett, and Tooby 2010, and Cosmides and Tooby 2013. Alternative explanations of performance on the selection task can be found in Oaksford and Chater 1994, and Sperber, Cara, and Girotto 1995. For more reading on the massive modularity hypothesis see the end of Chapter 10.

For specific references on the fMRI technology see the suggestions for further reading in Chapter 11. For a survey of some of the general issues in thinking about the neural correlates of the BOLD signal see Heeger and Ress 2002 and Raichle and Mintun 2006. Logothetis's single-authored 2001 paper in the *Journal of Neuroscience* is a good introduction to the general issues as well as to his own experiments. A more recent summary can be found in Goense, Whittingstall, and Logothetis 2012. For the Rees–Friston–Koch hypothesis, see Rees, Friston, and Koch 2000. For commentary on Logothetis see Bandettini and Ungerleider 2001. For an alternative view see Mukamel *et al*. 2005.

CHAPTER FIVE

Tackling the integration challenge

Overview

In Chapter 4 we saw that cognitive science confronts an *integration challenge*. The integration challenge emerges because cognitive science is an interdisciplinary enterprise. Cognition and the mind are studied from complementary perspectives in many different academic disciplines, using divergent techniques, methods, and experimental paradigms. Cognitive scientists usually have specialist training in a particular academic discipline. Many are psychologists, for example, or linguists. But as cognitive scientists their job is to look beyond the boundaries of their own disciplines and to build bridges to scientists and theoreticians tackling similar problems with different tools and in different theoretical contexts.

When we think about cognitive science as a whole, rather than simply about the activities of individual cognitive scientists, the fact of interdisciplinarity is its most characteristic and defining feature. The guiding idea of cognitive science is that the products of the different, individual "cognitive sciences" can somehow be combined to yield a unified account of cognition and the mind. The integration challenge is the challenge of explaining how this unity is going to arise. It is the challenge of providing a framework that makes explicit the common ground between all the different academic disciplines studying the mind and that shows how they are related to each other.

The last two sections of the previous chapter explored two examples of local integrations. These are cases where problems thrown up in one region of cognitive science have been tackled using tools and techniques from another region. In this chapter we move from the local to the global level. Instead of looking at particular examples of how bridges are built between two or more regions of cognitive science, we will be thinking about different models that have been proposed for achieving unity in cognitive science – for solving the integration challenge.

We begin in sections 5.1 and 5.2 with two models of integration that think about unity explicitly in terms of relations between levels of explanation (as discussed in section 4.2). One of these models is derived from the philosophy of science. It is the model of *intertheoretic reduction*, which (as applied to cognitive science) proposes to solve the integration challenge by reducing the various theories in cognitive science to a fundamental theory (just as theorists of the unity of science have proposed to unify the physical sciences by reducing them all to physics). The second model (discussed in section 5.2) is one that we have already encountered on several occasions. Many cognitive scientists have thought that Marr's tri-level hypothesis is the key to integrating the interdisciplinary and multi-level field of cognitive science. It turns out that there are serious problems with both levels-based proposals for solving the integration challenge in cognitive science.

The principal aim of this chapter is to introduce a more modest approach to the integration challenge. This is the *mental architecture* approach. The mental architecture approach looks for a general model of the organization of the mind and the mechanics of cognition that incorporates some of the basic assumptions common to all the disciplines and fields making up cognitive science. The basic idea of the mental architecture approach is introduced and placed in historical context in section 5.3. We will look at specific ways of implementing the approach in parts III and IV.

5.1   Intertheoretic reduction and the integration challenge

Cognitive science is not unique in confronting an integration challenge. The integration challenge in cognitive science bears many similarities to the problem of the unity of science that has been much discussed by philosophers of science.

What drives the problem of the unity of science is the basic assumption that all of science is a unified intellectual enterprise focused on giving a complete account of the natural world (just as what drives the integration challenge in cognitive science is the assumption that cognitive science is a unified intellectual enterprise that aims to give a complete account of the mind). Since the mind is a part of the natural world (or at least, if you don't believe that the mind is a part of the natural world you are unlikely to be reading a book on cognitive science), it is clear that the integration challenge in cognitive science is really just a part of the more general problem of the unity of science.

Unity of science theorists have tended to assume that the fundamental scientific disciplines are those dealing with the most basic levels of organization in the natural world. One level of organization is generally taken to be more basic than another if, roughly speaking, it deals in smaller things. So, the molecular level is less basic than the atomic level – which in turn is less basic than the sub-atomic level. Correspondingly, we can identify the most fundamental branches of science as those that deal with most basic levels of organization. Particle physics will come out as the most fundamental scientific discipline, since it deals with the elementary constituents of matter. The basic question for unity of science theorists, therefore, is how the non-fundamental scientific disciplines are related to the most fundamental one.

A traditional answer to this question (one that goes back to the group of philosophers from the 1920s and 1930s known as *logical positivists*) is that non-fundamental sciences can be *reduced* to more fundamental ones – and, ultimately, to the most basic science.

What is intertheoretic reduction?

Reduction is a relation that holds between theories that can be formulated as interconnected groups of laws. The classic example of a scientific theory is the collection of laws that make up classical thermodynamics. The laws of thermodynamics govern the flow and balance of energy and matter in thermodynamic systems (such as a steam engine, or a living organism). According to the First Law, for example, the amount of energy lost in a steady-state process cannot be greater than the amount of energy gained (so that the total quantity of energy in the universe remains constant), while the Second Law states that the total entropy of isolated systems tends to increase over time.

Exercise 5.1 Give another example of a scientific theory from your studies of other subjects and explain why it counts as a theory.

One reason that philosophers of science particularly like the example of thermodynamics is that the laws of thermodynamics can be written down as mathematical formulas. This means that we can think in a rigorous manner about what follows logically from those laws – and about what they themselves might follow logically from. When we have two or more theories that can be written down in a precise, mathematical way we can explore how they are logically related to each other. In particular, we can ask whether one can be *reduced* to the other.

As standardly understood in the philosophy of science, reduction is a relation between two theories, one of which is more fundamental than the other. We can give the label T1 to the less fundamental theory (the higher-level theory that is a candidate for being reduced) and T2 to the more fundamental theory (the lower-level theory to which T1 will be reduced). We have a reduction of T1 to T2 when two conditions are met.

Condition 1 There has to be some way of connecting up the vocabularies of the two theories so that they become *commensurable* (that is, so that they come out talking about the same things in ways that can be compared and integrated). This is standardly done by means of principles of translation (often called *bridging principles*) that link the basic terms of the two theories.

Condition 2 It has to be possible to show how key elements of the structure of T1 can be derived from T2, so that T2 can properly be said to explain how T1 works. As this is classically understood, the derivability requirement holds if, and only if, the fundamental laws of T1 (or, more accurately, analogs of the laws of T1 formulated in the vocabulary of T2) can be logically derived from the laws of T2. When this happens we can speak of T2, together with the bridging principles, entailing T1 – and hence of T1 being reduced to T2.

A classical example of reduction in the philosophy of science is the reduction of thermodynamics to the theory of statistical mechanics (which uses probability theory to study the behavior of large populations of microscopic entities). The laws of thermodynamics are formulated in terms of such macroscopic properties as temperature, energy, pressure, and volume. The laws of statistical mechanics, in contrast, are formulated in terms of the statistical properties of collections of widely separated, comparatively small, relatively independently moving molecules.

What makes the reduction possible is that there are bridge laws linking the two fundamentally different types of property. A famous example is the bridge law stating that temperature is mean molecular kinetic energy. This bridge law allows us to identify the temperature of a gas, say, with the average kinetic energy of the molecules that make it up. Given the bridge laws, it is possible to derive the laws of thermodynamics from the laws of statistical mechanics (or, at least, so the story goes – the details of the case are hotly disputed by historians and philosophers of science).

This gives a clear way of thinking about the unity of science. The relation of reduction between theories is transitive. That is, if T1 is reducible to T2 and T2 is reducible to T3, then T1 is reducible to T3. The vision of the unity of science, therefore, is that all the sciences (both the physical sciences and the so-called special sciences, such as psychology, economics, and sociology) will ultimately prove to be reducible to the most fundamental form of physics.

Is this model of intertheoretic reduction the answer to the integration challenge? Certainly, if it is an accurate model of the unity of science then it will be an important part of solving the integration challenge (since most of the different disciplines and sub-disciplines in cognitive science will be parts of the unified science). Unfortunately, it also works the other way round. If the model of intertheoretic reduction is not a good way of thinking about the integration challenge, then it is unlikely to be a good way of thinking about the unity of science in general.

The prospects for intertheoretic reduction in cognitive science

There are ongoing disputes in the philosophy of science about whether intertheoretic reduction is a viable model for thinking about the relation between the different physical sciences. But it is hard to see how one might even get started on applying the reductionist model to the cognitive sciences. Intertheoretic reduction is, in the last analysis, a relation between laws at different levels of explanation. One fundamental problem is that there are very few laws in cognitive science, and the laws that there are tend to function in a very different way from laws in the physical sciences.

Within the physical sciences laws play a fundamentally explanatory role. We explain events by citing laws under which they fall. It is much disputed by philosophers of science whether this is *all* that there is to explanation in, say, physics. But it certainly seems to be a very important part of explanation in physics.

Things are rather different in the cognitive sciences, however. Take psychology as an example. One place in psychology where we do find laws is *psychophysics* (which is the experimental study of how sensory systems detect stimuli in the environment). But these laws do not work in quite the same way as laws in the physical sciences. They predict how sensory systems behave, but they do not explain them.

As an illustration, consider the Stevens Law in psychophysics. This law can be written as follows.

$$\Psi = k\Phi^n$$

On the face of it, this looks rather like the fundamental laws of thermodynamics. It can be formulated as an equation of a familiar-looking type. In this equation Ψ is the perceived intensity of a stimulus and Φ is a physical measure of intensity (e.g. temperature according to some scale), while k and n are constants, with n depending on the type of stimulus (e.g. for temperature, $n = 1.6$; and for an electric shock, $n = 3.5$).

It is certainly true that the Stevens Law produces robust predictions of how subjects report the perceived intensity of a range of stimuli. It is hard to see, however, that we are given any *explanation* by being told that the extent to which someone yelps with pain on being burnt is fully in line with what we would expect from the Stevens Law. Many philosophers of science, most prominently Robert Cummins, have suggested instead that the Stevens Law and the other laws and generalizations to be found in psychology are not really laws in the sense that the laws of thermodynamics are laws. They are statistical regularities that are predictive, but not themselves explanatory. Generalizations such as the Stevens Law track robust phenomena (what psychologists often call *effects*). But effects are not explanations. Rather, they are phenomena that themselves need to be explained.

Exercise 5.2 Formulate in your own words the difference between an effect and a law. Can you identify any effects in the historical survey in Part I?

On Cummins's interpretation, which harks back to several of the themes that emerged in our historical survey in Part I, psychology is engaged in a very different sort of enterprise from physics (and so are the cognitive sciences more generally). Whereas identifying laws and showing how particular events fall under them is a very important part of explanation in physics and the physical sciences, Cummins sees the principal methodology of scientific psychology as *functional decomposition*.

Functional decomposition is the process of explaining a cognitive capacity by breaking it down into sub-capacities that can be separately and tractably treated. Each of these sub-capacities can in turn be broken down into further nested sub-capacities. As this process of functional decomposition proceeds we will move further and further down the hierarchy of explanation until we eventually arrive (so it is hoped) at capacities and phenomena that are not mysterious in any psychological or cognitive sense. As the process of functional analysis proceeds, the mechanisms identified get more and more "stupid" until we eventually arrive at mechanisms that have no identifiable cognitive dimension.

It is not hard to find examples of this type of functional decomposition in scientific psychology. One very nice example comes with how psychologists have studied memory. Although in ordinary life we tend to think of memory as a single, unified phenomenon, psychologists studying memory make a basic distinction into three distinct (although of course interrelated) processes. Memory involves *registering* information, *storing* that information, and then *retrieving* the information from storage. What drives this *decomposition* of memory into three distinct processes is the idea that each process has a very different *function*. Hence the term "functional decomposition."

The three-way distinction between registration, storage, and retrieval is just the beginning. The interesting questions arise when we start to enquire how those three functions might themselves be performed. For the sake of simplicity I shall concentrate on the function of information storage. The most basic functional decomposition in theorizing about how information is stored comes with the distinction between *short-term* and *long-term* memory (usually abbreviated STM and LTM respectively). The evidence for this distinction comes from two different sources. One important set of evidence derives from the study of brain-damaged patients. Experimental tests on patients during the 1960s uncovered a *double dissociation* between what appeared to be two separate types of information storage. A double dissociation between two cognitive abilities A and B is discovered when it is found that A can exist in the absence of B and B in the absence of A.

One patient, known by his initials as K.F. and originally studied by the neuropsychologists Timothy Shallice and Elizabeth Warrington, was severely impaired on memory tests that involve repeating strings of digits or words shortly after being presented with them. Nonetheless, he was capable of performing more or less normally on tasks that involved recalling material that he had read, recognizing faces, or learning over time to find his way around a new environment.

A diametrically opposed pattern of breakdown (a classical form of *amnesia*) has been observed in other patients. Patient H.M., for example, was originally studied by Brenda Milner. H.M., whose brain damage is depicted in Figure 5.1, was perfectly normal when it came to repeating strings of words or telephone numbers, but profoundly impaired at recalling information over longer periods (Milner 1966). Many researchers have concluded that there are two different types of information storage involved here, one involving storing information for a relatively short period of time and the other operating over much longer time periods.

But how should these two functional components themselves be understood? In the case of STM, one influential analysis has suggested a further functional decomposition into a complex multi-component system. According to the *working memory hypothesis* originally proposed by the psychologist Alan Baddeley, STM is composed of a variety of independent sub-systems, as illustrated in Figure 5.2. They identify a system whose functional role it is to maintain visual-spatial information (what they call the *sketchpad*) and another responsible for holding and manipulating speech-based information (the so-called *phonological loop*). Both of these sub-systems are under the control of an attentional control system (the *central executive*).

In the case of LTM, neuropsychological research has once again been very influential. Evidence from profoundly amnesic patients (such as H.M.) suffering from *antero-grade amnesia* (affecting memory of events after the onset of brain injury, as opposed to *retrograde amnesia*, which extends to events before the injury) has suggested that we need to make a distinction between *implicit* and *explicit* memory systems within

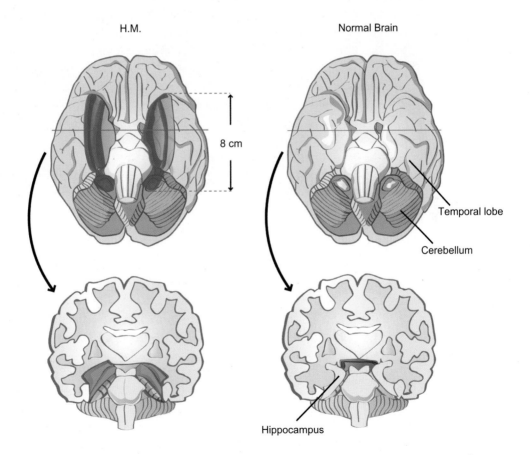

Figure 5.1 Two illustrations of the neural damage suffered by the amnesic patient H.M. The MRI scan (overleaf) was taken in 1998.

(Continues)

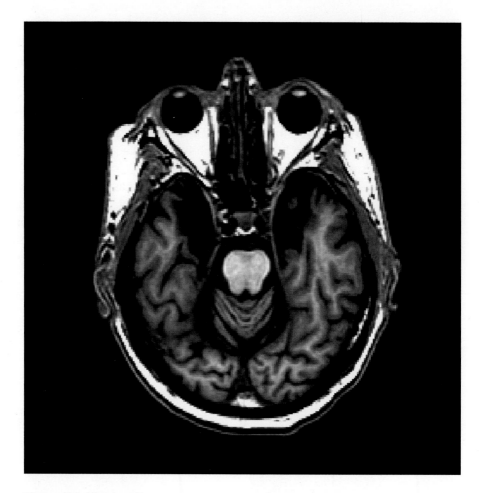

Figure 5.1 (*Continued*)

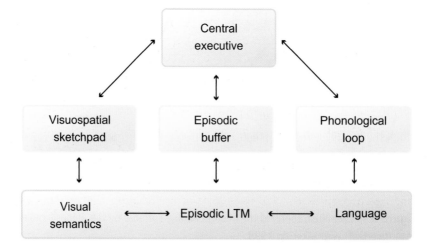

Figure 5.2 Baddeley's model of working memory.

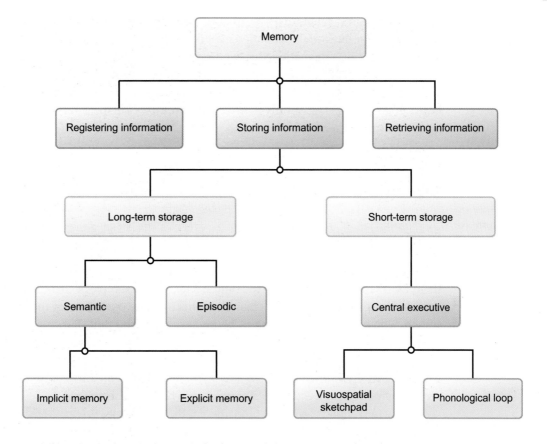

Figure 5.3 The initial stages of a functional decomposition of memory.

the general LTM system. Many such patients have shown normal levels of ability in acquiring motor skills and in developing conditioned responses, even though they have no explicit recollection of the learning process. The tasks on which they perform well are tasks such as manipulating a computer that do not require the patient to think back to an earlier episode. Anterograde amnesiacs are profoundly impaired on tasks of the second type, such as having to recall lists of words or numbers.

A further distinction suggested by the neuropsychological evidence (and indeed also by experimental evidence from normal subjects) is between episodic memory and semantic memory. Episodic memories are directed at temporally dated episodes or events and always have an autobiographical element, while the semantic memory system stores high-level conceptual information, including information about how to speak one's language as well as the various bodies of information that we all possess about the structure of the natural and social worlds.

Figure 5.3 is a diagram illustrating one way of representing the first stages of the functional decomposition of memory, as sketched out in the last few paragraphs.

For our purposes, what matters are not the details of this particular high-level decomposition, but rather the differences between this sort of model of explanation and the model of explanation that we find in the physical sciences. If this is indeed how we should think about the types of explanation in which psychologists are engaged, then it is clear that the idea of intertheoretic reduction cannot even begin to get a grip. This means that we need to look elsewhere for a solution to the integration challenge.

Exercise 5.3 Explain in your own words why intertheoretic reduction is not adequate for explaining functional decomposition of memory.

5.2   Marr's tri-level hypothesis and the integration challenge

We looked at Marr's theory of early visual processing in section 2.3. As was brought out there, Marr's theory was hailed at the time as a textbook example of cognitive science. Its renown was partly due to Marr's many insights into the operations of the early visual system, which was just beginning to be understood at the time. But there is a further reason why Marr has been so celebrated as an inspiration for cognitive science. Marr's book *Vision* is truly interdisciplinary, and the theoretical framework that he developed, what is generally known as the *tri-level hypothesis*, has seemed to many to provide a general framework and methodology for cognitive science in general.

We saw in section 2.3 that the fundamental theoretical idea driving Marr's discussion is that cognitive systems, such as the early visual system, have to be analyzed at three different levels. Marr's three levels differ in how abstract they are. The most abstract level of analysis is the computational level. Analyzing a cognitive system at the computational level is a matter of specifying the cognitive system's function or role. But this specification has to take a particular form.

Marr understands the role of a cognitive system in a very clearly defined and focused sense. We specify the role of a cognitive system by specifying the information-processing task that the system is configured to solve. The basic assumption is that cognitive systems are information-processing systems. They transform information of one type into information of another type. For Marr, we analyze a cognitive system at the computational level by specifying what that transformation is. Marr's computational analysis of the early visual system is, in essence, that its role is to transform information from the retina into a representation of the three-dimensional shape and spatial arrangement of an object.

The next level of analysis is the algorithmic level. The form of an analysis at the algorithmic level is dictated by the analysis given at the computational level. This is because, as its name suggests, an algorithmic analysis specifies an algorithm that performs the information-processing task identified at the computational level. Information-processing algorithms are step-by-step procedures for solving information-processing problems. We will be looking at algorithms in more detail in Chapters 6 through 9. For the moment the important points to notice are, first, that algorithms are finite sets of instructions. It must be possible to write them down. Second, it must be possible to execute an algorithm in a finite amount of time. Finally, algorithms must be mechanical and automatic. They cannot involve either guesswork or judgment.

We can think of a computer program as the paradigm of an algorithm. A computer program is a set of instructions that "tells" the computer what to do with any input it receives. If the program is well designed and contains no bugs, then it will always respond in the same way to the same inputs. Consider a spell-checker in a word-processing program, for example. A well-designed spell-checker will always flag exactly the same words every time it is presented with a given sentence. And it does not require any further information beyond the words that it is checking. All the relevant information is programmed into it.

Exercise 5.4 Give another example of an algorithm, preferably not one that has anything to do with computers. Explain why it counts as an algorithm.

The move from the computational level of analysis to the algorithmic level is the move from identifying what information-processing task a system is carrying out to identifying the procedure that the cognitive system uses to carry out the task. The first step in giving an analysis at the algorithmic level involves deciding how information is encoded in the system. Algorithms are procedures for manipulating information. In order to spell out how the algorithm works we need to specify what it is working on. Information needs to be encoded in a way that allows it to be mechanically (algorithmically) manipulated to solve the information-processing problem.

In earlier chapters we have seen some very different ways of thinking about how information is encoded. When we looked at artificial neural networks in section 3.3, for example, we looked at an artificial neural network trained to discriminate between mines and rocks. The information-processing problem that the network is trying to solve is the problem of distinguishing between sonar echoes that come from rocks and sonar echoes that come from mines. As we saw, the network solves this problem through the backpropagation learning algorithm. Backpropagation is algorithmic because it works in a purely mechanical, step-by-step manner to change the weights in the network in response to the degree of "mismatch" between the actual result and the intended result. (This is the error that is "propagated back" through the network.)

But the algorithm can only work if the sonar echo is encoded in the right sort of way. The algorithm cannot work directly on sound waves traveling through water. This is why, as was explained in section 3.3, the levels of activation of the input units are used to code each sonar echo into the network. The input units are set up so that each one fires in proportion to the levels of energy at a particular frequency. Once the input information is encoded in this way, it can flow *forwards* through the network. This feedforward process is itself algorithmic, since there are simple rules that determine the levels of activation of individual units as a function of the inputs to those units. During the training phase, the output from the network is compared to the desired output and the backpropagation algorithm used to adjust the weights.

Exercise 5.5 Thinking back to the historical survey in Part I, identify one other example of an algorithmic analysis of an information-processing problem.

In one sense an analysis of an information-processing problem at the algorithmic level is very concrete. If the analysis is complete, then it tells us all we need to know *from the perspective of task analysis*. That is, it gives us a blueprint for solving the task identified at the computational level. We know that all that the system needs to do is to follow the algorithm, however complicated it might be. Nonetheless, in another sense an algorithmic analysis remains very abstract. If one is an engineer, for example, trying to build a machine to solve a specific information-processing problem, then it is plainly not enough to be given an algorithm for the problem. One needs to know, not just what algorithm to run, but how to build a machine that actually runs the algorithm. Similarly, in analyzing a cognitive system, it is not enough simply to know what algorithm it is running. One also needs to know how it runs the algorithm.

This brings us to the final level of analysis in Marr's approach, namely, the implementational level. An analysis at the implementational level is an analysis of how the algorithm is realized in the cognitive system being studied. Analysis at the implementational level takes us from abstract characterizations of inputs, outputs, and information-processing operations to detailed accounts of how the brain actually executes the algorithm. At the implementational level we are dealing primarily with neurobiology, neurophysiology, and neuroanatomy. At the time at which Marr was writing, far less was known than is now about how information is processed in the brain (and this is reflected in the relatively small amount of space devoted to questions of implementation in his book *Vision*).

Figure 5.4 shows one of Marr's implementational proposals. It represents schematically how the brain might be configured to detect zero-crossings (which are sudden changes of light intensity on the retina, so called because they mark the point where the value of light intensity goes from positive to negative, and hence crosses zero). The proposal exploits the fact that some neurons fire when the centers of their receptive fields are stimulated (these are the on-center neurons), while others (the off-center neurons) fire when there is no stimulation in their receptive field. If there are two neurons, one on-center and one off-center, with receptive fields as depicted in Figure 5.4, then both will fire when there is a zero-crossing between them. The only other thing needed for a zero-crossing detector is a third neuron that will fire only when the off-center and on-center neurons are both firing. This neuron would be functioning as what computer scientists call an AND-gate.

Despite cognitive science's turn to the brain (described in Chapter 3), it remains the case that there are relatively few information-processing problems for which we have a

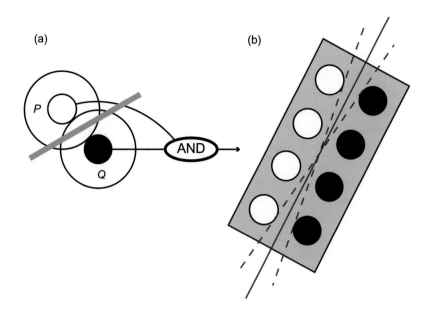

Figure 5.4 A mechanism for detecting oriented *zero-crossing segments*. In (a), if *P* represents an on-center geniculate X-cell receptive field, and *Q* an off-center, then a zero-crossing must pass between them if both are active. Hence, if they are connected to a logical AND gate as shown, the gate will detect the presence of the zero-crossing. If several are arranged in tandem as in (b) and are also connected by logical ANDs, the resulting mechanism will detect an oriented zero-crossing segment within the orientation bounds given roughly by the dotted lines. Ideally, we would use gates that responded by signaling their sum only when all their *P* and *Q* inputs were active. (Adapted from Marr and Hilldreth 1980)

fully worked out implementational level analysis. Fortunately we have already looked at some examples of implementational level analyses. One is the PET study of lexical processing explored in section 3.4.

Exercise 5.6 Redescribe the model of lexical processing reported in section 3.4 in terms of Marr's three levels of analysis.

The potential relevance of Marr's tri-level hypothesis to the integration challenge should be obvious. Marr is not simply suggesting a distinction between different levels of analysis. The key feature of his proposal for studying cognitive systems is that it gives us a way of connecting the different levels. The analyses at the three different levels are distinct but not independent of each other. Analysis at the computational level constrains and determines analysis at the algorithmic level. The aim of the algorithms identified at the algorithmic level is to solve the problems identified at the computational level. By the same token, analysis at the implementational level is dictated by analysis at the algorithmic level.

It is not surprising, therefore, that many cognitive scientists have seen Marr's tri-level hypothesis as the key to solving the problem of how to link together the different disciplines involved in cognitive sciences and the many different levels of organization that we find in human cognitive agents. We might think of high-level disciplines, such as cognitive psychology and cognitive neurospychology, as contributing to analysis at the computational level. Analysis at the algorithmic level might be carried out by computational neuroscientists, for example, or by researchers in artificial intelligence. Implementational level analysis might be thought of as the domain of neurophysiology and cellular neuroscience.

Certainly, this is often how cognitive science is presented – as an interdisciplinary activity unified by the fact that all its constituent disciplines and activities can be located at one or other level of Marr's hierarchy of levels of analysis. However, as I shall be suggesting in the remainder of this section, there is a very fundamental problem with any attempt to generalize Marr's theory into a global model for cognitive science.

This fundamental problem is a direct consequence of its most obvious and innovative feature – namely, the "recipe" that it gives for connecting up the different levels of analysis. As we have seen, the thread that ties the different levels together is the notion of an algorithm. In analyzing a cognitive system at the computational level, cognitive scientists have to be very precise and determinate about the information-processing problem that the system is configured to solve. They have to be precise and determinate because the information-processing problem has to be the sort of problem that can be solved algorithmically. Similarly, cognitive scientists working at the implementational level are not simply studying neurobiological systems. They are studying neurobiological systems as systems that are computing certain algorithmic procedures.

Problems with the tri-level hypothesis as a blueprint for cognitive science

A basic objection to taking Marr's tri-level hypothesis as a global model for cognitive science is that this type of algorithmic analysis seems best applicable to a limited and precisely identifiable type of cognitive system. If this is right, then the tri-level hypothesis really only applies to a relatively small part of the space of cognitive science.

It has become common among psychologists and cognitive scientists to draw a distinction between modular and non-modular cognitive systems. This is, in essence, a distinction between high-level cognitive processes that are open ended and involve bringing a wide range of information to bear on very general problems, and lower-level cognitive processes that work quickly to provide rapid solutions to highly specific problems. In more detail, modular systems are generally held to have most, if not all, of the following characteristics.

- *Domain-specificity.* They are highly specified mechanisms that carry out a very specific job with a fixed field of application.

■ *Informational encapsulation.* In performing this job modular systems are unaffected by what is going on elsewhere in the mind. Modular systems cannot be "infiltrated" by background knowledge and expectations.

■ *Mandatory application.* Modular systems respond automatically to stimuli of the appropriate kind. They are not under any executive control.

■ *Fast.* They transform input (e.g. patterns of intensity values picked up by photoreceptors in the retina) into output (e.g. representations of three-dimensional objects) quickly enough to be used in the online control of action.

■ *Fixed neural architecture.* It is often possible to identify determinate regions of the brain associated with particular types of modular processing.

■ *Specific breakdown patterns.* Modular processing can fail in highly determinate ways (as we saw in section 2.3 in Marr's discussion of Elizabeth Warrington's patients). These breakdowns can provide clues as to the form and structure of that processing.

We will return to the distinction between modular and non-modular systems in subsequent chapters (particularly in Chapter 10). The important idea for the moment is that there seem to be very close relations between a cognitive system being modular and it being susceptible to a Marr-style top-down analysis. This is so for two reasons.

The key to Marr's top-down approach to studying cognitive systems is that a computational level analysis will yield a determinate task or set of tasks that it is the job of the cognitive system to perform. This gives the first reason for thinking that a Marr-style analysis may best be suited to modular systems. It is certainly true that, *at some level of generality,* even non-modular cognitive processes can be described as performing a particular function. But the point of task analysis at the computational level is that the function or functions identified must be circumscribed and determinate enough for it to be feasible to identify an algorithm to compute them, and it is not obvious how this might be achieved for non-modular systems.

It is relatively easy to see how the right sort of functional analysis might emerge when we are dealing with a cognitive process that is domain-specific and specialized – the task of functional analysis is essentially the task of clarifying what exactly the system is specialized to do. But it is very unclear how this could work when the task can only be specified in very general terms (such as "deciding what to do"). And how can we be much more precise than this when we are dealing with systems that are not specialized for carrying out a particular function? It may well be that specialization, domain-specificity, and being susceptible to meaningful functional analysis go hand in hand.

A second reason for thinking that Marr's tri-level approach works best (and perhaps only) for modular systems is that algorithms must be computationally tractable. That is to say, it must be possible to implement them in an organism in a way that will yield useful results within the appropriate time frame (which might be very short when it comes, for example, to object recognition – particularly when the object might be a predator). If an algorithm is to be specified then there must only be a limited number of representational primitives and possible parameters of variation. Once again, it is easy to see why informational encapsulation will secure computational tractability. An informationally encapsulated module with have only a limited range of inputs on which to work.

In contrast, non-modular processing runs very quickly into versions of the so-called *frame problem*. This is the problem, particularly pressing for those developing expert systems in AI and designing robots, of building into a system rules that will correctly identify what information and which inferences should be pursued in a given situation. The problem is identifying what sort of information is relevant and hence needs to be taken into account. Daniel Dennett's classic article on the subject opens with the following amusing and instructive tale:

> Once upon a time there was a robot, named R1 by its creators. Its only task was to fend for itself. One day its designers arranged for it to learn that its spare battery, its precious energy supply, was locked in a room with a time bomb set to go off soon. R1 located the room, and the key to the door, and formulated a plan to rescue its battery. There was a wagon in the room, and the battery was on the wagon, and R1 hypothesized that a certain action which it called PULLOUT (Wagon, Room, t) would result in the battery being removed from the room. Straightaway it acted, and did succeed in getting the battery out of the room before the bomb went off. Unfortunately, however, the bomb was also on the wagon. R1 knew that the bomb was on the wagon in the room, but didn't realize that pulling the wagon would bring the bomb out along with the battery. Poor R1 had missed that obvious implication of its planned act.
>
> Back to the drawing board. "The solution is obvious," said the designers. "Our next robot must be made to recognize not just the intended implications of its acts, but also the implications about their side-effects, by deducing these implications from the descriptions it uses in formulating its plans." They called their next model, the robot-deducer, R1D1. They placed R1D1 in much the same predicament that R1 had succumbed to, and as it too hit upon the idea of PULLOUT (Wagon, Room, t) it began, as designed, to consider the implications of such a course of action. It had just finished deducing that pulling the wagon out of the room would not change the colour of the room's walls, and was embarking on a proof of the further implication that pulling the wagon out would cause its wheels to turn more revolutions than there were wheels on the wagon – when the bomb exploded.
>
> Back to the drawing board. "We must teach it the difference between relevant implications and irrelevant implications," said the designers, "and teach it to ignore the irrelevant ones." So they developed a method of tagging implications as either relevant or irrelevant to the project at hand, and installed the method in their next model, the robot-relevant-deducer, or R2D1 for short. When they subjected R2D1 to the test that had so unequivocally selected its ancestors for extinction, they were surprised to see it sitting, Hamlet-like, outside the room containing the ticking bomb, the native hue of its resolution sicklied o'er with the pale cast of thought, as Shakespeare (and more recently Fodor) has aptly put it. "Do something!" they yelled at it. "I am," it retorted. "I'm busily ignoring some thousands of implications I have determined to be irrelevant. Just as soon

as I find an irrelevant implication, I put it on the list of those I must ignore, and . . ." the bomb went off.

The greater the range of potentially relevant information, the more intractable this problem will be. This means that the tractability of the frame problem is in *inverse* proportion to the degree of information encapsulation. The more informationally encapsulated an informational system is, the less significant the frame problem will be. In the case of strictly modular systems, the frame problem will be negligible. In contrast, the less informationally encapsulated a system is, the more significant the frame problem will be. For non-modular systems, the frame problem has proven very hard indeed to tackle.

Exercise 5.7 Explain in your own words what the frame problem is, without reference to the robot example. Distinguish the three approaches to the problem that Dennett identifies in this passage (again without reference to the robot example) and explain the difficulty with each of them.

For these two reasons, then, it looks very much as if the type of top-down, algorithmic analysis proposed by Marr works best for cognitive systems that are specialized, domain-specific, and informationally encapsulated – that is, for modular systems. And even if it could be extended to systems that are non-modular, Marr's approach would still not be applicable to the mind as a whole. Whether or not it is possible to provide a functional specification susceptible to algorithmic formulation for high-level cognitive systems, it is hard to imagine what a functional specification would look like for the mind as a whole. But in the last analysis an understanding of the mind as a whole is what a solution to the integration challenge is ultimately aiming at.

5.3 Models of mental architecture

In this section we explore an alternative approach to the integration challenge – one that provides a much better fit with what is actually going on in contemporary cognitive science than either of the two global approaches we have been considering. The inter-theoretic reduction approach and the tri-level hypothesis both tackle the integration problem head-on. They take very seriously the idea that cognitive science spans different levels of explanation and they each propose a different model for connecting activity at those different levels. The approach we will be exploring in this section tackles the problem from a different direction. It starts off from a basic assumption common to all the cognitive sciences and then shows how different ways of interpreting that basic assumption generate different models of the mind as a whole. These different models of the mind as a whole are what I am calling different *mental architectures*. Each mental architecture is a way of unifying the different components and levels of cognitive science.

Modeling information processing

The basic assumption shared by all the cognitive sciences can be easily stated. It is that cognition is information processing. The terminology of information processing is ubiquitous in cognitive science, no matter what level of explanation or level of organization is being considered. Cognitive neuroscientists often describe individual neurons as information processors. Computational neuroscientists develop models of how the collective activity of many individual information-processing neurons allows neural systems to solve more complex information-processing tasks. Functional neuroimagers study the pathways and circuits through which information flows from one neural system to another. Cognitive psychologists treat the whole organism as an information processor – an information processor that takes as input information at the sensory periphery and whose outputs are behaviors, themselves controlled by complex forms of information processing. In short, information is the currency of cognitive science – as should already have become apparent from the historical survey in Part I.

Unfortunately, to say that information is the currency of cognitive science raises more questions than it answers. The concept of information is frequently used by cognitive scientists, but rarely explained. And there is certainly no guarantee that neurophysiologists mean the same by "information" as neuropsychologists or linguists. Or indeed that individual neurophysiologists (or neuropsychologists, or linguists) all use the word in the same way. One of the very few generalizations that can be made with any confidence about discussions of information in cognitive science is that (except for the most theoretical reaches of computer science) those discussions have little if anything to do with the well-studied mathematical theory of information inaugurated by Claude Shannon. The notion of information so central to cognitive science is not the notion studied by mathematicians.

In order to get more traction on the basic assumption that cognition is a form of information processing we can ask three very basic questions. Two of these are questions applicable to individual cognitive systems:

1 In what format does a particular cognitive system carry information?
2 How does that cognitive system transform information?

It is important that we ask these questions relative to individual cognitive systems (rather than asking in general how the mind carries and transforms information). This leaves open the possibility that they will be answered differently for different cognitive systems.

It may turn out to be the case that all cognitive systems carry and transform information in the same way. Certainly many discussions of mental architecture have assumed this to be the case – and some cognitive scientists, such as Jerry Fodor, have explicitly argued that it *has* to be the case, because it follows from the very nature of information processing (more details in Chapter 6). But it is unwise to take any such assumptions for granted at this stage in our investigations. We need to leave open the possibility that different cognitive systems carry and transform information in different ways.

Cognitive scientists have devoted much energy to thinking about how to answer these two questions. We will be considering the results in Part III, where we will look at the two dominant contemporary models of how information is processed, as well as a radical alternative that has recently been gaining ground with a number of cognitive scientists.

As emerged in Chapter 2, the early flowering of cognitive science as a distinct area of inquiry was very closely connected with the model of the mind as a digital computer. This model of the mind is built on a particular way of thinking about information processing, as the mechanical manipulation of symbols. We will be exploring this symbolic model of information processing in Chapters 6 and 7. Cognitive science's turn to the brain in the 1980s and 1990s was accompanied by a rather different approach to information processing, variously known as connectionism or parallel distributed processing (PDP). We encountered this approach in section 3.3 and will examine it in more detail in Chapters 8 and 9.

It would be very natural at this point to wonder what cognitive systems are, and how we can know that there are any such things. Unfortunately, it is very difficult, perhaps impossible, to explain what a cognitive system is without appealing to the notion of information processing. To a first approximation, cognitive systems are characterized by the information processing that they carry out. This is because we characterize cognitive systems in terms of the functions that they perform and, for cognitive scientists, these functions are typically information-processing functions. We looked at one way of thinking about cognitive systems in this way when we looked at Marr's tri-level hypothesis in sections 2.3 and 5.2. As we saw there, the information-processing function of a cognitive system is not always sufficiently circumscribed to determine an algorithm for carrying it out. But whenever we have a cognitive system, we have some information-processing function (however complex, open-ended, and difficult to spell out). This is what distinguishes cognitive systems from, say, anatomical systems. It is why we cannot read off the organization of the mind from a brain atlas.

As for the question of how we know that there are any cognitive systems, this can be easily answered. We know that there is at least one cognitive system – namely, the mind as a whole. The question of how many more cognitive systems there might be remains open. Certainly, if the modularity hypothesis is correct, then there will be many cognitive systems. And there will be very many indeed if it turns out to be correct to view individual neurons as information processors. But this brings us to our third question, and to a very different aspect of a mental architecture.

Modeling the overall structure of the mind

Specifying a mental architecture is a matter of answering three questions. The first two have to do with how information is stored and processed. In contrast, the third question has to do, not with how information is processed in individual cognitive systems, but rather with the structure and organization of the mind as a whole:

3   How is the mind organized so that it can function as an information processor?

What we are asking about here is the overall structure of the mind. Is the mind best viewed as a single, all-purpose information-processing system? Or do we need to break it down into different mechanisms and/or functions? If the latter, then what are the principles of organization?

Many textbooks in cognitive psychology reflect a particular answer to this question. They are often organized into what one might think of as distinct faculties. Psychologists and cognitive scientists often describe themselves as studying memory, for example, or attention. The guiding assumption is that memory and attention are distinct cognitive systems performing distinct cognitive tasks. In the case of memory, the task is (broadly speaking) the retention and recall of information, while in the case of attention the task is selecting what is particularly salient in some body of information. These faculties are generally taken to be *domain-general*. That is to say, there are no limits to the types of information that can be remembered, or to which attention can be applied. The faculties of attention and memory cut across cognitive domains.

We have already encountered a rather different way of thinking about the organization of the mind. According to the modularity hypothesis (introduced in the context of Marr's theory of vision in section 5.2), the mind contains cognitive systems specialized for performing particular information-processing tasks. In contrast to the more standard conception of domain-general mental faculties and mechanisms, the basic idea behind the modularity hypothesis is that many cognitive systems, particularly those involved in the initial processing of sensory information, are *domain-specific* and operate autonomously of other cognitive systems.

We can find good candidates for cognitive modules in the early stages of perceptual processing. Color and shape perception are often thought to be carried out by specialized cognitive systems (and, as we saw in Chapter 3, neuroscientists have had some success in locating these specialized systems within the visual cortex). But there are also higher-level candidates for modularity. It has been suggested that face recognition is carried out by a specialized cognitive system. Likewise for various different aspects of language processing, such as syntactic parsing.

Exercise 5.8 Explain in your own words how the modularity hypothesis differs from the faculty-based view of the mind's organization.

The modularity hypothesis comes in different forms. Some cognitive scientists have taken the idea of cognitive modules in a somewhat looser sense, and have suggested that even very sophisticated forms of cognition, such as understanding other people's mental states, are carried out by cognitive modules. And, as we saw in section 4.4, evolutionary psychologists have suggested a view of the mind on which it is composed of nothing but modules (the *massive modularity hypothesis*). We will be looking at different versions of the modularity hypothesis in Part IV.

Here again are the three key questions.

1   In what format does a particular cognitive system carry information?
2   How does that cognitive system transform information?
3   How is the mind organized so that it can function as an information processor?

What I am calling a mental architecture is a set of answers to these three questions. A mental architecture is a model of how the mind is organized and how it works to process information.

I am understanding mental architectures in a broader sense than the cognitive architectures discussed in some parts of cognitive science. When some cognitive scientists, particularly those with a background in computer science, talk about cognitive architectures they are talking about particular models of intelligent problem-solving. The term 'cognitive architecture' is sometimes used to describe very specific models of human problem-solving, such as ACT-R or Soar. We will look at ACT-R in more detail in section 10.4, but it is worth pointing out here that these are not examples of mental architectures in the sense that I am discussing them. Here is the difference. Just as programming languages give computer programmers a general set of tools that they can use to write specific programs, ACT and Soar provide researchers with a basic set of computational tools that they can use to construct models of particular cognitive activities. In a popular phrase, cognitive architectures in the narrow sense are "blueprints for intelligent agents." In contrast, in the broad sense in which we are thinking of cognitive architectures, a cognitive architecture is a set of very general assumptions about the form that such a blueprint might take – what you might think of as a set of design principles for an intelligent agent.

The computational tools used by each cognitive architecture reflect certain basic theoretical assumptions about the nature of information processing. In the terms that I am using, these theoretical assumptions can be seen as answers to the first two questions. They are assumptions about how information is carried and how it is processed. From the perspective I am developing, the assumptions shared between particular cognitive architectures are at least as important as the differences between them. Both ACT and Soar, for example, share a general commitment to the *physical symbol system hypothesis*.

This, as we shall see in more detail in Chapter 6, is the hypothesis that information processing is a matter of manipulating physical symbol structures through transformations that operate solely on the "formal" or "syntactic" properties of those symbol structures. Admittedly, ACT and Soar think about these physical symbol structures and how they are transformed in rather different ways. These reflect different conceptions of how to *implement* the physical symbol system hypothesis. In the case of ACT, for example, the proposed framework for implementing the physical symbol system hypothesis is partly based upon experimental data from cognitive neuroscience and cognitive psychology.

Many advocates of ACT and Soar (and other cognitive architectures) think that they are providing frameworks that can be applied to every form of cognition. If they are correct in thinking this, then there is in the last analysis no difference between cognitive architectures and mental architectures. But there is certainly no consensus in the AI community (let alone in the cognitive science community more generally) that either of these architectures is the last word. From the perspective of thinking about information processing in general it seems wise to leave open the possibility that the physical symbol system hypothesis might be implemented differently in different cognitive systems. Indeed, it seems wise to leave open the possibility that the physical symbol hypothesis might not be appropriate for some (or any?) cognitive systems.

This is why the third of our key questions is so important. There are, broadly speaking, two ways of answering the first two questions. There is the computational information-processing paradigm, associated with the physical symbol system hypothesis, and the connectionist information-processing paradigm, associated with research into artificial neural networks. We will be considering each of these in the chapters in Part III. Many supporters of each paradigm think that they have identified the uniquely correct model of how information is carried and processed in the mind. But there may not be any uniquely correct model of how information is carried and processed in the mind. It may be that information is processed differently in different types of cognitive systems. Information may be carried and processed one way in perceptual and motor systems, for example, and in a different way in systems dedicated to higher-level cognitive functions (such as reasoning about other people's psychological states, for example). One way of motivating this claim would be to argue that there is a genuine distinction to be drawn between modular and non-modular cognitive systems, and then to claim that information is processed differently in modular and non-modular systems.

In any event, on the definition of mental architecture that we will be working with for the remainder of this book, it is perfectly possible for there to be a single mental architecture that incorporates elements of two or more different information-processing paradigms. This would be a *hybrid* mental architecture. We will see an example of such a hybrid architecture, a version of ACT, in section 10.4.

Summary

Chapter 4 introduced the integration challenge and explored two examples of local integration – examples of cognitive scientists combining tools and data from different regions in the space of cognitive science. This chapter has focused on global responses to the integration. It began by assessing two approaches to unifying the cognitive sciences. One approach exploits models of intertheoretic reduction initially developed in the context of the physical sciences, while the second takes Marr's three-way distinction between different levels of analysis as a blueprint for cognitive science. Neither of these approaches seems likely to succeed. Important parts of cognitive science are engaged in a project of functional decomposition that does not really fit the model of intertheoretic reduction, while Marr's tri-level approach seems to work best for specialized, modular cognitive systems. The chapter proposed a new approach to solving the integration challenge – the mental architecture approach. Specifying a mental architecture involves (1) a model of how the mind is organized into cognitive systems, and (2) an account of how information is processed in (and between) different cognitive systems.

Checklist

Responses to the integration challenge

(1) The integration challenge can be tackled in a global manner.

(2) Global responses to the integration challenge seek to define relations either between different levels of explanation or between different levels of organization.

(3) The strategy of intertheoretic reduction is an example of the first approach.

(4) Marr's tri-level hypothesis is an example of the second approach.

Intertheoretic reduction as a response to the integration challenge

(1) The integration challenge would certainly be solved if it turned out that all the levels of explanation in cognitive science could be reduced to a single, fundamental level of explanation (in the way that unity of science theorists think that all of science can be reduced to physics).

(2) Reduction is a relation that holds between two theories when the laws of those theories are suitably related to each other.

(3) The basic problem in applying this model to cognitive science is that there are very few laws in cognitive science.

(4) In scientific psychology, for example, what seem at first glance to be laws are often better viewed as effects. Effects are not themselves explanatory, but rather things that need to be explained.

(5) The methodology of scientific psychology is often best viewed as one of functional decomposition.

Marr's tri-level hypothesis

(1) Marr's distinction between computational, algorithmic, and implementational levels of explanation has often been taken as a general framework for cognitive science in general.

(2) Marr does not just distinguish levels of explanation, but gives us a (top-down) way of connecting them, since analysis at the computational level is supposed to constrain analysis at the algorithmic level, which in turn constrains analysis at the implementational level.

(3) The basic problem with taking Marr's tri-level hypothesis as a general methodology for cognitive science is that the cognitive systems best suited to a Marr-style analysis seem to be modular.

(4)   Only for modular systems is it clear how to define computational tasks sufficiently circumscribed and determinate for there to be an algorithm that computes them.

(5)   The frame problem is particularly problematic for systems (such as non-modular systems) that are not informationally encapsulated.

The mental architecture approach to the integration challenge

(1)   The mental architecture approach is an alternative way of unifying the different components and levels of cognitive science.

(2)   The term "mental architecture" is being used here in a broader sense than is usual in, for example, artificial intelligence.

(3)   The starting-point for the mental architecture approach is the idea that all cognition is information processing.

(4)   A mental architecture involves (1) a model of how the mind is organized into cognitive systems, and (2) an account of how information is processed in (and between) different cognitive systems.

Further reading

There is an extensive literature on intertheoretic reduction in the philosophy of science. A good place to start is the *MITECS* entry on "Unity of science" (Bechtel 1999). The most developed proposal for using intertheoretic reduction to integrate cognitive science has come from Patricia Churchland (Churchland 1986). See also the references to Chapter 4. The functional decomposition model of psychological explanation has been developed by Robert Cummins. See Cummins 2000, reprinted in part in Bermúdez 2006.

The working memory hypothesis was first proposed in Baddeley and Hitch 1974. It has been much discussed and revised since then. The most systematic development is in Baddeley's recent book *Working Memory, Thought, and Action* (Baddeley 2007). For a shorter review of the main theoretical developments and principal experimental findings, see Baddeley 2003. Patient K.F. was first discussed in Shallice and Warrington 1970 and H.M. in Milner 1966. The distinction between episodic and semantic memory was first proposed in Tulving 1972. For current research in the psychological study of memory see the chapters in Roediger, Dudai, and Fitzpatrick 2007, as well as Rösler, Ranganath, Röder, and Kluwe, 2009.

See the suggested readings for section 2.3 for Marr. We will be looking at different ways of thinking about modularity in Chapter 10. For further reading see the suggestions at the end of that chapter. The long quote from Dennett is from Dennett 1984. This influential article has been reprinted in a number of places, including Boden 1990b and Bermúdez 2006 – as well as in Pylyshyn 1987, which collects a number of early papers on the frame problem. For a recent overview see Shanahan 2003. Shanahan also has an entry on the frame problem in the *Stanford Encyclopedia of Philosophy* (see online resources). The *MITECS* entry on "Cognitive architecture" (Sloman 1999) is helpful. Several of the AI cognitive architectures have dedicated websites that give helpful introductions and tutorials. See the online resources for the Soar and ACT-R websites. Lebiere 2003 and Ritter 2003 give brief overviews of ACT and Soar respectively. Laird 2012 also provides an overview of Soar and cognitive architectures more generally.

PART III

INFORMATION-PROCESSING MODELS OF THE MIND

INTRODUCTION

Thinking about the integration challenge in Part II reinforced one of the key themes in our historical survey in Part I. The fundamental principle of cognitive science is that cognition is information processing. In Part I we saw how cognitive science emerged when researchers from different disciplines, all tackling very different problems, ended up converging on this basic insight. In Part II I proposed thinking about the integration challenge in terms of different mental architectures, where a mental architecture involves (1) a model of how the mind is organized into different cognitive systems, and (2) an account of how information is processed within (and across) those cognitive systems. The chapters in Part III introduce different ways of thinking about the second of these – how information is processed. The overall organization of the mind will be the subject of Part IV.

The first way of thinking about information processing, explored in Chapters 6 and 7, is closely tied to what is often called the computational theory of mind. Its central organizing principle is the so-called *physical symbol system hypothesis*, originally proposed by Herbert Simon and Allen Newell. According to the physical symbol system hypothesis, cognitive information processing has to be understood in terms of the rule-governed transformation of physical symbols. This way of thinking about information processing is inspired by the metaphor of the mind as computer.

Chapter 6 explains the physical symbol system hypothesis and explores one way of developing the hypothesis into a concrete proposal about how the mind processes information. We look at the language of thought hypothesis, as developed by the philosopher Jerry Fodor, as well as at some of the theoretical objections that have been raised. In Chapter 7 we turn to three different implementations of the physical symbol system hypothesis. These include illustrations from machine learning and data-mining (the ID3 algorithm); the WHISPER program for detecting physical instabilities in a block world; and a mobile robot called SHAKEY that can operate and plan simple tasks in a real, physical environment.

In Chapter 3 we looked briefly at a second way of modeling cognitive information processing. This emerged from the connectionist networks and artificial neural networks that began to be intensively studied in the mid 1980s. The focus in artificial neural networks (and more generally in computational neuroscience) is in thinking about how information might be a distributed quantity (distributed, say, across a population of neurons) rather than a quantity carried by a physical symbol. This distributed model of information processing will be explored further in Chapters 8 and 9.

Chapter 8 introduces the main features of artificial neural networks, exploring the relation between real neurons and individual network units. We start off with single-unit networks and work up to the much more powerful multilayer networks. Both types of network are capable of learning, but multilayer networks exploit a learning algorithm (the backpropagation algorithm) that does not have the limitations associated with the algorithm used to train single-unit networks. These learning algorithms make artificial neural networks very suitable for modeling how cognitive abilities emerge and evolve. We look at two illustrations of this in Chapter 9. The first illustration shows how artificial neural networks can provide an alternative to seeing language learning and language mastery as fundamentally rule-based. We look at neural network models of how young children learn the past tenses of irregular English verbs. The second illustration also derives from child development. We explore neural network models of how children learn to recognize and reason about how objects behave when they are not actually being perceived.

CHAPTER SIX

Physical symbol systems and the language of thought

Overview

This chapter focuses on one of the most powerful ideas in cognitive science. This is the analogy between minds and digital computers. In the early days of cognitive science this analogy was one of cognitive science's defining ideas. As emerged in the historical overview in Part I, cognitive science has evolved in a number of important ways and what is often called the computational theory of mind is no longer "the only game in town." Yet the computational theory, and the model of information processing on which it is built, still commands widespread support among cognitive scientists. In this chapter we see why.

For a very general expression of the analogy between minds and computers we can turn to the physical symbol system hypothesis, proposed in 1975 by the computer scientists Herbert Simon and Allen Newell. According to this hypothesis, all intelligent behavior essentially involves transforming physical symbols according to rules. Section 6.1 spells out how this very general idea is to be understood. Newell and Simon proposed the physical symbol system hypothesis in a very programmatic way. It is more of a general blueprint than a concrete proposal about how the mind processes information. And so in section 6.2 we turn to the version of the physical symbol system hypothesis developed by the philosopher Jerry Fodor. Fodor develops a subtle and sophisticated argument for why symbolic information processing has to be linguistic. He argues that the architecture of the mind is built around a language of thought.

At the heart both of the very general physical symbol system hypothesis and the very detailed language of thought hypothesis is a sharp distinction between the syntax of information processing (the physical manipulation of symbol structures) and the semantics of information processing. The philosopher John Searle has developed a famous argument (the Chinese room argument) aiming to show that this distinction is fatally flawed. We look at his argument and at some of the ways of replying to it in section 6.3. In the same section we explore a more general problem for symbolic models of information processing – the so-called symbol-grounding problem.

6.1   The physical symbol system hypothesis

In 1975 the Association of Computing Machinery gave their annual Turing Award to two very influential computer scientists and pioneers of artificial intelligence - Herbert Simon and Allen Newell. Simon and Newell were recognized for their fundamental contributions to computer science. They created the Logic Theory Machine (1957) and the General Problem Solver (1956), two early and very important programs that developed general strategies for solving formalized symbolic problems. In the lecture that they delivered as one of the conditions of receiving the award Newell and Simon delivered a manifesto for a general approach to thinking about intelligent information processing - a manifesto that was intended to apply both to the study of the human mind and to the emerging field of artificial intelligence. Their manifesto hinged on what they called the *physical symbol system hypothesis*.

Newell and Simon start their lecture by observing that many sciences are governed by certain very basic principles (what they called *laws of qualitative structure*). So, for example, biology has the basic principle that the cell is the basic building block of all living organisms. Geology is governed by the basic principle (enshrined in the theory of plate tectonics) that geological activity on the surface of the earth is generated by the relative movement of a small number of huge plates.

In their lecture they propose the physical symbol system hypothesis as a comparable law of qualitative structure for the study of intelligence:

The physical symbol system hypothesis: A physical symbol system has the necessary and sufficient means for general intelligent action.

There are two claims here. The first (the necessity claim) is that nothing can be capable of intelligent action unless it is a physical symbol system. Since humans are capable of intelligent action, this means, of course, that the human mind must be a physical symbol system. In this sense, then, the physical symbol system hypothesis comes out as a constraint upon any possible mental architecture. The second (the sufficiency claim) is that there is no obstacle in principle to constructing an artificial mind, provided that one tackles the problem by constructing a physical symbol system.

The plausibility and significance of the claim depends on what a physical symbol system is. Here are Newell and Simon again:

> A physical symbol system consists of a set of entities, called symbols, which are physical patterns that can occur as components of another type of entity called an expression (or symbol structure). Thus a symbol structure is composed of a number of instances (or tokens) of symbols related in some physical way (such as one token being next to another). At any instant of time the system will contain a collection of these symbol structures. Besides these structures, the system also contains a collection of processes that operate on expressions to produce other expressions: processes of creation, modification, reproduction, and destruction. A physical symbol system is a machine that produces through time an evolving collection of symbol structures.

With this passage in mind we can break down Newell and Simon's characterization of physical symbol systems into four basic ideas.

1   Symbols are physical patterns.
2   These symbols can be combined to form complex symbol structures.
3   The physical symbol system contains processes for manipulating complex symbol structures.
4   The processes for generating and transforming complex symbol structures can themselves be represented by symbols and symbol structures within the system.

Before going on to explore these in more detail we should pause to note (without much surprise, given that the physical symbol system hypothesis is the brainchild of two computer scientists) that the description of a physical symbol system looks very much like an abstract characterization of a digital computer. We might think of the physical symbols mentioned in (1) as corresponding to the alphabet of a computer language. One very common computer alphabet is the binary alphabet {0, 1}. The symbols in the binary alphabet can be combined into strings of 0s and 1s that are the "words" of the computer language. Computers work in virtue of procedures for manipulating strings – as suggested in (3). Some of these procedures are very basic. These are the programs hard-wired into the computer and written in what is usually called machine language. But, as implied by (4), computers can run programs that "instruct" the basic procedures to operate in certain ways and in a certain order. These programs are written in higher-level programming languages.

We need to look in more detail at each of the basic ideas (1) through (4) before seeing how they might be combined in a particular model of information processing. Thinking about Turing machines will help bring out some of the issues here. Turing machines were introduced in section 1.2 as abstract models of computation. Newell and Simon make clear in their paper how Turing's work on Turing machines in the 1930s was the first step towards the physical symbol system hypothesis. Now would be a good moment to look back at section 1.2.

Symbols and symbol systems

We can start with ideas (1) and (2).

(1) *Symbols are physical patterns.* For Newell and Simon symbols are physical objects, just as the letters in the alphabet are physical objects. This is exactly how Turing machines work. The tape contains symbols and the Turing machine reads those symbols. What the machine does at any given moment is fixed by the state it is in and the symbol that is on the cell being scanned.

We should not take this too literally, however. The fact that a computer has an alphabet composed of the digits 0 and 1 does not mean that we will find any 0s and 1s in it if we open it up. If we dig down deep enough, all that there is to a computer is electricity flowing through circuits. When we talk about a computer alphabet we are already talking at several levels of abstraction above the physical machinery of the computer (its *hardware*). The physical symbol system hypothesis requires that there be, for each symbol in the alphabet, a corresponding physical object. But this physical object does not have to be, as it were, of the same shape as the symbol. If an electrical circuit functions as an on/off switch, then we can view that switch in symbolic terms as representing either a 0 (when it is off) or a 1 (when it is on). But there are no digits to be found in the circuit.

(2) *Symbols can be combined to form complex symbol structures.* Continuing the linguistic metaphor, the symbols in our alphabet can be combined to form word-like symbol structures and those word-like structures put together to form sentence-like structures. The processes of combining symbols into complex symbol structures are governed by strict rules. We can think of these strict rules as telling the symbol system which combinations of symbols count as grammatical. These rules are likely to be *recursive* in form. That means that they will show how to get from an acceptable combination of symbols to a more complex combination that is still acceptable. The definition of a *well-formed formula* in the branch of logic known as sentence logic or propositional logic is a useful example of a recursive definition. See Box 6.1.

Turing machines can only scan a single cell at a time, but they are capable of working with complex symbol structures because those complex symbol structures can be built up from individual symbols in adjacent cells (just as a well-formed formula in the propositional calculus is built up from individual symbols). The Turing machine needs to know two things: It needs to know what symbols can follow other symbols. And it needs some way of marking the end of complex symbols. The first can come from instructions in the machine table, while the second can be provided by symbols that serve as punctuation marks, effectively telling the scanner when it has arrived at the end of a complex symbol.

Solving problems by transforming symbol structures

We turn now to the core of the physical symbol system hypothesis, which is the idea that problem-solving should be understood as the rule-governed transformation of symbol structures.

BOX 6.1   Defining well-formed formulas (WFFs) in propositional logic

Propositional logic is the branch of logic that studies argument forms whose basic constituents are whole sentences or propositions. The basic building blocks of propositional logic (the alphabet) are infinitely many sentence symbols (P1, P2, P3 . . .), together with a small set of logical connectives (the precise set varies, since the logical connectives are interdefinable and different authors take different sets of connectives as basic). One connective ("$\neg$," read as "not-") is *unary* – that is, it applies to single formulas. Other connectives (such as "$\wedge$," "$\vee$," and "$\Rightarrow$," read as "and," "or," and "if . . . then . . ." respectively) are *binary* – they connect pairs of formulas. The legitimate combinations of symbols in the alphabet might typically be defined as follows.

(a) Any sentence symbol is a WFF.
(b) If φ is a WFF then $\neg\varphi$ is a WFF.
(c) If φ and ψ are WFFs, then $\varphi \wedge \psi$ is a WFF and so on for "$\vee$" and "$\Rightarrow$."

Note that φ and ψ can stand here for any formula, not just for sentence symbols. So this definition gives us a recipe for creating WFFs of unlimited complexity. (The technical way of describing this is to say that (b) and (c) are recursive rules.)

---

(3) *The physical symbol system contains processes for manipulating symbols and symbol structures.* We have already seen how a physical symbol system can contain processes for generating complex symbol structures from the basic building blocks provided by the system's alphabet. But what really matters is what the system does with those complex symbol structures – just as what really matters in propositional logic are the rules that allow one complex formula to be derived from another.

The physical symbol system hypothesis is a hypothesis about intelligence and intelligent action. This means that it has to explain what thinking consists in - whether in human beings or in machines. And here we have the distinctive claim of the physical symbol system hypothesis. This is that thinking is simply the transformation of symbol structures according to rules. Any system that can transform symbol structures in a sophisticated enough way will qualify as intelligent. And when we fully understand what is going on in agents that we uncontroversially take to be intelligent (such as human beings), what we will ultimately find is simply the rule-governed transformation of symbol structures.

This hypothesis about thinking is simple (and in many ways compelling). There are many different things that count as thinking. But not all of them really count as manifestations of intelligence. After all, even daydreaming is a type of thinking. Newell and Simon's fundamental claim is that the essence of intelligent thinking is the ability to solve problems. Intelligence consists in the ability to work out, when confronted with a range of options, which of those options best matches certain requirements and constraints.

Intelligence only comes into the picture when there is what might abstractly be called a search-space. The notion of a search-space is very general. One example might be the position of one of the players halfway through a chess game - as in the situation being

Figure 6.1 Allen Newell and Herbert Simon studying a search-space.

analyzed by Newell and Simon in Figure 6.1. Each chess player has a large number of possible moves and a clearly defined aim – to checkmate her opponent. The possible moves define the search-space and the problem is deciding which of the possible moves will move her closest to her goal.

Another example (much studied by computer scientists and mathematicians) is a traveling salesman who starts in a particular city (say, Boston) and has to visit twenty other cities as quickly and efficiently as possible before eventually returning to Boston. Here we can think about the search-space in terms of all the possible routes that start and end in Boston and go through the twenty cities (perhaps visiting some more than once). The diagram at the top in Figure 6.2 illustrates a simpler traveling salesman problem with only five cities.

Search-spaces are typically represented in terms of states. They are given by an initial state (the start state) and a set of permissible transformations of that start state. The search-space is composed of all the states that can be reached from the start state by applying the permissible transformations. The transformations can be carried out in any order. In the chess example, the start state is a particular configuration of the chess pieces and the permissible transformations are the legal moves in chess. In the traveling salesman example, the start state might be Boston, for example, and the permissible transformations are given by all the ways of getting directly from one city to another.

An instance of the traveling
salesman problem

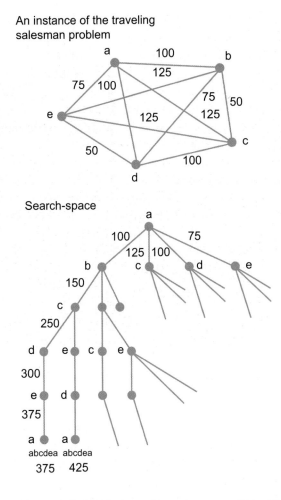

Figure 6.2 A typical traveling salesman problem. The top diagram depicts the problem.
A traveling salesman has to find the shortest route between five cities. The diagram below depicts
part of the search-space. A complete representation of the search-space would show twenty-four
different routes.

Computer scientists standardly represent search-spaces in terms of trees. So, for
example, the search-space for the traveling salesman problem is given by a tree whose
first node is the starting city. In Figure 6.2 the start city is *a*. There is a branch from the
first node to a node representing each of the cities to which the start city is directly
connected – i.e. cities *b*, *c*, *d*, and *e*. From each of those nodes there are further branches
connecting each city to all the other cities to which it is directly connected. And so on.
The diagram at the bottom of Figure 6.2 illustrates a part of the search-space for our five-
city version of the traveling salesman problem.

What counts as solving a problem? Solving a problem is a matter of identifying a
solution state. In the case of chess, the solution state is any configuration of the board on
which the opponent's king is in checkmate. In the traveling salesman case, the solution is

the shortest branch of the tree that ends with Boston and that has nodes on it corresponding to each of the twenty cities that the salesman needs to visit.

How should we think about the process of solving a problem? The most general characterization of problem-solving is as a process of searching through the search-space until a solution state is found. But everything here depends upon what counts as search. Brute force searches that follow each branch of the tree tend only to work for very simple problems. It does not take long for a problem-space to get so big that it cannot be exhaustively searched in any feasible amount of time.

The traveling salesman tree gets very complicated very quickly. If there are n cities, then it turns out that there are $(n - 1)!$ possible routes to take into account, where $(n - 1)! = (n - 1) \times (n - 2) \times (n - 3) \ldots$ This is not too many for the five-city version of the problem depicted in Figure 6.2 (it gives twenty-four different routes). But the problem gets out of control very quickly. In a twenty-city version there are approximately 6×10^{16} different ways for a traveling salesman to start in Boston and travel through the other nineteen cities visiting each exactly once. Checking one route per second, it would take more or less the entire history of the universe to search the problem-space exhaustively.

Here is a rather simpler example than the traveling salesman problem (which, by the way, computer scientists and mathematicians are still working on - no general solution is yet known). The foxes and the chickens problem is a version of a problem that Newell and Simon themselves used to illustrate their General Problem Solver (GPS) program.

The basic idea behind the GPS program is relatively straightforward. It uses the problem-solving technique known as *means–end analysis*. Means–end analysis is a three-stage process that is intended to converge on a solution state by reducing the difference between the current state and the goal state. Here is how it works.

1   Evaluate the difference between the current state and the goal state.
2   Identify a transformation that reduces the difference between current state and goal state.
3   Check that the transformation in (2) can be applied to the current state.
    3a. If it can, then apply it and go back to step (1).
    3b. If it can't, then return to (2).

Means–end analysis is an example of what Newell and Simon call *heuristic search*. Heuristic search techniques are techniques for searching through a search-space that do not involve exhaustively tracing every branch in the tree until a solution is found. Heuristic search techniques trim the search-space down to make the search process more tractable.

Exercise 6.1 Explain how means–end analysis trims down the search-space.

Here is the problem of the foxes and the chickens - a type of problem that Newell and Simon showed could be solved by their GPS program. Imagine that there are three chickens and three foxes on one side of a river and they all need to get over to the other side. The only way of crossing the river is in a boat that can only take two animals (or fewer). The boat can cross in either direction, but if at any moment the foxes outnumber the chickens then the outnumbered chickens will be eaten. The problem is to work out a way of getting all the chickens and foxes onto the other side of the river without any of the chickens being eaten.

We might think of each state as specifying which animals are on each bank and which in the boat (as well as the direction in which the boat is traveling). The start state obviously has all six on one bank (say the right bank) with nobody in the boat or on the other bank. The solution state is the state that has all six on the left bank, with nobody in the boat or on the other bank. The permissible transformations are defined by the rule that the boat cannot carry more than two animals.

The foxes and the chickens problem lends itself very clearly to the general approach to problem-solving that Newell and Simon propose. If we feed into the GPS program representations of the start state and the goal state(s), the program employs various strategies to transform the start state in a way that minimizes the difference from the goal state. The eventual solution is a series of representations, whose first member is a representation of the start state and whose final member is a representation of one of the goal states, and where each member is derived from its predecessor by a permissible transformation.

Each of these representations is itself a symbol structure. Newell and Simon's point is that the GPS program reaches a solution by modifying the original symbol structure (representing the start state) until it arrives at a symbol structure that coincides with one of the goal states. The trick in writing the GPS program, of course, is building into it search strategies and sub-routines that will ensure that it reaches the goal state as efficiently as possible.

Exercise 6.2 Find a solution to the foxes and the chickens problem. Show how your solution can be represented as a process of what Newell and Simon call heuristic search.

We should observe, finally, that these rule-governed transformations are *algorithmic* in the sense discussed in section 1.2. According to our official definition, an algorithm is a finite set of unambiguous rules that can be applied systematically to an object or set of objects. The rules transform the objects in definite and circumscribed ways. To put it another way, algorithms are purely mechanical procedures. They can be followed blindly, without any exercise of judgment or intuition. Elementary school arithmetic provides plenty of examples of algorithms, such as the algorithms for multiplying pairs of numbers and for long division.

The algorithm requirement is not explicitly mentioned by Newell and Simon, but it is clearly required by their overall project. Part of what they are trying to do is to explain what intelligence consists in. The physical symbol system hypothesis is what might be called a *reductive definition* of intelligence. Definitions are not very useful if they tacitly appeal to what they are trying to explain. But some degree of intelligence is required to follow any rule that is not purely algorithmic, and so any definition of intelligence that appeals to transformations that are not purely algorithmic will end up being circular.

Intelligent action and the physical symbol system

We turn now to the final strand in the physical symbol system hypothesis.

(4) *The processes for generating and transforming complex symbol structures can them-selves be represented by symbols and symbol structures within the system.* A fundamental feature of modern computers, so familiar that most of us never think about it, is the fact that a single computer (a single piece of hardware) can run many different programs, often simultaneously. It is this feature that distinguishes a general-purpose computer from a specialized computing machine such as a pocket calculator. And what makes it possible for computers to be programmable in this way is that they are able to contain symbol structures that encode information about, and instructions for, other symbol structures.

It is understandable why Newell and Simon should have thought that something like this feature of computers should be a necessary condition of intelligent action. It is natural to think that intelligence is a function of general problem-solving abilities and skills, rather than specialized ones. Pocket calculators, one might think, are too special-ized to count as intelligent. They contain highly specific routines for dealing with highly determinate problems, whereas genuine intelligence implies the kind of flexibility that involves being able to select which routine to apply to a particular problem.

In the background here is a very important theoretical discovery about Turing machines from mathematical logic. Turing machines are abstract models of a computing device. What we have been looking at so far are individual Turing machines. Each individual Turing machine has a set of instructions (its *machine table*) that programs it to carry out a particular task (such as computing a particular function).

One of the reasons why Turing machines are so significant is that Alan Turing proved that there is a special kind of Turing machine – what he called a *universal Turing machine.* A universal Turing machine can mimic any specialized Turing machine implementing a particular algorithm. A universal Turing machine is a special kind of general-purpose computer that can simulate any more specialized computer. We can think of the special-ized computers as software programs that run on the more general operating system of the universal Turing machine. To cut a long and complex story short, what makes universal Turing machines possible is that Turing machine tables can be encoded as numbers, and hence can be the inputs to Turing machines. The physical symbol system hypothesis builds something like this feature into the characterization of an intelligent system.

The physical symbol system hypothesis is a very general claim about the nature of intelligent action. It is more of a position statement than a concrete proposal. We have to remember, after all, that it was explicitly proposed as an analog to the cell doctrine in biology and to the theory of plate tectonics in geology – namely, as a set of basic principles to guide and direct research. Cognitive scientists, particularly those with a background in artificial intelligence, accept the physical systems hypothesis in much the same spirit as a particle physicist might accept the basic principle that subatomic par-ticles are the fundamental constituents of matter.

The physical symbol system hypothesis is too fundamental to be empirically testable. It is not formulated precisely enough to yield particular predictions that can be put to the test. But it is not, of course, above challenge. There is a very powerful argument, due to the philosopher John Searle, which purports to show that the physical symbol system hypothesis is fundamentally misconceived. Searle sets out to show that no amount of symbol manipulation could possibly give rise to intelligent action. The problem is not that we do not have sufficiently powerful ways of manipulating symbols, or that we have not yet worked out what the right symbols are or how they should be transformed. The problem is much more fundamental for Searle. His claim is that symbol manipulation is fundamentally unintelligent. It is just the wrong place to look for intelligence. We will look at Searle's argument in more detail in the final section of this chapter.

First, though, we need to have in front of us a more concrete example of how the physical symbol system hypothesis might actually be implemented. The physical symbol system hypothesis tells us that in the last analysis intelligent problem-solving is achieved by physically transforming symbolic structures. In order to move forwards with this idea we need a much more detailed account of what these symbolic structures are, how they are transformed, and how those transformations give rise to intelligent action of the sort that human beings might carry out. Until we do this we will not have worked out an account of what we have been calling mental architecture. We have used Turing machines and problems such as the problem of the foxes and the chickens to illustrate the basic ideas behind the physical symbol system hypothesis. But in order to see how physical symbol systems could serve as mental architectures we need to explore how they might serve as a model of human cognition. In the next section we will look at a much more detailed account of how information is processed in the human mind. This is the *language of thought hypothesis* developed by the philosopher and cognitive scientist Jerry Fodor.

6.2 From physical symbol systems to the language of thought

According to Fodor's language of thought hypothesis, the basic symbol structures in the mind that carry information are sentences in an internal language of thought (sometimes called Mentalese). Information processing works by transforming those sentences in the language of thought.

Our starting-point for exploring this idea is the basic fact that the mind *receives* information about its environment. Some of this information is carried by light waves arriving at the retina or sound waves hitting the eardrum. But in general our behavior is not *determined* by the information that we receive. Different people, or the same person at different times, react differently to the same situation. There is no standard response to the pattern of sound waves associated (in English) with a cry of "Help!" for example. How we behave depends upon what our minds do with the information that they receive – how they *process* that information. If I run to your assistance when you cry "Help!" it is because my mind has somehow managed to decode your utterance as a word in English, worked out what you are trying to communicate, and then decided how to respond. This is all complex processing of the initial information that arrived at my eardrum.

But how does this information processing take place? How do vibrations on the eardrum lead to the muscle contractions involved when I save you from drowning? The information has to be carried by something. We know how the information is carried in the auditory system. We know that vibrations in the eardrum are transmitted by the ossicles to the inner ear, for example. What happens the further away the information travels from the eardrum is not so well understood, but another integral part of the general picture of the mind as physical symbol system is that there are physical structures that carry information and, by so doing, serve as *representations* of the immediate environment (or, of course, of things that are more abstract and/or more remote). This is another basic assumption of cognitive science. Information processing is, at bottom, a matter of transforming these representations in a way that finally yields the activity in the nervous system that "instructs" my limbs to jump into the water.

Information processing involves many different kinds of representation. This is illustrated by the example just given. The whole process begins with representations that carry information about vibrations in the eardrum. Somehow these representations get transformed into a much more complex representation that we might describe as my *belief* that you are in danger. This belief is in an important sense the "motor" of my behavior (my jumping into the water to rescue you). But it is not enough on its own. It needs to interact with other representations (such as my belief that I can reach you before you drown, and my *desire* to rescue you) in order to generate what I might think of as an *intention* to act in a certain way. This intention in turn gives rise to further representations, corresponding to the motor instructions that generate and control my bodily movements.

Among all these different types of representation, Fodor is particularly interested in the ones that correspond to beliefs, desires, and other similar psychological states. These psychological states are often called *propositional attitudes* by philosophers. They are called this because they can be analyzed as attitudes to propositions. Propositions are the sorts of thing that are expressed by ordinary sentences. So, there is a proposition expressed by the sentence "That person will drown" or by the sentence "It is snowing in St. Louis." Thinkers can have different attitudes to those propositions. I might fear the first, for example, and believe the second.

One of Fodor's ways of motivating the language of thought hypothesis is by reflecting on the role that propositional attitudes play in our understanding of behavior. As many philosophers and psychologists have stressed, we are, by and large, successful in explaining and predicting other people's behavior in terms of what they believe about the world and what they want to achieve. This success is something that itself needs explanation. Why is it that our vocabulary of beliefs and desires (our *belief-desire psychology* or *propositional attitude psychology*) is so deeply ingrained and indispensable in our social interactions and social coordination?

According to Fodor, there can only be one possible explanation. Belief-desire psychology is successful because it is true. There really are such things as beliefs and desires.

They are physical items that cause us to behave in certain ways. Belief-desire explanations are successful when they correctly identify the beliefs and other states that caused us to act in the way that we did. If I say that someone jumped into the water because he believed that a child was drowning and wanted to save her, then what I am really claiming is that that person's bodily behavior was caused by internal items corresponding to the belief that someone is drowning and the desire to save her. This view is often called *intentional realism or realism about the propositional attitudes*. Fodor's argument for the language of thought hypothesis is, in essence, that the hypothesis is the only way of explaining how belief-desire explanations can work. We will see how the argument works in the next two sub-sections.

Exercise 6.3 Explain intentional realism in your own words.

Intentional realism and causation by content

Intentional realism treats beliefs and desires as the sorts of things that can cause behavior. But this is a special type of causation. There is a fundamental difference between my leg moving because I am trying to achieve something (perhaps the journey of a thousand miles that starts with a single step) and my leg moving because a doctor has hit my knee with his hammer. In the first case, what causes my movement is what the desire is a desire for – namely, the beginning of the journey of a thousand miles. This is what philosophers call the *content* of the desire. There is nothing corresponding to this when a doctor hits my knee with a hammer.

Beliefs and desires cause behavior by virtue of how they represent the world – by virtue of their content. Any satisfactory account of intentional realism must explain how this type of *causation by content* is possible. In particular it needs to do justice to the rational relations holding between belief and desires, on the one hand, and the behavior that they cause on the other. Beliefs and desires cause behavior that makes sense in the light of them. Moving my leg is a rational thing to do if I desire to begin the journey of a thousand miles and believe that I am pointing in the right direction.

Yet causation by content is deeply mysterious. In one sense representations are simply objects like any other – they might be patterns of sound waves, populations of neurons, or pieces of paper. Thought of in this way there is no more difficulty in understanding how representations can cause behavior than there is in understanding how the doctor's hammer can make my leg move. But the representations that we are interested in (the propositional attitudes) are also things that bear a special *semantic* relation to the world – they have meanings. The puzzle is not just how representations can have causal effects within the world – but rather how representations can have causal effects within the world as a function of their semantic properties, as a function of the relations in which they stand to other objects in the world (and indeed to objects that may not in fact even be in existence).

The great advantage of the language of thought hypothesis, for Fodor, is that it solves the puzzle of causation by content. In order to see why, we need to formulate the puzzle more precisely. Fodor, along with almost all cognitive scientists and the vast majority of philosophers, holds that the manipulations that the brain carries out on representations are purely physical and mechanical. Brains and the representations that they contain are physical entities and this means that they can only be sensitive to certain types of property in mental representations. My utterance of the word "cat" is ultimately no more than a particular pattern of sound waves. These sound waves have certain physical properties that can have certain effects on the brain. They have amplitude, wavelength, frequency, and so on. But the fact that those sound waves represent cats for English-speakers is a very different type of property (or at least, so the argument goes).

Let us call the physical properties that can be manipulated within brains *formal properties*. We call them this because they have to do with the physical *form* (i.e. the shape) of the representation. And let's call the properties by virtue of which representations represent, *semantic properties* – just as semantics is the branch of linguistics that deals with the meanings of words (how words represent). This gives us another way of putting our problem. How can the brain be an information-processing machine if it is blind to the semantic properties of representations? How can the brain be an information-processing machine if all it can process are the formal properties of representations?

Exercise 6.4 Explain the contrast between formal and semantic properties in your own words.

This is where we see the particular slant that Fodor is putting on the physical symbol system hypothesis. Computers essentially manipulate strings of symbols. A computer programmed in binary, for example, manipulates strings of 1s and 0s. This string of 1s and 0s might represent a natural number, in the way that in binary 10 represents the number 2 and 11 represents the number 3. Or it might represent something completely different. It might represent whether or not the individual members of a long series of pixels are on or off, for example. In fact, with a suitable coding, a string of 1s and 0s can represent just about anything. As far as the computer is concerned, however, what the string of 1s and 0s represents is completely irrelevant. The semantic properties of the string are irrelevant. The computer simply manipulates the formal properties of the string of 1s and 0s. We might say, in fact, that the computer operates on *numerals* rather than *numbers*. Numerals are just symbols with particular shapes. Numbers are what those numerals represent.

Nonetheless, and this is the crucial point, the computer is programmed to manipulate strings of 1s and 0s in certain ways that yield the right result relative to the interpretation that is intended, even though the computer is blind to that interpretation. If the computer is a calculator, for example, and it is given two strings of 0s and 1s it will output a third string of 1s and 0s. If the first two strings represent the numbers 5 and 7 respectively, then the third string will be a binary representation of the number 12. But these semantic properties are irrelevant to the mechanics of what the computer actually does. All that the computer is doing is mechanically manipulating 1s and 0s – numerals not numbers – operating on their formal properties. But it does this in a way that respects their semantic properties.

So, computers manipulate symbols in a way that is sensitive only to their formal properties while respecting their semantic properties. And this, Fodor argues, is exactly what brains have to do. Brains are physical systems that can be sensitive only to the formal properties of mental representations. But nonetheless, as information processing machines, they (like computers) have to respect the semantic properties of mental representations. We can understand Fodor's argument from intentional realism to the language of thought hypothesis as follows. Since brains and computers have to solve the same problem, and we understand how computers solve it, the easiest way to understand how brains solve it is to think of the brain as a kind of computer.

Exercise 6.5 Explain the analogy between brains and computers in your own words.

The computer model of the mind and the relation between syntax and semantics

But how exactly does the analogy work? The following three claims summarize Fodor's distinctive way of working out the computer model of the mind.

1 Causation through content is ultimately a matter of causal interactions between physical states.
2 These physical states have the structure of sentences, and their sentence-like structure determines how they are made up and how they interact with each other.
3 Causal transitions between sentences in the language of thought respect the rational relations between the contents of those sentences in the language of thought.

The second and third claims represent Fodor's distinctive contribution to the problem of causation by content. The second is his influential view that the medium of cognition is what he calls the language of thought. According to Fodor, we think in sentences, but these are not sentences of a natural language such as English. The language of thought is much more like a logical language, such as the propositional calculus (which we looked at briefly earlier in this chapter – see Box 6.1). It is supposed to be free of the ambiguities and inaccuracies of English.

The analogy between the language of thought and logical languages is at the heart of Fodor's solution to the problem of causation by content. It is what lies behind claim (3). The basic fact about formal languages that Fodor exploits is the clear separation that they afford between *syntax* and *semantics*.

Consider, for example, the *predicate calculus*. This is a logical language more powerful and sophisticated than the propositional calculus we looked at in Box 6.1. Unlike the propositional calculus (which only allows us to talk about complete sentences or propositions) the predicate calculus allows us to talk directly about individuals and their properties. In order to do this the predicate calculus has special symbols. These special symbols include individual constants that name particular objects, and predicate letters that serve to name properties. The symbols are typically identifiable by simple typographical features (such as upper case for predicate letters and lower case for individual constants) and they can be combined to make complex symbols according to certain rules.

Viewed syntactically, a formal language such as the predicate calculus is simply a set of symbols of various types together with rules for manipulating those symbols according to their types. These rules identify the symbols only in terms of their typographical features. An example would be the rule that the space after an upper-case letter (e.g. the space in "F—") can only be filled with a lower-case letter (e.g. "*a*"). Simplifying somewhat, this rule is a way of capturing at the syntactic level the intuitive thought that properties apply primarily to things – because upper-case letters (such as "F—") can only be names of properties, while lower-case letters (such as "*a*") can only be names of objects. The rule achieves this, however, without explicitly stating anything about objects and properties. It just talks about symbols. It is a matter purely of the *syntax* of the language.

The connection between the formal system and what it is about, on the other hand, comes at the level of *semantics*. It is when we think about the semantics of a formal language that we assign objects to the individual constants and properties to the predicates. We identify the particular object that each individual constant names, for example. To provide a semantics for a language is to give an interpretation to the symbols it contains – to turn it from a collection of meaningless symbols into a representational system.

Just as one can view the symbols of a formal system both syntactically and semantically, so too can one view the transitions between those symbols in either of these two ways. The predicate calculus typically contains a rule called existential generalization. This rule can be viewed either syntactically or semantically. Viewed syntactically, the rule states that if on one line of a proof one has a formula of the form Fa, then on the next line of the proof one can write the formula $\exists x$ Fx.

Viewed semantically, on the other hand, the rule states that if it is true that one particular thing is F then it must be true that something is F. This is because the expression "$\exists x$ Fx" means that there is at least one thing (x) that is F – the symbol "$\exists$" is known as the existential quantifier. All transitions in formal systems can be viewed in these two ways, either as rules for manipulating essentially meaningless symbols or as rules determining relations between propositions.

Exercise 6.6 Explain the distinction between syntax and semantics in your own words.

It is because of this that it is standard to distinguish between two ways of thinking about the correctness of inferential transitions in formal systems. From a syntactic point of view the key notion is *logical deducibility*, where one symbol is derivable from another just if there is a sequence of legitimate formal steps that lead from the second to the first. From the semantic point of view, however, the key notion is *logical consequence*, where a conclusion is the logical consequence of a set of premises just if there is no way of interpreting the premises and conclusion that makes the premises all true and the conclusion false. We have logical deducibility when we have a derivation in which every step follows the rules, while we have logical consequence when we have an argument that preserves truth (that is, one that can never lead from a true premise to a false conclusion).

Fodor's basic proposal, then, is that we understand the relation between sentences in the language of thought and their content (or meaning) on the model of the relation between syntax and semantics in a formal system. Sentences in the language of thought can be viewed purely syntactically. From the syntactic point of view they are physical symbol structures composed of basic symbols concatenated according to certain rules of composition. Or they can be viewed semantically in terms of how they represent the world (in which case they are being viewed as the vehicles of propositional attitudes). And so, by extension, transitions between sentences in the language of thought can be viewed either syntactically or semantically – either in terms of formal relations holding between physical symbol structures, or in terms of semantic relations holding between states that represent the world.

Putting the pieces together: Syntax and the language of thought

Let us go back to Fodor's claim (3). Suppose we think that the causal transitions holding between sentences in the language of thought are essentially syntactic, holding purely in virtue of the formal properties of the relevant symbols irrespective of what those symbols might refer to. Then we need to ask the following question:

> Why do the syntactic relations between sentences in the language of thought map onto the semantic relations holding between the contents of those sentences?

If we take seriously the idea that the language of thought is a formal system, then this question has a perfectly straightforward answer. Syntactic transitions between sentences in the language of thought track semantic transitions between the contents of those sentences for precisely the same reason that syntax tracks semantics in any properly designed formal system.

Fodor can (and does) appeal to well-known results in meta-logic (the study of the expressive capacities and formal structure of logical systems) establishing a significant degree of correspondence between syntactic derivability and semantic validity. So, for example, it is known that the first-order predicate calculus is sound and complete. That is to say, in every well-formed proof in the first-order predicate calculus the conclusion really is a logical consequence of the premises (*soundness*) and, conversely, for every argument in which the conclusion follows logically from the premises and both conclusion and premises are formulable in the first-order predicate calculus there is a well-formed proof (*completeness*).

Put in the terms we have been employing, the combination of soundness and completeness has the following important consequences. If a series of legitimate and formally definable inferential transitions lead from formula A to a second formula B, then one can be sure that A cannot be true without B being true – and, conversely, if A entails B in a semantic sense then one can be sure that there will be a series of formally definable inferential transitions leading from A to B.

Let's look at an example of how this is supposed to work. Suppose that we have two complex symbols. Each of these symbols is a sentence in the language of thought. Each has a particular syntactic shape. Let us say that these are G*a* and F*a* respectively. These syntactic shapes have meanings – and the particular meanings that they can have are a function of their shape. We know that "F–" and "G–" are symbols for *predicates*. Let us say that "F–" means "– has red hair" and "G–" means "– is tall." We also know that "*a*" is a *name* symbol. Let us say that "*a*" names Georgina. The meaning of "G*a*" is that Georgina is tall, while the meaning of "F*a*" is that Georgina has red hair. We can look now at how a very simple piece of thinking might be analyzed by the language of thought hypothesis.

SYMBOLS	TRANSFORMATION RULE	MEANING
1. G*a*		1. Georgina is tall
2. F*a*		2. Georgina has red hair
3. (F*a* & G*a*)	If complex symbols "S" and "T" appear on earlier lines, then write "(S & T)"	3. Georgina is tall and has red hair
4. ∃*x* (F*x* & G*x*)	If on an earlier line there is a complex symbol containing a name symbol, then replace the name symbol by "*x*" and write "∃*x* —" in front of the complex symbol	4. At least one person is tall and has red hair

In the table we see how two physical symbols "G*a*" and "F*a*" can be transformed in two inferential steps into the more complex physical symbol "∃*x* (G*x* & F*x*)." The rules that achieve this transformation are purely syntactic, in the sense that they are rules for manipulating symbol structures. But when we look at the relation between the meanings of "F*a*" and "G*a*," on the one hand, and the meaning of "∃*x* (F*x* & G*x*)" on the other, we see that those purely syntactic transformations preserve the logical relations between the propositions that the symbols stand for. If it is true that Georgina is tall and that Georgina has red hair, then it is certainly true that at least one person is tall and has red hair.

To draw the threads together, then, beliefs and desires are realized by language-like physical structures (sentences in the language of thought), and practical reasoning and other forms of thinking are ultimately to be understood in terms of causal interactions between those structures. These causal interactions are sensitive only to the formal, syntactic properties of the physical structures. Yet, because the language of thought is a formal language with analogs of the formal properties of soundness and completeness, these purely syntactic transitions respect the semantic relations between the contents of the relevant beliefs and desires. This is how (Fodor claims) causation by content takes place in a purely physical system such as the human brain. And so, he argues,

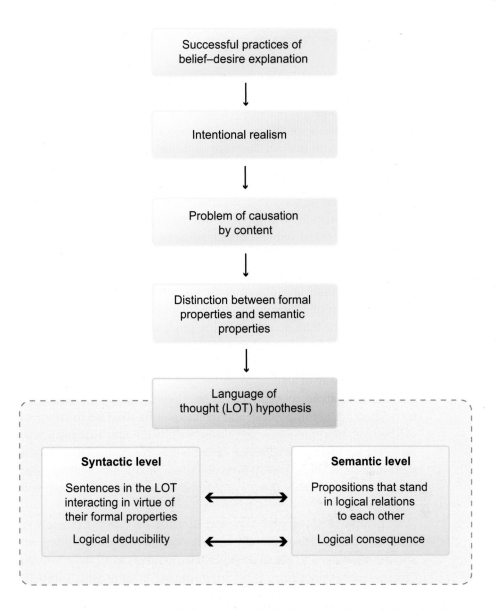

Figure 6.3 The structure of Fodor's argument for the language of thought hypothesis.

commonsense psychological explanation is vindicated by thinking of the mind as a computer processing sentences in the language of thought.

The line of reasoning that leads to the language of thought hypothesis is fairly complicated. To make it easier to keep track of the different steps, I have represented them diagrammatically in Figure 6.3.

Exercise 6.7 Use the flowchart in Figure 6.3 to explain Fodor's argument in your own words.

6.3 The Chinese room argument

The physical symbol system hypothesis holds that we have intelligent behavior when (and only when) we have systems that manipulate symbols according to rules. The language of thought hypothesis is a particular way of applying this model of intelligent behavior. It offers a specific proposal for how to understand the symbols. The symbols are sentences in an internal language of thought. The language of thought hypothesis also tells us what the rules are going to be like and how they will end up producing intelligent behavior. These rules are fundamentally syntactic in form, transforming the physical symbols in ways that depend solely on their physical/formal characteristics. These transformations will produce intelligent behavior because syntactic transformations of the physical symbols mimic semantic relations between the propositions that give meaning to the physical symbols.

We need now to stand back from the details of the language of thought hypothesis to consider a fundamental objection to the very idea of the physical symbol system hypothesis. This objection comes from the philosopher John Searle, who is convinced that no machine built according to the physical symbol system hypothesis could possibly be capable of intelligent behavior. He tries to show that the physical symbol system hypothesis is misconceived through a thought experiment. Thought experiments are a very standard way of arguing in philosophy. Thought experiments are intended to test our intuitions about concepts and ideas. They do this by imagining scenarios that are far-fetched, but not impossible, and then exploring what we think about them.

The basic idea that Searle takes issue with is the idea that manipulating symbols is sufficient for intelligent behavior - even when the manipulation produces exactly the right outputs. What he tries to do is describe a situation in which symbols are correctly manipulated, but where there seems to be no genuine understanding and no genuine intelligence.

Searle asks us to imagine a person in what he calls a Chinese room. The person receives pieces of paper through one window and passes out pieces of paper through another window. The pieces of paper have symbols in Chinese written on them. The Chinese room, in essence, is an input-output system, with symbols as inputs and outputs. The way the input-output system works is determined by a huge instruction manual that tells the person in the room which pieces of paper to pass out depending on which pieces of paper she receives. The instruction manual is essentially just a way of pairing input symbols with output symbols. It is not written in Chinese and can be understood and followed by someone who knows no Chinese. All that the person needs to be able to do is to identify Chinese symbols in some sort of syntactic way - according to their shape, for example. This is enough for them to be able to find the right output for each input - where the right output is taken to be the output dictated by the instruction manual.

The Chinese room is admittedly a little far-fetched, but it does seem to be perfectly possible. Now, Searle continues, imagine two further things. Imagine, first, that the

Figure 6.4 Inside and outside the Chinese room.

instruction manual has been written in such a way that the inputs are all questions in Chinese and the outputs are all appropriate answers to those questions. To all intents and purposes, therefore, the Chinese room is answering questions in Chinese. Now imagine that the person in the room does not in fact know any Chinese. All he is doing is following the instructions in the instruction manual (which is written in English). The situation is illustrated in Figure 6.4. What the Chinese room shows, according to Searle, is that it is perfectly possible for there to be syntactic symbol manipulation without any form of intelligence or understanding.

The Chinese room seems to be set up in accordance with the physical symbol system hypothesis. After all, the person in the Chinese room is manipulating symbols according to their formal/syntactic properties. Moreover, the Chinese room has been set up so that it produces the right output for every input. In the terms we used in the last section, the syntactic manipulation of the symbols preserves their semantic properties. The semantic properties of the input symbols are their meanings - i.e. certain questions. The semantic properties of the output symbols are answers to those questions. So, as long as the person in the Chinese room follows the instructions correctly, the semantic relations between input and output will be preserved. And yet, Searle argues, the Chinese room does not understand Chinese. How can it understand Chinese, given that the person in the room does not understand Chinese?

But if the Chinese room does not understand Chinese then, Searle argues, there is no sense in which it is behaving intelligently. To someone outside the room it might look as if there is intelligent behavior going on. The machine does, after all, respond to the questions it is asked with answers that make sense. But this is just an illusion of intelligence. The Chinese room cannot be behaving intelligently if it does not understand Chinese. And so it is a counter-example to the physical symbol system hypothesis - or so Searle argues.

The Chinese room and the Turing test

Before we look at ways of responding to Searle's Chinese room argument we need to relate it to another important idea in thinking about the relation between symbol manipulation and intelligence. This is the famous Turing test, proposed by Alan Turing in his paper "Computing machinery and intelligence" (Turing 1950). Turing proposed a test for machine intelligence, as a replacement for what he considered to be thorny and ultimately intractable debates about whether machines could think.

The Turing test is based on what he called the imitation game. The imitation game has three players - a man, a woman, and an interrogator. The interrogator is in a room separate from the other two players, but able to communicate with them by means of a printer (or some other technology that will not give any clues about the identity of the other player). The interrogator's job is to ask questions that will allow him to work out which of the other two players is male and which female.

Suppose, Turing proposed, that we replace one of the players by a machine and change the rules of the game so that the interrogator's job is now to work out which of the players is a machine and which human. If the interrogator makes no more mistakes in the machine version of the game than in the male-female version, then, Turing claimed, that is a sign that the machine is genuinely intelligent. So, as far as Turing was concerned, the aim of artificial intelligence was to build machines that would pass the Turing test.

Exercise 6.8 How plausible do you find the Turing test as a criterion of intelligence?

Taking the Turing test as a criterion of intelligence is much weaker than the physical symbol system hypothesis. This is because the Turing test places no constraints on *how* the machine manages to pass the test. All that matters is that the machine fool the interrogator, not that it achieve this result by manipulating symbols according to their syntactic properties. The Turing test really only requires that what comes out of the machine is appropriate, given what goes into it. What actually happens between input and output is completely irrelevant.

The way in which the Chinese room argument is formulated makes it an objection to taking the Turing test to be a criterion of intelligence, as well as an objection to the physical symbol system hypothesis. It seems plausible that a suitably constructed Chinese room would pass the Turing test – and so if Searle is right that the Chinese room does not display intelligent behavior, then passing the Turing test cannot be a sufficient condition for intelligent behavior. But it is perfectly possible to reject the Turing test as a criterion of intelligence while accepting the physical symbol system hypothesis. Someone who took this position might deny that the Chinese room argument is effective against the physical symbol system hypothesis, while still holding that there has to be more to intelligent behavior than simply passing the Turing test. Or, to put it another way, one can reject the Chinese room argument without endorsing the Turing test as a criterion of intelligence.

Responding to the Chinese room argument

The Chinese room argument has been much discussed by philosophers and cognitive scientists. My aim here is not to come out for or against the argument. It is simply to introduce you to some of the main moves that have been made (or might be made) in the debate – and so to to give you the tools to make your own assessment of its power and plausibility.

Many people have pointed out that there seems to be a crucial equivocation in the argument. The physical symbol system hypothesis is a hypothesis about how cognitive systems work. It says, in effect, that any cognitive system capable of intelligent behavior will be a physical symbol system – and hence that it will operate by manipulating physical symbol structures. The crucial step in the Chinese room argument, however, is not a claim about the system as a whole. It is a claim about part of the system – namely, the person inside the room who is reading and applying the instruction manual. The force of the claim that the Chinese room as a whole does not understand Chinese rests almost entirely on the fact that this person does not understand Chinese. According to what Searle and others have called the *systems reply* to the argument, the argument is simply based on a mistake about where the intelligence is supposed to be located. Supporters of the systems reply hold that the Chinese room as a whole understands Chinese and is displaying intelligent behavior, even though the person inside the room does not understand Chinese.

Here is one way of developing the systems reply in a little more depth. It is true, someone might say, that the person in the room does not understand Chinese.

Nonetheless, that person is still displaying intelligent behavior. It is no easy matter to apply the sort of instruction manual that Searle is envisaging. After all, using an English dictionary to look words up is not entirely straightforward, and what Searle is envisaging is more complex by many orders of difficulty. The person inside the room needs to be able to discriminate between different Chinese symbols – which is no easy matter, as anyone who has tried to learn Chinese well knows. They will also need to be able to find their way around the instruction manual (which at the very least requires knowing how the symbols are ordered) and then use it to output the correct symbols. The person inside the room is certainly displaying and exercising a number of sophisticated skills. Each of these sophisticated skills in turn involves exercising some slightly less sophisticated skills. Discriminating the Chinese characters involves exercising certain basic perceptual skills, for example.

A supporter of the systems reply could argue that we can analyze the ability to understand Chinese in terms of these more basic skills and abilities. This would be a very standard explanatory move for a cognitive scientist to make. As we have seen on several occasions, cognitive scientists often break complex abilities down into simpler abilities in order to show how the complex ability emerges from the simpler ones, provided that they are suitably organized and related. This is the source of the "boxological" diagrams and analyses that we have looked at, including the Broadbent model of attention (in section 1.4) and the Petersen model of lexical processing (in section 3.4). A cognitive scientist adopting this strategy could argue that the system as a whole has the ability to understand Chinese because it is made up of parts, and these parts individually possess the abilities that together add up to the ability to understand Chinese.

Searle himself is not very impressed by the systems reply. He has a clever objection. Instead of imagining yourself in the Chinese room, imagine the Chinese room inside you! If you memorize the instruction manual then, Searle says, you have effectively internalized the Chinese room. Of course, it's hard to imagine that anyone could have a good enough memory to do this, but there are no reasons to think that it is in principle impossible. But, Searle argues, internalizing the Chinese room in this way is not enough to turn you from someone who does not understand Chinese into someone who does. After all, what you've memorized is not Chinese, but just a complex set of rules for mapping some symbols you don't understand onto other symbols you don't understand.

Exercise 6.9 How convincing do you find this response to the systems reply?

Another common way of responding to the Chinese room argument is what is known as the robot reply. We can think about this as another way of developing the basic idea that we need to analyze in more detail what understanding Chinese actually consists in (in order to move beyond vague intuitions about understanding or its absence). Some writers have suggested that the Chinese room, as Searle describes it, is far too thinly described. The problem is not with what goes on inside the room, but rather with what goes into the room and comes out of it.

A supporter of the robot reply would agree with Searle that the Chinese room does not understand Chinese – but for very different reasons. The problem with the Chinese room has nothing to do with some sort of impassable gap between syntax and semantics. The problem, rather, is that it is embodied agents who understand Chinese, not disembodied cognitive systems into which pieces of paper enter and from which other pieces of paper come out. Understanding Chinese is a complex ability that manifests itself in how an agent interacts with other people and with items in the world.

The ability to understand Chinese involves, at a minimum, being able to carry out instructions given in Chinese, to coordinate with other Chinese-speakers, to read Chinese characters, and to carry on a conversation. In order to build a machine that could do all this we would need to embed the Chinese room in a robot, providing it with some analog of sensory organs, vocal apparatus, and limbs. If the Chinese room had all this and could behave in the way that a Chinese-speaker behaves then, a supporter of the robot reply would say, there is no reason to deny that the system understands Chinese and is behaving intelligently.

Again, Searle is unconvinced. For him the gulf between syntax and semantics is too deep to be overcome by equipping the Chinese room with ways of obtaining information from the environment and ways of acting in the world. An embodied Chinese room might indeed stop when it "sees" the Chinese character for "stop." But this would simply be something it has learnt to do. It no more understands what the character means than a laboratory pigeon trained not to peck at a piece of card with the same character on it. Interacting with the environment is not the same as understanding it. Even if the Chinese room does and says all the right things, this does not show that it understands Chinese. The basic problem still remains, as far as Searle is concerned: simply manipulating symbols does not make them meaningful and unless the symbols are meaningful to the Chinese room there is no relation between what it does and what a "real" Chinese-speaker might do.

Exercise 6.10 Explain the robot reply and assess Searle's response to it.

Clearly there are some very deep issues here. Searle's arguments go right to the heart, not just of the physical symbol system hypothesis, but also of the very question of how it is possible for an embodied agent to interact meaningfully with the world. Searle sometimes writes as if the problems he raises are specific to the enterprise of trying to build intelligent symbol manipulators. But it may be that some of his arguments against the physical symbol system apply far more widely. It may be, for example, that exactly the same questions that Searle raises for the robot reply can be asked of ordinary human beings interacting with the world. What exactly is it that explains the meaningfulness of our thoughts, speech, and actions? Some cognitive scientists have given this problem a name. They call it the *symbol-grounding problem*. It is the subject of the next section.

The symbol-grounding problem

We can see Searle's Chinese room argument as illustrating a more general problem. Searle's target is the physical symbol system hypothesis. The physical symbol system hypothesis is a hypothesis about the nature of information processing. It claims that the mind processes information by manipulating symbols. Searle uses the example of the Chinese room to argue that there is a huge and impassable gap between formal symbol manipulation, on the one hand, and genuine thought and understanding on the other. The force of the argument rests, of course, on the undeniable fact that we know what it is like to encounter meaningful symbols that we understand. We do this every time that we engage in a conversation in our native language, for example, and whenever we read a newspaper. Searle's argument trades on the powerful intuition that the way things are for the person in the Chinese room is fundamentally different from how they are for us when we answer questions in a language that we understand.

But the fact that the experience of manipulating symbols with understanding is so familiar should not blind us to the fact that it is really rather mysterious. How do symbols become meaningful? This is what is often called the *symbol-grounding problem*.

Exercise 6.11 State the symbol-grounding problem in your own words.

It is important to distinguish the symbol-grounding problem from another problem that seems on the face of it to be rather similar. Philosophers often use the word "intentionality" to refer to the property symbols have of being about things in the world. Philosophers of mind and philosophers of language have spent a lot of time exploring different ways of explaining the intentionality of thought and language. Like the symbol-grounding problem the *problem of intentionality* is a very deep problem. But the two problems are subtly different.

Exercise 6.12 State the problem of intentionality in your own words.

The symbol-grounding problem is a problem about how words and thoughts become meaningful to speakers and thinkers. The problem of intentionality is a problem about how words and thoughts connect up with the world. In order to see why these problems are different we can think back to the Chinese room. The person in the Chinese room is manipulating symbols. These symbols are, as it happens, symbols in Chinese that refer to objects and properties in the world. So we can ask: What makes it the case that those symbols refer to the objects and properties that they do?

One way of answering this question would be to appeal to the linguistic behavior of people in China. So we might say that what makes it the case that a given Chinese character refers to tables is that that is how it is used by people in China. If this is right (and it seems plausible) then we have a good answer to the question of how the symbols connect up with the world. But this does not tell us anything about the symbol-grounding problem. A correct account of the intentionality of the symbols cannot solve the symbol-grounding problem because (if Searle is right) the symbols are not grounded.

Exercise 6.13 Explain the difference between the symbol-grounding problem and the problem of intentionality in your own words.

For this reason, then, the symbol-grounding problem is more fundamental than the problem of intentionality. We can have a perfectly good answer to the problem of intentionality without having an answer to the symbol-grounding problem. But do we have any idea what an answer to the symbol-grounding problem might look like?

It depends on what type of symbol we are thinking about. When we think about linguistic symbols there seems to be an obvious answer to the symbol-grounding problem. Words in a language are meaningful for us because we attach meanings to them when we learn how to use them. If this is right then the meaningfulness of words in a public language comes from the meaningfulness of our own thoughts. But this of course just pushes the problem a step further back. What makes our thoughts meaningful?

This is not an easy question to answer. One problem is that a regress quickly threatens. It is fine to say that linguistic symbols become meaningful because in thinking about them we attach meanings to them. But we obviously can't say the same thing about thoughts. That would be trying to pull ourselves up by our bootstraps. The activity that we are appealing to in our explanation (meaningful thinking) is the very activity that we are trying to explain.

It seems very unsatisfying to say that thoughts are intrinsically meaningful. It is true that that is the way that things *seem* to us. Our thoughts always come to us already interpreted, as it were. But cognitive scientists cannot be content with appeals to intro-spection. Introspection gives us data, not explanations. But if we try to explain the meaningfulness of thoughts then it looks as if we run straight into the symbol-grounding problem again.

The basic principle of cognitive science is that the mind works by processing infor-mation. So thinking must, in the last analysis, be a form of information processing. If this information processing is symbolic, then the symbol-grounding problem immedi-ately raises its head. Many people who share the sort of intuitions that drive the Chinese room argument (and who are unimpressed by the systems and robot replies sketched out in the last section) would think that in order to solve the problem we need to do one of two things. We can either abandon the idea that cognition is a form of information processing (and with it abandon the idea that cognitive science can explain the mind). Or we can look for forms of information processing that are not symbolic.

Searle himself would, I suspect, take the first option. Before following him in this, however, we would do well to explore the second option! We will start doing this in Chapter 8, where we explore the neural networks approach to information processing. The neural networks approach offers a fundamentally different approach to information processing – one that is not based on the idea of symbol manipulation. First, though, we should take a step back from these objections to the physical symbol system hypothesis. We will be in a much better position to evaluate them when we have looked at some concrete examples of the hypothesis in action.

Summary

Chapter 5 introduced the concept of a mental architecture, which combines a model of how information is stored and processed with a model of the overall organization of the mind. This chapter has looked at one of the two principal models of information storage and processing – the physical symbol system hypothesis, originally proposed by Newell and Simon. After introducing the physical symbol system hypothesis we saw a particular application of it in the language of thought hypothesis developed by Jerry Fodor in order to solve problems associated with the psychological explanation of behavior. The chapter also discussed two objections to the physical symbol system hypothesis – the Chinese room argument and the symbol-grounding problem.

Checklist

The physical symbol system hypothesis states that a physical symbol system has necessary and sufficient means for general intelligent action. In more detail:
(1) These symbols are physical patterns.
(2) Physical symbols can be combined to form complex symbol structures.
(3) Physical symbol systems contain processes for manipulating complex symbol structures.
(4) The processes for manipulating complex symbol structures can be represented by symbols and structures within the system.
(5) Problems are solved by generating and modifying symbol structures until a solution structure is reached.

The physical symbol system hypothesis is very programmatic. Fodor's language of thought hypothesis is one way of turning the physical symbol system hypothesis into a concrete proposal about mental architecture.
(1) The language of thought hypothesis is grounded in realism about the propositional attitudes. Propositional attitudes such as belief and desire are real physical entities. These entities are sentences in the language of thought.
(2) It offers a way of explaining causation by content (i.e. how physical representations can have causal effects in the world as a function of how they represent the world).
(3) Fodor suggests that we understand the relation between sentences in the language of thought and their contents on the model of the relation between syntax and semantics in a formal system.
(4) The syntax of the language of thought tracks its semantics because the language of thought is a formal language with analogs of the formal properties of soundness and completeness.

The Chinese room argument is a thought experiment directed against the idea that the rule-governed manipulation of symbols is sufficient to produce intelligent behavior.
(1) The person in the Chinese room is manipulating symbols according to their formal/syntactic properties without any understanding of Chinese.

(2) According to the systems reply, the Chinese room argument misses the point, because the real question is whether the system as a whole understands Chinese, not whether the person in the room understands Chinese.

(3) According to the robot reply, the Chinese room does not understand Chinese. But this is not because of any uncrossable gap between syntax and semantics. Rather, it is because the Chinese room has no opportunity to interact with the environment and other people.

(4) The Chinese room argument can be viewed as an instance of the more general symbol-grounding problem.

Further reading

The paper by Newell and Simon discussed in section 6.1 is reprinted in a number of places, including Boden 1990b and Bermúdez 2006. A good introduction to the general ideas behind the physical symbol system hypothesis in the context of artificial intelligence is Haugeland 1985, particularly ch. 2, and Haugeland 1997, ch. 4. See also chs 1–3 of Johnson-Laird 1988, chs 4 and 5 of Copeland 1993, ch. 2 of Dawson 1998, and the *Encyclopedia of Cognitive Science* entry on Symbol Systems (Nadel 2005). Russell and Norvig 2009 is the new edition of a popular AI textbook. Also see Poole and Mackworth 2010, Warwick 2012, and Proudfoot and Copeland's chapter on artificial intelligence in *The Oxford Handbook of Philosophy of Cognitive Science* (Margolis, Samuels, and Stich 2012).

Fodor 1975 and 1987 are classic expositions of the language of thought approach from a philosophical perspective. For Fodor's most recent views see Fodor 2008. For a psychologist's perspective see Pylyshyn's book *Computation and Cognition* (Pylyshyn 1984) and his earlier target article in *Behavioral and Brain Sciences* (Pylyshyn 1980). More recent philosophical discussions of the language of thought can be found in Schneider 2011 and Schneider and Katz 2012. The *Encyclopedia of Cognitive Science* has an entry on the topic, as does the *Stanford Encyclopedia of Philosophy*. For a general, philosophical discussion of the computational picture of the mind Crane 2003 and Sterelny 1990 are recommended. Block 1995a explores the metaphor of the mind as the software of the brain. Fodor's argument for the language of thought hypothesis is closely tied to important research in mathematical logic and the theory of computation. Rogers 1971 is an accessible overview. For general introductions to philosophical debates about mental causation and the more general mind–body problem, see Heil 2004 and Searle 2004.

Searle presents the Chinese room argument in his "Minds, brains, and programs" (1980). This was originally published in the journal *Behavioral and Brain Sciences* with extensive commentary from many cognitive scientists. Margaret Boden's article "Escaping from the Chinese room" (Boden 1990a), reprinted in Heil 2004, is a good place to start in thinking about the Chinese room. The entry on the Chinese room argument in the online *Stanford Encyclopedia of Philosophy* is comprehensive and has a very full bibliography. The *Encyclopedia of Cognitive Science* has an entry as well. The symbol-grounding problem is introduced and discussed in Harnad 1990 (available in the online resources).

CHAPTER SEVEN

Applying the symbolic paradigm

Overview

Now that we have the theory behind the physical symbol system hypothesis clearly in view we can explore its application to particular information-processing problems. We have already looked at one example of what is often called the symbolic paradigm. This is the SHRDLU program written by Terry Winograd and discussed in section 2.1. SHRDLU inhabits a virtual micro-world. It uses a simple language program to describe that world and to receive instructions about what actions to perform. It would be a very useful exercise at this stage to go back to section 2.1 in the light of the discussion in the previous chapter and work out how and why SHRDLU illustrates the basic principles of the physical symbol system hypothesis.

In this chapter we look in detail at three more applications of the symbolic paradigm. The first comes from research in Artificial Intelligence (AI) into expert systems. This is one of the domains where the symbolic approach is widely viewed as very successful. Expert systems are designed to simulate human experts in highly specialized tasks, such as the diagnosis of disease. They standardly operate through decision trees. These decision trees can either be explicitly programmed into them or, as in the cases we are interested in, they can be constructed from a database by a *machine learning algorithm*. In section 7.1 we see how machine learning algorithms illustrate Newell and Simon's heuristic search hypothesis. In section 7.2 we explore in detail a particular machine learning algorithm – the ID3 algorithm developed by the computer scientist Ross Quinlan.

The ID3 machine learning algorithm is a very traditional application of the physical symbol system hypothesis. The physical symbol system hypothesis is standardly developed in ways that depend upon the physical symbols being essentially language-like. This is very clear, for example, in the language of thought hypothesis. But the physical symbol system hypothesis does not have to be developed in this way. Physical symbol systems can involve representations that are imagistic or pictorial. As we saw in section 2.2, there is experimental evidence that some cognitive information processing does involve imagistic representations. In section 7.3 we look at the WHISPER program developed by Brian Funt. This program exploits imagistic representations in order to solve problems of physical reasoning in a micro-world very much like that inhabited by SHRDLU.

Finally, in section 7.4 we look at one of the historic achievements of early cognitive science. This is SHAKEY, a mobile robot developed at the Artificial Intelligence Center at SRI (Stanford Research Institute). SHAKEY shows how the physical symbol system hypothesis can serve as a theoretical framework for bringing together language processing, computer vision, and robotic engineering. SHAKEY was designed to operate and perform simple tasks in a real, physical environment. The programs built into it permitted SHAKEY to plan ahead and to learn how to perform tasks better.

7.1 Expert systems, machine learning, and the heuristic search hypothesis

The physical symbol system hypothesis was first proposed by two of the founding fathers of AI – Allen Newell and Herbert Simon. In fact, workers in the field often think of the physical symbol system hypothesis as the basic doctrine of Good Old-Fashioned AI - or, as it is standardly abbreviated, GOFAI. (The contrast is with AI research inspired by neural networks, which we will be looking at in more detail in the next chapter.) Although "GOFAI" may not be the most flattering of terms, the enterprise of symbolic AI remains vigorous and many areas could be chosen to illustrate how the physical symbol system hypothesis can be applied. One particularly relevant area is the field of AI known as *expert systems* research, where researchers set out to write computer programs that will reproduce the performance of human beings who are expert in a particular domain.

Expert systems programs are typically applied in narrowly defined domains to solve determinate problems. Diagnosis of fairly specific medical disorders is a popular area for expert systems research. A well-known expert systems program called MYCIN was developed at Stanford University in the early 1970s. MYCIN was designed to simulate a human expert in diagnosing infectious diseases. MYCIN took in information from doctors on a particular patient's symptoms, medical history, and blood tests, asking for any required information that it did not already have. It then analyzed this information using a knowledge base of about 600 heuristic rules about infectious diseases derived from clinical experts and textbooks.

MYCIN produced a number of different diagnoses and recommendations for antibiotic treatments. It was able to calculate its degree of confidence in each diagnosis and so present its findings as a prioritized list. Although MYCIN was never actually used as the sole tool for diagnosing patients, a widely reported study at Stanford University's medical school found that it produced an acceptable diagnosis in 69 percent of cases. You may think that 69 percent is not very high, but it turns out to be significantly higher than infectious disease experts who were using the same rules and information.

Expert systems and decision trees

Expert systems have become very deeply entrenched in the financial services industry, particularly for mortgage loan applications and tax advice. Most banks these days have online "wizards" that will take mortgage applicants through a series of simple questions designed to lead to a decision on the applicant's "mortgage-worthiness." Mortgage wizards can be represented through *decision trees.* In the simplest form of decision tree each node corresponds to a question. Each node has several branches leading from it. Each branch corresponds to an answer to the question. The answer the mortgage applicant gives determines which branch the program goes down, and hence what the next question will be.

Figure 7.1 illustrates a very simple schematic expert system for a loan decision tree. Two features of this decision tree are worth highlighting. First, it offers a fixed decision procedure. Whatever answers the loan applicant gives to the fixed questions, the decision tree will eventually come up with a recommendation. Second, the presentation in tree form is completely inessential. We can easily convey what is going on in terms of explicit rules, such as the following:

IF income less than $40K THEN no loan

IF income greater than $75K AND no criminal record THEN loan

IF income between $40K and $75K AND applicant working for 1–5 years AND credit not good THEN no loan

(I have used upper-case letters to bring out the logical structure of the rules.) When the decision tree is written as a computer program it may well be written using explicit rules such as these.

Let us think now about what makes this decision tree work as well as it does. In one sense the answer is obvious. The decision tree works because of the questions that are asked at each node. When taken together the questions exhaust the space of possibilities. Each question partitions the possibility space in such a way that each branch of the tree

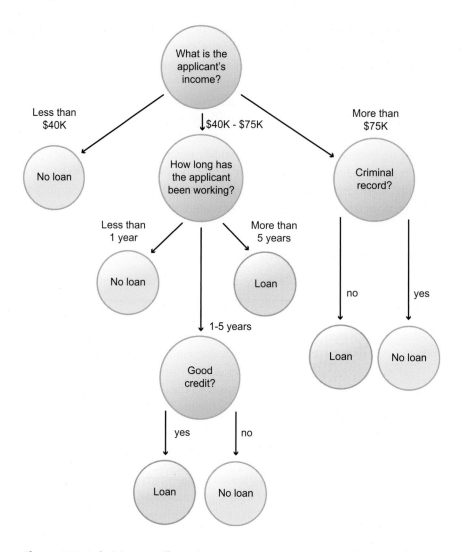

Figure 7.1 A decision tree illustrating a mortgage expert system. (From Friedenberg and Silverman 2006)

leads to a unique outcome (which computer scientists call a *terminal leaf or node*). But how are we supposed to get to these questions? How does the decision tree get designed, as it were?

One simple way of doing it would be to ask a team of mortgage loan officers to sit down and work out a decision tree that would more or less map onto the practices at their bank. This could then be used as the basis for writing a program in a suitable programming language. This would be fine, and it is no doubt how many expert systems programs are actually written (particularly in the mortgage area). But from the perspective of AI this would not be very interesting. It would be an expert system only in a very derivative sense. The real expert system would be the team of mortgage loan professionals. Much more interesting would be a program that was capable of producing its own decision tree – a program capable of imposing its own structure upon the problem and working out what would count as a solution. How would this work?

Here is a more precise way of characterizing the problem. Suppose that we have a huge database of all the loan decisions that the bank has taken over a long period of time, together with all the relevant information about the applicants – their income, work history, credit rating, and so on. If we can find a way of representing the bank's past decisions in the form of a decision tree, so that each branch of the tree ends either in the loan being given or the loan being declined, then we can use that decision tree to "process" new applications.

Machine learning and the physical symbol system hypothesis

We can put the same point the other way around. The decision tree in Figure 7.1 is a tool for analyzing new loan applications. The information that any applicant provides in response to the questions that the tree poses will steer the applicant down one of the branches and the applicant will end up with their application either being approved or turned down. So the challenge for the expert system is to come up with a decision tree like that in Figure 7.1 from a database of previous loan applicants, their personal information, and the decision that was eventually made.

This is a classic example of the type of problem tackled in the branch of AI known as *machine learning* (a sub-field in expert systems research). The challenge is to produce an algorithm that will organize a complex database in terms of some attribute we are particularly interested in (such as an applicant's loan-worthiness, in the example we are considering). The organization takes the form of a decision tree, which will determine whether or not the attribute holds in a given case (i.e. whether or not the applicant is loan-worthy).

In the case of the mortgage loan decision tree the target attribute is labeled as *Loan*. All the branches of the decision tree must end in terminal nodes that have a value for the target attribute (i.e. they must say *Yes* or *No*). The decision tree is constructed by classifying the database in terms of other features (such as *Good credit?* or *Earns more than $75K?*). Once the decision tree has been constructed, it can then be used to decide whether some new instance (i.e. some new mortgage applicant) has the target attribute or not (i.e. is approved for the loan or not).

In the next section we will look in some detail at how an influential machine learning algorithm works. But first let me make explicit the connection with the physical symbol system hypothesis. As we saw in section 6.1, the physical symbol system hypothesis involves four basic claims.

1 Symbols are physical patterns.
2 Symbols can be combined to form complex symbol structures.

3   The physical symbol system contains processes for manipulating symbols and symbol structures.

4   The processes for generating and transforming complex symbol structures can themselves be represented by symbols and symbol structures within the system.

We have already looked in some detail at these claims in the context of the language of thought hypothesis. The machine learning literature gives us another way of thinking about claims (3) and (4). These claims are closely associated with what Newell and Simon called the heuristic search hypothesis. This is the hypothesis that problems are solved by generating and modifying symbol structures until a suitable solution structure is found.

Machine learning algorithms certainly operate on symbol structures in the sense defined by (3) and (4). The programming languages used to write GOFAI learning algorithms are defined over precisely the sort of symbol structures that Newell and Simon had in mind. What is interesting about the algorithms is that they make very vivid how a problem can be solved by modifying and manipulating symbol structures. The symbol structures that the algorithm starts with are complex databases of the sort that we have been discussing – collections of information about, for example, mortgage loan applicants, their financial histories, and whether or not they were granted loans. The job of the learning algorithm is to transform this complex database into a different kind of symbol structure – namely, a set of IF … THEN … rules that collectively determine a decision tree.

What machine learning algorithms do, therefore, is transform symbol structures until they arrive at a solution structure (a decision tree that can be used to classify incoming data not already in the database). When we look in more detail at particular machine learning algorithms in the next section we will see how exactly this process of transforming symbol structures works. We will be looking at the physical symbol system hypothesis in action.

7.2   ID3: An algorithm for machine learning

This section explores an influential machine learning algorithm developed by the computer scientist Ross Quinlan. Quinlan developed the ID3 learning algorithm while working at the University of Sydney in Australia. He now runs a company called RuleQuest Research which is commercially marketing updated and more efficient versions of the ID3 algorithm.

Remember the basic problem that a machine learning algorithm is designed to solve. A machine learning algorithm works on a vast database of information. It looks for regularities in the database that will allow it to construct a decision tree. In order to specify what is going on more clearly we need a precise way of describing the information in a database. Machine learning algorithms such as ID3 only work on databases that take a very specific form. There are algorithms more advanced than ID3 that are less constrained than it is, but these more advanced algorithms have constraints of their own.

The basic objects in the database are standardly called *examples*. In the loan application decision tree that we looked at earlier, the examples are loan applicants. These loan applicants can be classified in terms of a certain number of *attributes*. Each example has a value for each attribute. So, for example, if the attribute is *Credit History?*, then the possible values are *Good or Bad* and each mortgage applicant is assigned exactly one of these values. We can call the attribute we are interested in the *target attribute*. In our example the target attribute is *Loan* and the two possible values are *Yes* and *No*. Again, every applicant either receives a loan or is turned down.

The attributes work to divide the examples into two or more classes. So, for example, the attribute at the top of the decision tree is *Income?*. This attribute divides the loan applicants into three groups. As we move down each branch of the tree each node is an attribute that divides the branch into two or more further branches. Each branch ends when it arrives at a value for the target attribute (i.e. when the decision is made on whether to give the loan or not).

From this brief description we see that the sort of databases we are considering have three basic features:

1 The examples must be characterizable in terms of a fixed set of attributes.
2 Each attribute must have a fixed set of values.
3 Every example has exactly one value for each attribute.

When we take these three features together they rule out any ambiguity or fuzziness in the database. They also make clear exactly what the machine learning algorithm is doing. It is learning in the sense that it is turning a complex database into a decision tree. This decision tree can then be applied to new examples, provided that we know the values that those examples have on every attribute except for their value for the target attribute.

This is the whole point of a machine learning algorithm. It makes it possible to extract from a database a procedure that can then be applied to new cases. The procedure is the decision tree and if the database has features (1) through (3) it will always be possible to extract a decision tree and then use that decision tree to determine how to deal with new cases.

So how does the learning algorithm turn a database with features (1) through (3) into a decision tree? The intuitive idea is not (too) hard to describe, although the details can get tricky. I'll sketch out the basic idea, and then we can look at an example to see how the details get worked out.

From database to decision tree

The ID3 algorithm exploits the basic fact that each attribute divides the set of examples into two or more classes. What it does is assign attributes to nodes. It identifies, for each node in the decision tree, which attribute would be most informative at that point. That is, it identifies at each node which attribute would divide the remaining examples up in the most informative way. Everything depends here on how we measure informativeness – and this is where the details start to get important.

The ID3 algorithm uses a statistical measure of informativeness. This measure is standardly called *information gain*. Informally, information gain is a measure of how much information we would acquire by being told that an example has the attribute in question. So, information gain measures how well a particular attribute classifies a set of examples.

At each node the algorithm has to choose one of the remaining attributes to assign to that node. (It does not have to worry about the attributes that have already been assigned at earlier nodes in the branch.) It does this by identifying, for each node in the tree, the information gain associated with each of the available attributes. The aim is to assign to each node the attribute with the highest information gain. The basic idea here is that we will learn more by categorizing our examples according to the attribute with the highest information gain.

The concept of information gain is itself defined in terms of a more fundamental measure called *entropy*. (Warning: You may have come across the concept of entropy in physics, where it features for example in the second law of thermodynamics. Entropy is defined somewhat differently in information theory than in physics and it is the information-theoretic use that we are interested in here.) We can think of entropy as a measure of uncertainty.

It is easiest to see what is going on with a very simple example. Imagine that you are about to pick a ball from an urn. You know that all the balls in the urn are black or white, but you can't see the color of the ball before you pick it. Let's say that the attribute you are interested in is *Black?* – i.e. whether the ball is black or not. How uncertain are you? And, relatedly, how much information would you acquire by picking a ball and seeing that it is black?

Everything depends on what information you have about the proportion of black balls in the urn. If you know that all the balls are black, then you already know that the next ball will be black. The entropy here is 0. Likewise if you know that none of the balls is black. Here too the entropy level is 0 – you have no uncertainty because you know that the next ball can't be black.

But if you know that exactly half of the balls are black, then you are in a state of maximal uncertainty about the color of the next ball. As far as you are concerned the outcome is completely random. The entropy level is as high as it can be. It is assigned a value of 1 (in the case where we are dealing with a binary attribute – an attribute that only has two values).

If you know that 60 percent of the balls are black then you are slightly better off. You will be a little less uncertain about the color of the next ball you pick out. So here the entropy level is somewhere between 1 and 0. The more the proportion of black balls in the urn departs from 50 percent, the lower the entropy will be. In fact, we can represent the entropy in a graph, as in Figure 7.2.

Exercise 7.1 Explain in your own words why the graph is symmetrical – i.e. why the entropy is the same when the probability of a black ball is 0.4 and when it is 0.6, for example.

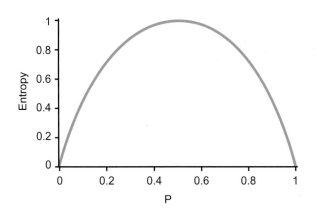

Figure 7.2 A graph illustrating the relation between entropy and probability in the context of drawing a ball from an urn as the probability of drawing a black ball varies. The *x*-axis gives the proportion of black balls in the urn. Entropy is on the *y*-axis.

Box 7.1 shows how to calculate the entropy of a set of examples relative to a binary attribute. Enthusiasts can go into the details. But all that we really need to know is that there is an algorithm for calculating an entropy value between 0 and 1 for a set of examples with respect to a binary attribute. The closer the entropy value is to 0, the lower the degree of uncertainty about the value of a particular example relative to a given attribute.

Once we have a formula for calculating entropy we can calculate information gain relative to a particular attribute. Since we are trying to measure information *gain*, we need to work out some sort of baseline. The ultimate aim of the algorithm is to produce a decision tree in which each branch ends in a value for the target attribute (i.e. the loan application is either accepted or declined). It makes sense to start, therefore, by considering the entropy of the total set of examples relative to the target attribute. We can call this set S. Calculating the entropy of S measures our degree of uncertainty about whether examples in S have the target attribute.

This starting-point allows us (or rather, the ID3 algorithm) to work out the first node of the decision tree. Basically, for each attribute, the algorithm works out how well the attribute organizes the remaining examples. It does this by calculating how much the entropy would be reduced if the set were classified according to that attribute. This gives a measure of the information gain for each attribute. Then the algorithm assigns the attribute with the highest information gain to the first node on the tree. Box 7.2 gives the formula for calculating information gain.

Once an attribute has been assigned to the first node we have a tree with at least two branches. And so we have some more nodes to which attributes need to be assigned. The algorithm repeats the procedure, starting at the leftmost node. The leftmost node represents a subset S* of the set of examples. So the algorithm calculates

BOX 7.1 Calculating entropy   OPTIONAL

Entropy in the information-theoretic sense is a way of measuring uncertainty. How do we turn this intuitive idea into a mathematical formula?

To keep things simple we will just calculate the entropy of a set of examples relative to a binary attribute. A binary attribute is one that has two possible values. The example in the text of *Black?* is a binary attribute, for example. We need some notation – as follows

S	the set of examples
$N(S)$	the number of examples in S
A	the (binary) attribute
$N(A^{YES})$	the number of examples with attribute A
$N(A^{NO})$	the number of examples lacking attribute A

So, the proportion of examples in S with attribute A is given by $\frac{N(A^{YES})}{N(S)}$ and the proportion of examples in S lacking attribute A is given by $\frac{N(A^{NO})}{N(S)}$. If we abbreviate these by $Prop(A^{YES})$ and $Prop(A^{NO})$ respectively, then we can calculate the entropy of S relative to A with the following equation

$$\textbf{Entropy } S/A = -\textbf{Prop}(A^{YES})\log_2 \textbf{Prop}(A^{YES}) - \textbf{Prop}(A^{NO})\log_2 \textbf{Prop}(A^{NO})$$

This is not as bad as it looks! We are working in base 2 logarithms because we are dealing with a binary attribute.

Exercise *To make sure that you are comfortable with this equation, refer to the example in the text and check:*

(a) *that the entropy is 1 when the proportion of black balls is 0.5*
(b) *that the entropy is 0.88 when the proportion of black balls is 0.7*

NB Your calculator may not be able to calculate logarithms to the base 2 directly. The log button will most likely be base 10. You may find the following formula helpful: $\log_2(x) = \log(x) \div \log(2)$ for any base.

the baseline entropy of S* relative to the target attribute. This is the starting point from which it can then calculate which of the remaining attributes has the highest information gain. The attribute with the highest information gain is selected and assigned to the node.

This process is repeated until each branch of the tree ends in a value for the target attribute. This will happen if the attributes on a particular branch end up narrowing the set of examples down so that they all have the same value for the target attribute. When every branch is closed in this way the algorithm halts.

BOX 7.2 Calculating information gain

OPTIONAL

We can measure information gain once we have a way of measuring entropy. Assume that we are starting at a node on the tree. It may be the starting node, but need not be. The node has associated with it a particular set S* of examples. If the node is the starting node then S* will contain all the examples – i.e. we will have S* = S. If the node is further down the tree then it will be some subset of S – i.e. we have S* ⊆ S.

The first step is to calculate the entropy of S* relative to the target attribute A – i.e. **Entropy (S*/A)**. This can be done using the formula in Box 7.1 and gives the algorithm its baseline again.

Now what we want to do is to calculate how much that uncertainty would be reduced if we had information about whether or not the members of S* have a particular attribute – say, B.

So, the second step is to calculate the entropy with respect to the target attribute of the subset of S* that has attribute B – what according to the notation we used in Box 7.1 we call B^{YES}. This can be done using the formula from Box 7.1 to give a value for **Entropy (B^{YES}/A)**.

The third step is the same as the second, but in this case we calculate the entropy of B^{NO} with respect to the target attribute – i.e. the subset of S* that does not have attribute B. This gives a value for **Entropy (B^{NO}/A)**.

Finally, the algorithm puts these together to work out the information gain in S* due to attribute B. This is given by the following formula:

Gain (S*, B) = Entropy (S*/A)

– Prop (B^{YES}) × Entropy (B^{YES}/A)

– Prop (B^{NO}) × Entropy (B^{NO}/A)

As in Box 7.1, Prop (A^{YES}) stands for the proportion of S* that has attribute A.

ID3 in action

We can illustrate how ID3 works by showing how it can produce a decision tree for solving a relatively simple problem - deciding whether or not the weather is suitable for playing tennis. In order to apply ID3 we need a database. So imagine that, as keen tennis players who seriously consider playing tennis every day, we collect information for two weeks. For each day we log the principal meteorological data and note whether or not we decide to play tennis on that day.

The target attribute is *Play Tennis?*. The other attributes are the general weather outlook, the temperature, the humidity, and the wind. Here they are with the values they can take.

Outlook?	{sunny, overcast, rain}
Temperature?	{hot, mild, cool}
Humidity?	{high, low, normal}
Wind?	{weak, strong}

Our careful recordkeeping results in the following database.

DAY	OUTLOOK?	TEMPERATURE?	HUMIDITY?	WIND?	PLAY TENNIS?
D1	Sunny	Hot	High	Weak	No
D2	Sunny	Hot	High	Strong	No
D3	Overcast	Hot	High	Weak	Yes
D4	Rain	Mild	High	Weak	Yes
D5	Rain	Cool	Normal	Weak	Yes
D6	Rain	Cool	Normal	Strong	No
D7	Overcast	Cool	Normal	Strong	Yes
D8	Sunny	Mild	High	Weak	No
D9	Sunny	Cool	Normal	Weak	Yes
D10	Rain	Mild	Normal	Weak	Yes
D11	Sunny	Mild	Normal	Strong	Yes
D12	Overcast	Mild	High	Strong	Yes
D13	Overcast	Hot	Normal	Weak	Yes
D14	Rain	Mild	High	Strong	No

Even this relatively small database is completely overwhelming. It is very hard to find any correlations between the target attribute and the other attributes. And certainly no decision tree springs to mind. It would be very hard to take an assignment of values to the four non-target attributes and then work out a value for the target attribute.

That is to say, if we found ourselves on a sunny but mild day with high humidity and strong wind, we would be hard pressed to extrapolate from the database to a decision

BOX 7.3   Calculating the baseline entropy for the set of examples   **OPTIONAL**

The entropy (S/A) of the set of examples S relative to the target attribute can be worked out using the formula in Box 7.1. Letting A stand for *Play Tennis?* we have:

$$\text{Entropy } S/A = -\text{Prop}(A^{YES})\log_2 \text{Prop}(A^{YES}) - \text{Prop}(A^{NO})\log_2 \text{Prop}(A^{NO})$$

Since we played tennis on nine of the fourteen days for which records were kept, we have $\text{Prop}(A^{YES}) = 9/14$ and $\text{Prop}(A^{NO}) = 5/14$. So, it is an easy matter for ID3 to compute that Entropy S/A = 0.94.

Exercise *Check that this is indeed the case. You can work out logarithms to base 2 by using the formula $\log_2(x) = \log_{10}(x) \div \log_{10}(2)$.*

whether or not to play tennis. Fortunately, though, this is exactly the sort of problem that ID3 can solve.

The first step is to identify an initial node. So, the ID3 algorithm needs to compare the information gain for each of the four non-target attributes. In order to do this it needs to establish a baseline. The baseline is provided by the entropy of the set of examples S relative to the target attribute. As it happens, this entropy is 0.94. The calculations that give this number are summarized in Box 7.3.

As suspected, the target attribute does not classify the set of examples very well. In order to do that we need to know more about the weather on that particular day. ID3 needs to construct a decision tree.

The first step in constructing the decision tree is working out what attribute to use at the first node. ID3 has four to choose from – *Outlook?*, *Temperature?*, *Humidity?*, and *Wind?*. Obviously, the most efficient thing to do would be to use the attribute that gives the most information – that reduces uncertainty the most. So, ID3 needs to find the attribute with the highest information gain. This is a lengthy process – but not for ID3. Box 7.4 illustrates some of the steps involved in calculating the information gain associated with the attribute *Outlook?*.

When ID3 calculates the information gain for all four attributes the results come out as follows:

Gain (S, *Outlook?*)	=	0.246	Gain (S, *Humidity?*)	=	0.151
Gain (S, *Temperature?*)	=	0.029	Gain (S, *Wind?*)	=	0.048

BOX 7.4 Calculating the information gain for *Outlook?* **OPTIONAL**

Let's run through the calculations for the attribute *Outlook?*. This is a little complicated because *Outlook?* is not a binary attribute. It has three possible values. So, abbreviating *Outlook?* by X, we need to work out values for the entropy of X^{SUNNY}, $X^{OVERCAST}$, and X^{RAIN}, all relative to the target attribute. Again, this is a cumbersome calculation, but exactly the sort of thing that computers are rather good at.

We can work it out for X^{SUNNY}. We are only interested here in the sunny days and how they performed relative to the target attribute. There are five sunny days and we played tennis on only two of them. So $Prop(A^{YES}) = 2/5$ and $Prop(A^{NO}) = 3/5$. The equation in Box 7.1 gives Entropy $X^{SUNNY}/A = 0.96$.

Exercise *Confirm this and calculate the entropy values for $X^{OVERCAST}$ and X^{RAIN}.*

Once we have all this information we can work out the information gain for *Outlook?* using the equation in Box 7.2 and the value for Entropy (S/A) that we derived in Box 7.3. Here is the equation, abbreviating the set of examples as S and *Outlook?* as X:

Gain (S, X) = Entropy (S/A)

– Prop (X^{SUNNY}/A) × Entropy (X^{SUNNY}/A)

– Prop ($X^{OVERCAST}/A$) × Entropy ($X^{OVERCAST}/A$)

– Prop (X^{RAIN}/A) × Entropy (X^{RAIN}/A)

Again, it won't take ID3 long to come up with a value. The value, as it happens, is 0.246.

Exercise *Check that this holds.*

So it is clear what ID3 will do. The information gain is highest for *Outlook?* and so that is the attribute it assigns to the first node in the decision tree. The decision tree looks like the one in Figure 7.3. Each of the three branches coming down from the first node corresponds to one of the three possible values for *Outlook?*. Two of the branches (Sunny and Rain) lead to further nodes, while the middle branch immediately ends.

Exercise 7.2 Explain why the decision tree takes this form.

In order to make further progress the ID3 algorithm needs to assign attributes to the two vacant nodes. It does this by running through a version of the same process that we have just traced. Or rather, the process is exactly the same: It is just that the inputs are a little different. For one thing, the range of possible attributes is smaller. The *Outlook?* attribute has already been taken care of. So ID3 only needs to compare *Temperature?*, *Wind?*, and *Humidity?*. For another, ID3 no longer needs to take into account all fourteen days for which records were kept. For the left node, for example, it only needs to take into

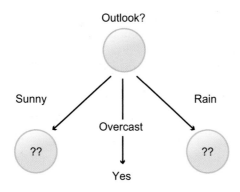

Figure 7.3 The first node on the decision tree for the tennis problem. *Outlook?* is the first node on the decision tree because it has the highest information gain. See the calculations in Box 7.4.

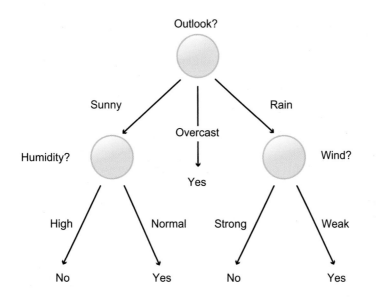

Figure 7.4 The complete decision tree generated by the ID3 algorithm.

account the five days on which it was sunny. To use the notation we employed earlier, instead of S, the ID3 algorithm now operates on the subset S*. The subset S* is the set {D1, D2, D8, D9, D11}.

What the algorithm has to do is calculate, for each of the three remaining attributes, the information gain of that attribute relative to S* - i.e. relative to the five days when the sun shone. With this information in hand, ID3 can then work out which attribute to assign to the vacant node reached from the base node by following the Sunny path. Likewise at the other vacant node (the one reached from the base node by following the Rain path). It turns out that assigning attributes to these two nodes is all that is required for a comprehensive decision tree - i.e. for a decision tree that will tell us whether or not to play tennis in any combination of meteorological conditions. The final decision tree is illustrated in Figure 7.4.

Admittedly, this is a "toy" example. We need a toy example to keep the calculations manageable. But there are plenty of "real-life" examples of how successful ID3 can be. Here is one.

In the late 1970s Ryszard Michalski and Richard Chilausky, two computer scientists at the University of Illinois (deep in the agricultural heartland of America's Midwest), used ID3 to devise an expert system for diagnosing diseases in soybeans, one of Illinois's most important crops. This is a rather more difficult problem, since there are nineteen common diseases threatening soybean crops. Each disease is standardly diagnosed in terms of clusters of thirty-five different symptoms. In this case, therefore, the target attribute has nineteen different possible values and there are thirty-five different attributes. Many of these attributes also have multiple possible values.

In order to appreciate how complicated this problem is, look at Figure 7.5. This is a questionnaire sent to soybean farmers with diseased crops. It gives values for each of the thirty-five attributes, together with a diagnosis. Completed questionnaires such as this one were one of the inputs to the initial database. They were supplemented by textbook analyses and lengthy consultations with a local plant pathologist. The total database on which ID3 was trained comprised 307 different examples.

Michalski and Chilausky were interested not just in whether ID3 could use the training examples to construct a decision tree. They wanted to compare the resulting decision tree to the performance of a human expert. After all, what better gauge could there be of whether they really had succeeded in constructing an expert system? And so they tested the program on 376 new cases and compared its diagnoses to those made by various experts on plant disease (including the author of the textbook that they had originally used to compile the database). As it turned out, the expert system did much better than the human expert on the same 376 cases. In fact, it made only two mistakes, giving it a 99.5 percent success rate, compared to the 87 percent success rate of the human experts.

ID3 and the physical symbol system hypothesis

Let me end this section by making explicit the connection between the ID3 machine learning algorithm and physical symbol system hypothesis. In presenting the machine learning algorithm and the way it solves classification problems I highlighted the idea of a decision tree. It is natural to think of decision trees in a visual way – as if they were graphs, for example. But this is just a convenience to make it easier to appreciate what is going on. There is nothing intrinsically graphic or pictorial about decision trees. As we have seen on several occasions, decision trees can be represented as sets of IF . . . THEN . . . instructions – or, in other words, as complex symbol structures.

Writing decision trees down as sets of IF . . . THEN . . . instructions makes it much easier to see why ID3 is a paradigm example of the physical symbol system hypothesis. What the ID3 algorithm does is transform one highly complex symbol structure into a much simpler symbol structure. The highly complex symbol structure it starts off with is the database – a symbolic representation of massive amounts of information about, for

Environmental descriptors
    Time of occurrence = July
    Plant stand = normal
    Precipitation = above normal
    Temperature = normal
    Occurrence of hail = no
    Number of years crop repeated = 4
    Damaged area = whole fields

Plant global descriptors
    Severity = potentially severe
    Seed treatment = none
    Seed germination = less than 80%
    Plant height = normal

Plant local descriptors
    Condition of leaves = abnormal
        Leafspots–halos = without yellow halos
        Leafspots–margin = without watersoaked margin
        Leafspot size = greater than ½"
        Leaf shredding or shot holding = present
        Leaf malformation = absent
        Leaf mildew growth = absent

    Condition of stem = abnormal
        Presence of lodging = no
        Stem cankers = above the second node
        Canker lesion color = brown
        Fruiting bodies on stem = present
        External decay = absent
        Mycelium on stem = absent
        Internal discoloration of stem = none
        Sclerotial–internal or external = absent

    Conditions of fruit-pods = normal
        Fruit spots = absent

    Condition of seed = normal
        Mould growth = absent
        Seed discoloration = absent
        Seed size = normal
        Seed shrivelling = absent

    Condition of roots = normal

Diagnosis:
    Diaporthe stem canker() Charcoal rot() Rhizoctonia
    root rot() Phytophthora root rot() Brown stem root rot()
    Powdery mildew() Downy mildew() Brown spot(x)
    Bacterial blight() Bacterial pustule() Purple seed stain()
    Anrhenorose() Phyllosticta leaf spot() Alternaria leaf
    spot() Frog eye leaf spot()

Figure 7.5 A sample completed questionnaire used as input to an ID3-based expert system for diagnosing diseases in soybean crops. (Adapted from Michalski and Chilausky 1980)

example, the physical characteristics of soybean plants, or the financial histories of mortgage applicants. The symbol structure it ends up with is the set of rules that define the decision tree.

Once the decision tree is in place, it then functions as a different kind of physical symbol system. It is now, in effect, a decision procedure. But it still works by transforming symbol structures. The complex symbol structure that it takes in is a set of specifications of values for the relevant attributes. The symbol structure might convey the information that the weather is sunny – with high temperatures, and low humidity – or the information about the plant's leaves, fruit pods, and so on. The output symbol structure is the symbol structure that conveys the "decision" whether or not to play tennis, or the diagnosis that the plant has a particular type of leaf spot. And the process of transforming inputs to outputs is essentially a process of manipulating symbol structures according to rules. The rules are precisely the IF ... THEN ... instructions produced by the ID3 learning algorithm.

7.3 WHISPER: Predicting stability in a block world

According to the physical symbol system hypothesis, information is processed by transforming physical symbol structures according to rules. According to the heuristic search hypothesis, problem-solving involves manipulating and transforming an initial symbol structure until it becomes a solution structure. The physical symbol structures that we have been looking at up to now all have something in common. We have been looking at different logical calculi, at the language of thought, and at numerical representations in databases. These are all basically language-based.

But there is nothing in the physical symbol system hypothesis that requires physical symbol structures to be language-like. The physical symbol system hypothesis is perfectly compatible with physical symbol structures being diagrams or images. This is particularly important in the light of all the experimental evidence seeming to show that certain types of information are stored in an image-like format. Think back, for example, to the mental rotation experiments by Shepard and Metzler that we looked at back in section 2.2.

As we saw in section 2.2, the mental rotation experiments can be understood both propositionally and imagistically. On the imagistic view, the mental rotation experiments show that certain types of information are stored and processed in an analog format. According to propositionalists, on the other hand, the experimental data are perfectly compatible with information being digitally encoded. It is important to recognize that the dispute here is a dispute *within* the scope of the physical symbol system hypothesis. It is a dispute about which sort of physical symbol structures are involved in particular types of information processing. It is not a dispute about the validity of the physical symbol system hypothesis.

Figure 7.6 illustrates how the dialectic works here. The physical symbol system hypothesis is one way of implementing the basic idea that cognition is information

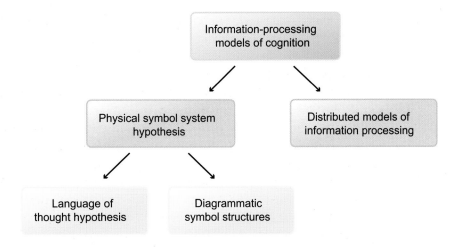

Figure 7.6 Classifying different information-processing models of cognition. Note that the physical symbol system hypothesis can be developed both propositionally (as in the language of thought hypothesis) and imagistically (as in the WHISPER program).

processing – this is the single most important idea at the heart of cognitive science. The physical symbol system hypothesis stands in opposition to the distributed models of information processing associated with connectionist modeling and artificial neural networks (that we briefly considered in section 3.3 and that we will look at in much more detail in Chapters 8 and 9). But there are different ways of implementing the physical symbol system hypothesis. The language of thought hypothesis is one way of implementing it. But it can also be implemented in systems with diagrammatic representations.

In this section we explore the diagrammatic approach to implementing the physical symbol system hypothesis. We will consider a computer problem-solving system known as WHISPER, which was developed in 1980 by the computer scientist Brian Funt. WHISPER shows in a very clear way how physical symbol structures can be diagrammatic, rather than language-like – and, moreover, how this can have a very definite pay-off in making information processing easier.

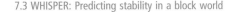 WHISPER: How it works

WHISPER is designed to work in a virtual block world, containing representations of blocks of different shapes and sizes on a flat surface. Funt designed WHISPER to perform a very specialized task. Its job is to assess the stability of structures in the block world and then work out how unstable structures will collapse. In the block world these structures are piles of blocks (or rather: representations of piles of blocks). But the problem that WHISPER is designed to solve is quite plainly a scaled-down and highly simplified version of a problem that engineers and builders confront on a daily basis.

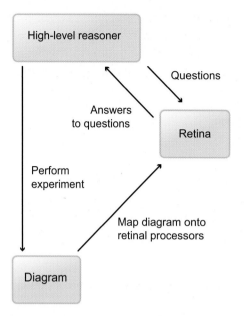

Figure 7.7 The basic architecture of WHISPER. The high-level reasoner (HLR) gets information about structures in the block world from a retina that functions as its perceptual system. It uses that information to construct and manipulate diagrams of block structures in order to work out how those structures will behave. (From Funt 1980)

WHISPER'S basic architecture is summarized in Figure 7.7. It has two components (or rather: it would have two components if anyone were actually to build it – WHISPER is just as virtual as the block world that it is analyzing). The first component is a high-level reasoner (HLR). The high-level reasoner is the top level of the system. It serves as a controller and has programmed into it knowledge of stability and object movement – a basic physics for the block world. The HLR gets information about structures in the block world from a retina that functions as its perceptual system. It uses that information to construct and manipulate diagrams of block structures in order to work out how those structures will behave. In effect, WHISPER works by having the retina "visualize" what happens when blocks in a particular structure start to rotate or slide.

WHISPER is given a diagram of the initial problem state. The diagram depicts a pile of blocks. WHISPER works by producing a sequence of diagrams (which Funt calls *snapshots*). It stops when it outputs a diagram in which all the blocks are perfectly stable – this is the solution diagram. We can already see how this fits the description of the heuristic search hypothesis. According to the heuristic search hypothesis, problem-solving involves starting with a symbol structure defining a particular information-processing problem and then transforming it until a solution structure is reached. In the case of WHISPER, the initial diagram is the problem structure. Each snapshot represents a transformation of the previous diagram. And the condition that a snapshot must satisfy in order to count as a solution structure is that none of the depicted shapes be unstable.

WHISPER's operation can be summarized algorithmically. Here is the algorithm (for the case where objects move only by rotating – allowing objects to slide introduces another layer of complexity):

Step 1 Determine all instabilities.

Step 2 Pick the dominant instability.

Step 3 Find the pivot point for the rotation of the unstable object.

Step 4 Find the termination condition of the rotation using retinal visualization.

Step 5 Call transformation procedure to modify diagram from Step 4.

Step 6 Output modified diagram as a solution snapshot.

Step 7 Restart from Step 1 using diagram from Step 6 as input.

In order to execute these steps WHISPER needs to be able to detect and analyze features of the starting diagram and the ensuing snapshots. It also needs to be able to transform those diagrams in certain specified ways. These features and transformations are WHISPER's *perceptual primitives*. The perceptual primitives include the following operations:

- Finding the center of area of a particular shape (and hence its center of gravity)
- Finding the point of contact between two shapes
- Examining curves for abrupt changes in slope
- Testing a shape for symmetry
- Testing the similarity of two shapes
- Visualizing the rotation of a shape (and potential conflicts with other shapes)

All of these perceptual primitives are themselves detected by algorithmic procedures that exploit design features of the retina.

We can get a sense of how WHISPER works (and of how it illustrates the physical symbol system hypothesis) by looking at how it solves a particular problem – the so-called *chain reaction problem*.

WHISPER solving the chain reaction problem

WHISPER is given as input the diagram represented in Figure 7.8. The diagram is in a standard format. It depicts a side view of the block structure. Each block has a different "color" to allow WHISPER to tell them apart easily. Each color is represented by a particular letter, and each block is built up from lines of that letter.

Numerals represent the boundaries of each block. Each block has its boundaries marked by a different numeral. The block at the bottom left, for example, is represented by lines of As, with its boundaries marked by 1s. This way of representing the blocks has

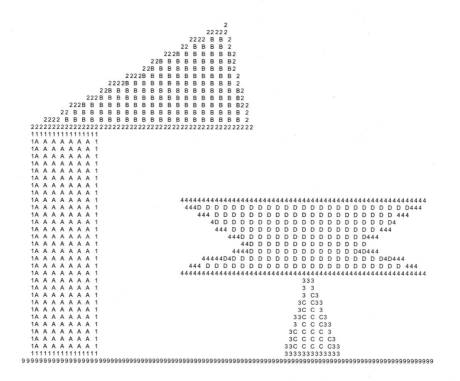

Figure 7.8 The starting diagram for the chain reaction problem. Each block has a particular "color" represented by a letter, and its boundaries are represented by a numeral. (From Funt 1980)

some useful features. It is easy to work out, for example, when two blocks are touching, since this will only occur when two numerals are adjacent to each other with no gap between them. We will see shortly how useful this is.

The first step in the algorithm requires identifying any instabilities in the structure depicted in the diagram. WHISPER works this out by breaking the complete structure down into its independent substructures – since the complete structure will only be stable if all its substructures are stable. This ultimately boils down to computing the stability of single blocks, which WHISPER does using a routine called SINGLE-STABLE. The routine evaluates, for example, how a block's center of gravity is related to its supports (either the surface, or other blocks) in order to determine whether it will rotate about a support point.

When WHISPER applies SINGLE-STABLE to the structure in Figure 7.8 it determines that B is the only unstable block. The background knowledge programmed into the HLR tells WHISPER that block B will rotate around the support point closest to its center of gravity. This takes care of Step 3 in the algorithm, because it identifies the pivot point of the dominant instability.

The next stage in the algorithm (Step 4) requires WHISPER to visualize the rotation and work out where block B will end up. WHISPER can make a rough calculation

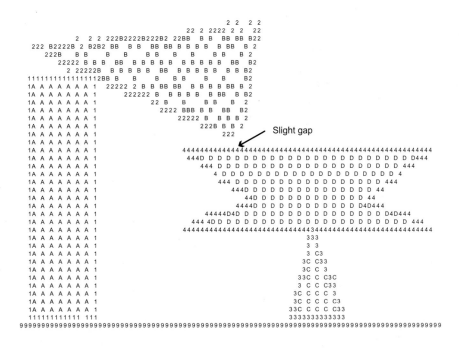

Figure 7.9 The result of applying WHISPER's rotation algorithm in order to work out the trajectory of block B. (From Funt 1980)

of the contact point between block B and block D. It then uses a trial and error method to compute the contact point exactly. WHISPER starts off by deliberately underestimating the contact point. It does this in order to avoid over-rotating block B so that it will (contrary to the laws of physics) overlap with block D. Using its rotation algorithm WHISPER comes up with a new diagram, which might look like Figure 7.9.

WHISPER directs the retina to examine this diagram, fixating it on the anticipated collision point. The retina "sees" that block B and block D are not touching – it is easy to do this, since the diagram is set up so that we only have two blocks touching when their respective numerals are adjacent to each other without any gaps between them. If WHISPER detects a gap then it extends the rotation and re-examines the diagram. This completes Steps 4 and 5 of the algorithm. WHISPER is now in a position to output its first solution snapshot. This is illustrated in Figure 7.10.

At this point the first application of the algorithm is complete. So WHISPER starts again from the beginning. It works out that block D is now unstable, since block B is pushing down on one of its sides. After finding the pivot point for block D's rotation (which is the point of contact between block C and block D), WHISPER visualizes what will happen to block D. Since the rotation of block D will leave block B unsupported, WHISPER applies the routine again to block B. We see the final snapshot in Figure 7.11.

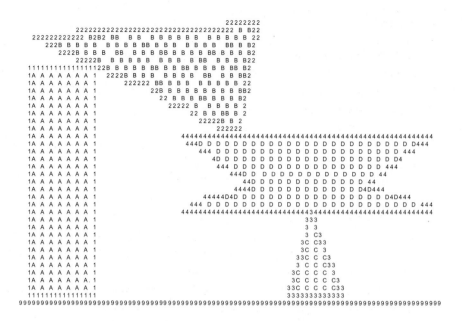

Figure 7.10 The first solution snapshot output by WHISPER. It represents the result of rotating block B around block A. This rotation reveals a new instability.

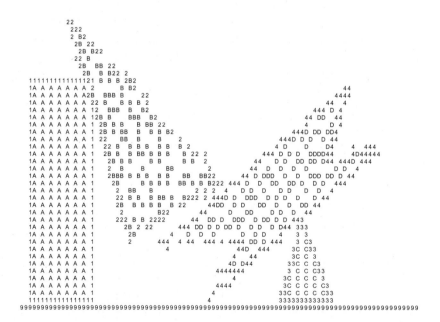

Figure 7.11 The final snapshot representing WHISPER's solution to the chain reaction problem. (From Funt 1980)

WHISPER: What we learn

Unsurprisingly, WHISPER does not work perfectly, even in the block world. There are certain types of instability that its algorithm cannot deal with. For example, it has nothing to say about structures containing moving blocks, or about what sort of impact could cause a stable structure to collapse. But our main reason for looking at WHISPER is not that it completely succeeds in solving problems about the stability of block structures. Even if WHISPER were perfectly successful at this, it would still only be a relatively minor achievement in the overall scheme of things.

What is really interesting about WHISPER is that it gives a very clear illustration of just how wide-ranging the physical symbol system hypothesis can be. When one first encounters the physical symbol system hypothesis, it is very natural to think of it in terms of the type of symbols with which we are most familiar – namely, words and sentences in a natural language. On this way of thinking about it, physical symbols are essentially language-like, and information processing is basically a matter of manipulating sentence-like structures. These might be sentences in an artificial language (such as the predicate calculus), or they might be sentences in something more like a natural language. Or, combining elements from both artificial and natural languages, they might be sentences in the language of thought (as we explored in section 6.3).

What we learn from WHISPER, however, is that there are other ways of thinking about the physical symbol system hypothesis. Physical symbol systems can use diagrams. Moreover (and in a sense this is the most important point), physical symbol systems that use diagrams to carry information can be engaged in information processing of exactly the same general type as systems that carry information in language-like representations.

Considered in the abstract, from a purely information-processing perspective, WHISPER does not differ in any significant way from the data-mining program ID3 that we looked at in the first section of this chapter. Both of them clearly illustrate the four basic tenets of the physical symbol system hypothesis. In addition, they both function in accordance with the heuristic search hypothesis. Both ID3 and WHISPER solve problems by generating and modifying physical symbol structures until a solution structure is reached.

Exercise 7.3 Construct a table to show, for each of the four basic claims of the physical symbol system hypothesis, how they are satisfied respectively by ID3 and WHISPER.

ID3 starts with a database and manipulates it until it arrives at a set of IF … THEN … rules that defines a decision tree. The decision tree is the solution structure. WHISPER starts with an input diagram and then transforms it according to the algorithm given earlier in this section. Again, WHISPER continues applying the algorithm until it reaches a solution structure. In this case the solution structure is a snapshot that contains no instabilities.

The two algorithms are very different. So are the symbols in which they operate. But both ID3 and WHISPER exemplify the same model of information processing. They are both implementations of the physical symbol system hypothesis.

7.4   Putting it all together: SHAKEY the robot

The physical symbol system hypothesis is a hypothesis about the necessary conditions of intelligent *action*. Up to now we have been talking about action only in a rather tenuous sense. ID3 performs the "action" of constructing decision trees from databases. WHISPER performs the "action" of assessing the stability of block structures in a virtual micro-world. We have seen how ID3 and WHISPER work by manipulating symbol structures. The next question to ask is whether symbol manipulation can give us a richer type of intelligent action – intelligent action that involves moving around and solving problems in a real, physical environment.

The best place to look for an answer to this question is the field of robotics. In this section we will look at a pioneering robot developed in the late 1960s and early 1970s in the Artificial Intelligence Center at what was then called the Stanford Research Institute (it is now called SRI International and no longer affiliated to Stanford University). This robot, affectionately called SHAKEY (because of its jerky movements), was the first robot able to move around, perceive, follow instructions, and implement complex instructions in a realistic environment (as opposed to virtual micro-worlds like those "inhabited" by SHRDLU and WHISPER). SHAKEY has now retired from active service and lives in the Robot Hall of Fame at Carnegie Mellon University in Pittsburgh, Pennsylvania.

Figure 7.12 depicts one of the physical environments in which SHAKEY operated. The name of each room begins with an "R." "RMYS" is a mystery room – i.e. SHAKEY has no information about its contents. Doorway names begin with a "D" and are labeled in a way that makes clear which rooms they are connecting. "DUNIMYS," for example, labels the door between RUNI (where SHAKEY starts) and RMYS. The environment is empty, except for three boxes located in RCLK (the room with the clock).

In thinking about SHAKEY the first place to start is with the physical structure itself. Figure 7.13 is a photograph of SHAKEY. The photo is clearly labeled and should be self-explanatory. The software that allows SHAKEY to operate is not actually run on the robot itself. It was run on a completely separate computer system that communicated by radio with SHAKEY (the radio antenna can be seen in the photo).

We are looking at SHAKEY as our third illustration of the physical symbol system hypothesis. So the first thing we need to do is to identify the basic symbols that are used in programming the robot, and that the robot uses in planning, executing, and monitoring its actions. The programs that run SHAKEY are examples of what is generally called *logic programming*. They incorporate a basic model of the environment together with a set of procedures for updating the model and for acting on the environment.

SHAKEY's basic model is given by a set of statements in the *first-order predicate calculus*. (The first-order predicate calculus is the logical language that allows us to talk about particular objects having particular properties, and also permits us to formulate generalizations either about all objects or about at least one object.) These statements are in a basic vocabulary that contains names for the objects in the robot's world – doors, blocks, walls, and so on – as well as predicates that characterize the properties those objects can

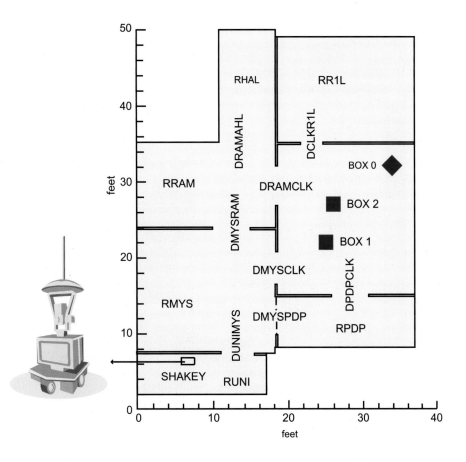

Figure 7.12 A map of SHAKEY's physical environment. Each room has a name. The room containing the boxes is called RCLK (an abbrevation for "Room with clock"). The total environment measures about 60 feet by 40 feet. (From Nilsson 1984)

have. The vocabulary also contains a name for SHAKEY and predicates that describe the robot's state - where it is, the angle at which its head is tilted, and so on. The software that SHAKEY uses to plan and execute its actions exploits this same vocabulary, supplemented by terms for particular actions.

SHAKEY's software I: Low-level activities and intermediate-level actions

In order to understand how SHAKEY's software works we need to go back to some ideas that we first encountered back in Chapter 1. We looked there at some of Lashley's influential (and at the time very innovative) ideas about the hierarchical organization of behavior. Reacting against the behaviorist idea that actions could be viewed as linked chains of responses, Lashley argued that many complex behaviors resulted from prior planning and organization. These behaviors are organized hierarchically (rather than linearly). An

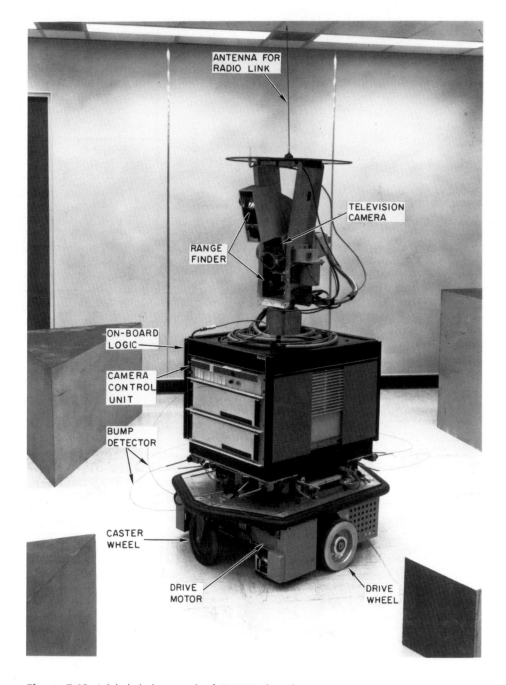

ANTENNA FOR
RADIO LINK

TELEVISION
CAMERA

RANGE
FINDER

ON-BOARD
LOGIC

CAMERA
CONTROL
UNIT

BUMP
DETECTOR

CASTER
WHEEL

DRIVE
MOTOR

DRIVE
WHEEL

Figure 7.13 A labeled photograph of SHAKEY the robot.

overall plan (say, walking over to the table to pick up the glass) is implemented by simpler plans (the walking plan and the reaching plan), each of which can be broken down into simpler plans, and so on. Ultimately we arrive at basic actions that don't require any planning. These basic actions are the components from which complex behaviors are built.

TABLE 7.1   SHAKEY'S five levels

LEVEL	FUNCTION	EXAMPLES
1 Robot vehicle and connections to user programs	To navigate and interact physically with a realistic environment	See the illustration of SHAKEY in Figure 7.13
2 Low-level actions (LLAs)	To give the basic physical capabilities of the robot	ROLL (which tells the robot to move forward by a specified number of feet) and TILT (which tells the robot to tilt its head upwards by a specified number of degrees)
3 Intermediate-level actions (ILAs)	Packages of LLAs	PUSH (OBJECT, GOAL, TOL) which instructs the robot to push a particular object to a specified goal, with a specified degree of tolerance
4 STRIPS	A planning mechanism constructing MACROPS (sequences of ILAs) to carry out specific tasks	A typical MACROP might be to fetch a block from an adjacent room
5 PLANEX	Executive program that calls up and monitors individual MACROPS	PLANEX might use the sensors built into the robot to determine that the block can only be fetched if SHAKEY pushes another block out of the way first – and then invoke a MACROP to fetch a block

SHAKEY's software packages are built around this basic idea that complex behaviors are hierarchically organized. We can see how this works in Table 7.1, which shows how we can think about SHAKEY as a system with five different levels. The bottom level is the hardware level, and there are four different levels of software. The software levels are hierarchically organized. Each level of software controls a different type of behavior. Going up the hierarchy of software takes us up the hierarchy of behavior.

The interface between the physical hardware of the robot and the software that allows it to act in a systematic and planned way is at the level of Low-Level Actions

TABLE 7.2 How SHAKEY represents its own state	
ATOM IN AXIOMATIC MODEL	**AFFECTED BY**
(AT ROBOT xfeet yfeet)	ROLL
(DAT ROBOT dxfeet dyfeet)	ROLL
(THETA ROBOT degreesleftofy)	TURN
(DTHETA ROBOT dthetadegrees)	TURN
(WHISKERS ROBOT whiskerword)	ROLL, TURN
(OVRID ROBOT overrides)	OVRID
(TILT ROBOT degreesup)	TILT
(DTILT ROBOT ddegreesup)	TILT
(PAN ROBOT degreesleft)	PAN
(DPAN ROBOT ddegreesleft)	PAN
(IRIS ROBOT evs)	IRIS
(DIRIS ROBOT devs)	IRIS
(FOCUS ROBOT feet)	FOCUS
(DFOCUS ROBOT dfeet)	FOCUS
(RANGE ROBOT feet)	RANGE
(TVMODE ROBOT tvmode)	TVMODE
(PICTURESTAKEN ROBOT± picturestaken)	SHOOT

(LLAs). The LLAs are SHAKEY's basic behaviors – the building blocks from which everything that it does is constructed. The LLAs exploit the robot's basic physical capabilities. So, for example, SHAKEY can move around its environment by rolling forwards or backwards. It can take photos with the onboard camera and it can move its head in two planes – tilting it up and down, and panning it from side to side. There are LLAs corresponding to all of these abilities. So, as we see in the table, ROLL and TILT are LLAs that tell the robot to move a certain number of feet either forward or back, and to tilt its head up or down a certain number of degrees.

As we saw earlier, SHAKEY has a model of its environment. This model also represents the robot's own state. Of course, executing an LLA changes the robot's state and so requires the model to be updated. Table 7.2 shows the relation between the LLAs that SHAKEY can perform and the way in which it represents its own state.

Some of these are more self-explanatory than others. SHAKEY has built into it eight tactile sensors that tell it if it is in contact with another object. These are the whiskers referred to in the fifth line. The last few lines all have to do with the various things that SHAKEY can do with its "visual system" – control the amount of light that comes through the lens, switch it from photograph mode to TV mode, focus the lens, and so on.

So, the LLAs fix SHAKEY's basic repertoire of movements. In themselves, however, LLAs are not much use for problem-solving and acting. SHAKEY's designers needed to build a bridge between high-level commands (such as the command to fetch a block from a particular room) and the basic movements that SHAKEY will use to carry out that command. As we saw from the table, the first level of organization above LLAs comes with Intermediate-Level Actions (ILAs). The ILAs are essentially action routines – linked sequences of LLAs that SHAKEY can call upon in order to execute specific jobs, such as navigating to another room, or turning towards a goal. Table 7.3 shows some ILAs.

ILAs are not just chains of LLAs (in the way that behaviorists thought that complex actions are chained sequences of basic responses). They can recruit other ILAs. So, for example, the GETTO action routine takes SHAKEY to a specific room. This action routine calls upon the NAVTO routine for navigating around in the room SHAKEY is currently in, as well as the GOTOROOM routine, which takes SHAKEY to the room it is aiming for. Of course, SHAKEY can only move from any room to an adjacent room. And so the GOTOROOM routine is built up from the GOTOADJROOM routine.

SHAKEY's hierarchical organization is very clear even at the level of ILAs. But in order to appreciate it fully we need to look at the next level up. Nothing that we have seen so far counts as planning. Both LLAs and ILAs allow SHAKEY to implement fairly low-level commands. But there is little here that would properly be described as problem-solving – or indeed, to go back to Newell and Simon, as intelligent action.

SHAKEY's software II: Logic programming in STRIPS and PLANEX

The real innovation in SHAKEY's programming came with the STRIPS planner ("STRIPS" is an acronym for "Stanford Research Institute Problem Solver"). The STRIPS planner (which, as it happens, was fairly closely related to Newell and Simon's General Problem Solver (GPS)) allows SHAKEY to do things that look much more like reasoning about its environment and its own possibilities for action. What STRIPS does is translate a particular goal statement into a sequence of ILAs.

In order to understand how STRIPS works we need to look a little more closely at how the environment is represented in SHAKEY's software. As we have seen, SHAKEY has an axiomatic model of its environment. The axioms are well-formed formulas in the predicate calculus, built up from a basic vocabulary for describing SHAKEY and its environment. These formulas describe both SHAKEY's physical environment and its own state. The model is updated as SHAKEY moves around and acts upon the environment.

TABLE 7.3   SHAKEY's intermediate-level routines

ILA	ROUTINES CALLED	COMMENTS
PUSH3	PLANOBMOVE*, PUSH2	Can plan and execute a series of PUSH2s
PUSH2	PICLOC*, OBLOC*, NAVTO, ROLLBUMP, PUSH1	Check if object being pushed slips off
PUSH1	ROLL*	Basic push routine; assumes clear path
GETTO	GOTOROOM, NAVTO	Highest level go-to routine
GOTOROOM	PLANTOUR*, GOTOADJROOM	Can plan and execute a series of GOTOADJROOMs
GOTOADJROOM	DOORPIC*, ALIGN, NAVTO, BUMBLETHRU	Tailored for going through doorways
NAVTO	PLANJOURNEY*, GOTO1	Can plan and execute a trip within one room
GOTO1	CLEARPATH*, PICDETECTOB*, GOTO	Recovers from errors due to unknown objects
GOTO	PICLOC*, POINT, ROLL2	Executes single straight-line trip
POINT	PICTHETA*, TURN2	Orients robot towards goal
TURN2	TURNBACK*, TURN1	Responds to unexpected bumps
TURN1	TURN*	Basic turn routine; expects no bumps
ROLL2	ROLLBACK*, ROLL1	Responds to unexpected bumps
ROLL1	ROLL*	Basic roll routine that expects no bumps
ROLLBUMP	ROLLBACK*, ROLL1	Basic roll routine that expects a terminal bump

The tasks that SHAKEY is given are presented in the same format. So, we would give SHAKEY the instruction to fetch a box from another room by inputting what the result of that action would be. If SHAKEY is, say, in room RUNI (as in the environment we looked at earlier), then the result of the action would be the presence of a box in room RUNI. This would be conveyed by the following formula:

$$(*)\,\exists\, x(\text{BOX}(x)\, \&\, \text{INROOM}(x, \text{RUNI}))$$

This formula says that there is at least one thing x, and that thing is a box, and it is in room RUNI. This is the state of affairs that SHAKEY needs to bring about.

Presenting the goal of the action in this way allows SHAKEY to exploit the inferential power of the first-order predicate calculus. The predicate calculus is a tool for deduction and what SHAKEY does, in essence, is to come up with a deduction that has the formula (*) as its conclusion. Certainly, if we assume that room RUNI does not currently have a box in it, then it will not be possible for SHAKEY to deduce (*) from its axiomatic model of the world. So what SHAKEY has to do is to transform its axiomatic model until it can deduce (*). How does SHAKEY transform its axiomatic model? By moving around its environment and updating the model! (Remember that SHAKEY is programmed continually to update its model of the world as it moves around and acts.)

The beauty of STRIPS is in how it works out which movements SHAKEY must make (and hence how its axiomatic model is to be updated). STRIPS represents each ILA in terms of three basic components:

The precondition formula. This represents the state of affairs that has to hold in order for the ILA to be applicable in a given environment. So, for example, the precondition formula for the GOTOADJROOM ILA is the formula stating that the door between the two rooms is open.

The add function. This represents the formulas that need to be added to the model of the environment when the ILA is carried out. So, for example, if the ILA takes SHAKEY from room RUNI to room RMYS, then the add function will add to SHAKEY's model the formula stating that SHAKEY is now in RMYS.

The delete function. This represents the formulas that have to be deleted from the model once the ILA has been carried out. If SHAKEY has moved from room RUNI to RMYS then the model can no longer contain the formula saying that SHAKEY is in RUNI.

SHAKEY has a repertoire of ILAs to choose from. Each of these ILAs has its precondition formula. What the STRIPS program does is to find an ILA that, when executed, will bring SHAKEY closer to its goal of being able to deduce the target formula (*).

In order to find an applicable ILA, STRIPS has to find an ILA whose precondition formula is satisfied in the current environment. That in turn requires finding an ILA whose precondition formula can be deduced from SHAKEY's current axiomatic model of the environment.

We can think about SHAKEY's planning process as involving a tree search. (Think back to the decision trees that we looked at in section 7.1.) The first node (the top of the tree) is SHAKEY's model of the current environment. Each branch of the tree is a sequence of ILAs. Each node of the tree is an updated model of the environment. A branch comes to an end at a particular node when one of two things happens.

At each node a branch splits into as many continuation branches as there are ILAs whose precondition formulas are satisfied at that node. Each continuation branch represents a different course of action that SHAKEY could follow. If there are no ILAs with precondition formulas that can be deduced from the last node on the branch, then the branch comes to an end. This is quite literally a dead-end. What STRIPS then does is to go back up the tree to the last point at which there is a continuation branch that it has not yet tried out. Then it goes down the new branch and keeps going.

A second possibility is that the target formula (*) can be deduced from the updated model at that node. If this happens then STRIPS has solved the problem. What it then does is instruct SHAKEY to follow the sequence of ILAs described in the branch that leads to the model entailing (*). SHAKEY does this, updating its model of the environment as it goes along.

There is no guarantee that this will always get SHAKEY to where it wants to go. The goal might not be attainable. Its model of the environment might not be correct. Someone might have moved the block without telling SHAKEY (and in fact researchers at SRI did do precisely that to see how SHAKEY would update its model). This is where the PLANEX level comes into play. The job of the PLANEX software is to monitor the execution of the plan. So, for example, PLANEX contains an algorithm for calculating the likely degree of error at a certain stage in implementing the task (on the plausible assumption that executing each ILA would introduce a degree of "noise" into SHAKEY's model of the environment). When the likely degree of error reaches a certain threshold, PLANEX instructs SHAKEY to take a photograph to check on its position. If a significant error is discovered, then PLANEX makes corresponding adjustments to the plan.

So, we can see now how STRIPS and PLANEX work and how they illustrate the physical symbol system hypothesis. The physical symbol structures are well-formed formulas in the predicate calculus. These symbols give SHAKEY's model of the environment, as well as the goals and sub-goals that SHAKEY is trying to achieve. And we can also see how those physical symbol structures are manipulated and transformed. The manipulations and transformations take one of two forms.

On the one hand formulas in the predicate calculus can be manipulated and transformed according to the rules of the predicate calculus itself. This is what happens when STRIPS tries to deduce a particular precondition formula from a given model of the environment. What STRIPS does is pretty much the same thing that you will do if you take a logic course. Basically, it tries to derive a contradiction from the axiomatic model together with the *negation* of the precondition formula. The problem is rather more complex than the exercises in the average logic text, but the fundamental idea is the same.

The second way of manipulating and transforming the symbol structures in SHAKEY's software is via the sort of algorithms that we have just been looking at – such as the algorithm that STRIPS uses to identify a sequence of ILAs that will lead to the required goal state. These algorithms are purely mechanical. And they do not require any exercise of judgment or intuition (which is fortunate, since they have to be programmed into a robot).

Finally, SHAKEY clearly illustrates the heuristic search hypothesis. The hypothesis says that intelligent problem-solving takes place by transforming and manipulating symbol structures until a solution structure is reached. The starting-point is given by SHAKEY's model of the environment, together with the target formula that represents the desired end-state. We have just looked at what the permissible transformations and manipulations are. And it is easy to see what the solution structure is. The problem is solved when the initial symbol structure has been transformed into a symbol structure from which the target formula can be deduced.

Summary

In Chapter 6 we looked at some of the central theoretical ideas behind the physical symbol system hypothesis. In this chapter we have looked at three different practical applications of the physical symbol system approach. Both the ID3 machine learning algorithm and the WHISPER program illustrate Newell and Simon's heuristic search hypothesis – the idea that intelligent problem-solving involves transforming physical symbol structures until a solution structure is reached. The ID3 algorithm operates on databases of information and uses those databases to construct decision trees, while WHISPER shows that physical symbols need not be language-like – they can be imagistic. The mobile robot SHAKEY illustrates the basic principles of logic programming and shows how the physical symbol system can be used to control and guide action in a physical (as opposed to a virtual) environment.

Checklist

Expert systems and machine learning

(1)   Expert systems are designed to reproduce the performance of human experts in particular domains (e.g. medical diagnosis and financial services).

(2)   Expert systems typically employ decision rules that can be represented in the form of a decision tree.

(3)   One problem studied in the field of machine learning is developing an algorithm for generating a decision tree from a complex database.

(4)   Generating a decision tree in this way is an example of Newell and Simon's heuristic search hypothesis.

The ID3 machine learning algorithm

(1)   ID3 looks for regularities in a database of information that allow it to construct a decision tree.

(2)   The basic objects in the database are called *examples*. These examples can be classified in terms of their *attributes*. Each feature divides the examples up into two or more classes.

(3)   ID3 constructs a decision tree by assigning attributes to nodes. It assigns to each node the attribute that is most informative at that point.

(4)   Informativeness is calculated in terms of *information gain*, which is itself calculated in terms of *entropy*.

(5)   The decision tree that ID3 generates can be written down as a set of IF . . . THEN . . . instructions.

(6)   ID3 illustrates the heuristic search hypothesis because it is a tool for the rule-governed transformation of a complex symbol structure (the initial database) into a solution structure (the decision tree).

The physical symbol system hypothesis does not require physical symbols to be logical formulas or numerical representations in databases. The WHISPER program illustrates how the physical symbol system hypothesis can work with diagrams.

(1)   WHISPER is designed to assess the stability of structures in a virtual block world.

(2)   It contains two components – a high-level reasoner (HLR) and a retina.

(3)   The HLR has programmed into it basic knowledge of stability and object movement. The retina is able to "visualize" what happens when blocks start to rotate or slide.

(4)   The solution structure for WHISPER is a diagram in which the retina can detect no instabilities.

The robot SHAKEY is an example of how a physical symbol system can interact with a real physical environment and reason about how to solve problems.

(1)   SHAKEY has a model of its environment given by a set of sentences in a first-order logical language. This model is updated as SHAKEY moves around.

(2)   SHAKEY's software is hierarchically organized into four different levels. At the most basic level are primitive actions (Low-Level Actions – LLAs). These LLAs are organized into action routines (Intermediate-Level Actions – ILAs). SHAKEY solves problems by constructing a sequence of ILAs that will achieve a specific goal.

(3)   The STRIPS problem-solving software is an example of logic programming. It explores the logical consequences of SHAKEY's model of its current environment in order to work out which ILAs can be applied in that environment.

(4)   STRIPS then works out how the model would need to be updated if each ILA were executed in order to develop a tree of possible ILA sequences. If one of the branches of the tree leads to the desired goal state then SHAKEY implements the sequence of ILAs on that branch.

Further reading

Much of the literature in this area is very technical, but there are some accessible introductions. Haugeland 1985 and Franklin 1995 remain excellent introductions to the early years of AI research. Russell and Norvig 2009 is much more up to date. Also see Poole and Mackworth 2010, Warwick 2012, and Proudfoot and Copeland's chapter on artificial intelligence in *The Oxford Handbook of Philosophy of Cognitive Science* (Margolis, Samuels, and Stich 2012). Medsker and Schulte 2003 is a brief introduction to expert systems, while Jackson 1998 is one of the standard textbooks. The *Encyclopedia of Cognitive Science* also has an entry on expert systems (Nadel 2005). See the online resources for a very useful collection of machine learning resources.

The application of ID3 to soybean diseases described in section 7.2 was originally reported in Michalski and Chilauski 1980. The database for the tennis example explored in section 7.2 comes from ch. 3 of Mitchell 1997. Wu *et al*. 2008 describes more recent extensions of ID3, including C4.5 and C5.0, as well as other data mining methods.

Funt's description of the WHISPER program (Funt 1980) was originally published in the journal *Artificial Intelligence*. It was reprinted in an influential collection entitled *Readings in Knowledge Representation* (Brachman and Levesque 1985), which also contains a paper on analogical representations by Aaron Sloman. Laird 2012 includes discussion of recent developments in navigating the block world. SHAKEY is very well documented in technical reports published by SRI. These can be downloaded at www.ai.sri.com/shakey/. Technical report 323 is particularly helpful. Also see the *Encyclopedia of Cognitive Science* entry on STRIPS. The logic-based approach to robot design exemplified by SHAKEY has been influentially criticized within contemporary robotics. We will look at some of these criticisms in sections 13.3 and 13.4 – see the suggested readings for Chapter 13.

CHAPTER EIGHT

Neural networks and distributed information processing

Overview

This chapter looks at a model of information processing very different from the physical symbol system hypothesis. Whereas the physical symbol system hypothesis is derived from the workings of digital computers, this new model of information processing draws on an idealized model of how neurons work. Information processing in artificial neural networks is very different from information processing in physical symbol systems, particularly as envisaged in the language of thought hypothesis. In order to understand what is distinctive about it we will need to go into some detail about how neural networks actually function. I will keep technicality to a minimum, but it may be helpful to begin by turning back to section 3.3, which contains a brief overview of the main features of artificial neural networks. As we work through the much simpler networks discussed in the first few sections of this current chapter, it will be helpful to keep this overview in mind.

The chapter begins in section 8.1 by reviewing some of the motivations for neurally inspired models of information processing. These models fill a crucial gap in the techniques that we have for studying the brain. They help cognitive scientists span the gap between individual neurons (that can be directly studied using a number of specialized techniques such as microelectrode recording) and relatively large-scale brain areas (that can be directly studied using functional neuroimaging, for example).

In section 8.1 we look at the relation between biological neurons and artificial neurons (the units in neural networks). We will see that the individual units in artificial neural networks are (loosely) modeled on biological neurons. There are also, as we will see further on in the chapter, parallels between the behavior of connected sets of artificial neurons (the networks as a whole) and populations of biological neurons.

The simplest kind of artificial neural network is a single-layer network – a network in which every unit communicates directly with the outside world. Section 8.2 explores what can be achieved with single-layer networks. We will see that single-layer networks are computationally very powerful, in the following sense. Any computer can be simulated by a suitably chained together set of single-layer networks (where particular networks take the outputs of other networks as inputs, and themselves provide inputs for other networks). The limitations of single-layer networks are all to do with learning. Single-layer networks are capable of learning, using rules such as the perceptron convergence rule, but (as we see in section 8.2) there are important limits to what they can learn to do.

Overcoming those limits requires moving from single-layer networks to multilayer networks (like those explored in section 3.3). In section 8.3 we look at the backpropagation algorithm used to train multilayer networks. Finally, in section 8.4 we look at some of the key features of information processing in multilayer artificial neural networks, explaining how it is thought to be different from the type of information processing involved in the physical symbol system hypothesis.

8.1   Neurally inspired models of information processing

We saw in Part I (particularly in Chapter 3) that detailed knowledge of how the brain works has increased dramatically in recent years. Technological developments have been very important here. Neuroimaging techniques, such as fMRI and PET, have allowed neuroscientists to begin establishing large-scale correlations between types of cognitive functioning and specific brain areas. PET and fMRI scans allow neuroscientists to identify the neural areas that are activated during specific tasks. Combining this with the information available from studies of brain-damaged patients allows cognitive scientists to build up a functional map of the brain.

Other techniques have made it possible to study brain activity (in non-human animals, from monkeys to sea-slugs) at the level of the single neuron. Microelectrodes can be used to record electrical activity both inside a single neuron and in the vicinity of that neuron. Recording from inside neurons allows a picture to be built up of the different types of input to the neuron, both excitatory and inhibitory, and of the mechanisms that modulate output signals. In contrast, extra-cellular recordings made outside the neuron allow researchers to track the activation levels of an individual neuron over extended periods of time and to investigate how it responds to distinct types of sensory input and how it discharges when, for example, particular movements are made.

None of these ways of studying the brain gives us direct insight into how information is processed in the brain. The problem is one of fineness of grain. Basically, the various techniques of neuroimaging are too coarse-grained and the techniques of single neuron recordings too fine-grained (at least for studying higher cognitive functions). PET and fMRI are good sources of information about which brain areas are involved in particular cognitive tasks, but they do not tell us anything about how those cognitive tasks are actually carried out. A functional map of the brain tells us very little about how the brain carries out the functions in question. We need to know not just *what* particular regions of the brain do, but *how* they do it. Nor will this information come from single neuron recordings. We may well find out from single neuron recordings in monkeys that particular types of neuron in particular areas of the brain respond very selectively to a narrow range of visual stimuli, but we have as yet no idea how to scale this up into an account of how vision works.

Using microelectrodes to study individual neurons provides few clues to the complex patterns of interconnection between neurons. Single neuron recordings tell us what the results of those interconnections are for the individual neuron, as they are manifested in action potentials, synaptic potentials, and the flow of neurotransmitters, but not about how the behavior of the population as a whole is a function of the activity in individual neurons and the connections between them. At the other end of the spectrum, large-scale information about blood flow in the brain will tell us which brain systems are active, but is silent about how the activity of the brain system is a function of the activity of the various neural circuits of which it is composed.

Everything we know about the brain suggests that we will not be able to understand cognition unless we understand what goes on at levels of organization between large-scale brain areas and individual neurons. The brain is an extraordinarily complicated set of interlocking and interconnected circuits. The most fundamental feature of the brain is its *connectivity* and the crucial question in understanding the brain is how distributed patterns of activation across populations of neurons can give rise to perception, memory, sensori-motor control, and high-level cognition. But we have (as yet) limited tools for directly studying how populations of neurons work.

It is true that there are ways of directly studying the overall activity of populations of neurons. Event-related potentials (ERPs) and event-related magnetic fields (ERFs) are cortical signals that reflect neural network activity and that can be recorded non-invasively from outside the skull. Recordings of ERPs and ERFs have the advantage over information derived from PET and fMRI of permitting far greater temporal resolution and hence of giving a much more precise sense of the time course of neural events. Yet information from ERPs and ERFs is still insufficiently fine-grained. They reflect the summed electrical activity of populations of neurons, but offer no insight into how that total activity level is generated by the activity of individual neurons.

In short, we do not have the equipment and resources to study populations of neurons directly. And therefore many researchers have taken a new tack. They have developed techniques for studying populations of neurons indirectly. The approach is via models that approximate populations of neurons in certain important respects. These models are standardly called neural network models.

Like all mathematical models they try to strike a balance between biological realism, on the one hand, and computational tractability on the other. They need to be sufficiently "brain-like" that we can hope to use them to learn about how the brain works. At the same time they need to be simple enough to manipulate and understand. The aim is to abstract away from many biological details of neural functioning in the hope of capturing some of the crucial general principles governing the way the brain works. The multilayered complexity of brain activity is reduced to a relatively small number of variables whose activity and interaction can be rigorously controlled and studied.

There are many different types of neural network models and many different ways of using them. The focus in *computational neuroscience* is on modeling biological neurons and populations of neurons. Computational neuroscientists start from what is known about the biology of the brain and then construct models by abstracting away from some biological details while preserving others. *Connectionist modelers* often pay less attention to the constraints of biology. They tend to start with generic models. Their aim is to show how those models can be modified and adapted to simulate and reproduce well-documented psychological phenomena, such as the patterns of development that children go through when they acquire language, or the way in which cognitive processes break down in brain-damaged patients.

For our purposes here, the differences between computational neuroscientists and connectionist modelers are less important than what they have in common. Neural network models have given rise to a way of thinking about information processing very different from the physical symbol system hypothesis and the language of thought hypothesis. Neural network models are distinctive in how they store information, how they retrieve it, and how they process it. And even those models that are not biologically driven remain neurally inspired. This neurally inspired way of thinking about information processing is the focus of this chapter.

Neurons and network units

Neural networks are made up of individual units loosely based on biological neurons. There are many different types of neuron in the nervous system, but they all share a common basic structure. Each neuron is a cell and so has a cell body (a *soma*) containing a nucleus. There are many root-like extensions from the cell body. These are called *neurites*. There are two different types of neurite. Each neuron has many dendrites and a single axon. The dendrites are thinner than the axon and form what looks like a little

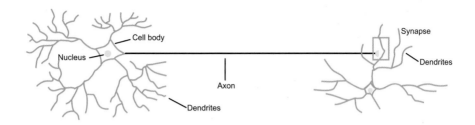

Figure 8.1 Schematic illustration of a typical neuron.

bush (as illustrated in Figure 8.1). The axon itself eventually splits into a number of branches, each terminating in a little *endbulb* that comes close to the dendrites of another neuron.

Neurons receive signals from other neurons. A typical neuron might receive inputs from 10,000 neurons, but the number is as great as 50,000 for some neurons in the brain area called the hippocampus. These signals are received through the dendrites, which can be thought of as the receiving end of the neuron. A sending neuron transmits a signal along its axon to a *synapse*, which is the site where the end of an axon branch comes close to a dendrite or the cell body of another neuron. When the signal from the sending (or *presynaptic*) neuron reaches the synapse, it generates an electrical signal in the dendrites of the receiving (or *postsynaptic*) neuron.

The basic activity of a neuron is to fire an electrical impulse along its axon. The single most important fact about the firing of neurons is that it depends upon activity at the synapses. Some of the signals reaching the neuron's dendrites promote firing and others inhibit it. These are called *excitatory and inhibitory* synapses respectively. If we think of an excitatory synapse as having a positive weight and an inhibitory synapse a negative weight, then we can calculate the strength of each synapse (by multiplying the strength of the incoming signal by the corresponding synaptic weight). Adding all the synapses together gives the total strength of the signals received at the synapses – and hence the total input to the neuron. If this total input exceeds the *threshold of the neuron* then the neuron will fire.

Neural networks are built up of interconnected populations of units that are designed to capture some of the generic characteristics of biological neurons. For this reason they are sometimes called artificial neurons. Figure 8.2 illustrates a typical network unit. The unit receives a number of different inputs. There are n inputs, corresponding to synaptic connections to presynaptic neurons. Signals from the presynaptic neurons might be excitatory or inhibitory. This is captured in the model by assigning a numerical weight W_i to each input I_i. Typically the weight will be a real number between 1 and −1. A positive weight corresponds to an excitatory synapse and a negative weight to an inhibitory synapse.

The first step in calculating the total input to the neuron is to multiply each input by its weight. This corresponds to the strength of the signal at each synapse. Adding all these individual signals (or *activation levels*) together gives the total input to the unit,

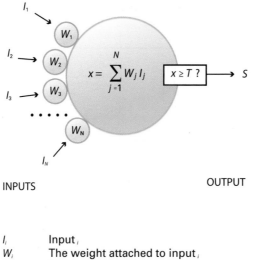

$$x = \sum_{j=1}^{N} W_j I_j \qquad x \geq T \ ?$$

INPUTS

OUTPUT

I_i	Input $_i$
W_i	The weight attached to input $_i$
T	The threshold of the neuron
X	The total input to the neuron
S	The output signal

Figure 8.2 An artificial neuron.

corresponding to the total signal reaching the nucleus of the neuron. This is represented using standard mathematical format in Figure 8.2. (A reminder – Σ is the symbol for summation (repeated addition). The N above the summation sign indicates that there are N many things to add together. Each of the things added together is the product of I_j and W_j for some value of j between 1 and N.) If the total input exceeds the threshold (T) then the neuron "fires" and transmits an output signal.

The one thing that remains to be specified is the strength of the output signal. We know that the unit will transmit a signal if the total input exceeds its designated threshold, but we do not yet know what that signal is. For this we need to specify an *activation function* – a function that assigns an output signal on the basis of the total input. Neural network designers standardly choose from several different types of activation function. Some of these are illustrated in Figure 8.3.

The simplest activation function is a linear function on which the output signal increases in direct proportion to the total input. (Linear functions are so called because they take a straight line when drawn on a graph.) The threshold linear function is a slight modification of this. This function yields no output signal until the total input reaches the threshold – and then the strength of the output signal increases proportionately to the total input. There is also a binary threshold function, which effectively operates like an on/off switch. It either yields zero output (when the input signal is below threshold) or maximum output (when the input signal is at or above threshold).

The threshold functions are intended to reflect a very basic property of biological neurons, which is that they only fire when their total input is suitably strong. The binary

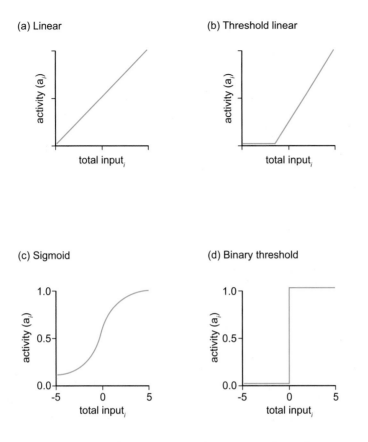

Figure 8.3 Four different activation functions. Each one fixes a neuron's activation level as a function of the total input to the neuron. (Adapted from McLeod, Plunkett, and Rolls 1998)

threshold activation function models neurons that either fire or don't fire, while the threshold linear function models neurons whose firing rate increases in proportion to the total input once the threshold has been reached.

The sigmoid function is a very commonly used nonlinear activation function. This reflects some of the properties of real neurons in that it effectively has a threshold below which total input has little effect and a ceiling above which the output remains more or less constant despite increases in total input. The ceiling corresponds to the maximum firing rate of the neuron. Between the threshold and the ceiling the strength of the output signal is roughly proportionate to the total input and so looks linear. But the function as a whole is nonlinear and drawn with a curve.

We see, then, how each individual unit in a network functions. The next step is to see how they can be used to process information. This typically requires combining units into neural networks. But before looking at how that works it will be useful to think about a restricted class of neural networks, standardly called *single-layer networks*.

8.2 Single-layer networks and Boolean functions

One way of thinking about information processing is in terms of *mapping functions*. Functions are being understood here in the strict mathematical sense. The basic idea of a function should be familiar, even if the terminology may not be. Addition is a function. Given two numbers as *inputs*, the addition function yields a third number as *output*. The output is the sum of the two inputs. Multiplication is also a function. Here the third number is the product of the two inputs.

Let us make this a little more precise. Suppose that we have a set of items. We can call that a *domain*. Let there be another set of items, which we can call the *range*. A mapping function maps each item from the domain onto exactly one item from the range. The defining feature of a function is that no item in the domain gets mapped to more than one item in the range. Functions are *single-valued*. The operation of taking square roots, for example, is not a function (at least when negative numbers are included), since every positive number has two square roots.

Exercise 8.1 Give another example of an arithmetical operation that counts as a function. And another example of an operation that is not a function.

Figure 8.4 gives an example of a mapping function. The arrows indicate which item in the domain is mapped to each item in the range. It is perfectly acceptable for two or more items in the domain to be mapped to a single item in the range (as is the case with A_1 and A_2). But, because functions are single-valued, no item in the domain can be mapped onto more than one item in the range.

The mapping function of addition has a domain made up of all the possible pairs of numbers. Its range is made up of all the numbers. In this case we can certainly have several different items in the domain mapping onto a single item in the range. Take A_1 to be the pair $\langle 1, 3 \rangle$ and A_2 to be the pair $\langle 2, 2 \rangle$. The addition function maps both A_1 and A_2 onto 4 (which we can take to be B_2).

Consider now a mapping function with two items in its range. We can think about this as a way of classifying objects in the domain of the function. Imagine that the

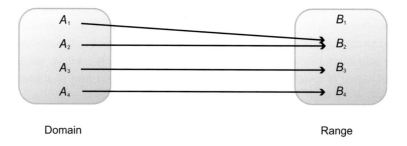

Figure 8.4 Illustration of a mapping function. A mapping function maps each item in its domain to exactly one item in its range.

domain of the function contains all the natural numbers and the range of the function contains two items corresponding to TRUE and FALSE. Then we can identify any subset we please of the natural numbers by mapping the members of that subset onto TRUE and all the others onto FALSE. If the subset that the function maps onto TRUE contains all and only the even numbers, for example, then we have a way of picking out the set of the even numbers. This in fact is how the famous mathematician Gottlob Frege, who invented modern logic, thought about concepts. He thought of the concept *even number* as a function that maps every even number to TRUE and everything else to FALSE.

Anybody who has taken a course in elementary logic will be familiar with an important class of mapping functions. These functions all have the same range as our even number function – namely, the set consisting of the two truth values TRUE and FALSE. Using the standard notation for sets we can write the range of the function as {TRUE, FALSE}. Instead of having numbers in the domain, however, the domain of these functions is made up of pairs of truth values. These functions, the so-called *binary Boolean functions*, take pairs of truth values as their inputs and deliver truth values as their outputs. They are called binary functions because the domain of the function consists of pairs (addition is also a binary function). They are called Boolean functions (after the nineteenth-century mathematician George Boole) because both the domain and range are built up from truth values.

Exercise 8.2 Give an example of a unary (one-place) Boolean function and an example of a ternary (three-place) Boolean function.

There are four different possible pairs of truth values. These pairs form the domain of the binary Boolean functions. The range, as with all Boolean functions, is given by the set {TRUE, FALSE}, as illustrated below:

DOMAIN	RANGE
FALSE, FALSE	
FALSE, TRUE	FALSE
TRUE, FALSE	TRUE
TRUE, TRUE	

Each binary Boolean function assigns either TRUE or FALSE to each pair of truth values.

It is easier to see what is going on if you think of a binary Boolean function as a way of showing how the truth value of a complex sentence is determined by the truth values of the individual sentences from which they are built up. Some of the Boolean functions should be very familiar. There is a binary Boolean function standardly known as AND, for example. AND maps the pair {TRUE, TRUE} to TRUE and maps all other pairs of truth values to FALSE. To put it another way, if you are given a sentence A and a sentence B, then the only circumstance in which it is true to claim A AND B is the circumstance in which both A and B have the value TRUE.

Similarly OR is the name of the Boolean function that maps the pair {FALSE, FALSE} to FALSE, and the other three pairs to TRUE. Alternatively, if you are given sentences A and B then the only circumstance in which it is false to claim A OR B is the circumstance in which both A and B have the value FALSE.

It is important that the OR function assigns TRUE to the pair {TRUE, TRUE}, so that A OR B is true in the case where both A and B are true. As we shall see, there is a Boolean function that behaves just like OR, except that it assigns FALSE to {TRUE, TRUE}. This is the so-called XOR function (an abbreviation of exclusive-OR). XOR *cannot* be represented by a single-layer network. We will look at this in more detail in section 8.2.

We can represent these functions using what logicians call a truth table. The truth table for AND tells us how the truth value of A AND B varies according to the truth value of A and B respectively (or, as a logician would say – as a *function* of the truth values of A and B).

A	B	A AND B
FALSE	FALSE	FALSE
FALSE	TRUE	FALSE
TRUE	FALSE	FALSE
TRUE	TRUE	TRUE

This truth table should come as no surprise. It just formalizes how we use the English word "and."

 Exercise 8.3 Give a truth table for the Boolean function OR.

What has this got to do with neural networks? The connection is that the network units that we looked at in section 8.1 can be used to represent some of the binary Boolean functions. The first step is to represent Boolean functions using numbers (since we need numbers as inputs and outputs for the arithmetic of the activation function to work). This is easy. We can represent TRUE by the number 1 and FALSE by 0, as is standard in logic and computer science. If we design our network unit so that it only takes 1 and 0 as inputs and only produces 1 and 0 as outputs then it will be computing a Boolean function. If it has two inputs then it will be computing a binary Boolean function. If it has three inputs, a ternary Boolean function. And so on.

Figure 8.5 A single-layer network representing the Boolean function AND.

It is easy to see how we design our network unit to take only 0 and 1 as input. But how do we design it to produce only 0 and 1 as output?

The key is to use a binary threshold activation function. As we saw in Figure 8.3, a binary threshold activation function outputs 0 until the threshold is reached. Once the threshold is reached it outputs 1, irrespective of how the input increases. What we need to do, therefore, if we want to represent a particular Boolean function, is to set the weights and the threshold in such a way that the network mimics the truth table for that Boolean function. A network that represents AND, for example, will have to output a 0 whenever the input is either (0, 0), (0, 1), or (1, 0). And it will have to output a 1 whenever the input is (1, 1).

The trick in getting a network to do this is to set the weights and the threshold appropriately. Look at Figure 8.5. If we set the weights at 1 for both inputs and the threshold at 2, then the unit will only fire when both inputs are 1. If both inputs are 1 then the total input is $(I_1 \times W_1) + (I_2 \times W_2) = (1 \times 1) + (1 \times 1) = 2$, which is the threshold. Since the network is using a binary threshold activation function (as described in the previous paragraph), in this case the output will be 1. If either input is a 0 (or both are) then the threshold will not be met, and so the output is 0. If we take 1 to represent TRUE and 0 to represent FALSE, then this network represents the AND function. It functions as what computer scientists call an AND-gate.

Exercise 8.4 Show how a network unit can represent OR and hence function as an OR-gate.

There are Boolean functions besides the binary ones. In fact, there are n-ary Boolean functions for every natural number n (including 0). But cognitive scientists are generally only interested in one non-binary Boolean function. This is the unary function NOT. As its name suggests, NOT A is true if A is false and NOT A is false if A is true. Again, this is easily represented by a single network unit, as illustrated in Figure 8.6. The trick is to set the weights and threshold to get the desired result.

Exercise 8.5 Explain why this network unit represents the unary Boolean function NOT.

We see, then, that individual neuron-like units can achieve a lot. A single unit can represent some very basic Boolean functions. In fact, as any computer scientist knows, modern digitial computers are in the last analysis no more than incredibly complicated systems of AND-gates, OR-gates, and NOT-gates. So, by chaining together individual network units into a network we can do anything that can be done by a digital

Figure 8.6 A single-layer network representing the Boolean function NOT.

computer. (This is why I earlier said that cognitive scientists are generally only interested in one non-binary Boolean function. AND, NOT, OR, and a little ingenuity are enough to simulate any *n*-ary Boolean function, no matter how complicated.)

There is something missing, however. As we have seen, the key to getting single units to represent Boolean functions such as NOT and OR lies in setting the weights and the threshold. But this raises some fundamental questions: How do the weights get set? How does the threshold get set? Is there any room for learning?

Thinking about these questions takes us to the heart of the theory and practice of neural networks. What makes neural networks such a powerful tool in cognitive science is that they are capable of learning. This learning can be *supervised* (when the network is "told" what errors it is making) or *unsupervised* (when the network does not receive feedback). In order to appreciate how neural networks can learn, however, we need to start with single-layer networks. Single-layer networks have some crucial limitations in what they can learn. The most important event in the development of neural networks was the discovery of a learning algorithm that could overcome the limitations of single-unit networks.

Learning in single-layer networks: The perceptron convergence rule

We can start with a little history. The discovery of neural networks is standardly credited to the publication in 1943 of a pathbreaking paper by Warren McCullough and Walter Pitts entitled "A logical calculus of the ideas immanent in nervous activity." One of the things that McCullough and Pitts did in that paper was propose that any digital computer can be simulated by a network built up from single-unit networks similar to those discussed in the previous section. They were working with fixed networks. Their networks had fixed weights and fixed thresholds and they did not explore the possibility of changing those weights through learning.

A few years later in 1949 Donald Hebb published *The Organization of Behavior* in which he speculated about how learning might take place in the brain. His basic idea (the idea behind what we now call *Hebbian learning*) is that learning is at bottom an associative process. He famously wrote:

> When an axon of a cell A is near enough to excite cell B or repeatedly or persistently takes part in firing it, some growth or metabolic change takes place in both cells such that A's efficiency, as one of the cells firing B, is increased.

Hebbian learning proceeds by synaptic modification. If A is a presynaptic neuron and B a postsynaptic neuron, then every time that B fires after A fires increases the probability that B will fire after A fires (this is what Hebb means by an increase in A's efficiency).

In its simplest form Hebbian learning is an example of unsupervised learning, since the association between neurons can be strengthened without any feedback. In slogan form, Hebbian learning is the principle that *neurons that fire together, wire together.* It has proved to be a very useful tool in modeling basic pattern recognition and pattern completion, as well as featuring in more complicated learning algorithms, such as the competitive learning algorithm discussed in section 8.3.

Hebb was speculating about real neurons, not artificial ones. And, although there is strong evidence that Hebbian learning does take place in the nervous system, the first significant research on learning in artificial neural networks modified the Hebbian model very significantly. In the 1950s Frank Rosenblatt studied learning in single-layer networks. In an influential article in 1958 he called these networks *perceptrons.*

Rosenblatt was looking for a learning rule that would allow a network with random weights and a random threshold to settle on a configuration of weights and thresholds that would allow it to solve a given problem. Solving a given problem means producing the right output for every input.

The learning in this case is supervised learning. So, whenever the network produces the wrong output for a given input, this means that there is something wrong with the weights and/or the threshold. The process of learning (for a neural network) is the process of changing the weights in response to error. Learning is successful when these changes in the weights and/or the threshold converge upon a configuration that always produces the desired output for a given input.

Rosenblatt called his learning rule the *perceptron convergence rule.* The perceptron convergence rule has some similarities with Hebbian learning. Like Hebbian learning it relies on the basic principle that changes in weight are determined solely by what happens locally – that is, by what happens at the input and what happens at the output. But, unlike Hebbian learning, it is a supervised algorithm – it requires feedback about the correct solution to the problem the network is trying to solve.

The perceptron convergence rule can be described with a little symbolism. We can assume that our networks are single-layer networks like those discussed earlier in this section. They have a binary threshold activation function set up so that they output either 1 or 0, depending on whether or not the total input exceeds the threshold. We assume also that the inputs to the network are always either 0 or 1 (so that the networks are really computing Boolean functions).

The perceptron convergence rule allows learning by reducing error. The starting-point is that we (as the supervisors of the network) know what the correct solution to the problem is, since we know what mapping function we are trying to train the network to compute. This allows us to measure the discrepancy between the output that the network actually produces and the output that it is supposed to produce. We can label that discrepancy δ (small delta). It will be a number – the number reached by subtracting the actual output from the correct output. So:

δ = INTENDED OUTPUT – ACTUAL OUTPUT

Suppose, for example, that we are trying to produce a network that functions as an AND-gate. This means that, when the inputs each have value 1, the desired output is 1 (since A AND B is true in the case where A is true and B is true). If the output that the network actually produces is 0, then δ = 1. If, in contrast, the inputs each have value 0 and the actual output is 1, then δ = −1.

It is standard when constructing neural networks to specify a learning rate. This is a constant number between 0 and 1 that determines how large the changes are on each trial. We can label the learning rate constant ε (epsilon). The perceptron convergence rule is a very simple function of δ and ε.

If we use the symbol Δ (big delta) to indicate the adjustment that we will make after each application of the rule, then the perceptron convergence rule can be written like this (remembering that T is the threshold; I_i is the i-th input; and W_i is the weight attached to the i-th input):

$$\Delta T = -\varepsilon \times \delta$$
$$\Delta W_i = \varepsilon \times \delta \times I_i$$

Let's see what's going on here. One obvious feature is that the two changes have opposite signs. Suppose δ is positive. This means that our network has undershot (because it means that the correct output is greater than the actual output). Since the actual output is weaker than required we can make two sorts of changes in order to close the gap between the required output and the actual output. We can *decrease* the threshold and we can *increase* the weights. This is exactly what the perceptron convergence rule tells us to do. We end up decreasing the threshold because when δ is positive, −ε × δ is negative. And we end up increasing the weights, because ε × δ × I_i comes out positive when δ is positive.

Exercise 8.6 What happens if the network overshoots?

An example may make things clearer. Let's consider the very simple single layer network depicted in Figure 8.7. This network only takes one input and so we only have one weight to worry about. We can take the starting weight to be −0.6 and the threshold to be 0.2. Let's set our learning constant at 0.5 and use the perceptron learning rule to train this network to function as a NOT-gate.

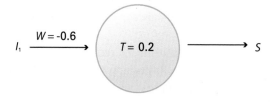

Figure 8.7 The starting configuration for a single-layer network being trained to function as a NOT-gate through the perceptron convergence rule. It begins with a weight of −0.6 and a threshold of 0.2.

Suppose that we input a 1 into this network (where, as before, 1 represents TRUE and 0 represents FALSE). The total input is $1 \times -0.6 = -0.6$. This is below the threshold of 0.2 and so the output signal is 0. Since this is the desired output we have $\delta = 0$ and so no learning takes place (since $\Delta T = -\varepsilon \times \delta = -0.5 \times 0 = 0$, and ΔW also comes out as 0). But if we input a 0 then we get a total input of $0 \times -0.6 = 0$. Since this is also below the threshold the output signal is 0. But this is not the desired output, which is 1. So we can calculate $\delta = 1 - 0 = 1$. This gives $\Delta T = -0.5 \times 1 = -0.5$ and $\Delta W = 0.5 \times 1 \times 0 = 0$. This changes the threshold (to -0.3) and leaves the weight unchanged.

This single application of the perceptron convergence rule is enough to turn our single-unit network with randomly chosen weight and threshold into a NOT-gate. If we input a 1 into the network then the total input is $1 \times -0.5 = -0.5$, which is below the threshold. So the output signal is 0, as required. And if we input a 0 into the network then the total input is $0 \times -0.5 = 0$, which is above the threshold of -0.3. So the output signal is 1, as required. In both cases we have $\delta = 0$ and so no further learning takes place. The network has *converged* on a solution.

The perceptron convergence rule is very powerful. In fact, it can be proved (although we shan't do so here) that applying the rule is guaranteed to converge on a solution in every case that a solution exists. But can we say anything about when there is no solution – and hence about which functions a network can learn to compute via the perceptron convergence rule and which will forever remain beyond its reach? It turns out that there is a relatively simple way of classifying the functions that a network can learn to compute by applying the perceptron convergence rule. We will see how to do it later in this section.

Linear separability and the limits of perceptron convergence

We have seen how our single-layer networks can function as AND-gates, OR-gates, and NOT-gates. And we have also seen an example of how the perceptron convergence rule can be used to train a network with a randomly assigned weight and a randomly assigned threshold to function as a NOT-gate. It turns out that these functions share a common property and that that common property is shared by every function that a single-layer network can be trained to compute. This gives us a very straightforward way of classifying what networks can learn to do via the perceptron convergence rule.

It is easiest to see what this property is if we use a graph to visualize the "space" of possible inputs into one of the gates. Figure 8.8 shows how to do this for two functions. The function on the left is the AND function. On the graph a black dot is used to mark the inputs for which the AND-gate outputs a 1, and a white dot marks the inputs that get a 0. There are four possible inputs and, as expected, only one black dot (corresponding to the case where both inputs have the value TRUE). The graph for AND shows that we can use a straight line to separate out the inputs that receive the value 1 from the inputs that receive the value 0. Functions that have this property are said to be *linearly separable*.

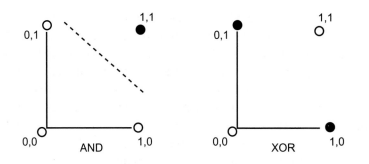

Figure 8.8 Graphical representations of the AND and XOR (exclusive-OR) functions, showing the linear separability of AND. Each of the four circles marked on the graph represents a possible combination of input truth values (as fixed by their respective coordinates). The circle is colored black just if the function outs 1 at that point.

Exercise 8.7 Draw a graph to show that OR is linearly separable.

It should not take long to see, however, that the function on the right is not linearly separable. This is the exclusive-OR function (standardly written as XOR). The OR function that we have been looking at up to now has the value TRUE except when both inputs have the value FALSE. So, A OR B has the value TRUE even when both A and B have the value TRUE. This is not how the word "or" often works in English. If I am offered a choice between A or B it often means that I have to choose one, but not both. This way of thinking about "or" is captured by the function XOR. A XOR B has the value TRUE only when exactly one of A and B has the value TRUE.

No straight line separates the black dots from the white dots in the graph of XOR. This means that XOR is not linearly separable. It turns out, moreover, that XOR cannot be represented by a single-layer network. This is easier to see if we represent XOR in a truth table. The table shows what the output is for each of the four different possible pairs of inputs – we can think of 1 as the TRUE input and 0 as the FALSE input.

I_1	I_2	OUTPUT
0	0	0
0	1	1
1	0	1
1	1	0

Now, think about how we would need to set the weights and the threshold to get a single-layer network to generate the right outputs. We need the network to output a 1 when the first input is 0 and the second input is 1. This means that W_2 (the weight for the second input) must be such that $1 \times W_2$ is greater than the threshold. Likewise for the case where the first input is 1 and the second input is 0. In order to get this to come out right we need W_1 to be such that $1 \times W_1$ is greater than the threshold. But now, with the weights set like that, it is inevitable that the network will output a 1 when both inputs are 1 - if each input is weighted so that it exceeds the threshold, then it is certain that adding them together will exceed the threshold. In symbols, if $W_1 > T$ and $W_2 > T$, then it is inevitable that $W_1 + W_2 > T$.

So, XOR fails to be linearly separable and is also not computable by a single-layer network. You might wonder whether there is a general lesson here. In fact there is. The class of Boolean functions that can be computed by a single-unit network is precisely the class of linearly separable functions. This was proved by Marvin Minsky and Seymour Papert in a very influential book entitled *Perceptrons* that was published in 1969.

Many cognitive scientists at the time saw this proof as a death sentence for the research program of neural networks. The problem does not seem too serious for binary Boolean functions. There are 16 binary Boolean functions and all but 2 are linearly separable. But things get worse when one starts to consider n-ary Boolean functions for n greater than 2. There are 256 ternary Boolean functions and only 104 are linearly separable. By the time we get to $n = 4$ we have a total of 65,536 quarternary Boolean functions, of which only 1,882 are linearly separable. Things get very much worse as n increases.

You may have been struck by the following thought. Earlier in this section I said that any Boolean function, no matter how complicated, could be computed by a combination of AND-gates, OR-gates, and NOT-gates. This applies both to those Boolean functions that are linearly separable and to those that are not. So, why does it matter that single-layer networks cannot compute Boolean functions that are not linearly separable? Surely we can just put together a suitable network of AND-gates, OR-gates, and NOT-gates in order to compute XOR – or any other Boolean function that fails to be linearly separable. So why did researchers react so strongly to the discovery that single-unit networks can only compute linearly separable Boolean functions?

This is a very good question. It is indeed not too hard to construct a network that will compute XOR. This had been known for a long time before Minsky and Papert published their critique of Rosenblatt's perceptrons – at least as far back as the 1943 article by McCullough and Pitts. Figure 8.9 shows a network that will do the job. This network is what is known as a multilayer network. Up to now we have been looking at single-layer networks. The units in single-layer networks receive inputs directly. Multilayer networks, in contrast, contain units that only receive inputs indirectly. These are known as *hidden units*. The only inputs they can receive are outputs from other units.

Exercise 8.8 There are two binary Boolean functions that fail to be linearly separable. The second is the reverse of XOR, which assigns 1 where XOR assigns 0 and 0 where XOR assigns 1. Construct a network that computes this function.

The presence of hidden units is what allows the network in Figure 8.9 to compute the XOR function. The problem for a single-unit network trying to compute XOR is that it

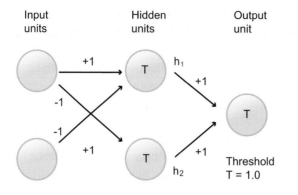

Input units   Hidden units   Output unit

Figure 8.9 A multilayer network representing the XOR (exclusive-OR) function. Note that, unlike the single-layer perceptrons that we have been considering up to now, this network has three layers. One of these layers is a hidden layer – it receives inputs only indirectly from other units. (Adapted from McLeod, Plunkett, and Rolls 1998)

can only assign one weight to each input. This is why a network that outputs 1 when the first input is 1 and outputs 1 when the second input is 1 has to output 1 when both inputs are 1. This problem goes away when a network has hidden units. Each input now has its own unit and each input unit is connected to two different output units. This means that two different weights can now be assigned to each input.

Multilayered networks can compute any computable function – not just the linearly separable ones. But what stopped researchers in their tracks in 1969 was the fact that they had no idea how to train multilayered networks. The reason that so much weight was placed on single-layer networks was that there were rules for training those networks to converge on patterns of weights and thresholds that would compute certain functions – the best known of those rules being the perceptron convergence rules explained above. Single-layer networks do not have to be completely programmed in advance. They can learn.

The perceptron convergence rule cannot be applied to multilayer networks, however. In order to apply the rule we need to know what the required output is for a given unit. This gives us the δ value (the error value), and without that value we cannot apply the rule. The problem is that there is no required output for hidden units. If we know what function we are trying to compute then we know what the required output is. But knowing the function does not tell us what any hidden units might be supposed to do. And even if we do know what the hidden units are supposed to be doing, adjusting the thresholds and weights of the hidden units according to the perceptron convergence rule would just throw our updating algorithm for the output unit completely out of step.

The situation after Minsky and Papert's critique of perceptrons was the following. It was known (a) that any computable function could be computed by a multilayer network and (b) that single-layer networks could only compute linearly separable functions. The basic problem, however, was that the main interest of neural networks for cognitive scientists was that they could learn. And it was also the case (c) that the learning algorithms that were known applied only to single-layer networks. The great break-through came with the discovery of an algorithm for training multilayer networks.

8.3 Multilayer networks

Paul Werbos is one of the great unsung heroes of cognitive science. The dissertation he submitted at Harvard University in 1974 for his PhD degree contained what is generally thought to be the earliest description of a learning algorithm for multilayer networks. Unfortunately, as with most PhD theses, it languished unread for many years. Werbos published an extended version of the dissertation in 1994, but (as discussed in section 3.3) the start of neural network research in cognitive science is generally credited to the publication in 1986 of a very influential two-volume collection of papers edited by Jay McClelland and David Rumelhart and entitled *Parallel Distributed Processing: Explorations in the Microstructure of Cognition*. The papers in the collection showed what could be done by training multilayer neural networks. It was the start of a new way of thinking about information processing in cognitive science.

Before giving an informal account of the learning algorithm we need to remind ourselves of some basic facts about how multilayer networks actually function. Multi-layer networks are organized into different layers. Each layer contains a number of units. The networks in each layer are typically not connected to each other. All networks contain an input layer, an output layer, and a number (possibly 0) of what are called *hidden layers*. The hidden layers are so called because they are connected only to other network units. They are hidden from the "outside world."

Information enters the network via the input layer. Each unit in the input layer receives a certain degree of activation, which we can represent numerically. Each unit in the input layer is connected to each unit in the next layer. Each connection has a weight, again representable numerically. The most common neural networks are *feedforward* networks. As the name suggests, activation spreads forward through the network. There is no spread of activation between units in a given layer, or backwards from one layer to the previous layer.

Information processing in multilayer networks is really a scaled-up version of infor-mation processing in single-unit networks. The activation at a given input unit is transmitted to all of the units to which it is connected in the next layer. The exact quantity of activation transmitted by each unit in the input layer depends upon the weight of the connection. The total input to a given unit in the first hidden layer is determined exactly as in the single-unit case. It is the sum of all the quantities of activation that reach it. If the total input to the unit reaches the threshold then the unit fires (i.e. transmits its own activation). The amount of activation that each unit transmits is given by its activation function.

The process is illustrated in Figure 8.10, which illustrates the operation of a sample hidden unit in a simple network with only one layer of hidden units. (Note that the diagram follows the rather confusing notation standard in the neural network literature.

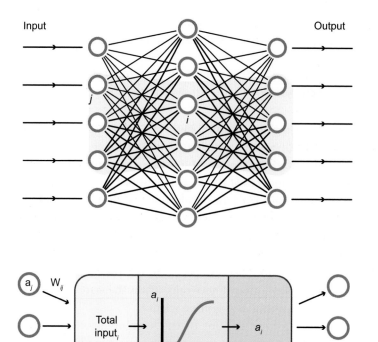

Integrate input   Transform total   Transmit activity
from previous   input to activity   level to units in next
layer   level (a_i)   layer

Figure 8.10 The computational operation performed by a unit in a connectionist model. Upper: General structure of a connectionist network. Lower: A closer look at unit i. Its operation can be broken into three steps: (1) Integrate all the inputs from the previous layer to create a total input. (2) Use an activation function to convert the total input to an activity level. (3) Output the activity level as input to units in the next layer. (Adapted from McLeod, Plunkett, and Rolls 1998)

The usual practice is to label a particular unit with the subscript i. So we write the name of the unit as u_i. If we want to talk about an arbitrary unit from an *earlier* layer connected to u_i, we label that earlier unit with the subscript j and write the name of the unit as u_j. Just to make things as difficult as possible, when we label the weight of the connection from u_j to u_i we use the subscript ij, with the label of the later unit coming first. So, w_{ij} is the weight of the connection that runs *from u_j to u_i*.)

As we see in the figure, our sample unit u_i integrates the activation it receives from all the units in the earlier layer to which it is connected. Assume that there are n units connected to u_i. Multiplying each by the appropriate weight and adding the resulting numbers all together gives the total input to the unit - which we can write as total input (i). If we represent the activation of each unit u_j by a_j, then we can write down this sum as

$$\text{Total input} = \sum_{j=1}^{N} w_{ij}\, a_j$$

We then apply the activation function to the total input. This will determine the unit's activity level, which we can write down as a_i. In the figure the activation function is a sigmoid function. This means that a_i is low when total input (i) is below the threshold. Once the threshold is reached, a_i increases more or less proportionally to total input. It then levels out once the unit's ceiling is reached.

Once we understand how a single unit works it is straightforward to see how the whole network functions. We can think of it as a series of n time steps where n is the number of layers (including the input, hidden, and output layers). In the first time step every unit in the input layer is activated. We can write this down as an ordered series of numbers – what mathematicians call a *vector*. At step 2 the network calculates the activation level of each unit in the first hidden layer, by the process described in the previous paragraph. This gives another vector. And so on until at step n the network has calculated the activation level of each unit in the output layer to give the output vector.

The backpropagation algorithm

This tells us what the network is doing from a mathematical point of view. But what the network is doing from an information-processing point of view depends on how we interpret the input and output units. In section 3.3 we looked at a network designed to distinguish between sonar echoes from rocks and sonar echoes from mines. The activation levels of the input units represent the energy levels of a sonar echo at different frequencies, while the activation levels of the two output units represent the network's "confidence" that it is encountering a rock or a mine. In the previous section we looked at a network computing the Boolean XOR function. Here the inputs and outputs represent truth values. In the next chapter we will look at other examples of neural networks. In order to appreciate what all these networks are doing, however, we need to understand how they are trained. This takes us back to Paul Werbos's learning algorithm.

Werbos called his algorithm the *backpropagation algorithm*. The name has stuck and it is very revealing. The basic idea is that error is propagated backwards through the network from the output units to the hidden units. Recall the basic problem for training multilayer networks. We know what the target activation levels are for the output units. We know, for example, that a network computing XOR should output 0 when the inputs are both 1. And we know that a mine/rock detector should output (1, 0) when its inputs correspond to a mine and (0, 1) when its inputs correspond to a rock. Given this we can calculate the degree of error in a given output unit. But since we don't know what the target activation levels are for the hidden units we have no way of calculating the degree of error in a given hidden unit. And that seems to mean that we have no way of knowing how to adjust the weights of connections to hidden units.

The backpropagation algorithm solves this problem by finding a way of calculating the error in the activation level of a given hidden unit even though there is no explicit activation level for that unit. The basic idea is that each hidden unit connected to an output unit bears a degree of "responsibility" for the error of that output unit. If, for example, the activation level of an output unit is too low, then this can only be because insufficient activation has spread from the hidden units to which it is connected. This gives us a way of assigning error to each hidden unit. In essence, the error level of a hidden unit is a function of the extent to which it contributes to the error of the output unit to which it is connected. Once this degree of responsibility, and consequent error level, is assigned to a hidden unit, it then becomes possible to modify the weights between that unit and the output unit to decrease the error.

This method can be applied to as many levels of hidden units as there are in the network. We begin with the error levels of the output units and then assign error levels to the first layer of hidden units. This allows the network both to modify the weights between the first layer of hidden units and the output units and to assign error levels to the next layer of hidden units. And so the error is *propagated* back down through the network until the input layer is reached. It is very important to remember that activation and error travel through the network in opposite directions. Activation spreads forwards through the network (at least in *feed forward* networks), while error is propagated backwards.

How biologically plausible are neural networks?

I began this chapter by describing artificial neural networks as responding to a need for a neurally inspired approach to modeling information processing. But just how biologically plausible are neural networks? This is a question to which computational neuroscientists and connectionist modelers have devoted considerable attention.

There are certainly some obvious and striking dissimilarities at many different levels between neural networks and the brain. So, for example, whereas neural network units are all homogeneous, there are many different types of neuron in the brain - twelve different types in the neocortex alone. And brains are nowhere near as massively parallel as typical neural networks. Each cortical neuron is connected to a roughly constant number of neurons (approximately 3 percent of the neurons in the surrounding square millimeter of cortex). Moreover, the scale of connectionist networks seems wrong. The cortical column is an important level of neural organization. Each cortical column consists of a population of highly interconnected neurons with similar response properties. A single cortical column cuts vertically across a range of horizontal layers (*laminae*) and can contain as many as 200,000 neurons - whereas even the most complicated artificial neural networks rarely have more than 5,000 units. This "scaling up" from artificial neural networks to cortical columns is likely to bring a range of further disanalogies in its wake. In particular, genuine neural systems will work on data that are far less circumscribed than the inputs to artificial neural networks.

But the real problems come with the type of learning that artificial neural networks can do. Some of these are practical. As we have seen, artificial neural networks learn by modifying connection weights and even in relatively simple networks this requires hundreds and thousands of training cycles. It is not clear how much weight to attach to this. After all, the principal reason why training a network takes so long is that networks tend to start with a random assignment of weights and this is not something one would expect to find in a well-designed brain.

But much more significant are the problems posed by the training methods for artificial neural networks. There is no evidence that anything like the backpropagation of error takes place in the brain. Researchers have failed to find any neural connections that transmit information about error. What makes backpropagation so powerful is that it allows for a form of "action at a distance." Units in the hidden layers have their weights changed as a function of what happens at the output units, which may be many layers away. Nothing like this is believed to occur in the brain.

Moreover, most neural networks are supervised networks and only learn because they are given detailed information about the extent of the error at each output unit. But very little biological learning seems to involve this sort of detailed feedback. Feedback in learning is typically diffuse and relatively unfocused. The feedback might simply be the presence (or absence) of a reward – a long way away from the precise calibration of degree of error required to train artificial neural networks.

It is important to keep these arguments in perspective, however. For one thing, the backpropagation of error is not the only learning algorithm. There are others that are much more biologically plausible. Computational neuroscientists and connectionist modelers have a number of learning algorithms that are much more realistic than the backpropagation algorithm. These algorithms tend to be what are known as *local algorithms*.

In local learning algorithms (as their name suggests) an individual unit's weight changes directly as a function of the inputs to and outputs from that unit. Thinking about it in terms of neurons, the information for changing the weight of a synaptic connection is directly available to the presynaptic axon and the postsynaptic dendrite. The Hebbian learning rule that we briefly looked at earlier is an example of a local learning rule. Neural network modelers think of it as much more biologically plausible than the backpropagation rule.

Local learning algorithms are often used in networks that learn through unsupervised learning. The backpropagation algorithm requires very detailed feedback, as well as a way of spreading an error signal back through the network. *Competitive networks*, in contrast, do not require any feedback at all. There is no fixed target for each output unit and there is no external teacher. What the network does is classify a set of inputs in such a way that each output unit fires in response to a particular set of input patterns.

The key to making this work is that there are inhibitory connections between the output units. This is very much in contrast to standard feedforward networks, where there are typically no connections between units in a single layer. The point of these inhibitory connections is that they allow the output units to compete with each other. Each output unit inhibits the other output units in proportion to its firing rate. So, the unit that fires the most will win the competition. Only the winning unit is "rewarded" (by having its weights increased). This increase in weights makes it more likely to win the competition when the input is similar. The end result is that each output ends up firing in response to a set of similar inputs.

As one might imagine, competitive networks are particularly good at classification tasks, which require detecting similarities between different input patterns. They have been used, for example, to model visual pattern recognition. One of the amazing properties of the visual system is its ability to recognize the same object from many different angles and perspectives. There are several competitive network models of this type of *position-invariant object recognition*, including the VisNet model of visual processing developed by Edmund Rolls and T. T. Milward. VisNet is designed to reproduce the flow of information through the early visual system (as sketched in section 3.2). It has different layers intended to correspond to the stages from area V1 to the inferior temporal cortex. Each layer is itself a competitive network, learning by a version of the Hebbian rule.

In short, there are many ways of developing the basic insights in neural network models that are more biologically plausible than standard feedforward networks that require detailed feedback and a mechanism for the backpropagation of error. And in any case, the question of whether a given artificial neural network is biologically plausible needs to be considered in the context of whether it is a good model. Neural network models should be judged by the same criteria as other mathematical models. In particular, the results of the network need to mesh reasonably closely with what is known about the large-scale behavior of the cognitive ability being modeled. So, for example, if what is being modeled is the ability to master some linguistic rule (such as the rule governing the formation of the past tense), one would expect a good model to display a learning profile similar to that generally seen in the average language learner. In the next chapter we will look at two examples of models that do seem very promising in this regard. First, though, we need to make explicit some of the general features of the neural network approach to information processing.

8.4 Information processing in neural networks: Key features

So far in this chapter we have been looking at the machinery of artificial neural networks – at how they work, how they learn, what they can do, and the ways they relate to networks of neurons in the brain. It is easy to get lost in the details. But it is important to remember why we are studying them. We are looking at neural networks because we are interested in mental architectures. In particular we are interested in them as models of information processing very different from the type of models called for by the physical symbol system hypothesis. From this perspective, the niceties of different types of network and different types of learning rule are not so important. What are important are certain very general features of how neural networks process information. This section summarizes three of the most important features.

Distributed representations

According to the physical symbol system hypothesis, representations are distinct and identifiable components in a cognitive system. If we examine a cognitive system from the outside, as it were, it will be possible to identify the representations. This is because physical symbol structures are clearly identifiable objects. If the information a physical symbol carries is complex, then the symbol is itself complex. In fact, as emerges very clearly in the language of thought hypothesis, the structure and shape of the physical symbol structure is directly correlated with the structure and shape of the information it is carrying.

This need not be true in artificial neural networks. There are some networks for which it holds. These are called *localist* networks. What distinguishes localist networks is that each unit codes for a specific feature in the input data. We might think of the individual units as analogs of concepts. They are activated when the input has the feature encoded that the unit encodes. The individual units work as simple feature-detectors. There are many interesting things that can be done with localist networks. But the artificial neural networks that researchers have tended to find most exciting have typically been *distributed* networks rather than localist ones. Certainly, all the networks that we have looked at in this chapter have been distributed.

The information that a distributed network carries is not located in any specific place. Or rather, it is distributed across many specific places. A network stores information in its pattern of weights. It is the particular pattern of weights in the network that determines what output it produces in response to particular inputs. A network learns by adjusting its weights until it settles into a particular configuration - hopefully the configuration that produces the right output! The upshot of the learning algorithm is that the network's "knowledge" is distributed across the relative strengths of the connections between different units.

No clear distinction between information storage and information processing

According to the physical symbol system hypothesis all information processing is rule-governed symbol manipulation. If information is carried by symbolic formulas in the language of thought, for example, then information processing is a matter of transforming those formulas by rules that operate only on the formal features of the formulas. In the last analysis, information is carried by physical structures and the rules are rules for manipulating those symbol structures. This all depends upon the idea that we can distinguish within a cognitive system between the representations on which the rules operate and the rules themselves - just as, within a logical system such as the propositional or predicate calculus, we can distinguish between symbolic formulas and the rules that we use to build those symbolic formulas up into more complex formulas and to transform them.

Exercise 8.9 Look back at Box 6.1 and Figure 6.3 and explain how and why the distinction between rules and representations is central to the physical symbol system and language of thought hypotheses.

Consider how AND might be computed according to the physical symbol system hypothesis. A system for computing AND might take as its basic alphabet the symbol

"0" and the symbol "1." The inputs to the system would be pairs of symbols and the system would have built into it rules to ensure that when the input is a pair of "1"s then the system outputs a "1," while in all other cases it outputs a "0." What might such a rule look like?

Well, we might think about the system along the lines of a Turing machine (as illustrated in section 1.2). In this case the inputs would be symbols written on two squares of a tape. Assume that the head starts just to the left of the input squares. The following program will work.

Step 1 Move one square R.

Step 2 If square contains "1" then delete it, move one square R and go to Step 6.

Step 3 If square contains "0" then delete it, move one square R and go to Step 4.

Step 4 Delete what is in square and write "0."

Step 5 Stop.

Step 6 If square contains "0" then stop.

Step 7 If square contains "1" then stop.

The tape ends up with a "1" on it only when the tape started out with two "1"s on it. If the tape starts out with one or more "0"s on it then it will stop with a "0." The final state of the tape is reached by transforming the initial symbol structure by formal rules, exactly as required by the physical symbol system hypothesis. And the rules are completely distinct from the symbols on which they operate.

Exercise 8.10 Write a program that will compute the function XOR.

There is no comparable distinction between rules and representations in artificial neural networks. The only rules are those governing the spread of activation values forwards through the network and those governing how weights adjust. Look again at the network computing XOR and think about how it works. If we input two 1s into the network (corresponding to a pair of propositions, both of which are true), then the information processing in the network proceeds in two basic stages. In the first stage activation spreads from the input layer to the hidden layer and both hidden units fire. In the second stage activation spreads from the hidden units to the output unit and the output unit fires.

The only rules that are exploited are, first, the rule for calculating the total input to a unit and, second, the rule that determines whether a unit will fire for a given total input (i.e. the activation function). But these are exactly the same rules that would be activated if the network were computing AND or OR. These "updating rules" apply to all feedforward networks of this type. What distinguishes the networks are their different patterns of weights. But a pattern of weights is not a rule, or an algorithm of any kind. Rather a particular pattern of weights is what results from the application of one rule (the learning algorithm). And it is one of the inputs into another rule (the updating algorithm).

⬛💿 The ability to learn from "experience"

Of course, talk of neural networks learning from experience should not be taken too seriously. Neural networks do not experience anything. They just receive different types of input. But the important point is that they are not fixed in how they respond to inputs. This is because they can change their weights. We have looked at several different ways in which this can take place – at several different forms of learning algorithm. Supervised learning algorithms, such as the backpropagation algorithm, change the weights in direct response to explicit feedback about how the network's actual output diverges from intended output. But networks can also engage in unsupervised learning (as we saw when we looked briefly at competitive networks). Here the network imposes its own order on the inputs it receives, typically by means of a local learning algorithm, such as some form of Hebbian learning.

This capacity to learn makes neural networks a powerful tool for modeling cognitive abilities that develop and evolve over time. We will look at examples of how this can be done in the next chapter.

Summary

This chapter has explored a way of thinking about information processing very different from the physical symbol system hypothesis discussed in Chapters 6 and 7. Artificial neural networks are constructed from individual units that function as highly idealized neurons. We looked at two very different types of network. In the first part of the chapter we looked at single-layer networks and saw how they can learn via the perceptron convergence rule. Unfortunately, single-layer networks are limited in the functions that they can compute. It has been known for a long time that multilayer networks built up from single-layer networks can compute any function that can be computed by a digital computer, but it was not until the emergence of the backpropagation learning algorithm that it became possible to train multilayer neural networks. The chapter ended by considering the biological plausibility of neural networks and summarizing some of the crucial differences between artificial neural networks and physical symbol systems.

Checklist

Neurally inspired information processing

(1) A fundamental question in thinking about how the brain processes information is how the activities of large populations of neurons give rise to complex sensory and cognitive abilities.

(2) Existing techniques for directly studying the brain do not allow us to study what happens inside populations of neurons.

(3) Computational neuroscientists use mathematical models (neural networks) to study populations of neurons.

(4)   These neural networks are made up of units loosely based on biological neurons. Each unit is connected to other units so that activation levels can be transmitted between them as a function of the strength of the connection.

Single-layer networks

(1)   We can use single-layer networks to compute Boolean functions such as AND, OR, and NOT.
(2)   Any digital computer can be simulated by a network of single-layer networks appropriately chained together.
(3)   Single-layer networks can learn by adjusting their weights to minimize their degree of error (the δ signal) according to the perceptron convergence rule.
(4)   Single-layer networks can only learn to compute functions that are linearly separable.

Multilayer networks

(1)   Multilayer networks have hidden units that are neither input units nor output units.
(2)   The presence of hidden units enables multilayer networks to learn to compute functions that cannot be learnt by single-layer networks (including functions that are not linearly separable).
(3)   The backpropagation learning algorithm for multilayer networks adjusts the weights of hidden units as a function of how "responsible" they are for the error at the output units.

Biological plausibility

(1)   Neural network units are much more homogeneous than real neurons. And real neural networks are likely to be both much larger and less parallel than network models.
(2)   The backpropagation algorithm is not very biologically plausible. There is no evidence that error is propagated backwards in the brain. And nature rarely provides feedback as detailed as the algorithm requires.
(3)   However, there are other learning algorithms. Competitive networks using Hebbian learning do not require explicit feedback, and there is evidence for local learning in the brain.

Information processing in neural networks

(1)   Representation in neural networks is distributed across the units and weights, rather than being encoded in discrete symbol structures, as in the physical symbol system hypothesis.
(2)   There are no clear distinctions to be drawn within neural networks either between information storage and information processing or between rules and representations.
(3)   Neural networks are capable of sophisticated forms of learning, which makes them particularly suitable for modeling how cognitive abilities are acquired and how they evolve.

Further reading

The Handbook of Brain Theory and Neural Networks (Arbib 2003) is the most comprehensive single-volume source for different types of computational neuroscience and neural computing, together with entries on neuroanatomy and many other "neural topics." It contains useful introductory material and "road maps." Stein and Stoodley 2006 and Trappenberg 2010 are user-friendly introductions to neuroscience and computational neuroscience respectively. Arbib 1987 surveys the theoretical issues in modeling the brain from a mathematical perspective.

The classic source for connectionism is the two volumes of Rumelhart, McClelland, and the PDP Research Group 1986. Churchland and Sejnowski 1992 is an early manifesto for computational neuroscience. See also Bechtel and Abrahamsen 2002 and the relevant chapters of Dawson 1998. There are useful article-length presentations in Rumelhart 1989 (reprinted in Haugeland 1997) and Churchland 1990b (reprinted in Cummins and Cummins 2000). McLeod, Plunkett, and Rolls 1998 covers both the theory of neural networks and their modeling applications, including the VisNet model of visual processing originally presented in Rolls and Milward 2000. The first chapter is reprinted in Bermúdez 2006. Dawson 2005 is a "hands-on" introduction to connectionist modeling. For a survey of applications of connectionist networks in cognitive psychology, see Houghton 2005. See also Thomas and McClelland's chapter on connectionist modeling in Sun (2008). A more recent discussion of connectionism can be found in McClelland *et al.* 2010, with commentary and target articles from others in the same issue.

The biological plausibility of artificial neural networks has been much discussed and researchers have developed a number of learning algorithms that are less biologically implausible than the backpropagation algorithm. O'Reilly and Munakata 2000 is a good place to start in finding out about these. Warwick 2012 is a more recent alternative. See Bowers 2009 and Plaut and McClelland 2010 for an exchange concerning biological plausibility as well as local and distributed representations. The perceptron convergence learning rule discussed in section 8.2 is also known as the delta rule. It is very closely related to the model of associative learning in classical (Pavlovian) conditioning independently developed by the psychologists Robert Rescorla and Allen Wagner in the 1970s. For more on reward learning and the delta rule see ch. 6 of Trappenberg 2010. The *Encyclopedia of Cognitive Science* also has an entry on perceptrons (Nadel, 2005). For more on McCullough and Pitts see ch. 2 of Arbib 1987, and Piccinini 2004, as well as Schlatter and Aizawa 2008.

One of the key distinguishing features of neural networks is that their "knowledge" is distributed across units and weights. This raises a number of issues, both practical and theoretical. Rogers and McClelland 2004 develops a distributed model of semantic knowledge. Philosophers have explored the relation between distributed representations and standard ways of thinking about propositional attitudes and mental causation. Some of the points of contact are explored in Clark 1989 and 1993. Macdonald and Macdonald 1995 collects some key papers, including an important debate between Smolensky and Fodor about the structure of connectionist networks. Other collections include Davis 1993 and Ramsey, Stich, and Rumelhart 1991.

Not all neural networks are distributed. There are also localist networks. Whereas in distributed networks it is typically not possible to say what job an individual unit is doing (and when it is possible, it usually requires knowing a lot about what other units are doing), units in localist networks can be interpreted independently of the states of other units. For a robust defense of the localist approach see Page 2000 and the papers in Grainger and Jacobs 1998.

One topic not discussed in the text is the computational power of artificial neural networks. It is sometimes suggested that connectionist networks are computationally equivalent to digital computers (in virtue of being able to compute all Turing-computable functions), which might be taken to indicate that connectionist networks are simply implementations of digital computers. The implementation thesis is canvassed by both opponents of connectionism (Fodor and Pylyshyn 1988) and by leading connectionist modelers (Hinton, McClelland, and Rumelhart 1986). Siegelmann and Sontag 1991 present a neural network that can simulate a universal Turing machine. For skeptical discussion see Hadley 2000.

CHAPTER NINE

Neural network models of cognitive processes

Overview

The last chapter explored the theory behind the neural networks approach to information processing. We saw how information processing works in single-unit networks and then looked at how the power of neural networks increases when hidden units are added. At the end of the chapter we considered some of the fundamental differences between artificial neural networks and the sort of computational systems to which the physical symbol system hypothesis applies. In particular, we highlighted the following three differences.

- Representation in neural networks is distributed across the units and weights, whereas representations in physical symbol systems are encoded in discrete symbol structures.
- There are no clear distinctions in neural networks either between information storage and information processing or between rules and representations.
- Neural networks are capable of sophisticated forms of learning. This makes them very suitable for modeling how cognitive abilities are acquired and how they evolve.

In this chapter we will explore how these differences in information processing give us some very different ways of thinking about certain very basic and important cognitive abilities. We will focus in particular on language learning and object perception. These are areas that have seen considerable attention from neural network modelers – and also that have seen some of the most impressive results.

In section 9.1 we explore some of the basic theoretical challenges in explaining how we understand and learn languages. Since language is a paradigmatically rule-governed activity, it can seem very plausible to try to make sense of the information processing involved in understanding and learning language along the lines proposed by the physical symbol system hypothesis. This gives a rule-based conception of language mastery, which is very compatible with the language of thought hypothesis. Section 9.2 explores an alternative to the rule-based conception. We look at neural network models of past tense learning and show how their learning trajectory bears striking resemblances to the learning trajectory of human infants.

In the next two sections we turn to object perception (and what developmental psychologists call object permanence). Research in recent years has shown that the perceptual universe of human infants is far more complex and sophisticated than was traditionally thought. From a very early age human infants seem to be sensitive to certain basic properties of physical objects. They have definite (and often accurate) expectations about how objects behave and interact. Some of this research is presented in section 9.3, where we see how it can very naturally be interpreted in computational terms, as involving an explicitly represented and quasi-theoretical body of rules and principles (a *folk physics*). In section 9.4, however, we show how some of the very same data can be accommodated without this type of explicit, symbolic representation. We look at some neural network models that share some of the basic behaviors of the infants in the experiments without having any rules or principles explicitly coded into them. This opens the door to a different way of thinking about infants' knowledge of the physical world.

9.1 Language and rules: The challenge for information-processing models

Language is a highly sophisticated cognitive achievement. Without it our cognitive, emotional, and social lives would be immeasurably impoverished. And it is a truly remarkable fact that, with a very small number of unfortunate exceptions, all human children manage to arrive at more or less the same level of linguistic comprehension and language use. Unsurprisingly, cognitive scientists have devoted an enormous amount of research to trying to understand how languages are learnt. In this section we will introduce one very fundamental issue that arises when we start to think about language learning. This is the role that learning rules plays in learning a language.

It is clear that language is a paradigmatically rule-governed activity. At a most basic level, every language is governed by grammatical rules. These rules, painfully familiar to anyone who has tried to learn a second language, govern how words can be put together to form meaningful sentences. But grammatical rules such as these are only the tip of the iceberg. Linguists devote much of their time to trying to make explicit much more fundamental rules that govern how languages work. (These additional rules are more fundamental in the sense that they are supposed to apply to all languages, irrespective of the particular grammar of the language.)

Back in section 1.3 we looked very briefly at the version of transformational grammar proposed by Noam Chomsky in the 1950s. In effect, what Chomsky was proposing were rules that governed how a sentence with one type of grammatical structure could be legitimately transformed into a sentence with a different grammatical structure but a similar meaning. The example we looked at in section 1 was the pair of sentences "John has hit the ball" and "The ball has been hit by John." Here we have two sentences with very different surface grammatical structures, but that convey similar messages in virtue of having the same deep (or phrase) structure. Chomsky's insight was that we can understand what is common to these sentences in terms of the transformational rules that allow one to be transformed into the other. Chomsky's view on what these rules actually are has changed many times over the years, but he has never abandoned the basic idea that the deep structure of language is governed by a body of basic rules.

The rule-governed nature of language makes thinking about language a very interesting test case for comparing and contrasting the physical symbol system hypothesis and the neural network model of information processing. One of the fundamental differences between these two models of information processing has to do with the role of rules. As we saw in Chapter 6, the basic idea behind the physical symbol system hypothesis is that information processing is a matter of manipulating physical symbol structures according to rules that are explicitly represented within the system. In contrast, in Chapter 7 we learnt that it is not really possible to distinguish rules and representations in artificial neural networks (apart from the algorithm that governs how the network updates its activation levels). Information processing in artificial neural networks does not seem to involve rule-governed symbol manipulation.

Nonetheless, the fact that languages are governed by rules does not automatically mean that the information processing involved in understanding and learning languages has to involve manipulating symbol structures according to rules. If we are to arrive at that conclusion it will have to be through some combination of theoretical argument and empirical evidence. In the remainder of this section we will look at some of the theoretical reasons that have been given for thinking that the physical symbol system hypothesis (particularly in its language of thought incarnation) is the only way of making sense of the complex phenomenon of linguistic comprehension and language learning. In the next section we will test the power of those arguments by looking at connectionist models of specific aspects of language learning.

What is it to understand a language?

We need to start by thinking about the nature of linguistic comprehension. What is it to understand a language? In a very general sense, there are two different dimensions to linguistic comprehension. One dimension is understanding what words mean. There is no language without vocabulary. But words on their own are not much use. The basic unit of communication is not the word, but rather the sentence. The logician and philosopher Gottlob Frege famously remarked that only in the context of a sentence do words have meaning. This takes us to the rules that govern how words can be put together to form meaningful sentences. As we have already seen, these rules are likely to fall into two groups. On the one hand there are the rules that tell us which combinations of words are grammatical. On the other there are the rules that govern the deep structure of language.

So, understanding a language is partly a matter of understanding what words mean, and partly a matter of understanding the rules by which words are combined into sentences. What does this understanding consist in? The default hypothesis is that understanding a language is fundamentally a matter of mastering rules. This applies to the vocabulary of a language no less than to its grammar and deep structure. We can think of understanding the meaning of a word in terms of mastery of the rule that governs its application – the rule, for example, that the word "dog" refers to four-legged animals of the canine family and the rule that the word "square" applies to four-sided shapes with sides of equal size and each corner at an angle of 90 degrees.

The default hypothesis does not, however, tell us very much. Everything depends on how we think about mastering a rule. At one extreme is the view that there is no more to mastering a linguistic rule than being able to use words in accordance with the rule. There is no need for competent language users to represent the rule in any way. All they need to be able to do is to distinguish applications of the word that fit the rule from applications that do not. This is a very minimalist conception of linguistic understanding. It makes linguistic understanding much more of a practical ability than a theoretical achievement.

Many theorists, in contrast, think that this way of thinking about mastery of rules is far too weak. After all, the rock that falls in accordance with Newton's law of gravity cannot in any sense be said to have mastered that law. Mastering linguistic rules certainly requires using words in accordance with the rule, but it is not just a practical ability. Many theorists take the view that we cannot take linguistic abilities as given. They have to be explained in some way. And one explanation many have found plausible is that language users are capable of using words in accordance with linguistic rules because they represent those rules. These representations are thought to guide the language user's use of language. Language users use words in accordance with the rule because they somehow manage to compare possible sentences with their internalized representations of the rules. This is the other extreme. It makes linguistic understanding much more of a theoretical achievement than a practical ability – or rather, it takes linguistic understanding to be a practical ability grounded in a theoretical achievement.

So, the default hypothesis that linguistic understanding consists in mastery of linguistic rules can be understood in many different ways, depending on where one stands in between these two extremes. And this has significant implications for how one thinks about the information processing involved in understanding and using a language. The more importance one attaches to the explicit representation of rules, the more likely one is to think that this information processing must be understood through the physical symbol system hypothesis. This is because the physical symbol system hypothesis allows rules to be explicitly represented within the system. In fact, it not only *allows* rules to be explicitly represented. It *depends upon* rules being explicitly represented.

Conversely, the more one thinks of linguistic understanding as a practical ability, the more one will be inclined to think of language-related information processing along neural network lines. Artificial neural networks do not have rules explicitly represented in them. The only rules operative in neural networks are the arithmetical rules that govern how activation spreads through the network, on the one hand, and how weights are changed on the other. As we shall see later on in the chapter, artificial neural networks can be built that certainly behave in accordance with rules governing particular aspects of linguistic understanding, even though they do not in any sense represent those rules.

The question of how languages are learnt is very closely tied to the question of what it is to understand a language. This is not surprising, since the aim of learning a language is to end up in the position of understanding the language. And so cognitive scientists will have different views on how languages are acquired depending on their views about what it is to understand a language. If understanding a language is thought to be primarily a theoretical achievement, then learning that language will be a theoretical process. Conversely, if one thinks of linguistic understanding in practical terms, then one will favor a practical account of language acquisition. On this view, learning a language is much more like learning to ski than it is like learning arithmetic.

Since learning a language is an information-processing achievement, it is something that we need to think about in terms of a particular model of information processing. The question of which model will occupy us for this section and the next. What I want to do now is sketch out a powerful line of argument suggesting that we should think about language learning in terms of the physical symbol system model – and, in particular, in terms of the language of thought hypothesis. This argument is due to the philosopher Jerry Fodor, although its basic thrust is, I think, one that many cognitive scientists would endorse and support.

Language learning and the language of thought: Fodor's argument

Fodor starts off with a strong version of the rule-based conception of language learning. He thinks of the process of acquiring a language as a lengthy process of mastering the appropriate rules, starting with the simplest rules governing the meaning of everyday words, moving on to the simpler syntactic rules governing the formation of sentences, and then finally arriving at complex rules such as those allowing sentences to be embedded within further sentences and the complex transformational rules discussed by Chomsky and other theoretical linguists.

How does Fodor get from the rule-based conception of language learning to the existence of a language of thought? His argument is in his book *The Language of Thought*.

It starts off from a particular way of thinking about the rules governing what words mean. According to Fodor these rules are what he calls *truth rules.* They are called truth rules because they spell out how words contribute to determining what it is for sentences in which they feature to be true. Understanding truth rules may not be all that there is to understanding a language. But Fodor is emphatic that we will not be able to understand a language without understanding truth rules. Truth rules may not be sufficient, but they are certainly necessary (he claims).

Let us take a very simple sentence to illustrate how truth rules work. Consider, for example, the sentence "Felicia is tall." This sentence is what logicians call an atomic sentence. It is made up simply of a proper name ("Felicia") and a predicate ("___ is tall," where the gap indicates that it needs to be "completed" by a name of some sort). Proper names are names of individuals and predicates are names of properties. And so this gives us a very straightforward way of thinking about what makes an atomic sentence such as "Felicia is tall" true. The sentence is true just if the individual named by the proper name (i.e. Felicia) does indeed have the property named by the predicate (i.e. the property of being tall). So, the atomic sentence "Felicia is tall" is true just if Felicia is tall. It is standard to call this the *truth condition* of the sentence.

You may well think, though, that the truth condition cannot be much help to us in thinking about what it is to understand the sentence "Felicia is tall," or about how one might learn how to use the expressions "Felicia" and "___ is tall." Here is the truth condition:

TC "Felicia is tall" is true just if Felicia is tall

Surely, you might say, someone can only understand the truth condition (TC) if they already understand the sentence "Felicia is tall" (because this very sentence features in the truth condition, both inside and outside quotation marks. But then the truth condition can only be intelligible to someone who already understands the expressions "Felicia" and "___ is tall." It cannot help us to make sense of how someone can learn to use those expressions.

This is why Fodor thinks that we need something more than truth conditions such as TC in order to make sense of linguistic comprehension and language learning. We need rules that will tell us which individual the name "Felicia" refers to, and which property is named by the predicate "___ is tall." If these rules are to be learnable then they must be stated in terms of expressions that the language user is already familiar with. In fact, we really need something like the following rule.

TC* "Felicia is tall" is true just if X is G

Here "X" stands for another name for Felicia - one that the language user already understands (perhaps "X" might be "George's sister"). Likewise "G" stands for another way of naming the property of being tall (perhaps "G" might be "greater than average in height"). This is what Fodor calls a truth rule.

Exercise 9.1 Explain in your own words the difference between the truth condition TC and the truth rule TC*.

So, putting all this together, Fodor argues that learning a language has to involve learning truth rules. He thinks that this places some very fundamental constraints on any information-processing account of language learning. Learning a truth rule such as TC* is, he thinks, a matter of forming hypotheses about what the expressions "Felicia" and "____ is tall" mean. These hypotheses are then tested against further linguistic data and revised if necessary. Learning that George has no sisters, for example, would force me to revise my first version of the Felicia truth rule.

This is where the language of thought is required, Fodor argues. Learning a public language such as English, even if it is your first language, requires you to formulate, test, and revise hypotheses about the truth rules governing individual words. These hypotheses have to be formulated in some language. A truth rule is, after all, just a sentence. But which language are truth rules formulated in?

Fodor thinks that it cannot be the language being learnt. You cannot use the language that you are learning to learn that language. That would be pulling yourself up by your own bootstraps! And since Fodor takes his account to apply to children learning their first language no less than to people learning a second language, the language cannot be any sort of public language. It can only be the language of thought, as described in Chapter 6.

Is this the best way to think about language learning and language mastery? One way of querying the argument would be to challenge the strongly rule-based conception of language learning on which it rests. This might be done on theoretical grounds. As pointed out earlier, there are all sorts of ways in which mastery of a linguistic rule might be implicit rather than explicit, so that one learns to follow the rule without formulating a series of increasingly refined versions of it. It is far from obvious that the ability to use words in accordance with a rule should be understood as a matter of in some sense *internalizing* the rule.

This is not a *purely* theoretical issue. We are discussing the process of language learning and there is an empirical fact of the matter about the form that this process takes. It is natural, then, to wonder whether there might be any relevant empirical evidence. Are there any facts about how languages are learnt that could point us towards one or other way of thinking about how linguistic rules are mastered? There are some very suggestive results from neural network models of language learning that are potentially very relevant. We will look at these in the next section.

9.2 Language learning in neural networks

This section explores some influential and important studies on how neural networks can model types of language acquisition. Looking at these networks will help us to see that there is an alternative to the rule-based conception of language comprehension and learning discussed in section 9.1.

Much of the discussion of language learning has been very theoretical, based on arguments (such as *poverty of the stimulus arguments*) about what it is possible for a cognitive system to learn. Some of these arguments are technical and explore the learn-ability of formal languages studied by computer scientists. Others are more intuitive (based, for example, on the type of evidence that language learners are assumed to have). In either case, however, there is room for trying to test the arguments by constructing systems that have certain constraints built into them (such as the constraint, for example, that they only ever receive positive evidence) and then seeing how successful those systems are at learning fragments of language. Neural networks have proved to be very important tools in this project and neural network models of linguistic processes have made contributions to our understanding of language learning.

One contribution network models of linguistic processes have made is to show that neural networks can indeed model complex linguistic skills without having any explicit linguistic rules encoded in them. So, for example, the simple recurrent networks developed by Jeff Elman have been successfully trained to predict the next letter in a sequence of letters, or the next word in a sequence of words. This in itself is very important in thinking about the information processing involved in language learning. At the very least it casts doubt on claims that we can only think about language in terms of rule-based processing.

But researchers in this area have also made a second, very important, contribution, one that speaks more directly to issues about the psychological plausibility of neural network models. Developmental psychologists and psycholinguists have carefully studied pat-terns in how children learn languages. They have discovered that, in many aspects of language acquisition, children display a very typical trajectory. So, for example, children make very similar types of error at similar stages in learning particular grammatical constructions. Neural network researchers have explored the extent to which their models can reproduce these characteristic patterns. They have found some striking analogies between how children learn and how neural networks learn.

The challenge of tense learning

One of the most formidable problems confronting children learning a language such as English is that it has both regular and irregular verbs. Some verbs behave in very predictable ways. So, for example, their past tenses are formed according to straightfor-ward rules. Consider the verb "to bat," for example. This is a regular verb. In the present tense we have "I bat." In the past tense this becomes "I batted." There is a very simple rule here. For regular verbs we form the past tense by adding the suffix "-ed" to the stem of the verb. The stem of "to bat" is "batt-." For regular verbs, then, all that one needs to know in order to be able to put them in the past tense is their stem.

Contrast regular verbs with irregular verbs. We have "I give" in the present tense. This becomes "I gave" in the past tense - not "I gived," as the simple rule might suggest. Likewise for "I take," which becomes "I took." Irregular verbs, by their very nature, are not easily summarized by simple rules. It is true that there are observable regularities in how the past tenses of irregular verbs are formed. So, for example, we see that both "I ring" and "I sing" have similar past tenses ("I rang" and "I sang"). It would be unwise, however, to take this as a general rule for verbs ending in "-ing." The past tense of "I bring" is most certainly not "I brang." Anyone who has ever learnt English as a second language will know that the corpus of irregular verbs is full of "false friends" such as these.

Yet somehow more or less all young children in the English-speaking world manage to find their way through this minefield. How do they do it? There are robust data indicating that children go through three principal stages in learning how to use the past tense in English. Researchers such as the psychologist Stan Kuczaj have studied the grammaticality judgments that children made about sentences involving past tense verbs in order to test their understanding of the past tense. The test sentences included both correct past tense forms (such as "brought" and "gave") and incorrect ones (such as "brang" and "gived"). The incorrect ones were typically constructed either by treating irregular verbs as if they were regular (as in "gived"), or by exploiting "false friends" (as in "brang"). Looking at patterns of grammaticality judgments across populations of children aged from 3 to 11 has led researchers to hypothesize that children go through three distinct stages in learning the past tense.

In the first stage young language learners employ a small number of very common words in the past tense (such as "got," "gave," "went," "was," etc.). Most of these verbs are irregular and the standard assumption is that children learn these past tenses by rote. Children at this stage are not capable of generalizing from the words that they have learnt. As a consequence they tend not to make too many mistakes. They can't do much, but what they do they do well.

In the second stage children use a much greater number of verbs in the past tense, some of which are irregular but most of which employ the regular past tense ending of "-ed" added to the root of the verb. During this stage they can generate a past tense for an invented word (such as "rick") by adding "-ed" to its root. Surprisingly, children at this stage take a step backwards. They make mistakes on the past tense of the irregular verbs that they had previously given correctly (saying, for example, "gived" where they had previously said "gave"). These errors are known as *over-regularization* errors.

In the third stage children cease to make these over-regularization errors and regain their earlier performance on the common irregular verbs while at the same time improving their command of regular verbs. Table 9.1 shows the basic trajectory.

TABLE 9.1   The stages of past tense learning according to verb type

	STAGE 1	STAGE 2	STAGE 3
Early verbs	Correct	Over-regularization errors	Correct
Regular verbs		Correct	Correct
Irregular verbs		Over-regularization errors	Improvement with time
Novel		Over-regularization errors	Over-regularization errors

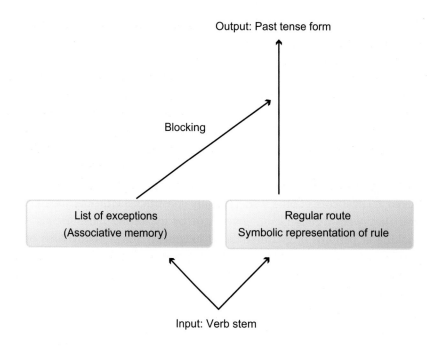

Figure 9.1 The dual route model of past tense learning in English proposed by Steven Pinker and Alan Prince.

At first sight, this pattern of performance seems to support something like Fodor's rule-governed conception of language learning. One might think, for example, that what happens in the second stage is that children make a general hypothesis to the effect that all verbs can be put in the past tense by adding the suffix "-ed" to the root. This hypothesis overrides the irregular past tense forms learnt earlier by rote and produces the documented regularization errors. In the transition to the third stage, the general hypothesis is refined as children learn that there are verbs to which it does not apply and, correspondingly, begin to learn the specific rules associated with each of these irregular verbs.

The cognitive scientists Steven Pinker and Alan Prince have in fact proposed a model of understanding the English past tense that fits very well with this analysis. Their model has two components and, correspondingly, two information-processing routes. These are illustrated in Figure 9.1.

One route goes via a symbolic representation of the rule that the past tense is formed by adding "-ed" to the stem of the verb. The symbolic component is not sensitive to the particular phonological form of the verb. It does not recruit information that, for example, the present tense of the verb ends in "-ing." It simply applies the rule to whatever input it gets.

The second route, in contrast, goes via an associative memory system that is sensitive to the phonological form of the verb stem. It is responsible for storing exceptions to the general rule. It classifies and generalizes these exceptions in terms of their phonological similarity. One would expect this mechanism to pick up very quickly on the similarity, for example, between "sing" and "ring."

The two routes are in competition with each other. The default setting, as it were, is the symbolic route. That is, the system's "default assumption" is that it is dealing with a verb where the past tense is formed by adding "-ed" to the stem. But this default setting can be overridden by a strong enough signal coming from the associative memory system that keeps track of exceptions. What makes signals from the override system strong is that they have been suitably reinforced through experience. If I have had plenty of exposure to the "sing-sang" and "ring-rang" pairs, then this will strengthen the signal for "bring-brang." But the more exposure I have to the "bring-brought" pair, the weaker the signal for "bring-brang." Gradually, as I become increasingly exposed to different irregular forms, the signals that are reinforced end up being generally correct.

The model proposed by Pinker and Prince is certainly compatible with the general trajectory of how children learn the English past tense. It is also supported by the general considerations we looked at earlier. But should we accept it (or some other rule-based model like it)?

Exercise 9.2 Explain how this two-component model of past tense understanding is compatible with the stages identified earlier in young children's learning of the past tense in English.

This is where artificial neural networks come back into the picture, because researchers in neural network design have devoted considerable attention to designing networks that reproduce the characteristic pattern of errors in past tense acquisition without having programmed into them any explicit rules about how to form the past tense of verbs, whether regular or irregular.

Neural network models of tense learning

The pioneering network in this area was designed by David Rumelhart and Jay McClelland and appeared in their 1986 collection of papers on parallel distributed processing. It was a relatively simple network, without any hidden units (and hence not requiring backpropagation), but nonetheless succeeded in reproducing significant aspects of the learning profile of young children. The network is illustrated in Figure 9.2.

There are really three different networks here. The first network takes as input a phonological representation of the root form of a verb. That is, it takes as input a sequence of phonemes. Phonemes are what linguists take to be the most basic meaningful constituents of words. An example is the phoneme /n/, which is the final sound in the words "tin" and "sin." The first network translates this sequence of phonemes into a representational format that will allow the network to detect relevant similarities between it and other verb roots - as well as between the root forms and the correct past tense forms.

This representational format exploits an ingenious device that Rumelhart and McClelland call *Wickelfeatures* (after the cognitive psychologist Wayne Wickelgren, whose ideas

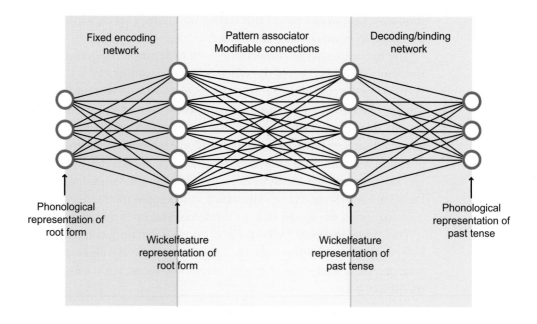

Figure 9.2 Rumelhart and McClelland's model of past tense acquisition. (Adapted from Rumelhart, McClelland, and PDP Research Group 1986)

they adapted). The details are very complex, but the basic idea is that a Wickelfeature representation codes phonetic information about individual phonemes within a word and their context. The aim is to represent verb stems in a way that can capture similarities in how they sound (and hence better represent the sort of stimuli to which young children are exposed).

The first network (the network converting phonological representations into Wickelfeature representations) is fixed. It does not change or learn in any way. The learning proper takes place in the second network. As the diagram shows, this network has no hidden units. It is a simple *pattern associator* mechanism. It associates input patterns with output patterns. The output patterns are also Wickelfeature representations of words, which are then decoded by the third network. This third network essentially reverses the work done by the first network. It translates the Wickelfeature representations back into sequences of phonemes.

The network was initially trained on 10 high-frequency verbs, to simulate the first stage in past tense acquisition, and then subsequently on 410 medium-frequency verbs (of which 80 percent were regular). To get a sense of the amount of training required for an artificial neural network, the initial training involved 10 cycles with each verb being presented once in each cycle. The subsequent training involved 190 cycles, with each cycle once again involving a single presentation of each of the 420 verbs (the 410 medium-frequency verbs together with the 10 original high-frequency verbs).

The learning algorithm used by the network is the perceptron convergence rule that we studied back in section 8.2. At the end of the training the network was almost errorless

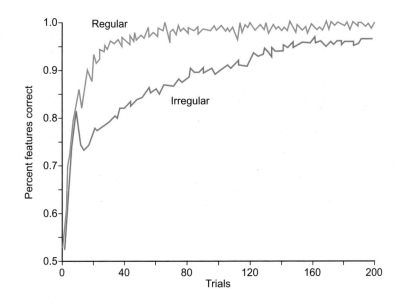

Figure 9.3 Performance data for Rumelhart and McClelland's model of past tense learning. The graph shows the success rates for both regular and irregular verbs. The line for irregular verbs clearly indicates the over-regularization phenomenon. (Adapted from Rumelhart, McClelland, and PDP Research Group 1986)

on the 420 training verbs and generalized quite successfully to a further set of 86 low-frequency verbs that it had not previously encountered (although, as one might expect, the network performed better on novel regular verbs than on novel irregular verbs).

One significant feature of the Rumelhart and McClelland network is that it reproduced the over-regularization phenomenon. This is shown in Figure 9.3, which maps the network's relative success on regular and irregular verbs. As the graph shows, the network starts out rapidly learning both the regular and the irregular past tense forms. There is a sharp fall in performance on irregular verbs after the eleventh training cycle, while the degree of success on regular verbs continues to increase. While the network's performance on irregular verbs is "catching up" with its performance on regular verbs, the characteristic errors involve treating irregular verbs as if they were regular. The network seems to be doing exactly what young children do when they shift from the correct "gave" to the incorrect "gived" as the past tense of "give."

Exercise 9.3 Explain in your own words why it is significant that the Rumelhart and McClelland network produces the over-regularization phenomenon.

Although the results produced by the Rumelhart and McClelland network are very striking, there are some methodological problems with the design of their study. In particular, as was pointed out in an early critique by Steven Pinker and Alan Prince, the over-regularization effect seems to be built into the network. This is because the training

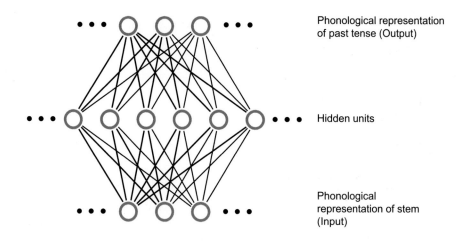

Figure 9.4 The network developed by Plunkett and Marchman to model children's learning of the past tense. The network has a layer of thirty hidden units and is trained using the backpropagation learning algorithm. (Adapted from Plunkett and Marchman 1993)

set is so dramatically expanded after the tenth cycle. And since the expanded training set is predominantly made up of regular verbs, it has seemed to many that something like the over-regularization phenomenon is inevitable.

Nonetheless, it is significant that a series of further studies have achieved similar results to Rumelhart and McClelland with less question-begging assumptions. Kim Plunkett and Virginia Marchman, for example, have produced a network with one layer of hidden units that generates a close match with the learning patterns of young children. The network is illustrated in Figure 9.4.

The Plunkett and Marchman network is in many ways a much more characteristic neural network. Whereas the Rumelhart-McClelland network is a simple pattern associator using the perceptron convergence learning rule, the Plunkett-Marchman model has hidden units. Their model has twenty input and twenty output units. Between them is a single hidden unit layer with thirty units. The network uses the backpropagation learning algorithm. One advantage of this is that it removes the need to translate the initial phonological representation into Wickelfeatures.

Unlike the McClelland and Rumelhart model, the first stage of the training schedule was on twenty verbs, half regular and half irregular. After that the vocabulary size was gradually increased. There was no sudden increase – and hence no "predisposition" towards regularization errors. The percentage of regular verbs in the total vocabulary was 90 percent, which matches more or less the relative frequency of regular verbs in English. And yet the network did indeed display the characteristic trajectory, including the regularization errors characteristic of stage 2 learning in children. Plunkett and Marchman correctly guessed that the simple presence in the training set of both regular and irregular verbs would be enough to generate regularization errors during the second stage of training.

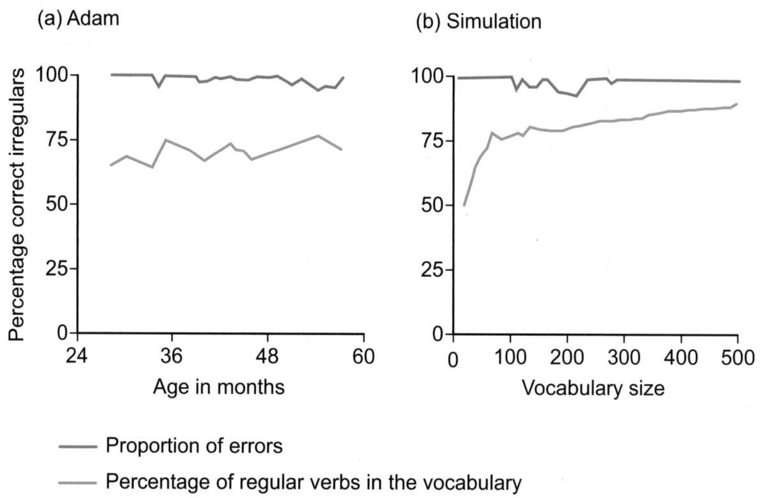

Figure 9.5 A comparison of the errors made by Adam, a child studied by the psychologist Gary Marcus, and the Plunkett–Marchman neural network model of tense learning. Unlike the Rumelhart–McClelland model, this model uses hidden units and learns by backpropagation. (Adapted from McLeod, Plunkett, and Rolls 1998)

It is interesting to compare the learning profile of the Plunkett and Marchman network with the detailed profile of the learning pattern of a child studied by the psychologist Gary Marcus. The graph in Figure 9.5 compares the percentage of correctly produced irregular past tenses in the Plunkett and Marchman simulation and in a child whose past tense acquisition was studied by Marcus and colleagues. As we see in this graph, the percentage of correctly produced irregular past tenses drops in both the network and the child as the vocabulary size increases. This seems to correspond to the second of the three stages identified earlier and to be correlated with the predominance of over-regularization errors.

Certainly, there are huge differences between children learning languages and artificial neural networks learning to correlate verb stems with the correct versions of the past tense. And even when taken on their own terms, neural network models of language acquisition are deeply controversial. And this is before we take into account concerns about the biological plausibility of neural networks. But even with these caveats, using artificial neural networks to model cognitive tasks offers a way of putting assumptions about how the mind works to the test - the assumption, for example, that the process of learning a language is a process of forming and evaluating hypotheses about linguistic rules.

The aim of neural network modeling is not to provide a model that faithfully reflects every aspect of neural functioning, but rather to explore alternatives to dominant conceptions of how the mind works. If, for example, we can devise artificial neural networks that reproduce certain aspects of the typical trajectory of language learning without having encoded into them explicit representations of linguistic rules, then that at the very least suggests that we cannot automatically assume that language learning is a matter of forming and testing hypotheses about linguistic rules. We should look at artificial neural networks not as attempts faithfully to reproduce the mechanics of cognition, but rather as tools for opening up new ways of thinking about how information processing might work. In this spirit we turn now to our second set of studies. These are focused on the development of physical reasoning abilities in infancy. As we see in the next section, this is an area that raises questions and problems very similar to those raised by language acquisition.

9.3 Object permanence and physical reasoning in infancy

What is it like to be a human infant? Until very recently most developmental psychologists were convinced that the infant experience of the world is fundamentally different from our own. The famous psychologist and philosopher William James (brother of the novelist Henry James) coined the memorable phrase "a blooming, buzzing, confusion" to describe what it is like to be a newborn infant (a *neonate*, in the jargon of developmental psychologists). According to James, neonates inhabit a universe radically unlike our own, composed solely of sensations, with no sense of differentiation between self and objects or between self and other, and in which the infant is capable only of reflex actions. It takes a long time for this primitive form of existence to become the familiar world of people and objects and for reflexes to be replaced by proper motor behavior.

The most famous theory within the traditional view was developed by the Swiss psychologist Jean Piaget. According to Piaget, infants are born with certain innate, reflex-like sensori-motor schemas that allow them to perform very basic acts such as sucking a nipple. Infants gradually bootstrap these basic schemas into more complex behaviors (what Piaget called circular reactions) and gradually come to learn that they inhabit a world containing other objects and other individuals. According to Piaget, infants are born highly egocentric and it is not until the end of what he called the sensori-motor stage (at around 2 years of age) that they come fully to appreciate the distinctions between self and other and between the body and other physical objects.

In recent years, however, researchers have developed new techniques for studying the cognitive abilities of neonates and older infants. These techniques have led to a radical revision of the traditional view. As a consequence, many developmental psychologists now think that the world of the human infant is much less of a "blooming, buzzing, confusion" than James thought. Researchers have developed techniques for exploring the expectations that infants have about how objects will behave. It is now widely held that even very young infants inhabit a highly structured and orderly perceptual universe. The most famous technique in this area is called the *dishabituation paradigm* (which was originally developed for studying human infants, but has now proved a useful tool for studying non-human animals).

Infant cognition and the dishabituation paradigm

The basic idea behind the dishabituation paradigm is that infants look longer at events that they find surprising. So, by measuring the amount of time that infants look at events of different types experimenters can work out which events the infants find surprising and then use this to work backwards to the expectations that the infants have about different types of events.

This basic idea is applied in practice in a number of ways. One technique is to habituate infants to a given type of event (i.e. presenting the infants with examples until they lose interest) and then to present them with events that differ from the original one in certain specified ways. Looking-time measures can then be used to identify which of the new events capture the infants' attention, as measured by the amount of time the infants spend looking at them. This allows experimenters to detect which features of the events the infants find surprising – and hence to work out how the infants expected the events to unfold. This way of identifying "violation of expectations" is called the dishabituation paradigm.

The developmental psychologist Renée Baillargeon devised a very influential set of experiments using the dishabituation paradigm. We can use her *drawbridge* experiments to illustrate how the paradigm works and what we can learn from it about the perceptual universe of the human infant. In one set of experiments, Baillargeon habituated her infants (who were all about 4.5 months old) to a screen (the drawbridge) rotating 180 degrees on a table. She was interested in how the infants would react when an object was hidden within the drawbridge's range of motion, since this would be a way of finding out whether the infant had any expectations about objects it could not directly perceive.

In order to investigate this, Baillargeon contrived a way of concealing the object so that, although it could not be seen by the infant, any adult or older child looking at the apparatus could easily work out that it would obstruct the movement of the screen. She then presented infants with two different scenarios. In the first scenario the screen rotated as it had done before until it got to the place where the obstructing box would be – and then it stopped, exactly as you or I would expect it to. In the second scenario, the screen kept on rotating for the full 180 degrees and hence apparently passed through the obstructing box. The experiments are illustrated in Figure 9.6.

Baillargeon found that the infants looked significantly longer in the second scenario. They were, it seemed, surprised that the screen looked as if it was passing straight through the obstructing box. In essence, her assumption was that infants look longer when their expectations are violated. The experiments show that infants do not expect the screen to keep on rotating through the place where the obstructing box would be. So, Baillargeon concluded that, although the infants could not see the obstructing box, in some sense they nonetheless "knew" that the box was there – and that the screen could not pass through it.

This result is very interesting because it has direct implications for a long-running debate in developmental psychology. Developmental psychologists have long been concerned with the question: At what stage, in early childhood or infancy, is it

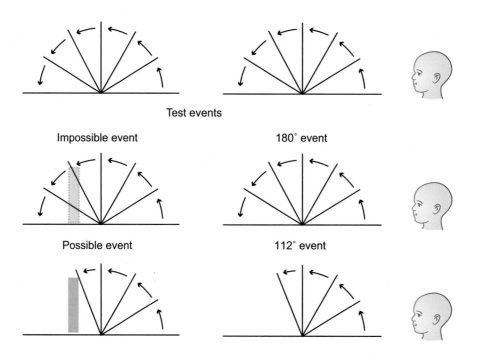

Test events

Impossible event   180° event

Possible event   112° event

Figure 9.6 Schematic representation of the habituation and test conditions in Baillargeon's drawbridge experiments. After habituation to a drawbridge moving normally through 180 degrees, infants were tested both on an impossible event (in which the drawbridge's movement would require it to pass through a hidden object) and a normal event (in which the drawbridge halts at the point where it would make contact with the hidden object). Baillargeon found that 4.5-month-old infants reliably looked longer in the impossible condition. (Adapted from Baillargeon 1987)

appropriate to ascribe a grasp that objects exist even when not being perceived? (Or, as developmental psychologists often put it, at what stage in development does *object permanence* emerge?) On the traditional view, derived ultimately from Piaget, object permanence does not appear until relatively late in development, at about 8 or 9 months. What Baillargeon's drawbridge experiments seem to show, however, is that object permanence emerges much earlier than Piaget (and others) had thought.

But there is more going on here than simply object permanence. After all, it is not just that the infants are in some sense aware that the obstructing box is there even though they cannot see it. Their surprise at the second scenario shows that they have expectations about how objects behave. And, in particular, about how objects should interact. In fact, Baillargeon's drawbridge experiments, together with other experiments using the same paradigm, have been taken to show that even very young infants have the beginnings of what is sometimes called *folk physics* (or *naïve physics*) – that is to say, an understanding of some of the basic principles governing how physical objects behave and how they interact.

Habituation

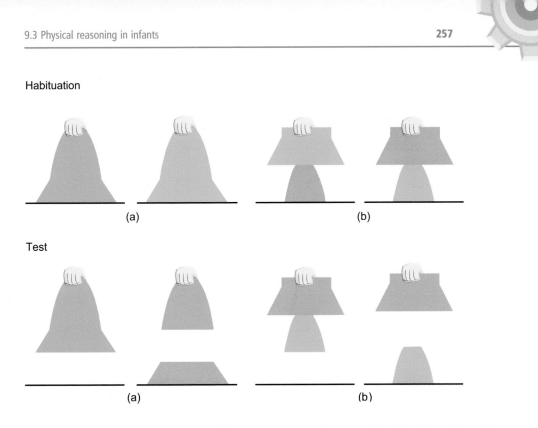

Test

Figure 9.7 Schematic representation of an experiment used to test infants' understanding of object boundaries and sensitivity to what Spelke calls the principle of cohesion (that surfaces lie on a single object if they are in contact). (Adapted from Spelke and Van de Walle 1993)

Elizabeth Spelke is another pioneer in using dishabituation experiments to study the perceptual universe of human infants. She has argued with considerable force that from a very young age infants are able to parse the visual array into spatially extended and bounded individuals that behave according to certain basic principles of physical reasoning. She thinks that four of these principles are particularly important.

The first of the four principles is the *principle of cohesion*, according to which surfaces belong to a single individual if and only if they are in contact. It is evidence for the principle of cohesion, for example, that infants do not appear to perceive the boundary between two objects that are stationary and adjacent, even when the objects differ in color, shape, and texture. Figure 9.7 illustrates how sensitivity to the principle of cohesion might be experimentally tested. Three-month-old infants are habituated to two objects, one more or less naturally shaped and homogeneously coloured, and the other a gerry-mandered object that looks rather like a lampshade. When the experimenter picks up the objects, they either come apart or rise up cleanly. Infants show more surprise when the object comes apart, even if (as in the case of the lampshade) the object does not have the Gestalt properties of homogeneous colour and figural simplicity. The conclusion drawn by Spelke and other researchers is that the infants perceive even the gerrymandered object as a single individual because its surfaces are in contact.

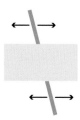

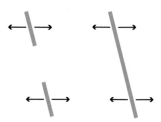

Test

Figure 9.8 Schematic representation of an experiment testing infants' understanding of the principle that only surfaces in contact can move together. (Adapted from Spelke and Van de Walle 1993)

The principle of cohesion clearly suggests that infants will perceive objects with an occluded center as two distinct individuals, since they cannot see any connection between the two parts. And this indeed is what they do – at least when dealing with objects that are stationary. Thus it seems that infants do not perceive an occluded figure as a single individual, *if the display is static.* After habituation to the occluded figure they showed no preference for either of the test displays.

On the other hand, however, infants do seem to perceive a center-occluded object as a single individual if the object is in motion (irrespective, by the way, of whether the motion is lateral, vertical, or in depth). According to Spelke this is because there is another principle at work, which she terms the *principle of contact.* According to the principle of contact, only surfaces that are in contact can move together. When the principle of cohesion and the principle of contact are taken together they suggest that, since the two parts of the occluded object move together, they must be in contact and hence in fact be parts of one individual. This is illustrated in Figure 9.8.

Exercise 9.4 Explain how an infant who understands the principles of cohesion and contact might respond to the two test situations depicted in Figure 9.8.

Spelke identifies two further constraints governing how infants parse the visual array. A distinctive and identifying feature of physical objects is that every object moves on a single trajectory through space and time, and it is impossible for these paths to intersect in a way that would allow more than one object to be in one place at a time. One might test whether infants are perceptually sensitive to these features

(a) No violation

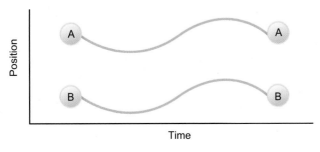

(b) Continuity violation

(c) Solidity violation

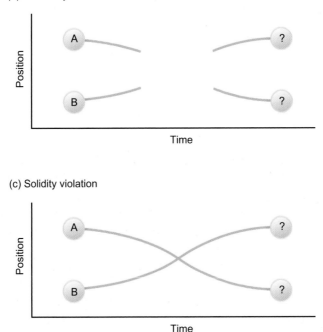

Figure 9.9 Schematic depiction of events that accord with, or violate, the continuity or solidity constraints. Solid lines indicate each object's path of motion, expressed as changes in its position over time. Each object traces (a) exactly one connected path over space and time, (b) no connected path over space and time, or (c) two connected paths over space and time. (Adapted from Spelke and Van de Walle 1993)

by investigating whether they are surprised by breaches of what Spelke calls the *solidity* and *continuity* constraints. The drawbridge experiment that we have just discussed is a good example of reasoning according to the solidity constraint, since it shows that infants are sensitive to the impossibility of there being more than one object in a single place at one time. Figure 9.9 is a schematic representation of an experiment to test whether infants parse their visual array in accordance with the continuity and solidity constraints.

These are just some of the experiments that have been taken to show that even very young infants have a surprisingly sophisticated understanding of the physical world. Spelke herself has some very definite views about what this understanding consists in. According to Spelke, even very young infants have a theoretical understanding of physical objects and how they behave. Infants are able to represent principles such as those that we have been discussing – the principles of continuity, solidity, and so on. They can use these principles to make predictions about how objects will behave. They show surprise when those predictions are not met – and lose interest (as measured by looking times) when they are met.

How should the dishabituation experiments be interpreted?

What the infants are doing, according to Spelke (and many others), is not fundamentally different in kind from what scientists do. The infants are making inferences about things that they cannot see on the basis of effects that they can see – just as scientists make inferences about, say, sub-atomic particles on the basis of trails in a cloud chamber. Infants are little scientists, and the perceptual discriminations that they make reflect their abilities to make inferences about the likely behavior of physical objects; inferences that in turn are grounded in a stored and quasi-theoretical body of knowledge about the physical world – what is sometimes called infant folk physics.

So, what sort of information processing underlies infant folk physics? As we have seen on many occasions in Part 3, the physical symbol system hypothesis gives us a natural way of thinking about how rules might be explicitly represented and applied. The idea here would be that the basic principles of infant folk physics (such as the principle of continuity) are symbolically represented. These symbolically represented principles allow the infants to compute the probable behavior and trajectory of the objects in the dishabituation experiments. They show surprise when objects do not behave according to the results of the computations.

This view is perfectly consistent with the idea that infant folk physics is importantly different from adult folk physics. Infant folk physics has some puzzling features. Developmental psychologists have found, for example, that infants tend to place more weight on spatiotemporal continuity than on featural continuity. For infants, movement information dominates information about features and properties. Their principal criterion for whether or not an object persists over time is that it should maintain a single trajectory, even if its perceptible properties completely change. This is why, for example, infants who otherwise perceive differences between the color and form of objects still tend not to show surprise when one object disappears behind a screen and another completely different object emerges at the other side of the screen. For adults, on the other hand, featural constancy is often more important. This is elegantly expressed by the developmental psychologists Alison Gopnik and Andrew Meltzoff:

As adults we individuate and reidentify objects by using both place and trajectory information and static-property information. We also use property information to predict and explain appearances and disappearances. If the same large, distinctive white rabbit appears in the box and later in the hat, I assume it's the same rabbit, even if I don't immediately see a path of movement for it. In fact, I infer an often quite complex invisible path for the object. If I see the green scarf turn into a bunch of flowers as it passes through the conjuror's hand while maintaining its trajectory, I assume it is a different object. On the other hand, if an object changes its trajectory, even in a very complex way, while maintaining its properties, I will assume it is still the same object. (Gopnik and Meltzoff 1997: 86)

So, there are some important differences between infant folk physics and adult folk physics. The important point, though, is that for Spelke (and indeed for Gopnik and Meltzoff) both should be understood as theories. Here is how Spelke described her findings in an influential early paper.

I suggest that the infant's mechanism for apprehending objects is a mechanism of thought: an initial *theory* of the physical world whose four principles jointly define an initial *object concept*. (Spelke 1988: 181)

It is no easy matter to say what a theory actually is, but as Spelke states, the simplest way of thinking about theories is in terms of laws or principles. Laws and principles can be linguistically expressed. This means that they can easily be represented by physical symbol structures. In this respect thinking about naïve physics as a theory is rather like thinking of grammatical knowledge in terms of rules. In both cases we have cognitive capacities (knowledge of a theory in the one case, and the ability to apply rules in the other) that lend themselves to being modeled in computational terms – as suggested by the physical symbol system hypothesis.

As we saw in the case of grammatical knowledge, however, there are alternatives to this type of computational approach. We can think about knowledge in non-symbolic ways, exploiting neural network technology. Some of the possibilities are sketched out in the next section.

9.4 Neural network models of children's physical reasoning

A number of neural network modelers have explored alternatives to the theoretical model of infant cognitive abilities outlined at the end of the previous section. They have tried to show how a neural network can simulate the behavior of human infants in experiments using the dishabituation paradigm without any principles or rules being explicitly coded into it.

One researcher who has done a considerable amount of work in this area is the psychologist Yuko Munakata, working with a number of collaborators, including the distinguished connectionist modeler Jay McClelland (who, together with David Rumelhart, edited the two-volume *Parallel Distributed Processing*, which gave such a huge impetus to connectionist approaches to cognitive science). Here is how Munakata and her co-authors describe the basic idea behind their approach, and how it differs from the theoretical model:

> Because infants seem to behave in accordance with principles at times, there might be some use to describing their behavior in these terms. The danger, we believe, comes in the tendency to accept these descriptions of behavior as mental entities that are explicitly accessed and used in the production of behavior. That is, one could say that infants' behavior in a looking-time task accords with a principle of object permanence, in the same way one could say that the motions of the planets accord with Kepler's laws. However, it is a further – and we argue unfounded – step to then conclude that infants actually access and reason with an explicit representation of the principle itself.

The connectionist modelers accept that the dishabituation experiments show that human infants are sensitive to (and react in accordance with) certain basic physical principles (such as the principles of solidity and continuity). But they reject the way that computational theorists interpret this basic fact. The computational approach and the theoretical model of infant cognition both assume that a cognitive system (whether a human infant, or a computational model) can only act in accordance with, say, the principle of continuity if that principle is explicitly represented in it in a symbolic form. But, according to Munakata and her collaborators, this assumption is wrong – and it can be shown to be wrong by constructing a neural network model that acts in accordance with the principle of continuity even though it does not have that principle symbolically encoded in it. They continue:

> We present an alternative approach that focuses on the adaptive mechanisms that may give rise to behavior and on the processes that may underlie change in these mechanisms. We show that one might characterize these mechanisms as behaving in accordance with particular principles (under certain conditions); however, such characterizations would serve more as a shorthand description of the mechanism's behavior, not as a claim that the mechanisms explicitly consult and reason with these principles. (Munakata *et al.* 1997: 687)

The alternative proposal that they develop is that infants' understanding of object permanence is essentially practical. The fact that infants successfully perform object permanence tasks does indeed show that they know, for example, that objects continue to exist even when they are not being directly perceived. But this knowledge is not explicitly stored in the form of theoretical principles. In fact, it is not explicitly stored at all. Rather, it is implicitly stored in graded patterns of neural connections that evolve as a function of experience.

According to the neural networks approach to object permanence, the expectations that infants have about how objects will behave reflect the persistence of patterns of neural activation – patterns that vary in strength as a function of the number of neurons firing, the strength and number of the connections between them, and the relations between their individual firing rates. The mechanisms that explain the type of perceptual sensitivity manifested in dishabituation paradigms are essentially associative mechanisms of pattern recognition of precisely the type well modeled by connectionist networks.

Here, in a nutshell, is how the process works. As infants observe the "reappearance" of occluded objects, this strengthens the connection between two groups of neurons – between the group of neurons that fire when the object first appears, on the one hand, and the group that fires when it reappears, on the other. As a result the representations of perceived objects (i.e. the patterns of neural activation that accompany the visual perception of an object) persist longer when the object is occluded. So, according to Munakata *et al.*, the infant's "knowledge" of object permanence should be understood in terms of the persistence of object representations, rather than in terms of any explicitly coded principles. This "implicit" understanding of object permanence is the foundation for the theoretical understanding that emerges at a much later stage in development.

One advantage of their approach is the explanation it gives of well-documented behavioral dissociations in infant development. There is good evidence that infants' abilities to act on occluded objects lag a long way behind their perceptual sensitivity to object permanence, as measured in preferential looking tasks. Although perceptual sensitivity to object permanence emerges at around 4 months, infants succeed in searching for hidden objects only at around 8 months. Munakata *et al.* argue (and their simulations illustrate) that it is possible for a visual object representation to be sufficiently strong to generate expectations about the reappearance of an occluded object, while still being too weak to drive searching behavior.

Modeling object permanence

One of the networks studied by Munakata *et al.* is designed to simulate a simple object permanence task involving a barrier moving in front of a ball and occluding the ball for a number of time steps. Figure 9.10 shows the inputs to the network as the barrier moves in front of the ball and then back to its original location. The input units are in two rows. The two rows jointly represent the network's "field of view." The bottom layer represents the network's view of the barrier, while the top layer represents the network's view of the ball. As we see in the figure, when the barrier moves in front of the ball there is no input in the ball layer. When the barrier moves to one side, revealing the previously occluded

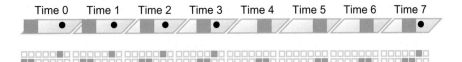

Figure 9.10 A series of inputs to the network as a barrier moves in front of a ball and then back to its original location. The top row shows a schematic drawing of an event in the network's visual field; the bottom row indicates the corresponding pattern of activation presented to the network's input units, with each square representing one unit. Learning in the network is driven by discrepancies between the predictions that the network makes at each time step and the input it receives at the next time step. The correct prediction at one time step corresponds to the input that arrives at the next time step. (Adapted from Munakata *et al.* 1997)

ball, the ball layer is correspondingly activated again. What the network has to do is to learn to represent the ball even when there is no activation in the input layer corresponding to the ball – it needs to find a way of representing the ball even when the ball cannot directly be seen.

In order to design a network that can do this Munakata and her collaborators used a type of network that we have not yet looked at. They used a particular type of *recurrent network*. Recurrent networks are rather different from the feedforward and competitive networks that we have been considering up to now. Like feedforward and competitive networks they have hidden units whose weights are modified by algorithmic learning rules. But what distinguishes them is that they have a feedback loop that transmits activation from the hidden units back to themselves. This transmission works before the learning rule is applied. This feedback loop allows the network to preserve a "memory" of the pattern of activation in the hidden units at the previous stage.

So, in the network that Munakata and collaborators used to model object permanence, the level of activation in the hidden units at any given temporal stage is determined by two factors. The first factor (as in any neural network) is the pattern of activation in the input units. The second factor (distinctive to this type of recurrent neural network, known as an Elman network after its inventor Jeff Elman) is the pattern of activation in the hidden units at the previous temporal stage. This second factor is crucial for allowing the network to learn object permanence.

Figure 9.11 is a schematic representation of their recurrent network. The network has two distinctive features. The first is the set of recurrent weights from the hidden layer back to itself. These function as just described – to give the network information about what happened at the previous temporal stage. The second is a set of connections, with corresponding weights, running from the hidden units to the input units. These weighted connections allow the network to send a prediction to the input units as to what the next set of inputs will be. The network's learning (which works via the standard backpropagation rule) is driven by the discrepancy between the actual input and the predicted input.

We can think about the network's "understanding" of object permanence in terms of its sensitivity to the ball's reappearance from behind the occluder. This sensitivity can in turn be measured in terms of the accuracy of the network's "prediction" when the ball does eventually reappear. (An accurate prediction is one where the predicted pattern exactly matches the input pattern.) As training progresses the network becomes increasingly proficient at predicting the reappearance of occluded objects over longer and longer periods of occlusion.

Informally, what makes this possible is the recurrent connection from the hidden layer back to itself. The activation associated with the "sight" of the ball at a given temporal stage is transmitted to the next stage, even when the ball is not in view. So, for example, at temporal stages 4, 5, and 6 in Figure 9.10, there is no activation in the input units representing the ball. But, once the network's training has progressed far enough, the weights will work in such a way that the memory from the earlier stages is strong enough that the network will correctly predict the reappearance of the ball at temporal stage 7.

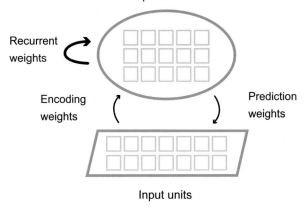

Figure 9.11 Recurrent network for learning to anticipate the future position of objects. The pattern of activation on the internal representation units is determined by the current input and by the previous state of the representation units by means of the encoding weights and the recurrent weights respectively. The network sends a prediction back to the input units to predict the next state of the input. The stimulus input determines the pattern of activation on the input units, but the difference between the pattern predicted and the stimulus input is the signal that drives learning. (Adapted from Munakata *et al.* 1997)

How exactly does this work? One way to find this out is to analyze the patterns of hidden unit activation to find out how the network represents the occluded ball. The strategy adopted by Munakata and colleagues was to identify which of the fifteen hidden units are sensitive to the ball. This can be done by identifying which hidden units showed the greatest difference in activation between stimuli with and without balls. Once it is known which hidden units are sensitive to the ball, it then becomes possible to analyze the activation of those hidden units during the period when the ball was occluded.

The researchers found that improved sensitivity to object permanence is directly correlated with the hidden units representing the ball showing similar patterns of activation when the ball is visible and when it is occluded. In effect, they claim, the network is learning to maintain a representation of an occluded object. The network's "understanding" of object permanence is to be analyzed in terms of its ability to maintain such representations. And this comes in degrees. As further simulations reported in the same paper show, a network can maintain representations sufficiently strong to drive perceptual "expectations" but too weak to drive motor behavior. Sensitivity to object permanence is, they suggest, a graded phenomenon – a function of strengthened connections allowing maintained activation patterns – rather than a theoretical achievement.

Exercise 9.5 Explain and assess the significance of this network model for thinking about the information processing underlying object permanence.

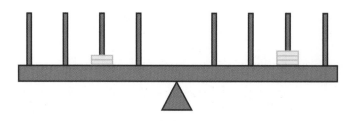

Figure 9.12 A balance beam. Weights can be added at different distances from the fulcrum. Children are asked whether the beam is in balance and, if not, which side will go down.

Modeling the balance beam problem

We turn now to a second example of how connectionist models can provide alternatives to theory-based accounts of infant cognitive development. This is the balance beam problem. It is particularly interesting because the task being modeled is very similar to a task that we looked at in detail in the context of the physical symbol system hypothesis.

Children are shown a balance beam as in Figure 9.12. The balance beam has a fulcrum and weights at varying distances from the fulcrum. The children are asked whether the beam is in balance and, if not, which side will go down. In different trials the weights are varied, but the children are not given any feedback on whether their answers are correct or not. The problem here is very similar to the problem that WHISPER was designed to solve (see section 7.3). In both cases what needs to be worked out is how different forces will interact. If they are in equilibrium then the balance beam and WHISPER's blocks will remain where they are. If not, then the infant and WHISPER have to work out where the operative forces will leave the beam/blocks.

Research by the developmental psychologist Bob Siegler has shown that children typically go through a series of stages in tackling the balance beam problem – rather like young children learning the past tense of English verbs. And, as in the past tense case, these stages can be summarized in terms of some relatively simple rules. There are four stages and corresponding rules. Siegler identifies these as follows:

Stage 1 The rule in the first stage is that the side with the greatest number of weights will go down, irrespective of how those weights are arranged. If there are equal numbers of weights on both sides, then the beam is judged to be in balance.

Stage 2 The rule in the second stage is that, when the weights on each side of the fulcrum are equal, the side on which the weights are furthest away will go down. If this doesn't hold then children either use the first rule or guess.

Stage 3 In the third stage children use the correct rule, in accordance with the general principle that downwards force is a function both of weight and of the distance from the fulcrum. But they only manage to do this when the two sides differ in respect *either* to weight *or* to distance, but not both.

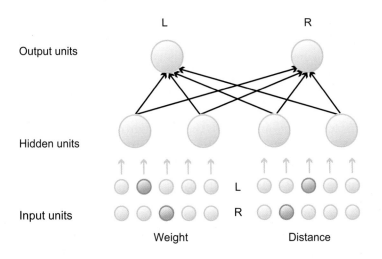

Figure 9.13 The architecture of the McClelland and Jenkins network for the balance beam problem. (Adapted from Elman *et al*. 1996)

Stage 4 It is usually not until adolescence that children acquire a general competence for balance beam problems – and even then not all of them do.

The situation here is very similar to the past tense case. And, as in that case, it seems initially plausible to model the child's learning process as a matter of learning a series of rules. These rules might be implemented in some sort of rule-based architecture, along the lines of WHISPER. This way of looking at the child's emerging naïve physics is fully in line with the physical symbol system hypothesis.

As we saw in section 9.2, however, there are other ways of thinking about this type of developmental progression. Even though children progress through a series of discrete stages, and their performance can be characterized in terms of a progression of rules, it does not follow that the cognitive systems actually carrying out the relevant information processing take the form of a rule-based architecture. As before, artificial neural networks offer an alternative way of looking at the phenomenon, illustrating how the appearance of rule-based learning can emerge from a system that does not exploit any explicit rules.

Jay McClelland and E. Jenkins designed an artificial neural network to model children's performance on the balance beam problem. The network is designed to reflect the different types of potential input in solving balance beam-type tasks. The network is illustrated in Figure 9.13. It has four different groups of input units, receiving input about weights and distances for each side of the fulcrum. It is important to realize that the information the network gets is actually quite impoverished. One group of input units will get information corresponding to, say, the weights to be found on one side of the beam. Another group of units will get information corresponding to the distances of those weights from the fulcrum. But these are separate pieces of information. The network needs to work out during training that the two groups of units are carrying information about the same side of the balance beam. The weights are initially set at random.

As we see in Figure 9.13, the weight units are connected to a pair of hidden units. Likewise for the distance units. There are no connections between the two pairs of hidden units, but each hidden unit projects to both the output units. The network predicts that the balance beam will come down on the left-hand side when the activation on the left output unit exceeds the activation on the right output unit.

The McClelland-Jenkins network learns by backpropagation. The discrepancy between the correct output and the actual output on given iterations of the task is propagated backwards through the network to adjust the weights of the connections to and from the hidden units.

As the training went on, the network went through a sequence of stages very similar to those that Siegler identified in children. The training initially focused on weights – that is, the initial training examples showed much more variation in weight than in distance. This was intended to reflect the fact that children are more used to using weight than distance in determining quantities like overall heaviness. As an artifact of the training schedule, therefore, the network's early discriminations all fell into Siegler's stage 1. As training progressed, the network learnt to use distance to solve problems with equal numbers of weights on each side – as per Siegler's stage 2. The final stages of the training saw the network move to Siegler's stage 3, correctly using both weight and distance provided that the two sides differed only on one dimension, but not on both. The McClelland-Jenkins network did not arrive at Siegler's stage 4. But a similar network designed by Jay McClelland did end up showing all four stages.

The moral to be drawn from this example is rather similar to the moral of the tense-learning networks we looked at in section 9.2. Like tense learning, progress on the balance beam problem can be characterized as a step-like progression. Each step seems to involve exploiting a different rule. The most natural way of modeling this kind of learning pattern would be via a model that had these rules explicitly wired into it – exactly the sort of model that would be suggested by the physical symbol system hypothesis. The qualitative progression between different stages would be explained by the transition from one rule to another.

Neural network models show us, however, that step-like progressions can emerge without the network learning explicit rules. The network learns, and its progress falls into discernible stages that can be described in terms of rules, but there are no rules to be found in the network. The learning is purely quantitative. It simply involves adjusting weights in response to feedback according to the backpropagation rule. There are only two rules explicitly programmed into the network – the activation rule governing the spread of activation forwards throughout the network, and the backpropagation rules governing the spread of error backwards through the network. There is nothing in the network corresponding to the rules in terms of which it might be described. Nor are there any sharp boundaries between the type of learning at different stages, even though its actual performance on the task has a clearly identifiable step-like structure.

9.5 Conclusion: The question of levels

This chapter has explored artificial neural network models of a range of cognitive abilities – from mastering the past tense of English verbs to understanding what objects are and how they behave. These models have revealed some of the great strengths of artificial neural networks – in particular, their ability to model the complicated trajectories by which cognitive abilities are learnt. We have seen how representations in neural networks are distributed across different hidden units, and how hard it can be to find any sort of straightforward mapping between what is going on inside the network and the task that the network is performing. In this final section we will step back from the details of individual neural network models to look briefly at a very important concern that some cognitive scientists have raised about the whole enterprise of neural network modeling.

In order to appreciate the issues here we need to think back to a distinction between different levels of explanation that we first encountered in section 2.3. This is Marr's tri-level hypothesis. Recall that Marr distinguished between three different levels at which cognitive scientists can think about a given cognitive system. Cognitive scientists are trying to do different things at each level. A quick reminder:

- *The computational level* provides a general characterization of the information-processing task that the system is trying to perform.
- *The algorithmic level* identifies a particular algorithm or set of algorithms that can carry out the task identified at the computational level.
- *The implementational level* explains how the algorithm is actually realized in the system.

We can illustrate the three-way distinction with the example of trying to build a Turing machine that can perform multiplication. We can think about this machine at three different levels. A computational-level analysis machine will identify the general information-processing task that the machine is performing. This is the task of computing an arithmetical function that maps pairs of numbers to single numbers (2 and 3 to 6, for example). An analysis at the algorithmic level will come up with a specific machine table that will compute this function. When we turn to the implementational level what we are interested in is how to build a physical system that will run that algorithm.

The difference between the algorithmic and implementational levels is very important. The implementational level is the level of engineering and machinery. In contrast, the algorithmic level is the level of discrete information-processing steps, each governed by specific rules. Our Turing machine might take the form of a digital computer. In this case the algorithmic-level analysis would correspond to the program that the computer is running, while the implementational analysis would explain how that program is realized in the hardware of the computer.

Physical symbol theorists have tended to be very explicit about the level at which their accounts are pitched. As one would expect, given the emphasis on algorithms and rules for manipulating symbol structures, the physical symbol system hypothesis is aimed squarely as an algorithmic-level account. It is not an engineering-level account of information-processing machinery. Rather, it needs to be supplemented by such an account.

This immediately raises the question of how we should think about artificial neural networks. If we have an artificial neural network model of, say, past tense learning, should we think about it as an algorithmic-level account? Or should we think about it as an account offered at the implementational level? Do artificial neural networks tell us about the abstract nature of the information-processing algorithms that can solve particular types of cognitive task? Or do they simply give us insight into the machinery that might run those information-processing algorithms?

The issue here is absolutely fundamental to how one evaluates the whole project of artificial neural networks. Because artificial neural networks will only count as alternatives to physical symbol systems if they turn out to be algorithmic-level accounts. The whole contrast that we have been exploring in the last two chapters between neural network models of information processing and physical symbol system models depends upon understanding neural networks at the algorithmic level.

A number of physical symbol theorists (most prominently Jerry Fodor and Zenon Pylyshyn) have used this point to make a powerful objection to the whole enterprise of artificial neural network modeling. In effect, their argument is this. We can think about artificial neural networks either at the implementational or at the algorithmic level. If we think about them at the implementational level then they are not really an alternative to the physical symbol system hypothesis at all. They are simply offering models of how physical symbol systems can be implemented.

But, Fodor and Pylyshyn continue, the prospects for taking artificial neural networks as algorithmic-level accounts are not very promising. Their reasons for saying this rest upon the sort of considerations that we looked at in Chapter 6 – particularly in the argument for the language of thought theory that we explored in section 6.3. For language of thought theorists, such as Fodor and Pylyshyn, cognition should be understood in terms of the rule-governed transformation of abstract symbol structures – a manipulation that is sensitive only to the formal, syntactic features of those symbol structures. That these symbol structures have the appropriate formal features is a function of the fact that they are composed of separable and recombinable components.

In contrast, there do not seem to be any such separable and recombinable components in artificial neural networks. On the face of it, the evolution of an artificial neural network takes a fundamentally different form. Since each distinct unit has a range of possible activation levels, there are as many different possible dimensions of variation for the network as a whole as there are units. Let us say that there are n such units. This means that we can think of the state of the network at any given moment as being a position in an n-dimensional space – standardly called the *activation space* of the system.

This activation space contains all possible patterns of activation in the network. Since both inputs and outputs are themselves points in activation space, computation in an artificial neural network can be seen as a movement from one position in the network's activation space to another. From a mathematical point of view any such trajectory can be viewed as a vector-to-vector transformation (where the relevant vectors are those giving the coordinates of the input and output locations in activation space).

Once we start to think of the states of artificial neural networks in terms of positions in multidimensional activation space and the vectors that give the coordinates of those positions, it becomes very plausible that the notion of structure cannot really be applied. A point on a line does not have any structure. Nor does a point on the plane (i.e. in two-dimensional space). By extension one would not expect a point in n-dimensional space where $n > 2$ to have any structure.

This is where we can see the force of Fodor and Pylyshyn's argument. We can put it in a slightly different way – in the form of a dilemma. Either neural networks contain representations with separable and recombinable components, or they do not. If they do contain such representations, then they are not really alternatives to the physical symbol system hypothesis. In fact, they will just turn out to be ingenious ways of implementing physical symbol systems. But if, on the other hand, they do not contain such representations, then (according to Fodor and Pylyshyn) they have absolutely no plausibility as algorithmic-level models of information processing. Here is the argument, represented schematically.

1   Either artificial neural networks contain representations with separable and recombinable components, or they do not.
2   If they do contain such representations, then they are simply implementations of physical symbol systems.
3   If they do not contain such representations, then they cannot plausibly be described as algorithmic information processors.
4   Either way, therefore, artificial neural networks are not serious competitors to the physical symbol system hypothesis.

This argument is certainly elegant. You may well feel, though, that it is begging the question. After all, the whole point of the neural network models we have been looking at in this chapter has been to try to show that there can be information processing that does *not* require the type of rule-governed symbol manipulation at the heart of the physical symbol system hypothesis. In a sense, the models themselves are the best advertisement for artificial neural networks as genuine alternative models of information processing – rather than simply implementations of physical symbol systems.

In any case, there is no reason why cognitive scientists cannot be broad-minded about the nature of information processing. There is no law that says that there is only one type of information processing. Perhaps the physical symbol system approach and the neural networks approach can co-exist. It may turn out that they are each suitable for different information-processing tasks. When we explored the language of thought hypothesis, for example, we placed considerable emphasis on the role of propositional attitudes such as belief and desire in causing behavior. The interplay of syntax and semantics in the language of thought was intended to capture the idea that beliefs and desires could bring about behavior in virtue of how they represent the world. But the types of task we have been looking at in this chapter seem on the face of things to be very different. Language learning and physical reasoning are in many ways much closer to perception and pattern recognition than to abstract symbol manipulation. It may turn out that different types of cognitive task require fundamentally different types of information processing.

In order to carry this general idea forward we need to think more about the overall organization of the mind. It may well be that some cognitive systems process information via symbol manipulation, while others work more like artificial neural networks. On this view the mind would have what is sometimes called a hybrid architecture. We will return to this idea at the end of the next chapter, in section 10.4.

Summary

This chapter has shown how the neural networks approach to information processing can be applied to model a range of cognitive phenomena. As we saw in Chapter 8, one of the great strengths of neural network models is that they are capable of learning. The models in this chapter are all models of how cognitive abilities are acquired in the normal course of human development. We began with the problem of how children learn the past tense of English verbs and saw how neural network models of tense learning offer an alternative to the idea that grammar is learnt by internalizing explicitly represented grammatical rules. We then moved on to how infants learn to represent objects and how they behave. After reviewing some relevant experiments, we looked at neural network models of object permanence and physical reasoning (as manifested in the balance beam problem). These models present an alternative to theory-based models of infants' understanding of the physical world. The chapter ended by considering a famous dilemma that Fodor and Pylyshyn have posed for neural network models.

Checklist

Language and rules

(1) Language is a paradigmatically rule-governed activity (not just grammatical rules, but also rules giving the meanings of individual words and governing the deep structure of sentences).

(2) The default hypothesis in thinking about language learning is that it is a matter of learning the rules that govern the meanings of words and how they combine into meaningful units.

(3) Fodor has built on the default hypothesis to argue that learning a language requires learning *truth rules*, which must be stated in the language of thought.

(4) One way to challenge such arguments is to construct models that simulate the trajectory of human language learning without explicitly representing any rules.

Modeling the acquisition of the English past tense

(1)   Children learning the English past tense go through three easily identifiable stages:
Stage 1 They employ a small number of verbs with (mainly irregular) past tenses.
Stage 2 They employ many more verbs, tending to construct the past tense through the standard
      stem + -ed construction (including verbs they had formerly got right).
Stage 3 They learn more verbs and correct their over-regularization errors.

(2)   This pattern of past tense acquisition can be accommodated by a symbolic model.
(3)   But connectionist models of past tense acquisition have been developed that display a similar
      trajectory without having any rules explicitly coded in them.

Modeling the emergence of object permanence in infancy

(1)   According to the traditional view, the perceptual universe of the infant is a "blooming, buzzing,
      confusion" with infants only coming to understand object permanence (i.e. that objects continue
      to exist when they are not directly perceived) at the age of 8 months or so.

(2)   Recent studies using the dishabituation paradigm have led many developmental psychologists to
      revise this view and to claim that even very young infants inhabit a highly structured and orderly
      perceptual universe.

(3)   Researchers such as Elizabeth Spelke have argued that young infants are able to parse the visual
      array into objects that behave according to certain basic physical principles.

(4)   One way of modeling the information processing that this involves is symbolically, on the
      assumption that infant perceptual expectations result from computations that exploit explicitly
      represented physical principles.

(5)   Connectionist models of object permanence have lent support, however, to the idea that
      understanding object permanence is a matter of having representations of objects that persist
      when the object is occluded, rather than explicitly representing physical principles.

The Fodor–Pylyshyn dilemma

(1)   Either artificial neural networks contain representations with separable and recombinable
      components, or they do not.
(2)   If they do contain such representations, then they are simply implementations of physical symbol
      systems.
(3)   If they do not contain such representations, then they cannot plausibly be described as algorithmic
      information processors.
(4)   Either way, Fodor and Pylyshyn argue, artificial neural networks are not serious competitors to the
      physical symbol system hypothesis.
(5)   *But* – this seems to be begging the question, since the central claim of the neural networks is that
      information processing need not require the type of rule-governed symbol manipulation at the
      heart of the physical symbol system hypothesis.

Further reading

The second volume of *Parallel Distributed Processing* (McClelland, Rumelhart, and the PDP Research Group 1986) contains a number of papers applying the theoretical framework of connectionism to different cognitive abilities. Some of these applications are explored further in McLeod, Plunkett, and Rolls 1998 and Plunkett and Elman 1997. For more general discussion of modeling within a connectionist framework see Dawson 2004. Paul Churchland has been a tireless proponent of the power of connectionist networks. See, for example, the papers in Churchland 2007 for a wide range of applications. See also McClelland et al. 2010.

Ch. 18 of the original PDP collection (Rumelhart and McClelland 1986) was the first salvo in what has become a lengthy debate about how to model past tense learning. Pinker and Prince 1988a made some telling criticisms of Rumelhart and McClelland's model (Pinker and Prince 1988b, reprinted in Cummins and Cummins 2000, is more condensed). A number of researchers took up Pinker and Prince's challenge – see, for example, Plunkett and Marchman 1993. The work by Marcus described in the text is presented in Marcus *et al*. 1992. For a more recent exchange see Pinker and Ullman 2002 and the reply in McClelland and Patterson 2002. Connectionist models have been applied to many different aspects of language. Plaut, Banich, and Mack 2003 describes applications to phonology, morphology, and syntax. Christiansen and Chater 2001 is an interdisciplinary collection of papers in the emerging field of connectionist psycholinguistics. Westermann and Ruh 2012 provides a review of different approaches to past tense learning, including connectionist approaches. Perhaps the most famous formal result in the theory of language learning is Gold's theorem, which places constraints upon the class of languages that can be learnt with purely positive feedback. Gold's theorem is clearly presented in Johnson 2004. Doug Rohde and David Plaut have used neural network models to argue that Gold's theorem cannot straightforwardly be applied in cognitive science (Rohde and Plaut 1999).

The drawbridge experiments described in section 9.3 were first present in Baillargeon 1986 and 1987. They have been extensively discussed and developed since then. For a recent model see Wang and Baillargeon 2008. Spelke's experiments using the dishabituation paradigm are reviewed in many places – e.g. Spelke *et al*. 1995. A general discussion of habituation methodology can be found in Oakes 2010. Spelke and Kinzler 2007 reviews evidence for infant "core knowledge" in understanding objects, actions, number, and space. Susan Carey and Renée Baillargeon have extended Spelke's "core knowledge" in a number of ways. Summaries can be found in Baillargeon and Carey 2012, Baillargeon, Li, Gertner, and Wu 2010, Carey 2009, and Carey and Spelke 1996. Woodward and Needham 2009 is a collection of review articles on the state of the art in studying infant cognition. Hespos and van Marle 2012 provide a summary pertaining specifically to infants' knowledge of objects. The "child as little scientist" theory is engagingly presented in Gopnik and Meltzoff 1997. One of the first papers exploring connectionist approaches to object permanence was Mareschal, Plunkett, and Harris 1995. See further Mareschal and Johnson 2002. The papers discussed in the text are Munakata *et al*. 1997, Munakata 2001, and Munakata and McClelland 2003. For a book-length treatment of the power of connectionist approaches in thinking about cognitive development see Elman *et al*. 1996 – which also contains a detailed account of the balance beam network discussed in section 9.4 (originally presented in McClelland and Jenkins 1991). Plunkett and Elman 1997 is an accompanying workbook with software. Marcus 2003 attempts to integrate connectionist and symbolic approaches. Elman 2005 is another good review. A critical view can be found in Quinlan, van der Maas, Jansen, Booij, and Rendell 2007.

The Fodor and Pylyshyn argument discussed in section 9.5 can be found in Fodor and Pylyshyn 1988. It has been widely discussed. A number of important papers are collected in Macdonald and Macdonald 1995. See ch. 9 of Bermúdez 2005 for a general discussion and further references.

PART IV

THE ORGANIZATION OF THE MIND

INTRODUCTION

This book's approach to cognitive science has focused on what I have called mental architectures, which are ways of carrying forward the basic principle that cognition is information processing. A mental architecture incorporates both a model of the overall organization of the mind and an account of how information is actually processed in the different components of the architecture. The emphasis in Part III was on different ways of looking at information processing. We examined both the computer-inspired physical symbol hypothesis and the neurally inspired artificial neural networks approach. In Part IV we turn our attention to the overall organization of the mind.

The concept of modularity is one of the basic concepts in theoretical cognitive science, originally proposed by the philosopher Jerry Fodor. Fodor's principle is that many information-processing tasks are carried out by specialized sub-systems (modules) that work quickly and automatically, drawing only upon a proprietary database of information. Those parts of cognition not carried out by specialized modules he describes as central processing. As we see in Chapter 10, Fodor is very pessimistic about cognitive science's prospects for understanding central processing. The massive modularity hypothesis (also considered in Chapter 10) offers one way of dealing with Fodor's concerns. According to the massive modularity hypothesis, there is no such thing as central processing. All cognition is modular and carried out by specialized sub-systems.

There are close connections between what I am calling mental architectures and what are known as cognitive architectures in computer science. At the end of Chapter 10 we look at one of these cognitive architectures. This is ACT-R/PM, developed by John R. Anderson and colleagues at Carnegie Mellon University. ACT-R/PM is a hybrid architecture that incorporates a modular approach and combines both symbolic and subsymbolic information processing.

Many cognitive neuroscientists think that the brain is, broadly speaking, organized along modular lines. They hold that the brain is organized at a neuroanatomical level into distinct neural populations that are segregated from each other. This is a basic fact about brain anatomy. They also typically hold that, at the functional level, distinct types of cognitive functioning involve the coordinated activity of networks of different brain areas. Cognitive neuroscientists can use a range of different techniques and technologies to study the relation between neuroanatomical structure and cognitive function. These include functional neuroimaging, human encephalography, and animal electrophysiology. Chapter 11 explains some of the key elements of the cognitive neuroscientist's toolkit and explores how they can be used to study the overall organization of the mind.

Chapter 12 works through a case study to illuminate how some of the general ideas about modularity that emerged in Chapter 10 have been put into practice. We look at research by psychologists and neuroscientists into what is known as mindreading – the complex of skills and abilities that allow us to make sense of other people and to coordinate our behavior with theirs. We explore ways of understanding mindreading as a modular activity, looking at different proposals for understanding what some psychologists have called the theory of mind system. We look at a non-modular approach to mindreading (associated with what is known as the simulation theory) and explore how some of the tools and techniques discussed in Chapter 11 bear upon these different ways of thinking about mindreading.

CHAPTER TEN

How are cognitive systems organized?

Overview

Cognitive science is the study of mental architecture, based on the fundamental assumption that cognition is information processing. In this book we are thinking of mental architectures in terms of three basic questions. Here they are again.

1   In what format does a particular cognitive system carry information?
2   How does that cognitive system transform information?
3   How is the mind organized so that it can function as an information processor?

In Part III we looked in detail at the two most important models of information processing – the physical symbol system hypothesis and the model associated with neurally inspired computing. We turn now to different ways of thinking about the third question.

Our topic in this chapter is the overall organization of the mind. We start thinking about this in section 10.1 by taking a detour through what are known as *agent architectures* in AI. Agent architectures are blueprints for the design of artificial agents. Artificial agents can be anything from robots to internet bots. Looking at different architectures allows us to see what is distinctive about cognitive systems (as opposed, for example, to reflex systems, or reflex agents). Reflex systems are governed by simple production rules that uniquely determine how the system will behave in a given situation. In contrast, cognitive systems deploy information processing between the input (sensory) systems and the output (effector) systems.

Intelligent agents in AI are standardly built up from sub-systems that perform specific information-processing tasks. This illustrates a very standard way of thinking about the mind in cognitive science. Cognitive scientists tend to think of the mind (at least in part) as an organized collection of specialized sub-systems carrying out specific information-processing tasks. The earliest sustained development of this idea from a theoretical point of view came in a book entitled *The Modularity of Mind*, written by the philosopher Jerry Fodor. We look at Fodor's modularity thesis in section 10.2. Fodor divides information processing in the mind into two categories. The mind contains both specialized information-processing modules that engage only limited types of information, and a non-specialized central processing system.

In section 10.2 we see how Fodor's modularity thesis leads him to what he provocatively calls "Fodor's First Law of the Non-Existence of Cognitive Science." Fodor claims that cognitive science is best suited to understanding modular processes. It can tell us very little about central processing. There are many ways of responding to Fodor's pessimism about central processing. One very radical way is to deny that there is any such thing as non-modular central processing! This is the path taken by advocates of the massive modularity hypothesis, which we examine in section 10.3.

Finally, in section 10.4 we look at the relation between mental architectures and what are known as cognitive architectures in AI. We look at an example of a hybrid architecture combining the two different approaches to information processing that we looked at in Part III. This is the ACT-R/PM architecture, developed by John R. Anderson and colleagues at Carnegie Mellon University.

10.1   Architectures for intelligent agents

One of the aims of AI researchers is to build intelligent agents. In thinking about how to achieve this computer scientists have come up with an interesting range of different *agent architectures*. An agent architecture is a blueprint that shows the different components that make up an agent and how those components are organized. Looking at different agent architectures is a very useful way to start thinking about how the human mind might be organized.

In this section we will look at three different types of agent architecture:

- A simple reflex agent
- A goal-based agent
- A learning agent

This will set the scene for thinking about the organization of the mind in the rest of the chapter. It does this by showing us what is distinctive about cognitive agents, as opposed to simpler, non-cognitive agents. The agent architectures we will be looking at range from the plainly non-cognitive to the plainly cognitive. As we go through them we get a better picture of the basic functions that any cognitive system has to perform.

First, we need to know what an agent is. The quick definition is that an agent is a system that perceives its environment through *sensory systems* of some type and acts upon that environment through *effector systems*. There are many different types of AI agents. The first things that probably come to mind when thinking about intelligent agents are robotic agents – the robot SHAKEY that we looked at in Chapter 7, for example. Robots are built to operate in real, physical environments. Their sensory systems are made up of cameras and distance sensors, while their effector systems involve motors and wheels. But many agents are designed to function in virtual environments. Shopping bots are good examples. Some shopping bots are designed to travel around the internet comparing prices for a single item, while others trawl through sites such as Amazon finding items that you might be likely to buy (perhaps because they have been bought by customers who bought some items that you bought).

The basic challenge for a computer scientist programming an agent (whether a software agent or a robotic agent) is to make sure that what the agent does is a function of what the agent perceives. There need to be links between the agent's sensory systems and its effector systems. What distinguishes different types of agent is the complexity of those links between sensory systems and effector systems.

Three agent architectures

The simplest type of agent explored within agent-based computing is the *simple reflex agent*. In simple reflex agents there are direct links between sensory and effector systems – the outputs of the sensory systems directly determine the inputs to the effector systems. These direct links are achieved by what are known as *condition-action rules* or *production rules*. Production rules take the form IF *condition C holds* THEN *perform action A*. It is the job of the sensory systems to determine whether or not condition C holds. Once the sensory systems have determined whether condition C holds, then the behavior of the simple reflex agent is fixed. Figure 10.1 shows a schematic representation of the architecture of a simple reflex agent.

Simple reflex agents are not, by any stretch of the imagination, cognitive systems. This is widely accepted by cognitive scientists. It is not too hard to see why simple reflex agents fail to qualify, given our discussion earlier in the book. The central principle of cognitive science, as we have been exploring it, is that cognition is information processing. This works both ways. On the one hand, the principle tells us that any cognitive activity is carried out by some information-processing mechanism – and so tells us that whenever we are trying to understand some cognitive system we need to look for an information-processing explanation. But, in the other direction, the principle also tells us that no system that is not processing information can count as a cognitive system. This is why simple reflex systems are not

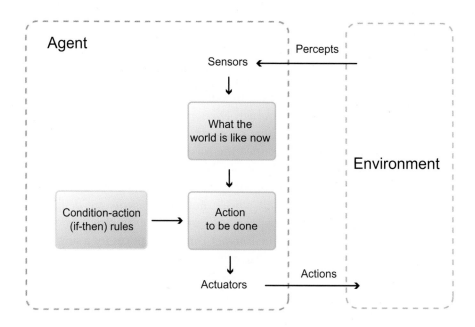

Figure 10.1 The architecture of a simple reflex agent. Production rules are all that intervenes between sensory input and motor output. (Adapted from Russell and Norvig 2009)

cognitive systems. They are not processing information. They are simply acting upon it. (Of course, as we will see later, this is not to say that there is no information processing going on in generating the sensory inputs and motor outputs. What I am emphasizing here is that there is no information processing *between* sensory input and motor output.)

Cognition and information processing come into the picture when there are no direct links between (perceptual) input and (motor) output. Cognitive systems represent the environment. They do not simply react to it. In fact, cognitive systems can react differently to the same environmental stimulus. This is because their actions are determined not just by environmental stimuli, but also by their goals and by their stored representations of the environment. Human agents, for example, sometimes act in a purely reflex manner. But more often we act as a function of our beliefs and desires – not to mention our hopes, fears, dislikes, and so on.

A primitive type of cognitive system is captured in the schematic agent architecture depicted in Figure 10.2. This is a *goal-based agent*. As the diagram shows, goal-based agents do not simply act upon environmental stimuli. There are no simple production rules that will uniquely determine how the agent will behave in a given situation. Instead, goal-based agents need to work out the consequences of different possible actions and then evaluate those consequences in the light of their goals. This is done by the specialized cognitive systems labeled in Figure 10.2.

There is still something missing from goal-based agents, however. As so far presented they have no capacity to learn from experience. Yet this, surely, is one of the most

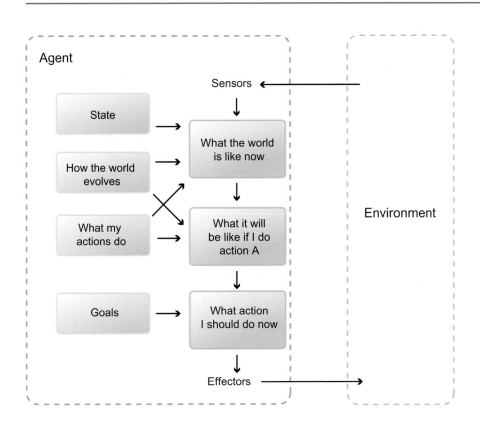

Figure 10.2 The architecture of a goal-based agent. There are information-processing systems intervening between input and output. (Adapted from Russell and Norvig 2009)

fundamental aspects of human mental architecture; and, one might reasonably think, a necessary condition for any agent to count as an intelligent agent. A sample architecture for a *learning agent* is presented in Figure 10.3.

The learning agent has certain standards that it wants its actions to meet. These are one of the inputs to the Critic sub-system, which also receives inputs from the sensory systems. The Critic's job is to detect mismatches between sensory feedback and the performance standard. These mismatches feed into the Learning sub-system which determines learning goals and makes it possible for the system to experiment with different ways of achieving its goals.

As the example of the learning agent shows, computer scientists designing intelligent agents typically build those agents up from sub-systems that each perform specific information-processing tasks. This way of thinking about cognitive systems (as organized complexes of sub-systems) has proved very influential in cognitive science. It raises a number of very important issues. So, for example, the schemas for both the goal-based agent and the learning agent seem to have built into them a sharp distinction between the sub-systems that place the agent in direct contact with the environment (the sensory systems and the action systems) and those sub-systems that operate,

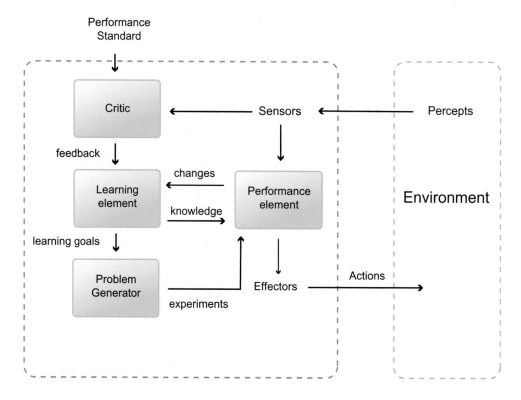

Figure 10.3 The architecture of a learning agent. Mismatches between sensory feedback and the performance standards are detected by the Critic sub-system. The Learning sub-system determines learning goals and allows the system to experiment with different ways of achieving its goals. (Adapted from Russell and Norvig 2003)

as it were, inside the agent (the Critic sub-system, for example). One might ask the following questions:

- How are we to identify and distinguish cognitive sub-systems?
- Are there any important differences between the sub-systems responsible for sensory processing and motor behavior, on the one hand, and those that operate between those input and output sub-systems?
- Do all the sub-systems in a cognitive system process information in the same way? Do they all involve the same type of representations?
- How "autonomous" are the different sub-systems? How "insulated" are they from each other?

These questions are fundamental to our understanding of mental architecture. In order to explore them further and in a broader context we need to turn away from agent-based AI to one of the most influential ideas in contemporary cognitive science. This is the modular analysis of cognitive sub-systems proposed by the philosopher and cognitive scientist Jerry Fodor in his well-known book *The Modularity of Mind*, published in 1983. We will explore Fodor's arguments in the next section.

10.2 Fodor on the modularity of mind

Computer scientists designing intelligent agents build them up from sub-systems performing relatively specific and determinate tasks. How helpful is this in thinking about the overall organization of the human mind? It all depends on how literally we take this idea of cognitive sub-systems and how we apply it to human agents.

Certainly there are ways of thinking about the organization of the mind that do not think of it in terms of cognitive sub-systems at all. At various times the history of psychology has been dominated by the idea that all cognition is carried out by a single mechanism. During the eighteenth century, for example (before psychology had become established as an intellectual discipline in its own right), the philosophers known as the British empiricists proposed an associationist picture of the mind, according to which all thinking is grounded in the strength of associations between ideas. The stimulus-response psychology at the heart of psychological behaviorism is a recognizable descendant of this view and so too, some have argued, is the increasing popularity of appeals to artificial neural networks. In none of these ways of thinking about the machinery of cognition is there any room for seeing the mind as an organized collection of sub-systems.

For a counterbalance we can turn to one of the most influential books in cognitive science – Jerry Fodor's *The Modularity of Mind*, published in 1983. We have already encountered Fodor in Chapter 6, as the principal architect of the language of thought hypothesis (and we briefly encountered the modularity thesis in section 5.2). In *The Modularity of Mind* he delivers a powerful defense of the idea that the mind contains autonomous cognitive sub-systems.

In a characteristically provocative maneuver, Fodor presents his main thesis in *The Modularity of Mind* as a defense of the type of faculty psychology proposed by the phrenologist Franz Joseph Gall. Gall was one of the first neuroanatomists to try to pin specific mental functions down to particular locations in the brain (as shown in the phrenological map of the skull depicted in Figure 10.4b).

Although Fodor has no plans to rehabilitate Gall's completely discredited idea that character traits and propensities to criminality can be read off the shape of the skull, he argues that Gall was basically correct to think of the mind as made up of semi-autonomous cognitive faculties. Gall was wrong to think of these cognitive faculties as individuated in terms of their location in the brain, but (according to Fodor) he was quite right to argue that they are specialized for performing particular cognitive tasks.

Gall's faculty psychology is an alternative, Fodor argues, not just to the monolithic conception of cognitive architecture that we find in stimulus–response behaviorism, but

Figure 10.4a Franz Joseph Gall (1758–1828). Courtesy of Smithsonian Institution Libraries, Washington DC.

also to what he calls *horizontal faculty psychology.* Horizontal faculty psychology is endemic, he claims, in much contemporary psychology and cognitive science. Although they tend not to use the language of faculties, psychologists and cognitive scientists often describe themselves as studying memory, for example, or attention. These are taken to be separate cognitive mechanisms that can each be studied on their own terms. We see this reflected, for example, in the chapter headings for introductory textbooks in psychology, and in the titles for research grant programs put out by funding agencies.

The fact that the experimental study of memory is independent of the experimental study of attention is not simply an artifact of how textbooks are organized and research grants allocated. Behind it lies the assumption that memory and attention are distinct cognitive mechanisms performing distinct cognitive tasks. In the case of memory, the task is (broadly speaking) the retention and recall of information, while in the case of attention the task is selecting what is particularly salient in some body of information. What makes this a version of *horizontal* faculty psychology, according to Fodor, is that these faculties are *domain-general.* Any form of information can be retained and recalled, irrespective of what it is about. And anything that can be perceived is a candidate for attention.

For Fodor, Gall's great insight was the existence of what he terms *vertical* cognitive faculties. As Fodor develops the idea, these cognitive systems are *domain-specific,* as opposed to domain-general. They carry out very specific types of information-processing

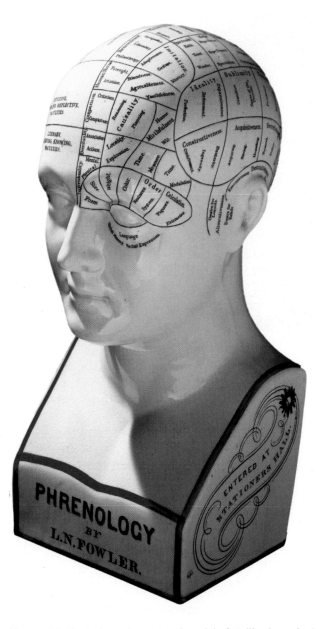

Figure 10.4b A three-dimensional model of Gall's phrenological map developed by the American phrenologist Lorenzo Niles Fowler (1811–96).

tasks. They might be specialized for analyzing shapes, for example, or for recognizing conspecifics. Moreover, they have a second important property. They are *information-ally encapsulated*. It is not just that they only perform certain types of task. They can only call upon a very limited range of information in doing so. Each vertical cognitive faculty has its own database of information relevant to the task it is performing,

Figure 10.4c Jerry Fodor (1935–).

and it can use only information in this database. These vertical cognitive faculties are what Fodor calls *cognitive modules*.

Characteristics of modular processing

Building on this idea, Fodor makes a general distinction between modular and non-modular cognitive processes. This is, in essence, a distinction between high-level cognitive processes that are open-ended and that involve bringing a wide range of information to bear on very general problems, and lower-level cognitive processes that work quickly to provide rapid solutions to highly determinate problems. In more detail, modular processes have the following four characteristics:

- *Domain-specificity.* Modules are highly specialized mechanisms that carry out very specific and circumscribed information-processing tasks.
- *Informational encapsulation.* Modular processing remains unaffected by what is going on elsewhere in the mind. Modular systems cannot be "infiltrated" by background knowledge and expectations, or by information in the databases associated with different modules.
- *Mandatory application.* Cognitive modules respond automatically to stimuli of the appropriate kind, rather than being under any executive control. It is evidence that certain types of visual processing are modular that we cannot help but perceive visual illusions, even when we know them to be illusions.

- *Speed.* Modular processing transforms input (e.g. patterns of intensity values picked up by photoreceptors in the retina) into output (e.g. representations of three-dimensional objects) quickly and efficiently.

In addition to these "canonical" characteristics of modular processes, Fodor draws attention to two further features that sometimes characterize modular processes.

- *Fixed neural architecture.* It is sometimes possible to identify determinate regions of the brain associated with particular types of modular processing. So, for example, an area in the fusiform gyrus (the so-called fusiform face area) is believed to be specialized for face recognition, which is often described as a modular process.
- *Specific breakdown patterns.* Modular processing can fail in highly determinate ways. These breakdowns can provide clues as to the form and structure of that processing. Prosopagnosia is a highly specific neuropsychological disorder that affects face recognition abilities, but not object recognition more generally.

Fodor's reason for downplaying these last two characteristics is that he identifies and individuates cognitive modules in terms of their function (the information-processing task that they carry out), instead of their physiology. This is one of the points where he parts company with Gall. A cognitive module has to perform a single, circumscribed, domain-specific task. But it is not necessary that it map onto a particular part of the brain. Some modules do seem to be localizable, but for others we have (as yet) no evidence either way. Certainly there does not seem to be any incoherence in the idea that the information processing involved in a cognitive module should be plastic – i.e. carried out by different neural systems, depending on contextual and other factors.

Cognitive modules form the first layer of cognitive processing. They are closely tied to perceptual systems. Here are some mechanisms that Fodor thinks are likely candidates for cognitive modules:

- Color perception
- Shape analysis
- Analysis of three-dimensional spatial relations
- Visual guidance of bodily motions
- Face recognition
- Grammatical analysis of heard utterances
- Detecting melodic or rhythmic structure of acoustic arrays
- Recognizing the voices of conspecifics

Some of these candidate modules are close to the sensory periphery. That is to say, relatively little information processing occurs between the sense organs and the module. This is clearly the case for color perception. Other systems are much further "downstream." An example here would be the face recognition system. Moreover, some cognitive modules can take the outputs of other modules as inputs. It is likely that information about the rhythmic structure of an acoustic array will be relevant to identifying the voice of a conspecific.

▚▞ Central processing

Not all cognition can be carried out by modular mechanisms, however. Fodor is emphatic that there have to be psychological processes that cut across cognitive domains. He stresses the distinction between what cognitive systems compute and what the organism believes. The representations processed within cognitive modules are not the only kind of representation in cognitive systems. The very features of cognitive modules that make them computationally powerful, such as their speed and informational encapsulation, mean that their outputs are not always a good guide to the layout of the perceived environment. Appearances can be deceptive. This means that there has to be information processing that can evaluate and correct the outputs of cognitive modules. As Fodor puts it,

> Such representations want correction in light of background knowledge (e.g., information in memory) and of the simultaneous results of input analysis in other domains. Call the process of arriving at such corrected representations "the fixation of perceptual belief." To a first approximation, we can assume that the mechanisms that effect this process work like this: they look simultaneously at the representations delivered by the various input systems and at the information currently in memory, and they arrive at a best (i.e., best available) hypothesis about how the world must be, given these various sorts of data. (Fodor 1983: 102)

As he immediately points out, systems that can do all this cannot be either domain-general nor informationally encapsulated. So, there must be non-modular processing – or what Fodor and others often call central processing, to distinguish it from modular processing, which is peripheral.

Central processing, Fodor suggests, has two distinguishing features. It is *Quinean* and *isotropic*. What he means by describing central processing as Quinean (after the philosopher Willard von Orman Quine, who famously proposed a holistic view of knowledge and confirmation) is that central processing aims at certain knowledge properties that are defined over the propositional attitude system as a whole. Fodor sees each organism's belief system as, in important respects, analogous to a scientific theory. It is, in fact, the organism's theory of the world. As such it shares certain important properties with scientific theories. It is the belief system as a whole that is evaluated for consistency and coherence, for example. We cannot consider how accurate or well confirmed individual beliefs are in isolation, since how we evaluate individual beliefs cannot be divorced from how we think about other elements of the system in which they are embedded.

The isotropic nature of central processing is in many ways a corollary of its Quinean property. To say that central processing is isotropic is, in essence, to say that it is *not* informationally encapsulated. In principle any part of the belief system is relevant to confirming (or disconfirming) any other. We cannot draw boundaries within the belief system and hope to contain the process of (dis)confirmation within those boundaries.

We can map this distinction between modular and non-modular processing back onto the agent architectures that we looked at in section 10.1. Fodor's cognitive modules are mainly located at the interface between cognitive system and environment. Most of the modules that he discusses are involved in perceptual information processing, but it seems likely that many motor tasks are also carried out by modules. Planning even the simplest reaching movement involves calibrating information about a target object (a glass, say) with information about hand position and body orientation. This calibration will involve coding the location of the glass on a hand-centered coordinate system (as opposed to one centered on the eyes, for example). Executing the movement requires, first, calculating a trajectory that leads from the start location to the end location, and then calculating an appropriate combination of muscle forces and joint angles that will take the arm along the required trajectory. These are all highly specialized tasks that seem not to depend upon background information or central processing – prime candidates for modular processing, on Fodor's analysis.

Suppose that Fodor is right about the role that cognitive modules play in sensory and motor processing. This still only covers a small number of the cognitive sub-systems identified in the agent architectures that we looked at in the previous section. And there are very many (and very important!) information-processing tasks that cannot be performed by cognitive modules, as Fodor understands them – all the information-processing tasks that Fodor delegates to what he calls central processing. How should we think about these information-processing tasks? What can cognitive science say about them? In the next section we see that Fodor himself is very pessimistic about cognitive science's prospects for understanding central processing.

Modularity and cognitive science

The basic distinction that Fodor made in *The Modularity of Mind* between modular and non-modular processing has received far more attention than one of the morals that he drew from the distinction. The chapter of the book devoted to central processing contains what Fodor provocatively refers to as "Fodor's First Law of the Nonexistence of Cognitive Science." Basically, "the more global (i.e. the more isotropic) a cognitive process is, the less anybody understands it. *Very* global processes, like analogical reasoning, aren't understood at all" (1983: 107). Cognitive science, Fodor argues, is really best suited to understanding modular processes. It can tell us very little about central processes – about all the processing that takes place in between sensory systems and motor systems.

This claim is so strong that it is surprising that it has not received more attention. In *The Modularity of Mind* Fodor's controversial claim about the limits of cognitive science is not backed up by argument. To the extent that it is backed up at all, Fodor justifies it with some rather controversial claims about contemporary cognitive science – such as the claim that the traditional AI project of developing a general model of intelligent problem-solving had come to a dead end and that relatively little serious work was any longer being done on building an intelligent machine. Unsurprisingly, enthusiasts for AI and cognitive science were not much moved by his polemical claims. In more recent work, however, Fodor has, in effect, provided an argument for his "First Law."

The basic problem, for Fodor, is that there is a tension between the language of thought hypothesis and the nature of central (non-modular) processing. What causes the problem are the features of central processing that we noted at the end of the previous section. Central processing is Quinean and isotropic. The job of central processing is not to construct, for example, a single representation of the environment, or to parse a heard sentence. What central processing does is to interpret what is going on in the environment, or what a particular person is trying to achieve by uttering a particular sentence. These are tasks of a very different kind. For one thing, anything that a system knows might potentially be relevant to solving them. Think about what it takes to understand a joke, for example, or the lateral thinking often required to solve practical problems. The information processing that each of these involves cannot be informationally encapsulated. And it often depends upon working out what is and what is not consistent with one's general beliefs about how people behave or how the world works.

Why do these features show that central processing is intractable from the perspective of cognitive science? In order to appreciate the difficulty we need to think back to Chapter 6 where we first encountered Fodor's ideas about the language of thought. The language of thought hypothesis is an implementation of the physical symbol structure hypothesis, and so it is committed to the basic idea that problem-solving and thinking involve manipulating physical symbol structures. What is distinctive about the language of thought hypothesis is how it understands both the physical symbol structures themselves and the way that they are manipulated and transformed in information processing.

According to the language of thought hypothesis, information processing is defined over sentences in the language of thought. The physical symbols are described as sentences because they have a syntactic structure. The syntactic structure of a sentence in the language of thought is determined solely by its physical properties. As Fodor suggestively puts it, the syntactic structure of a sentence in the language of thought is like the shape of a key – it determines how the sentence behaves in much the same way as the shape of a key determines which locks the key will unlock. So, the syntactic properties of a sentence in the language of thought are intrinsic, physical properties of that physical structure.

This idea that syntactic properties are intrinsic, physical properties of sentences in the language of thought is at the heart of Fodor's solution to the problem of causation by content. (To remind yourself how this works, look back to section 6.2 and, for a quick summary, to Figure 6.3.) Fodor proposes to solve the problem by arguing that the intrinsic physical properties of sentences move in tandem with their non-intrinsic semantic properties – in an analogous way to how transformations of the physical shapes of symbols in a logical proof move in tandem with the interpretation of those symbols.

A natural question to ask at this point is how exactly "intrinsic" is to be understood. It seems plausible that the intrinsic properties of mental representations cannot be context sensitive. That is to say, the intrinsic properties of a mental representation cannot vary with the cognitive processes in which it is involved and/or the other mental representations to which it is responsive. The analogy with logic is helpful once again. The interdependence of derivability and validity would be completely undermined if the shape of a logical symbol on one line of a proof varied according to what is going on in earlier or later lines of that proof.

Putting all this together, we can conclude that syntactic properties have to be context-*in*sensitive. And this is the source of Fodor's skepticism about cognitive science's prospects for understanding central processing. The basic problem is that context-insensitivity goes hand in hand with informational encapsulation. Saying that information processing is context-insensitive is really just another way of saying that it rests upon relatively little contextual and background information. Yet, the information processing associated with propositional attitude psychology is a paradigm example of processing that is not informationally encapsulated. According to Fodor, non-modular processing is Quinean and isotropic. But, because non-modular processing is Quinean and isotropic, it is typically context-sensitive.

Here is an example. Many of the beliefs that we form are instances of inference to the best explanation (also known as *abduction*), as when I see my friend's car in her drive and conclude that she is at home. Beliefs reached by inference to the best explanation are not *entailed* by the evidence on which they are based. There is no way of *deducing* the belief from the evidence. It is perfectly possible that my friend has left home without her car. But, given what I know of her, it just seems more likely that she is still at home. This belief does a better job of explaining the evidence than any of the alternatives. But what does "better" mean here?

In many cases, an explanation is better because it is simpler than the alternatives. In other cases, an explanation is better because it explains other phenomena that the alternatives cannot explain. In still other cases, an explanation is better because it is more conservative (it requires the believer to make fewer adjustments to the other things that she believes). What all these considerations (of simplicity, explanatory power, and conservativeness) have in common is that they are dependent upon global properties of the belief system. But this dependence on global properties is a form of context sensitivity. And we cannot, Fodor thinks, understand context-sensitive processing in computational terms.

We can now see the fundamental tension between the theory of the representational mind and the way that Fodor characterizes the distinction between modular and non-modular processing. The language of thought hypothesis at the heart of the theory of the representational mind requires that transitions between sentences in the language of thought be a function purely of the syntactic properties of those sentences. These syntactic properties must be context-sensitive. But this conflicts with the characteristics of the central processing that Fodor highlights in drawing the distinction between modular and non-modular processing. When we are dealing with sentences in the language of thought corresponding to beliefs and other propositional attitudes, we have transitions between sentences in the language of thought that are context-sensitive. Because these transitions are context-sensitive they cannot be determined purely by

TABLE 10.1   Why we cannot use the language of thought hypothesis to understand central processing: A summary of Fodor's worries
1. The best model we have for understanding information processing is the language of thought model.
2. According to the language of thought model, information is carried by sentences in the language of thought and information processing is a matter of manipulating and transforming those representations.
3. The possibilities for transforming and manipulating a sentence in the language of thought are determined solely by its syntactic properties.
4. The syntactic properties of a sentence in the language of thought are intrinsic, physical properties.
5. The way in which representations are manipulated and transformed in central processing depends upon global properties of the system's "theory" of the world (such as consistency, explanatory power, conservativeness, and so on).
6. These global properties are not intrinsic, physical properties of an individual representation, even though they determine the behavior of that representation.
7. Hence, central processing cannot be understood on the language of thought model.

the syntactic properties of the mental representations involved. But then this means that we cannot apply our model of information processing to them, since that model only applies when we have purely syntactic transitions. Table 10.1 summarizes the reasons Fodor has for being skeptical about the prospects of developing an information-processing model of central processing.

If Fodor is right, then this is obviously very bad news for cognitive science. But there are several ways of trying to avoid his argument. One possible strategy is to reject the idea that there are completely domain-general forms of information processing that can potentially draw upon any type of information. It is this way of thinking about central processing that causes all the difficulties, since it brings into play the global properties of belief systems (such as consistency, coherence, explanatory power, and so on) that cannot be understood in a physical or syntactic way. But perhaps it is wrong.

There is an alternative way of thinking about central processing. On this alternative conception, there is no real difference in kind between modular and central processing. In fact, there is no such thing as central processing in the way that Fodor discusses it, because all processing is modular. This is the *massive modularity hypothesis*. We encountered it for the first time in section 4.3. We will explore it further in the next section.

10.3   The massive modularity hypothesis

The concept of modularity is very important to cognitive science, and it has been understood in a number of different ways. Jerry Fodor's version is very strict. In order to qualify as a Fodorean module a cognitive system needs to have a number of very definite features. Fodorean modules are domain-specific, informationally encapsulated, mandatory, and fast – and they may well have a fixed neural architecture and specific patterns of breakdown. On this very strict definition of a module, there are many types of cognitive information processing that cannot be modular. After all, not all information processing is mandatory and fast. And so Fodor is led to a general distinction between modular information processing and non-modular information processing (what he calls central processing).

As we have seen, however, there is a tension between, on the one hand, how Fodor thinks about central processing and, on the other, the language of thought model of information processing. The tension is generated by certain features of central processing, as Fodor understands it – in particular, by the fact that central processing is not informationally encapsulated in any way. It is because central processing is not informationally encapsulated that it needs to be sensitive to global properties of the organism's theory of the world. It is those global properties that cannot be accommodated on Fodor's model of information processing.

One way of getting around this problem is to develop an alternative way of thinking about central processing. Supporters of the massive modularity hypothesis claim that the mind does not really do any central processing of the type that Fodor discusses. Whereas Fodor makes a sharp distinction between modular and non-modular processing, massive modularity theorists think that all information processing is essentially modular. They understand modules in a much less strict way than Fodor does. But the upshot of their position is certainly that there is no such thing as central processing of the type that Fodor discusses.

We have already encountered the massive modularity hypothesis. Back in section 4.4 we looked at an exciting example of a local integration – of what happens when theories and tools from one area of cognitive science are brought into play to explain results and findings in a different area. We explored the interface between experiments in the psychology of reasoning, on the one hand, and evolutionary psychology, on the other.

From reasoning experiments to Darwinian modules

The starting-point is a collection of well-known experiments on reasoning with conditionals (sentences that have an IF … THEN … structure). These experiments, often using variants of the Wason Selection Task (discussed in section 4.4), have been widely interpreted as showing that humans are basically very poor at elementary logical reasoning. It turns out, however, that performance on these tasks improves drastically when they are reinterpreted to involve a particular type of conditional. These are so-called *deontic conditionals*. Deontic conditionals have to do with permissions, requests, entitlements, and so on. An example of a deontic conditional would be: If you are drinking beer then you must be over 21 years of age.

The evolutionary psychologists Leda Cosmides and John Tooby came up with a striking and imaginative explanation for the fact that humans tend to be very good at reasoning involving deontic conditionals – and much better than they are at reasoning involving ordinary, non-deontic conditionals. According to Cosmides and Tooby, when people solve problems with deontic conditionals they are using a specialized module for monitoring social exchanges and detecting cheaters. They propose an ingenious explanation for why there should be such a thing as a cheater detection module.

This explanation is evolutionary. Basically, they argue that the presence of some sort of cheater detection module is a very natural corollary of one very plausible explanation for the emergence of co-operative behavior in evolution. This is the idea that co-operative behavior evolved through people applying strategies such as TIT FOR TAT in situations that have the structure of a prisoner's dilemma. We need to be very good at detecting cheaters (free riders, or people who take benefits without paying the associated costs) in order to apply the TIT FOR TAT algorithm, because the TIT FOR TAT algorithm essentially instructs us to co-operate with anyone who did not cheat on the last occasion we encountered them. According to Cosmides and Tooby, this created pressure for the evolutionary selection of a cognitive module specialized for detecting cheaters (and, more generally, for navigating social exchanges).

The cheater detection module gives massive modularity theorists a model for thinking about how the mind as a whole is organized. They hold that the human mind is a collection of specialized modules, each of which evolved to solve a very specific set of problems that were confronted by our early ancestors – by hunter-gatherers in the Pleistocene period. These modules have come to be known as *Darwinian modules*.

What sort of Darwinian modules might there be? Evolutionary psychologists have tended to focus primarily on modules solving problems of social coordination, such as problems of cheater detection, kin detection, and mate selection. But massive modularity theorists are also able to appeal to evidence from many different areas of cognitive science pointing to the existence of specialized cognitive systems for a range of different abilities and functions. These include:

- Face recognition
- Emotion detection
- Gaze following
- Folk psychology
- Intuitive mechanics (folk physics)
- Folk biology

Many different types of evidence are potentially relevant here. In section 9.3 we looked briefly at some influential experiments on prelinguistic infants using the dishabituation paradigm. These experiments show that infants are perceptually sensitive to a number of basic principles governing the behavior of physical objects – such as the principle that objects follow a single continuous path through space and time. As we saw, these experiments have been taken to show that infants possess a basic theory of the physical world.

This basic theory is held by many to be the core of adult folk physics, which itself is the domain of a specialized cognitive system.

Another type of evidence comes from neurological impairments. The possibility of selective impairments is often taken as evidence for specialized cognitive systems. *Prosopagnosia*, also known as face blindness, is a good example. Patients with prosopagnosia are unable to recognize faces, even though their general object recognition capacities are unimpaired. Prosopagnosia is often connected to injury to a specific brain area – the part of the fusiform gyrus known as the fusiform face area. Many cognitive scientists think that there is a specialized face recognition system located in the fusiform face area.

Certainly, it is perfectly possible to believe in one or more of these candidate functional specializations without accepting the massive modularity hypothesis. After all, one can perfectly well think that there are specialized systems for folk physics and folk biology while at the same time thinking that there is a completely domain-general reasoning system – and in fact, something like this is probably the dominant view among cognitive scientists. Massive modularity theorists are certainly happy to take any evidence for specialized cognitive systems as evidence in support of the massive modularity hypothesis. But the case for massive modularity rests on more general theoretical considerations.

Some of these theoretical arguments are brought out in an important paper by Cosmides and Tooby that appeared in a 1994 collection of essays entitled *Mapping the Mind: Domain Specificity in Cognition and Culture.* As its title suggests, the collection was a manifesto for thinking about the organization of the mind in terms of specialized cognitive systems. In their contribution, Cosmides and Tooby gave two arguments for thinking that there is nothing more to the mind than a collection of specialized subsystems. These are:

1 The argument from error
2 The argument from statistics and learning

Both arguments have an evolutionary flavor. The basic assumptions (surely both correct) are that the human mind is the product of evolution, and that evolution works by natural selection. These two basic assumptions give us a fundamental constraint upon possible mental architectures. Any mental architecture that we have today must have evolved because it was able to solve the adaptive problems that our ancestors encountered. Conversely, if you can show that a particular mental architecture could not have solved those adaptive problems, then it could not possibly be the architecture that we now have – it would have died out long ago in the course of natural selection.

In this spirit, the two arguments set out to show that evolution could not have selected a domain-general mental architecture. No domain-general, central-processing system of the type that Fodor envisages could have been selected, because no such processing system could have solved the type of adaptive problems that fixed the evolution of the human mind.

The argument from error

It is a sad fact that organisms tend to learn by getting things wrong. Learning requires feedback and negative feedback is often easier to come by than positive feedback. But how do we know when we have got things wrong, and so be able to work out that we need to try something different? In some cases there are obvious error signals – pain, hunger, for example. But such straightforward error signals won't work for most of what goes on in central processing. We need more abstract criteria for success and failure. These criteria will determine whether or not a particular behavior promotes fitness, and so whether or not it will be selected.

But, Cosmides and Tooby argue, these fitness criteria are domain-specific, not domain-general. What counts as fit behavior varies from domain to domain. They give the example of how one treats one's family members. It is certainly not fitness-promoting to have sex with close family members. But, in contrast, it is fitness-promoting to help family members in many other circumstances. But not in every circumstance. If one is in a social exchange with a prisoner's dilemma-type structure and is applying something like the TIT-FOR-TAT algorithm, then it is only fitness-promoting to help family members that are cooperating – not the ones that are taking the benefit without paying the costs.

So, because there are no domain-general fitness criteria, there cannot (according to Cosmides and Tooby) be domain-general cognitive mechanisms. Domain-general cognitive mechanisms could not have been selected by natural selection because they would have made too many mistakes – whatever criteria of success and failure they had built into them would have worked in some cases, but failed in many more. Instead, say Cosmides and Tooby, there must be a distinct cognitive mechanism for every domain that has a different definition of what counts as a successful outcome.

Exercise 10.1 State the argument from error in your own words and evaluate it.

The argument from statistics and learning

Like the previous argument, the argument from statistics and learning focuses on problems in how domain-general cognitive systems can discover what fitness consists in. The basic difficulty, according to Cosmides and Tooby, is that domain-general architectures are limited in the conclusions that they can reach. All that they have access to is what can be inferred from perceptual processes by general cognitive mechanisms. The problem is that the world has what Cosmides and Tooby describe as a "statistically recurrent domain-specific structure." Certain features hold with great regularity in some domains, but not in others. These are not the sort of things that a general-purpose cognitive mechanism could be expected to learn.

The example they give is the equation for kin selection proposed by the evolutionary biologist W. D. Hamilton. The problem of kin selection is the problem of

Figure 10.5 The evolutionary biologist W. D. Hamilton (1936–2000). © Jeffrey Joy

explaining why certain organisms often pursue strategies that promote the reproduct-ive success of their relatives, at the cost of their own reproductive success. This type of self- sacrificing behavior seems, on the face of it, to fly in the face of the theory of natural selection, since the self-sacrificing strategy seems to diminish the organism's fitness. This problem is a special case of the more general problem of explaining the evolution of co-operation – a problem that evolutionary psychologists have also explored from a rather different perspective in the context of the prisoner's dilemma.

Hamilton's basic idea is that there are certain circumstances in which it can make good fitness-promoting sense for an individual to sacrifice herself for another individual. From an evolutionary point of view, fitness-promoting actions are ones that promote the spread of the agent's genes. And, Hamilton argued, there are circumstances where an act of self-sacrifice will help the individual's own genes to spread and thereby spread the kin selection gene. In particular, two conditions need to hold:

Condition 1 The self-sacrificer must share a reasonable proportion of genes with the individual benefiting from the sacrifice.

Condition 2 The individual benefiting from the sacrifice must share the gene that promotes kin selection.

What counts as a reasonable proportion? This is where Hamilton's famous kin selection equation comes in. According to Hamilton, kin selection genes will increase when the following inequality holds:

$$R_{xy} B_y > C_x$$

Here the x subscript refers to the self-sacrificer and the y subscript to the beneficiary of the sacrifice. The term R_{xy} is a measure of how related x and y are. The term C_x measures the reproductive cost of kin selection to x, while B_y measures the reproductive benefit to y. In English, therefore, Hamilton's kin selection equation says that kin selection genes will spread when the reproductive benefit to the recipient of the sacrifice, discounted by the recipient's degree of relatedness to the self-sacrificer, exceeds the reproductive cost to the self-sacrificer.

Typically, two sisters will share 50 percent of their genes – or, more precisely, 50 percent of the variance in their genes (i.e. what remains after taking away all the genetic material likely to be shared by any two randomly chosen conspecifics). So, if x and y are sisters (and we measure relatedness in this way – evolutionary biologists sometimes use different measures), then we can take $R_{xy} = 0.5$. This tells us that it is only fitness-promoting for one sister to sacrifice her reproductive possibilities to help her sister when her sister will thereby do twice as well (reproductively speaking!) as she herself would have done if she hadn't sacrificed herself. So, the sacrifice will be fitness-promoting if, for example, the self-sacrificing sister could only have one more child, while the sacrifice enables her sister to have three more.

So much for the kin selection equation. Why should this make us believe in the massive modularity hypothesis? Cosmides and Tooby think that massive modularity is the only way of solving a fundamental problem raised by Hamilton's theory of kin selection. The problem has to do with how an organism learns to behave according to the kin selection equation. Simply looking at a relative will not tell the organism how much to help that relative. Nor will she be able to evaluate the consequences of helping or not helping. The consequences will not be apparent until long after the moment of decision. The kin selection equation exploits statistical relationships that completely outstrip the experience of any individual. According to Cosmides and Tooby, then, no domain-general learning mechanism could ever pick up on the statistical generalizations that underwrite Hamilton's kin selection law.

So how could the kin selection law get embedded in the population? The only way that this could occur, they think, is for natural selection to have selected a special-purpose kin selection module that has the kin selection law built into it.

Exercise 10.2 State the argument from statistics and learning in your own words and evaluate it.

Evaluating the arguments for massive modularity

It is plain from what we have seen of the massive modularity hypothesis that Darwinian modules are very different from Fodorean modules. This is not very surprising, since Darwinian modules were brought into play in order to explain types of information processing that could plainly not be carried out by Fodorean modules. Let us look again at the list of six key features of Fodorean modules:

- Domain-specificity
- Informational encapsulation
- Mandatory application
- Speed
- Fixed neural architecture
- Specific breakdown patterns

Of these six features, only the first seems clearly to apply to Darwinian modules. The second applies only in a limited sense. If I am deciding whether or not to help a relative, there are many things that might come into play besides the calculations that might be carried out in a Darwinian kin selection module – even though those calculations themselves might be relatively informationally encapsulated. I need to make a complex cost-benefit analysis where the costs and the benefits can take many different forms. There is no proprietary database that I might appeal to in solving this problem.

Darwinian modules do not seem to be mandatory – it is unlikely that the kin selection module will be activated every time that I encounter a relative. Neither of the two arguments we have considered has anything to say about neural architecture or break-down patterns (and nor does the example of the cheater detection module that we worked through in section 4.4). There may be a sense in which Darwinian modules are fast, but this is a rather fuzzy concept to apply without a specific measure of computational complexity – and we cannot apply any measure of computational complexity without some understanding of the algorithms that Darwinian modules might be running.

But given these fundamental differences between Darwinian modules and Fodorean modules, it is natural to ask why it is that Darwinian modules are modules at all. That is, in what sense are Darwinian modules dedicated cognitive sub-systems of the sort that might be identifiable components of individual mental architectures? One natural criticism of the arguments we have looked at (as well as the specific example of the cheater detection module) is that they seem perfectly compatible with a much weaker conclusion. Both the argument from error and the argument from statistics and learning are compatible with the idea that human beings (not to mention other animals) are born with certain innate bodies of domain-specific *knowledge*. This is a weaker requirement because information processing can exploit domain-specific knowledge without being modular.

In fact, the second argument is really a version of a very standard way of arguing for the existence of innate knowledge. It is a *poverty of the stimulus argument* – an argument which maintains that certain types of knowledge must be innate, as the stimuli that we encounter are too impoverished to allow us to acquire that knowledge. The best-known poverty of the stimulus argument is Chomsky's argument for the innateness of syntactic knowledge.

Evolutionary psychologists are not always as precise as they could be in distinguishing between domain-specific modules and domain-specific bodies of knowledge. When we are thinking about the organization of the mind, however, the distinction is fundamentally important. When we formulate the massive modularity hypothesis in terms of cognitive modules it is a bold and provocative doctrine about mental architecture. It says that there is no such thing as a domain-general information-processing mechanism and that the mind is nothing over and above a collection of independent and quasi-autonomous cognitive sub-systems.

But when we formulate the massive modularity thesis in terms of domain-specific bodies of knowledge it is much less clear what the claim actually is. The idea that we (and quite possibly other animals) are born with innate bodies of knowledge dedicated to certain domains is not really a claim about the architecture of cognition. As we saw at the beginning of this section, cognitive scientists have proposed such innate bodies of knowledge in a number of different areas – such as numerical competence, intuitive mechanics, and so on.

The distinctive feature of the massive modularity hypothesis, as developed by Cosmides and Tooby, is its denial that there is any such thing as domain-general central processing. But this is a claim about information processing and mental architecture. If we think instead in terms of innate bodies of knowledge then the only way I can think of reformulating the denial is as the claim that there are no domain-general learning mechanisms.

On the face of it there do appear to be obvious counter-examples to this claim. Don't classical conditioning and instrumental conditioning (as discussed in section 1.1) count as learning mechanisms? They certainly seem to be domain-general. Cosmides and Tooby surely cannot be denying that classical and instrumental conditioning are possible. That would be to fly in the face of over a century of experimental evidence and theoretical analysis. All that they could plausibly be saying is that we know things that we could not have learnt by applying domain-general learning mechanisms. This may or may not be true. Certainly many people believe it. But the important point is that it is a much weaker claim than the massive modularity hypothesis advertises itself as making.

So, the case for the massive modularity thesis is compatible with a much weaker and less controversial conclusion. But that still does not give us a reason to *reject* the stronger version of the massive modularity thesis as an account of information-processing mental architecture. Let me end this section by proposing two arguments that aim to show that the massive modularity thesis cannot be true. These arguments set out to show that there *must* be domain-general reasoning and domain-general information processing. According to these arguments there cannot be a completely modular cognitive system, and so the massive modularity thesis must be false.

The first argument is due to Jerry Fodor who is, as one might expect, a fierce opponent of the massive modularity thesis. His book attacking the thesis is provocatively entitled *The Mind Doesn't Work That Way*. The title is a reference to an earlier book by Steven Pinker entitled *How the Mind Works*. Pinker's book was an enthusiastic endorsement of massive modularity.

Fodor's critique starts off from the obvious fact that any modular system, whether Darwinian or Fodorean, takes only a limited range of inputs. So, one question anyone proposing a modular cognitive capacity has to answer is how that limited range of inputs is selected. In particular, is any information processing involved in identifying the relevant inputs and discriminating them from inputs that are not relevant?

For Fodorean modules the answer is straightforward. Modules responsible for low-level tasks such as early visual processing and syntactic parsing are supposed to operate directly on sensory inputs and it is usual to postulate sensory systems (so-called *transducers*) that directly filter the relevant inputs. These filters ensure, for example, that only information about light intensity feeds into the earliest stages of visual processing.

But Darwinian modules and Fodorean modules operate on fundamentally different types of input. Inputs into the cheater detection module, for example, must be representations of social exchanges of the sort that may be exploited by cheaters. So some processing is required to generate the appropriate inputs for the cheater detection module. It does not make sense to postulate the existence of social exchange transducers. There has to be some sort of filtering operation that will discriminate all and only the social exchanges.

This is where Fodor's objection strikes. According to the massive modularity hypothesis, the processing involved in this initial filtering must be modular. Clearly, the filtering process will only work if the filtering module has a broader range of inputs than the module for which it is doing the filtering. But, on the other hand, since the filtering process is modular, it must have a limited range of inputs. The filtering process is itself domain-specific, working to discriminate the social exchanges from a slightly broader class of inputs – perhaps a set of inputs whose members have in common the fact that they all involve more than one person.

So the same question arises again. How is this set of inputs generated? Presumably a further set of processing will be required to do the filtering. It follows from the massive modularity hypothesis that this processing must itself be modular. But the same question now arises again. What are the inputs to this filtering module? These inputs must be drawn from a wider pool of potential inputs – which makes this filtering module less domain-specific than the last one. The process repeats itself until we eventually arrive at a pool of potential inputs that includes everything. The filtering here involves processing so domain-general that it cannot be described as modular at all. A similar line of argument will apply, Fodor claims, to all the other Darwinian modules. The massive modularity hypothesis collapses, because it turns out that massive modularity requires complete domain-generality.

Fodor's argument is bottom-up. It analyzes the *inputs* into Darwinian modules. There is also room for a broadly parallel line of argument that is top-down, directed at the *outputs* of Darwinian modules.

It is very likely that some situations will fall under the scope of more than one module. So, for example, something might be a social exchange when looked at from one point of view, but a potentially dangerous situation when looked at from another. Let us call this situation S. Under the first description S would be an input for the cheater detection module, while under the second description S might be relevant to, say, the kin selection module. In this sort of case one might reasonably think that a representation of S will be processed by both modules in parallel.

But this will often create a processing problem. The outputs of the relevant modules will need to be reconciled if, for example, the kin selection module "recommends" one course of action and the cheater detection module another. The cognitive system will have to come to a stable view, prioritizing one output over the other. This will require further processing. And the principles of reasoning used in this processing cannot be domain-specific. This is because these principles need to be applicable to both of the relevant domains, and indeed to any other domains that might be potentially relevant.

The general thought here is really rather straightforward. According to the massive modularity hypothesis the mind is a complex structure of superimposed Darwinian modules that have evolved at different times to deal with different problems. Given the complexities of human existence and human social interactions, there will have to be a considerable number of such modules. Given those very same complexities, moreover, it seems highly unlikely that every situation to which the organism needs to react will map cleanly onto one and only one Darwinian module. It is far more likely that in many situations a range of modules will be brought to bear. Something far closer to what is standardly understood as central processing will be required to reconcile conflicting outputs from those Darwinian modules. This central processing will have to be domain-general.

So, what can we take out of this discussion of the massive modularity hypothesis? On the one hand, the strongest version of the hypothesis (on which it is a hypothesis about the organization and wiring of the mind) seems much stronger than is required to do justice to the two arguments for massive modularity that we considered. The argument from error and the argument from statistics and learning certainly fall short of establishing a picture of the mind as composed solely of domain-specific and quasi-autonomous cognitive sub-systems. At best those arguments show that there must be some domain-specific modules – which is a long way short of the controversial claim that there cannot be any domain-general processing. And we have also looked at two arguments trying to show that the strong version of the massive modularity hypothesis cannot possibly be true.

But, on the other hand, even if one rejects the massive modularity hypothesis in its strongest form, it still makes some very important points about the organization of the mind. In particular, it makes a case for thinking that the mind might be at least partially organized in terms of cognitive sub-systems or modules that are domain-specific without having all the characteristics of full-fledged Fodorean modules. Cognitive scientists have taken this idea very seriously and we will be exploring it further in the next two chapters.

In Chapter 11 we will look at how the techniques of cognitive neuroscience can be used to study the organization of the mind, focusing in particular on the strengths and limits of using imaging techniques to map the mind. In Chapter 12 we will work through a case study that brings the theoretical discussions about modularity to life. We will look at a debate that is very much at the forefront of contemporary cognitive science – the controversial question of whether there is a module responsible for reasoning about the mental states of others, or what many cognitive scientists have come to call the theory of mind module.

First, though, we will look at a way of thinking about the mind that brings the discussion of modularity in this chapter into contact with the discussion in earlier chapters of two competing ways of modeling information processing. In the next section we will look at hybrid mental architectures that have both symbolic components (as per the physical symbol system hypothesis) and subsymbolic components (as per the artificial neural networks approach).

10.4 Hybrid architectures

Up to now we have been thinking separately about the different aspects of mental architecture. We looked in detail in Chapters 6 through 9 at the two principal models of information storage and information processing – the symbolic paradigm associated with the physical symbol system hypothesis, and the distributed paradigm associated with artificial neural networks. In this chapter we have been looking at two different ways of thinking about the overall organization of the mind. We began with several different models of agent architectures and then went on to study both Fodor's sharp distinction between modular processing and central processing, and the massive modularity thesis associated with the evolutionary psychologists Leda Cosmides and John Tooby. In this section we will bring these two different aspects of mental architectures into contact. We will look at how the symbolic and distributed paradigms have been combined in a model of the overall organization of the mind – the ACT-R/PM cognitive architecture associated with the psychologist John R. Anderson and his research team at Carnegie Mellon University.

It may have occurred to you that the distinction between physical symbol systems and artificial neural networks is not all-or-nothing. As we saw when we looked at specific examples and models, symbolic and distributed information processing seem to be suited for different tasks and different types of problem-solving. The type of problems tackled by GOFAI physical symbol systems tend to be highly structured and sharply defined – playing checkers, for example, or constructing decision trees from databases. The type of problems for which artificial neural networks seem particularly well suited tend to be perceptual (distinguishing mines from rocks, for example, or modeling how infants represent unseen objects) and involve recognizing patterns (such as patterns in forming the past tense of English verbs).

The extreme version of the physical symbol system hypothesis holds that *all* information processing involves manipulating and transforming physical symbol structures.

It may be that Newell and Simon themselves had something like this in mind. There is a comparable version of the artificial neural networks approach, holding that physical symbol structures are completely redundant in modeling cognition – artificial neural networks are all we need. There seems to be room, though, for a more balanced approach that tries to incorporate both models of information processing. Anderson's ACT-R/PM cognitive architecture is a good example.

We have talked a lot about mental architectures in this book. Mental architectures, as we have been thinking about them, are theoretical in orientation – they incorporate theoretical models of information processing and how the mind is organized (whether it is modular, for example, and if so how). The notion of a cognitive architecture, as used by computer scientists and psychologists, is a more practical notion. A cognitive architecture is similar to a programming language. It gives researchers the tools to construct cognitive models using a common language and common toolkit.

One of the first cognitive architectures was actually developed by Allen Newell, working with John Laird and Paul Rosenbloom. It was originally called SOAR (for State Operator And Result). The current incarnation is known as Soar. Soar is very closely tied to the physical symbol system hypothesis. It is based on the means–end and heuristic search approaches to problem-solving that we looked at in Chapter 6. Soar is intended to be a unified model of cognition. It does not incorporate any elements corresponding to artificial neural networks. All knowledge is represented in the same way in the architecture, and manipulated in a rule-governed way.

The ACT-R/PM (Adaptive Control of Thought – Rational/Perceptual–Motor) cognitive architecture is the latest installment of a cognitive architecture that was first announced under the name ACT in 1976. It is a development of the ACT-R architecture, which itself develops the ACT* architecture. ACT-R/PM is less homogeneous than Soar. It counts as a hybrid architecture because it incorporates both symbolic and subsymbolic information processing. One of the things that makes ACT-R interesting from the perspective of this chapter is that it is a modular cognitive architecture. It has different modules performing different cognitive tasks and the type of information processing depends upon the type of task.

The ACT-R/PM architecture

The basic structure of ACT-R/PM is illustrated in Figure 10.6. As the diagram shows, the architecture has two layers – a perceptual-motor layer and a cognitive layer. It is the addition of the perceptual-motor layer that distinguishes ACT-R/PM from its predecessor ACT-R. Each layer contains a number of different modules.

The modules within each layer are generally able to communicate directly with each other. Communication between modules on different layers, on the other hand, only takes place via a number of *buffers*. A buffer is rather like a workspace. It contains the "sensory" input that is available for processing by the central cognitive modules. The cognitive modules can only access sensory information that is in the relevant buffer (visual information in the visual buffer, and so on).

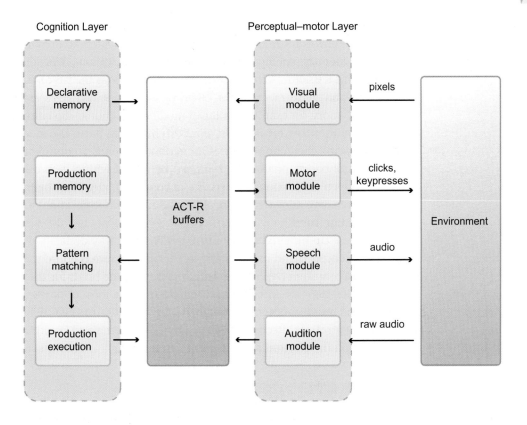

Cognition Layer   Perceptual–motor Layer

Figure 10.6 The ACT-R/PM cognitive architecture. The architecture has two layers – a cognitive layer and a perceptual–motor (PM) layer. By permission of Lorin Hochstein.

The cognition layer is built upon a basic distinction between two types of knowledge – declarative and procedural. In philosophy this is often labeled the distinction between *knowledge-that* (declarative) and *knowledge-how* (procedural) – between, for example, knowing that Paris is the capital of France and knowing how to speak French. The first type of knowledge involves the storage and recall of a very specific piece of information. The second is a much more general skill, one that is manifested in many different ways and in many different types of situations.

Declarative and procedural knowledge are both represented symbolically, but in different ways. Declarative knowledge is organized in terms of "chunks." A chunk is an organized set of elements. These elements may be derived from the perceptual systems, or they may be further chunks. The basic ideas behind chunking as a way of representing the content of declarative memory are directly related to the physical symbol system hypothesis. We can think of chunks as symbol structures (say the equation "7 + 6 = 13") built up in rule-governed ways from physical symbols (corresponding to "7," "6," "+," "1," and "3"). These chunks are stored in the declarative memory module. The chunks in declarative memory might encode objects in the environment. Or they might encode goals of the system.

ACT-R/PM represents procedural knowledge in terms of *production rules*. Production rules are also known as Condition-Action Rules. As this alternative name suggests, production rules identify specific actions for the system to perform, depending upon which condition it finds itself in. When a production rule fires (as the jargon has it) in a given condition, it can perform one of a range of actions. It can retrieve a chunk from declarative memory, for example. Or it can modify that chunk – updating its representation of the environment, for example, or modifying a goal. It can also modify its environment. In this case the action really is an action – it sends a command to the motor module. And of course production rules can be nested within each other, so that the output of a given production rule serves as a condition triggering the firing of another production rule. This allows complex abilities (such as multiplication) to be modeled as sets of production rules.

So far there is nothing hybrid about ACT-R/PM. The way declarative and procedural knowledge is encoded and manipulated in the architecture is entirely in line with the physical symbol system hypothesis. And in fact the same holds for the perceptual and motor modules. Here too information is encoded in the form of physical symbols. The perceptual and motor modules are designed on the basis of the EPIC (Executive Process/ Interactive Control) architecture developed by David Kieras and David Meyer. EPIC falls squarely within the physical symbol system approach.

ACT-R/PM as a hybrid architecture

What makes ACT-R/PM a hybrid architecture is that this symbolic, modular architecture is run on a subsymbolic base. In order to appreciate what is going on here, take another look at Figure 10.6. In many ways the overall organization looks very Fodorean. There are input modules and output modules. These modules are all encapsulated. They communicate only via the buffer systems. And yet there is something missing. There is no system responsible for what Fodor would call central processing. But nor, on the other hand, is ACT-R/PM massively modular. It does not have dedicated, domain-specific modules.

So, a natural question to ask of ACT-R/PM is: How does it decide what to do? If a given production rule or set of production rules is active, then there is no difficulty. The system follows the "instructions" provided by the production rules – it performs the actions triggered by the conditions in which it finds itself. But how does it decide which production rules to apply? ACT-R/PM is designed to operate serially. At any given moment, only one production rule can be active. But most of the time there are many different production rules that could be active. Only one of them is selected. In a Fodorean architecture, this job would be done by some type of central processing system that operates symbolically. In ACT-R/PM, in contrast, the process of selection takes place subsymbolically. This is what makes it a hybrid architecture.

The job of selecting which production rule is to be active at a given moment is performed by the pattern-matching module. This module controls which production rule gains access to the buffer. It does this by working out which production rule has the highest utility at the moment of selection. The concept of utility is directly derived from the theory of rational choice (as developed, for example, in statistics, decision theory, and economics) – this is why the "R" in ACT-R/PM stands for "rational."

Utility can be understood in many different ways, but the basic idea is that the production rule with the highest utility is the rule whose activation will best benefit the cognitive system. The notion of benefit here is understood with reference to the system's goals – or rather, to the system's current goal. The utility of a particular production rule is determined by two things. The first is how likely the system is to achieve its current goal if the production rule is activated. The second is the cost of activating the production rule.

So, the pattern-matching module essentially carries out a form of cost-benefit analysis in order to determine which production rule should gain access to the buffer. The entire process takes place without any overseeing central system. It is a type of "winner-take-all" system. All the work is done by the equations that continually update the cost and utility functions. Once the numbers are in, the outcome is determined.

The designers of ACT-R/PM describe these calculations as *subsymbolic*. This is a very important concept that is also standardly used to describe how artificial neural networks operate. Each production rule is purely symbolic. Production rules are built up in rule-governed ways from basic constituent symbols exactly as the physical symbol system hypothesis requires. The compositional structure of production rules determines how the production rule behaves once it is activated, but it does not play a part in determining whether or not the rule is activated. For that we need to turn to the numbers that represent the production rule's utility. These numbers are subsymbolic because they do not reflect the symbolic structure of the production rule.

ACT-R/PM has other subsymbolic dimensions. The architecture also uses subsymbolic equations to model the accessibility of information in declarative memory. It is a very basic fact about cognition that memories are not all created equal. Some are easier to access than others. Cognitive psychologists studying memory have discovered all sorts of different effects when they study how memories are accessed and retrieved. An architecture such as ACT-R/PM has to find a way of modeling this type of variability.

The accessibility and retrievability of memories in ACT-R/PM is modeled subsymbolically. Recall that the basic units of declarative memory are chunks – as opposed to the production rules that are the basic units of procedural memory. Each chunk has associated with it a particular activation level. This activation level can be represented numerically. The higher the activation level, the easier it is to retrieve the chunk from storage.

The activation levels of chunks in declarative memory are determined by equations. These equations are rather similar to the equations governing the utilities of production .rules. There are two basic components determining a chunk's overall activation level. The first component has to do with how useful the chunk has been in the past. Usefulness is understood in terms of utility, which in turn is understood in terms of how the chunk has contributed to realizing the system's goals. The second component has to do with how relevant the chunk is to the current situation and context.

Again, we can draw the same basic contrast here between symbolic and subsymbolic dimensions. Chunks themselves are symbolic ways of carrying information. They are

TABLE 10.2   Comparing the symbolic and subsymbolic dimensions of knowledge representation in the hybrid ACT-R/PM architecture

	PERFORMANCE MECHANISMS		LEARNING MECHANISMS	
	SYMBOLIC	**SUBSYMBOLIC**	**SYMBOLIC**	**SUBSYMBOLIC**
Declarative chunks	Knowledge usually facts) that can be directly verbalized	Relative activation of declarative chunks affects retrieval	Adding new declarative chunks to the set	Changing activation of declarative chunks and changing strength of links between chunks
Production rules	Knowledge for taking particular actions in particular situations	Relative utility of production rules affects choice	Adding new production rules to the set	Changing utility of production rules

built up from basic symbols, and the way they function within the architecture is determined by this symbolic structure. But they cannot do anything while they are stored in the declarative memory module. In order to function within the architecture they need to be retrieved from storage and placed in the buffer. This process is governed by the subsymbolic equations that fix each chunk's activation level as a function of its past usefulness and current relevance. These equations are subsymbolic because they are completely independent of the chunk's internal symbolic structure. Table 10.2 summarizes the relation between the symbolic and subsymbolic dimensions of ACT-R/PM.

What ACT-R/PM reveals, therefore, is the possibility of an approach to thinking about the overall organization of the mind that combines elements of the two different approaches to information processing that we have been considering – the symbolic approach associated with the physical symbol system hypothesis, on the one hand, and the subsymbolic approach associated with the artificial neural network approach, on the other. Knowledge is represented in ACT-R/PM in the form of physical symbol structures – either as chunks of declarative knowledge, or as production rules in procedural memory. Once these items of knowledge reach the buffer, and so become available for general processing within the system, they operate purely symbolically. But the processes that govern when and how they reach the buffer are subsymbolic.

It is true that the designers of ACT-R/PM do not see these types of subsymbolic processing as being implemented by artificial neural networks – artificial neural networks do not have a monopoly on subsymbolic information processing. So, the distinction between symbolic and subsymbolic information processing in this architecture does not map precisely onto the distinction between physical symbol systems and artificial neural networks. But there are (at least) two very important lessons to be learnt from ACT-R/PM.

The first lesson is the very close connection between debates about the organization of the mind and debates about the nature of information processing. Thinking properly about the modular organization of the mind requires thinking about how the different modules might execute their information-processing tasks. The second lesson follows directly on from this. Different parts of a mental architecture might exploit different models of information processing. Some tasks lend themselves to a symbolic approach. Others to a subsymbolic approach. The debate between models of information processing is not all-or-nothing.

Summary

This chapter has focused on the third of the questions that a mental architecture has to answer: How is the mind organized so that it can function as an information processor? We began by looking at three different architectures for intelligent agents in AI, in order to see what distinguishes the organization of cognitive agents from that of simple reflex agents. Cognitive agents are standardly modeled in terms of quasi-autonomous information-processing systems, which raises the question of how those systems should be understood. Pursuing this question we looked at Jerry Fodor's analysis of modular information-processing systems and explored his reasons for thinking that cognitive science is best suited to explaining modular systems, as opposed to non-modular, central information-processing systems. We then examined an alternative proposed by massive modularity theorists, who hold that all information processing is modular. Finally we turned to the hybrid architecture ACT-R/PM, which brings the discussion of modularity into contact with the discussion of information processing in Part III. ACT-R/PM is a modular system that combines the symbolic approach associated with the physical symbol system hypothesis and the subsymbolic neural networks approach.

Checklist

Computer scientists building intelligent agents distinguish different types of agent architectures

(1) Simple reflex agents have condition-action rules (production rules) that directly link sensory and effector systems.

(2) Simple reflex agents are not cognitive systems, unlike goal-based agents and learning agents.

(3) Goal-based agents and learning agents are built up from sub-systems that perform specific information-processing tasks.

(4) This general approach to agent architecture raises theoretical questions explored in discussions of modularity.

Fodor's modularity thesis

(1) The thesis is built on a rejection of horizontal faculty psychology (the idea that the mind is organized in terms of faculties such as memory and attention that can process any type of information).

(2)   It proposes the existence of specialized information-processing modules that are:
domain-specific
informationally encapsulated
mandatory
fast

(3)   These modules may also have a fixed neural architecture and specific breakdown patterns.

(4)   Modules are employed for certain, basic types of information processing (e.g. shape analysis, color perception, and face recognition).

(5)   Modules provide inputs to non-modular, central processing – the realm of belief fixation and practical decision-making, among other things.

(6)   Central processing is Quinean (i.e. holistic) and isotropic (i.e. not informationally encapsulated).

According to "Fodor's First Law of the Nonexistence of Cognitive Science," cognitive science is best suited for understanding modular processes

(1)   Non-modular information processing has to be context-sensitive, and so involves the non-intrinsic properties of mental representations (such as how consistent they are with other mental representations).

(2)   The language of thought hypothesis, however, depends upon the idea that syntactic transformations of mental representations are defined over their intrinsic, physical properties.

(3)   Fodor's argument is reviewed in Table 10.1.

According to the massive modularity hypothesis, all information processing is modular. There is no domain-general information processing.

(1)   The human mind is claimed to be a collection of specialized modules, each of which evolved to solve a specific set of problems encountered by our Pleistocene ancestors.

(2)   Examples of these Darwinian modules are the cheater detection module (discussed in section 4.4) and modules proposed for folk psychology (theory of mind) and folk physics (intuitive mechanics).

(3)   According to the argument from error, domain-general cognitive mechanisms could not have evolved because there are no domain-general fitness criteria.

(4)   According to the argument from statistics and learning, domain-general learning mechanisms cannot detect statistically recurrent domain-specific patterns (such as the kin selection equation proposed by W. D. Hamilton).

(5)   Both of these arguments can be satisfied with the much weaker claim that there are innate, domain-specific bodies of knowledge.

(6)   It is possible to argue that there has to be domain-general information processing, in order (a) to filter inputs to Darwinian modules, and (b) to reconcile conflicts between them.

ACT-R/PM is an example of a hybrid architecture that combines both symbolic and subsymbolic elements

(1)   Knowledge in ACT-R/PM is represented in two different ways – declarative knowledge is represented in chunks, while procedural knowledge is represented through production rules.

(2)   Items of knowledge become available for general information processing when they appear in one of the buffers. This general information processing is fundamentally symbolic in character.

(3)   In contrast, the processes that determine whether a particular item of knowledge ends up in a buffer are subsymbolic – equations, for example, that calculate how useful a given production rule might be in a particular context.

(4)   These processes are subsymbolic because they do not exploit or depend upon the internal symbolic structure of the item of knowledge.

Further reading

There is a useful introduction to intelligent agents in Russell and Norvig 2009, particularly ch. 2. An earlier version of this chapter (from the book's first edition) is available in the online resources. A good review can also be found in Poole and Mackworth 2010. See the online resources for other helpful collections pertaining to agent architectures.

Fodor's modularity thesis is presented in his short book *The Modularity of Mind* (Fodor 1983). A summary of the book, together with peer commentaries was published in the journal *Behavioral and Brain Sciences* (Fodor 1985). The summary is reprinted in Bermúdez 2006. For critical discussion of the modularity of face perception see Kanwisher, McDermott, and Chun 1997, and Kanwisher 2000. Cosmides and Tooby have written an online evolutionary psychology primer, available in the online resources. More recent summaries of Cosmides and Tooby's research can be found in Cosmides, Barrett, and Tooby 2010, and Cosmides and Tooby 2013. Their 1994 paper discussed in the text is reprinted in Bermúdez 2006. It was originally published in Hirschfeld and Gelman 1994. This influential collection contains a number of other papers arguing for a modular approach to cognition. There is a useful entry on Biological Altruism in the online *Stanford Encyclopedia of Philosophy*. For Hamilton's theory of kin selection, see Dawkins 1979 (available in the online resources).

Pinker 1997 develops a view of the mind that integrates the massive modularity hypothesis with other areas of cognitive science. Pinker is a particular target of Fodor's discussion of massive modularity in Fodor 2000. Pinker responds to Fodor in Pinker 2005 (available in the online resources).

Carruthers 2006 is a book-length defense of a version of the massive modularity thesis. The journal *Mind and Language* published a precis of the book (Carruthers 2008b), together with three commentaries – Machery 2008, Wilson 2008, and Cowie 2008. Carruthers replies in the same issue (Carruthers 2008a). A good review of modularity research can be found in Barrett and Kurzban 2006. Also see Richard Samuels's chapter on massive modularity in Margolis, Samuels, and Stich 2012. The *Stanford Encyclopedia of Philosophy* also has an entry on modularity.

The homepage for the ACT architecture is the best place to start (see online resources). It contains a comprehensive bibliography with links to PDF versions of almost every referenced paper. For a brief overview of the general ACT approach, see Lebiere 2003. For a longer introduction to ACT-R see Anderson *et al*. 2004. To see how ACT-R can be implemented neurally see Zylberberg, Dehaene, Roelfsema, and Sigman 2011.

CHAPTER ELEVEN

Strategies for brain mapping

Overview

Most cognitive scientists think that, *in some sense*, the mind is organized into cognitive sub-systems. But there are many different ways of thinking about how this organization might work in practice. We looked at some of these in the last chapter. Fodor's modularity doctrine is one example. The massive modularity thesis a rather different one. But, if we accept the general picture of the mind as organized into cognitive sub-systems, two questions immediately arise:

1   How do the individual cognitive sub-systems work?
2   How are the individual sub-systems connected up with each other?

In Chapters 6–10 we have been focusing on the first question. In this chapter we turn to the second question. What we are interested in now is how the individual sub-systems fit together – or, to put it another way, what the wiring diagram of the mind looks like.

This question is more tricky than initially appears. Neuroanatomy is a very good place to start in thinking about the organization of the mind, but neuroanatomy can only take us so far. The wiring diagram that we are looking for is a cognitive wiring diagram, not an anatomical one. We are trying to understand how information flows through the mind, and whether certain types of information processing are carried out in specific brain areas. This takes us beyond anatomy, because we certainly cannot take it for granted that cognitive functions map cleanly onto brain areas. Section 11.1 looks in more detail at the theoretical and practical issues that arise when we start to think about the interplay between *structure* and *function* in the brain.

Many neuroscientists think that we can *localize* particular cognitive functions in specific brain areas (or networks of brain areas). Their confidence is in large part due to the existence of powerful techniques for studying patterns of cognitive activity in the brain. These techniques include

- PET (positron emission tomography)
- fMRI (functional magnetic resonance imaging)
- EEG (electroencephalography) for measuring ERPs (event-related potentials)

Section 11.2 introduces these techniques and their respective strengths, while the case studies in sections 11.3 and 11.4 show how the different techniques can be combined to shed light on the complex phenomenon of attention.

Neuroimaging techniques do not in any sense provide a direct "window" on cognitive functions. They provide information about blood flow (in the case of PET) or the blood oxygen level dependent (BOLD) signal (in the case of fMRI). How we get from there to models of cognitive organization depends upon how we interpret the data. In section 11.5 we will look at some of the challenges that this raises.

11.1 Structure and function in the brain

From an anatomical point of view the brain has some conspicuous landmarks. Most obviously, it comes in two halves – the left hemisphere and the right hemisphere. The division between them goes lengthwise down the middle of the brain. Each of these hemispheres is divided into four lobes. As we saw in section 3.2, each of the four lobes is thought to be responsible for a different type of cognitive functioning. The frontal lobe is generally associated with reasoning, planning, and problem-solving, for example. Anatomically speaking, however, the lobes are distinguished by large-scale topographic features known as *gyri* and *sulci* (the singular forms are *gyrus* and *sulcus* respectively).

If you look at a picture of the surface of the brain you will see many bumps and grooves. The bumps are the gyri and the grooves are the sulci. The sulci are also known as fissures. Many of these bumps and grooves have names. Some of the names are purely descriptive. The parieto-occipital sulcus, for example, separates the parietal lobe from the occipital lobe. Some of the names are more interesting. The Sylvian sulcus (which is marked in Figure 11.1 as the lateral cerebral sulcus) divides the temporal lobe from the lobe in front of it (the frontal lobe) and from the lobe above it (the parietal lobe). It is named after Franciscus Sylvus, who was a seventeenth-century professor of medicine at the University of Leiden in the Netherlands.

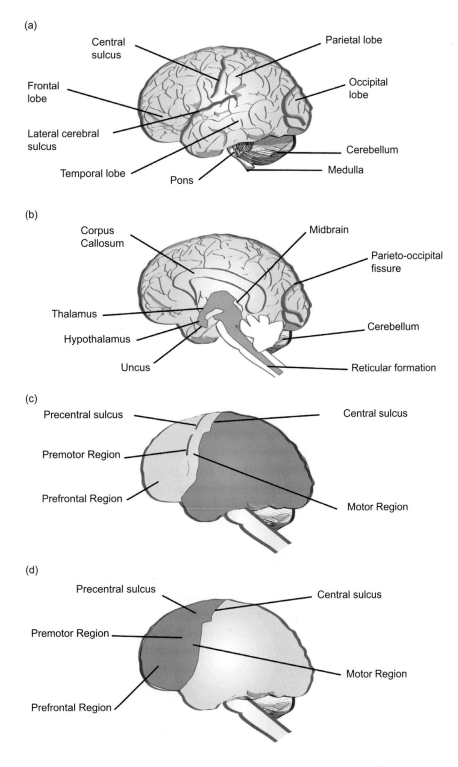

Figure 11.1 Luria's 1970 diagram of the functional organization of the brain. The top diagram is anatomical, while the other three depict functional networks. (Adapted from Luria 1970)

The diagram in Figure 11.1a is drawn from a review article published in *Scientific American* in 1970 by the famous Russian neuropsychologist Alexander Luria. It illustrates some of the most prominent large-scale features of the anatomy of the brain's surface. My main interest in reproducing it, however, is to contrast it with the other three diagrams in Figure 11.1. Each of these depicts one of what Luria thought of as the three main *functional networks* in the brain. Luria called these networks "blocks." They are colored brown in the diagrams.

According to Luria, each block has very different roles and responsibilities. Figure 11.1b is the most primitive block, made up of the brain stem and the oldest parts of the cortex. (This would be a good moment to look back at the first few paragraphs of section 3.2.) According to Luria, this system regulates how awake and responsive we are. The second block (in Figure 11.1c) regulates how we code, control, and store information, while the third block (Figure 11.1d) is responsible for intentions and planning.

The specific details of Luria's analysis are not particularly important. What he was reviewing in 1970 is no longer state of the art now. We are looking at Luria's diagram because it is a particularly clear example of two things. The first is the difference between anatomy and cognitive function. The diagram in Figure 11.1a is an anatomical diagram. It organizes the brain in terms of large-scale anatomical features (such as the lobes and the sulci). It divides the brain into regions, but it has nothing to say about what those regions actually do. The other three diagrams, however, are not purely anatomical. They mark many of the same anatomical regions, but they are organized in functional terms. This is particularly clear in Figures 11.1c and d, corresponding to Luria's second and third blocks. Here we have regions picked out in terms of what they are thought to do (in terms of the cognitive function that they serve). So, for example, a particular section of the frontal lobe is identified as the motor region (responsible for planning voluntary movements).

This distinction between anatomy and cognitive function is fundamentally important in thinking about the brain. But the second thing that we learn from Luria's diagram is how easy it is to slide from talking about anatomical areas to talking about functional areas (and vice versa). When we talk about the Sylvian sulcus we are talking about an anatomical feature of the brain. When we talk about the motor region, in contrast, we are talking about a region of the brain identified in terms of its function. But it is very common to have (as we have here) diagrams and maps of the brain that use both types of label. And in fact, the same area can have two very different names depending on how we are thinking about it. The precentral gyrus, for example, is an anatomical feature located just in front of the central sulcus. It is also called the primary motor cortex, because neuroscientists have discovered that directly stimulating this area causes various parts of the body to move.

Exploring anatomical connectivity

Large-scale anatomical features of the brain, such as the lobes, sulci and gyri, are readily apparent simply from looking at the brain (or pictures of it). Neuroscientists are also interested in identifying anatomical regions on a smaller scale. In order to do this neuroscientists and neuroanatomists need to use special techniques. Some of these techniques were developed in the early days of neuroscience. As was briefly mentioned in section 3.2, neuroscientists still use a classification of anatomical areas in the cerebral cortex developed by the great German neuroanatomist Korbinian Brodmann in the late nineteenth and early twentieth century.

Brodmann's basic insight was that different regions in the cerebral cortex can be distinguished in terms of the types of cell that they contain and how densely those cells occur. In order to study the distribution of cells in the cortex Brodmann used recently discovered techniques for staining cells. Staining methods are still used by neuroscientists today. They involve dipping very thin slices of brain tissue into solutions that allow details of cellular structure to be seen under a microscope. Brodmann used the Nissl stain, developed by the German neuropathologist Franz Nissl. The Nissl stain turns all cell bodies a bright violet color.

By using the Nissl stain to examine the distribution of different types of neuron across the cerebral cortex, Brodmann identified over fifty different cortical regions. Figure 11.2 gives two views of the brain with the four lobes and the different Brodmann areas clearly marked. The top view is a lateral view (from the side) while the lower one is a medial view (down the middle).

It is a remarkable fact about neuroanatomy that the classification of cortical regions developed by Brodmann on the basis of how different types of neuron are distributed can also serve as a basis for classifying cortical regions according to their function (according to the types of information that they process and the types of stimuli to which they respond). In section 3.2 we looked at some of the brain areas involved in processing visual information. For example, the primary visual cortex, also known as area V1, is the point of arrival for information from the retina. In anatomical terms it is Brodmann area 17. Somatosensory information about the body gained through touch and body sense arrives in a region of the postcentral gyrus known as the primary somatosensory cortex. This is Brodmann area 3. We have already mentioned the primary motor cortex (the precentral gyrus). This is Brodmann area 4.

The process of localizing cognitive functions in specific brain areas is complex and controversial, particularly when we move away from basic sensory processing (such as that carried out in the primary visual cortex and the primary somatosensory cortex). We will be looking at some of the techniques that neuroscientists use to localize functions in the remainder of this chapter.

One of the most fundamental principles of neuroscience is the *principle of segregation*. This is the idea that the cerebral cortex is divided into segregated areas with distinct neuronal populations. Again, this is an idea that can be interpreted both anatomically and functionally. Anatomical explorations such as those carried out by Brodmann reveal anatomical segregation. Much of contemporary neuroscience is devoted to identifying functional segregation in the brain. Later sections of this chapter will be exploring the evidence for and implications of functional segregation. For the rest of this section we will explore the idea of anatomical segregation a little further.

Brodmann Areas

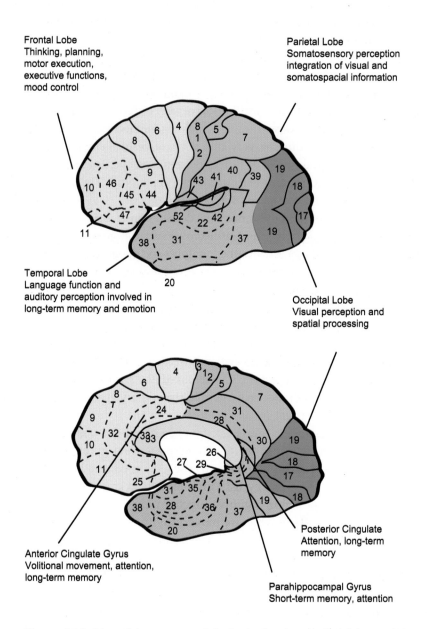

Frontal Lobe
Thinking, planning,
motor execution,
executive functions,
mood control

Parietal Lobe
Somatosensory perception
integration of visual and
somatospacial information

Temporal Lobe
Language function and
auditory perception involved in
long-term memory and emotion

Occipital Lobe
Visual perception and
spatial processing

Anterior Cingulate Gyrus
Volitional movement, attention,
long-term memory

Posterior Cingulate
Attention, long-term
memory

Parahippocampal Gyrus
Short-term memory, attention

Figure 11.2 Map of the anatomy of the brain showing the four lobes and the Brodmann areas. The captions indicate general functional specializations. The top view is a lateral view (from the side) while the lower one is a medial view (down the middle). Reproduced courtesy of appliedneuroscience.com

Even from an anatomical point of view, identifying segregated and distinct cortical regions can only be part of the story. We also need to know how the cortical regions are connected with each other. This would give us what we can think of as an anatomical wiring diagram of the brain - or, to use the terminology more standard in neuroscience, a map of *anatomical connectivity*.

Exploring anatomical connectivity requires a whole new set of techniques. One very influential technique is called *tract tracing*. Tract tracing involves injecting a chemical that works as a marker into a particular brain region. Typical markers are radioactive amino acids or chemicals such as horseradish peroxidase (HRP). When the marker is injected near to the body of a nerve cell it is absorbed by the cell body and then transported along the cell's axon. Looking to see where the marker ends up allows neuroanatomists to identify where the cell projects to - and doing this for enough cells allows them to work out the connections between different brain regions.

Tract tracing is what is standardly called an invasive technique. It is only possible to discover where HRP has been transported to by examining sections of the cortex through a microscope. This cannot be done on living creatures. And so neuroanatomists have primarily worked on the brains of non-human animals - primarily macaque monkeys, rats, and cats. Their results are often represented using *connectivity matrices*. Figure 11.3 is an example, from a very influential set of data on the visual system of the macaque monkey published in 1991 by Daniel J. Felleman and David Van Essen. The brain regions are abbreviated in a standard way. We can read off the matrix the regions to which any given region projects. Find the region you are interested in on the first column and then work your way across. If there is a "1" in the column corresponding to another brain region, then there is a connection going from the first to the second. If there is a "0" then no connection has been found. The gaps in the matrix indicate a lack of information.

The same data can be presented in a form that makes it look much more like a wiring diagram. We see this in Figure 11.4. The wiring diagram format makes it a little easier to visualize what is going on, but it doesn't give quite as much information as the connectivity matrix.

Exercise 11.1 What type of information about anatomical connectivity do we get from a connectivity matrix but not from a wiring diagram?

Unquestionably, connectivity matrices and anatomical wiring diagrams are a vital part of understanding how the brain works and how it processes information. This is so for the very simple reason that information can only travel from one brain region to another if there is a neural pathway connecting them. Nonetheless, there are several important limitations on what we can learn from information about anatomical connectivity.

One difficulty is that data about anatomical connectivity are largely derived from animal studies, whereas the brains that we are really interested in are our own. We need to be very careful about extrapolating from animal brains to human brains. The

	V1	V2	V3	VP	V3A	V4	VOT	V4T	MT	FST	PITd	PIT	PITv	CITd	CIT	CITv	AITd	AITv	STPp	STP	STPa	TF	TH	MSTd	MSTl	PO	PP	LP	VIP	MIP	MDP	DP	7a	FEF	46
V1		1	1	0	1	1	0	0	1	0	0		0	0		0	0	0	0		0	0	0	0		1	1	0	0	0	0	0	0	0	0
V2	1		1	1	1	1	1	1	1	1	0		0	0		0	0	0	0		0	0	0	1	1	1	1	0	1	0	0	0	0		0
V3	1	1			1	1	0	1	1	1	0		0	0		0	0	0	0		0	1	0	1	0	1	1	1	1	0	0		0		0
VP	0	1	1		1	1	1	0	1	1	0		0	0		0	0	0	0		0	1	0	1	0	1	1		1	0	0		0		0
V3A	1	1	1	1		1			1	1	0		0	0		0	0	0	0		0	0	0	1	1	1				0	0	1	0		0
V4	1	1	1	1	1			1	1	1	1		1	1		1	0	1	0		0	1	1	0	0	0	1	1	0	0	0	1	0		1
VOT	0	1	0	1		1					1		1																						
V4t	1		1	0		1			1	1														0	1	1									
MT	1	1	1	1	1	1		1		1	0		0	0		0	0	0	0		0	0	0	1	1		1	1	1	0	0	0	0	1	
FST	0	0	1	0	1	1		1	1			1		0		0	0	0	1			1		1	1	0	0	1	1				1	1	0
PITd	0	0	0	0	0	1			0							1	1	1							0	0	0	0	0				0		
PIT										1														1										1	1
PITv	0	0	0	0	0	1			0							1		1							0	0	0		0				0		
CITd	0	0	0	0	0	1			0				1				1	1						0	0	0	0	0	0				0		
CIT																																		1	1
CITv	0	0	0	0	0	1			0				1				1	1						0	0	0	0	0	0				0		
AITd	0	0	0	0	0	0			0	0			1			1								0	0	0	0	0	0	0	0		1	1	1
AITv	0	0	0	0	0	1			0	0			1			1					0	1	1	0	0	0	0	0	0	0	0				
STPp	0	0	0	0	0	0			0	1					1		0				1	1	1	1	1	0	0	0	0	0	0			1	1
STP																																	1		
STPa	0	0	0	0	0	0			0								1	0	1			1	1			0	0	0	0	0	0				1
TF	0	0	1	1	0	1			0	1			1			1	1	1	1		1			1		0	0		0	0	0		1		1
TH	0	0	0	0	0	1			0				1		1		1	1	1		1			0	0	0	0	0	0	0	0		1		1
MSTd	0	1	1	1	1	0		1	1	1		1		0		0	0	0	1							1		1	1			1	1	1	
MST1	0	1	0	0	1	0		0	1	1	0	0	0	0		0	0	0	1							1	0		1			0	0	1	
PO	1					0			1	0	0		0	0		0	0	0	0		0	0	0	1	1			1	1			1	1		
PIP	1		1	1		1			1		0		0	0		0	0	0	0		0					1						1	1		
LIP	0		1	1	1	1			1	1	0		1	0		0	0	0				1	0	1	1	1			1			1	1	1	1
VIP	0		1						1	1	0		0	0		0	0	0						1	1	1		1					1	1	
MIP	0	0	0	0	0	0			0	0	0		0	0		0	0	0						0	0	1							1		
MDP	0	0	0	0	0	0			0	0	0		0	0		0	0	0						0	0	1							1		
DP	0	0	0	0	1	1			0	1	0		0	0		0	0	0	0		0	0	0	1	1	1	1	1					1		1
7a	0	0	0	0	0	0			0		0		0	0		0	1			1		1	1	1		1		1				1		1	1
FEF	0									1					1		1		1					1	1	1		1	1			1	1		1
46	0	0	0	0	0					0					1		1		1		1	1	1	0								1	1	1	

Figure 11.3 A connectivity matrix for the visual system of the macaque monkey. (Adapted from Felleman and Van Essen 1991)

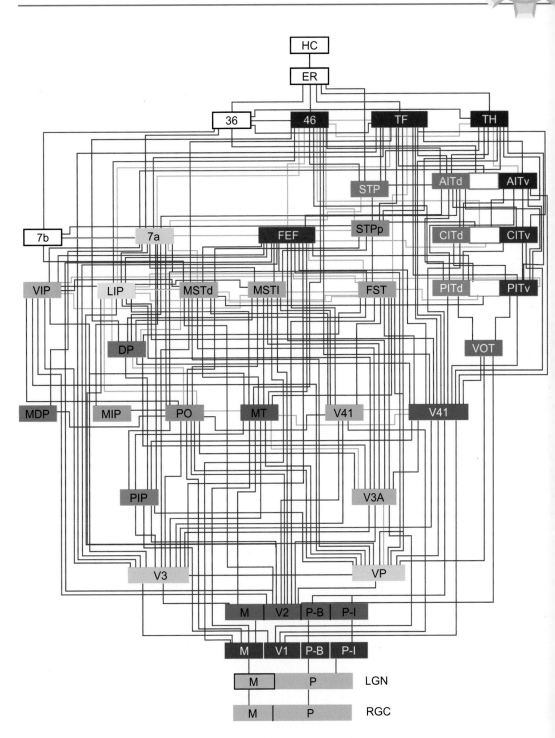

Figure 11.4 An anatomical wiring diagram of the visual system of the macaque monkey. (Adapted from Felleman and Van Essen 1991)

information that we have about anatomical connectivity specifically in humans is largely derived from post-mortem studies of human brains. Techniques for studying human anatomical connectivity *in vivo* are being developed. What is known as *diffusion tractography* exploits the technology of magnetic resonance imaging (which we will be looking at in much more detail in the next section) in order to study how water diffuses in the brain. Mapping how water diffuses allows neuroanatomists to identify the barriers that block the free flow of the liquid. Since these barriers are typically bundles of axons, the technique can yield valuable information about anatomical connectivity. The fact remains, however, that this way of studying anatomical connectivity in humans is in its infancy – and much of the detailed information we have still comes from animal studies.

A second issue is that anatomical wiring diagrams do not carry any information about the direction of information flow between and across neural regions. There are typically at least as many feedback connections as feedforward connections. This can be seen even in the visual cortex. Back in section 3.2 we looked at the hypothesis that there are two different systems for processing visual information. Each of these systems exploits a different anatomical pathway. The "where" system is served by the dorsal pathway, while information processed by the "what" system travels along the ventral pathway. The ventral pathway begins in area V1 and then progresses through areas V1, V2, and V4 on its way to the inferotemporal cortex. When we think about the ventral pathway in information-processing terms it is natural to think of information as starting out in V1 and then moving along the pathway. From an anatomical point of view, however, this "directionality" is not apparent. As you can see from the connectivity matrix in Figure 11.3, each of the three areas is connected to each of the others in both directions.

Exercise 11.2 Check that this is the case.

Finally, and most obviously, anatomical connectivity is studied almost completely independently of cognitive functioning. An anatomical wiring diagram tells us which brain regions are in principle able to "talk" directly to each other. But it does not tell us anything about how different brain regions might form circuits or networks to perform particular information-processing tasks. For that we need to turn to some very different techniques and technologies – techniques and technologies that allow us to study brain connectivity when it is actually carrying out different types of task.

11.2 Studying cognitive functioning: Techniques from neuroscience

In the last section we explored the anatomical basis for what is often called the *principle of segregation* in thinking about the brain. This is the principle that the brain is organized into distinct neural populations that are segregated from each other. We saw how neuroscientists have used techniques such as Nissl staining in order to identify these areas. Most neuroscientists also accept a *principle of integration*. This is the idea that cognitive functioning involves the coordinated activity of networks of different brain areas, with different types of task recruiting different networks of brain areas.

It is because of the principle of integration that it is so important to look at patterns of connectivity in the brain. We made a start on this in the last section by looking at connectivity from an anatomical perspective. As we saw, though, there are limits to what we can learn about cognition from an anatomical wiring diagram of the brain. In order to make further progress in understanding how cognition works we need to supplement information about anatomical connectivity with information about what actually goes on in the brain when it is performing specific cognitive tasks. Neuroscientists have developed a number of techniques for doing this. In this section we will briefly survey them. In sections 11.3 and 11.4 we will look at a case study involving four of the principal techniques – EEG and electrophysiology in section 11.3 and PET and fMRI in section 11.4.

The techniques that we are currently interested in are those that can most easily be used to study the cognitive organization of the mind. Sadly, there is no way of measuring cognitive activity directly. All that neuroscientists can do is to track certain things going on in the brain and the nervous system that they have good reason to think are correlated with cognitive activity. The two most obvious candidates are the brain's electrical activity and how blood behaves in the brain. In fact, the techniques we will look at fall into two general categories, depending upon which type of brain activity they measure. The first set of techniques are focused on the brain's electrical activity. The second set of techniques study the flow and oxygen levels of blood in the brain.

Mapping the brain's electrical activity: EEG and MEG

When neurons fire they send electrical impulses down their axons. These electrical impulses are called *action potentials*. Action potentials are transmitted to the dendrites of other neurons at *synapses*. Electrical synapses transmit electrical signals directly, while chemical synapses transmit chemicals called neurotransmitters. The precise details of how this works are not important for now. Two things are important. The first is that this electrical activity is a good index of activity in neurons. What neurons do is fire, and when they fire they generate electricity. The second is that there is a range of different techniques for measuring this activity.

Microelectrodes can be used to measure the electrical activity in individual neurons. Neurophysiologists can record the discharge of action potentials by placing a microelectrode close to the cell being recorded. (For an illustration see section 4.5.) This technique has been used to identify neurons that are sensitive to particular stimuli. The recent discovery of what are known as *mirror neurons* is a very good example. A group of neuroscientists led by Giacomo Rizzolatti in Parma, Italy, have identified neurons in monkeys that fire both when the monkey performs a specific action and when it observes that action being performed by an observer. This is illustrated in Figure 11.5.

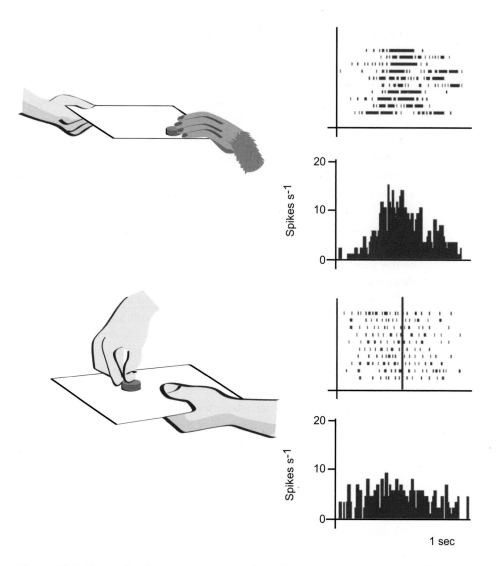

Figure 11.5 The results of single-neuron recordings of a mirror neuron in area F5 of the macaque inferior frontal cortex. The neuron fires both when the monkey grasps food (top) and when the monkey observes the experimenter grasping the food (bottom). Each horizontal line in the top diagram represents a single trial and each nick the firing of a neuron. Neural activity is summed over trials in the two histograms. (Adapted from Iacoboni and Dapretto 2006)

This type of single-unit recording is fundamentally important for studying individual neurons. In order to study the brain's organization and connectivity, however, we need to turn to tools that will allow us to study what is going on on a much larger scale. We need to look at the electrical activity of populations of neurons, rather than single neurons. As we saw in section 4.5, microelectrodes can be used to study electrical activity in clusters of neurons very near to the tip of the electrode (within 2 mm or so). But this is still too fine-grained to help us map the relations between neural activity in different brain areas.

Human encephalography (EEG) is one way of studying the activity of larger populations of neurons. EEG is a very straightforward procedure. It requires little complicated machinery or disturbance to the subject. EEG uses electrodes attached to the skull and wired up to a computer. Each electrode is sensitive to the electrical activity of thousands of neurons, with the neurons nearest the electrode making the largest contribution to the output signal.

The coordinated activity of these neural populations can be seen in EEGs as oscillatory waves at different frequencies. These frequencies are typically labeled in terms of bands. The bands are named with letters from the Greek alphabet – from alpha through to gamma. Confusingly, the alpha band is neither the lowest frequency nor the highest. The lowest frequency activity takes place in the delta band. Delta band activity is seen in very deep sleep (sometimes called slow wave sleep).

In fact, different stages in the sleep cycle are associated with activity in different bands – and sleep specialists use EEG to identify and study sleep disorders. EEGs can be used for other forms of medical diagnosis. So, for example, epilepsy is associated with a distinctive, "spikey" wave, as can be seen in Figure 11.6.

As far as studying the organization and connectivity of the brain is concerned, EEGs are particularly important because they give a reliable way of measuring what are known as *event-related potentials* (ERPs). An ERP is the electrical activity provoked by a specific stimulus.

The reason that EEGs are so useful for studying ERPs is that EEGs have a very fine temporal resolution – or, in other words, they are sensitive to very small differences in elapsed time. So, EEG recordings can trace the subtle dynamics of the brain's electrical activity as it processes information in response to a particular stimulus. We will look in more detail at EEGs and ERPs in the next section, but the basic idea is that when the electrical signals from many different trials are averaged out it becomes possible to filter out the electrical activity specific to the particular stimulus from the background electrical activity constantly going on in the brain.

EEGs are not the only way of studying the electrical activity of large populations of neurons. But it is the most widespread technique and (not coincidentally, one imagines) the least expensive. The other principal technology is *magnetoencephalography* (MEG). Magnetoencephalography measures the same electrical currents as are measured by EEG. It measures them through the magnetic fields that they produce. This allows a finer spatial resolution than is possible with EEGs. It is also much less susceptible to distortion due to the skull than EEG. But, on the other hand, it brings with it all sorts of technical issues. For example, it can only be carried out in a room specially constructed to block all alien magnetic influences, including the earth's magnetic field. MEG is relatively little used in research neuroscience (as opposed to medical diagnosis).

Name and example	Description
Delta 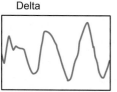	Delta is the slow wave characteristic of deep, unconscious sleep. It is less than 4 Hz, and similar EEG frequencies appear in epileptic seizures and loss of consciousness, as well as some comatose states. It is therefore thought to reflect the brain of an unconscious person. The delta frequency tends to have the highest amplitude and the slowest frequency. Delta waves increase with decreasing awareness of the physical world.
Theta 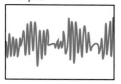	Theta activity has a frequency of 3.5 to 7.5 Hz. Theta waves are thought to involve many neurons firing synchronously. Theta rhythms are observed during some sleep states, and in states of quiet focus, for example meditation. They are also manifested during some short-term memory tasks, and during memory retrieval. Theta waves seem to communicate between the hippocampus and neocortex in memory encoding and retrieval.
Alpha 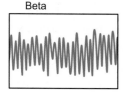	Alpha waves range between 7.5 and 13 Hz and arise from synchronous (in-phase) electrical activity of large groups of neurons. They are also called Berger's waves in memory of the founder of EEG. Alpha waves are predominantly found in scalp recordings over the occipital lobe during periods of relaxation, with eyes closed but still awake. Conversely alpha waves are attenuated with open eyes as well as by drowsiness and sleep.
Beta 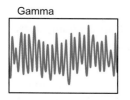	Beta activity is 'fast' irregular activity, at low voltage (12–25 Hz). Beta waves are associated with normal waking consciousness, often active, busy, or anxious thinking and active concentration. Beta is usually seen on both sides of the brain in symmetrical distribution and is most evident frontally. It may be absent or reduced in areas of cortical damage.
Gamma	Gamma generally ranges between 26 and 70 Hz, centered around 40 Hz. Gamma waves are thought to signal active exchange of information between cortical and other regions. They are seen during the conscious state and in REM dreams (Rapid Eye Movement Sleep). Note that gamma and beta activity may overlap in their typical frequency ranges, because there is still disagreement on the exact boundaries between these frequency bands.

Figure 11.6 Typical patterns of EEG waves, together with where/when they are typically found. (From Baars and Gage 2012)

Mapping the brain's blood flow and blood oxygen levels: PET and fMRI

The principal alternative to measuring electrical activity in the brain is looking at what happens to the blood in the brain during particular cognitive tasks. The main techniques for doing this are PET and fMRI. PET scans track the movement of radioactive water in the brain in order to map cerebral blood flow. fMRI, in contrast, measures the levels of blood oxygenation.

Both PET and fMRI are based on the well-established idea that the quantity of blood flowing to a particular brain region increases when the region is active. PET measures blood flow directly. fMRI measures blood flow indirectly through blood oxygen levels in particular brain regions. Blood oxygen level is a good index of regions with high blood flow. This is because the increased neural activity in those areas does not consume all of the oxygen in the blood that reaches them. As a consequence, the ratio of oxyhemoglobin to deoxyhemoglobin increases in areas that see increased blood flow. This gives rise to the so-called BOLD (*blood oxygen level dependent*) signal.

We have already looked at both of these techniques earlier in the book. In section 3.4 we looked at experiments that used PET to explore the information processing involved in reading single words. In section 4.5 we looked at experiments exploring the relation between data about electrical activity derived from microelectrode recordings and data about the BOLD signal derived from fMRI. It would be a good idea at this point to look back to those sections and review some of the basic principles of these two types of neuroimaging.

Both PET and fMRI have high spatial resolution and relatively poor temporal resolution. That means that they are much more sensitive to spatial change and variation than they are to change and variation over time. In this respect they are very different from EEG and MEG, both of which have relatively poor spatial resolution and high temporal resolution. What this means, in practical terms, is that these two neuroimaging techniques are much better at telling us about how cognitive activity is distributed across the brain over a period of time than they are at telling us about the precise sequence of events as information is processed.

The standard use of functional neuroimaging is to identify networks of neural areas that are involved in carrying out cognitive tasks of a particular kind – those exploiting short-term memory, for example. This does not require a particularly fine temporal resolution. It simply requires being able to identify which neural regions are simultaneously active when the task is being performed. And the spatial resolution has to be sufficiently fine-grained for the results to be interpretable in terms of standard anatomical maps of the brain. The technology has to have sufficient spatial resolution to be able to pinpoint, for example, activity in the premotor cortex (Brodmann area 6), or in the orbitofrontal cortex (Brodmann area 11). Only thus will we be able to make a bridge between cognitive functioning and our anatomical wiring diagram.

We can end this section with Table 11.1, which summarizes some of the key features of these different techniques.

TABLE 11.1 Comparing techniques for studying connectivity in the brain			
	DIRECTLY MEASURES	TEMPORAL RESOLUTION	SPATIAL RESOLUTION
Single unit recording	Potentials in individual neurons and very small populations of neurons	High	High
EEG (electroencephalography)	Electrical activity of larger populations of neurons	High	Low
MEG (magnetoencephalography)	Magnetic fields produced by electrical activity of larger populations of neurons	High	Low
PET (positron emission tomography)	Cerebral blood flow in particular brain regions	Low	High
fMRI (functional magnetic resonance imaging)	Levels of blood oxygen in particular brain regions	Low	High

In the next two sections we will look at how these different techniques and technologies can be combined and calibrated with each other.

11.3   Combining resources I: The locus of selection problem

We experience the world in a highly selective way. At any given moment we effectively ignore a huge amount of the information that our perceptual systems give us. We saw an example of this in Chapter 1 – the so-called cocktail party phenomenon. At a lively party we can often hear many different conversations. There is often background noise and other distractions. And yet somehow we manage to screen all the conversations and noise except the particular conversation that we are interested in. The same thing holds for vision. At any given moment our field of vision is about 180 degrees in the horizontal plane and 135 degrees in the vertical plane. In principle, therefore, we can see things that are more or less level with our ears. Yet we are barely aware of much of our so-called peripheral vision. It is only when something in the periphery "catches our eye" that we realize quite how far our field of vision extends.

This selectivity is a very basic feature of perception. We only *focus on* or *attend to* a small proportion of what we actually see, hear, touch, and so on. Psychologists label the mechanism responsible for this very general phenomenon *attention*. As we saw in Chapter 1, one of the key steps towards what we now think of as cognitive science was taken when cognitive psychologists such as Donald Broadbent began to explore attention experimentally and then used the results of those experiments to develop information-processing models of how attention might work.

The key idea in Broadbent's model of attention is that attention functions as a filter. Information coming from the sensory systems passes through a selective filter that screens out a large portion of the information. What the filter lets through depends upon what the cognitive system as a whole is trying to achieve. In a cocktail party situation, for example, the filter might be tuned to the sound of a particular individual's voice.

On Broadbent's model attention comes out as a low-level process. Attention does its screening relatively early on in perceptual processing. The selective filter screens out all the sounds that don't correspond to the voice of the person I am talking to long before my auditory systems get to work on parsing the sounds into words and then working out what is being said. Attention is applied to very low-level properties of the auditory stimulus – such as pitch, for example, or timbre. Semantic processing comes much later, as does identifying who the voice actually belongs to.

Broadbent thinks of attention as occurring at the early stages of perceptual processing. His model is what is known as an *early selection model*. Other models claim that attention operates at a much later stage. These are *late selection models*. According to late selection models, important parts of perceptual processing are complete before attention comes into play. In vision, for example, late selection models think that attention only comes into play once representations of sensory features (such as color, shape, and so on) have already been combined into representations of objects and those objects identified.

The late selection approach is taken, for example, in the object-based model of attention developed by the cognitive psychologist John Duncan in the 1980s. At the heart of Duncan's theory (which has, by now, gone through a number of different versions) is the idea that attention is applied to representations of objects. The initial impetus for this way of thinking about attention came from experiments showing that subjects are much better at identifying visual features within a single object than when the features belong to two or more objects. Duncan's idea was that identification is facilitated by attention and that the experiments show that attention does not work well when distributed across two or more objects. But there would be no reason for this to hold unless attention were selecting between representations of objects.

The *locus of selection problem* is the problem of determining whether attention is an early selection phenomenon or a late selection phenomenon. For a long time models of attention were derived primarily from behavioral data – from experiments developed by psychophysicists and cognitive psychologists. Behavioral data are not sufficient to resolve the locus of selection problem, however. In order to get real traction on the problem, what is required is some way of measuring what is going on in visual information processing in order to determine when attention comes into play.

⊠ Combining ERPs and single-unit recordings

The locus of selection problem is at bottom a problem about the temporal organization of information processing. The key question is whether the processing associated with selective attention takes place before or after the processing associated with object recognition. One way of getting traction on this problem is to use EEGs to measure the ERPs evoked by visual information processing. As we observed in the previous section, EEGs have a very high temporal resolution. They are sensitive at the level of milliseconds.

Something that makes ERPs particularly relevant to tackling the locus of attention problem in the case of vision is that quite a lot is known about two important things. First, we have good information about how the shape of the wave of electrical activity following a visual stimulus reflects processing in different cortical areas in the visual system. Second, we have good information about what type of information processing those different cortical areas actually carry out. These two types of information make it much easier to interpret what is going on in the ERP data and to apply to it to tackle the locus of selection problem.

First, we need a little more detail on what sort of information we actually get from ERP experiments. Remember that EEG, which is electroencephalography, is the general technique, while an ERP, which is an evoked reaction potential, is what the technique actually measures when it is *time-locked* with the onset of a particular stimulus. What we get from an ERP experiment is a wave that measures the electrical activity in the period of time immediately following the onset of the stimulus. The time is standardly measured in milliseconds (thousandths of a second), while the electrical activity is measured in microvolts (millionths of a volt).

We see a typical example in Figure 11.7b. The graph displaying the ERP typically has a number of spikes and troughs. These are known as the *components* of the ERP and represent voltage deflections. The voltage deflections are calculated relative to a pre-stimulus baseline of electrical activity – which might, for example, be derived by measuring electrical activity at the tip of the nose.

In order to interpret these spikes and troughs properly we need to bear in mind a very confusing feature of ERP graphs. The *y*-axis represents negative activations above positive ones. This is very counter-intuitive because it means that, when the line goes up the electrical activity is actually going down! And vice versa.

The time that elapses between stimulus onset and a particular spike or trough is known as the *latency* of the particular component. The components of the ERP for vision have been well studied. The earliest component is known as the C1 component. It is a negative component and appears at 50–90 ms after the appearance of the stimulus. There is a standard labeling for subsequent components. These are labeled either P or N, depending upon whether they are positive or negative. And they are given a number, which represents either their position in the ERP or their latency.

The P1 component, for example, is the first positive component, while the P300 is a positive component that occurs 300 ms (i.e. 0.3 seconds) after the stimulus is detected.

(a)

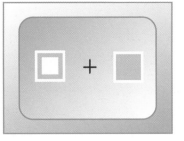

Figure 11.7a Common experimental design for neurophysiological studies of attention. The outline squares are continuously present and mark the two locations at which the solid square can be flashed.

(b)

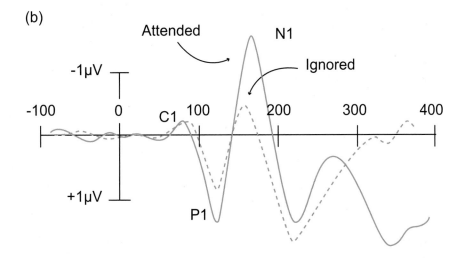

Figure 11.7b Example of the occipital ERPs recorded in a paradigm of this nature. Note that the C1 wave (generated in area V1) shows no attention effect, whereas the P1 and the N1 waves (generated in extrastriate cortex) are larger for the attended stimuli.

The P300 typically occurs in response to unexpected or novel stimuli. It is often taken as a sign that higher cognitive processes, such as attention, are involved in processing the stimulus. The graph in Figure 11.7b has the C1, N1, and P1 components marked. It is also possible to see the P200 component and a (slightly delayed) P300.

The key to understanding how measuring ERPs can help with the locus of selection problem is that the ERP wave displays an *attention effect*. Certain components of the wave change depending upon whether or not the subject is attending to the stimulus. Figure 11.7a illustrates a typical experiment used to elicit the attention effect. The subject is asked to attend to one of two boxes in a screen. Stimuli are presented at various places in the screen and the ERPs are measured both for the case where the stimulus is in the box being attended to and the case where it is elsewhere.

(c)

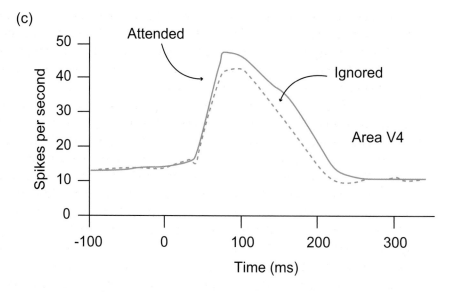

Figure 11.7c Single-unit responses from area V4 in a similar paradigm. Note that the response is larger for attended compared with ignored stimuli.

(d)

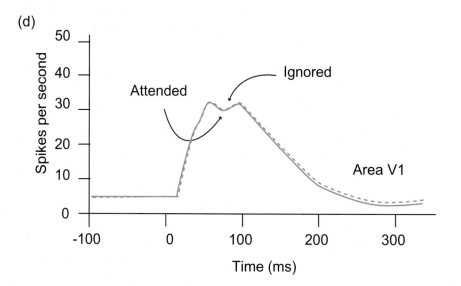

Figure 11.7d Single-unit responses from area V1 showing no effect of attention. (Adapted from Luck and Ford 1998)

The results of these experiments are striking. They are illustrated in Figure 11.7b. The solid line shows the ERP when subjects are attending and the dotted line when subjects are not attending. There are important differences in two of the components – together with an important non-difference in one component. The non-difference first – there is no significant difference in the C1 component between the attended and the unattended cases. But there are significant differences in the P1 and N1 components. The P1 component is the first significant positive component and the N1 the first significant negative component. Both the P1 component and the N1 component are larger when the subject is attending to the box in which the stimulus appears.

This looks significant. But what does it show? And in particular, how is it relevant to the locus of selection problem? If we accept that the shape and dimensions of the ERP wave are correlated with information processing, then we can certainly conclude that there is something different going on in the attended case from the unattended case. And in fact, if we accept that a higher P1 component and a lower N1 component are signs that more information processing is going on, then we can conclude that there are two additional bursts of information processing taking place roughly 100 and 200 ms after stimulus onset. It is plausible to conclude that this additional information processing is associated with the exercise of attention – since the only difference between the two cases has to do with where attention is directed. But how does it help us to decide whether attention is an early selection phenomenon or a late selection phenomenon?

The ERP data on their own cannot settle this question. In order to make progress we need independent information that will allow us to map the C1, P1, and N1 components onto activity in the brain. Fortunately, we can triangulate ERP data with data derived from different sources. As we have seen on several occasions, neurophysiologists have used a variety of techniques in order to identify a number of different areas in the visual system of the macaque monkey. It is generally thought that object identification exploits the so-called ventral pathway that begins in V1 (the *striate cortex*) and then progresses through areas V2 and V4 en route to the inferotemporal cortex.

Electrophysiological studies have shown that (in the macaque brain, at least) these different areas in the visual system process different types of information. V1 is the origin both of the ventral (vision for identifying objects) pathway and the dorsal (vision for locating and acting upon objects) pathway. It is generally thought that V1 is responsible for processing basic shape information – information that is obviously relevant both to identifying objects and to locating and acting upon them. Visual areas V2 and V4 (which is an *extrastriate* area) are thought to process more advanced information about shape, together with information about color, texture, and so on.

On standard understandings, the different areas in the object identification pathway process different types of information separately but in parallel. There is a very real question as to how this separately processed information is combined to form representations of objects. This problem is known as the *binding problem*. For the moment we can simply note that the information processing in V1, V2, and V4 is standardly thought to take place *upstream* of wherever the process of binding takes place. In other words, all the information processing in the early visual areas such as V1, V2, and V4 takes place *before* the visual system is working with representations of objects.

This gives a clear criterion for thinking about the locus of selection problem. Recall that the issue is whether attention is an early selection phenomenon or a late selection phenomenon. We said earlier that if attention is a late selection phenomenon then it only comes into play when the visual system has generated (and perhaps identified) representations of objects – that is to say, well after the process of binding is complete. The processing in areas V1, V2, and V4 is upstream of the binding process. Therefore, any evidence that the exercise of attention affects processing in the early visual areas will be evidence that attention is an early selection phenomenon.

This is why the ERP data are so significant. There is a range of evidence connecting different components of the ERP wave to processing in different visual areas. The C1 component, for example, is thought to reflect processing in the striate cortex (V1). Since the C1 component is constant across both the attended and the unattended conditions, we can conclude that processing in V1 is not modulated by attention. On the other hand, however, there is evidence connecting the P1 and N1 components with processing in the extrastriate cortex (i.e. in areas such as V2 and V4). This evidence comes from experiments calibrating ERP data with PET scans. So, although the EEG technology used in measuring ERPs has a low spatial resolution when considered on its own, combining it with other techniques can overcome this limitation.

There is more information that can be brought to bear here. Single-unit recording using microelectrodes is a technique that has both high spatial resolution and high temporal resolution. It can give us very accurate information about what is going on over short periods of time at very specific areas in the brain. Although single-unit recording is highly invasive and so can only be used on non-human animals, it still gives us a way of triangulating the ERP data. The diagrams in Figures 11.7c and d show the results of making recordings in areas V1 and V4 while monkeys are performing a task similar to that depicted in Figure 11.7a. As the graphs show, there is no difference between levels of activity in V1 across the attended and unattended conditions. But there are significant differences in V4. This is certainly consistent with the hypothesis that attention is an early selection phenomenon.

There is a clear "take-home message" here. Although there are no techniques or technologies for studying cognitive activity directly and although each of the techniques has significant limitations, we can overcome many of the limitations by combining and triangulating the different techniques. The high temporal resolution of EEG complements the high spatial resolution of imaging technologies such as PET. And predictions from studies of humans using these techniques can be calibrated with electrophysiological studies on monkeys.

In the example of attention that we have been considering, combining ERP and PET generates predictions that can be tested using single-unit recordings on monkeys. The studies on humans predict that activity in V1 is not going to be modulated by attention, while activity in V4 will be modulated by attention. These predictions are borne out. The result of combing all these techniques is a picture of how attention can operate in early stages of visual processing.

11.4 Combining resources II: Networks for attention

The previous section explored the locus of selection problem. As we saw, the key question in the locus of selection problem is whether attention operates in the early stages of perceptual processing, or whether it only comes into play once perceptual processing is essentially completed. The data that we reviewed seem to suggest that attention is an early selection phenomenon. This certainly tells us something very important about attention. It tells us that attention can intervene in early perceptual processing. But it doesn't tell us very much about what attention actually is. It leaves many, very important questions unanswered. For example:

- Which brain areas are involved in attention?
- How is attention related to other cognitive processes, such as memory and action-planning?
- How does the brain direct attention to particular objects and particular places?

We will be exploring these questions in this section. This will allow us to see some of the power of experiments using functional neuroimaging – and also, to continue one of the themes of this chapter, to explore how neuroimaging data can be calibrated and reinforced with the results of electrophysiological experiments.

There are many different types of selective attention. Attention operates in all the sensory modalities. We can attend to sounds, smells, and tactile surfaces, as well as things that we see. The visual modality has probably been studied more than any other – although, as we saw in Chapter 1, experiments on auditory attention were very important in developing Broadbent's model of attention.

Even within vision there are different varieties of attention. We can attend to one object among others – to the unfamiliar bird in the flock of sparrows, for example. Or we can attend to one part of an object rather than another – to the bird's head or beak rather than its wings. Alternatively we can attend to places – to the place where we expect the bird to fly to next.

The experiments that we looked at in the previous section focused on the last of these types of visual attention. Subjects were asked to focus on a particular location on the screen (marked by a box) – a location at which a stimulus might or might not appear. Neuroscientists and psychologists call this phenomenon *spatially selective attention* (or *visuospatial attention*).

Let us start with the first of the questions identified earlier. Which brain areas are involved in spatially selective attention? Long before the discovery of fMRI, PET, or any of the other techniques we have been looking at, there was good evidence that spatial attention was under the control of brain areas in the frontal and parietal cortices. Much of this evidence came from patients with brain damage. Patients with unilateral spatial neglect (also known as *hemineglect*) have severe difficulties keeping track of and attending to objects on their left (including their own bodies). Hemineglect is most often seen after damage to the parietal cortex on the right side of the brain (with patients having difficulty attending to the *contralesional* side – the side opposite the damaged hemisphere). Animals that had had their parietal cortices lesioned showed similarly disturbed behaviors.

By its very nature, however, brain damage is an imprecise tool for locating cognitive functions in the brain. The damage is often very widespread and brings with it all sorts of other cognitive and motor problems. Animal studies are valuable but it is not always clear what they tell us about information processing in the human brain. The development of imaging technology gave neuroscientists a much more precise tool.

A number of studies carried out during the 1990s permitted researchers to identify a network of cortical areas implicated in visuospatial attention. The specific tasks varied, but all of the experiments involved subjects directing attention to stimuli in the periphery of their visual field without moving their eyes. This is very important. Typically, we attend to different objects in the visual field by making very quick (and unconscious) eye movements known as *saccadic eye movements*. Experimenters studying visuospatial attention, however, are interested in attention as a mechanism that operates independently of eye movements – a mechanism that can be directed at different peripheral areas while gaze is fixated on a central point. Researchers call this *covert attention*.

All of these experiments were carried out with PET. So, what was being measured was blood flow (as an indirect measure of cognitive activity). In order to identify the cortical areas specifically involved in attention, experimenters needed to separate out the blood flow associated with attention from the blood flow associated with visually processing the stimulus and the blood flow associated with planning and making the behavioral response required in the experiments. The standard way of doing this is by considering only differences in blood flow between experimental conditions and control conditions. The experimental conditions are the tasks designed to elicit the subject's attention. The control conditions might be simply asking the subject to fixate on the fixation point without directing their attention or presenting any stimuli, and/or presenting the stimuli without requiring any response.

Figure 11.8 summarizes a number of these studies. It identifies a network of areas in the parietal and frontal areas that are active during tasks that require subjects to direct covert attention to peripheral areas in the visual field. The existence of this frontoparietal cortical network is widely accepted among researchers into attention and has been confirmed by retrospective analyses of PET and fMRI data.

The simple fact of identifying a network of brain areas involved in the information processing associated with visuospatial attention does not in itself tell us much about how attention works, however. It answers the first of the three questions we identified at the beginning of this section, but not the second or the third. It does not tell us about how attention is related to other cognitive processes, such as memory or action-planning. And it does not tell us anything about how exactly the brain directs attention to particular locations in space.

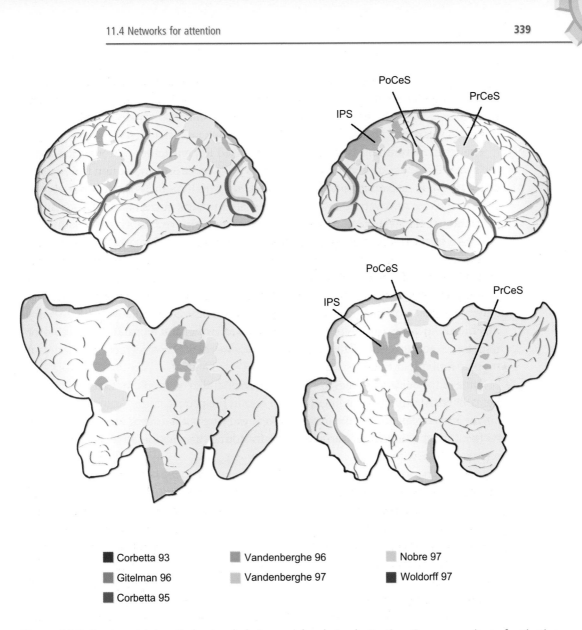

Figure 11.8 Frontoparietal cortical network during peripheral visual attention. Common regions of activation across studies include the intraparietal (IPS), postcentral (PoCeS), and precentral sulcus (PrCeS). (Adapted from Gazzaniga 2000)

Two hypotheses about visuospatial attention

In order to move beyond thinking about *where* the control of visuospatial attention takes place to thinking about *how* it takes place we need to start testing specific hypotheses. There are two dominant hypotheses about how visuospatial attention works.

The first hypothesis is that visuospatial attention exploits certain memory mechanisms. The basic idea here is that, in order to attend to a specific location, we need actively to remember that location. If this is right, then we would expect brain networks associated with spatial working memory to be active during tasks that involve attention.

The second hypothesis is that attention is linked to preparatory motor signals. Here the idea is that there are very close connections between directing attention to a particular location and preparing to move to that location. This hypothesis is intended to apply even in the case of covert attention. In covert attention the focus of attention changes even though the eyes do not move. The intention to move here is, presumably, the intention to move the eyes. The prediction generated by this hypothesis is that brain areas associated with motor planning will be active in tasks that exploit visuospatial attention.

The two hypotheses are not necessarily exclusive. The existence of a correlation between spatial working memory and the allocation of visuospatial attention does not rule out there being a close connection between attention and preparatory visuomotor responses – nor vice versa. This is fortunate, because there is considerable experimental support for both of them.

Some of the evidence comes from single-neuron studies on monkeys. Carol Colby and her collaborators made recordings from an area in the parietal cortex known as LIP (the *lateral intraparietal* area) while monkeys were carrying out a *delayed saccade task*. LIP is widely thought to play an important role in storing information about location over relatively short intervals.

In an ordinary saccade task the monkeys are trained to make a saccade (i.e. quickly move both eyes) from a central fixation point to a stimulus as soon as the stimulus appears. In a delayed saccade task the monkeys are trained not to make the saccade until the fixation point disappears – by which time the stimulus has disappeared (see Figure 11.9). When the fixation point disappears they then have to make a saccade to the location where the stimulus originally appeared. Success on the delayed saccade task

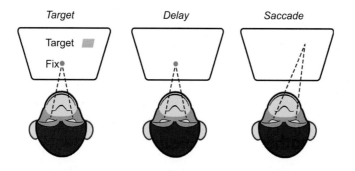

Figure 11.9 An illustration of a typical delayed saccade task. The monkeys are trained to withhold their saccade to the visual target until the fixation point disappears. Note that the head does not move during the task. (From White and Snyder 2007)

requires the monkeys to remember where the stimulus appeared if they are to make a successful saccade. This type of short-term memory about spatial location is typically called *spatial working memory*.

It turns out that the firing rates of neurons in LIP go up both when monkeys are performing delayed saccade tasks (and so exercising spatial working memory) and when they are carrying out peripheral attention tasks such as those discussed in the previous section. This electrophysiological evidence from monkeys is backed up by a wide range of neuroimaging studies carried out on humans. Both PET and fMRI studies have shown significant overlap between the brain areas activated in visuospatial attention tasks and those active during tasks that require subjects to store and manipulate in working memory information about spatial locations. The results of these studies are depicted in the two diagrams on the left-hand side in Figure 11.10.

We see very clearly in the diagram that, while there seem to be separate cortical networks for visuospatial attention and spatial working memory, these networks overlap very significantly in the parietal cortex. This is highly consistent with the results from the electrophysiological experiments.

We turn now to the relation between visuospatial attention and preparatory motor responses. The two diagrams on the right-hand side of Figure 11.10 report cross-experiment analyses. The experiments reported here all explored the relation between covert attention and saccadic eye movements. The diagrams superimpose the cortical networks thought to be involved in visuospatial attention onto the cortical networks implicated in saccadic eye movements. Research carried out in Maurizio Corbetta's laboratory at Washington University in St. Louis, for example, scanned subjects both during conditions that required them to shift attention while maintaining their gaze fixed on a fixation point and during conditions in which gaze and attention shifted simultaneously. As the diagrams show, there is significant overlap across the covert attention and the saccadic eye movement tasks both in the parietal and in the precentral region (where the overlap is much stronger than in the working memory experiments).

These results raise many interesting questions, which are currently being tackled both by neuroimagers and by electrophysiologists. The study of visuospatial attention is a very fast-moving, cutting-edge area. One reason for this is that it lends itself to the sort of triangulated approach that I have been trying to illustrate in this section and the previous one.

Visuospatial attention has different facets, and different techniques are better suited to some rather than others. Researchers are interested in the *time course* of visuospatial attention – that is to say, in tracing how attention is initiated and then develops over time. They are also interested in the *neural correlates* of attention – that is, in identifying which brain areas are involved when visuospatial attention is exercised. For studying the time course of attention we need to use techniques with a high temporal resolution. These include EEG and single-unit electrophysiology. In contrast, the high spatial resolution of neuroimaging techniques such as PET and fMRI makes them much more useful for studying the neural correlates of attention.

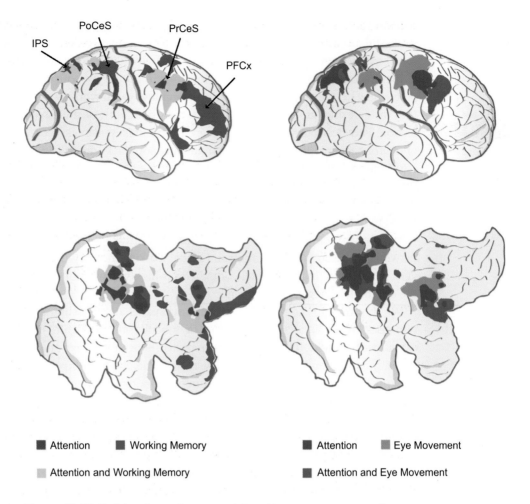

Figure 11.10 Peripheral attention vs. spatial working memory vs. saccadic eye movement across studies. Left: Regions active for peripheral attention (red), regions active for spatial working memory (blue), and regions of overlap (yellow). Note the remarkable overlap in parietal cortex, partial overlap in precentral region, and exclusive activation of prefrontal cortex (PFCx) for spatial working memory. Right: Comparison between peripheral attention (red) and saccadic eye movements (green). Note the strong overlap (magenta) in both parietal and precentral region. There is no activation in prefrontal cortex. (Adapted from Gazzaniga 2000)

What should have emerged very clearly from our discussion of visuospatial attention is that progress in this area depends upon combining and calibrating what is learnt from each of these techniques. We do not have any *direct* measures of cognitive activities such as visuospatial attention. But we do have the next best thing, which is a wide range of *indirect* measures. Single unit recordings, PET, fMRI, and EEG all give us very different perspectives on visuospatial attention. We can use some techniques to compensate for the weaknesses of others. And we have powerful tools for cross-checking and integrating information from different sources. We have seen how this works in the case of visuospatial attention. This is an excellent case study in how neuroscientists are moving towards the goal of providing a cognitive wiring diagram of the brain.

11.5 From data to maps: Problems and pitfalls

Working through our case study of visuospatial attention brought out some of the extraordinary power of neuroimaging techniques such as PET and fMRI. It is important not to get carried away, however. Neuroimaging has yielded unparalleled insight into the structure and organization of the mind – perhaps more so than anything else in the neuroscientist's toolkit. But, as I have stressed on several occasions, it is a tool that needs to be used with caution. We need to recognize that neuroimaging is *not* a direct picture of cognitive activity. It is easy to be seduced by the brightly colored images that emerge from software packages for interpreting neuroimaging data. These images look very much like maps of the brain thinking. And so it is easy to think that neuroimaging gives us a "window on the mind." In this section we will see why we need to be much more cautious.

From blood flow to cognition?

As we have stressed on a number of occasions, neuroimaging technologies only measure cognitive activity indirectly. FMRI measures the BOLD signal, while PET measures cerebral blood flow. There is nothing wrong with indirect measures per se. After all, large parts of science study the behavior of things that are too small to be directly observed. Think of sub-atomic particles such as electrons, neutrinos, or quarks, for example. Physicists can only measure the behavior of sub-atomic particles indirectly – by examining what happens in cloud chambers, linear accelerators, or particle colliders.

The issue with neuroimaging is not simply that it is indirect. The problem is that very little is known about the connections between what we can observe directly (the BOLD signal, for example) and what we are trying to measure indirectly (information processing in the brain). As we saw in some detail in section 4.5, there is a lively debate within neuroscience about the neural correlates of the BOLD signal. Researchers are calibrating fMRI data with electrophysiological techniques in order to try to work out whether the BOLD signal is correlated with the firing rates of populations of neurons, or whether it is correlated with the local field potentials (which are thought to reflect the inputs to neurons, rather than their outputs). We looked at some experimental evidence (from Logothetis and his collaborators) that seems to point to the second possibility.

But even if we had a conclusive answer to this question, we would still be a long way from a clear picture of the relation between variation in the BOLD signal and information processing in the brain. This is because we do not have any generally accepted models of how populations of neurons process information in particular brain areas – either as a function of their firing rates or as a function of their local field potentials. We do have models of neurally inspired information processing (derived from connectionist AI and computational neuroscience) that might point us in the right direction, but there remains a very significant theoretical gap between what we can measure directly and what we are trying to understand. One illustration of this is that the BOLD signal gives us no indication whether the activity it measures is excitatory or inhibitory – something that would presumably be rather important to the type of information processing being carried out.

Noise in the system?

One of the great strengths of neuroimaging technology is the spatial resolution it yields. In the case of fMRI, the basic spatial unit is called the *voxel*. We can think of this as a three-dimensional version of a pixel (the name is a combination of the words "volume" and "pixel"). The basic unit of data obtained from fMRI is the BOLD signal in each voxel. The spatial resolution is directly correlated with the size of the voxels – the smaller the voxel, the higher the spatial resolution. The problem, though, is that the strength of the signal is directly correlated with the size of the voxel – the smaller the voxel, the lower the signal strength.

For some brain areas, particularly those involving basic perceptual processing or simple motor behaviors (such as finger tapping), experimenters can design tasks that elicit strong signals even when the voxel size is small. Things are not so straightforward, however, for more complex types of processing – particularly those performed by distributed networks of neural areas. Here it is often necessary to increase the voxel size in order to capture smaller fluctuations in the BOLD signal. Unsurprisingly, this decreases the spatial resolution. But it also has a less expected consequence.

Increasing the voxel size increases the range of different types of brain tissue occurring in each voxel. Ideally, a voxel would simply contain the cell bodies of individual neurons. This would allow us to conclude that changes in the BOLD signal in a particular voxel are directly generated by activity in those neurons. Things are much messier, however, if the voxel includes extraneous material, such as white matter or cerebrospinal fluid. This can distort the signal, giving rise to what are known as *partial volume effects*. It can also happen that a single voxel contains more than one cell type, whereas neuroimaging data are standardly interpreted on the tacit assumption that voxels are homogeneous.

There are other ways in which noise can get into the system. One of the key culprits here is the fact that everybody's brain is subtly different. If neuroscientists are to be able to compare fMRI data across subjects, or to make meaningful comparisons across different subjects, the data need to be *normalized* – that is, the data from each subject need to be reinterpreted on a brain atlas that uses a common coordinate system, or what is known as a *stereotactic map*. This requires very complicated statistical techniques, which themselves may introduce distortion in the data.

It should also be noted that there are many different brain atlases, such as the Talairach–Tournoux atlas, the MNI atlas from the Montreal Institute of Neurology, and the Population-Average, Landmark and Surface-Based (PALS) atlas recently developed by David Van Essen at Washington University in St. Louis. Since different research groups often use a different atlas, this can make the business of comparing and contrasting different studies a tricky undertaking.

Functional connectivity vs. effective connectivity

One of the main reasons that neuroscientists are interested in neuroimaging techniques such as fMRI and PET is that they make it possible to identify networks and circuits of brain areas involved in particular tasks. As we saw earlier in this chapter, current research in neuroscience is governed by two basic principles. According to the *principle of segregation*, the cerebral cortex is divided into segregated areas with distinct neuronal populations. These different areas perform different information-processing tasks. According to the *principle of integration*, on the other hand, most information-processing tasks are carried out by distributed networks of brain areas.

The fundamental importance of neuroimaging techniques to modern neuroscience is directly associated with these two principles. The high spatial resolution of PET and fMRI allows neuroscientists to focus on anatomically segregated brain areas. At the same time, PET and fMRI allow neuroscientists to examine the whole brain while patients are performing specific tasks. This allows them to examine what is going on in different brain areas simultaneously and hence to identify the distributed neural networks that are recruited by the task the subject is performing. We saw a very good example of this earlier in the chapter when we looked at how researchers have isolated a frontoparietal cortical network that seems to be specialized for visuospatial attention. Further experiments were then able to explore the relation between this network of brain areas and the networks involved in, for example, the control of saccadic eye movements and short-term memory for spatial locations.

This is how neuroimaging helps us to understand the *connectivity* of the brain. It allows us to visualize how information processing is distributed across different brain areas. The type of connectivity involved here is very different from the anatomical connectivity that we looked at earlier. The anatomical connectivity of the brain is a matter of anatomical connections between different brain areas – which brain areas project to which others. Neuroimaging, in contrast, allows neuroscientists to study the connectivity of the brain when it is actually processing information. To continue with the wiring diagram metaphor that we used earlier, studying functional connectivity gives a wiring diagram of the brain as an information-processing machine.

But the wiring diagram that we get from fMRI and PET is still not quite the kind of diagram that we are looking for. The basic idea of cognitive science is that cognition is information processing. This offers a very natural way of understanding the principle of integration. Why does performing specific tasks involve a particular network of brain areas? Because different brain areas perform different parts of the overall information-processing task. This is very clear in the visual cortex, where (as we have seen several times) different anatomical areas seem to be specialized for processing different types of information.

This way of thinking about how information is processed in the brain brings with it the idea that information flows through a distributed brain network. Again, we have seen examples of this in the neuroscience of vision. The distinction between the dorsal pathway (specialized for action) and the ventral pathway (specialized for object identification and recognition) is a distinction between two different routes along which information from the retina can travel through the brain.

It is very important to realize, however, that neither PET nor fMRI tells us anything *directly* about how information flows through the brain. A single experiment can tell us which brain areas are simultaneously active while subjects are performing a particular task, but this does not tell us about how information flows through those different areas. It does not tell us, for example, about the order in which the areas are active, or about the direction that the information takes. The diagrams that present the results of neuroimaging experiments only show which areas "light up together." They identify a network of areas that are simultaneously active when certain tasks are performed. But they do not tell us anything about how information is processed within that network. The diagrams only identify correlations between the activity levels of different brain areas.

Neuroimaging is a very useful tool for studying the connectivity of the brain as an information-processing machine, but we need to recognize that it has limitations. Some of these limitations are captured in a very useful distinction made within the neuroimaging community. This is the distinction between *functional connectivity and effective connectivity.*

Functional connectivity is a statistical notion. It is standardly defined in terms of statistical correlations between levels of activity in physically separate parts of the brain. We can unpack this a little by looking at some of the basic principles of analyzing fMRI experiments. Simplifying somewhat, we can identify two basic steps. The first step is to identify, for each individual voxel, how changes in level of the BOLD signal within that voxel are correlated with changes in some experimentally controlled variable. This experimentally controlled variable is determined by the particular information-processing task that experimenters are trying to study. In, for example, the studies of attention that we looked at in the previous section the experimentally controlled variable is how the subject allocates attention. So, the first step in analyzing the data coming out of the scanner in those experiments is to work out, for each voxel, the degree to which changes in the level of the BOLD signal are correlated with important changes in how the subject allocates attention.

Once the correlations have been worked out for individual voxels, the next step is to develop what is called a *statistical parametric map* (SPM). The SPM shows which voxels have BOLD signal levels significantly correlated with the task being performed. It is important to look closely at how SPMs are created. One very important feature is that the connections between specific voxels are not taken into account in creating the SPM. The analysis is based purely on the correlations between each voxel and the experimental variables. What the SPM identifies are system elements (voxels and, derivatively, the brain areas that they make up) that are correlated in the same way with the task. This tells us nothing about how those system elements are related to each other.

At best, therefore, functional connectivity is a matter of statistical correlations between distinct brain areas. We need more than functional connectivity if we are to have a wiring diagram of how the brain works as an information-processing machine. What we really need is what neuroscientists call *effective connectivity*. Effective connectivity is a measure of how neural systems actually interact. Studying effective connectivity is studying the influence one neural system exerts on another. These notions of interaction and influence are *causal* notions. They capture the idea that information processing is a causal process. Information flows through different brain areas in a particular order. What happens to the information at earlier stages affects how it is processed at later stages.

Neuroimaging is much better at telling us about functional connectivity than about effective connectivity. This is just a simple fact about the technology and how the data it produces are interpreted, widely recognized within the neuroimaging community, but not as well known as it should be outside that community. PET and fMRI are tools specialized for studying correlation, not causation.

This does not mean that neuroimaging data cannot be used to develop models of effective connectivity. Quite the contrary. There are all sorts of ways in which neuroimaging data can contribute to our understanding of effective connectivity in the brain. One way of deriving conclusions about effective connectivity from neuroimaging data is to design a series of experiments in a way that yields information about the flow of information. We looked at a very nice example of this back in section 3.4. Steve Petersen and his collaborators were able to draw significant conclusions about the stages of lexical processing from a series of PET experiments using the paired-subtraction paradigm. The model that they developed is plainly a contribution to our understanding of the effective connectivity of the brain.

Exercise 11.3 Look back at the lexical processing experiments described in section 3.4 and explain in your own words how the experimental design overcomes some of the problems raised by the distinction between functional and effective connectivity.

It is also the case that statisticians and economists have developed a number of theoretical tools to try to extract information about causation by comparing what are known as time-series data – i.e. data about how a particular system evolves over time. Statistical methods such as Granger causality can be used to try to work out the extent to which the evolution of one time series (such as the BOLD signal from a given neural area) predicts the evolution of another time series (the BOLD signal from a different neural area). If certain background conditions are satisfied, these methods can be used to give information about the effective connectivity between the two areas – on the assumption that predictability is likely to be explained by a causal connection. Neuroscientists are starting to use these statistical techniques to explore effective connectivity in the brain – see the further reading section for an example.

Moreover, as I have been stressing throughout this chapter, the results of neuroimaging can always be calibrated and triangulated with other tools and techniques, such as EEG and electrophysiology. Our discussion of the locus of selection problem showed how data from neuroimaging, EEG, and electrophysiology can be combined to develop a model of the effective connectivity of covert attention.

Nonetheless, we do have to be careful in how we interpret the results of neuroimaging experiments. In particular, we need to be very careful not to interpret experiments as telling us about effective connectivity when they are really only telling us about functional connectivity. We must be very careful not to draw conclusions about the causal relations between brain areas and how information flows between them from data that only tell us about correlations between BOLD signal levels in those areas.

Summary

This chapter has continued our exploration of the large-scale organization of the mind. Whereas Chapter 10 focused on issues of modularity, this chapter has looked at some of the ways in which cognitive neuroscience can help us to construct a wiring diagram for the mind. We began by highlighting the complex relations between functional structure and anatomical structure in the brain and then looked at some of the techniques for tracing anatomical connections between different brain areas. Completely different tools are required to move from anatomical connectivity to functional connectivity. We looked at various techniques for mapping the brain through measuring electrical activity and blood flow and blood oxygen levels. These techniques all operate at different degrees of temporal and spatial resolution. As we saw in two case studies, each having to do with a different aspect of the complex phenomenon of attention, mapping the functional structure of the brain requires combining and calibrating different techniques. At the end of the chapter we reviewed some of the pitfalls in interpreting neuroimaging data.

Checklist

It is a basic principle of neuroscience that the cerebral cortex is divided into segregated areas with distinct neuronal populations (the *principle of segregation*)

(1) These different regions are distinguished in terms of the types of cell they contain and the density of those cells. This can be studied using staining techniques.

(2) This *anatomical* classification of neural areas can serve as a basis for classifying cortical regions according to their function.

(3) Neuroscientists can study *anatomical connectivity* (i.e. develop an anatomical wiring diagram of the brain) by using techniques such as tract tracing or diffusion tractography.

(4) Most of the evidence comes from animal studies. Neuroscientists have developed well worked out models of anatomical connectivity in macaque monkeys, rats, and cats.

Neuroscientists also adopt the *principle of integration* – that cognitive functioning involves the coordinated activity of networks of different brain areas

(1) Identifying these networks requires going beyond anatomical activity by studying what goes on in the brain when it is performing particular tasks.

(2) Some of the techniques for studying the organization of the mind focus on the brain's electrical activity. These include electrophysiology, EEG, and MEG.

(3) These techniques all have high temporal resolution – particularly EEG when it is used to measure ERPs. But the spatial resolution is lower (except for electrophysiology using microelectrodes).

(4) Other techniques measure blood flow (PET) and levels of blood oxygen (fMRI). These techniques have high spatial resolution, but lower temporal resolution.

The *locus of selection* problem is the problem of determining whether attention operates early in perceptual processing, or upon representations of objects. It provides a good illustration of how neuroscientists can combine different techniques

(1) The problem has been studied using EEG to measure ERPs. Attentional effects appear relatively early in the ERP wave following the presentation of a visual stimulus.

(2) These results can be calibrated with PET studies mapping stages in the ERP wave onto processing in particular brain areas. This calibration reveals attentional effects in areas such as V2 and V4, which carry out very basic processing of perceptual features.

(3) This resolution of the locus of selection problem seems to be confirmed by single-unit recordings in monkeys.

The locus of selection problem focuses on spatially selective (or visuospatial) attention. Neuroimaging techniques can help identify the neural circuits responsible for attention

(1) Preliminary evidence from brain-damaged patients (e.g. with hemispatial neglect) points to the involvement of frontal and parietal areas in visuospatial attention.

(2) This has been confirmed by many experiments on covert attention using PET and fMRI.

(3) PET and fMRI experiments on humans, together with single-neuron experiments on monkeys, have shown that tasks involving visuospatial attention also generate activation in brain networks responsible for planning motor behavior and for spatial working memory.

The discussion of attention shows that neuroimaging is a very powerful tool for studying cognition. It is not a "window on the mind," however, and neuroimaging data should be interpreted with caution

(1) Neuroimaging techniques can only measure cognitive activity indirectly. PET measures blood flow and fMRI measures the BOLD signal. There is a controversy in neuroscience about what type of

neural activity is correlated with the BOLD signal (see section 4.5) – and no worked out theory about how that neural activity functions to process information.

(2) There are many opportunities for noise to get into the system in neuroimaging experiments. Partial volume effects can occur when the voxel size is large and distortions can occur when data are being normalized to allow comparison across subjects.

(3) Neuroimaging techniques are much better at telling us about *functional connectivity* (correlations between activation levels in different brain areas as a task is performed) than about *effective connectivity* (how information flows between different brain areas and how they influence each other).

Further reading

The explosion of interest in cognitive neuroscience in the last couple of decades has generated a huge literature. For keeping up to date with contemporary research, the journal *Trends in Cognitive Science* regularly contains accessible survey articles. Authoritative review articles on most of the key topics studied by cognitive neuroscientists can be found in *The Cognitive Neurosciences III*, edited by Michael Gazzaniga (Gazzaniga 2004). The two earlier editions (Gazzaniga 1995 and 2000) also contain much useful material. Gazzaniga is one of the authors of an influential textbook on cognitive neuroscience (Gazzaniga, Ivry, and Mangun 2008 – the third edition). Ch. 4 is a useful introduction to the methods of cognitive neuroscience. Also see Baars and Gage 2010.

Zeki 1978 was one of the first papers to identify functional specialization in the primate visual system. David Van Essen's work is accessibly presented in Van Essen and Gallant 2001. The much-cited paper discussed in the text is Felleman and Van Essen 1991. Reviews of other classic work can be found in Colby and Goldberg 1999 and Melcher and Colby 2008. Orban, Van Essen, and Vanduffel 2004 is an interesting discussion of the challenges in comparing the neurobiology of cognitive function across humans and macaque monkeys. Also see Passingham 2009. An interesting trend in recent discussions of anatomical connectivity has been the use of mathematical tools from graph theory – in particular the idea of small-world networks. There is a very useful introduction in Bassett and Bullmore 2006. Jirsa and McIntosh 2007 is a collection of up-to-date surveys of different aspects of neural connectivity. For article-length surveys see Ramnani *et al*. 2004 and Bullmore and Sporns 2009. Bressler *et al*. 2008 uses Granger causality to explore effective connectivity in the neural basis of visual-spatial attention.

There has been much discussion of the pitfalls and advantages of using neuroimaging techniques to study cognitive function in the human mind. In addition to research on the neural basis of the BOLD signal discussed in Chapter 4 (see the references there), researchers have focused on the methodology of inferring cognitive function from selective patterns of activation. See, for example, Henson 2006 and Poldrack 2006. For a recent review of the current state of fMRI from a leading researcher see Logothetis 2008. Also see Ashby 2011, Charpac and Stefanovic 2012, Machery 2012, and Poldrack, Mumford, and Nichols 2011.

For a recent survey of research into selective attention see Hopfinger, Luck, and Hillyard 2004. Experimental work reported in section 11.3 is described more fully in Luck and Ford 1998. Stephen Luck is the author of an important textbook on ERP techniques (Luck 2005). The introductory chapter can be downloaded from the online resources. See also his co-edited volume Luck and Kappenman 2011.

Humphreys, Duncan, and Treisman 1999 contains many useful papers on the psychology and neuroscience of attention, as does Posner 2004. For more details of the findings discussed in section 11.4 see Chelazzi and Corbetta 2000. Other good reviews on a wide variety of attention phenomena can be found in chapters 8 and 10 of Baars and Gage 2010, Carrasco 2011, and Chun, Golomb, and Turk-Browne 2011.

CHAPTER TWELVE

A case study: Exploring mindreading

Overview

The two previous chapters in this section have explored a key question in thinking about the architecture of the mind: What is the large-scale organization of the mind? In Chapter 10 we looked at different models of modularity. The basic idea of modularity is that the mind is organized into dedicated cognitive systems (modules) that perform specialized information-processing tasks. In this chapter we explore a particular cognitive system that has received an enormous amount of attention from cognitive scientists in recent years – both from those sympathetic to ideas of modularity and from those opposed to it. We will look at what is often called *mindreading*. We can think of this as a very general label for the skills and abilities that allow us to make sense of other people and to coordinate our behavior with theirs. Our mindreading skills are fundamental to social understanding and social coordination.

Cognitive scientists have developed a sophisticated information-processing model of mindreading. This model emerged initially from studies of pretending in young children. Section 12.1 presents the information-processing model of pretense proposed by the developmental psychologist Alan Leslie. According to Leslie, pretending exploits the same information-processing mechanisms as mindreading. Section 12.2 looks at some experimental evidence supporting Leslie's model. Some of this evidence comes from the *false belief task*, testing young children's understanding that other people can have mistaken beliefs about the world.

The central feature of Leslie's model is what he calls the *theory of mind mechanism* (TOMM). The TOMM's job is to identify and reason about other people's *propositional attitudes* (complex mental states, such as beliefs, desires, hopes, and fears). In section 12.3 we look at a model of the entire mindreading system developed by the developmental psychologist and autism specialist Simon Baron-Cohen in response to a wide range of experimental data both from normal development and from autism and other pathologies.

In section 12.4 we focus on the question of why it takes so long for children to succeed on the false belief task if, as Leslie believes, the TOMM mechanism emerges when children start to engage in pretend play. We look at two different explanations – one from Leslie and one from Josef Perner (who originally developed the false belief task).

Section 12.5 introduces an alternative way of thinking about mindreading. This alternative view holds that mindreading takes place via processes of simulation. Instead of having dedicated information-processing systems for identifying and reasoning about other people's mental states, we make sense of their behavior by running our "ordinary" information-processing systems offline in order to simulate how other people will solve a particular problem, or react to a particular situation.

Finally, in section 12.6 we turn to the cognitive neuroscience of mindreading. We explore how some of the techniques and technologies presented in Chapter 11 have been used to test and refine the different approaches to mindreading discussed in earlier sections.

12.1   Pretend play and metarepresentation

Developmental psychologists think that the emergence of pretend play is a major milestone in cognitive and social development. Children start to engage in pretend play at a very young age, some as early as 13 months. Normal infants are capable of engaging in fairly sophisticated types of pretend play by the end of their second year. The evidence here is both anecdotal and experimental. Developmental psychologists such as Jean Piaget have carried out very detailed longitudinal studies of individual children over long periods of time. There have also been many experiments exploring infants' emerging capacities for pretend play.

The development of pretend play in infancy appears to follow a fairly standard trajectory. The most basic type is essentially *self-directed* – with the infant pretending to carry out some familiar activity. The infant might, for example, pretend to drink from an empty cup, or to eat from a spoon with nothing on it. The next stage is *other-directed*, with the infant pretending that some object has properties it doesn't have. An example of this might be the infant's pretending that a toy vehicle makes a sound, or that a doll is saying something. A more sophisticated form of pretense comes with what is sometimes called *object substitution*. This is when the infant pretends that some object is a different object and acts accordingly – pretends that a banana is a telephone, for example, and talks into it. Infants are also capable of pretense that involves imaginary objects. Imaginary friends are a well-known phenomenon.

Pretend play engages some fairly sophisticated cognitive abilities. Some forms of pretend play are linguistic in form and so exploit the young infant's emerging linguistic abilities. Others exploit the infant's understanding of the different functions that objects can play. A common denominator in all instances of pretend play is that in some sense the infant is able to represent objects and properties not perceptible in the immediate environment – or at least, not perceptible in the object that is the focus of the pretense (since there may be a telephone elsewhere in the room, for example).

The significance of pretend play

Alan Leslie calls the infant's basic representations of the environment its *primary representations*. Primary representations include both what the infant perceives, and its stored knowledge of the world. All the evidence is that infants, both language-using and prelinguistic, have a sophisticated representational repertoire. Without this sophisticated representational repertoire, pretend play would be impossible.

Leslie's model of infant pretense starts off from three basic observations:

1 *Pretend play in the infant depends crucially on how the infant represents the world (and hence on her primary representations).* If an infant pretends that a banana is a telephone then she must be representing the banana to start with. The infant is in some sense taking her representation of a banana and making it do the job of a representation of a telephone. Similarly, the infant cannot represent a toy car as making a noise unless she is representing the car.

2 *We cannot explain what is going on in pretend play simply with reference to the infant's primary representations.* We cannot assume that the infant is somehow coordinating her banana representation and her telephone representation. The problem is that the primary representation and the pretend representation typically contradict each other. After all, the banana is a banana, not a telephone.

3 *The pretend representations must preserve their ordinary meanings in pretend play.* During pretend play the infant cannot lose touch of the fact that, although she is pretending that it is a telephone, what she has in front of her is really a banana. Likewise, representing the banana as a telephone requires representing it as having the properties that telephones standardly have.

Combining these three ideas leads Leslie to the idea that, although representations featuring in pretend play have to preserve their usual meaning, they cannot in other respects be functioning as primary representations. Pretend representations are somehow "quarantined" from ordinary primary representations. If this sort of quarantining did not take place, then the infant's representations of the world would be completely chaotic – one and the same cup would be both empty and contain water, for example. The key problem is to explain how this quarantining takes place.

Leslie's explanation of how primary representations are quarantined exploits a very basic parallel between how representations function in pretend play and how they function when we are representing other people's mental states in mindreading. When we represent what other people believe or desire, we do so with representations that are also quarantined from the rest of our thinking about the world.

Suppose, for example, that I utter the sentence "Sarah believes that the world is flat." I am asserting something about Sarah – namely, that she believes that the world is flat. But I am certainly not saying that the world is flat. If I were to utter the words "the world is flat" on their own, then I would standardly be making an assertion about the world. But when those very same words come prefixed by the phrase "Sarah believes that …" they function very differently. They are no longer being used to talk about the world. I am using them to talk about Sarah's state of mind. They have become *decoupled* from their usual function.

Leslie on pretend play and metarepresentation

Let us look at this in more detail. When I describe Sarah as believing that the world is flat the phrase "the world is flat" is being used to describe how Sarah herself represents the world. Philosophers and psychologists typically describe this as a case of *metarepresentation*. Metarepresentation occurs when a representation is used to represent another representation, rather than to represent the world. The fact that there is metarepresentation going on changes how words and mental representations behave. They no longer refer directly to the world. But they still have their basic meaning – if they lost their basic meaning then they couldn't do the job of capturing how someone else represents the world.

The basic picture is summarized in Figure 12.1. As the figure shows, my primary representations can serve two functions. They can represent the world *directly*. This is the standard, or default use. But they can also be used to metarepresent someone else's primary representations. This is what goes on when we engage in mindreading.

The heart of Leslie's model of pretend play is the idea that primary representations function in exactly the same way when they are used in pretend play and when they are used to metarepresent someone else's state of mind. In both cases, primary representations are decoupled from their usual functions. In fact, Leslie argues, the mechanism that decouples primary representations from their usual functions in the context of pretend play is exactly the same mechanism that decouples primary representations from their usual functions in mindreading. For Leslie, pretend play is

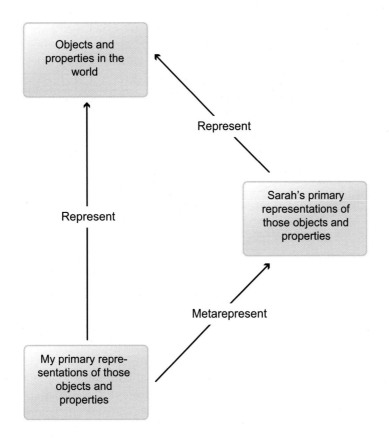

Figure 12.1 An example of metarepresentation. Metarepresentation involves second-order representations of representations. In this example I am representing Sarah's representations of certain objects and properties in the world.

best understood as a type of metarepresentation. The structure of Leslie's model is outlined in Figure 12.2.

He develops the model in a way that falls neatly within the scope of the physical symbol system hypothesis, as developed in Part III. The physical symbol system hypothesis tells us how to think about primary representations. It tells us that those primary representations are physical symbol structures, built up out of basic symbols. It also tells us that information processing is achieved by manipulating and transforming those representations.

So, suppose that we have an account of what those physical symbols are and the sort of operations and transformations that can be performed on them. Suppose that this account is adequate for explaining what goes on when primary representations are being used in their usual sense. This will give us a physical symbol system model of the left-hand side of Figure 12.2. How might this be extended to a model of the right-hand side of Figure 12.2? How can we extend a model of how primary representations work to a model of metarepresentation that will work for pretend play?

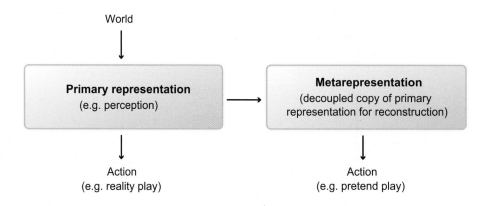

Figure 12.2 The general outlines of Leslie's model of pretend play. (Adapted from Leslie 1987)

Leslie thinks that we need to supplement our account of how primary representations function with two extra components. Adding these two extra components will give us an information-processing model of pretend play. The first component is a way of marking the fact that a primary representation has been decoupled and is now being used for pretend play. The second is a way of representing the relation between agents and decoupled representations.

Leslie proposes that the first of these is achieved by a form of quotation device. In ordinary language we use quotation marks to indicate that words are being decoupled from their normal function. In fact, we often do this when we are reporting what other people have said. So, for example, the following two ways of reporting what Sarah said when she expressed her belief that the world is flat are more or less equivalent:

(1) Sarah said that the world is flat.
(2) Sarah said: "The world is flat."

The second report contains a device that makes explicit the decoupling that is achieved implicitly in the first report. His suggestion, then, is that the physical symbol system responsible for pretend play contains some sort of quotation device that can be attached to primary representations to mark that they are available for pretend play.

Exercise 12.1 (1) and (2) are not completely equivalent. Explain why not.

How are decoupled primary representations processed in pretend play? As we saw from our three observations, the relation between decoupled primary representations and ordinary representations in pretend play is very complex. When an infant pretends that a banana is a telephone, she is not transforming the banana representation into a telephone representation. Her banana representation remains active, but it is not functioning in the way that banana representations usually do. Likewise for her telephone representation, which is in some way quarantined from her knowledge that telephones are not usually banana-shaped.

Leslie's solution is that the metarepresention system contains a special operation, which he calls the PRETEND operation. The subject of the PRETEND operation is an agent (which may be the pretending infant himself). The PRETEND operation is applied to decoupled primary representations. But these are not pure decoupled representations. The essence of pretend play is the complex interplay between ordinary primary representations and decoupled primary representations. Leslie's model aims to capture this with the idea that decoupled representations are, as he puts it, *anchored* to parts of primary representations.

Let's go back to our example of the infant pretending that the banana is a telephone. What happens here is that the infant's representation of the banana is decoupled and then anchored to her primary representation of a telephone. Leslie would represent what is going on here in the following way:

I PRETEND "*This banana*: it is a telephone."

The object of the PRETEND operation is the complex representation: "*This banana*: it is a telephone." As the quotation marks indicate, the complex representation as a whole is decoupled. But it is made up of two representations – a (decoupled) representation of a banana and an ordinary representation of a telephone. The ordinary representation of the telephone is the anchor for the decoupled representation of the banana.

The details of Leslie's model of pretense can be seen in Figure 12.3. As we see, information goes from central cognitive systems into what Leslie calls the Expression Raiser.

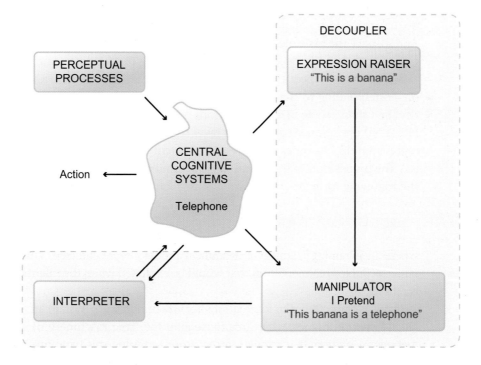

Figure 12.3 Leslie's Decoupler model of pretense. This model makes explicit how the right-hand side of Figure 12.2 is supposed to work. (Adapted from Leslie 1987)

This is the system that decouples primary representations – by placing them within some analog of quotation marks. Decoupled primary representations can then be fed into the Manipulator, which applies the PRETEND operation as described earlier. The job of the Interpreter is to relate the output of the Manipulator to what the infant is currently perceiving. The Interpreter essentially controls the episode of pretend play. Pretend play requires certain inferences (for example – the inference that, since the telephone is ringing, I must answer it). These are implemented in the Interpreter, using general information about telephones stored in central systems.

One important feature of Leslie's model is that it explains both how infants can engage in pretend play, and how they can understand pretense in other people. In Figure 12.3 the infant herself is the agent of the PRETEND operation, but the agent could equally be someone else. This allows the infant to engage in collaborative pretend play – and, moreover, gives her an important tool for making sense of the people she is interacting with.

The link to mindreading

Understanding that other people are pretending is itelf a form of mindreading. In this sense, therefore, Leslie's model of pretense is already a model of mindreading. But, as Leslie himself points out, the basic mechanism of metarepresentation at the heart of the model can be applied much more widely to explain other forms of mindreading. This is because many forms of mindreading exploit decoupled representations, as we saw earlier. And so, once the basic mechanism of decoupling is in place, being able to perform other types of mindreading depends upon understanding the corresponding operations.

So, we might expect there to be operations BELIEVE, DESIRE, HOPE, FEAR, and so on, corresponding to the different types of mental state that a mindreader can identify in other people. These operations will all function in the same way as the PRETEND operation. At an abstract level these operations are all applied to decoupled representations. In order to represent an agent as believing a particular proposition (say, the proposition that it is raining), the mindreader needs to represent something of the following form:

Agent BELIEVES "It is raining."

where "it is raining" signifies a decoupled primary representation. This is exactly the same decoupled representation that would be exploited when the infant pretends that it is raining.

If this is right, then the foundations for the mindreading system are laid during the second year of infancy, when infants acquire the basic machinery of decoupling and metarepresentation. It is a long journey from acquiring this basic machinery to being able to mindread in the full sense. Mindreading is a very sophisticated ability that continues to develop throughout the first years of life. Many of the operations that are exploited in older children's and adults' mindreading systems are much harder to acquire than the PRETEND operation. There is robust evidence, for example, that young children only acquire the ability to represent other people's beliefs at around the age of 4 – we will look at this evidence in more detail in section 12.4. And it is not really until late childhood or early adolescence that children even begin to grasp the psychological complexities that are regularly exploited by novelists and filmmakers.

12.2 Metarepresentation, autism, and theory of mind

Before going on (in the next section) to explore in more detail the developmental trajectory of mindreading, we need to look at some of the empirical evidence for Leslie's model of pretense. After all, we need to have some reason to think that the model actually captures what is going on in infancy. The basic idea behind Leslie's model is that pretend play involves metarepresentation. But why should we believe that?

In developing his model Leslie placed considerable weight on studies of children with autism. Autism is a developmental disorder that has been increasingly discussed and studied in recent years. Autism typically emerges in toddlers and the symptoms are often detectable before the age of 2. The disorder is strongly suspected to be genetic in origin, although its genetic basis remains poorly understood. For psychologists and cognitive scientists, autism is a very interesting disorder because it typically involves deficits in social understanding, social coordination, and communication. But these social and communicative problems are not typically accompanied by general cognitive impairments. Autistic subjects can have very high IQs, for example. Their problems seem to be relatively circumscribed, although autistics often have sensory and motor problems, in addition to difficulties with language.

One feature of autism that particularly sparked Leslie's attention is that autistic children have well-documented problems with pretend play. This has been revealed by many studies showing that pretend play in autistic children is very impoverished, in comparison both with much younger normal children and with mentally retarded children of the same age. In fact, the phenomenon is so widespread in autism that it has become a standard diagnostic tool. Parents are often first alerted to autism in their children by their apparent inability to engage in pretense and make-believe – and by the child's inability to understand what other people are up to when they try to incorporate the child into pretend play. And one of the first questions that clinicians ask when parents suspect that their child has autism is whether the child engages in pretend play.

This well-documented fact about autistic children is particularly interesting in the context of the other problems that autistic children have. These problems cluster around the very set of abilities in social understanding and social coordination that we are collectively terming mindreading. In 1985 Leslie was one of the authors of a very influential paper arguing that autistic children had a very specific mindreading deficit – the other two authors were Simon Baron-Cohen and Uta Frith.

Using the false belief task to study mindreading

Baron-Cohen, Leslie, and Frith studied three populations of children. The first group were autistic, aged between 6 and 16 (with a mean of 11;11 – i.e. 11 years and 11 months). The second group of children suffered from Down syndrome, which is a chromosomal disorder usually accompanied by mental disability, often severe. The Down syndrome children varied from 7 to 17 years old (with a mean of 10). The third group (the control group) were children with no cognitive or social disorders, aged from 3;5 to 6, with a mean of 4;5.

It is very interesting to look at the overall cognitive ability of the three different populations, as measured on standard tests of verbal and nonverbal mental age, such as the British Picture Vocabulary test (which measures the ability to match words to line drawings) and the Leiter International Performance Scale (which measures nonverbal abilities such as memory and visualization). The normal children scored lowest on the nonverbal measures. The normal children's mean nonverbal mental age of 4;5 compared to a mean nonverbal mental age of 5;1 for the Down syndrome group and 9;3 for the autistic group. The Down syndrome group had the lowest verbal mental age (with a mean of 2;11). The verbal skills of the autistic group were significantly ahead of the normal children (with a mean verbal mental age of 5;5). These numbers are all depicted in Table 12.1.

Baron-Cohen, Leslie, and Frith tested the mindreading abilities of the three groups by using a very famous experimental paradigm known as the *false belief test*. The false belief test was first developed by the developmental psychologists Heinz Wimmer and Joseph Perner in an article published in 1983.

There are many different versions of the false belief test, but they all explore whether young children understand that someone might have mistaken beliefs about the world. There is a very basic contrast between belief, on the one hand, and knowledge, say, on the other. Consider knowledge. There is no way in which I can know that some state of affairs holds without that state of affairs actually holding. Knowledge is an example of what philosophers sometimes call *factive* states.

Exercise 12.2 Can you give examples of other mental states that are factive in this sense?

TABLE 12.1 The three groups studied in Baron-Cohen, Leslie, and Frith 1985		
POPULATION	**MEAN VERBAL MENTAL AGE**	**MEAN NONVERBAL MENTAL AGE**
Normal group	4;5	4;5
Down syndrome group	2;11	5;1
Autistic group	5;5	9;3

In contrast, beliefs are not factive. I cannot have false knowledge, but I can (all too easily) have false beliefs. This has implications for what is involved in understanding what belief is. If a young child does not understand the possibility that someone might have false beliefs about the world, then there seems to be no sense in which they understand what is involved in believing something. They cannot possess the concept of belief. And this, in turn, tells us something about their mindreading skills. Children who do not understand the concept of belief are lacking a fundamental component of the mindreading toolkit.

But how do we test whether children understand the possibility of false belief? This is where the false belief test comes into the picture. The experimental set-up used by Baron-Cohen, Leslie, and Frith is a variant of Wimmer and Perner's original false belief test. It is depicted in Figure 12.4. The child being tested is seated in front of an experimenter, who

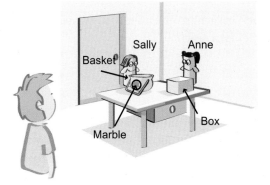

(a) Sally places her marble in basket.

(b) Exit Sally.

(c) Anne transfers Sally's marble to box.

(d) Re-enter Sally. The experimenter asks: Where will Sally look for the marble?

Figure 12.4 The task used by Baron-Cohen, Leslie, and Frith to test for children's understanding of false belief. (Adapted from Baron-Cohen, Leslie, and Frith 1985)

has two puppets, Sally and Anne. Between the child and the experimenter is a table with a basket and box. In front of the child, Sally places a marble in the basket and then leaves the room. While she is away Anne transfers the marble from the basket to the box. Sally then returns. The experimenter asks the child: "Where will Sally look for her marble?" (or, in some versions of the test, "Where does Sally think the marble is?").

The point of the experiment is that, although the child saw the marble being moved, Sally did not. So, if the child has a clear grip on the concept of belief and understands that it is possible to have false beliefs, then she will answer that Sally will look in the basket, since nothing has happened that will change Sally's belief that the marble is in the basket. If, on the other hand, the child fails to understand the possibility of false belief, then she will answer that Sally will look for the marble where it in fact is – namely, in the box.

Exercise 12.3 Explain in your own words the logic behind the false belief task. Do you think it succeeds in testing a young child's understanding of false belief?

Interpreting the results

The results of the experiment were very striking. The main question that the experimenters asked was the obvious one, which they called the Belief Question: "Where will Sally look for her marble?" But they also wanted to make sure that all the children understood what was going on. So they checked that each child knew which doll was which and asked two further questions:

"Where was the marble in the beginning?"   (the Memory Question)
"Where is the marble really?"   (the Reality Question)

Exercise 12.4 Explain in your own words the purpose of asking these two extra questions.

Baron-Cohen, Leslie, and Frith found that all the children understood the experimental scenario. None of them failed either the Memory Question or the Reality Question. But there was a very significant difference in how the three groups fared with the Belief Question. Both the Down syndrome group and the normal group were overwhelmingly successful – with correct answers from 86 percent and 85 percent respectively. This is despite the fact that the Down syndrome group had a mean verbal mental age of less than 3. In very striking contrast, the autistic group (with a mean verbal mental age of 5;5) performed extremely poorly. In fact, 80 percent of the autistic children failed the Belief Question, despite a relatively high level of general intelligence.

The conclusion the experimenters drew was that autistic children have a highly specific mindreading deficit. As they put it in the original paper, "Our results strongly support the hypothesis that autistic children as a group fail to employ a theory of mind.

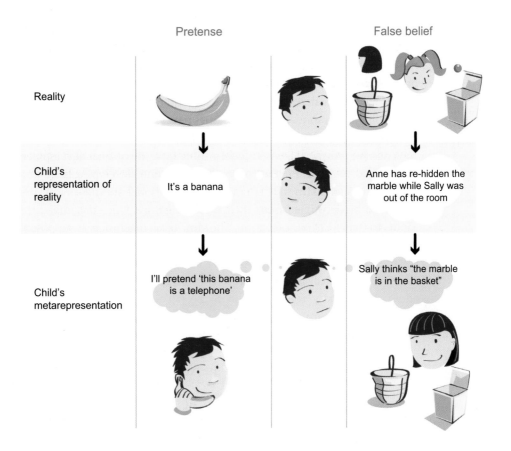

Figure 12.5 Illustration of the connection between pretend play and success on the false belief task.

We wish to explain this failure as an inability to represent mental states. As a result of this the autistic subjects are unable to impute beliefs to others and are thus at a grave disadvantage when having to predict the behavior of other people" (Baron-Cohen *et al.* 1985: 43).

Notice the specific diagnosis of why the autistic children fail the false belief task. It is described as a failure in the ability to represent mental states – in metarepresentation. This connection with Leslie's theory of pretend play is illustrated in Figure 12.5.

Leslie's theory allows us to connect two things that seem on the face of it to be completely unconnected. The first is the fact that autistic children have severe problems with pretend play. The second is that autistic children have serious difficulties with the false belief task – and so, many have concluded, with mindreading more generally. These two things turn out to be very closely connected if we think that both pretend play and mindreading critically depend upon metarepresentation. Autistic children's difficulties with pretend play and with mindreading turn out to have a common cause and a common explanation – namely, a deficit in metarepresentation.

This way of thinking about what is going wrong in the social development of the autistic child goes hand in hand with a model of how social development progresses for the normal child. On Leslie's model, as reinforced by the experimental studies we have been examining, pretend play has a crucial role to play in the emergence of metarepresentation. In autistic children, for reasons that are not yet understood, the process of developing metarepresentational abilities never really gets going. The ideas here are very powerful. But they still leave open a number of very fundamental questions.

When we presented Leslie's model we saw how the normal developmental progression is supposed to work. Pretend play rests upon and develops a basic portfolio of metarepresentational abilities. These metarepresentational abilities permit primary representations to be decoupled from their usual functions. Once decoupled they can serve as inputs to the PRETEND operation. The same basic machinery is supposed to be exploited in mindreading more generally. When young children (or adults, for that matter) successfully pass the false belief task, they are (according to the model) starting with their memory of the ball being placed in the basket. The metarepresentational mechanisms allow this primary representation to be decoupled from its usual role (so that, for example, it is not invalidated by watching Anne transfer the marble from the basket to the box). This allows the child to form a representation along these lines:

Sally BELIEVES "The marble is in the basket."

There is still a very important gap in the account, however. The problem is chronological. Pretend play emerges during the second year of life. But children do not typically pass the false belief test until they are nearly 4. There is a very clear sense, therefore, in which the BELIEVES operation must be much harder to acquire than the PRETENDS operation. But why is this? And what is the developmental progression that takes the normal child from pretend play to successful mindreading, as evidenced by success on the false belief task? We turn to these questions in the next two sections. First, though, we need to consider some important experiments suggesting that children may be able to understand false beliefs significantly earlier than suggested by the standard false belief task.

Implicit and explicit understanding of false belief

The false belief task originally proposed by Baron-Cohen, Leslie, and Frith is a verbal task. Children are explicitly asked about where they think Sally will look, or where they think the marble is. But it may be that these explicit questions introduce additional computational demands that muddy the waters. Perhaps young children fail the false belief task because they cannot cope with these extra computational demands, rather than because they do not understand false belief.

One way of exploring this possibility would be to develop a less demanding false belief test. This was done by Kristine Onishi and Renée Baillargeon in a famous set of experiments first published in 2005. Instead of explicitly asking children about how the characters they were observing would behave, or what they believed, Onishi and Baillargeon used a violation of expectations paradigm that measured looking times. Their set-up was very similar to the Baron-Cohen set-up. Fifteen-month-old infants were familiarized with an actor searching for a toy in one of two boxes (yellow and green, respectively). They were then presented with different conditions. In one condition the toy was moved from one box to the other with the actor clearly watching. In a second condition the toy was moved in the absence of the actor. After the toy was moved the actor then looked for the toy in one of the two baskets.

Onishi and Baillargeon hypothesized that the length of time that the infants looked at each of the scenarios would be a guide to their implicit understanding of false belief. Consider the second scenario, where the toy is moved without the actor seeing. Suppose that the toy was moved from the green box to the yellow box without the actor observing. Then the actor would presumably have a false belief about the toy's location, thinking it to still be in the green box when it is really in the yellow box. If infants understand this then they will presumably expect the actor to search in the green box. This expectation will be violated if the actor searches in the yellow box. So, on the assumption that looking time increases when expectations are violated, Onishi and Baillargeon predicted the infants would look significantly longer when the actor did not behave as expected. The robust effect that they discovered is that infants looked significantly longer when the actor searched in the yellow box than when the actor searched in the green box. Even though the toy was really in the green box, Onishi and Baillargeon claim that the infants were surprised that the actor did not act on the basis of his (false) belief that the toy was still in the green box. So, they conclude, infants have an understanding of false belief much earlier than suggested by the traditional false belief task.

The Onishi and Baillargeon results are very robust, and have been replicated and expanded by other researchers. At the same time, however, there has been considerable debate about how to interpret them. Some cognitive scientists, including Onishi and Baillargeon themselves, think that the results show that young infants have a full understanding of false belief, directly refuting the standard claim that children do not arrive at a full understanding of false belief until around 4 years of age. Others take a more measured approach. This is what we shall do here.

The original Perner and Wimmer, and Baron-Cohen, Leslie, and Frith experiments seem to be testing for a cognitive ability considerably more sophisticated than could be revealed by the Onishi and Baillargeon experiments. The earlier experiments are directly targeting explicit conceptual abilities manifested in verbal responses and explicit reflection. Children are asked about what agents will do and what they believe. What the experiments are getting at is mastery of the concept of belief, together with the complicated vocabulary and other baggage that goes with it. In contrast, the Onishi and Baillargeon experiments are probing the nonverbal expectations that young children have about behavior and how behavior is affected by what an agent has and has not observed. It is clear that these are related in at least one important sense. Nobody who lacked the nonverbal expectations identified in the Onishi and Baillargeon experiments could possibly pass the much more sophisticated false belief test. At the same time, though, the dependence doesn't seem to hold in the opposite direction. It seems perfectly possible to have the right nonverbal expectations without being able to articulate them in the right sort of way to pass the false belief test. In fact, all the experimental evidence seems to suggest that this is what happens to most children between 1.5 and 4 years of age.

Perhaps the best way to look at the situation is this. The Onishi and Baillargeon experiments identify an *implicit* understanding of false belief, whereas the standard false belief tasks are testing for an *explicit* understanding of false belief. By an explicit understanding I mean one that is verbally articulated and reflective, developed as part of high-level explanations of behavior in terms of beliefs and other mental states. An implicit understanding, in contrast, is predominantly practical, focused primarily on aligning one's behavior with that of others and correctly predicting how others will behave as a function of what they have or have not seen.

In the remainder of this chapter we will be focusing primarily on what it takes for a child to understand false belief explicitly. As we have already seen, there is evidence from (for example) pretend play suggesting that young children are capable of forms of metarepresentation considerably before they have an explicit understanding of false belief. The Onishi and Baillargeon experiments add an additional data point by showing that young children can have an implicit understanding of false belief more than two years earlier. One very interesting question that this raises is how an implicit understanding of false belief fits into the overall development of what cognitive scientists call the mindreading system. In the next sections we will look in more detail at the mindreading system and how it emerges.

12.3   The mindreading system

Sections 12.1. and 12.2 have explored some of the connections between mindreading and pretend play. The principal link between them, according to the model first proposed by Alan Leslie and developed by many others, is that both exploit metarepresentational skills. The model is built around the idea that mindreading and pretend play have a common information-processing structure. Both involve a "decoupling" of representations from their usual functions. In pretend play these decoupled representations serve as inputs to the PRETEND operation. In mindreading the theory of mind system uses these decoupled representations to make sense of what is going on in other people's minds.

However, as we saw when we looked at the false belief task, some of the more complex types of mindreading emerge much later in cognitive development than pretend play, even though they both involve a sophisticated type of information processing that involves representing representations. Young children start to engage in pretend play well before they are 2 years old, but it is not until the age of around 4 that they have a rich enough understanding of belief to pass the false belief task. This raises two sets of questions. The first set of questions has to do with how mindreading emerges in the course of development.

- Are the mindreading skills of normal human children built on a foundation of more primitive cognitive abilities?
- If so, then what does this tell us about the architecture of the mind?
- What can we learn from the developmental progression of normal human children about the origins and causes of mindreading deficits such as those suffered by autistic children?

A second set of questions has to do directly with the gap between belief and pretense. If we accept Leslie's model, then we have to accept that children as young as 2 years of age are basically capable of metarepresentational information processing. But then we need to explain why it takes so long for them to learn how to perform the false belief task.

- What is it about understanding belief that makes it so hard for young children to perform the false belief task?
- Are there alternative explanations of why it takes so long for young children to understand the possibility of false beliefs?

These two sets of questions are closely connected. As we will see, some distinguished developmental psychologists (including Josef Perner, who invented the false belief task) think that it is wrong to describe young children as being capable of metarepresentation until they pass the false belief task. For these theorists, the theory of mind system does not emerge before the age of 4.

First steps in mindreading

The developmental psychologist Simon Baron-Cohen was one of the co-authors of the 1985 paper that we looked at in the last section – the paper that first drew the connection between autism and problems in mindreading. Since then he has developed and fine-tuned a model of how mindreading emerges in infants and young children.

The theory of mind mechanism (TOMM) identified by Alan Leslie is the culmination of this process. But there are several stepping-stones on the way. Each of these stepping-stones opens up a different type of mindreading to the young infant. For Baron-Cohen, mindreading is a highly complex suite of abilities. It emerges in stages, with each stage building on its predecessors. Baron-Cohen has developed and fine-tuned his model over the years. The basic components of the latest version of the model are illustrated in Figure 12.6. As this shows, Baron-Cohen's model sees the foundations of mindreading emerging in the earliest months of infant development. The most basic mindreading skills are all in place by the time a normal infant is 9 months old. These basic mindreading skills are all essentially perceptual in nature. They involve the infant becoming perceptually sensitive to behavioral manifestations of psychological states. The *intentionality detector* (ID) is a mechanism that allows the infant to identify purposeful movements. When an agent makes a self-propelled movement, ID codes the movement as being goal-driven – it allows the infant to identify her mother's arm movement as a

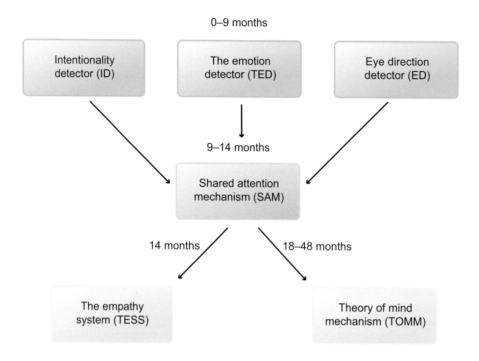

Figure 12.6 Baron-Cohen's model of the mindreading system.

reaching, for example. At a more fundamental level, ID allows the infant to distinguish the animate, goal-driven entities from the other objects it encounters.

A good way of finding out the apparent goal of a purposeful movement is to check where the agent is looking – since agents tend to keep their eyes on the target. So one of the most fundamental tools for making sense of the social world is the ability to track other people's eye movements. This is the function of the *eye direction detector* (EDD). Whereas ID enables the infant to detect purposeful movements, the job of EDD is to help the infant identify the goals of the movement. The two mechanisms are highly complementary. There is little point in knowing that a movement is purposeful unless one has some idea what the goal is.

But there is more to making sense of people's movements than identifying purposeful movements and their goal. Young infants beginning to negotiate the social world need to be sensitive to the motivations and moods of the people with whom they are interacting – complete strangers, as well as their caregivers and other family members. This is the job of the *emotion detector* (TED). The emotion detector allows infants to understand not just that agents make movements towards particular goals, but also *why* those movements are being made and what sort of movements they are. Are they playful movements, for example, or protective ones? Sensitivity to moods and emotions is a first step towards understanding the complexities of psychology.

According to Baron-Cohen, the three basic components of the mindreading system are all in place by the time the infant is 9 months old. Well before the end of their first year human infants are capable of distinguishing animate objects from inanimate ones, of tracking where other people are looking, and of picking up on their moods. All of these skills have something important in common. They are all primarily perceptual. What the infant is learning to do is to pick up clues about people's psychology from what she can perceive of their physical characteristics and movements. Moods are revealed in facial expressions, and in tone of voice. Animate beings move in very different ways from inanimate objects – their movements are much less regular and much harder to predict, for example. The orientation of the head is a good clue to eye gaze. In all these cases the infant is decoding the perceived environment in terms of some very basic psychological categories.

From an information-processing point of view, the three basic systems (ID, TED, and EDD) all involve very simple types of representation. They all involve representing other agents as having certain fairly basic features. TED, for example, involves "tagging" other agents with primitive representations of their moods (happy, sad, angry, frightened). EDD involves identifying a *dyadic* relation between an agent and an object (*Dad sees the cup*, for example). Dyadic relations have two parts. The dyadic relation of seeing is a relation between an agent and an object. ID also produces representations of dyadic relations between agents and objects. The dyadic relations here all involve intentional movements, such as reaching, or following, or pushing.

From dyadic to triadic interactions: Joint visual attention

Between the ages of 9 and 14 months a very important transformation takes place in the young infant's mindreading skills. In the first 9 months of life infants are capable of understanding people and interacting with them in certain very basic ways. They are also capable of understanding objects and manipulating them. But for the very young infant these are two separate activities. Starting at the age of 9 months the infant learns to combine them. Infants become capable of employing their interactions with people in their interactions with objects, and vice versa. This is illustrated in the much-studied phenomenon of *joint visual attention.*

Joint visual attention occurs when infants look at objects (and take pleasure in looking at objects) because they see that another person is looking at that object – and because they see that the other person sees that they are looking at the object. Joint visual attention is a collaborative activity. The infant does not just represent a dyadic relation between her mother and a cup, for example. The infant learns to represent different *triadic* (or three-way) relations between herself, the mother, and the cup – as well as to initiate them with pointing and other gestures. In joint visual attention the infant exploits representations such as the following:

Mother SEES (I SEE the cup)
I SEE (Mother SEES the cup)

What makes joint visual attention possible is that the infant becomes capable of embedding representations – of representing that an agent (whether herself, or someone else) is representing someone else's representation. This is a very different type of information processing from the information processing involved in detecting eye direction or sensitivity to moods. It makes possible a whole range of coordinated social behaviors in which infants and their caregivers take enormous pleasure in collaborative games – games that involve and exploit an awareness of what others are doing and how they too are participating in the game.

This distinctive kind of information processing is carried out in what Baron-Cohen has termed the *shared attention mechanism* (SAM). The emergence of the shared attention mechanism is a crucial stage in the development of the young child's mindreading skills. The connections with autism are very suggestive here too. We saw in the last section that autistic children have well-documented problems both with advanced mindreading (of the sort required for successful performance on the false belief task) and with pretend play. It turns out that autistic children also have difficulties with joint attention – and that there is a strong correlation between the severity of their social impairments and their inability to engage in joint attention.

The shared attention mechanism is also very important for language development. Pointing to objects is a very important way of teaching children what words mean. But in order for children to pick up on the cues that they are being given they need to be able to understand that they and the person pointing are jointly attending to the very same thing. Without this children cannot understand the instructions that they are being given.

TESS and TOMM

In Baron-Cohen's model, SAM is a crucial foundation for the final two components of the mindreading system. We have already encountered one of these components – the theory of mind mechanism (TOMM). Earlier versions of Baron-Cohen's model contained only TOMM after SAM. Recently, however, he has added an additional component, which he calls TESS (for *the empathizing system*). For normal social development it is not enough simply to be able to identify other people's emotional states and moods. The developing child needs to learn to respond appropriately to those emotional states and moods. This is where empathy comes in.

Psychosocial disorders such as psychopathy suggest that TOMM and TESS can come apart (and hence that there are two distinct and separable mechanisms carrying out the different tasks of identifying other people's mental states and developing affective responses to those mental states). Psychopaths have profound social problems, but these problems are very different from those suffered by autistic people. Psychopaths are typically very good at working out what is going on in other people's heads. The problem is that they tend not to care about what they find there – and in fact they use their understanding to manipulate other people in ways that a normal person would find unacceptable. Diagnosing psychopathy is a very complex business, but psychiatrists typically put a lot of weight on basic failures of empathy - on failure to feel sympathy when someone else is in pain or obvious distress, for example.

TESS emerges once the basic capacity for shared attention is in place. In many ways empathy is a matter of being able to put oneself in someone else's position - to imagine what it would be like to be someone else, and to find oneself in the situation that they find themselves in. Shared attention basically exploits the same ability, it is just being applied in a much more limited sphere. The child engaged in joint visual attention or collaborative play is able to adopt someone else's visual perspective, to represent how things look to someone else. As they do this more and more they eventually bootstrap themselves into the ability to understand someone else's emotional perspective on the world - to understand not just how a situation looks to someone, but how that situation affects them.

The possibility of psychopathy shows (according to Baron-Cohen) that TESS and TOMM are distinct, although they both emerge from a common foundation in SAM. They develop more or less in parallel, with TESS emerging a little earlier, but TOMM taking much longer to emerge completely. The first stages in the development of TOMM are taken as early as 18 months, which is when typical young children start to engage in pretend play. But full-fledged TOMM does not emerge until much later in development - at around the age of 4, which is when young children tend on average to pass the false belief test.

This brings us to the second cluster of questions that we identified earlier:

- What is it about understanding belief that makes it so hard for young children to pass the false belief test?
- Are there alternative explanations of why it takes so long for young children to understand the possibility of false beliefs?

On the face of it there is a puzzle here. Look back at the diagram of the mindreading system in Figure 12.6. The evolution of TOMM is a lengthy process. It begins at around 14 months (when the infant starts to engage in pretend play) and is not complete until the child is around 4 years old (when the young child acquires the understanding of complex mental states tested in the false belief task). But why does this process take so long? On Leslie's analysis (as discussed in section 12.2) information processing in the TOMM essentially exploits the machinery of metarepresentation and "decoupled" primary representations. The same machinery is involved both in pretend play and in the attribution of beliefs. When an infant pretends that it is raining, Leslie analyzes his metarepresentational state as follows (remember that the quotation marks are signs that the representation has been decoupled:

I PRETEND "It is raining."

And when a much older child represents her mother as believing that it is raining, Leslie gives the following analysis:

Mother BELIEVES "It is raining."

The two analyses look structurally identical. So why are infants able to engage in pretend play so much earlier than they are capable of understanding beliefs and passing the false belief task? We explore this question in the next section.

12.4 Understanding false belief

Leslie and his collaborators have a subtle solution to the problem of explaining the long time lag between when they think that the capacity for metarepresentation first emerges (during the second year) and when children generally pass the false belief test (towards the end of the fourth year).

Leslie thinks that there are two very different abilities here. The first is the ability to attribute true beliefs to someone else. The second is the ability to attribute false beliefs. These two abilities emerge at very different times in development. On Leslie's model, young children are able to attribute true beliefs from a relatively early age. In fact, the default setting of the theory of mind mechanism is to attribute true beliefs. This is why they cannot pass the false belief task until they are very much older. Success on the false belief task only comes when young children learn to "switch off," or inhibit, the default setting. According to Leslie, this requires the development of a new mechanism. He calls this mechanism the *selection processor*.

The selection processor hypothesis

Let us go back to the basic false belief task, as illustrated in Figure 12.4. According to Leslie, the TOMM generates two candidate beliefs in response to the experimental situation (remember that the marble really is in the box, although Sally did not see it being moved and so should still think that it is in the basket).

Sally BELIEVES "The marble is in the basket."   [the *false belief* candidate]
Sally BELIEVES "The marble is in the box."   [the *true belief* candidate]

The selection processor is set up to favor true beliefs. This makes very good sense for a number of reasons. Generally speaking, people have more true beliefs than they have false beliefs, and so, unless there are specific countervailing reasons, a system that attributes true beliefs by default will at least be right more times than it is wrong. And identifying true beliefs is much easier than identifying false beliefs. There are all sorts of ways in which a person can have a false belief, but only one way of having a true belief – true beliefs have to match the facts, but anything goes for false ones. For these reasons, unless the system has specific evidence to the contrary, it is sensible for the system to work backwards from the way the world is to the beliefs that other people are likely to have.

So, the selection processor's default setting favors the true belief candidate – the belief that Sally believes that the marble is in the box. But in this case there is evidence to the contrary. Given how the experiment is set up, the child knows that Sally did not see the marble being moved from the basket to the box. In order for this countervailing evidence to be effective, however, the selection processor's default setting needs to be overridden. This is what separates children who pass the false belief task from children who fail. The ones who pass are able to inhibit the bias in favor of the true belief candidate.

So, Leslie and his collaborators think that young children *fail* on tasks requiring an understanding of false belief because they are *not* able to inhibit the selection processor's default bias, and when children succeed on the task it is because they become capable of switching off the default bias. The problem, they think, lies not with TOMM itself. TOMM is in place from the pretend play stage. It is just that it initially only works to attribute true beliefs. Success on the false belief task comes only when the young child acquires a more general capacity for executive control. Is there any way of testing this general hypothesis?

According to Leslie and his group, we can test this hypothesis by altering the false belief task to increase the executive control component, thereby making greater demands on mechanisms of inhibitory control. If the task makes greater demands on inhibitory control, and inhibitory control is the factor that explains success rather than failure on the false belief task, then one would expect that success rates on the altered task would be lower than on the original task.

Exercise 12.5 Explain and assess this reasoning in your own words. Can you think of other ways to test the hypothesis?

A study published by Leslie and Pamela Polizzi in 1998 reported a number of experiments adopting this general strategy. Here is a representative example. Children are presented with a scenario in which a girl (let's call her Sally, for continuity) is asked to place food in one of two boxes. The twist to the tale is that one of the boxes contains a sick kitten. Because eating the food might make the kitten worse, Sally wants to avoid putting the food into the box with the kitten in it. So Sally has what Leslie, German, and Polizzi term an *avoidance-desire*. The significance of this, they claim, is that avoidance-desires are inhibitory. An avoidance-desire is a desire *not* to do something.

There were two conditions – a true belief condition and a false belief condition. In the true belief condition, the kitten is moved from Box A to Box B in front of Sally. In the false belief condition, the kitten is moved without Sally seeing. Children undergoing the experiment in each condition are asked to predict which box Sally will put the food in. There is no question here about whether the children understand false belief. All the children were able to pass the standard false belief task and all of them answered correctly when they were asked where Sally thought the kitten was (in Box B in the true belief condition, and in Box A in the false belief condition).

In the true belief condition the child knows that the kitten is in Box B (since she saw the kitten being moved there) and she knows that Sally wants to avoid putting the kitten and the food in the same box. So she needs to predict that Sally will put the food in Box A. Arriving at this prediction requires the child to think about Sally's avoidance-desire. The box with the kitten in it is salient, but the child needs to understand that Sally actively wants to avoid the salient box. So the child does need to be able to make sense of Sally's inhibition of what most people would normally want to do – which is to give food to a kitten. It turned out that a very high percentage (well over 90 percent) of the children in the experiment were able successfully to predict where Sally would put the food in the true belief condition.

Now consider the false belief condition. The child still knows that the kitten is in Box B and she still knows that Sally wants to make sure that the kitten does not get the food. But now she also needs to take on board the fact that Sally did *not* see the kitten being moved from Box A to Box B. So, as on the standard false belief task, she needs to *inhibit* her own knowledge of where the kitten is. All the children in the task were able to pass the false belief task. They all knew that Sally thought that the kitten was still in Box A. But the problem here is that the children are being asked to do two things at once – to inhibit their own knowledge of where the kitten is, as well as to make sense of Sally's inhibition of the normal desire to give food to a kitten. There is a *double inhibition* required.

According to Leslie, German, and Polizzi this is why the success rate in the false belief condition is so much lower than in the true belief condition. It turned out that only 14 percent of children in the study succeeded in the false belief condition (as opposed to 94 percent in the true belief condition). Their hypothesis is that the double inhibition places much higher demands on the selection processor than the ordinary false belief tasks.

Exercise 12.6 Explain the reasoning behind this experiment in your own words and assess it.

Exercise 12.7 Is the selection processor hypothesis compatible with the Onishi and Baillargeon data suggesting an implicit understanding of false belief in 15-month-old infants? If so, how? If not, why not?

An alternative model of theory of mind development

Leslie and his collaborators have an ingenious way of reconciling their theory with the developmental data. Their theory holds that TOMM is in place from the early days of pretend play (well before the average infant is 2 years old). Data from the false belief task seem to suggest, however, that full-fledged TOMM does not emerge until much later. According to Leslie and his research group, this delay occurs because the young child needs to develop a selection processor capable of overruling the initial bias towards true beliefs. But this is not the only way of looking at how young children's mindreading skills develop. We will end this section by looking at an alternative picture, developed by the developmental psychologist Joseph Perner (one of the two authors of the original paper that presented the false belief task).

Perner's thinking about mindreading is very much informed by influential theories in philosophy about the nature of belief, and other mental states that philosophers collectively label *propositional attitudes*. Belief is called a propositional attitude because it involves a thinker taking an attitude (the attitude of belief) towards a proposition. So, if I believe that it is now raining, then I am taking the attitude of belief to the proposition *it is now raining*. For many philosophers, the distinguishing feature of propositions is that they can be true or false. If I believe the proposition *it is now raining* then I am, in effect, making a claim about the world. This claim can be true (if indeed it is now raining), or false (if it is not).

What are propositions? This is a question that has greatly exercised philosophers, who have come up with a bewildering array of different theories. Some have argued that propositions are essentially abstract objects like numbers, for example. Others think of them as sets of possible worlds. Fortunately we don't need to go into these debates. What we are interested in at the moment is what it is for someone (particularly a young child between the ages of 3 and 4) to understand another person's belief. For that we can simply think of propositions as representations of the world that can be either true or false. This means that if a young child (or anyone else, for that matter) is to attribute a belief to someone else, she must represent that person as standing in the belief relation to a representation of the world *that can be either true or false*.

Understanding propositions in this way leads Joseph Perner and others to a very different way of thinking about young children's mindreading skills *before* they pass the false belief task. Perner rejects Leslie's claim that there could be a theory of mind mechanism that only attributes true beliefs. Leslie may well be right that young children are attributing to others some sort of psychological state that is always true (from the child's perspective). But, according to Perner, that psychological state cannot be the state of belief. Beliefs are just not the sort of thing that can always be true.

The issue here is not purely terminological – it is not just a matter of what one calls beliefs. For Perner there is something much deeper going on, something to do with the type of metarepresentation that is available to young children before they pass the false belief task. Recall that metarepresentation is a matter of representing representations. In order to engage in metarepresentation a child needs to be able to represent a representation. In the case of beliefs (and other propositional attitudes) this target representation is a proposition – something that can be either true or false. So, in order for a child to attribute a belief to Sally, for example, she needs to be able to represent the object of Sally's belief (what it is that Sally believes) as something that can be either true or false.

But if we put all these ideas together we see that they are incompatible with Leslie's model of the theory of mind mechanism. If, as Leslie thinks, TOMM is not capable of attributing false beliefs until the child is capable of passing the false belief task, then it looks very much as if TOMM is not attributing beliefs until that happens. In order to understand the concept of belief, the child needs to understand the possibility of false belief. But this possibility is exactly what the child does not grasp until she passes the false belief task.

Exercise 12.8 State in your own words and assess this objection to Leslie's model of the TOMM.

In fact, a stronger conclusion follows, according to Perner. If the psychological states that the child attributes are always true (from the child's perspective), then the child is not really engaged in metarepresentation at all. The child is certainly representing another person as being in a psychological state. But they can do that without engaging in metarepresentation. Since the content of the psychological state tracks what the child considers to be the state of the world, the child does not need to deploy any resources over and above the resources that she herself uses to make sense of the world directly.

One way of understanding what is going on here is to compare belief with perception. Perception is a psychological state that represents the world as being a certain way. And so to represent someone as perceiving something is to represent them as being in a representational psychological state. But this is a very different matter from representing them as believing something. As we saw when we first encountered the false belief task in section 12.2, perception is what philosophers call *factive*. I can only perceive that things are a certain way if they really are that way. I can only perceive that it is raining if it really is raining. The factive nature of perception carries across to what happens when we represent someone else as perceiving something. I cannot represent someone else as perceiving things a certain way unless I also take things to be that way. Or, to put it the other way round, I can read the contents of someone else's perceptual state off from what I myself take the world to be. I can represent what is going on in their head simply by representing the world.

Figures 12.7 and 12.8 make it easier to see what is going on here. In Figure 12.7 we see full-blown metarepresentation. The structure of metarepresentation is triadic. A metarepresenting subject has to represent another psychological subject, a psychological relation such as belief, and the proposition that is believed. The proposition represents a particular state of affairs in the world (the state of affairs of the marble being in the box, or of the cat being on the mat). It can be either true or false. But, as far as the accuracy of metarepresentation is concerned, what matters is not whether or not the proposition is true, but rather whether or not the metarepresenting subject has identified it correctly.

In Figure 12.8, in contrast, we see what is going on when a psychological subject represents another psychological subject's perceptual state. Here there is no need for a proposition to be identified. There is no need for metarepresentation in the strict sense. All that the person representing the psychological state needs to do is to represent directly a relation between the perceiver and the state of affairs in the world that the perceiver is perceiving.

On Perner's view of mindreading, therefore, metarepresentation in the full sense of the word does not appear until fairly late in development. In fact, he doesn't think it is right to describe children as engaged in metarepresentation until they are able to pass the false

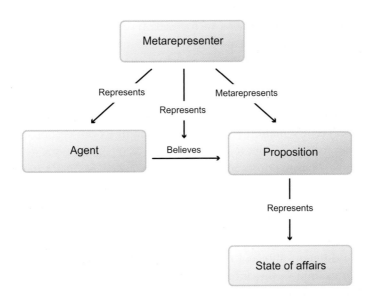

Figure 12.7 What goes on in representing belief. Note that representing belief requires metarepresentation.

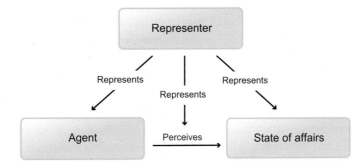

Figure 12.8 What goes on in representing perception. Note that representing perception does *not* require metarepresentation.

belief test. It is only when children start to understand the possibility of false belief that we see the emergence of what Perner calls the *representational mind*.

This brings us right back to where we started. We began our exploration of mindreading in section 12.1 with the idea that pretend play is metarepresentational and exploits the very same information-processing mechanisms that are deployed in sophisticated types of mindreading. If Perner is right, however, that metarepresentation does not emerge until children pass the false belief test, then we need to find another way of interpreting what is going on in pretend play.

Perner's book *Understanding the Representational Mind*, published in 1991, also makes a distinction between primary representations and secondary representations. For Perner, as for Leslie, primary representations are focused on the world. And (again like Leslie) he also thinks that secondary representations come about when primary representations are "decoupled" from reality. But, according to Perner, the fact that primary representations can be decoupled from reality does not necessarily mean that there is metarepresentation going on. Metarepresentation, as we have seen, involves representing a representation. Passing the false belief test requires metarepresentation because it requires representing another subject's representation of the world. But thinkers can decouple primary representations from reality without representing them as representations.

One example of this occurs in what is often called *counterfactual thinking*. We engage in counterfactual thinking when we think about how things might be (but are not). (Counterfactual reasoning used to be called contrary-to-fact reasoning, which may make clearer what is going on.) If I am wondering whether I have made the right choice of restaurant I might start to think about how things might have turned out had I made a different choice. I might imagine how things would be in a different restaurant, for example – the different things that I could have ordered, the different clientele. The representations that I use in this sort of counterfactual thinking are decoupled in the sense that they are being used to think about how things might be, rather than about how they are. But they do not involve metarepresentation. When I think about the steak that I might now be having in the restaurant over the street, my representation of the steak is decoupled from reality (because, after all, I am not thinking about any particular steak). But I am not engaged in metarepresentation – I am thinking about the steak that I could be having, not about my representation of the steak.

Here is a way of putting the basic distinction. Metarepresentation is a matter of *thinking about* decoupled representations (thinking that is directly focused on representations, rather than on the world). But counterfactual thinking is a matter of *thinking with* decoupled representations (using decoupled representations to think about the world). We can certainly think with decoupled representations without thinking about them. It is not hard to see why Leslie and Perner both agree that passing the false belief test requires thinking about decoupled representations. They also agree that pretend play exploits decoupled representations. But Perner thinks that we can understand what is going on in pretend play without holding that the child is thinking about those decoupled representations. When the child pretends that the banana is a telephone, she is decoupling her primary representations of the telephone and applying them to the banana. But at no point is she representing those primary representations – and so she is not engaged in metarepresentation.

A cognitive scientist who adopts Perner's interpretation of pretend play can nonetheless adopt many of Leslie's specific proposals about the information processing in pretend play. She could also adopt the model of the complete mindreading system proposed by Simon Baron-Cohen (although the emergence of the TOMM would have to be dated somewhat later). Because of this, one might well think that there is much more agreement than disagreement between Leslie and Perner. In fact, this turns out to be exactly right when we look at a very different model of mindreading that some cognitive scientists and developmental psychologists have proposed. This is the *simulationist* model that we will examine in section 12.5.

Exercise 12.9 Go back to section 12.1 and identify how Leslie's basic model of pretend play would need to be modified in order to accommodate Perner's interpretation.

Exercise 12.10 Is Perner's interpretation compatible with the Onishi and Baillargeon data suggesting an implicit understanding of false belief in 15-month-old infants? If so, how? If not, why not?

12.5 Mindreading as simulation

The last section focused primarily on the differences between the models of mindreading developed by Alan Leslie and Joseph Perner. These differences have to do primarily with the role of metarepresentation and when it emerges in cognitive development. Leslie finds metarepresentation in pretend play and thinks that a basic metarepresentational capacity is present in normal children before they are 2 years old. For Perner, in contrast, metarepresentation is a much more sophisticated cognitive achievement that emerges only towards the end of the child's fourth year. These significant differences should not obscure to us the very considerable common ground that Leslie and Perner share. They are both committed to the view that mindreading is basically a theoretical accomplishment. It requires bringing a specialized body of knowledge (theory of mind) to bear in order to explain and predict the behavior of others.

In this respect, then, both Leslie and Perner provide a very clear illustration of one of the basic principles that we have identified as lying at the heart of cognitive science. This is the principle that much of cognition exploits dedicated, domain-specific information processing. In this section we explore an alternative to their shared view. This alternative comes from simulation theory. According to simulation theory, the core of the mindreading system does indeed exploit a specialized cognitive system, but this cognitive system is not actually dedicated to information processing about beliefs, desires, and other propositional attitudes. There is no specialized theory of mind mechanism. Instead, theory of mind processing is carried out by the very same systems that are responsible for ordinary decision-making and for finding out about the world.

Different versions of the simulation theory all share a single basic idea. This is the idea that we explain and predict the behavior of other agents by projecting ourselves into the situation of the person whose behavior is to be explained/predicted and then using our own mind as a model of theirs. Suppose that we have a reasonable sense of the beliefs and desires that it would be appropriate to attribute to someone else in a particular situation, so that we understand both how they view the situation and what they want to achieve in it. And suppose that we want to find out how they will behave. Instead of using specialized knowledge about how mental states typically feed into behavior to predict how that person will behave, the simulationist thinks that we use our own decision-making processes to run a simulation of what would happen if we ourselves had those beliefs and desires. We do this by running our decision-making processes *offline*, so that instead of generating an action directly they generate a description of an action or an intention to act in a certain way. We then use this description to predict the behavior of the person in question.

Standard simulationism

There are, broadly speaking, two ways of developing this basic idea. One way was originally proposed by the developmental psychologist Paul Harris and subsequently developed by the philosopher Alvin Goldman. We can call their theory *standard simulationism*. According to standard simulationism, the process of simulation has to start with the mindreader *explicitly* (although not necessarily consciously) attributing beliefs and desires to the person being simulated. The mindreader has to form explicit judgments about how the other person represents the relevant situation and what they want to achieve in that situation. These judgments serve as the input to the ordinary decision-making system. A schematic version of this general model is illustrated in Figure 12.9.

Both Goldman and Harris think of these judgments as "pretend" beliefs and "pretend" desires. The decision-making system processes pretend beliefs and desires in exactly the same way that it processes "genuine" beliefs and desires. By doing this the mindreader simulates the person whose behavior she is trying to predict. The mindreader reads the prediction off the outputs of the decision-making system when it is operating in simulation mode with pretend inputs.

You might ask where these pretend inputs come from. Goldman has developed the most sophisticated response to this question. For Goldman we identify other people's beliefs and desires by analogy with our own beliefs and desires. We know which beliefs we tend to form in response to particular situations. And so we assume that others will form the same beliefs, unless we have specific evidence to the contrary. This might be evidence, for example, about how they have acted in the past, or about temperamental differences – or about the different information that they have available to them. When we do have such additional evidence we make the necessary adjustments before forming the pretend beliefs and pretend desires that then go into the decision-making process. We make the necessary adjustments by thinking about what we would do if we had those temperamental features or that extra information.

There is a sense in which this simply pushes the problem back a step, and also weakens the basic force of simulationism. On Goldman's model, knowledge of others rests upon self-knowledge. The simulationist has to work outwards from her own psychological states to those of others. Without this there will be no inputs to the decision-making system. But, one might ask, where does this self-knowledge come from? How do we know what we ourselves believe and desire?

Goldman thinks that we have a special mechanism for finding out about our own beliefs, desires, and other propositional attitudes – a self-monitoring mechanism that

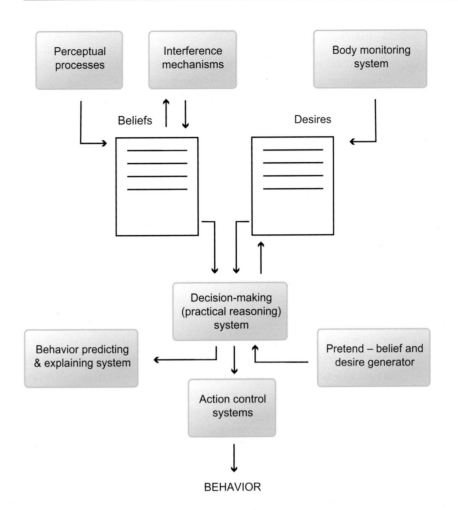

Figure 12.9 A schematic version of standard simulationism. Note that the ordinary decision-making system is being run offline with pretend inputs. (Adapted from Nichols *et al*. 1996)

philosophers call *introspection* or *inner sense*. Philosophers have developed many different theories of introspection. Fortunately, we don't need to go into them. The key thing to bear in mind for now is that standard simulationists are typically committed to the following two basic principles:

1   We understand the psychological states of others by analogy with our own psychological states.
2   We have a special self-monitoring mechanism for keeping track of our own psychological states.

These two basic principles explain how we arrive at the pretend beliefs and desires that are the inputs for simulating other people.

Radical simulationism

There is a second way of developing the basic simulationist idea – what is often called *radical simulationism*. Radical simulationism has been developed primarily by the philosophers Robert Gordon and Jane Heal. The intuitive idea behind radical simulationism is that, instead of coming explicitly to the view that the person whose behavior I am trying to predict has a certain belief (say, the belief that *p*), what I need to do is to imagine how the world would appear from her point of view.

According to standard simulationism, I can only simulate another person by forming pretend beliefs and pretend desires. These pretend beliefs and pretend desires are, in effect, beliefs about another person's beliefs and desires. They are metarepresentations. According to radical simulationism, on the other hand, what the simulator is thinking about is the world, rather than the person they are simulating. The simulator is thinking about the world *from the perspective of the person being simulated*, rather than thinking about their beliefs, desires, and other psychological states. The spirit of this "world-directed" way of thinking about psychological explanation comes across in the following passage from Jane Heal (although she prefers to talk about *replication*, rather than *simulation*):

> On the replicating view psychological understanding works like this. I can think about the world. I do so in the interests of taking my own decisions and forming my own opinions. The future is complex and unclear. In order to deal with it I need to, and can, envisage possible but perhaps non-actual states of affairs. I can imagine how my tastes, aims, and opinions might change, and work out what would be sensible to do or believe in the circumstances. My ability to do these things makes possible a certain sort of understanding of other people. I can harness all my complex theoretical knowledge about the world and my ability to imagine to yield an insight into other people *without any further elaborate theorizing about them*. Only one simple assumption is needed: that they are like me in being thinkers, that they possess the same fundamental cognitive capacities and propensities as I do. (Heal 1986, reprinted in Davies and Stone 1995b: 47)

Radical simulationism is intended to offer the possibility of mindreading without metarepresentation. This is because it is world-directed, rather than mind-directed. And as a result it gives a very different account of what is going wrong when children fail the false belief test. For the radical simulationist, children who fail the false belief test lack imaginative capacities. Their capacity to project themselves imaginatively into someone else's position is not sufficiently developed. They are not yet able to form beliefs *from a perspective other than their own*. They are capable of imaginative perceiving. That is, they can adopt someone else's perceptual perspective on the world – they can appreciate how things *look* to Sally. But they are not capable of imaginatively working their way into the beliefs that someone might have about the world.

Exercise 12.11 We have now looked at four different ways of thinking about the false belief task. Draw up a table indicating the four different proposals that have been made for explaining what it is that the false belief task is testing for.

12.6 The cognitive neuroscience of mindreading

So far in this chapter we have been looking at relatively high-level theories of mind-reading. We began with Leslie's information-processing model of metarepresentation in pretend play and explored several different ways of thinking about how metarepresentation might (or might not) be involved in different types of mindreading. The evidence that we have been looking at is primarily psychological – evidence from the false belief task and from studies of pretend play in children. In this section we consider what we can learn about mindreading using the techniques of cognitive neuroscience, such as functional neuroimaging (in human adults and children) and single-unit recordings (in monkeys). The neuroscience of mindreading has become a very hot topic in recent years and we can only scratch the surface here. But we can focus the issues by concentrating on three questions that emerge from our earlier discussion.

Several of the models of mindreading that we have been looking at start off from the working hypothesis that there is a dedicated, multi-component theory of mind system. The clearest articulation of this is the model proposed by Simon Baron-Cohen (see Figure 12.6). Baron-Cohen's theory of mind system has a number of different components. The centerpiece of the model is what he, following Leslie, calls the theory of mind mechanism (TOMM). TOMM is the information-processing system responsible for reasoning about other people's beliefs, desires, and other propositional attitudes. What characterizes it from an information-processing point of view is that it exploits metarepresentation. So, a natural question to ask is:

Question 1 Is there any evidence at the neural level for the existence of a TOMM?

In section 12.5 we looked at an alternative way of thinking about mindreading. On this alternative approach mindreading is an exercise in simulation. It does not exploit systems specialized for mindreading. Instead, the information processing in mindreading is carried out by cognitive systems that also do other things. We can call these *co-opted systems*. On Goldman's version of simulationism, for example, we reason about other people's mental states by co-opting our ordinary decision-making system – we run it offline with pretend beliefs and desires as inputs. Again, we can ask whether there is any evidence at the neural level for this way of thinking about mindreading.

There are really two different questions here, depending upon the type of mind-reading one is thinking about. On Baron-Cohen's model the mindreading system is complex with six different components. We can think about this in functional terms. We might say, for example, that the overall task of mindreading involves six different sub-tasks. But there is no particular reason why those different mindreading tasks should be carried out by information-processing systems of the same type. Some might be carried out by co-opted mechanisms and others not.

The theory of mind mechanism has a distinctive position within the mindreading system as a whole. It is the only part of the mindreading system that is thought to deploy metarepresentation, for one thing. So, we can make a distinction between low-level mindreading and high-level mindreading. Low-level mindreading involves detecting emotions, identifying goal-driven actions, sensitivity to eye gaze, and so on. High-level mindreading involves identifying and reasoning about beliefs, desires, and other psychological states. This gives us two further questions:

> *Question 2* Is there evidence at the neural level that *low-level mindreading* is a process of simulation involving co-opted systems?
>
> *Question 3* Is there evidence at the neural level that *high-level mindreading* is a process of simulation involving co-opted systems?

Neuroimaging evidence for a dedicated theory of mind system?

We looked in some detail at neuroimaging techniques in Chapter 11. Neuroimaging allows cognitive scientists to map activity in the brain while subjects are performing specific tasks. Assuming that the BOLD signal is a good index of cognitive activity, neuroimaging can give us a picture of which neural regions are recruited for particular types of information-processing tasks. On the face of it, therefore, this offers an excellent opportunity to tackle the first of our three questions – the question of whether there is any evidence at the neural level for the existence of a dedicated theory of mind system. As emerged in Chapter 11, neuroimaging is a powerful tool, but one to be used with caution. As with all experiments, much depends upon the exact question that is being asked. So what exactly would count as evidence for a dedicated theory of mind system? In order to focus the issue neuroscientists have concentrated primarily on beliefs. They have tried to uncover whether there are any neural areas that are dedicated to reasoning about beliefs. This allows them to draw on (and adapt) the vast amount of research that has been done on young children's understanding of false belief. It should be noted, though, that very little neuroimaging has been done on children. Almost all of the experiments have been done on adults.

Experimenters have looked for brain regions that have the following two characteristics:

1 They show increased activity in response to information-processing tasks that require the subject to attribute beliefs.
2 These increased activation levels are specific to tasks involving belief attribution – as opposed, for example, to reflecting demands on general reasoning, or the fact that people (rather than inanimate objects) are involved.

As far as (1) is concerned, it is very important that a candidate TOMM region should show increased activation both for false belief tasks and for true belief tasks. What (2) is asking for is evidence that the neural systems are engaged in domain-specific processing. In order to establish that (2) holds, experimenters need to make sure that they have controlled for domain-general processes (such as language or working memory).

Neuroimaging studies have identified a number of brain regions as showing increased activation in tasks that seem to require reasoning about beliefs. Most of these studies have involved versions of the false belief test, although some have explored different paradigms. The cognitive psychologist Vinod Goel, for example, ran a series of studies in which he asked subjects to decide whether Christopher Columbus would have been able to work out the function of an object from a picture – the idea being that this task requires subjects to reason about the sort of beliefs that a fifteenth-century explorer would have been likely to have. Other studies had subjects read a short story and then answer questions on it. Some of the questions required making inferences about the beliefs of characters in the story and others not.

Studies such as these have identified a number of brain regions as potentially forming part of a dedicated theory of mind system. These include (working more or less from front to back):

- medial prefrontal cortex
- anterior cingulate cortex
- orbitofrontal cortex
- temporal pole
- Broca's area
- anterior superior temporal sulcus
- fusiform gyrus
- temporoparietal junction
- posterior superior temporal sulcus

This is a long list and, as we see in Figure 12.10, these regions collectively cover a large area of the brain.

The list includes a number of brain areas thought to be specialized for other information-processing functions. Broca's area, for example, is widely held to be involved in aspects of language processing, while the fusiform gyrus includes the fusiform face area (which has been hypothesized as a dedicated face-processing system). This is not particularly surprising. The various tasks that have been used to explore belief attribution inevitably bring other capacities and abilities into play. In order to narrow the list down we need to see which (if any) of these areas satisfy (1) and (2) above.

The first stage, corresponding to (1), is to check whether particular neural regions show activation both in false belief and in true belief conditions. This is particularly important, since many neuroimaging studies follow the developmental studies in focusing only on false belief conditions. This emphasis on false belief is fine for looking at the development of mindreading in children – since the crucial developmental measure is standardly taken to be success on false belief tasks. But if we are looking for a neural substrate for belief reasoning we need to consider true belief conditions as well as false ones – after all, perhaps some of the activation in the false belief condition is due to the falsity of the belief attributed, rather than to its being a belief.

Rebecca Saxe and Nancy Kanwisher carried out a set of false belief experiments with a true belief condition as a control. We will look at these experiments in more detail below

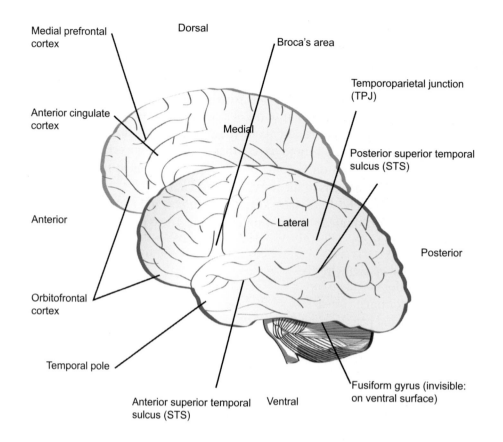

Figure 12.10 Schematic representation of brain regions associated with the attribution of mental states. (Adapted from Saxe, Carey, and Kanwisher 2004)

(in the context of identifying mechanisms specialized for theory of mind tasks). For the moment we need only note what happened when they did a more detailed statistical analysis of the patterns of activation within individual subjects. They found three brain regions where both true and false belief attribution tasks elicited activation in the very same voxels. (Recall that a voxel is a *volumetric pixel* representing a small volume within the brain.) These regions are:

- medial prefrontal cortex (MPFC)
- superior temporal sulcus (STS)
- temporoparietal junction (TPJ)

Applying (1), then, significantly narrows down the field. What happens when we apply (2)?

In order to apply (2) we need to find a way of controlling for some of the other types of domain-general information processing that might be generating activation in the candidate areas. Saxe and Kanwisher introduced two control conditions, based on their analysis of what is required in order to succeed on tasks involving belief attribution.

Their first observation is that when we attribute beliefs to other people we are effectively identifying hidden causes. This is because we typically attribute beliefs when we are trying to explain or predict behavior, and we cannot do so in terms of what is immediately observable. So, in order to make sure that activation in the candidate theory of mind areas really does reflect domain-specific theory of mind reasoning, we need to rule out the possibility that what is going on is really just domain-general reasoning about hidden causes. To do this, Saxe and Kanwisher developed a set of stories depending on non-psychological hidden causes. Here are two:

- The beautiful ice sculpture received first prize in the contest. It was very intricate. Unfortunately, the temperatures that night hit a record high for January. By dawn, there was no sculpture.
- The night was warm and dry. There had not been a cloud anywhere for days. The moisture was certainly not from rain. And yet, in the early morning, the long grasses were dripping with cool water.

Call this the hidden causes condition.

Saxe and Kanwisher also wanted to rule out the possibility that activation is due to general reasoning about false representations – as opposed to false *beliefs*. There is nothing psychological about a false representation such as a misleading map, for example. In order to rule out the possibility that the neural areas active in belief attribution are specialized for information processing to do with representations in general rather than theory of mind, Saxe and Kanwisher used a version of the *false photograph task* originally proposed by the developmental psychologist Debbie Zaitchik.

Here is a false photograph version of the false belief task. As before, the subject is presented with a story in which Sally places a marble in the basket. A photograph is taken of the contents of the basket and placed face down. After the photograph is taken, Anne moves the marble from the basket to the box. Everything is exactly as in the false belief task – except that the subjects are asked where the object appears in the photograph. The idea behind the task is that a subject who does not understand the possibility of false representations will think that the object's location in the photograph will be where it really is – and so the photograph will depict the marble as being in the box.

Exercise 12.12 Assess the reasoning behind the false photograph task.

Experimental subjects were presented with a number of short stories and questions in each of the three conditions. Saxe and Kanwisher found that there was significant activation in the three regions identified earlier (MPFC, STS, and TPJ) in the belief attribution condition, but not in the false representation or hidden causes conditions. They concluded that these three regions satisfy the constraints that we have numbered (1) and (2).

The Saxe and Kanwisher experiments seem to support the claim that there is a neural system or circuit dedicated to theory of mind reasoning. Unsurprisingly, though, some cognitive scientists have disagreed. Some cognitive scientists have suggested that Saxe and Kanwisher did not control for all the domain-general processes potentially involved in belief attribution tasks – such as memory or language. Saxe and Kanwisher (and others) have responded by developing new experimental paradigms and refining those already in existence. Although the experiments described here were first published in 2003, this has already become one of the most exciting and productive areas of social neuroscience.

It is important to realize, however, that this debate is fairly circumscribed relative to our discussion earlier in this chapter. What is at stake here is simply the existence of brain regions specialized for processing information about mental states such as belief. Although the issue is standardly framed in terms of a dedicated *theory of mind* system, the experiments we have been looking at tell us little about how information is processed in that system (if indeed there does turn out to be one). For that we need to turn to our second and third questions.

Neuroscientific evidence for simulation in low-level mindreading?

Look back at Simon Baron-Cohen's model of the mindreading system in Figure 12.6. The theory of mind mechanism (TOMM) is a relatively small part of the overall mindreading system – just one out of six components. At least until recently, this part of the mindreading system has received by far the most attention from cognitive scientists. This is not very surprising, since it is in many ways the most sophisticated and visible tool that we have for navigating the social world. But, as the model brings out, we have a range of other tools besides explicit reasoning about beliefs, desires, and other propositional attitudes. So, for example, we are sensitive to other people's emotional states, to where their eyes are directed, and to what the targets of their actions are.

Important recent work in cognitive neuroscience has shed light on some of the mechanisms responsible for these more primitive forms of mindreading. Supporters of the simulationist approach to mindreading have argued that a number of results support their ideas about how mindreading works. One of the basic claims of simulation theorists is that mindreading is carried out by what they call *co-opted mechanisms*. These are information-processing systems that normally serve another function and that are then recruited to help make sense of the social world. A number of experiments have been interpreted by simulation theorists as showing that co-opted mechanisms play a fundamental role in mindreading.

One very basic form of mindreading is the ability to read emotions off perceptible bodily states. Facial expressions are the most obvious example, but tone and timbre of voice are often good guides to emotions, as are global features of posture (the vitality and energy of someone's movements, for example). Young children start to develop their skills in this form of mindreading at a very early age. It is an automatic and unconscious process for normal people – fundamental to our interactions with other people, and of course to how we respond to pictures and films. In Baron-Cohen's model it is the job of a dedicated component: the emotion detector.

On the simulationist view, the emotion detector is likely to be a co-opted mechanism (or set of mechanisms). What sort of co-opted mechanisms? The most obvious candidates are the very same mechanisms that allow people to experience emotions. The simulationist approach to mindreading holds that there is a single set of emotion mechanisms that come into play both when agents are experiencing emotional states and when they detect emotions in others. Is there any evidence that this is so? Some suggestive results have come from the study of brain-damaged patients. The simulation theory does generate some fairly clear predictions about possible patterns of brain damage.

These predictions emerge because there is evidence from neuroimaging studies that certain brain areas play specific roles in mediating particular emotions. So, for example, many studies have found that a region of the temporal lobe known as the *amygdala* plays an important role in mediating fear. The experience of disgust, in contrast, is much more closely correlated with activity in the *insula*, which lies in the lateral sulcus, separating the temporal lobe from the parietal cortex. (Both the amygdala and the insula form part of the *limbic system.*)

According to simulation theory, the very same mechanism that mediates the experience of a particular emotion is recruited when the subject recognizes that emotion in someone else. So, for example, a simulationist would expect the amygdala to be active both when someone is undergoing fear and when they identify that fear in others. And, conversely, a simulationist would expect damage to the amygdala to result in a patient having problems *both* with the experience of fear and with identifying fear in others. The prediction, therefore, is that damage to brain regions that play a significant role in mediating particular emotions will result in *paired deficits* - in problems with experiencing the relevant emotion and in identifying it in others.

There is evidence of paired deficits for several different emotional states.

- *Fear.* Ralph Adolphs and his colleague have studied a number of patients with damage to the amygdala. The patient S.M., for example, had her amygdala destroyed on both sides of the brain by Urbach–Wiethe disease. She is, quite literally, fearless - although she knows what fear is, she does not experience it. She is also significantly impaired on tests that require identifying fear on the basis of facial expression. Psychopathic patients are known to have both smaller amygdalas than normal subjects and reduced capacities for experiencing fear. It turns out that they are also much less good than normal controls at identifying fear in others.
- *Anger.* The neurotrasmitter *dopamine* is thought to play an important role in the experience of anger. Experiments on rats, for example, have shown that levels of aggression can be directly manipulated by raising/lowering the rat's dopamine levels. In humans, dopamine production can be temporarily blocked with a drug called *sulpiride.* Experiments have shown that subjects whose dopamine levels have been lowered in this way are significantly worse than controls in recognizing anger from facial expression - but do not have problems with other emotions.
- *Disgust.* The brain area most associated with the experience of disgust is the insula. Neuroimaging studies have shown that this area is also activated when subjects observe

facial expressions of disgust. This result is confirmed by studies of brain-damaged patients. N.K., a much-studied patient suffering from damage to the insula and basal ganglia, has severe problems both in experiencing disgust and in recognizing it in others. He performs no differently from controls, however, with regard to other basic emotions (such as surprise and fear).

Supporters of the simulationist approach to mindreading have also found evidence for co-opted mechanisms in some much-publicized experiments on "mirror neurons." We looked briefly at mirror neurons in section 11.2, as an example of what we can learn from recording electrical activity in single neurons. (This would be a good moment to look back at Figure 11.5 to see mirror neurons in action.)

Mirror neurons were first discovered in macaque monkeys by an Italian research group led by Giacomo Rizzolatti in the mid-1990s. Rizzolatti and his colleagues were recording the responses of neurons that showed selective activation when the monkey made certain hand movements (such as reaching for a piece of food) when they noticed completely by chance that the same neurons fired when the monkey saw an experimenter making the same movement.

In monkeys the mirror neuron system is located in area F5 in the ventral premotor cortex, as well as in the inferior parietal lobe. There has been considerable discussion about whether mirror neurons exist in humans. No mirror neurons have ever been directly detected in humans – not surprisingly, since it is not usually possible to make single-cell recordings in humans. The evidence for mirror neurons in humans comes primarily from fMRI studies. Studies have found a brain system that appears to have the basic "mirroring" feature – that is, its elements show activation both when the subject performs certain actions and when others are observed making that action. Researchers have dubbed this system the mirror neuron system. The mirror neuron system is illustrated in Figure 12.11 and described in the accompanying caption.

A number of cognitive scientists have suggested that the mirror neuron system functions as an *empathy* system. It allows people to *resonate* to the psychological states of other people. So, for example, studies have shown that areas in the mirror neuron system are activated both when the subjects feel pain and when they observe a loved one undergoing a painful stimulus. In terms of the models that we have been using, this would mean that the mirror neuron system could serve as a neural substrate both for TED (the emotion detector system) and TESS (the empathy system). And, as the caption to Figure 12.11 brings out, it is also thought that the mirror neuron system is part of what makes imitation possible.

Some of the stronger claims that have been made in this area should be treated with caution. Quite apart from any skepticism about whether there actually are any mirror neurons in humans, there are definite limits to the explanatory power of mirror neurons. Macaque monkeys are not very sophisticated mindreaders, to put it mildly, and so one might reasonably wonder about the role that can be played in mindreading by neural mechanisms present both in humans and monkeys.

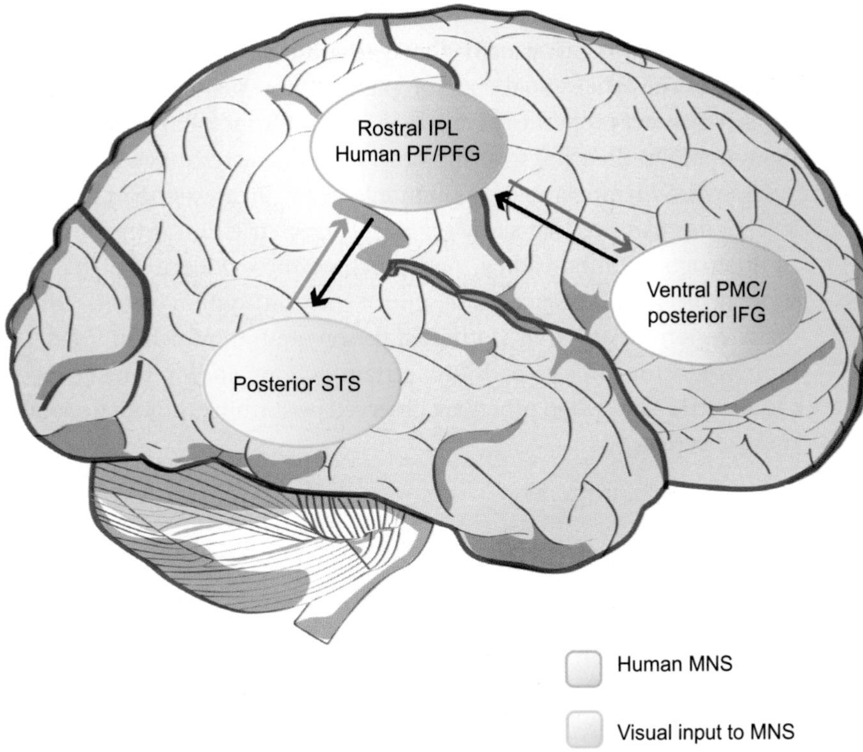

Figure 12.11 Schematic overview of the frontoparietal mirror neuron system (MNS) (pink) and its main visual input (yellow) in the human brain. An anterior area with mirror neuron properties is located in the inferior frontal cortex, encompassing the posterior inferior frontal gyrus (IFG) and adjacent ventral premotor cortex (PMC). A posterior area with mirror neuron properties is located in the rostral part of the inferior parietal lobule (IPL), and can be considered the human homolog of area PF/PFG in the macaque. The main visual input to the MNS originates from the posterior sector of the superior temporal sulcus (STS). Together, these three areas form a "core circuit" for imitation. The visual input from the STS to the MNS is represented by an orange arrow. The red arrow represents the information flow from the parietal MNS, which is mostly concerned with the motoric description of the action, to the frontal MNS, which is more concerned with the goal of the action. The black arrows represent efference copies of motor predictions of imitative motor plans and the visual description of the observed action. (Adapted from Iacoboni and Dapretto 2006)

The most likely application for mirror neurons is the information processing associated with understanding basic forms of goal-driven action – what Baron-Cohen calls the intentionality detector. Certainly, there is some evidence that mirror neurons are sensitive to goals (rather than simply to bodily movements). A study published in 2001 by Alessandra Umilta and colleagues showed that mirror neurons fire even when the monkey cannot see the final stages of the action. They used a screen to hide the experimenter's hand when it actually grasped the object and found that about 50 percent of the mirror neurons usually tuned to grasping actions were activated even in the absence of the usual visual cues for grasping. It seems that mirror neurons are sensitive to fairly abstract properties of movements – to the fact that they are goal-directed, rather than simply to their physical and observable characteristics.

In any event, mirror neurons in monkeys are direct examples at the most basic neural level of mechanisms that show the *dual purpose* structure at the heart of the simulationist approach to mindreading. And much of the evidence that has been produced in support of the existence of a mirror neuron system points to the existence of brain regions that serve both first-person and third-person roles. They are active both when the subject performs certain actions and/or undergoes experiences of a certain type – and when others are observed performing those actions and/or undergoing those experiences.

Neuroscientific evidence for simulation in high-level mindreading?

The issues are much less clear when we turn to high-level mindreading – the type of mindreading that involves attributing beliefs, desires, and other propositional attitudes. There is far less direct evidence for simulation in high-level mindreading than in the lower-level processes that we have just been discussing. Nonetheless, there are some suggestive results.

As we saw earlier, simulationists differ on how exactly the process of simulation is supposed to work. For standard simulationists, the process of simulation requires some form of *inference by analogy*. In essence, the simulator works out what she would do in a given situation and then infers (analogically) that the person she is trying to predict will do the same thing. Radical simulationists, in contrast, think that simulation can take place without this type of inference from oneself to others. They hold that simulation is fundamentally a matter of adopting another person's perspective – putting oneself into their shoes, as it were.

There is a prediction here. If standard simulation is a correct way of thinking about mindreading then mindreading should be both a first-person and a third-person process. The basic engine of simulation is the simulator running her own decision-making processes offline and identifying her own mental states. The results of this first-person simulation are then applied to the person being simulated. The prediction from standard simulation, therefore, is that regions of the brain specialized for what is sometimes called *self-reflection* (i.e. identifying one's own psychological attributes, abilities, and character traits) will be active during tasks that require mindreading.

There is some evidence bearing this prediction out. A number of studies have shown that self-reflection tasks elicit activation in an area of the brain thought to be involved in high-level mindreading – the medial prefrontal cortex (MPFC – illustrated in Figure 12.10). So, for example, in one set of studies (published by William Kelly and collaborators in

2002) subjects were presented with various written adjectives and asked some questions about them. These questions were either perceptual ("Is this adjective written in italics?"), self-directed ("Does this adjective describe you?"), or other-directed ("Does this adjective describe the President?"). The self-directed questions consistently generated greater activation in MPFC.

Further support for this apparent connection between self-reflection and mindreading came from a study published by Jason Mitchell, Mazharin Banaji, and Neil Macrae in 2005. The experimenters scanned subjects while they were presented with photographs of other people and asked questions about them. Some questions required mindreading ("How pleased is this person to have their photograph taken?"), while others did not ("How symmetrical is this person's face?"). After a short delay the subjects were presented with the photographs again and asked how similar they thought the other person was to themselves. This question is important for simulation theorists because simulation is likely to work best for people whom one thinks are similar to oneself.

The experimenters came up with two significant results. The first was further evidence that MPFC is important in high-level mindreading – MPFC showed much higher activation levels on the mindreading version of the task than on the other version. More significant was what happened when the experimenters compared activation in MPFC on the mindreading version of the task with the subjects' subsequent judgments when they were asked how similar they perceived the other person to be to themselves. It turned out that there was a significant correlation between activation in MPFC while the subjects were answering the mindreading questions and the degree of similarity that subjects subsequently observed between themselves and the person in the photograph. The greater the perceived similarity with the person in the photograph, the higher the level of activation in the subject's MPFC.

The cognitive neuroscience of mindreading is clearly a fascinating and thriving area. We have reviewed a number of important findings and experiments. It is far too early to draw any definite conclusions. But even this brief review illustrates very clearly two important points that emerged in earlier chapters:

- The cognitive neuroscience of mindreading involves careful calibration of results from different technologies. This comes across very clearly in the way experimenters have worked through the potential implications of mirror neurons for thinking about mindreading in humans. Single-neuron studies in monkeys have been calibrated by functional neuroimaging in humans.
- Neuroscientists interested in mindreading are not simply exploring the neural implementation of cognitive information-processing models developed in abstraction from details about how the brain works. It is true that much of the discussion in this area is driven by psychological experiments such as the false belief task and the cognitive models that have been produced in response to them, but participants at all levels in the debate clearly recognize that techniques from neuroscience have a crucial role to play in testing, confirming, and developing cognitive models.

Summary

This chapter explored a case study in how cognitive scientists think about the mind in terms of dedicated information-processing systems. The overarching theme for the chapter was the idea that there is a dedicated system for mindreading – for understanding other minds and navigating the social world. The chapter began by reviewing Leslie's theory that mindreading exploits a set of basic abilities that are also deployed in pretend play. These are abilities for metarepresentation – for representing representations. We looked at a famous set of experiments using the false belief task that seemed to show that autistic children (who are known to be deficient in pretend play) are also impaired in tasks involving reasoning about other people's beliefs. Mindreading is a complex phenomenon and we looked at a model of mindreading that sees it as made up of six distinct components, emerging at different stages in cognitive development. We compared two different ways of thinking about how mindreading develops and then explored an alternative model of mindreading. According to simulationists, there is no dedicated mindreading system. Instead mindreading is carried out by our "ordinary" cognitive systems running offline with pretend inputs. Finally, we reviewed a range of evidence from cognitive neuroscience, including research bearing on the question of whether there is a dedicated mindreading system.

Checklist

Alan Leslie's model of mindreading in young children is based on an analogy wwith the information processing involved in pretend play

(1) The emergence of pretend play in the second year of life is a major milestone in cognitive and social development.

(2) In pretend play some of an infant's *primary representations* of the world and other people become "decoupled" from their usual functions while preserving their ordinary meaning.

(3) Leslie thinks that primary representations function in the same way in pretend play as in mindreading. Both pretend play and mindreading exploit *metarepresentation*.

(4) Children with autism have significant problems both with mindreading and with pretend play.

(5) The false belief task (developed by Heinz Wimmer and Joseph Perner) is a standard test of mindreading abilities in children. It tests whether children are able to abstract away from their own knowledge to understand that someone else can have different (and mistaken) beliefs about the world.

High-level mindreading involves attributing *propositional attitudes* (such as beliefs and desires) to other people. But high-level mindreading depends upon a complex system of lower-level mechanisms – as in Simon Baron-Cohen's model of the overall mindreading system

(1) The *intentionality detector* is responsible for perceptual sensitivity to purposeful movements.

(2) The *eye direction detector* makes it easier to identify the goals of purposeful movements and to see where other people's attention is focused.

(3) The *emotion detector* gives a basic sensitivity to emotions and moods, as revealed in facial expressions, tone of voice, etc.

(4) The *shared attention mechanism* makes possible a range of coordinated social behaviors and collaborative activities.

(5) The *empathizing system* is responsible for affective responses to other people's moods and emotions (as opposed to simply identifying them).

Young children do not typically pass the false belief task before the age of 4, although other parts of the mindreading system come onstream much sooner. Different explanations have been given of this time lag

(1) Leslie argues that the theory of mind mechanism emerges during the infant's second year. But its default setting is to attribute true beliefs. Overcoming that default setting requires the emergence of an inhibitory mechanism that he calls the *selection processor*.

(2) Support for the selection processor interpretation comes from *double inhibition experiments*.

(3) For Perner, in contrast, children do not understand belief, properly speaking, until they pass the false belief task. Understanding belief requires the possibility of metarepresentation, and an inability to metarepresent explains failure on the task.

(4) Perner (and others) have developed accounts of pretend play on which it does not involve metarepresentation.

Perner and Leslie (and many other cognitive scientists) are committed to the idea that there is a dedicated theory of mind system responsible for identifying and reasoning about other people's beliefs, desires, and other propositional attitudes. This basic assumption is challenged by the simulationist approach to mindreading

(1) Simulationists think that mindreading is carried out by "ordinary" information-processing systems that are co-opted for mindreading. We use our own mind as a model of someone else's mind.

(2) According to standard simulationism, we predict other people's behavior, for example, by running our decision-making processes offline, with pretend beliefs and desires as inputs.

(3) Radical simulationists hold that mindreading does not involve representing another person's psychological states. Rather, it involves representing the world from their perspective.

Cognitive neuroscientists have used a range of techniques, including single-neuron recording and functional neuroimaging, in order to test and refine cognitive models of mindreading. These are early days in the cognitive neuroscience of mindreading, but some suggestive results have already emerged. For example:

(1) Neuroimaging studies have identified a number of brain areas that show increased activation during mindreading tasks. Experiments by Saxe and Kanwisher, for example, have highlighted the medial prefrontal cortex, the superior temporal sulcus, and the inferior parietal lobule. This is consistent with the claim that there is a dedicated theory of mind system.

(2) There is evidence that co-opted mechanisms are used in low-level mindreading (as predicted by the simulation theory). Areas active during the experience of basic emotions such as fear, disgust, and anger are also active when those emotions are identified in others.

(3)   Mirror neurons in area F5 of the macaque brain respond both when the monkey performs an action and when the monkey observes an experimenter or conspecific perform that action. A number of researchers have hypothesized a mirror neuron system in the human brain. This may play an important role in understanding goal-directed action.

(4)   There is evidence consistent with the simulation-driven processing in high-level mindreading. Experiments have shown that areas specialized for self-reflection are also implicated in mindreading (as predicted by standard simulationism).

Further reading

Leslie first presented his metarepresentational theory of pretend play and mindreading in Leslie 1987. The theory has been considerably modified and developed since then (as discussed in section 12.4). See Leslie and Polizzi 1998, Leslie, Friedman, and German 2004, and Leslie, German, and Polizzi 2005 for updates. The false belief task discussed in the text was first presented in Wimmer and Perner 1983. It has been much discussed (and criticized). For powerful criticisms see Bloom and German 2000. Perner's own theory of mindreading is presented in his book *Understanding the Representational Mind* (Perner 1993). There are numerous recent reviews discussing both implicit and explicit false belief understanding (Baillargeon, Scott, and He 2010, Beate 2011, Low and Perner 2012, Luo and Baillargeon 2010, Perner and Roessler 2012, and Trauble, Marinovic, and Pauen 2010). For a recent philosophical discussion of this research see Carruthers 2013.

The idea that autism is essentially a disorder of mindreading was first presented in Baron-Cohen, Leslie, and Frith 1985. For a book-length discussion of autism as "mindblindness" see Baron-Cohen 1995. This interpretation of autism has been challenged – see, for example, Boucher 1996. The papers in Baron-Cohen, Tager-Flusberg, and Cohen 2000 discuss autism from the perspective of developmental psychology and cognitive neuroscience. For a more recent survey see Baron-Cohen 2009.

Mindreading was one of the earliest fields to see sustained interactions and collaborations between philosophers and psychologists. A number of influential early papers, including Heal 1986 and Gordon 1986, are gathered in two anthologies edited by Davies and Stone (1995a and 1995b). Both have very useful introductions. The dialog is continued in the papers in Carruthers and Smith 1996. Much of this debate focuses on comparing simulationist approaches to mindreading (as presented in section 12.5) with the more traditional approach discussed in earlier sections (what is often called the theory theory model of mindreading). Goldman 2006 is a book-length defense of simulationism, written by a philosopher but with extensive discussions of the empirical literature.

Recent studies on the cognitive neuroscience of mindreading include Apperly *et al*. 2004, Samson *et al*. 2004, Samson *et al*. 2005, Saxe and Kanwisher 2005, Saxe, Carey, and Kanwisher 2004, Tamir and Mitchell 2010, and Waytz and Mitchell 2011. Recent reviews can be found in Abu-Akel and Shamay-Tsoory 2011, Adolphs 2009, Carrington and Bailey 2009, Frith and Frith, 2012, and Saxe 2009. Claims about the modularity of mindreading are critically discussed in Apperly, Samson, and Humphreys 2005. For skepticism about the false photograph task see Perner and Leekam 2008.

Research into mirror neurons has been reported in many papers – see, for example, Rizzolatti, Fogassi, and Gallese 2001. The findings are presented for a general audience in Rizzolatti, Fogassi, and Gallese 2006 (article) and Rizzolatti, Singaglia, and Andersen 2008 (book). For a more recent review see Rizzolatti and Sinigaglia 2010.

For more information on empirical findings about emotion recognition in brain-damaged and normal patients see Adolphs *et al*. 1994, Phillips *et al*. 1997, Adolphs and Tranel 2000, and Wicker *et al*. 2003.

PART V

NEW HORIZONS

INTRODUCTION

Investigating the interdisciplinary origins of cognitive science in Part I highlighted a theme that was one of the guiding ideas in this new discipline and throughout the book – that cognition is a form of information processing. Part II reinforced this theme by examining the integration challenge, and proposed thinking about this challenge in terms of different mental architectures. A mental architecture is a way of thinking about the overall organization of the mind in terms of different cognitive systems, together with a model of how information is processed within and across these systems. In Part III we explored different models of information processing, focusing on both the computer-inspired physical symbol hypothesis and the neurally inspired artificial neural networks approach. Part IV explored the concept of modularity, the idea that many information-processing tasks are carried out by specialized sub-systems (modules).

In the final section of this book we turn to new and different ways of modeling cognitive abilities and will look ahead at some of the challenges and opportunities facing cognitive science at this exciting time.

Chapter 13 describes how some cognitive scientists have used the mathematical and conceptual tools of dynamical systems theory to develop what they see as an alternative to thinking of cognition as information processing, modeling cognitive subjects instead as components of complex dynamical systems that evolve over time. We will look at concrete examples from child development. The second part of the chapter looks at the situated cognition movement, which has also proposed alternatives to the information-processing model, based on studying simple biological organisms and using that as a guide to build robots very different from those envisioned by traditional AI.

Chapter 14 explores the cognitive science of consciousness – a fast-moving and exciting area that raises fundamental questions about the potential limits of explanation in cognitive science. Some philosophers and cognitive scientists have argued that some aspects of experience cannot be fully explained through scientific tools and techniques. We will look at those arguments in the context of the thriving research program that exists in the cognitive science of consciousness, focusing in particular on studies of the differences between conscious and non-conscious information processing, and on what this tells us about the role and function of consciousness and how it might be neutrally implemented.

The final chapter previews exciting areas such as the Human Connectome Project and President Obama's BRAIN initiative; understanding what happens in the brain while it is in its default resting state; considering whether prostheses for the brain are possible; developing learning technologies; and the possibility of broadening cognitive science to include disciplines such as economics and law.

CHAPTER THIRTEEN

New horizons: Dynamical systems and situated cognition

Overview

Throughout this book we have been working through some of the basic consequences of a single principle. This is the principle that cognition is information processing. It is in many ways the most important framework assumption of cognitive science. The historical overview in Part I explored how researchers from a number of different disciplines converged on the information-processing model of cognition in the middle of the twentieth century. In Part III we looked at different ways of thinking about information processing – the physical symbol system hypothesis and the neural networks model. Despite their very significant differences, the physical symbol system and neural network approaches share a fundamental commitment to the idea that cognitive activity is essentially a matter of transforming representational states that carry information about the agent and about the environment.

In this chapter we turn to some of the new horizons opened up by two different ways of modeling cognitive abilities. Sections 13.1 and 13.2 explore how some cognitive scientists have proposed using the mathematical and conceptual tools of dynamical systems theory to model cognitive skills and abilities. One of the particular strengths of dynamical systems theory is the time-sensitivity that it offers. Dynamical models can be used to plot how a system evolves over time as a function of changes in a small number of system variables.

As we see in section 13.1, dynamical systems models differ in certain fundamental respects from the information-processing models we have been looking at. In section 13.2 we explore two examples of how dynamical systems models can shed light on child development. Dynamical systems theory offers fresh and distinctive perspectives both on how infants learn to walk and on infants' expectations about objects that they are no longer perceiving (as revealed in the so-called A-not-B error).

The second half of the chapter looks at the situated cognition movement in robotics. Situated cognition theorists are also dissatisfied with traditional information-processing approaches to cognitive science and have developed a powerful toolkit of alternatives. Some of the most exciting developments in situated cognition have come in artificial intelligence and robotics. This is what we will focus on here.

Section 13.3 brings out some of the complaints that situated cognition theorists level at traditional GOFAI (good old-fashioned AI) and illustrates some of the engineering inspiration that these theorists have drawn from studying very simple cognitive systems such as insects. In section 13.4 we look at how these theoretical ideas have been translated into particular robotic architectures, focusing on the subsumption architectures developed by Rodney Brooks, and at an example of what Maja Matarić has termed behavior-based robotics.

13.1 Cognitive science and dynamical systems

According to the dynamical systems hypothesis, cognitive science needs to be freed from its dependence on the ideas that we have been studying in earlier chapters. We can understand how organisms can respond to the environment and orient themselves in it without assuming that there are internal cognitive systems that carry out specific information-processing tasks. The basic currency of cognitive science is not the information-carrying representation, and nor are computations and algorithms the best way to think about how cognition unfolds.

So how should we think about mind, brain, and behavior, if we are not allowed to talk about representations and computations? It is not easy even to understand the suggestion. Anyone who has got this far through the book will most likely think that the idea of cognition without representations or computation is almost a contradiction in terms. But in fact dynamical systems theorists have very powerful theoretical machinery that they can bring to bear. Their basic idea is that cognitive scientists need to use the tools of dynamical systems theory in order to understand how perceivers and agents are embedded in their environments. And the study of dynamical systems has been pursued in physics and other natural sciences for many centuries.

What are dynamical systems?

In the broadest sense a dynamical system is any system that evolves over time in a law-governed way. The solar system is a dynamical system. So are you and I. So is a dripping tap. And so, for that matter, are Turing machines and artificial neural networks. There must be more to the dynamical systems hypothesis than the observation that cognitive agents are dynamical systems. This observation is both trivial and perfectly compatible with either of the two dominant information-processing approaches to cognition.

What distinguishes the dynamical systems hypothesis is the idea that cognitive systems should be studied with the tools of dynamical modeling. Dynamical modeling exploits powerful mathematical machinery to understand the evolution of certain types of natural phenomena. Newtonian mechanics is perhaps the most famous example of dynamical modeling, but all dynamical models have certain basic features.

Dynamical models typically track the evolving relationship between a relatively small number of quantities that change over time. They do this using calculus and differential or difference equations. Difference equations allow us to model the evolution of a system that changes in discrete steps. So, for example, we might use difference equations to model how the size of a biological population changes over time – each step being a year, for example. Differential equations, in contrast, allow us to model quantities that change continuously, such as the acceleration of a falling object.

One of the basic theoretical ideas in dynamical systems modeling is the idea of a *state space*. The state space of a dynamical system is a geometric way of thinking about all the possible states that a system can be in. A state space has as many different dimensions as it has quantities that vary independently of each other – as many different dimensions as there are degrees of freedom in the system. Any state of the dynamical system will involve the system having a particular value in each dimension. And so we can uniquely identify the state of the system in terms of a particular set of coordinates in the system's state space. The state space of an idealized swinging pendulum, for example, has two dimensions – one corresponding to its angle and one corresponding to its angular velocity. So, every possible state that the pendulum can be in can be represented by a pair of numbers, which in turn can be represented as a point in a two-dimensional space.

If we add another dimension to the state space to represent time then we can start thinking about the evolution of the pendulum in terms of a *trajectory* through state space. A trajectory through state space is simply a sequence of points in the multidimensional space. This sequence of points represents the successive states of the pendulum. Abstracting away from velocity, the state space of a simple pendulum is illustrated in Figure 13.1.

One of the basic aims of dynamical systems modeling is to write equations governing the evolution of the system – that is, governing the different possible trajectories that the system can take through state space, depending upon where the system starts (the system's *initial conditions*).

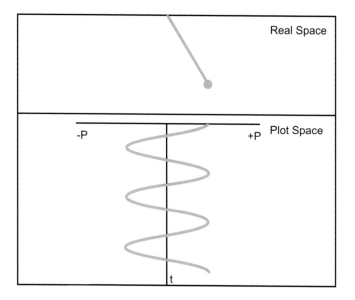

Figure 13.1 The trajectory through state space of an idealized swinging pendulum. The pendulum's position is its angle of displacement from the vertical (positive to the right and negative to the left). The time axis goes vertically downwards. By permission of M. Casco Associates

In the case of a simple pendulum, its position is determined solely by its amplitude (its initial angle of displacement) and the length of time it has been swinging. The equation is $p = A \times \sin(t)$. The trajectory, and corresponding equations, get much more complicated as we remove the simplifying conditions (by allowing for friction, for example) and taking more variables into account. If we reintroduce velocity and allow for energy loss due to friction, for example, the state space might look like Figure 13.2.

Exercise 13.1 Explain in your own words the difference between Figures 13.1 and 13.2.

But what, you may reasonably ask, has this got to do with cognitive science?

The dynamical systems hypothesis: Cognitive science without representations?

We can see how and why dynamical systems could be relevant to cognitive science by looking at a famous illustration introduced by the philosopher Tim Van Gelder, one of the early proponents of the dynamical systems hypothesis. Van Gelder introduces us to two ways of thinking about an engineering problem whose solution was a vital step in the Industrial Revolution. One way of solving the problem is structurally very similar to the information-processing approach to thinking about how the mind solves

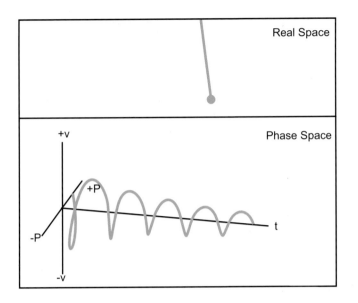

Figure 13.2 The state space of a swinging pendulum in a three-dimensional phase space. By permission of M. Casco Associates

problems. The other way, which is how the problem was actually solved, reveals the power of the dynamical systems approach.

Van Gelder's basic point is that cognitive scientists are essentially engaged in reverse engineering the mind – they are trying to work out how the mind is configured to solve the problems that it deals with. Cognitive scientists have tended to tackle this *reverse engineering* problem in a particular way – by assuming that the mind is an information-processing machine. But what Van Gelder tries to show is that this approach is neither the only way nor the best way. He does this by looking at an example from engineering itself – the Watt governor.

The development of the steam engine is very closely associated with the name of the Scottish engineer James Watt. The first steam engines were only capable of a reciprocating pumping motion. One of Watt's most significant contributions was designing a gearing system that allowed steam engines to drive a flywheel and hence to produce rotational power. This gearing system made it possible to use steam engines for weaving, grinding, and other industrial applications.

Unfortunately there was still a problem. The type of applications for which steam power was needed required the power source to be as uniform as possible. This, in turn, required the speed of the flywheel to be as constant as possible. But this was very hard to achieve because the speed of the flywheel depended upon two things that were constantly changing – the pressure of the steam driving the engine and the amount of work that the engine was doing. What was needed (and what Watt ended up inventing) was a *governor* that would regulate the speed of the flywheel.

The problem is clear, but how could it be solved? Van Gelder identifies one possible approach. This approach employs the sort of task analysis that we have encountered many times in this book. It breaks the task of regulating the speed of the flywheel into a series of sub-tasks, assumes that each of those sub-tasks is carried out in separate stages, and works out an algorithm for solving the problem by successively performing the sub-tasks. This approach gives what Van Gelder terms the *computational governor*, following something like the following algorithm:

1 Measure the speed of the flywheel
2 Compare the actual speed S_1 against the desired speed S_2
3 If $S_1 = S_2$, return to step 1
4 If $S_1 \neq S_2$ then
   (a) measure the current steam pressure
   (b) calculate the required alteration in steam pressure
   (c) calculate the throttle adjustment that will achieve that alteration
5 Make the throttle adjustment
6 Return to step 1

The computational governor has certain features that should be very familiar by now. It is *representational*, for example. It cannot work without some way of representing the speed of the flywheel, the pressure of the steam, and the state of the throttle valve. It is *computational*. The algorithm is essentially a process for comparing, transforming, and manipulating representations of speed, steam pressure, and so on. It is *sequential*. It works in a discrete, step-by-step manner. And finally, it is *decomposable* (or, as Van Gelder puts it, *homuncular*). That is to say, we can think of the computational governor as made up of distinct and semi-autonomous sub-systems, each responsible for a particular sub-task – the speed measurement system, the steam measurement system, the throttle adjustment system, and so on.

When we put all these features together we see that the computational governor is an application of some of the basic principles that cognitive scientists use to understand how the mind works. And it certainly seems to be a very natural way of solving the problem. The basic fact of the matter, though, is that Watt went about things in a very different way.

The Watt governor, which Watt developed using basic principles already exploited in windmills, has none of the key features of the computational governor. It does not involve representations and hence, as a consequence, cannot be computational. It is not sequential. And it is not decomposable. It is in fact, as Van Gelder points out, a dynamical system that is best studied using the tools of dynamical systems modeling. In order to see why we need to look more closely at how the Watt governor works.

The Watt governor is illustrated in Figure 13.3. The diagram at the top illustrates the Watt governor. The flywheel is right at the bottom. Coming up from the flywheel is a rotating spindle. The spindle rotates at a speed determined by the speed of the flywheel. It has two metal balls attached to it. As the speed of the spindle's rotation increases, centrifugal force drives the metal balls upwards. As the speed decreases the balls drop down. Watt's key idea was to connect the arms from which the metal balls are suspended directly to the throttle valve for the steam engine. Raising the arms closes down the throttle valve, while the valve is opened up when the arms fall.

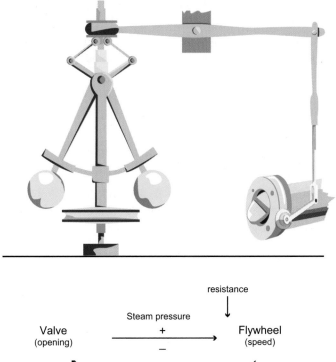

Figure 13.3 Illustration of the Watt governor, together with a schematic representation of how it works.

This ingenious arrangement allows the governor to regulate the speed by compensating almost instantaneously whether the speed of the flywheel is overshooting or undershooting. The lower part of Figure 13.3 illustrates the feedback loop.

Van Gelder stresses four very important features of the Watt governor:

- *Dynamical system.* The best way to understand the Watt governor is through the tools of dynamical systems theory. It is relatively straightforward to write a differential equation that will specify how the arm angle changes as a function of the engine speed. The system is a typical dynamical system because these equations have a small number of variables.
- *Time-sensitivity.* The Watt governor is all about timing. It works because fluctuations in the speed of the flywheel are almost instantly followed by variation in the arm angle. The differential equations governing the evolution of the system track the relation over time between flywheel speed and arm angle.
- *Coupling.* The Watt governor works because of the interdependence between the arm angle of the governor, the throttle valve, and the speed of the flywheel. The arm angle is a

parameter fixing the speed of the flywheel. But by the same token, the speed of the flywheel is a parameter fixing the angle of the arm. The system as a whole is what dynamical systems theorists call a coupled system characterized by feedback loops.

■ *Attractor dynamics.* For any given engine speed there is an equilibrium arm angle - an angle that will allow the engine to continue at that speed. We can think about this equilibrium arm angle as an attractor - a point in state space to which many different trajectories will converge. (See Box 13.1.)

BOX 13.1   Basins of attraction in state space

A particular dynamical system evolves through time along a trajectory in state space. The particular trajectory that it takes is typically a function of its initial conditions. So, the trajectory of the swinging pendulum, for example, is typically determined by its initial amplitude, together with the way that allowances for friction are built into the system.

But not all regions of state space are created equal. There are some regions of state space to which many different trajectories converge. These are called *basins of attraction*. In the case of a swinging pendulum subject to friction, there is a region of state space to which all trajectories converge – this is the point at which the pendulum is stationary.

Many dynamical systems have a number of basins of attraction – these are the *nonlinear dynamical* systems. There is a two-dimensional example in Figure B13.1.

The figure illustrates a range of different possible trajectories. The trajectories are marked by arrows, with the length of the arrow indicating the speed of the attraction (and hence the strength of the attraction). The state space has two basins of attraction.

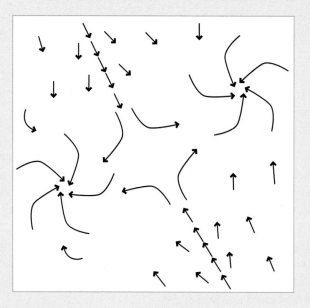

Figure B13.1

BOX 13.1   (cont.)

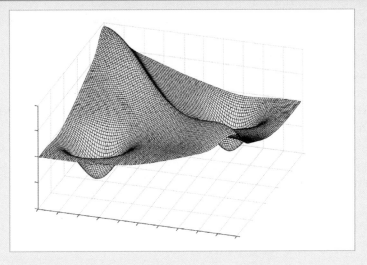

Figure B13.2

Figure B13.2 gives a different way of representing basins of attraction, in terms of what is often called an energy landscape. This gives a different way of visualizing how a system evolves through state space.

The undulating surface represents the space of possible trajectories. The two basins of attraction are represented by depressions in the surface. Since dynamical systems evolve towards a reduction in energy, trajectories will typically "roll" downhill until they end up in one of the two basins of attraction. In fact in this particular dynamical system any trajectory must begin on one side of the dividing "ridge" or the other – and so will end up in the corresponding basin of attraction.

So, the Watt governor can be characterized using the tools of dynamical systems theory. It is a coupled system that displays a simple version of attractor dynamics, because it contains basins of attraction (as described in Box 13.1). Unlike the computational governor, it does not involve any representation, computation, or decomposable sub-systems. Finally, the Watt governor works in real time. The adjustments are made almost instantaneously, exactly as required. It is very hard to see how the computational governor would achieve this.

But again, what has this got to do with the mind? It is not news, after all, that steam engines are not cognitive systems.

One fundamental point that Van Gelder and other supporters of the dynamical systems hypothesis are making is that the same basic tools that can be used to explain how the Watt governor works can be used to illuminate the workings of the mind. But the issue is not just about explanation. Dynamical systems theorists think that the explanations work because they track the basic design principles of the mind. They think not only that the mind is a dynamical system, but also that when we look at the relation between the organism and the environment what we see is a coupled system. The organism–environment complex is a system whose behavior evolves as a function of a small number of variables.

Certainly, the real test of this idea must come in concrete applications. The plausibility of the dynamical systems hypothesis cannot rest solely on an analogy between the mind and a steam engine – however suggestive that analogy may be. Some very exciting work has been done by cognitive scientists on giving dynamical systems models of particular cognitive abilities. Much of the most interesting research has been done on motor skills and motor learning. Dynamical systems theory has proved a powerful tool for understanding how children learn to walk, for example. In the next section we look at two applications of the dynamical systems approach to child development.

13.2 Applying dynamical systems: Two examples from child development

One of the key features of the dynamical systems approach is its time-sensitivity. Dynamical models can track the evolution of a system over time in very fine detail. This suggests that one profitable area to apply them is in studying how children learn new skills and abilities. In this section we look at two concrete examples of how episodes in child development can be modeled by dynamical systems theory. The dynamical systems approach certainly sheds light on things that look mysterious from the perspective of more standard information-processing approaches.

Two ways of thinking about motor control

Our first example is from the domain of motor control. It has to do with how infants learn to walk. The issue here is in many ways directly analogous to the example of the Watt governor. The dominant approach to understanding how movements are planned and executed is the computational model of motor control. This is the motor control equivalent of the computational governor. The dynamical systems approach offers an alternative – a non-computational way of thinking about how movements are organized and how motor skills emerge.

We can illustrate the computational model of motor control with a simple example. Consider the movement of reaching for an object. According to the computational model, planning this movement has to begin with the central nervous system calculating both the position of the target object and the position of the hand. These calculations will involve input both from vision and from different types of proprioception (such as sensors in the arm detecting muscle flexion). Planning the movement requires calculating a trajectory from the starting position to the goal position. It also involves computing a sequence of muscle movements that will take the hand along that trajectory. Finally,

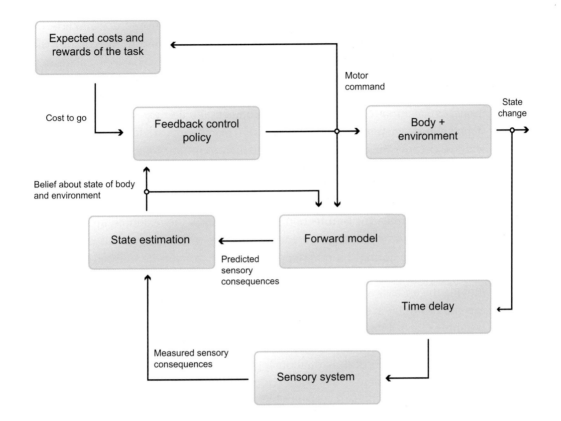

Figure 13.4 An example of the computational approach to motor control. This boxological model incorporates both forward mechanisms (that generate predictions about the sensory consequences of particular movements) and comparator mechanisms (that compare the predictions with actual sensory feedback). (Adapted from Shadmehr and Krakauer 2008)

executing the movement requires calculating changes in the muscle movements to accommodate visual and proprioceptive feedback. So, we have a multi-stage sequence of computations that seems tailor-made for algorithmic information processing. Figure 13.4 illustrates a computational model of motor control that fits this general description. It is a standard information-processing diagram – a boxological diagram.

But computational approaches to motor control are not the only possibility, as the psychologists Esther Thelen and Linda Smith have argued with specific reference to the case of infant walking.

Thelen and Smith make a powerful case that walking is not a planned activity in the way that many cognitive scientists have assumed, following the computational approach to motor control. It does not involve a specific set of motor commands that "program" the limbs to behave in certain ways. Rather, the activity of walking emerges out of complex interactions between muscles, limbs, and different features of the environment. There are many feedback loops controlling limb movements as a function of variation in both body and environment.

Concrete evidence for Thelen and Smith's position comes from studies on how infants learn to walk. Most normal infants start learning to walk towards the end of their first year – at around 11 months. For the first few months infants are capable of making stepping movements. They stop making these movements during the so-called "non-stepping" window. The movements obviously reappear when the infant starts walking. The traditional explanation for this U-shaped developmental trajectory is that the infant's initial stepping movements are purely reflexive. They disappear during the non-stepping window because the cortex is maturing enough to inhibit reflex responses – but is not sufficiently mature to bring stepping movements under voluntary control.

Thelen and Smith came up with a range of experimental evidence challenging this approach. They discovered that stepping movements could be artificially induced in infants by manipulating features of the environment. So, for example, infants in the non-stepping window will make stepping movements when they are suspended in warm water. Stepping during the non-stepping window can also be induced by placing the infants on a treadmill. The treadmill has the effect of increasing the leg strength by moving the leg backwards and exploiting its spring-like properties. Stepping movements can also be inhibited before the start of the non-stepping window – attaching even small weights to the baby's ankles will do the trick.

These possibilities for manipulating infant stepping movements present considerable difficulties for the cortical maturation approach – since they show that stepping movements vary independently of how the cortex has developed. And they also point towards a dynamical systems model by identifying the crucial parameters in the development of infant walking – parameters such as leg fat, muscle strength, gravity, and inertia. The brain and the rest of the central nervous system do not have a privileged position in generating this complex behavior. Instead we have a behavior that can in principle be modeled by equations tracking the interdependence of a small number of variables. Thelen and Smith have worked this idea out in great detail with a wealth of experimental studies and analyses.

Still, although walking is certainly a highly complex activity, it is not a very cognitive one. Is there support for the dynamical systems approach in a more cognitive sphere? Several examples suggest that there is. The dynamical systems approach has been profitably applied to the study of human decision-making, for example. The Decision Field Theory developed by Jerome R. Busemeyer and James T. Townsend sets out to explain certain experimental results in behavioral economics and the psychology of reasoning in terms of the interplay of seven parameters. Another example, and one that we will look at in more detail, also derives from the work of Thelen and Smith on infant development. Thelen and Smith have developed a dynamical systems approach to how young infants understand objects.

Dynamical systems and the A-not-B error

We looked at the emergence of what developmental psychologists call object permanence in sections 9.3 and 9.4. Object permanence is the infant's understanding that objects continue to exist when they are no longer being perceived. As we saw back in Chapter 9, object permanence emerges in stages and is intimately connected with the infant's emerging "naïve

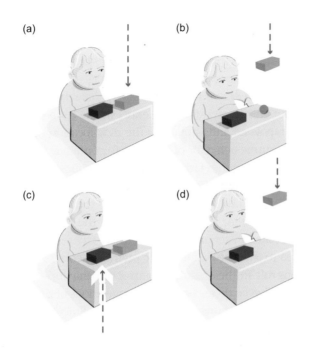

Figure 13.5 The stage IV search task, which typically gives rise to the A-not-B-error in infants at around the age of 9 months. The experimenter hides an object in the left-hand box (a). The infant searches successfully (b). But when the experimenter moves the object in full view of the infant (c), the infant searches again at the original location (d). (Adapted from Bremner 1994)

physics" – with its sensitivity to the basic principles governing how physical objects behave. One of the first to study the development of object permanence was the famous Swiss developmental psychologist Jean Piaget. In his highly influential 1954 book *The Construction of Reality in the Child* Piaget described a very interesting phenomenon.

One way to explore infants' understanding of object permanence is by looking at whether and how they search for hidden objects. Up to the age of around 7 months infants are very poor at searching for objects even immediately after they have seen them being hidden. For the very young infant, out of sight seems to be, quite literally, out of mind. From 12 months or so onwards, infants search normally. But between the ages of 7 months and 12 months young infants make a striking error that Piaget termed the stage IV error and that is now generally known as the A-not-B error. Figure 13.5 illustrates a typical experiment eliciting the A-not-B error.

Infants are placed in front of two containers – A and B. They see a toy hidden in container A and reach for the toy repeatedly until they are habituated to its presence in container A. Then, in plain view, the experimenter hides the toy in container B. If there is a short delay between hiding and when the infants are allowed to reach, they will typically reach to container A, rather than to container B (even though they have just seen the toy hidden in container B).

Piaget's own explanation of the A-not-B error tied it to the infant's developing representational abilities. He suggested that it is not until they are about 12 months old that infants are able to form abstract mental representations of objects. Before that age their actions are driven by sensori-motor routines. In the first stage of the task, searching for the toy in container A allows the infant to discover the spatial relationship between the toy and the container. But this knowledge only exists in the form of a sensori-motor routine. It cannot be extrapolated and applied to the new location of the toy. And so infants simply repeat the routine behavior of reaching to container A.

Other cognitive and neural interpretations have been proposed. On one common interpretation, the key factor is the infant's ability to inhibit her reaching response to container A. The first part of the task effectively conditions the infant to make a certain response (reaching for container A) and it is only when the infant becomes able to override that response that she can act on her knowledge of where the toy is. This ability to inhibit responses is tied to the maturation of the prefrontal cortex, which is generally held to play an important role in the executive control of behavior.

For Smith and Thelen, however, these cognitive interpretations of the A-not-B error fall foul of exactly the same sort of experimental data that posed difficulties for the cognitive interpretation of infant stepping movements. It turns out that infant performance on the task can be manipulated by changing the task. It is well known, for example, that the effect disappears if the infants are allowed to search immediately after the toy is hidden in container B. But Smith, Thelen, and other developmental psychologists produced a cluster of experiments in the 1990s identifying other parameters that had a significant effect on performance:

- Drawing infants' attention to the right side of the their visual field (by tapping on a board on the far right side of the testing table, for example) significantly improves performance. Directing their attention the other way has the opposite effect.
- The most reliable predictor of infant performance is the number of times the infants reach for the toy in the preliminary A trials.
- The error can be made to disappear by changing the infant's posture – 8-month-old infants who are sitting during the initial A trials and then supported in a standing position for the B test perform at the same level as 12-month-old infants (see Figure 13.6).

If the A-not-B error were primarily a cognitive phenomenon, due either to the infants' impoverished representational repertoire or their undeveloped cortical executive system, then we would not expect infants' performance to be so variable and so easy to manipulate. It is hard to think of a cognitive/neural explanation for why standing up should make such a drastic difference.

As in the infant walking case, Smith, Thelen, and their collaborators propose a dynamical systems model – what they call the *dynamic field model.* The dynamic field represents the space in front of the infant – the infant's visual and reaching space. High levels of activation at a specific point in the dynamic field are required for the infant to reach to that point. Thelen and Smith think about this in terms of a threshold. Movement occurs when the activation level at a particular point in the dynamic field is higher than the threshold.

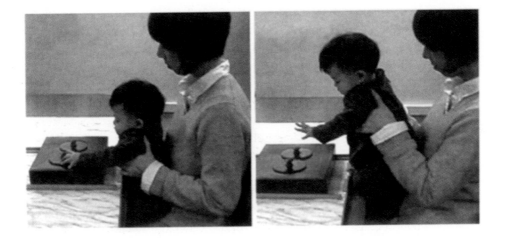

Figure 13.6 An infant sitting for an A trial (left) and standing for a B trial (right). This change in posture causes younger infants to search as 12-month infants do. (Adapted from Smith and Thelen 2003)

Since the model is dynamical, it is critically time-sensitive. The evolution of the field has what Smith and Thelen term continual dynamics. That is, its state at any given moment depends upon its immediately preceding states. So the activation levels evolve continuously over time. They do not jump from one state to another. What the model does is trace the evolution of activation levels in the dynamic field over time as a function of three different types of input.

- *Environmental input.* This might reflect, for example, features of the layout of the environment, such as the distance to the containers. This parameter represents the constraints the environment poses on the infant's possible actions. It will vary, for example, according to whether the infant is sitting or standing. The environmental input parameters also include the attractiveness and salience of the target, as well as contextual features of the environment, such as visual landmarks.
- *Task-specific input.* This reflects the specific demands placed upon the infant – the experimenter drawing attention to the target, for example.
- *Memory input.* The strength of this input is a function of the infant's previous reaching behavior. Since reaching behavior is partly a function of environmental input and task-specific input, the memory input reflects the history of these two types of input. And, as one would expect, it is weighted by a decay function that reflects how time diminishes memory strength.

All of these parameters are coded in the same way, in terms of locations in the movement/visual field. This allows them all to contribute to raising the activation level above threshold for a specific location (either container A or container B).

And this, according to Smith and Thelen, is exactly what happens in the A-not-B error. The perseverative reaching takes place, they claim, when the strength of the memory input overwhelms the other two inputs. This is illustrated in Figure 13.7.

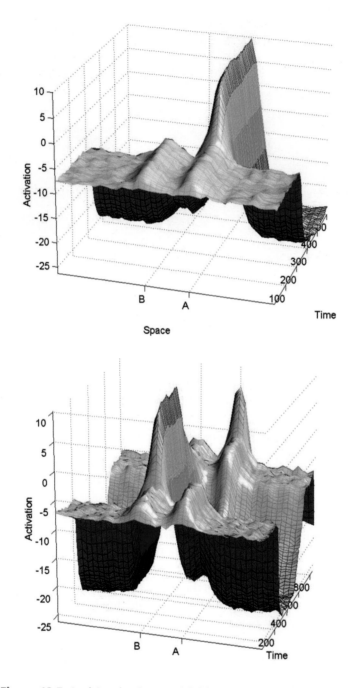

Figure 13.7 Applying the dynamical field model to the A-not-B error. (a) The time evolution of activation in the planning field on the first A trial. The activation rises as the object is hidden and, owing to self-organizing properties in the field, is sustained during the delay. (b) The time evolution of activation in the planning field on the first B trial. There is heightened activation at A before the hiding event, owing to memory for prior reaches. As the object is hidden at B, activation rises at B, but as this transient event ends, owing to the memory properties of the field, activation at A declines and that at B rises.

Their explanation makes no general appeal to cortical maturation, executive control, or the infant's representational capacities. And it is very sensitive to how the initial conditions are specified. If the strength of the memory input is allowed to diminish (by increasing the delay before the infant is allowed to reach, for example) then one would expect the error to diminish correspondingly – as indeed happens. Likewise for the other experimental manipulations that Smith and Thelen have uncovered. These manipulations all subtly change the inputs and parameters in the model, resulting in changes in the activation levels and hence in the infant's reaching behavior.

Assessing the dynamical systems approach

The experiments and models produced by Smith, Thelen, and other dynamical systems theorists clearly give us very powerful tools for studying the evolution of cognition and behavior. The explanations that they provide of the A-not-B error and how infants learn to walk seem to be both more complex and simpler than the standard type of information-processing explanations current in cognitive science. They seem more complex because they bring a wide range of factors into play that cognitive scientists had not previously taken into account, and they steer us away from explanation in terms of a single information-processing mechanism towards time-sensitive complex systems with subtle interdependencies and time-sensitivity. At the same time, though, their explanations seem simpler because they do not invoke representations and computations.

We started out, though, with the idea that the dynamical systems approach might be a radical alternative to some of the basic assumptions of cognitive science – and in particular to the idea that cognition essentially involves computation and information processing. Some proponents of the dynamical systems approach have certainly made some very strong claims in this direction. Van Gelder, for example, has suggested that the dynamical systems model will in time completely supplant computational models, so that traditional cognitive science will end up looking as quaint (and as fundamentally misconceived) as the computational governor.

There is a very important sense, though, in which claims such as these ignore one of the most basic and important features of cognitive science. As we have seen throughout this book, cognitive science is both interdisciplinary and multi-level. The mind is too complex a phenomenon to be fully understood through a single discipline or at a single level. This applies to the dynamical systems hypothesis no less than to anything else. There is no more chance of gaining a complete picture of the mind through dynamical systems theory than there is of gaining a complete account through neurobiology, say, or AI. All of these disciplines and approaches give us deep, but partial, insights. The real job for cognitive science is to integrate all these insights into a unified and comprehensive picture of the mind.

The contrast that Van Gelder draws between the computational governor and the Watt governor is striking and thought-provoking, but it cannot be straightforwardly transferred from engineering to cognitive science. The computational governor and the Watt governor do seem to be mutually exclusive. If we are trying to solve that particular engineering problem we need to take one approach or the other – but not both. Nothing like this holds when it comes to cognition, however. Dynamical systems models are perfectly compatible with information-processing models of cognition.

Dynamical systems models operate at a higher level of abstraction. They allow cognitive scientists to abstract away from details of information-processing mechanisms in order to study how systems evolve over time. But even when we have a model of how a cognitive system evolves over time we will still need an account of what makes it possible for the system to evolve in those ways.

Let me give an analogy. Dynamical systems theory can be applied in all sorts of areas. So, for example, traffic jams have been modeled as dynamical systems. Physicists have constructed models of traffic jams that depend upon seeing traffic jams as the result of interactions between particles in a many-particle system. These models have proved surprisingly effective at predicting phenomena such as stop-and-go traffic and the basic fact that traffic jams often occur before a road's capacity has been reached.

This certainly gives us a new way of thinking about traffic, and new predictive tools that make it easier to design roads and intersections. But no one would ever seriously propose that this new way of thinking about the collective movement of vehicles means that we no longer have to think about internal combustion engines, gasoline, spark plugs, and so on. Treating a traffic jam as an effect in a multi-particle system allows us to see patterns that we couldn't see before. This is because it gives us a set of tools for abstracting away from the physical machinery of individual vehicles. But "abstracting away from" is not the same as "replacing." Cars can be modeled as particles in a multi-particle system – but these models only make sense because we know that what are being modeled are physical objects powered by internal combustion engines.

With our analogy in mind, look again at the dynamical field model in Figure 13.7. This model may well accurately predict the occurrence of the A-not-B error in young infants. But look at what it leaves out. It says nothing about how memory works, how the infant plans her movement, how she picks up the experimenter's cues, and so on. We don't need answers to these questions in order to construct a dynamical system model. But nor can we simply leave them unanswered. The dynamical systems approach adds a powerful tool to the cognitive scientist's toolkit, but it is unlikely ever to be the only tool.

13.3 Situated cognition and biorobotics

Dynamical systems theory offers a new way of analyzing and predicting cognitive systems. Instead of information processing, it proposes that we think in terms of coupled systems. Instead of representations, it offers variables evolving through state space in real time. Instead of abstracting away from the physical details of how cognitive systems actually work, it suggests that those physical details can play all sorts of unsuspected but vitally important roles in determining how a cognitive system changes and evolves over time.

Dynamical systems theory is closely related to the movement in cognitive science often called *situated* or *embodied cognition.* Proponents of situated cognition (as I will call it henceforth, using the term to cover and include embodied cognition theorists) sometimes make very strong claims about what they are trying to achieve, rather similar to some of the claims made by dynamical systems theorists such as Van Gelder. Situated cognition is sometimes presented as a radical alternative to information-processing models of cognitive science – as a rejection of the basic idea that cognition is information processing, for example.

It is certainly true that situated cognition theorists have built models that do not seem to involve computational information processing of the type that we have been looking at throughout this book. In fact, we will look at some of these models shortly. But, as with dynamical systems models, there is room for a more measured approach. The fact that a cognitive system can be modeled at one level without any explicit mention of information processing does not rule out viewing it at another level as an information-processing system. And even if there are some systems that can be modeled in non-information-processing terms, this hardly gives us grounds for abandoning the whole idea of information processing!

The situated cognition movement is best seen as a reaction against some of the classic tenets of cognitive science. It offers a useful alternative to some assumptions that cognitive scientists have tended to make, often without realizing that they are making them. It is not an alternative to the information-processing paradigm in cognitive science. But, as is the case with dynamical systems theory, it does offer a powerful new set of tools and approaches. We will look at some of them in this section. In order to keep the discussion focused we will restrict attention to the field of robotics – a field where it is easy to see the force of the theoretical ideas behind situated cognition, and also where some of the most significant practical applications of those ideas have been made.

The challenge of building a situated agent

The principal objection that situated cognition theorists make to traditional cognitive science is that it has never really come to terms with the real problems and challenges in understanding cognition. For present purposes (since we will be focusing primarily on robotics) we can take traditional cognitive science to be the GOFAI approach to building artificial agents.

We looked in detail at two of the early successes of GOFAI robotics in earlier chapters. In section 2.1 we looked at Terry Winograd's SHRDLU program for natural language understanding. SHRDLU is a virtual robot, reporting on and interacting with a virtual micro-world. In section 7.4 we encountered SHAKEY, a real robot developed at what was then the Stanford Research Institute. Unlike SHRDLU, which "inhabited" a micro-world composed of blocks and boxes, SHAKEY was programmed to navigate and interact with a realistic environment.

A good way to understand the worries that situated cognition theorists have about GOFAI is via a criticism often leveled at SHRDLU and other micro-world programs. The

basic complaint is that SHRDLU only works because its artificial micro-world environment has been stripped of all complexity and challenge. Here is a witty expression of the
worry from the philosopher and cognitive scientist John Haugeland (although he is not
himself a promoter of the situated cognition movement):

> SHRDLU performs so glibly only because his domain has been stripped of anything that
> could ever require genuine wit or understanding. Neglecting the tangled intricacies of
> everyday life while pursuing a theory of common sense is not like ignoring friction while
> pursuing the laws of motion; it's like throwing the baby out with the bathwater. A round
> frictionless wheel is a good approximation of a real wheel because the deviations are
> comparatively small and theoretically localized: the blocks-world "approximates" a
> playroom more as a paper plane approximates a duck. (Haugeland 1985: 190)

One might wonder whether Haugeland is being completely fair here. After all, Winograd
did not really set out to provide "a theory of common sense," and there probably
are situations in which a paper plane is a useful approximation of a duck. But the basic
point is clear enough. There are many challenges that SHRDLU simply does not have
to deal with.

SHRDLU does not have to work out what a block is, for example - or how to
recognize one. There is very little "physical" challenge involved in SHRDLU's (virtual)
interactions with its micro-world environment, since SHRDLU has built into
it programs for picking up blocks and moving them around, and the robot-hand
is expressly designed for implementing those programs. Likewise, SHRDLU's
language-understanding achievements are partly a function of its artificially limited
language and the highly circumscribed conversational context. The major problems in
language understanding (such as decoding ambiguity and working out what a speaker
is really trying to say) are all factored out of the equation. Finally, SHRDLU is not
autonomous - it is a purely reactive system, with everything it does a response to
explicit instructions.

In other words, SHRDLU is not properly *situated* in its environment - or rather, the
way in which SHRDLU is situated in its environment is so radically different from how
we and other real-life cognitive agents are embedded in our environments that we can
learn nothing from SHRDLU about how our own cognitive systems work. In fact (the
argument continues), SHRDLU's environment is so constrained and devoid of meaning
that it is positively misleading to take it as a starting-point in thinking about human
cognition. The call for situated cognition, then, is a call for AI to work on systems that
have all the things that SHRDLU lacks - systems that are properly embodied and have
real autonomy. These systems need to be embedded in something much more like the
real world, with ambiguous, unpredictable, and highly complex social and physical
contexts.

But it is not just SHRDLU that fails to meet the basic criteria proposed by situated
cognition theorists. Their target is much wider. The researchers who designed and
built SHAKEY may have thought that they were programming something much
closer to an embodied and autonomous agent. After all, SHAKEY can navigate the

environment, and it is designed to solve problems, rather than to be purely reactive. But, from the perspective of situated cognition theorists, SHAKEY is really no better than SHRDLU.

For situated cognition theorists, SHAKEY is not really a situated agent, even though it propels itself around a physical environment. The point for them is that the real work has already been done in writing SHAKEY's program. SHAKEY's world is already defined for it in terms of a small number of basic concepts (such as BOX, DOOR, and so forth). Its motor repertoire is built up out of a small number of primitive movements (such as ROLL, TILT, PAN). The problems that SHAKEY is asked to solve are presented in terms of these basic concepts and primitive movements (as when SHAKEY is asked to fetch a BOX).

The robot has to work out a sequence of basic movements that will fulfill the command, but that is not the same as a real agent solving a problem in the real world. SHAKEY already has the basic building blocks for the solution. But working out what the building blocks are is perhaps the most difficult part of real-world problem-solving. Like SHRDLU, SHAKEY can only operate successfully in a highly constrained environment. Situated cognition theorists are interested in building agents that will be able to operate successfully even when all those constraints are lifted.

Situated cognition and knowledge representation

There is a very close relation between how a cognitive system's knowledge is pro-grammed and represented and the type of problem-solving that it can engage in. This connection is brought out by Rodney Brooks, a very influential situated cognition theorist, in a paper called "Intelligence without representation" that is something of a manifesto for the situated cognition movement. Brooks points out that classical AI depends crucially on trimming down the type and number of details that a cognitive system has to represent. Here is his illustration:

Consider chairs, for example. While these two characterizations are true

(CAN (SIT-ON PERSON CHAIR))

and

(CAN (STAND-ON PERSON CHAIR))

there is really much more to the concept of a chair. Chairs have some flat (maybe) sitting place, with perhaps a back support. They have a range of possible sizes, and a range of possibilities in shape. They often have some sort of covering material – unless they are made of wood, metal or plastic. They sometimes are soft in particular places. They can come from a range of possible styles. In sum, the concept of what a chair is is hard to characterize simply. There is certainly no AI vision program that can find arbitrary chairs in arbitrary images; they can at best find one particular type of chair in arbitrarily selected images. (Brooks 1997: 399)

Recognizing and interacting with chairs is a complicated business. But the programmer can remove the complications more or less at a stroke – simply by programming into the system a very narrow characterization of what a chair is. The beauty of doing this is that it can make certain types of chair interactions very simple.

If, to continue with Brooks's example, the system has to solve a problem with a hungry person seated on a chair in a room with a banana just out of reach, then the characterization in the program is just what's required. But of course, if the system solves the problem, then this is largely because it has been given all and only the right sort of information about chairs – and because the problem has been presented in a way that points directly to a solution! Here is Brooks again:

> Such problems are never posed to AI systems by showing them a photo of the scene. A person (even a young person) can make the right interpretation of the photo and suggest a plan of action. For AI planning systems, however, the experimenter is required to abstract away most of the details to form a simple description of atomic concepts such as PERSON, CHAIR, and BANANA.
>
> But this abstraction process is the essence of intelligence and the hard part of the problem being solved. Under the current scheme, the abstraction is done by the researchers, leaving little for the AI programs to do but search. A truly intelligent program would study the photograph, perform the abstraction itself, and solve the problem. (Brooks 1997: 399)

This gives us a much clearer view of what situated cognition is supposed to be all about. It's not just a question of designing robots that interact with their environments. There are plenty of ways of doing this that don't count as situated cognition. The basic idea is to develop AI systems and to build robots that don't have the solutions to problems built into them – AI systems and robots that can learn to perform the basic sensory and motor processes that are a necessary precondition for intelligent problem-solving.

Biorobotics: Insects and morphological computation

Situated cognition theorists, like dynamical systems theorists, believe that it pays to start small. Dynamical systems theorists often focus on relatively simple motor and cognitive behaviors, such as infant stepping and the A-not-B error. Cognitive scientists in situated robotics are often inspired by cognitively unsophisticated organisms. Insects are very popular. We can get the flavor from the title of another one of Rodney Brooks's influential articles – "Today the earwig, tomorrow man?"

Instead of trying to model highly simplified and scaled-down versions of "high-level" cognitive and motor abilities, situated cognition theorists think that we need to focus on much more basic and *ecologically valid* problems. The key is simplicity without simplification. Insects solve very complex problems. Studying how they do this, and building models that exploit the same basic design principles will, according to theorists such as

Brooks, pay dividends when it comes to understanding how human beings interact with their environment. We need to look at humans as scaled-up insects, not as scaled-down supercomputers.

One of the basic design principles stressed by situated cognition theorists is that there are direct links between perception and action. This is an alternative to the classical cognitive science view of thinking about organisms in terms of distinct and semi-autonomous sub-systems that can be analyzed and modeled independently of each other. On a view like Marr's, for example, the visual system is an autonomous input–output system. It processes information completely independently of what will happen to that information further downstream. When we look at insects, however, we see that they achieve high degrees of "natural intelligence" through clever engineering solutions that exploit direct connections between their sensory receptors and their effector limbs.

Some researchers in this field have described what they are doing as *biorobotics*. The basic idea is usefully summarized in Figure 13.8. Biorobotics is the enterprise of designing and building models of biological organisms that reflect the basic design principles built into those organisms.

Bioroboticists look to biology for insights into how insects and other simple organisms solve adaptive problems, typically to do with locomotion and foraging. On this basis they construct theoretical models. These models are modified in the light of what happens when they are physically implemented in robots – robots whose construction is itself biologically inspired.

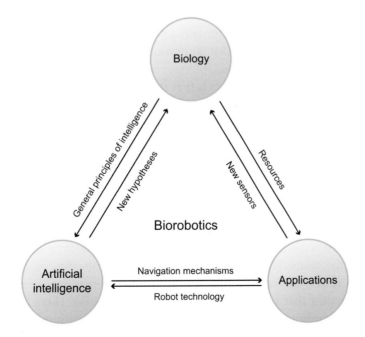

Figure 13.8 The organizing principles of biorobotics – a highly interdisciplinary enterprise.

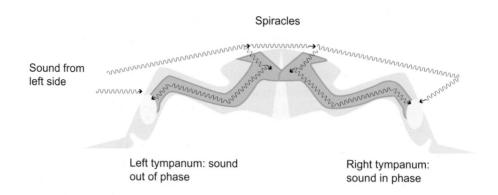

Figure 13.9 The cricket's ears are on its front legs. They are connected to each other via a tracheal tube. The spiracles are small openings that allow air into the tracheal tube. The arrows show the different routes that a single sound can take to each ear. (Adapted from Clark 2001)

A famous example of biorobotics in action is the work of Edinburgh University's Barbara Webb on how female crickets locate males on the basis of their songs – what biologists call cricket phonotaxis. The basic datum here is that female crickets are extremely good at recognizing and locating mates on the basis of the song that they make. On the face of it this might seem to be a problem that can only be solved with very complex information processing – identifying the sound, working out where it comes from, and then forming motor commands that will take the cricket to the right place. Webb observed, however, that the physiology of the cricket actually provides a very clever solution. This solution is a nice illustration of what can be achieved with direct links between perception and action.

One remarkable fact about crickets is that their ears are located on their legs. As we see in Figure 13.9, the cricket's ears are connected by a tube (the *tracheal tube*). This means that a single sound can reach each ear via different routes – a direct route (through the ear itself) and various indirect routes (via the other ear, as well as through openings in the tracheal tube known as spiracles). Obviously, a sound that takes the indirect route will take longer to arrive, since it has further to travel – and can't go faster than the speed of sound.

According to Barbara Webb, cricket phonotaxis works because of two very basic design features built into the anatomy of the cricket. The first is that the vibration is highest at the ear nearest the source of the sound, which provides a direct indication of the source of the sound. The second is that this vibration directly controls the cricket's movements. Crickets are *hard-wired* to move in the direction of the ear with the highest vibration (provided that the vibration is suitably cricket-like). There is no "direction-calculating mechanism," no "male cricket identification mechanism," and no "motor controller."

Webb and her co-workers have used this model of cricket phonotaxis to build robot crickets that can actually perform a version of phonotaxis. In fact, not only can they find the sources of artificial cricket sounds, but they perform successfully when set to work on real crickets. Webb's robot crickets nicely illustrate one of the basic themes of biorobotics and situated cognition. Input sensors are directly linked to output effectors via clever engineering solutions that make complicated information processing unnecessary.

One of the key design features of Webb's robot cricket (reflecting how real crickets have evolved) is that the cricket's body is a contributing factor in the computation. Cricket phonotaxis works by comparing two different signals. The availability of these two different signals is a direct function of the cricket's bodily layout, as illustrated in Figure 13.9. This can be seen as an early example of what subsequently emerged as the *morphological computation* movement in robotics.

Morphology (in this context) is body shape. The basic idea behind morphological computation is that organisms can exploit features of body shape to simplify what might otherwise be highly complex information-processing tasks. Morphological computation in robotics is a matter of building robots that share these basic properties, minimizing the amount of computational control required by building as much of the computation as possible directly into the physical structure of the robot. In essence, morphological computation is a research program for designing robots in which as much computation as possible is done for free.

The morphological computation movement is a very recent development. The first morphological computation conference was only held in 2005. But there have already been some very interesting developments. Here are two examples from the AI Lab in the Department of Informatics at the University of Zurich.

The first example is a fish called WANDA, illustrated in Figure 13.10. WANDA is designed with only one degree of freedom. The only thing WANDA can do is wiggle its tail from side to side at varying amplitudes and frequencies - i.e. WANDA can vary the speed and the degree with which its tail moves. And yet, due to the power of morphological computation, variation in tail wiggling allows WANDA to carry out the full range of fish movements in all three planes - up-down and left-right as well as forwards. Part of the trick here is WANDA's buoyancy, which is set so that slow tail wiggling will make it sink, while fast tail wiggling will make it rise. The other key design feature is the possibility of adjusting the zero point of the wiggle movement, which allows for movement to the left or right. Figure 13.11 shows WANDA swimming upwards.

A second example of morphological computation also comes from the realm of motor control. (We can think of both examples as ways of counterbalancing the appeal of the computational approach to motor control briefly discussed in section 13.2 and illustrated in Figure 13.4.) The robot hand devised by Hiroshi Yokoi in Figure 13.12 is designed to avoid the need for making explicit computations in carrying out grasping movements.

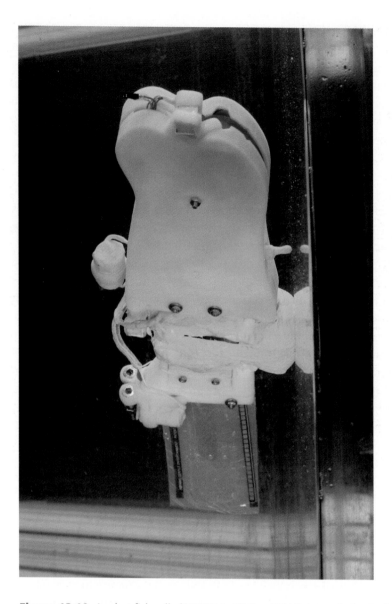

Figure 13.10 A robot fish called WANDA. All that WANDA can do is wiggle its tail fin. Yet, in an illustration of morphological computation, WANDA is able to swim upwards, downwards, and from side to side.

On the computational approach, grasping an object requires computing an object's shape and configuring the hand to conform to that shape. Configuring the hand, in turn, requires sending a set of detailed instructions to the tendons and muscles determining the position of the fingers and palm. None of this is necessary, however, in controlling the Yokoi hand. The hand is constructed from elastic and deformable materials (elastic tendons and deformable fingertips and spaces between the fingers). This morphology does the work that would otherwise be done by complex calculations within some sort of motor control unit. What

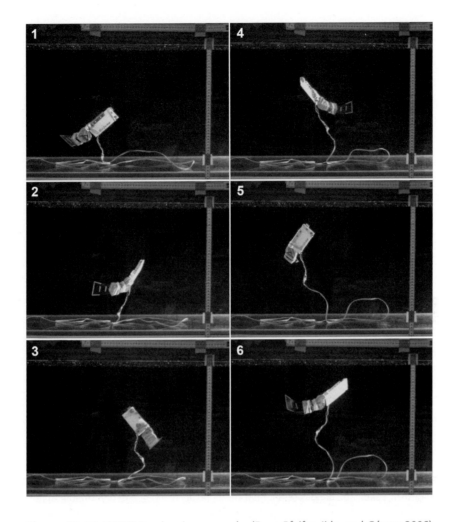

Figure 13.11 WANDA swimming upwards. (From Pfeifer, Iida, and Gómez 2006)

happens is that the hand's flexible and elastic morphology allows it to adapt itself to the shape of the objects being grasped. We see an example in Figure 13.13.

As with the robot cricket example, most work in morphological computation has focused on the realm of motor control and sensori-motor integration. It is worth pointing out, though, that these are areas in which traditional AI, and indeed traditional cognitive science, have often been thought to be deficient. These are not cognitive tasks in any high-level sense. But they are often thought to require information processing, which is why they come into the sphere of cognitive science.

The real question, though, must be how the type of insights that we can find in biorobotics and morphological computation can be integrated into models of more complex agents. Some very suggestive ideas come from the field of behavior-based robotics, to which we turn in the next section.

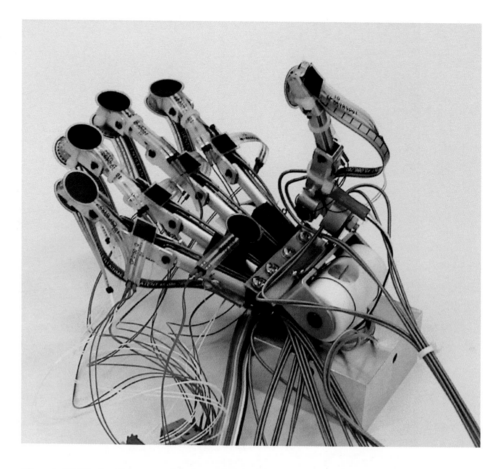

Figure 13.12 Another example of morphological computation: The robot hand designed by Hiroshi Yokoi. The hand is partly built from elastic, flexible, and deformable materials. The tendons are elastic, and both the fingertips and the space between the fingers are deformable. This allows the hand to adapt its grasp to the object being grasped.

13.4 From subsumption architectures to behavior-based robotics

Rodney Brooks has provided a general AI framework for thinking about some of the agents discussed in the previous section. Webb's robot crickets are examples of what Brooks calls *subsumption architectures*. In this book so far we have been looking primarily at modular architectures. The basic principle of a modular architecture is that cognitive agents are cognitively organized into sub-systems that are distinguished from each other in functional terms. There might, for example, be an early vision sub-system, a face recognition sub-system, and a place-learning sub-system – just to pick out three function-ally individuated sub-systems that have been much discussed by cognitive scientists.

Subsumption architectures are organized very differently from modular architectures. They are not made up of functional sub-systems. Instead, their basic components are

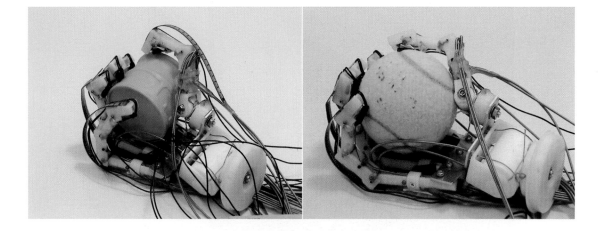

Figure 13.13 The Yokoi hand grasping two very different objects. In each case, the control is the same, but the morphology of the hand allows it to adapt to the shapes it encounters. (From Pfeifer, Iida, and Gómez 2006)

activity-producing sub-systems. Webb's hypothesized system for cricket phonotaxis is an excellent example of an activity-producing sub-system. Brooks calls these sub-systems *layers*. Subsumption architectures are made up of layers. The bottom level of the architecture is composed of very simple behaviors. Brooks's favorite example is obstacle avoidance, which is obviously very important for mobile robots (and living organisms). The obstacle-avoidance layer directly connects perception (sensing an obstacle) to action (either swerving to avoid the obstacle, or halting where the obstacle is too big to go around).

Whatever other layers are built into the subsumption architecture, the obstacle-avoidance layer is always online and functioning. This illustrates another basic principle of subsumption architectures. The layers are autonomous and work in parallel. There may be a "higher" layer that, for example, directs the robot towards a food source. But the obstacle-avoidance layer will still come into play whenever the robot finds itself on a collision course with an obstacle. This explains the name "subsumption architecture" – the higher layers subsume the lower layers, but they do not replace or override them.

This makes it easier to design creatures with subsumption architectures. The different layers can be grafted on one by one. Each layer can be exhaustively debugged before another layer is added. And the fact that the layers are autonomous means that there is much less chance that adding a higher layer will introduce unsuspected problems into the lower layers. This is obviously an attractive model for roboticists. It is also, one might think, a very plausible model for thinking about how evolution might work.

Subsumption architectures: The example of Allen

Rodney Brooks's lab at MIT has produced many robots with subsumption architectures exemplifying these general principles. One of the first was Allen, illustrated in Figure 13.14.

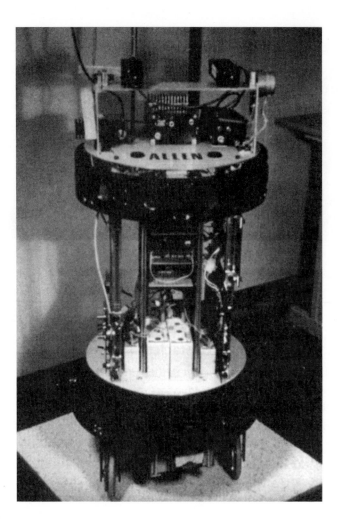

Figure 13.14 Rodney Brooks's robot Allen, his first subsumption architecture robot.
(From Brooks 1997)

At the hardware level, Allen does not, at least to my eye, look very dissimilar to SHAKEY. But the design principles are fundamentally different. At the software level, Allen is a subsumption architecture, built up in the standard layered manner. Over time, more and more layers were added to Allen's basic architecture. The first three layers are depicted in Figure 13.15.

The most basic layer is the obstacle avoidance layer. As we see from the diagram, this layer is itself built up from a number of distinct sub-systems. These do pretty much what their names suggest. The COLLIDE sub-system scans the sensory input for obstacles. It sends out a halt signal if it detects one. At the same time the FEELFORCE system works out the overall force acting upon the robot (using information from the sensors and the assumption that objects function as repulsive forces). These feed into systems responsible for steering the robot – systems that are directly connected to the motor effectors.

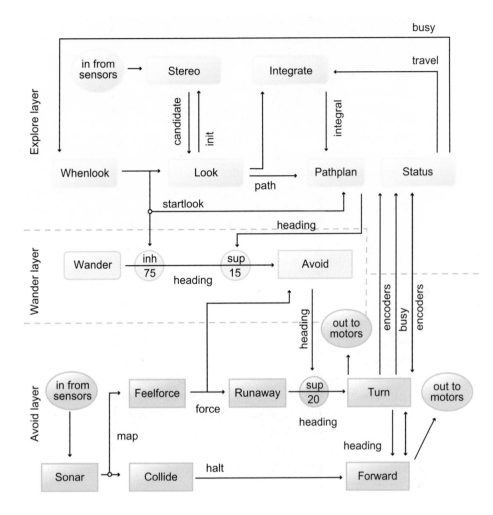

Figure 13.15 The layers of Allen's subsumption architecture. Allen has a three-layer architecture. The layers communicate through mechanisms of inhibition (inh) and suppression (sup). (From Brooks 1997)

The wander and explorer layers are constructed in the same way. In the middle layer the WANDER component generates random paths for Allen's motor system, while the AVOID component feeds back down into the obstacle avoidance layer to ensure that following the random path does not lead Allen to crash into anything. Allen is actually pretty successful at this. The robot can successfully navigate environments with both stationary obstacles and other moving objects. And it is not just wandering around at random. The sub-systems in the top layer (the explorer layer) work together to allow Allen to pursue goals in a self-directed way. These sub-systems receive input from the sensory systems and allow Allen to plan routes towards specific visible locations. As the wiring diagram in Figure 13.15 shows, the PATHPLAN sub-system feeds into the AVOID sub-system. This allows for the plan to be modified as the robot is actually moving towards the goal.

Drawing all this together, we can identify three basic features of subsumption architectures, as developed by Brooks and other AI researchers:

- *Incremental design.* Subsumption architecture robots are built to mimic how evolution might work. New sub-systems are grafted on in layers that typically don't change the design of the existing sub-systems.
- *Semi-autonomous sub-systems.* The sub-systems operate relatively independently of each other, although some sub-systems are set up to override others. The connections between the sub-systems are hard-wired. There is typically no central "controller."
- *Direct perception-action links.* Subsumption architectures trade as much as possible on sub-systems that deliver immediate motor responses to sensory input. They are designed for real-time control of action.

The contrast with traditional AI approaches is sharp. Traditional AI robots (such as SHAKEY) are designed in a very top-down way. There is typically a central planner maintaining a continuously updated model of the world, updated by incorporating information received through its sensors. The planner uses this model of the world to work out detailed action plans, which are transmitted to the effectors. The action plans tend to be multi-stage and leave little scope for modification. (For a nice example of this sort of approach, look back at the example of SHAKEY in section 7.4.)

Proponents of GOFAI robotics are likely to say that the basic features of subsumption architectures are very good design principles for robots that are intended to be no more than mechanical insects – basically capable only of moving around the environment and reacting in simple ways to incoming stimuli. But subsumption architectures are not going to help us with complex intelligent behavior. Recall the physical symbol system hypothesis, which we looked at in detail in Chapters 6 and 7. The physical symbol system hypothesis is a hypothesis about the necessary and sufficient conditions of *intelligent action.* But how intelligent is Allen, or the robot crickets and cockroaches that bioroboticists have developed?

GOFAI enthusiasts are likely to concede that we can learn much about online motor control and perceptual sensitivity from looking at insects and modeling simple behaviors using subsumption architectures. But, they will continue, if we are trying to model intelligent behavior (cognitive systems, rather than reactive systems) then there is no alternative to the sort of top-down approach that we find in SHAKEY and other traditional robots.

The problem is that subsumption architectures don't seem to have any decision-making processes built into them. Potential conflicts between different layers and between individual sub-systems within a layer are resolved by precedence relations that are built into the hardware of the robot. Conflict resolution is purely mechanical. But what makes a system intelligent, one might reasonably think, is that it can deal with conflicts that cannot be resolved by applying independent sub-systems in some predetermined order. Subsumption architectures lack intelligence almost by definition.

There are different ways in which a situated cognition theorist might try to respond to this challenge. One way is to try to combine the two approaches. There are hybrid architectures that have a subsumption architecture for low-level reactive control, in combination with a more traditional central planner for high-level decision-making. So, for example, Jonathan Connell, a researcher at IBM's T. J. Watson Research Center in Yorktown Heights, New York, has developed a three-level hybrid architecture that he calls SSS. It is easy to see where the acronym comes from, when we look at what each of the layers does. SSS contains:

- a **S**ervo-based layer that controls the robot's effectors and processes raw sensory data
- a **S**ubsumption layer that reacts to processed sensory input by configuring the servo-based layer (as is standard in a subsumption architecture, the different sub-systems are organized in a strict precedence hierarchy)
- a **S**ymbolic layer that maintains complex maps of the environment and is capable of formulating plans; the symbolic layer configures the subsumption layer

The hybrid architecture approach abandons some of the basic ideas behind situated cognition and biorobotics. To return to a phrase used earlier, situated cognition theorists like to think of sophisticated cognitive systems as scaled-up insects, whereas GOFAI theorists think of them as scaled-down supercomputers. The hybrid architecture approach, as its name suggests, looks for a middle way – it sets out to build scaled-up insects with scaled-down supercomputers grafted onto them.

But some situated cognition theorists have tried to meet the challenge without compromising on the basic principles of situated cognition. *Behavior-based robotics* moves beyond basic subsumption architectures in a way that tries to build on the basic insights of the situated cognition movement.

Behavior-based robotics: TOTO

Behavior-based architectures are designed to be capable of representing the environment and planning complex actions. Subsumption architectures (and insects, for that matter) are purely reactive – they are designed to respond quickly to what is happening around them. These responses are typically fairly simple – such as changing the robot's direction, or putting it into reverse when a collision is anticipated. These responses tend to be explicitly programmed in the system. Behavior-based robots, in contrast, are capable of more complex behaviors that need not be explicitly specified within the system. These are what are sometimes called *emergent* behaviors (because they emerge from the operation and interaction of lower-level behaviors). Moreover, this additional cognitive sophistication is gained without a central planner that works symbolically.

Behavior-based architectures incorporate some of the basic design features of subsumption architectures. They are typically built up from semi-autonomous sub-systems in a way that mimics the incremental approach that evolution seems to take. But they have two additional features that separate them from subsumption architectures.

- *Distributed representations:* Behavior-based architectures represent their environments and use those representations in planning actions. This distinguishes them from most subsumption architectures. But, unlike symbolic and hybrid architectures, those representations are not centralized or centrally manipulated. There is no central planning system that gathers together all the information that the robot has at its disposal.
- *Real-time functioning:* Like subsumption architectures, behavior-based architectures are designed to operate in real time. That is, they make plans on a timescale that interfaces directly with the robot's movements through the environment. This contrasts with symbolic planners and hybrid architectures, where planning is done offline and then needs to be integrated with the robot's ongoing behavior.

We can appreciate how these features work by looking at two examples from the work of Maja Matarić, one of the pioneers of behavior-based robotics. One of the very interesting features of Matarić's work is how she applies the behavior-based approach to programming collections of robots. We will look in some detail at an example of multi-agent programming. First, though, let's look briefly at how behavior-based robotics works for single robots.

A fundamental design feature of behavior-based architectures is the distinction between *reactive rules* and *behaviors*. Subsumption architectures are basically built up from reactive rules. A reactive rule might, for example, tell the robot to go into reverse when its sensors detect a looming object. The reactive rules exploit direct perception-action links. They take inputs from the robot's sensors and immediately send instructions to the robot's effectors. Behaviors, in contrast, are more complex. Matarić defines a behavior as *a control law that satisfies a set of constraints to achieve and maintain a particular goal.* The relevant constraints come both from the sensed environment (which might include other robots) and from the robot itself (e.g. its motor abilities).

So, the challenge for behavior-based robotics is to find a way of implementing behaviors in a mobile agent without incorporating a symbolic, central planner. Matarić's robot TOTO, which she designed and constructed together with Rodney Brooks, illustrates how this challenge can be met for a very specific navigation behavior. This is the behavior of finding the shortest route between two points in a given environment. Matarić and Brooks were inspired by the abilities of insects such as bees to identify short-cuts between feeding sites. When bees travel from their hive they are typically capable of flying directly to a known feeding site without retracing their steps. In some sense they (and many other insects, foraging animals, and migrating birds) are constructing and updating maps of their environment. This is a classic example of an apparently complex and sophisticated behavior being performed by creatures with very limited computational power at their disposal – exactly the sort of thing that behavior-based robotics is intended to model.

TOTO is designed to explore and map its environment (an office-like environment where the principal landmarks are walls and corridors) in a way that allows it to plan and execute short and efficient paths to previously visited landmarks. TOTO has a three-layer architecture. The first layer comprises a set of reactive rules. These reactive rules allow it to navigate effectively and without collisions in its environment. The second layer (the landmark-detector layer) allows TOTO to identify different types of landmark. In the third layer, information about landmarks is used to construct a distributed map of the environment. This map is topological, rather than metric. It simply contains information as to whether or not two landmarks are connected – but not as to how far apart they are. TOTO uses the topological map to work out in real time the shortest path back to a previously visited landmark (i.e. the path that goes via the smallest number of landmarks).

One of TOTO's key features is that its map is distributed (in line with the emphasis within behavior-based robotics on distributed representations) and the processing works in parallel. There is no single data structure representing the environment. Instead, each landmark is represented by a procedure that categorizes the landmark and fixes its compass direction. The landmark procedures are all linked together to form a network. Each node in the network corresponds to a particular landmark, and if there is a direct path between two landmarks then there is an edge connecting them in the network. This network is TOTO's topological map of the environment. It is distributed because it exists only in the form of connections between separate landmark procedures.

Behavior-based roboticists do not object to representations per se. They recognize that any robot capable of acting in complex ways in a complex environment must have some way of storing and processing information about its environment. Their real objection is to the idea that this information is stored centrally and processed symbolically. TOTO is an example of how there can be information processing that is not centralized and is not symbolic.

TOTO's network is constantly being expanded and updated as TOTO moves through the environment detecting new landmarks. This updating is done by activation spreading through the network (not dissimilar to a connectionist network). When the robot is at a particular landmark the node corresponding to that landmark is active. It inhibits the other nodes in the network (which is basically what allows TOTO to know where it is), at the same time as spreading positive activation (expectation) to the next node in the direction of travel (which allows TOTO to work out where it is going).

This distributed map of the environment is not very fine-grained. It leaves out much important information (about distances, for example). But for that very reason it is flexible, robust, and, most importantly, very quick to update. Matarić and Brooks designed an algorithm for TOTO to work out the shortest path between two nodes on the distributed map. The algorithm works by spreading activation. Basically, the active node (which is TOTO's current location) sends a call signal to the node representing the target landmark. This call signal gets transmitted systematically through the network until it arrives at the target node. The algorithm is designed so that the route that the call signal takes through the network represents the shortest path between the two landmarks. Then TOTO implements the landmark procedures lying on the route to navigate to the target landmark.

In TOTO, therefore, we have a nice example of the key features of behavior-based robotics. TOTO is not simply a reactive agent, like Barbara Webb's robot cricket. Nor does it have a central symbolic planner like Jonathan Connell's SSS. It is capable of fairly sophisticated navigation behavior because it has a distributed map of the environment that can be directly exploited to solve navigational problems. The basic activation-spreading mechanisms used for creating and updating the map are the very same mechanisms used for identifying the shortest paths between two landmarks. The mechanisms are somewhat rough-and-ready. But that is what allows them to be used efficiently in the real-time control of behavior – which, after all, is what situated cognition is all about.

Multi-agent programming: The Nerd Herd

For a second example of behavior-based robotics we can look at some of the work that Matarić has done with collections of robots. Multi-agent programming is highly demanding computationally, particularly if it incorporates some sort of centralized planner or controller. A central planner would need to keep track of all the individual robots, constantly updating the instructions to each one to reflect the movements of others – as well as the evolution of each robot's own map of the environment. The number of degrees of freedom is huge. The multi-agent case presents in a very stark way the fundamental challenges of robotics. How can one design a system that can reason about its environment without a complete combinatorial explosion? It is very instructive to see what happens when the challenge is tackled through the behavior-based approach.

Matarić built a family of twenty mobile robots – the so-called Nerd Herd, illustrated in Figure 13.16. Each robot was programmed with a set of basis behaviors. These basis behaviors served as the building blocks for more complex *emergent* behaviors that were not explicitly programmed into the robots.

Table 13.1 shows the five basis behaviors that Matarić programmed into the robots in the Nerd Herd. These behaviors could be combined in two ways. The first way is through summation. The outputs from two or more behaviors are summed together and channeled towards the relevant effector (e.g. the wheels of the robot). This works because all of the behaviors have the same type of output. They all generate velocity vectors, which can easily be manipulated mathematically. The second combination is through switching. Switching inhibits all of the behaviors except for one.

Each of these basis behaviors is programmed at the level of the individual robot. None of the basis behaviors is defined for more than one robot at a time and there is no communication between robots. What Matarić found, however, was that combining the basis behaviors at the level of the individual robots resulted in emergent behaviors at the level of the group. So, for example, the Nerd Herd could be made to display flocking behavior by summing basis behaviors in each individual robot. The group flocked together as a whole if each robot's control architecture summed the basis behaviors Disperson, Aggregation, and Safe-wandering. Adding in Homing allowed the flock to move together towards a particular goal.

TABLE 13.1	The five basis behaviors programmed into Matarić's Nerd Herd robots
Safe-wandering	Ability to move around while avoiding collisions with robots and other objects
Following	Ability to move behind another robot retracing its path
Dispersion	Ability to maintain a *minimum* distance from other robots
Aggregation	Ability to maintain a *maximum* distance from other robots
Homing	Ability to find a particular region or location

Figure 13.16 The Nerd Herd, together with the pucks that they can pick up with their grippers.

The principal activity of the robots in the Nerd Herd is collecting little pucks. Each robot has grippers that allow it to pick the pucks up. Matarić used the control technique of switching between different basis behaviors in order to generate the complex behavior of foraging. If the robot doesn't have a puck then all the basis behaviors are inhibited except Safe-wandering. If Safe-wandering brings it too close to other robots (and hence to potential competitors) then the dominant behavior switches to Dispersion. If it has a puck then the control system switches over to Homing and the robot returns to base.

You may be wondering just how intelligent these complex behaviors really are. It is true that flocking and foraging are not explicitly programmed into the system. They are emergent in the sense that they arise from the interaction of basis behaviors. But the mechanisms of this interaction are themselves programmed into the individual robots using the combinatorial operators for basis behaviors. They are certainly not emergent in the sense of being unpredictable. And one might think that at least one index of intelligence in robots or computers more generally is being able to produce behaviors that cannot simply be predicted from the wiring diagram.

It is significant, therefore, that Mataric's behavior-based robots are capable of learning some of these complex behaviors without having them explicitly programmed. She showed this with a group of four robots very similar to those in the Nerd Herd. The learning paradigm she used was reinforcement learning. What are reinforced are the connections between the states a robot is in and actions it takes.

Recall that the complex behavior of foraging is really just a set of condition–behavior pairs – if the robot is in a certain condition (e.g. lacking a puck) then it yields total control to a single behavior (e.g. Safe-wandering). So, learning to forage is, in essence, learning these condition–behavior pairs. This type of learning can be facilitated by giving the robot a reward when it behaves appropriately in a given condition, thus reinforcing the connection between condition and behavior. Mataric worked with two types of reinforcement – reinforcement at the completion of a successful behavior, and feedback while the robot is actually executing the behavior. Despite the complexity of the environment and the ongoing multi-agent interactions, Mataric found that her four robots successfully learnt group foraging strategies in 95 percent of the trials.

Obviously, these are early days for behavior-based robotics. It would be most unwise to draw sweeping conclusions about how behavior-based architectures will scale up. It is a long way from groups of robots foraging for hockey pucks in a closed environment to anything recognizable as a human social interaction. But behavior-based robotics does at least give us a concrete example of how some of the basic insights behind the situated cognition movement can be carried forward. Perhaps it is time to change Rodney Brooks's famous slogan: "Yesterday the earwig. Today the foraging robot. Tomorrow man?"

Summary

This chapter has looked at some of the possibilities opened up by two more recent ways of modeling cognitive abilities. We began by examining how some cognitive scientists have used the mathematical and conceptual tools of dynamical systems theory to model cognitive skills and abilities. These models exploit the time-sensitivity that dynamical models offer in order to plot how a system evolves over time as a function of changes in a small number of systems variables. We looked at two examples of dynamical systems models of child development. Dynamical systems theory offers fresh and distinctive perspectives both on how infants learn to walk and on infants' expectations about objects that they are no longer perceiving (as revealed in the so-called A-not-B error). The second half of the chapter looked at the situated cognition movement in robotics. After reviewing some of the objections that situated cognition theorists level at traditional GOFAI we explored how these theorists have been inspired by very simple cognitive systems such as insects. We then considered how these theoretical ideas have been translated into particular robotic architectures, focusing on the subsumption architectures developed by Rodney Brooks and on Maja Matarić's behavior-based robotics.

Checklist

Some cognitive scientists have turned to dynamical systems theory as an alternative to traditional information-processing models of cognition

(1) A dynamical system is any system that evolves over time in a law-governed way, but what distinguishes the dynamical systems approach in cognitive science is the idea of studying cognitive systems with the tools of dynamical systems theory.

(2) Dynamical models use calculus-based methods to track the evolving relationship between a small number of variables over time – a trajectory through state space.

(3) Dynamical systems often display coupling (interdependencies between variables) and an attractor dynamics (there are points in the system's state space on which many different trajectories converge).

(4) Cognitive systems modeled using dynamical systems theory do not display many of the classic features of information-processing systems. Dynamical models typically are not representational, computational, sequential, or homuncular.

Dynamical systems theory permits time-sensitive models of learning and skill acquisition in children

(1) Case studies include learning to walk in infancy, as well as performance on the A-not-B search task.

(2) Support for the dynamical systems approach comes from experiments showing that performance can be drastically altered by manipulating factors that would typically be ignored by computational models.

(3) The explanatory power of the dynamical systems approach does not mean that it should *replace* information-processing approaches to cognitive science.

(4) The dynamical systems approach sheds light on cognitive systems at a particular level of organization. There is no reason to think that the level of explanation it provides should be the only one in cognitive science.

Situated cognition theorists also react against some of the fundamental tenets of cognitive science. The force of the situated cognition approach can be seen very clearly in AI and robotics

(1) AI programs such as SHRDLU and robots such as SHAKEY can interact with their environments. But situated cognition theorists argue that they are not properly situated in their environments. The

real work of putting intelligence into SHRDLU and SHAKEY is not done by the systems themselves, but by the programmers.

(2) SHAKEY's world is already defined for it in terms of a small number of basic concepts. Likewise for its motor repertoire. This avoids the real problems of decoding the environment and reacting to the challenges it poses.

(3) Situated cognition theorists think that instead of focusing on simplified and scaled-down versions of "high-level" tasks, cognitive scientists should look at how simple organisms such as insects solve complex but ecologically valid problems.

(4) Biorobotics is the branch of robotics that builds models of biological organisms reflecting the basic design principles that have emerged in evolution. A good example is Barbara Webb's work on cricket phonotaxis.

Subsumption architectures are a powerful tool developed by situated cognition theorists such as Rodney Brooks

(1) Subsumption architectures are not made up of functional sub-systems in the way that modular architectures are. Instead they are built up from layers of semi-autonomous sub-systems that work in parallel.

(2) Subsumption architectures are built to mimic how evolution might work. New systems are grafted on in layers that typically don't change the design of the existing systems.

(3) Subsumption architectures trade as much as possible on direct perception–action links that allow the online control of action.

Subsumption architectures do not typically have decision-making systems built into them. Problems of action selection are solved by predefined precedence relations among sub-systems. Situated cognition theorists have to work out a more flexible solution to the action selection problem

(1) One approach is to develop a hybrid architecture, combining a subsumption architecture for low-level reactive control with a more traditional symbolic central planner for high-level decision-making.

(2) Behavior-based robotics takes another approach, more in the spirit of situated cognition. Behavior-based architectures (such as that implemented in TOTO) represent their environments and use those representations to plan actions. But these representations are not centralized or centrally manipulated.

(3) In addition to reactive rules such as those in subsumption architectures, behavior-based robots have basis behaviors programmed into them. These basis behaviors are more complex and temporally extended than reactive rules. They can also be combined.

(4) Behavior-based robots can exhibit emergent behaviors that have not been programmed into them (e.g. the flocking and foraging behaviors displayed by Matarić's Nerd Herd). Behavior-based robots have also been shown to be capable of learning these emergent behaviors through reinforcement learning.

Further reading

Timothy Van Gelder has written a number of articles promoting the dynamical systems approach to cognitive science. See, for example, Van Gelder 1995 and 1998. The papers in Port and Van Gelder's *Mind and Motion: Explorations in the Dynamics of Cognition* (Port and Van Gelder 1995) contain some influential dynamically inspired studies and models (including Townsend and Busemeyer's model of decision-making), as well as theoretical statements. Thelen and Smith's 1993 edited volume *A Dynamical Systems Approach to the Development of Cognition and Action* provides more detail on their studies of infant walking, as well as contributions from other dynamical systems theorists. Their BBS article (Thelen *et al*. 2001) presents the model of the A-not-B error. Smith and Thelen 2003 is a more accessible introduction. For overviews and assessments of the dynamical systems approach to cognitive science, see Eliasmith 1996, Clark 1998, Clark 2001 ch. 7, Weiskopf 2004, Clearfield, Dineva, Smith, Diedrich, and Thelen 2009, Spencer, Thomas, and McClelland 2009, Needham and Libertus 2011, Spencer, Perone, and Buss 2011, Riley and Holden 2012, and Spencer, Austin, and Schutte 2012. For a recent application of the dynamical systems approach to different areas of cognitive psychology see Spivey 2007.

The philosopher Andy Clark is a very clear expositor of situated cognition and biorobotics – see particularly his book *Being There* (Clark 1997) and ch. 6 of Clark 2001, as well as his book *Supersizing the Mind* (Clark 2008) and a discussion of the book in *Philosophical Studies* (Clark 2011). For more on morphological computation, including the two examples discussed in the text, see Pfeifer, Iida, and Gómez 2006. Clancey 1997 is a general survey of situated cognition from the perspective of an AI specialist. Several of Rodney Brooks's influential papers are reprinted in his book *Cambrian Intelligence* (Brooks 1999), which also contains some more technical papers on specific architectures. Brooks 1991 is also reprinted in Haugeland 1997. For early versions of some of the criticisms of GOFAI made by situated cognition theorists see Dreyfus 1977. For a very different way of thinking about situated cognition (in terms of situatedness within a social environment) see Hutchins 1995. The *Cambridge Handbook of Situated Cognition* (Robbins and Aydede 2008) is a very useful and comprehensive resource, with a strong emphasis on the philosophical underpinnings of the situated cognition movement. For more on embodied cognition see Shapiro 2007, Chemero 2009, Adams and Aizawa 2010, Shapiro 2011, Anderson, Richardson, and Chemero 2012, and Lawrence Shapiro's chapter in Margolis, Samuels, and Stich 2012.

Arkin 1998 is a comprehensive textbook on behavior-based robotics. For a more programming-oriented survey, see Jones and Roth 2003. Winfield 2012 is a more recent introduction. Maja Matarić has written many papers on behavior-based robotics (see online resources). Matarić 1997 and 1998 are good places to start. Readers interested in building their own mobile robots will want to look at her book *The Robotics Primer* (Matarić 2007).

CHAPTER FOURTEEN

The cognitive science of consciousness

Overview

The main part of this book has explored different ways of thinking about and developing the basic idea that cognition is a form of information processing. As we have discussed, there are different models of information processing, and so different ways of developing this fundamental framework assumption of cognitive science. From the perspective of classical cognitive science, digital computers are the best models we have of how information can be processed. And so, from the perspective of classical cognitive science, we need to think about the mind as a very complex digital computer that processes information in a step-by-step, serial manner. From a more neurally inspired perspective, in contrast, information processing is a parallel rather than serial process. Neural networks can be used to model information processing and problem-solving through the simultaneous activation of large populations of neuron-like units.

Chapter 13 explored alternative ways of analyzing and predicting the behavior of cognitive systems. The dynamical systems approach is one alternative, analyzing cognition in terms of variables evolving through state space, rather than the physical manipulation of symbols carrying information about the environment. Closely related to the dynamical systems approach is the situated cognition movement. This second alternative to information-processing models is inspired by studies of how insects and other low-level organisms solve complex ecological problems, and by illustrations from robotics of how complex behaviors can emerge in individuals and groups from a small repertoire of hard-wired basic behaviors.

Both the dynamical systems approach and the situated cognition movement are in effect raising questions about the *necessity* of modeling cognition as information processing. They provide many examples, some very compelling, of cognitive achievements and behaviors that can apparently be analyzed and predicted without building in assumptions about information processing. Generalizing from these examples, dynamical systems and situation cognition theorists raise the general question: Do we really need the framework assumption that cognition is information processing in order to understand the full range of behaviors and achievements of which cognitive agents are capable?

In this chapter we turn to a very different objection to information-processing models of cognition. This is not a challenge to the claim that it is *necessary* to assume that cognition is information processing. Rather, it is a challenge to the idea that this assumption is *sufficient*. In essence, what is being asked is: If we understand the mind as an information-processing machine, is there something missing? In recent years the most powerful attack on the explanatory adequacy of cognitive science has come from those who think that cognitive science cannot fully explain consciousness. At the same time, the scientific study of consciousness has proved one of the most exciting and fertile areas in cognitive science. This chapter reviews both sides of the debate.

Sections 14.1 and 14.2 review two classic articulations of the challenge that consciousness poses for science – the first from the seventeenth-century philosopher Gottfried Wilhelm Leibniz and the second from the contemporary philosopher Frank Jackson. In section 14.3 we begin reviewing the cognitive science of consciousness by looking at the differences between conscious and non-conscious information processing, as revealed in priming experiments and by studying the behavior of brain-damaged patients. Section 14.4 draws on these findings to explore theories about the function of consciousness, on the principle that we can explain consciousness by understanding its functional contribution to cognition. In section 14.5 we look at two powerful arguments objecting to that whole way of proceeding. According to these arguments, functional approaches to consciousness cannot help us understand what is truly mysterious about consciousness – at best they can shed light on what are sometimes called the "easy" problems of consciousness. Section 14.6 presents the other side of the coin by reviewing one of the best-established approaches to the functional role of consciousness – the so-called global workspace theory.

14.1   The challenge of consciousness: Leibniz's Mill

We can think about the challenge here through two different perspectives on cognitive agents. The dominant approach within cognitive science has been to look at cognitive agents from the third-person perspective. Cognitive scientists typically work backwards from observable behaviors and capacities to information-processing mechanisms that could generate those behaviors and support those capacities. As we have seen in earlier chapters, they do this using a range of experimental techniques and tools, including psychological experiments, functional neuroimaging, and computational modeling. In adopting this third-person perspective, what cognitive scientists do is broadly continuous with what physicists, chemists, and biologists do.

From this third-person perspective what cognitive scientists are working with and trying to explain are publicly observable phenomena – reaction times, levels of blood oxygen, verbal reports, and so forth. But there is another perspective that we have not yet discussed. This is the first-person perspective. Human cognitive agents have sensations. They experience the distinctive smell of a rose, the distinctive sound of chalk on a blackboard, the distinctive feel of cotton against the skin. They react emotionally to events and to each other. They regret the past and have hopes and fears for the future. From the first-person perspective we have a rich, conscious life, full of feelings, emotions, sensations, and experiences. These are all vital parts of what make us human. How can we make sense of them within the information-processing model of the mind?

We can see this challenge as a contemporary expression of a tension that has often been identified between the scientific perspective on the world and the psychological reality of conscious life. Here is a very famous articulation of the problem from the great seventeenth-century philosopher and inventor of the calculus, Gottfried Wilhelm Leibniz. In his 1714 essay *Monadology* Leibniz wrote:

> Moreover, we must confess that the perception, and what depends on it, is inexplicable in terms of mechanical reasons, that is, through shapes and motions. If we imagine that there is a machine whose structure makes it think, sense, and have perceptions, we could conceive it enlarged, keeping the same proportions, so that we could enter into it, as one enters into a mill. Assuming that, when inspecting its interior, we will only find parts that push one another, and we will never find anything to explain a perception.

This argument is known as Leibniz's Mill Argument.

Exercise 14.1 Formulate Leibniz's Mill Argument in your own words. Suggestion: Think of an example more relevant to cognitive science than a mill.

Here is one way to formulate what Leibniz thinks his argument shows. Nothing that we can observe "from the outside" can explain the distinctive nature of seeing, for example, a colorful sunset. We can explain all of the mechanical events that go on when we see a sunset. We can trace the route that light rays take through the lens of the eye to the retina. We can explain how those light rays are transformed into electrical impulses by rods and cones in the retina. And then we can give a compelling account of how information about the environment is extracted from those electrical impulses. But, Leibniz claimed, in that entire process "we will never find anything to explain a perception."

What Leibniz meant by this, I believe, is that there is nothing in the story we tell about how information carried by light rays is extracted and processed that will capture or explain the distinctive experience of seeing a sunset. We can trace the physiological events that take place, and conceptualize them in information-processing terms to understand how the organism represents what is going on around it. But this is all from the third-person perspective – from the outside looking in. It does not shed any light on what is going on from the first-person point of view of the person seeing the sunset. It does not capture the distinctive character of that person's experience. So, for example, it does not explain why people typically value the experience of seeing a sunset – why they would prefer to look at a sunset than to look at a blank sheet of paper.

Exercise 14.2 Do you agree with Leibniz's conclusion? Evaluate his reasoning.

In the next section we will look at a contemporary argument that comes to conclusions very similar to Leibniz's, but is much more focused on contemporary cognitive science.

14.2 Consciousness and information processing: The Knowledge Argument

The last section introduced the general challenge that conscious experience poses for information-processing models of the mind. In this section we will bring some of the problems into clearer focus through a thought experiment originally proposed by the philosopher Frank Jackson. It is usually called the Knowledge Argument.

Here is the Knowledge Argument in Jackson's own words:

Mary is confined to a black-and-white room, is educated through black-and-white books and through lectures relayed on black-and-white television. In this way she knows everything there is to know about the physical nature of the world. She knows all the physical facts about us and our environment, in a wide sense of "physical" which includes everything in *completed* physics, chemistry, and neurophysiology...

It seems, however, that Mary does not know all that there is to know. For when she is let out of the black-and-white room or given a color television, she will learn what it is to see something red ...

After Mary sees her first ripe tomato, she will realize how impoverished her conception of the mental life of *others* has been *all along*. She will realize that there was, all the time she was carrying out her laborious investigations into the neurophysiologies of others, something about these people she was quite unaware of. All along their experiences (or many of them, those got from tomatoes, the sky, ...) had a feature conspicuous to them, but until now hidden from her. (Jackson 1986, original emphasis)

When Jackson originally formulated the Knowledge Argument he offered it as a refutation of the philosophical theory known as physicalism (or materialism). According to physicalism, all facts are physical facts. Physicalism must be false, Jackson argued, because in her black-and-white room Mary knew all the physical facts that there are to know and yet there is a fact that she discovers when she leaves the room – the fact about what it is like for someone to see red.

Exercise 14.3 State physicalism in your own words. Do you think that Jackson's Knowledge Argument gives a compelling reason to reject physicalism?

Jackson no longer believes that the Knowledge Argument refutes physicalism, however, and so we will not pursue that issue here. For our purposes what is important is that the Knowledge Argument can also be used to argue that information-processing models of the mind are inadequate. The argument would go like this.

1 In her black-and-white room Mary has complete knowledge of how information is processed in the brain.
2 So in her black-and-white room Mary knows everything that there is to know about the information processing going on when a person has the experience of seeing red.
3 When she leaves the black-and-white room, Mary acquires new knowledge about what goes on when a person has the conscious experience of seeing red.
4 Therefore, there must be some aspects of what goes on when a person has the conscious experience of seeing red that cannot be understood in terms of how information is processed in the brain.

The Knowledge Argument raises a powerful challenge to the basic framework assumption of cognitive science that we can give a complete information-processing account of the mind. Little is more salient to each of us than our first-person conscious experience of the world. If, as the Knowledge Argument claims, this is something that cannot be captured in an information-processing account of the mind, then we will have to do a very fundamental rethink of the limits and scope of cognitive science.

For some cognitive scientists, the problem of consciousness is the "last, great frontier." For many outside the field, in contrast, consciousness reveals the fatal flaw in cognitive science. We will certainly not settle the issue in this book. But the remainder of this chapter surveys some important and exciting research in contemporary cognitive science in the context of this challenge to the very possibility of a cognitive science of consciousness.

14.3 Information processing without conscious awareness: Some basic data

We often understand things by understanding what they do and what they can be used for. Cognitive scientists have typically tackled consciousness by thinking about its function. A good way to start is to look at the types of information processing and problem-solving that can take place without consciousness and compare them with those that cannot, as a way of studying the difference that consciousness makes. We will look at two important sources of data about the differences between conscious and non-conscious information processing.

Cognitive scientists have learnt many things from *priming experiments*. These experiments typically have the following structure. Subjects are exposed very briefly to some stimulus – an image on a screen, perhaps, or a sound. The time of exposure is short enough that the subjects do not consciously register the stimulus. Nonetheless, the exposure to the stimulus affects their performance on subsequent tasks – how they complete word fragments, for example, or how quickly they can perform a basic classification. Since the information processing between initial exposure and subsequent task performance takes place below the threshold of consciousness, looking at the relation between the initial stimulus and the subsequent task can be very informative about the types of information processing that can be carried out non-consciously.

A second important source of information about non-conscious information processing comes from looking at how cognitive abilities can be damaged and impaired. Cognitive neuropsychologists study the structure of cognition – what underlies particular cognitive abilities and capacities, and how they depend upon each other. One way they do this is by carefully studying cognitive disorders, primarily those generated by brain damage. The guiding principle for this type of investigation is that we can work backwards from what happens when things go wrong to how they function in the normal case. So, for example, if in one type of brain damage we see ability A functioning more or less normally while ability B is severely impaired, then we can infer that in some sense A and B are independent of each other – or, as cognitive neuropsychologists call it, we can infer a *dissociation* between them. A *double dissociation* occurs when we have a dissociation in each direction – that is, in one disorder we have ability A functioning normally with B significantly impaired, while in a second disorder we have ability B functioning normally with A significantly impaired. Double dissociations provide stronger evidence that A and B are independent of each other.

Exercise 14.4 Explain in your own words why a double dissociation is a better sign of independence than a single dissociation.

Cognitive psychologists studying psychological disorders caused by brain trauma have identified very interesting dissociations involving consciousness. There are surprisingly many tasks that can be carried out non-consciously by brain-damaged patients, even though they are typically performed with conscious awareness by normal subjects.

Consciousness and priming

Figure 14.1 illustrates a very common type of priming experiment, known as a masked priming experiment. Masks are used to reduce the visibility of the priming stimulus. In masked priming experiments subjects are typically presented with a neutral mask for a

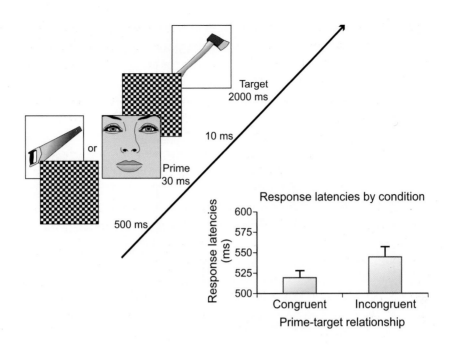

Figure 14.1 An illustration of a typical congruence priming experiment. The images above the arrow depict the sequence and timing of each stimulus when a tool is the target. The graph shows that people who were presented with a congruent prime were faster to identify the target than people who were presented with an incongruent prime. (From Finkbeiner and Forster 2008)

short period of time. The mask is presented long enough for subjects to be aware of it. The prime is then presented, too quickly for the subject to be aware of it. After an even briefer second presentation of the mask subjects see the target stimulus and can begin carrying out the required task.

The experiment depicted in Figure 14.1 is a congruence priming experiment. Subjects are asked to categorize the target as either a face or a tool. There are two different types of prime. One type is congruent with the target (e.g., another tool, if the target is a tool). The other is not congruent (e.g., a tool, if the target is a face). The experiment measures the response latency (the time it takes the subject to classify the target correctly). As the graph illustrates, the experimenters found a significant priming effect for congruent prime–target pairs.

What does this priming effect reveal? Think about what counts as a congruent prime–target pair. Figure 14.1 gives one example – a saw and a hammer. These are congruent because they both fall under a single category. Non-congruent prime–target pairs fall under different categories. So, what the priming effect appears to show is that the information processing required to carry out basic categorization can take place non-consciously. The processing time for correctly classifying a congruent target is less than for a non-congruent target, the standard explanation runs, because the subject is already thinking non-consciously about the relevant category.

BOX 14.1 A typical semantic priming experiment

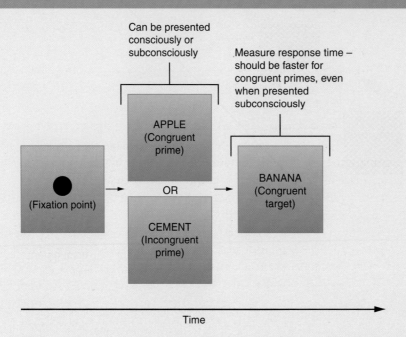

Time

There are many variations. Sometimes the words are presented in different languages, as discussed below, and sometimes the semantic congruence varies for the target instead of the prime. Participants can be asked to hit a button simply when they see the target word or make some more difficult judgment about the word (e.g., whether it is in fact a word).

Priming experiments have proved controversial. A number of cognitive scientists have raised important methodological objections to the whole paradigm. There has been very vigorous discussion, for example, about how to show that primes really are invisible and so that priming effects reflect non-conscious processing. A typical method of doing this is to identify a threshold by progressively lowering the presentation time of a stimulus until subjects identify it at chance. This is supposed to show that any stimulus presented for a length of time at or below the threshold will be non-visible and non-conscious. But one problem with this is that the threshold of visibility can vary. There is some evidence that primes become more visible when they are followed by congruent targets. Varying the mask can also alter the threshold of visibility.

More recent studies have been very sensitive to these methodological issues, and the majority view now is that priming effects do occur, and hence that there are some kinds of non-conscious information processing. The crucial question is: How "smart" is this non-conscious information processing? One of the most important areas where priming effects have been studied is language processing. In these experiments primes and targets are both words. The most controversial experiments have focused on what is known as *semantic priming* (as illustrated in Box 14.1). Semantic priming occurs when there is a priming effect that can only be explained through information processing about the meaning of words – as opposed, for example, to their phonology (how they are pronounced) or their orthography (how they are spelled).

Some interesting evidence for semantic priming comes from studies with bilingual subjects where prime and target are in different languages, particularly where those languages are in very different scripts (Chinese and English, for example). Many studies have shown robust priming effects when subjects are asked to decide whether or not a target string of letters is a proper word or not (what is called the *lexical decision task*). Interestingly, the priming effect tends to occur only when the prime is in the dominant (first) language (L1) and the target is in the second language (L2).

Semantic priming is potentially very significant, because of the longstanding and widely held view that semantic processing is very high-level and dependent upon conscious awareness. As we saw in detail in Chapter 10, cognitive scientists have often distinguished modular from non-modular (or central) information processing. Modular processes are quintessentially "dumb." They are hard-wired, quick, and automatic. In linguistic processing, for example, basic phonological processing has typically been taken to be modular, as have basic forms of syntactic analysis. Modular processing has always been thought to take place below the threshold of consciousness. And so priming effects that can be explained in terms of modular processing would not be much of a surprise. Semantic processing has typically been thought to be non-modular. This is why semantic priming is so important. It seems to show that there can be information processing that is both non-modular and non-conscious.

Non-conscious processing in blindsight and unilateral spatial neglect

Semantic priming provides good evidence that relatively high-level information processing takes place below the threshold of consciousness in normal subjects. We turn now to look at another very different source of evidence – the large body of information about non-conscious information processing that has emerged from studying brain-damaged patients with neuropsychological disorders. In particular we will look at two much-studied disorders – blindsight and unilateral spatial neglect. In each of these disorders we see something very striking – brain-damaged subjects are able to perform a variety of visual tasks even though they report themselves being completely unaware of the visual stimuli to which they are reacting.

Unilateral spatial neglect (also known as *hemiagnosia* or *hemineglect*) is a relatively common neuropsychological disorder. It typically occurs after damage to the right hemisphere, particularly damage to the parietal and frontal lobes. The defining feature of spatial neglect is that patients lack awareness of sensory events on the contralesional side of space (on the opposite side of the world to the side of the brain that is damaged). In the vast majority of cases, the neglected side is the left-hand side.

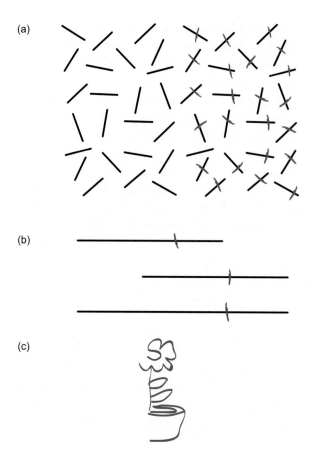

Figure 14.2 Examples of deficits found in patients with left spatial neglect (damage to the right hemisphere of the brain). In (a), unilateral neglect patients typically fail to mark the lines on the contralesional (here, left) side of a sheet of paper. In (b), patients are asked to bisect each line. Their markings are typically skewed to the right, as if they do not see the leftmost segment. In (c), patients are either asked to draw something from memory or to copy another illustration placed in front of them. In both cases, unilateral neglect patients tend to omit parts on the contralesional side. (From Driver and Vuilleumier 2001)

The neglect phenomenon was very strikingly illustrated by two Italian neuropsychologists in 1978. Eduardo Bisiach and Claudio Luzzatti asked two neglect patients to describe from memory the central square in Milan with the famous Duomo (cathedral). The patients were initially asked to describe the square as if they were standing in front of the Duomo. As predicted, the patients failed to describe the houses and shops on the left-hand side of the square (from their vantage-point in front of the Duomo). Bisiach and Luzzatti then asked the patients to orient themselves differently, so that they were imagining themselves on the edge of the square looking at the Duomo. Now the patients accurately described the houses and shops they had previously neglected, and instead missed out the side of the square that they had previously described. Figure 14.2 shows further examples of typical visual deficits in neglect patients.

Neglect also affects action. A neglect patient might only shave or apply make-up to one side of their face, for example. Or they might eat only from one side of a plate.

The blindsight patients who have been most studied report little to no awareness in one side of their visual field. They have what is called a *scotoma* (a region of very diminished visual acuity that does not occupy the whole visual field). In both blindsight and unilateral spatial neglect, patients report themselves to be unaware of what is going on in part of their visual field. The aetiology (cause) is different, however. The impairment in blindsight is typically due to lesions in the primary visual cortex (V1, or the striate cortex).

For our purposes, the interesting feature of both blindsight and unilateral spatial neglect is that patients appear to have surprising residual visual functioning despite reporting a more or less complete lack of visual awareness. Blindsight patients can respond to stimuli in the scotoma, and visual neglect patients can respond to stimuli in the neglected region of space.

One challenge in exploring the residual abilities of blindsight patients is that they will often find the experiments absurd. Ernst Pöppel, whose important 1973 article coauthored with Douglas Frost and Richard Held was one of the first to study blindsight, reported a patient irritatedly saying "How can I look at something that I haven't seen?" when asked to direct his eyes to a target in his blind field. This seems a perfectly reasonable response. The puzzling thing, though, is that the patient was in fact able to carry out the request, even while denying any awareness of the target.

In order to overcome this challenge, experiments have used nonverbal forced choice tests. In essence, patients are forced to guess in situations where they feel that they have no basis to make a judgment or to perform an action. The choices are usually binary – is the stimulus moving or stationary, is it high or low in the visual field, is it horizontal or vertical? Experimenters often find that blindsight patients perform significantly better than chance, even when the patients describe themselves as guessing (and so would be expected to perform at chance levels). There is strong evidence that blindsight patients can localize unseen stimuli in the blind field, that they can discriminate orientation, and that they can detect moving and stationary figures randomly interspersed with blank trials.

Neuropsychologists have also found that blindsight patients are capable of some types of form perception. Here is an example from a striking set of experiments performed by Ceri Trevethan, Arash Sahraie, and blindsight pioneer Larry Weiskrantz, working with a patient known by his initials D.B. Figure 14.3 depicts line drawings of animals that were presented within D.B.'s blind field.

The figures were shown at very low contrast (2 percent – although they are depicted in high contrast in Figure 14.3). The patient was told that he was being shown a picture of an animal and asked to guess which animal it was. The figure indicates the responses given, with correct answers underlined. As illustrated, D.B. achieved 89 percent accuracy, despite reporting no awareness whatsoever of any of the figures.

Spatial neglect patients also have considerable residual abilities. A famous example identified by neuropsychologists John Marshall and Peter Halligan is illustrated in

Figure 14.3 D.B.'s responses to pictures of animals presented in his blind field. Correct answers are underlined. (From Trevethan, Sahraie, and Weiskrantz 2007)

Figure 14.4. Marshall and Halligan showed P.S., a neglect patient, the two pictures in the diagram – one of a normal house and one of a house on fire. Since the flames were on the left-hand side of the picture, P.S. did not report seeing any difference between the two pictures. Nonetheless, when asked which house she would prefer to live in, P.S. reliably chose the house that was not on fire (9 times out of 11).

Figure 14.4 An illustration of the two houses presented to P.S. The houses are identical except that one has flames shooting out of its left side. Because P.S. possesses left-side spatial neglect, she reported not being able to see the flames, but still consistently selected the other house when asked which house she would prefer to live in. (From Marshall and Halligan 1988)

The Halligan and Marshall experiments indicate that neglect patients are capable of relatively high-level processing in their blind field. This conclusion is reinforced by experiments carried out by Italian neuropsychologists Anna Berti and Giacomo Rizzolatti. Berti and Rizzolatti (1992) used a semantic priming paradigm to explore whether neglect patients could identify semantic categories in their neglected field. Neglect patients were presented with priming stimuli in their neglected visual field and then asked to categorize objects presented in the normal field. As discussed above in section 14.3, the guiding principle for priming experiments is that, when the prime stimulus and the target stimulus are congruent (i.e., from the same category), then categorization will be easier and quicker, provided that the prime stimulus is processed. Berti and Rizzolatti found the predicted effect in patients who denied all awareness of the prime stimuli and so concluded that semantic information is processed in the neglected visual field.

14.4 So what is consciousness for?

We have reviewed experiments on both brain-damaged and normal subjects indicating that a large number of information-processing tasks can be performed without conscious awareness – or, to be more precise, can be performed by subjects who do not report any conscious awareness of the discriminations and selections that they are making. This leaves us with a puzzle. What exactly does consciousness contribute? Why do we need it? In order to make progress on this we need to look, not just at what blindsight and neglect patients can do, but also at what they can't do.

What is missing in blindsight and spatial neglect

The fact that blindsight and neglect patients have considerable residual abilities that can be teased out with careful experiments should not obscure the massive differences between these patients and normal subjects. These differences can give important clues about what conscious awareness contributes to cognition and behavior.

One very striking fact about the brain-damaged patients we have been looking at is just how difficult it is to elicit the residual abilities. As discussed earlier, the only way to do this is essentially to force patients to make choices and discriminations. Neither blindsight nor neglect patients will voluntarily do things in their blind or neglected fields. From a behavioral point of view this is most obvious in neglect patients. What characterizes the disorder is not just that patients report a complete lack of awareness of what is going on in the neglected visual field. It is also that they do not direct any actions within those regions of space that fall within the neglected visual field. This is the case both for their own personal, bodily space (so that male patients do not shave on the neglected side of their face) and for external space (so that they do not direct actions at objects located on the neglected side of the world as they perceive it). The same holds for blindsight patients, who never initiate actions towards the blind field, despite being able to point to stimuli in the blind field (when forced to do so).

This suggests a hypothesis about the difference between conscious and non-conscious information processing. Both normal and brain-damaged subjects receive many different types of non-conscious information about the world and about their own bodies. This information can be used in a number of ways. It can influence decision-making (as we saw in the Halligan and Marshall experiments). It can feed into judgments, as evidenced by the possibility of semantic priming in normal subjects and in the blind field of blindsight patients. The information can also guide motor behavior, as we see in blindsight patients who are able to point, grasp, and make saccades to objects in their blind field. But subjects can only initiate voluntary actions on the basis of information that is conscious. Only conscious information allows subjects to identify targets and to plan actions towards them.

Many aspects of action are controlled non-consciously. So, for example, whenever you reach out to grasp something, your hand non-consciously prepares itself for the grasping action, so that the fingers are at an appropriate aperture. This involves complex information processing, including estimates of the likely size of the object, taking into account distance and so forth. The online correction of movement, compensating for environmental change or initial errors of trajectory, is also typically non-conscious. But, according to the hypothesis, actually initiating deliberate action requires conscious information about the environment.

Milner and Goodale: Vision for action and vision for perception

The neuropsychologists David Milner and Melvyn Goodale have developed a sophisticated theory of vision that is built around this idea that one of the roles of consciousness is to permit voluntary and deliberate action. Their theory is based on the existence of two anatomical pathways carrying visual information in the primate brain. We looked at some of the neurophysiological evidence for these two anatomical pathways in section 3.2 when we reviewed the important Mishkin and Ungerleider experiments. Visual information takes two different routes from the primary visual cortex. One pathway, the ventral pathway, projects to the temporal lobe. A second pathway, the dorsal pathway, carries information to the posterior parietal lobe. (See Figure 3.5 for an illustration of the two pathways.)

The two pathways have very different functions. For Mishkin and Ungerleider, as we saw in Chapter 3, the crucial functional distinction is between the "what" system, concerned with object identification and subserved by the ventral pathway, and the "where" system, concerned with locating objects in space. Milner and Goodale have a related but somewhat different interpretation. They distinguish two types of vision, which they term *vision for action* and *vision for perception*. Both systems are involved in initiating and controlling action, but in very different ways. Here is the distinction in their own words:

> So what do we mean by "action" and what are the roles of the two streams in the guidance of action? The key contribution of the perceptual mechanisms in the ventral stream is the identification of possible and actual goal objects – and the selection of an appropriate course of action to deal with those objects. But the subsequent implementation of that action is the job of the dorsal stream. This stream plays no role in selecting appropriate actions, but is critical for the detailed specification and online control of the constituent movements that form the action, making use of metrical visual information that maps directly onto the action in the "here and now." ...

> The role of the ventral stream in action, then, is to provide visual information to enable the identification of a goal object such as a coffee cup, and to enable other cognitive systems to plan the action of picking up that cup. This would include the selection of the class of hand postures appropriate to the particular task at hand (whether that be taking a sip of coffee, for example, or putting the cup in the sink). But action planning of this sort is quite abstract, and the final movements that constitute the action could take many different forms. It is the dorsal stream's job to use the current visual information about the size, shape, and disposition of the object in egocentric coordinates (in the case of the coffee cup, with respect to the hand) to program and control the skilled movements needed to carry out the action. (Milner and Goodale 2008, 775–6)

In sum, then, the distinction is between initiating and planning an action, on the one hand, and the detailed execution of the action on the other. The first is performed using information from the ventral stream. The second uses information from the dorsal stream.

So, according to Milner and Goodale, actions have two very different aspects, which require very different types of information. These different types of information are processed separately. For our purposes, what is particularly interesting about this analysis of vision is that Milner and Goodale explicitly hold that only information relevant to what they call vision for action is actually conscious. Conscious awareness is restricted to the ventral pathway while the dorsal stream governs the visual control of movement non-consciously. This is consistent with the suggested hypothesis that one of the key functions of consciousness is to enable the initiation and planning of action.

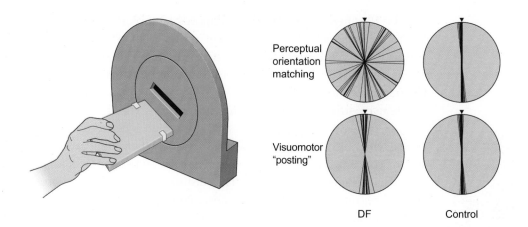

Figure 14.5 In this experiment subjects were asked either to "post" a card into a slot or to rotate another hand-held card to match the orientation of the slot. The angle of the slot varied across trials, although in each case the diagrams have been normalized so that the correct result is vertical. Normal subjects can perform both tasks with little difficulty. Patient D.F., in contrast, can carry out the visuomotor task almost as well as normal subjects, but her responses in the explicit matching task are almost random. (From Milner and Goodale 1998)

The Milner and Goodale interpretation relies heavily on experimental studies of both normal and brain-damaged patients. Here are two examples that illustrate how consciousness is and is not involved in vision.

Milner and Goodale's patient D.F. is one of the most studied and important neuropsychological patients. After carbon monoxide inhalation, D.F. developed what is known as *visual form agnosia*, substantially impaired visual perception of shape and orientation. The neural damage underlying her agnosia involved very serious damage to the central pathway. In a lengthy series of studies Milner, Goodale, and colleagues demonstrated a striking dissociation between D.F.'s visuomotor skills and her conscious awareness of shape and orientation, as evidenced by her verbal reports and performance on explicit tasks.

D.F. is able to perform many visuomotor tasks successfully, even though she is unable to recognize or identify the relevant features in her environment. Figure 14.5 illustrates a much-discussed example of two tasks where D.F. performs very differently. When asked to "post" a card into a slot D.F. was able to match her movements to the orientation of the slot and performed almost as successfully as normal subjects. But when asked to make an explicit judgment about the slot's orientation D.F.'s responses were almost random. This was the case whether she was asked to describe the orientation verbally or non-verbally (by rotating a card to match the orientation). According to Milner and Goodale, D.F. is receiving non-conscious information about orientation through the dorsal pathway, but because of damage to her ventral pathway is not consciously aware of the orientation.

Visual illusions provide another source of evidence for the dissociation between (non-conscious) vision for action and (conscious) vision for perception. Visual illusions affect how subjects consciously perceive the size and shape of objects. A number of experimenters have found, however, that the illusion does not carry over to visuomotor behavior. Subjects will report seeing an illusion, but when asked to make appropriate movements they will configure their grip and make other adjustments according to the correct dimensions of the relevant objects, not the dimensions that they report perceiving. So conscious perception (vision for perception) dissociates from (non-conscious) information relevant to the control of visuomotor behavior (vision for action). Figure 14.6 illustrates the

Figure 14.6 In the Ebbinghaus illusion two circles are illusorily seen as differently sized, depending on what surrounds them. The figure illustrates experiments published by Aglioti, DeSouza, and Goodale in 1995. The experimenters measured the size of the opening between fingers and thumb when subjects were asked to pick up two discs that they reported as being differently sized. They found no significant differences in grip aperture, suggesting that this aspect of the fine-grained control of grasping draws on different types of visual information than those that yield conscious awareness of the discs.

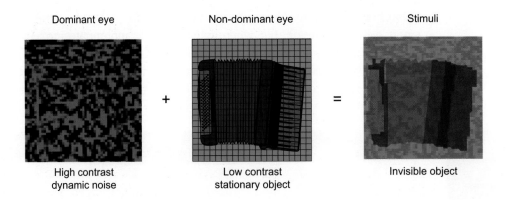

Dominant eye	Non-dominant eye	Stimuli

High contrast
dynamic noise

Low contrast
stationary object

Invisible object

Figure 14.7 Fang and He's interocular suppression task. The clear image presented to participants' non-dominant eye is rendered invisible by the unclear image presented to participants' dominant eye. (Adapted from Fang and He 2005)

experiment used by Aglioti, DeSouza, and Goodale to identify this dissociation, utilizing what is known as the Ebbinghaus illusion.

In addition to these (and many other) behavioral illustrations of the dissociation between (conscious) vision for perception and (non-conscious) vision for action, there is interesting supporting evidence from functional neuroimaging. Neuroimaging studies, such as those published by Fang Fang and Shen He in 2005, suggest that ventral stream activity is correlated with consciousness, while activity in the dorsal stream is not. Fang and He compared activation levels in areas known to be very involved in object processing in the dorsal and ventral streams respectively. They used a technique known as *interocular suppression* in which one eye is presented with an image of an object while the other eye is presented simultaneously with a high-contrast pattern that blocks conscious awareness of the presented image.

This paradigm enabled Fang and He to examine activation levels in the dorsal and ventral streams in the absence of conscious awareness and to compare those levels with activation levels when conscious awareness of the image was not suppressed. They found robust levels of activity in the dorsal stream even in the non-conscious conditions. In contrast, ventral stream activation was confined to the conscious condition.

In conclusion, Milner and Goodale's distinction between (conscious) vision for perception and (non-conscious) vision for action, together with the evidence supporting it from brain-damaged and normal subjects, both supports and clarifies the hypothesis that consciousness is important for initiating action. If Milner and Goodale are correct, then conscious awareness is key for identifying targets and for macro-level planning for how to effect actions. But conscious awareness is not typically involved in the fine-grained, online control of bodily movements.

What is missing in masked priming

We explored the extent of non-conscious information processing by looking at masked priming experiments. The masked priming paradigm provides powerful evidence that semantic processing can be non-conscious. At the same time, though, masked priming reveals very significant differences between how information is processed consciously and how it is processed non-consciously. This provides further important clues about the function of consciousness, complementing the discussion earlier in this section.

The key finding here is that the retention of information is very impaired in the absence of consciousness. So, although we find semantic information being processed below the threshold of consciousness in masked priming experiments, the processing is very transitory and short-lived. Here is an illustration from experiments published by Anthony Greenwald, Sean Draine, and Richard Abrams in 1996. The authors used a typical categorization task, asking subjects to identify first names as male or female or to classify words as pleasant or unpleasant in meaning. They succeeded in eliciting a robust priming effect when subjects were presented with a congruent masked prime. This effect was present both when the prime was presented subliminally and when it was presented supraliminally (above the threshold of consciousness). This allowed Greenwald, Draine, and Abrams to study the differences between subliminal priming and supraliminal priming. The particular dimension they explored was what happened when they varied the time between prime and trial (the so-called *stimulus-onset asynchrony*, SOA).

The SOA was varied between 67 ms and 400 ms in each of the two conditions (subliminal and supraliminal). Greenwald, Draine, and Abrams found a significant difference. In supraliminal cases, where the subjects were conscious of the prime, the priming effect was robust across all SOAs. The length of the delay between prime and target did not make a significant difference. In contrast, in the subliminal cases, with the subjects not consciously perceiving the prime, the effect was robust only at the shortest intervals and disappeared completely once the SOA went above 100 ms.

This experiment suggests an additional hypothesis about the function of conscious awareness – namely, that consciousness allows information to be explicitly retained and maintained. According to this hypothesis, information that is picked up non-consciously can indeed be deployed in relatively sophisticated tasks, but it can be used only within a very limited time horizon. Conscious information, in contrast, is more transferable and flexible. It can be used beyond the here-and-now. There are definite parallels between this idea and the idea of vision for action that Goodale and Milner propose. Vision for action is restricted to the online control and fine-tuning of behavior. It does not persist in the way that conscious visual information persists. That is one reason why Goodale and Milner think that the conscious vision-for-perception system is required for high-level action-planning.

14.5 Two types of consciousness and the hard problem

Sections 14.3 and 14.4 looked at a range of experimental evidence from normal and brain-damaged subjects in order to explore the scope and limits of non-conscious information processing. We reviewed key findings from blindsight and unilateral neglect patients, as well as the results of masked priming experiments and the more general two visual systems hypothesis proposed by Goodale and Milner. Two related ideas emerged about the function of consciousness. The first is that conscious awareness seems extremely important for planning and initiating action (as opposed to the online control of behavior, which can be carried out through non-conscious information processing). The second is that conscious information persists longer than non-conscious information. In the next section we will look at one example of a theory of consciousness that can accommodate these two ideas. First, though, we need to consider some important concerns about this whole way of proceeding that have been raised by the philosophers Ned Block and David Chalmers.

The philosopher Ned Block has cautioned cognitive scientists to be very careful about drawing conclusions about the nature and function of consciousness from neuropsychological disorders such as blindsight and unilateral spatial neglect. He thinks that these conclusions rest on flawed inferences. What causes the problem, according to Block, is a confusion between two very different concepts of consciousness. He calls these *phenomenal consciousness* and *access consciousness*. Here is how he characterizes the two notions, which he terms P-consciousness and A-consciousness respectively:

Phenomenal consciousness
P-consciousness is experience ... We have P-conscious states when we see, hear, smell, taste, and have pains. P-conscious properties include the experiential properties of sensations, feelings, and perceptions, but I would also include thoughts, wants, and emotions. (Block 1995b)

Access consciousness
A state is A-conscious if it is poised for direct control of thought and action. To add more detail, a representation is A-conscious if it is poised for free use in reasoning and for direct "rational" control of action and speech. (The rational is meant to rule out the kind of control that obtains in blindsight.) (Block 1995b)

Exercise 14.5 Give your own examples of A-consciousness and P-consciousness and describe the difference between them in your own words.

Exercise 14.6 Look back to the discussion of the Knowledge Argument in section 14.2. Is this argument about A-consciousness or P-consciousness?

Block often uses a famous paradigm developed by the cognitive psychologist George Sperling in 1960 to illustrate the difference between phenomenal and access consciousness. In Sperling's original experiment, subjects were briefly presented with a matrix containing three rows of four letters. They were then asked (in the *free recall* condition) to recall the letters they had seen. Typically subjects could only recall around 35 percent of the twelve letters in the matrix. Sperling was convinced that this free recall report was not a good guide to what the subjects had actually seen and so he asked subjects to report on their experience using an explicit cue. In the *cued recall* condition, subjects heard a tone shortly after the matrix. The frequency of the tone (high, medium, or low) cued a particular row in the matrix and subjects were asked to recall which letters they had seen in the cued row. In this condition performance improved dramatically, from 35 percent to around 75 percent. Sperling concluded that what subjects consciously perceive dramatically outstrips what they are able freely to recall. In Block's terminology, phenomenal consciousness dramatically outstrips access consciousness – what subjects are phenomenally conscious of remains constant, but what is available to access consciousness varies as the modes of access are varied (by switching from free recall to cued recall, for example).

From Block's perspective, the real problem of consciousness is the problem of understanding P-consciousness. All of the things that we have been looking at in the previous section, however, are really examples of A-consciousness. This is the "confusion" that he identifies in the title of his influential paper "On a confusion about a function of consciousness."

Here is a way of putting Block's point. We began this chapter by looking at the idea that consciousness presents a challenge to the guiding assumption of cognition science, namely, that the mind is an information-processing machine. We find this challenge encapsulated in the Knowledge Argument. Mary in her black-and-white room knows everything there is to know about the information processing that goes on when someone sees red, but she has not had the experience of seeing red and so does not know what it is like from a subjective point of view actually to see red. This subjective experience is what (according to the Knowledge Argument) cognitive science cannot explain. In Block's terminology, this subjective experience is P-consciousness.

A-consciousness, on the other hand, is something very different. It is not really a matter of how and why we experience the world in the way that we do, but rather of the difference between conscious information processing and non-conscious information processing. So, by definition, A-consciousness is a matter of information processing.

According to Block, the experiments and studies discussed in the previous section ultimately only inform us directly about the function of A-consciousness. They do not directly address the function of P-consciousness. The two hypotheses that were put forward about the function of consciousness were hypotheses about the difference between conscious information processing and non-conscious information processing. This all has to do with how information is used and whether or not it can be reported. It does not get to the heart of what Block sees as the real problem of consciousness, which has to do with how and why we experience the world the way we do.

The distinction that Block draws between A-consciousness and P-consciousness is related to further distinctions drawn by the philosopher David Chalmers in his influential book *The Conscious Mind* and other writings. Chalmers thinks that there is no single problem of consciousness. Instead, he thinks that we need to make a distinction between a cluster of relatively easy problems and a single, really difficult problem – what he calls the "hard problem" of consciousness.

Here are some examples of what Chalmers provocatively identifies as easy problems of consciousness:

- explaining an organism's ability to discriminate, categorize, and react to environmental stimuli;
- explaining how a cognitive system integrates information;
- explaining how and why mental states are reportable;
- explaining how a cognitive system can access its own internal states;
- explaining how attention gets focused;
- explaining the deliberate control of behavior;
- explaining the difference between wakefulness and sleep.

In Block's terminology these are different aspects of understanding A-consciousness. In the last analysis, they are all problems to do with how an organism accesses and deploys information.

Chalmers recognizes that "easy" is a relative term. None of the so-called easy problems has yet been solved, or even partially solved. The reason he calls them easy problems is that at least we have some idea of what a solution would look like. The easy problems are all problems that are recognizable within the basic framework of cognitive science and scientific psychology. People write papers about them, reporting relevant experiments and constructing theories.

According to Chalmers, though, no amount of progress on the easy problems of consciousness will help with the hard problem. Here is how he characterizes the hard problem:

> The really hard problem of consciousness is the problem of *experience*. When we think and perceive, there is a whir of information-processing, but there is also a subjective aspect. As Nagel (1974) has put it, there is *something it is like* to be a conscious organism. This subjective aspect is experience. When we see, for example, we *experience* visual sensations: the felt quality of redness, the experience of dark and light, the quality of depth in a visual field. Other experiences go along with perception in different modalities: the sound of a clarinet, the smell of mothballs. Then there are bodily sensations, from pains to orgasms; mental images that are conjured up internally; the felt quality of emotion, and the experience of a stream of conscious thought. What unites all of these states is that there is something it is like to be in them. All of them are states of experience.

> It is undeniable that some organisms are subjects of experience. But the question of how it is that these systems are subjects of experience is perplexing. Why is it that when our cognitive systems engage in visual and auditory information-processing, we have visual or auditory experience: the quality of deep blue, the sensation of middle C? How can we explain why there is something it is like to entertain a mental image, or to experience an emotion? . . .

> If any problem qualifies as *the* problem of consciousness, it is this one.

Exercise 14.7 In your own words characterize the proposed distinction between what Chalmers calls the easy problems of consciousness and what he calls the hard problem.

Looking at Chalmers's description, there are clear parallels with Block's distinction between A-consciousness and P-consciousness. In brief, Chalmers's hard problem is the problem of explaining Block's P-consciousness.

We can put all this together and relate it back to the discussion in the previous section. There we looked at different aspects of the function of consciousness through illustrations from both normal and brain-damaged subjects. The aim was to explore the differences between conscious and non-conscious information processing, which would in turn tell us about the function of consciousness and hence allow it to be studied scientifically. Block and Chalmers deliver a challenge to this whole way of proceeding. In effect they are saying that it completely misses the point. In Chalmers's phrase, looking at what happens in masked priming experiments or at the differences between normal subjects and blindsight patients can only help with the easy problems of consciousness. None of these things can possibly help with the hard problem of consciousness. The differences between normal subjects and patients suffering from blindsight or spatial neglect, or between subliminal and supraliminal, are differences in access to information. They cannot help us understand the nature of experience or what it is to be phenomenally conscious. In fact, Chalmers draws a very drastic conclusion from his distinction between easy and hard problems. He thinks that the hard problem of consciousness is in principle intractable to cognitive science (or any other kind of science).

A natural question to ask of Block and Chalmers is how they can be so confident that there is such a gulf between understanding access consciousness and understanding phenomenal consciousness, on the one hand, or between solving the easy problems and solving the hard problem, on the other. How can we be sure that we cannot understand P-consciousness by understanding the difference between conscious and non-conscious information processing? How can we be sure that P-consciousness is not ultimately a matter of A-consciousness? Similarly, how can we be sure that once we've solved all the easy problems we won't discover that we've solved the hard problem?

These questions raise some of the most involved and difficult issues discussed by contemporary philosophers. The basic contours of the discussion are relatively clear, however. In essence, what Chalmers, Block, and their supporters argue is that there is a *double dissociation* between access consciousness and phenomenal consciousness, between the easy (information-processing) aspects of consciousness and the hard (experiential) aspect. There can be phenomenal consciousness without access consciousness, and there can be access consciousness without phenomenal consciousness. This means that there are two different things, and so understanding one of them cannot be all that there is to understanding the other. There is what the philosopher Joseph Levine calls an *explanatory gap.*

Let's focus in particular on the idea that there may be access consciousness without phenomenal consciousness. Block accepts that there may not be any actual real-life examples of A-consciousness without P-consciousness. Blindsight patients, for example, do have experiences when they pick up information in their blind field. They have the experience of just guessing – an experience very different from the experience they have of picking up information in their sighted field. But, Block says, we can imagine patients with what he calls *super-blindsight*:

> A real blindsight patient can only guess when given a choice from a small set of alternatives (X/O; horizontal/vertical; etc.). But suppose … that a blindsight patient could be trained to prompt himself at will, guessing what is in the blind field without being told to guess. The super-blindsighter spontaneously says "Now I know that there is a horizontal line in my blind field even though I don't actually see it." Visual information from his blind field simply pops into his thoughts in the way that solutions to problems we've been worrying about pop into our thoughts, or in the way some people just know the time or which way is north without having any perceptual experience of it. The super-blindsighter himself contrasts what it is like to know visually about an X in his blind field and an X in his sighted field. There is something it is like to experience the latter, but not the former, he says. It is the difference between *just knowing* and knowing via a visual experience. (Block 1995 in Block, Flanagan, and Güzeldere 1997: 385)

Chalmers in effect generalizes the super-blindsight thought experiment. It is at least logically possible, he argues, that you could have a *zombie twin*. Your zombie twin behaves exactly like you; talks exactly like you; reacts to stimuli in exactly the same way that you do; has a brain and central nervous system identical to yours. In almost every physical and psychological respect your zombie twin is indistinguishable from you. The only difference is that your zombie twin has no experiences. There is nothing it is like to be your zombie twin – the lights are out.

Here in essence is how Chalmers reasons from these thought experiments:

1 Super-blindsighters and zombies are logically possible.
2 If super-blindsighters and zombies are logically possible, then it is possible to have access consciousness without phenomenal consciousness.
3 If it is possible to have access consciousness without phenomenal consciousness then we cannot explain phenomenal consciousness through explaining access consciousness.
4 The tools and techniques of cognitive science can only explain access consciousness.
5 The tools and techniques of cognitive science cannot explain phenomenal consciousness.

Exercise 14.8 Think about each step in this argument. Are there any steps you find unconvincing? If so, explain what is wrong with them. If not, are you prepared to accept the conclusion?

As indicated earlier, the issues here are incredibly complex, raising fundamental issues about the nature of explanation and indeed the nature of possibility. Are zombies really logically possible? Even if they are logically possible, what has that got to do with how we explain how things actually are (as opposed to how they could be in some abstract logical sense). These and other questions continue to be hotly debated and philosophers are far from agreement or resolution.

Without trying to settle the matter one way or the other, it seems plausible that progress is going to depend upon having a better idea of what an information-processing account of access consciousness might look like. Discussing the limits that there might or might not be to a particular type of explanation will be much easier when there is a particular example on which to focus. In the next section we will look at the *global workspace theory of consciousness*, which is an interesting candidate for an information-processing solution to some of the problems that Chalmers identifies as the easy problems of consciousness.

14.6 The global workspace theory of consciousness

In this final section we will review a prominent contemporary theory of consciousness – the global workspace theory. Global workspace theory was originally proposed by the psychologist and cognitive scientist Bernard Baars in his book *A Cognitive Theory of Consciousness*, published in 1988. Since then it has been taken up and developed by many others, including the neuroscientists Antonio Damasio and Stanislas Dehaene, as well as the philosopher Peter Carruthers. More recent presentations (in line with the general turn towards the brain in cognitive science) have emphasized the neural dimension of global workspace theory.

Global workspace is not, of course, the only theory currently being discussed by cognitive scientists. But it fits very naturally with many of the topics that we have been discussing in this chapter (and indeed throughout the book). In Block's terminology, global workspace theory is a theory of access consciousness – a theory of how information is made available for high-level cognition, action-planning, and speech. The theory is based on an analysis of the function of consciousness that directly addresses many of what Chalmers identifies as "easy" problems of consciousness. And finally, it draws on ideas that we have discussed earlier in the book – including the idea that the mind has both modular and non-modular components and the idea that attention serves a "gatekeeper" function in controlling what crosses the threshold of conscious awareness.

We will focus on the version of global workspace theory presented by Stanislas Dehaene and collaborators. They base the theory on two sets of factors. The first is a set of experimentally supported hypotheses about the function of consciousness. The second is a set of hypotheses about the basic mental architecture of the conscious mind. We will then look at their version of the global workspace theory and why they think it is the best model fitting all these experiments and hypotheses. Finally, we will look at some intriguing data suggesting a potential neural implementation of the global workspace theory (or, as Dehaene sometimes terms it, the global *neuronal* workspace theory).

The building blocks of global workspace theory

Stanislas Dehaene and Lionel Naccache give a very clear account of the theoretical underpinnings of the global workspace theory in their 2001 article "Towards a cognitive neuroscience of consciousness: Basic evidence and a workspace framework." They propose the theory as the best way of making sense of the basic functional benefits of consciousness within a framework set by some widely accepted assumptions about the architecture of the mind.

They focus in particular on three different things that they believe consciousness makes possible. These are:

■ the intentional control of action
■ durable and explicit information maintenance
■ the ability to plan new tasks through combining mental operations in novel ways

The first and second of these have been discussed at some length in section 14.4. We looked at the role of consciousness in the intentional control of action in the context of neuropsychological disorders such as blindsight and unilateral neglect, as well as in the two visual systems hypothesis proposed by Goodale and Milner. The significance of conscious awareness in durable and explicit information maintenance emerged from the discussion of masked priming.

For completeness we can review a study that Dehaene and Naccache cite to illustrate the role of consciousness in allowing several mental operations to be combined to carry out new tasks. In a paper published in 1995, the psychologists Philip Merikle, Stephen Joordens, and Jennifer Stolz developed a paradigm to study how routine behaviors can be inhibited and how automatic effects can be reversed. They focused on a version of the Stroop effect. The classical Stroop effect illustrates how reaction times in a color-naming task can be manipulated. If subjects are asked to name the color in which a word is printed, they are much slower when the word is the name of a different color (when the word "green" is printed in red ink, for example) than when the word names the color in which it is printed (when the word "green" is printed in green ink). Merikle, Joordens, and Stolz identified a priming version of the effect. Subjects were asked to classify a string of words as printed either in green or in red. Reaction times were significantly quicker when they were primed with the name of the correct color (with the word GREEN when the string was printed in green, for example) than when the prime and color were incongruent. This effect is exactly what one would expect.

Interestingly, though, the experimenters found that the Stroop effect could be reversed. When the percentage of incongruent trials was increased to 75 percent, the increased predictability of the incongruent color allowed reaction times to become quicker for *in*congruent trials than for congruent ones – so that subjects responded more quickly when green strings of words were primed with the word RED then when they were primed with the word GREEN. This reversed Stroop effect illustrates how an automatic effect can be strategically and intentionally reversed. But, and this is the important point, the strategic reversal can only take place when subjects are conscious of the prime. When a mask is used to keep the prime below the threshold of awareness, the reversal effect disappears. Dehaene and Naccache conclude: "We tentatively suggest, as a generalization, that the strategic operations which are associated with planning a novel strategy, evaluating it, controlling its execution, and correcting possible errors cannot be accomplished unconsciously" (Dehaene and Naccache 2001: 11).

Dehaene and Naccache consider these three hypothesized functions of consciousness within a framework set by two basic theoretical postulates about mental architecture and the large-scale organization of the mind.

The first theoretical postulate is a version of the modularity theory that we explored at length in Chapter 10. As originally presented by the philosopher Jerry Fodor, the modularity theory involves a distinction between two fundamental different types of cognitive processes – modular processes and non-modular processes. Modular processes have two key features. They are *domain-specific* and *informationally encapsulated*. That is to say, they are each dedicated to solving circumscribed types of problem that arise in very specific areas and in solving those problems they typically work with restricted databases of specialized information. A module specialized for one task (say, face recognition) cannot draw upon information available to a different module specialized for a different task. Many cognitive tasks involve a series of modules – executing an action is a good example – but, according to the classical version of modularity theory, there are some cognitive tasks that cannot be carried out by modular systems. These are tasks that are domain-general (they span a range of cognitive domains) and that can only be solved by drawing upon the full range of information that the organism has available to it. The global workspace is in essence a metaphorical name for this type of domain-general information processing.

Exercise 14.9 Review the discussion of modularity in Chapter 10.

Dehaene and Naccache take the basic distinction between modular and non-modular information processing and in effect extend it to a general hypothesis about the nature of consciousness. Within the overall architecture of a mind organized into domain-specific specialized processors and a domain-general global workspace, they suggest that the distinction between the conscious and non-conscious minds maps onto the distinction between modular processing and non-modular processing. Consciousness is restricted to information within the global workspace.

The second theoretical postulate has to do with how information becomes available to the global workspace. Attention is the key mechanism here. It functions as a gatekeeper, allowing the results of modular information processing to enter the global workspace. For the global workspace theory, attention and consciousness are very closely linked. This way of thinking about the role of attention has a long pedigree within cognitive science, going back to the pioneering work of Donald Broadbent, reviewed in section 1.4. Attention is thought of both as a *filter* (screening out unnecessary information, as in the cocktail party effect) and as an *amplifier* (allowing information that would otherwise have been unconscious to become available to consciousness).

▟▛◢▘ The global neuronal workspace theory

We have reviewed a small number of basic principles at the heart of the global workspace theory. Some of these have to do with the function of consciousness – with the idea that consciousness permits information to be explicitly and durably maintained for additional processing and reasoning, and with the idea that consciousness is necessary for initiating deliberate action. Other basic principles have to do with a basically modular approach to the architecture of the mind – with the idea that conscious information processing is non-modular and that attention controls how information from modular systems crosses the threshold of consciousness.

These basic principles can be developed in different ways. Three versions of the global workspace theory are illustrated in Figure 14.8, which shows how the workspace idea has evolved over the last thirty years.

An early antecedent was the theory of attention originally proposed by Donald Norman and Tim Shallice. As the figure illustrates, attention performs what Norman and Shallice term *contention scheduling*. Contention scheduling is required when different cognitive systems propose competing responses (whether cognitive or behavioral) to a single set of stimuli. Contention scheduling effectively resolves the competition to select a single response, which can either be an output to the action systems or can be fed back into the cognitive systems. The terminology of global workspace was introduced by Bernard Baars in the late 1980s. One version of his theory is depicted in the figure, showing very clearly how the global workspace is envisioned as a conscious window between non-conscious inputs and conscious outputs.

A much more recent version of the theory is depicted on the right side of Figure 14.8. It was developed by Stanislas Dehaene, Michel Kerszberg, and Jean-Pierre Changeux. This shares some features with the other two versions, particularly the idea that the global workspace receives inputs from different cognitive modules and then sends outputs to motor systems. What is particularly interesting about the Dehaene, Kerszberg, and Changeux theory, however, is that it is strongly grounded in hypotheses about neural implementation and connectivity – which is why they call their theoretical construct the *global neuronal workspace*, rather than simply the global workspace. This emerges even more clearly in Figure 14.9.

Figure 14.9 makes plain the distributed nature of the global neuronal workspace, as envisaged by Dehaene and his collaborators. They see the modular part of the mind as composed of many interconnecting modules that feed into each other in a hierarchical manner. (The hierarchy is depicted by concentric circles, and the closer the circles to the center the higher their place in the hierarchy.) Some of the hierarchical modules form fully automatic and non-conscious networks. Others in contrast have amplified levels of activity that allow them to feed into the global workspace. The global neuronal workspace itself is not a single neural location (as the metaphor of a workspace might initially suggest), but rather a distributed network of high-level processors that are highly connected to other high-level processes. The candidate areas identified include the prefrontal, parieto-temporal, and cingulate cortices – all areas that we have discussed in the context of different types of high-level cognition at various points in this book. The lower portion of Figure 14.9 includes a neural network simulation of the global neuronal workspace and when it

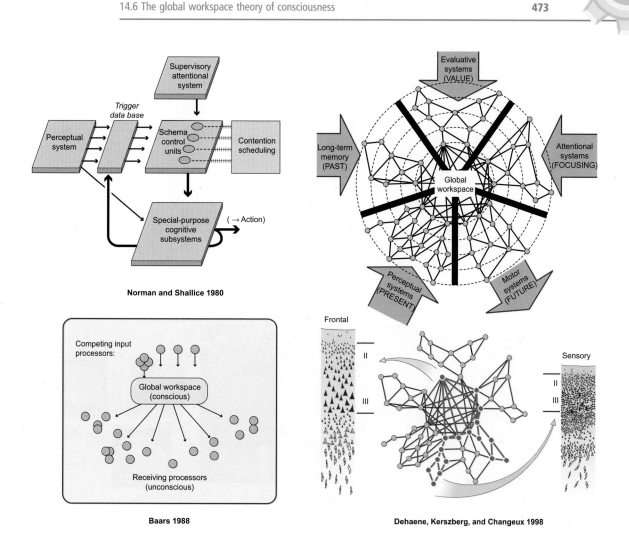

Figure 14.8 In the Norman and Shallice (1980) model (top left), conscious processing is involved in the supervisory attentional regulation, by prefrontal cortices, of lower-level sensori-motor chains. According to Baars (1989), conscious access occurs once information gains access to a global workspace (bottom left), which broadcasts it to many other processors. The global neuronal workspace (GNW) hypothesis (right) proposes that associative perceptual, motor, attention, memory, and value areas interconnect to form a higher-level unified space where information is broadly shared and broadcasted back to lower-level processors. The GNW is characterized by its massive connectivity, made possible by thick layers II/III with large pyramidal cells sending long-distance cortico-cortical axons, particularly dense in prefrontal cortex. (From Dehaene and Changeux 2011)

becomes engaged, in addition to an fMRI diagram indicating activation levels across the hypothesized network during high-level conscious tasks such as mental arithmetic.

The global neuronal workspace is thought to be generated by the activities of a particular type of neurons called pyramidal neurons. Pyramidal neurons are very wide-spread in the mammalian cortex and particularly dense in the prefrontal, cingulate, and parietal regions (all hypothesized to be important in the global neuronal workspace).

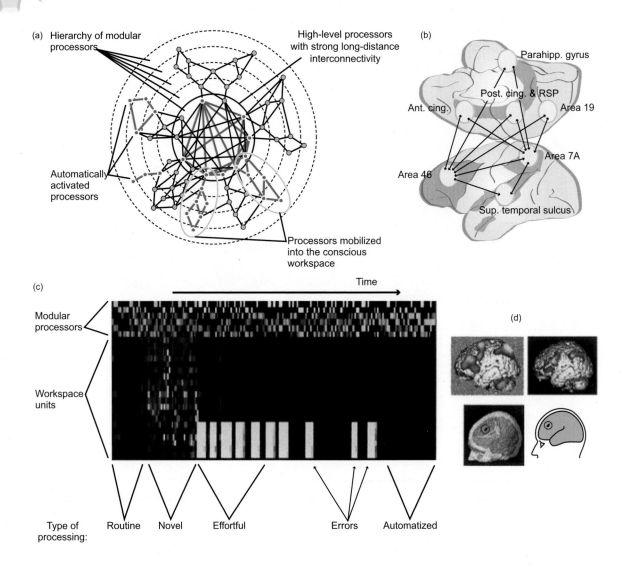

Figure 14.9 The neural substrates of the global workspace. (a) depicts the hierarchy of connections between different processors in the brain. Note the strong long-distance connections possessed by the higher levels. (b) depicts the proposed anatomical substrate of the global workspace. This includes a network linking the dorsolateral prefrontal, parietal, temporal, and anterior cingulate areas with other subcortical regions (RSP = retrosplenial region). (c) depicts the neural dynamics of the global workspace, derived from a neural simulation of the model shown in (a). The activation levels of various processor units (top lines) and workspace units (bottom lines) are shown as a function of time. (d) depicts different parts of the global workspace network activated by different tasks, including generation of a novel sequence of random numbers, effortful arithmetic, and error processing. (From Dehaene and Naccache 2001)

They are characterized by a single long axon and heavily branched dendrites, which allow them to communicate with many other neurons and with distant brain areas. Dehaene and collaborators hypothesize that networks of pyramidal neurons connect specialized modular processes and allow their outputs to be broadcast across the brain so that they are available for action-planning, verbal report, and other high-level cognitive processes.

Exercise 14.10 Explain in your own words how the global neuronal workspace theory incorporates the hypotheses about the function of consciousness identified in section 14.4.

14.7 Conclusion

This chapter has explored two very different approaches to consciousness. On the one hand there are those who think that consciousness is a mystery that we have no idea how to tackle with the tools and methods of cognitive science. On the other hand we have thriving research programs that study different aspects of the conscious mind and how consciousness contributes to action and cognition.

The "mysterians," as they are sometimes called, hold that the various research programs we have looked at only touch upon the "easy" aspects of the problem of consciousness – at best they can only explain access consciousness, as opposed to the really tough problem of explaining how and why we are phenomenally conscious. The global neuronal workspace theory was primarily developed to explain how consciousness can make a difference to cognition. The theory gives an account of why some information becomes conscious and how that information has a distinctive role to play in higher-level cognition. Mysterians will say that this account is all well and good, but cannot come to grips with the "hard problem" of explaining the distinctive experience of being conscious.

In response, cognitive scientists working on consciousness may well respond that the so-called hard problem of consciousness will disappear once we have a good enough understanding of the various phenomena lumped together under the label "access consciousness." This is the view taken by the philosopher Daniel Dennett, whose books *Content and Consciousness* and *Consciousness Explained* have been very influential in discussions of consciousness. The arguments that we looked at from Block, Jackson, and others all traded on the single basic intuition that we can give a complete account of access consciousness (the functional aspect of consciousness) that leaves phenomenal consciousness (the experiential aspect of consciousness) unexplained. But why should we accept that intuition? Thought experiments such as the Knowledge Argument or the alleged possibility of super-blindsighters or zombies are hardly decisive. If you do not accept the intuition then you will most likely reject the Knowledge Argument and deny that zombies or super-blindsighters are possible. Perhaps the source of the problem is that we do not have any real idea of what a complete account of access consciousness would look like. As its originators would be the first to admit, the global neuronal workspace theory is programmatic in the extreme. So are its competitors. It may well be that if we were in possession of something much more like a complete theory our intuitions would be very different. What makes the intuitions seem compelling is that our knowledge is so incomplete and our investigations of the cognitive science of consciousness at such an early stage.

It may be helpful to look at the analogy with debates in the nineteenth and early twentieth century about vitalism in biology. Vitalists such as the philosopher Henri Bergson and the biologist John Scott Haldane believed that the mechanist tools of biology and chemistry were in principle incapable of explaining the difference between living organisms and the rest of the natural world. Instead, we need to posit a vital force, or *élan vital*, that explains the distinctive organization, development, and behavior of living things. Certainly, vitalism has no scientific credibility today. The more that was discovered about the biology and chemistry of living things, the less work there was for an *élan vital*, until finally it became apparent that it was an unnecessary posit because there was no problem to which it might be a solution. But historians of science argue that debates about vitalism served an important role in the development of biology, by forcing biologists to confront some of the explanatory deficiencies of the models they were working with – both by developing new models and by developing new experimental tools. Perhaps mysterianism about the cognitive science of consciousness will have a similar role to play?

Certainly, that would be consistent with how cognitive science has evolved up to now. Many of the advances that we have explored have emerged in response to challenges that on the face of things are no less dramatic than the challenges posed by those who think that consciousness is scientifically inexplicable – the challenge to show how a machine can solve problems, for example; to show how neural networks can learn; or to show how systems can engage in sophisticated emergent behaviors without explicit information processing.

In any event, consciousness is one of the most active and exciting topics in contemporary cognitive science. Whether it will ultimately reveal the limits of cognitive scientific explanation or not, it continues to generate an enormous range of innovative experiments and creative theorizing.

Summary

This chapter reviewed basic challenges to the study of consciousness and introduced some promising theories of consciousness within cognitive science. We started by looking at the basic challenge for cognitive science raised by first- and third-person approaches to consciousness. We also saw how this challenge is present in Leibniz's Mill, Jackson's Knowledge Argument, Block's A- and P-consciousness, and Chalmers's distinction between the easy problems and hard problem of consciousness. Despite this challenge, consciousness research has made numerous interesting discoveries about the way our minds work. Priming studies and cases of neurological damage indicate that a great deal of information processing occurs below the threshold of consciousness. Milner and Goodale's research on the two visual streams, as well as other related studies, indicate that consciousness is important for planning and initiating actions. We concluded by looking at the global workspace theory of consciousness, which tied together a number of themes in this chapter and throughout the book. The global workspace theory shows how unconscious information reaches consciousness as well as how modular information is transmitted throughout the brain for use in high-level cognition.

Checklist

The challenge of consciousness

(1) We can take either a first-person or a third-person approach to consciousness.
(2) Leibniz's Mill and Jackson's Knowledge Argument illustrate the challenges to third-person approaches to consciousness.
(3) The contrast between the first- and third-person approaches points to the potential inadequacy of cognitive science for studying consciousness.

Information processing without conscious awareness

(1) There are two primary ways of understanding unconscious information processing: priming experiments and studies of patients with neurological damage.
(2) Semantic priming studies show that basic categorization can be accomplished unconsciously. Since semantic categorization is generally thought to be non-modular, these tasks also suggest that there can be non-modular unconscious processing.
(3) Blindsight and unilateral neglect indicate that high-level processing can be applied even to areas of the visual field that, due to damage, are not consciously perceived.

The function of consciousness

(1) Milner and Goodale's research reveals a basic functional distinction in the visual system: vision for perception and vision for action. The ventral visual stream is for perception and is conscious, while the dorsal visual stream is for action and is unconscious.
(2) Experiments on the Ebbinghaus illusion and interocular suppression provide support for Milner and Goodale's dual stream hypothesis.
(3) Milner and Goodale's research indicates that consciousness is functionally important for planning and initiating action.
(4) Priming studies show that consciously perceived primes are retained better and have greater impact on other cognitive processes.

The hard problem of consciousness

(1) Ned Block's distinction between access consciousness (or A-consciousness) and phenomenal consciousness (or P-consciousness) can be used to generate a dilemma for the cognitive science of consciousness: cognitive science seems to be informative only for understanding A-consciousness.
(2) Block claims that there is a double dissociation between A- and P-consciousness. This produces an explanatory gap.
(3) The Sperling task seems to indicate that what we experience phenomenally outstrips what we are able to report.
(4) The conflict between A- and P-consciousness can be understood in terms of what David Chalmers calls the hard problem of consciousness.
(5) The super-blindsight and zombie twin examples have been taken to show that it is logically possible to have A-consciousness but not P-consciousness. This further suggests that the traditional tools of cognitive science might only help us understand A-consciousness but not P-consciousness.

The global workspace theory of consciousness

(1)   The global workspace theory holds that attention makes low-level modular information available for conscious control in the "global workspace", from where the information is then "broadcast" to other areas of the brain.

(2)   The global workspace theory draws from two basic ideas: (a) consciousness permits information to be explicitly and durably maintained for additional processing and reasoning, and (b) consciousness is necessary for initiating deliberate action.

(3)   Information processing in the global workspace is a type of domain-general process, selecting among competing modular inputs.

(4)   There is some neurological support for the global workspace theory. Pyramidal neurons, for instance, may be responsible for connecting specialized modular processes and broadcasting their outputs throughout the brain for other cognitive processes.

Further reading

There has been an explosion of research on consciousness in the last decade or so, only a small portion of which can be covered in a single chapter. Good places to start to learn more are recent books by Jesse Prinz 2012 and Timothy Bayne 2012. Though written by philosophers, both books place heavy emphasis on empirical research, and synthesize a wide swath of recent studies of consciousness. Robert Van Gulick's chapter in Margolis, Samuels, and Stich 2012 also provides a good summary of both philosophical and neuroscientific theories of consciousness. Zelazo, Moscovitch, and Thompson 2007 is another excellent resource. Baars and Gage 2010 discusses a lot of the most recent research, including figures and descriptions of the most popular methods used to study consciousness.

Interpreting Leibniz's Mill argument has been the source of great debate among Leibniz scholars. Recent discussions can be found in Blank 2010 and Duncan 2011. Frank Jackson's Knowledge Argument was first presented in Jackson 1982. His more recent views can be found in Jackson 2003. A series of essays on the Mary thought experiment can be found in Ludlow, Nagasawa, and Stoljar 2004.

Prominent accounts of how unconscious information processing operates and how information becomes conscious include Dehaene, Changeux, Naccache, Sackur, and Sergent 2006, and Kouider, Dehaene, Jobert, and Le Bihan 2007. There are many excellent reviews of research on priming. Kouider and Dehaene 2007 is a good survey of the history of masked priming. On primes becoming more visible when followed by congruent primes see Bernstein, Bissonnette, Vyas, and Barclay 1989. Good resources on bilingual semantic priming are Kiran and Lebel 2007, Kotz 2001, and Schoonbaert, Duyck, Brysbaert, and Hartsuiker, 2009. Classic studies of unilateral neglect include Driver and Mattingly 1998, Driver and Vuilleumier 2001, and Peru, Moro, Avesani, and Aglioti 1996. A recent meta-analysis of the critical lesion locations involved in unilateral neglect can be found in Molenberghs, Sale, and Mattingley 2012. On the function of the parietal cortex in visual perception see Husain and Nachev 2007.

A summary of the two visual streams can be found in Milner and Goodale 2008. A recent critique of the two-stream account (with commentary from Milner, Goodale, and others) can be found in Schenk and McIntosh 2010. See Milner 2012 for a recent study on the two visual streams and consciousness. Goodale and Milner 2013 also provides a good review of the visual system. There are many studies on the Ebbinghaus illusion and the differences between vision for action and vision for perception. Aglioti, DeSouza, and Goodale 1995 is a classic study. For responses and follow-up studies see Glover and Dixon 2001, and Franz, Gegenfurtner, Bülthoff, and Fahle 2000.

The literature on access consciousness and phenomenal consciousness is quite large now. Block 1995b is the classic article on the topic. Block's more recent views can be found in Block 2007, where he proposes different neural structures underlying A- and P-consciousness, and Block 2011, where he responds to a number of criticisms of his account. The original Sperling experiment can be found in Sperling 1960. A criticism of Block's interpretation of the Sperling experiment, as well as discussion of phenomenal consciousness more generally, can be found in Kouider, de Gardelle, Sackur, and Dupoux 2010. For more on the putative explanatory gap between A- and P-consciousness see Levine 1983. Other well-known books on these topics include Carruthers 2000 and Dennett 1991. For classic formulations of the hard problem and easy problems of consciousness, see Chalmers 1995 and 1996.

For early formulations of the global workspace theory of consciousness, see Baars 1988 and 2002. Perhaps the most influential discussion of the theory is Dehaene and Naccache 2001. The most up-to-date summary of the theory can be found in Dehaene and Changeux 2011, including responses to critics.

Two popular topics in consciousness research that have been mentioned only briefly, but have their own burgeoning literatures, are attention, which was discussed in Chapter 11, and the neural correlates of consciousness. Posner 1980 is a classic early study on attention and consciousness. It was the first to convincingly demonstrate that gaze can be fixed while attention wanders. Lamme 2003 provides a concise summary of the reasons for separating attention from consciousness. Lavie 2005 is an influential account of how unattended stimuli are processed. Mack and Rock 1998 discusses a series of now-classic experiments on what is called "inattentional blindness." Simons and Chabris 1999 is another classic series of studies in this area. These experiments rely on selective looking, where people's selective attention alters what they see in a visual array. See Simons and Rensink 2005 for a review of these studies. Other reviews of how attention relates to consciousness can be found in Koch and Tsuchiya 2007, Martens and Wyble 2010, and Van den Bussche, Hughes, Humbeeck, and Reynvoet 2010.

Many trace the most recent wave of research into the neural correlates of consciousness (NCC) to Baars 1988 and Koch 2004. The global workspace theory is one prominent account of the NCC. An influential idea utilized by global workspace theorists is that of neural synchrony. This idea, popularized by Singer 1999, holds that groups of neurons must fire in sync in order to produce consciousness. Womelsdorf *et al*. 2007 is a more recent paper on this phenomenon. Crick and Koch 2003 is a widely cited review of different problems with the search for NCC, including arguments against the importance of neural synchrony for consciousness. An increasingly popular tool for identifying the NCC is to track brain activation in patients during and after being in a vegetative state. Steven Laureys's studies are some of the best-known. Laurey 2005 is an influential article describing the various brain areas that appear to be deactivated as a result of being in a vegetative state. Owen *et al*. 2006 and Hohwy 2009 are other important articles. Good reviews on the search for the NCC include Lamme 2006, Metzinger 2000, and Tononi and Koch 2008.

CHAPTER FIFTEEN

Looking ahead:
Challenges and applications

Cognitive science has already given us many important insights into the human mind. We have explored a good number of these in this book. As I have tried to bring out, these insights all stem from the single basic idea governing cognitive science as the interdisciplinary science of the mind. This is the idea that mental operations are information-processing operations.

This book began by looking at how this way of thinking about the mind first emerged out of developments in seemingly disparate subjects, such as mathematical logic, linguistics, psychology, and information theory. Most of the significant early developments in cognitive science explored the parallel between information processing in the mind and information processing in a digital computer. As cognitive scientists and cognitive neuroscientists developed more sophisticated tools for studying and modeling the brain, the information-processing principle was extended in new directions and applied in new ways.

Later chapters explored in detail the two computing approaches to information processing that have dominated the development of cognitive science. According to the physical symbol system hypothesis, we need to think about information processing in terms of the rule-governed transformation of physical structures. These physical structures are information-carrying representations.

Neural network modelers think of information processing somewhat differently. Information in neural networks does not have to be carried by discrete and independent structures. It can be distributed across patterns of weights and connectivity in a neural network. And information processing seems to work differently. The algorithms that update neural networks and allow them to learn are very different from the rules invoked by the physical symbol system hypothesis.

These two ways of thinking about information processing are neither exclusive nor exhaustive. There are ways of thinking about the overall architecture of the mind that combine both. The mind might turn out to have a hybrid architecture. It may be, for example, that certain information-processing tasks are carried out by manipulating physical symbol systems, while others are performed subsymbolically, by mechanisms that look much more like artificial neural networks. The sample applications that we looked at in Part III for the two approaches certainly seemed to suggest that they might each be best suited for rather different types of information-processing tasks.

As emerged in Chapter 13, recent developments in embodied and situated cognition, together with the mathematical tools provided by dynamical systems theory, have expanded the cognitive scientist's toolkit. These exciting research programs offer new ways of thinking about information processing – as well as new ways of thinking about how information-processing systems interact with their environments.

The interdisciplinary enterprise of cognitive science is now in excellent health. There are more contributing disciplines than ever before. Cognitive scientists have an ever-expanding range of theoretical models to work with. And there is a constant stream of technological advances in the machinery that cognitive scientists can use to study the brain. It is hard not to have a sense of optimism – a sense that cognitive science is getting close to a fundamental breakthrough in understanding cognition and the mind.

It is true that all these new developments make the integration challenge even more pressing. The more tools that cognitive scientists have, and the more models that they can use to interpret their findings, the more important it becomes to find a theoretical framework that will integrate them. But we have spent enough time on the integration challenge in this book. What I want to do now is to look ahead at some of the challenges and opportunities facing cognitive science at this exciting time. What follows is a small and highly personal selection of these challenges and potential applications.

15.1 Exploring the connectivity of the brain: The connectome and the BRAIN initiative

The successful completion of the Human Genome Project was one of the most significant scientific events of the last few decades. For the first time scientists succeeded in identifying and mapping the 20,000 to 25,000 genes in the human gene pool, giving unprecedented insights into human genetic make-up. The Human Genome Project was so successful that it focused the minds of funding agencies on huge, collaborative projects. In July 2009 the National Institutes of Health (NIH) announced what is in effect a cognitive science equivalent of the Human Genome Project – the *Human Connectome Project*. According to the funding opportunity announcement, "The overall purpose of this five year Human Connectome Project (HCP) is to develop and share knowledge about the structural and functional connectivity of the human brain." This collaborative and multi-site effort will directly tackle some of the theoretical issues that we have highlighted at various points in this book – such as the relation between different types of brain connectivity, and the importance of calibrating different tools for studying the brain. The NIH are confident that this $30 million initiative will generate fundamental insights into the wiring and functional make-up of the human brain. And it is likely that it will take cognitive scientists many more than five years to assimilate the data that emerge.

A new impetus for understanding brain connectivity came with the announcement by President Barack Obama in April 2013 of the BRAIN initiative. The acronym stands for Brain Research through Advanced Neurotechnologies. President Obama, explicitly comparing the initiative to the Human Genome Project, called for "the invention of new technologies that will help researchers produce real-time pictures of complex neural circuits and visualize the rapid-fire interactions of cells that occur at the speed of thought." The BRAIN initiative is spearheaded by the National Institutes for Health, the National Science Foundation, and DARPA (the Defense Advanced Research Projects Agency), in partnership with the Allen Institute for Brain Science, the Howard Hughes Medical Institute, the Kavli Foundation, and the Salk Institute for Biological Studies.

15.2 Understanding what the brain is doing when it appears not to be doing anything

Neuroimaging and electrophysiological experiments typically explore what happens in the brain when certain very specific tasks are being carried out. So, for example, neuro-imaging experiments typically identify the different brain areas where the BOLD contrast is highest during a given task. This is the basis for inferences about localization of function in the brain. But, some researchers have argued, task-specific activation is simply the tip of the iceberg. Marcus Raichle and colleagues at Washington University in St. Louis have argued that we shouldn't just pay attention to departures from the baseline set by the brain's default mode of operation. There is a huge amount of activity going on in the brain even when subjects are resting with their eyes closed, or passively looking at a fixed stimulus. This default mode of brain function has not yet been systematically studied by neuroscientists, but may be quite fundamental to understanding cognition. Concentrating solely on task-dependent changes in the BOLD signal may turn out to be like trying to understand how tides work by looking at the shape of waves breaking on the shore.

What is now often called the *default mode network* (DMN) can be studied in pure resting state experiments, where subjects are imaged while not performing any directed task. The brain areas most frequently identified in such experiments include the medial posterior cortex, particularly the posterior cingulate cortex and the precuneus, and the medial frontal cortex, in addition to areas around the temporoparietal junction area (TPJ). One very interesting possibility that is starting to be explored is that cognitive disorders and diseases may be correlated with impaired functioning of the DMN. A longitudinal study of patients suffering from Alzheimer's disease recently published (August 2013) in *JAMA Neurology* by neuroscientists at Washington University in St. Louis observed significant correlations between deteriorating connectivity of the DMN over time and two well-known markers of early Alzheimer's - rising levels of amyloid beta (the key component of brain plaques in Alzheimer's) and falling levels of tau protein.

Schizophrenia and autism are other disorders where impaired functioning of the DMN may be important.

15.3 Building artificial brain systems?

Suppose that, as many cognitive scientists think, important cognitive functions are carried out by functionally specialized systems that are themselves implemented in specific neural locations. Wouldn't it then be possible to build mechanical devices that could replace a damaged system in the brain, reversing the effects of disease or injury? Cognitive science certainly predicts that this type of *neuroprosthesis* ought to be possible. If cognitive systems are computational devices, whose job is basically transforming a certain type of input into a certain type of output, then the crucial thing is to work out how the input and output are represented in the brain, and what the basic transformations are. If this can be done, then the only obstacles to building neuroprostheses are technological.

In fact, some types of neuroprostheses are already widely used. Cochlear implants can restore hearing to individuals with hearing problems – even to the profoundly deaf. They work by providing direct electrical stimulation to the auditory nerve (doing the job that would otherwise be done by hair cells in the cochlea, which is in the inner ear). Neuroscientists, working together with biomechanical engineers, have produced motor prostheses that restore some movement to paralyzed patients. And scientists at the University of Southern California are working to develop an implant that will restore normal functioning when the hippocampus is damaged (the hippocampus plays an important role in forming and storing memories). The aim is to develop a device that will measure electrical inputs to the hippocampus; calculate what outputs would typically be generated in normal subjects; and then stimulate areas of the hippocampus to mimic a normally functioning brain. As of August 2013 an early prototype hippocampal prosthetic has been tested in rats and in macaque monkeys.

15.4 Enhancing education

Education is another area where cognitive science continues to have significant applications. Cognitive scientists continue to study how learning takes place and how knowledge is stored, organized, and recalled. The better these complex processes are understood the easier it will be to propose and evaluate specific tools for communicating knowledge effectively. This is one of the reasons why educational psychology is such a well-developed field. There are further promising possibilities more specific to cognitive science, however. One example would be learning technologies that are derived from specific models of cognitive architecture.

We looked at a recent version of the ACT-R (Adaptive Control of Thought – Rational) cognitive architecture in Chapter 10. This architecture is the basis for a series of cognitive tutors that exploit the assumptions about human cognition built into the ACT-R architecture in order to work out the specific problems that students are likely to have in, for example, learning mathematics and then to suggest learning strategies for overcoming those difficulties. The basic principle of ACT-R is that successful learning depends upon combining declarative knowledge (of facts) with procedural knowledge (of skills). Cognitive tutors, such as Carnegie Learning's Cognitive Tutor, are based on computer simulations of problem-solving in areas such as algebra and geometry, using those simulations to monitor and enhance student learning. Interactive mathematics software developed by ACT-R researchers at Carnegie Mellon University, together with experienced mathematics teachers, is currently being used in over 2,600 schools in the United States.

15.5 Building bridges to economics and the law

The intensely interdisciplinary nature of cognitive science has been a recurring theme in this book. We have looked at how cognitive science has been molded by contributions from psychology, philosophy, neuroscience, linguistics, computer science, and mathematics – to give just a partial list. But the list of disciplines to which cognitive science is potentially relevant is even longer. Two areas where the dialog with cognitive science is gaining momentum are economics and the law.

The interface between cognitive science, neuroscience, and economics has got its own name – neuroeconomics. Economists have always been interested in descriptive questions of how people actually make economic decisions, and one strand of neuroeconomics applies techniques such as neuroimaging to explore phenomena such as discounting over time, as well as to try to work out what is going on when people make decisions that seem to contravene the principles of economic rationality. Another strand in neuroeconomics works in the opposite direction – using the tools of economic theory to try to understand types of behavior that seem on the face of it to have nothing to do with economic behavior. Researchers have discovered, for example, that neurons in the parietal cortex seem to be sensitive to probabilities and utilities – the basic quantities in economic models of rational decision-making.

There are many points of contact between cognitive science and the law. Eyewitness testimony is a good example. It is a fundamental pillar of almost every legal system, and yet there is strong evidence that eyewitness testimony is both unreliable and manipulable. Memory and perceptual processes have been intensely studied by cognitive scientists. The challenge is to put these studies to practical use to develop procedures that will minimize errors and unsafe convictions – procedures, for example, for evaluating testimony in court and for identifying subjects in line-ups. Likewise there is enormous scope for using models of decision-making from cognitive science to study how jurors and judges reach decisions.

These are just some of the exciting challenges and opportunities opening up for cognitive scientists in the years ahead. I hope that readers of this book will pursue these – and develop others.

GLOSSARY

abduction (abductive reasoning): a form of reasoning in which one derives a conclusion as the best explanation of given evidence, even though it is not entailed by the evidence that it explains.

absolute judgment: a judgment about the intrinsic properties of a stimulus (e.g. naming a color or identifying the pitch of a particular tone), as opposed to a relative judgment comparing two stimuli.

access consciousness (or A-consciousness): information available or "poised" for conscious thought and action.

action potentials: electrical impulses fired by neurons down their axons to other neurons.

activation function: a function that assigns an output signal to a neural network unit on the basis of the total input to that unit.

algorithm: a finite set of unambiguous rules that can be systematically applied to an object or set of objects to transform it or them in definite ways in a finite amount of time.

anatomical connectivity: the anatomical connections between different brain regions.

anterograde amnesia: the loss of memory of events after the onset of a brain injury.

artificial neural network (connectionist network): an abstract mathematical tool for modeling cognitive processes that uses **parallel processing** between intrinsically similar units (artificial neurons) organized in a single- or multilayer form.

attractor: a region in the state space of **dynamical systems** on which many different trajectories converge.

backpropagation algorithm: a learning algorithm in multilayer neural networks in which error is spread backwards through the network from the output units to the hidden units, allowing the network to modify the weights of the units in the hidden layers.

behavior-based robotics: movement in robot design that moves beyond purely reactive **subsumption architectures** by allowing robots to represent their environment and to plan ahead.

behaviorism: the school of psychology holding that psychologists should only study observable phenomena and measurable behavior. Behaviorists maintain that all learning is the result of either **classical/Pavlovian** or **operant conditioning**.

binding problem: the problem of explaining how information processed in separate neural areas of the information-processing pathway is combined to form **representations** of objects.

biorobotics: the enterprise of designing and building models of biological organisms that reflect the basic design principles of those organisms.

bit: a measure of the information necessary to decide between two equally likely alternatives. For decisions between n alternatives, the number of bits $= \log_2 n$.

blindsight: a neurological disorder typically resulting from lesions in the primary visual cortex (V1, or the striate cortex). Like unilateral spatial neglect patients, blindsight patients report little to no awareness in one side of their visual field.

BOLD signal: the Blood Oxygen Level Dependent (BOLD) signal measures the contrast between oxygenated and deoxygenated hemoglobin in the brain, generally held to be an index of cognitive activity. The increase in blood oxygen can be detected by an fMRI scanner because oxygenated and deoxygenated hemoglobin have different magnetic properties.

Boolean function: a function that takes sets of truth values as input and produces a single truth value as output.

Brodmann areas: different regions of the cerebral cortex identified by the neurologist Korbinian Brodmann. The primary visual cortex, for example, is Brodmann area 17.

cerebral cortex: the parts of the brain, popularly called "grey matter," that evolved most recently.

channel capacity: the maximum amount of data that an **information channel** can reliably transmit.

chatterbot: a program set to respond to certain cues by making one of a small set of preprogrammed responses; these programs cannot use language to report on or navigate their environments because they do not analyze the syntactic structure or meaning of the sentences they encounter.

cheater detection module: hypothetical cognitive system specialized for identifying a "free rider" in a social exchange (i.e. a person who is reaping benefits without paying the associated costs).

Chinese room argument: John Searle's thought experiment that attempts to refute the **physical symbol system hypothesis** by showing that there can be syntactic symbol manipulation without any form of intelligence or understanding.

chunking: Miller's method of relabeling a sequence of information to increase the amount of data that the mind can reliably transmit. For example, relabeling sequences of digits with single numbers. i.e. 1100100 becomes "one-one hundred-one hundred."

Church–Turing thesis: the thesis that the algorithmically calculable functions are exactly the functions that can be computed by a **Turing machine**.

classical/Pavlovian conditioning: the process of creating an association between a reflex response and an initially neutral stimulus by pairing the neutral stimulus (e.g. a bell) with a stimulus (e.g. food) which naturally elicits the response (e.g. salivation).

competitive network: an example of an **artificial neural network** that works by unsupervised learning.

computation: purely mechanical procedure for manipulating information.

computational neuroscience: the use of abstract mathematical models to study how the collective activities of a population of neurons could solve complex information-processing tasks.

congruence priming: a priming task in which the basic category of a prime (e.g. a tool) enhances the salience of other stimuli matching that category (e.g. other tools).

connectionist network: see **artificial neural network**.

connectivity, anatomical: physiological connections between segregated and distinct cortical regions.

contralateral organization: occurs when each hemisphere of the brain processes input information from the opposite side of space (e.g. when an auditory stimulus presented to the right ear is processed by the left hemisphere of the brain).

co-opted system: according to **simulation theory**, a system specialized for a specific cognitive task that is then used to perform related mindreading tasks.

corpus callosum: the large bundle of fibers connecting the two hemispheres of the brain.

counterfactual: a statement about what would have happened, had things been different.

covert attention: the possibility of directing attention at different peripheral areas while gaze is fixated on a central point.

cross-lesion disconnection experiments: experiments designed to trace connections between cortical areas in order to determine the pathways along which information flows. These experiments take advantage of the fact that the brain is divided into two hemispheres with the major cortical areas being the same on each side.

cross-talk: the process in which separate sub-systems collaborate in solving information-processing problems using each other's outputs as inputs.

decision trees: a branching representation of all possible paths through a problem space starting from an initial point.

deep structure: in Chomskyan linguistics the deep structure of a sentence is its "real" syntactic structure, which serves as the basis for fixing its meaning. Two sentences with different **surface structures** can have the same deep structure (e.g. "John kissed Mary" and "Mary was kissed by John").

dichotic listening experiments: experiments in which subjects are presented with information in each ear in order to investigate selective attention in the auditory system.

dishabituation paradigm: a method for studying infant cognition that exploits the fact that infants look longer at events that they find surprising.

distributed representation: occurs when (as in many connectionist networks) objects or properties are represented through patterns of activation across populations of neurons – rather than through individual and discrete symbols.

domain-specific: term used to characterize cognitive mechanisms (modules) that carry out a very specific information-processing task with a fixed field of application.

dorsal pathway: the neural pathway believed to be specialized for visual information relevant to locating objects in space. This pathway runs from the **primary visual cortex** to the posterior parietal lobe.

double dissociation: experimental discovery that each of two cognitive functions can be performed independently of the other.

dynamical systems hypothesis: radical proposal to replace information-processing models in cognitive science with models based on the mathematical tools of dynamical systems theory.

dynamical systems theory: branch of applied mathematics using difference or differential equations to describe the evolution of physical systems over time.

early selection model: a cognitive model of attention in which attention operates as a filter early in the perceptual process and acts on low-level physical properties of the stimulus.

EEG (electroencephalography): experimental technique for studying the electrical activity of the brain.

effective connectivity: the causal flow of information between different brain regions.

entropy: a measure of how well a particular attribute classifies a set of examples. The closer the entropy is to 0, the better the attribute classifies the set.

event-related potentials (ERPs)/event-related magnetic fields: cortical signals that reflect neural network activity that can be recorded non-invasively using **EEG** or **MEG**.

expert systems research: a field of artificial intelligence that aims to reproduce the performance of human experts in a particular domain.

false belief task: an experimental paradigm first developed by psychologists Heinz Wimmer and Joseph Perner, exploring whether young children understand that someone might have mistaken beliefs about the world.

feedforward network: a connectionist network in which activation spreads forward through the network; there is no spread of activation between units in a given layer, or backwards from one layer to the previous layer.

fixed neural architectures: the identification of determinate regions of the brain associated with particular types of modular processing.

fMRI (functional magnetic resonance imaging): technology for functional neuroimaging that measures levels of blood oxygen as an index of cognitive activity.

folk physics: an intuitive understanding of some of the basic principles governing how physical objects behave and interact.

formal property: a physical property of a representation that is not semantic (e.g. a formal property of the word "apple" is that it is composed of six letters of the English alphabet).

frame problem: the problem of developing expert systems in AI and building robots that can build into a system rules that will correctly identify what information and which inferences are relevant in a given situation.

functional connectivity: the statistical dependencies and correlations between activation in different brain areas.

functional decomposition: the process of explaining a cognitive capacity by breaking it down into sub-capacities that can be analyzed separately. Each of these sub-capacities can in turn be broken down into further nested sub-capacities, until the process bottoms out in non-cognitive components.

functional neuroimaging: a tool that allows brain activity to be studied non-invasively while subjects are actually performing experimental tasks (e.g. **PET, fMRI**).

functional system: a system that can be studied and understood primarily in terms of the role it plays and the task that it executes, irrespective of the mechanism of implementation. These systems are studied only at the computational level and are multiply realizable. (See **multiple realizability**.)

global workspace theory of consciousness: a leading theory of how mental states become conscious. According to this theory, attention makes low-level modular information available to conscious control (the "global workspace") where the information is then "broadcast" to other areas of the brain.

GOFAI: good old-fashioned Artificial Intelligence – as contrasted, for example, with **artificial neural networks**.

graceful degradation: the incremental deterioration of cognitive abilities that is imperceptible within small time frames.

halting problem: the problem first raised by David Hilbert of algorithmically determining whether or not a computer program will halt (i.e. deliver an output) for a given input.

hard problem of consciousness: the problem of explaining phenomenal consciousness by appealing to physical processes in the brain and using the traditional tools of cognitive science.

Hebbian learning: Donald Hebb's model of associative process according to which "neurons that fire together, wire together."

heuristic search hypothesis: Newell and Simon's hypothesis that problems are solved by generating and algorithmically transforming symbol structures until a suitable solution structure is reached.

hidden layer: a layer of **hidden units** in an **artificial neural network**.

hidden unit: a unit (artificial neuron) in an **artificial neural network** whose inputs come from other units and whose outputs go to other units.

information channel: a medium that transmits information from a sender to a receiver (e.g. a telephone cable or a neuron).

informational encapsulation: property of modular systems that operate with a proprietary database of information and are insulated from background knowledge and expectations.

integration, principle of: fundamental idea of neuroscience stating that cognitive function involves the coordinated activity of networks of different brain areas, with different types of tasks recruiting different types of brain areas.

integration challenge: the ultimate goal for cognitive science of providing a unified account of cognition that draws upon and integrates the many different disciplines and techniques used to study cognition.

intentional realism: the thesis that propositional attitudes (e.g. beliefs and desires) can cause behavior.

intentionality: property in virtue of which symbols represent objects and properties in the world.

interocular suppression: a technique used to study consciousness, in which one eye is presented with an image of an object while the other eye is presented simultaneously with a high-contrast pattern that blocks conscious awareness of the presented image.

joint visual attention: occurs when infants look at objects, and take pleasure in doing so, because they see that another person is both looking at that object and noticing that the infant is also looking at the object.

Knowledge Argument: a thought experiment proposed by Frank Jackson and featuring a neuroscientist called Mary who is confined to a black-and-white room and has never experienced colors. Mary knows all the physical facts there are to be known, and yet, according to Jackson, there is a fact that she discovers when she leaves the room – the fact about what it is like for someone to see red.

language of thought hypothesis: a model of information processing developed by Jerry Fodor, which holds that the basic symbol structures that carry information are sentences in an internal language of thought (sometimes called Mentalese) and that information processing works by transforming those sentences in the language of thought.

late selection model: a cognitive model of attention in which attention operates as a filter on representations of objects after basic perceptual processing is complete.

Leibniz's Mill: a thought experiment used by Gottfried Wilhelm Leibniz to draw a contrast between understanding the physical parts of the mind and understanding the distinctive nature of conscious perceptions.

lexical access: the processing involved in understanding single words.

linear separability: characteristic of **Boolean functions** that can be learnt by neural networks using the **perceptron convergence learning rule**.

local algorithm: a learning algorithm in a connectionist network in which an individual unit weight changes directly as a function of the inputs to and outputs from that unit (e.g. the **Hebbian learning rule**).

local field potential (LFP): the local field potential is an electrophysiological signal believed to be correlated with the sum of inputs to neurons in a particular area.

locus of selection problem: the problem of determining whether attention is an **early selection** phenomenon or a **late selection** phenomenon.

logical consequence: a conclusion is the logical consequence of a set of premises just if there is no way of interpreting the premises and conclusion that makes the premises all true and the conclusion false.

logical deducibility: one formula is logically deducible from another just if there is a sequence of legitimate formal steps that lead from the second to the first.

machine learning: the production of an algorithm that will organize a complex database in terms of some target attribute by transforming symbol structures until a solution structure, or decision tree that will clarify incoming data, is reached.

machine learning algorithm: an algorithm for constructing a **decision tree** from a vast database of information.

mandatory application: a feature of modular processes where cognitive modules respond automatically to stimuli of the appropriate kind. They are not under any level of executive control.

masked priming: a priming task in which a stimulus is made invisible through presenting a second stimulus (the mask) in rapid succession.

massive modularity hypothesis: holds that all information processing is carried out by specialized modules that emerged in response to specific evolutionary problems (e.g. **cheater detection module**).

MEG (magnetoencephalography): brain imaging technique that measures electrical activity in the brain with magnetic fields.

mental architecture: a model of the mind as an information processor that answers the following three questions: In what format is information carried in a cognitive system? How is information in the cognitive system transformed? How is the mind organized to function as an information processor?

metarepresentation: metarepresentation occurs when a **representation** is used to represent another representation, rather than to represent the world (e.g. a representation of another person's mental state).

micro-world: an artificially restrictive domain used in AI in which all objects, properties, and events are defined in advance.

mirror neurons: neurons in monkeys that fire both when the monkey performs a specific action and when it observes that action being performed by an observer.

module: cognitive system dedicated to performing a domain-specific information-processing task. Typically held to be informationally encapsulated, but not necessarily to have a fixed neural architecture.

morphological computation: a research program in robotics for minimizing the amount of computational control required in a robot by building as much as possible of the computation directly into its physical structure.

multilayer network: an **artificial neural network** containing one or more **hidden layers.**

multiple realizability: a characteristic of functional systems whose tasks can be performed by a number of different physical manifestations. For example, a heart, when viewed as a functional system, is multiply realizable because human hearts and mechanical hearts can perform the same function.

neurotransmitters: neurochemicals that are transmitted across **synapses** in order to relay, amplify, and modulate signals between a neuron and another cell.

object permanence: the knowledge that an object exists even when it is not being perceived – an important milestone in children's development.

operant conditioning: a type of conditioning in which an action (e.g. pushing a lever) is reinforced by a reward (e.g. food).

over-regularization errors: systematic mistakes that children make during the process of language acquisition as they begin to internalize basic grammar rules. Children apply rules (such as adding the suffix "-s" to nouns to make them plural) to words that behave irregularly (e.g. saying "foots" instead of "feet").

paired-image subtraction paradigm: an experimental technique that allows neuroimagers to identify the brain activation relevant to a particular task by filtering out activation associated with other tasks.

parallel processing: simultaneous activation of units in an **artificial neural network** that causes a spread of activation through the layers of the network.

perceptron: a single-unit (or single-layer) **artificial neural network**.

perceptron convergence rule (delta rule): a learning algorithm for perceptrons (single-unit networks). It changes a perceptron's threshold and weights as a function of the difference between the unit's actual and intended output.

PET (positron emission tomography): a functional neuroimaging technique in which localization of cognitive activity is identified by measuring blood flow to specific areas of the brain.

phenomenal consciousness (or P-consciousness): the experiential or "what it's like" aspect of consciousness (e.g. the distinctive experience of smelling a rose or touching a piece of velvet cloth).

phrase structure grammar: describes the syntactic structure of a natural language sentence in terms of categories such as verb phrase and noun phrase. Permissible combinations of syntactic categories are given by phrase structure rules - e.g. the rule stating that every sentence must contain both a verb phrase and a noun phrase.

physical symbol system: a set of symbols (physical patterns) that can be combined to form complex symbol structures and contains processes for manipulating symbol structures. These processes can themselves be represented by symbols and symbol structures within the system.

physical symbol system hypothesis: Newell and Simon's hypothesis that a physical symbol system has the necessary and suffcient means for general intelligent action.

poverty of stimulus argument: maintains that certain types of knowledge must be innate, as they are too complicated to be learnt from the impoverished stimuli to which humans are exposed (e.g. Chomsky's argument for Universal Grammar).

pragmatics: the branch of linguistics concerned with the practical implication of language and what is actually communicated in a given context.

predicate calculus: formal system for exploring the logical relations between formulas built up from symbols representing individuals, properties, and logical operations. Unlike the **propositional calculus**, the predicate calculus includes quantifiers (ALL or SOME) that allow representations of generality.

prestriate cortex: an area in the occipital and parietal lobes which receives cortical output from the **primary visual cortex**.

primary visual cortex: the point of arrival in the cortex for information from the retina; also called the striate cortex and Brodmann area 17.

priming: an experimental technique, particularly useful in studying consciousness, where a stimulus (often not consciously perceived) influences performance on subsequent tasks.

principle of cohesion: principle of infant **folk physics**, according to which two surfaces are part of the same object if and only if they are in contact.

principle of contact: principle of infant **folk physics**, according to which only surfaces that are in contact can move together.

principle of continuity: principle of infant **folk physics**, according to which objects can only move on a single continuous path through space-time.

principle of solidity: one of the basic principles of infant **folk physics**, according to which there cannot be more than one object in a place at one time.

prisoner's dilemma: any social exchange interaction between two players where a player benefits most if she defects while her opponent co-operates and suffers most when she co-operates and her opponent defects. If each player is rational and works backwards from what her opponent might do, she will always reason that the best choice is to defect.

propositional attitude: a psychological state that can be analyzed into a proposition (e.g. the proposition that it is snowing in St. Louis) and an attitude to that proposition (e.g. the attitude of belief, or the attitude of hope).

propositional calculus: formal system for exploring the logical relations between formulas built up from symbols for complete propositions using logical operators (such as NOT, OR, and AND).

psychophysics: the branch of psychology that studies the relationship between physical stimuli and how subjects perceive and discriminate them.

recurrent network: an **artificial neural network** that has a feedback loop serving as a memory of what the **hidden layer** was doing at the previous time step.

recursive definition: process for defining a set of objects by starting with a set of base cases and specifying which transformations of objects preserve membership in the set. So, for example, a recursive definition of a **well-formed formula** in the **propositional calculus** starts with propositional symbols (the base cases) and indicates which logical operations (e.g. negation) create new formulas from existing formulas.

reduction: the process of showing how higher-level parts of science (e.g. thermodynamics) can be understood in terms of more basic parts of science (e.g. statistical mechanics).

representation: structure carrying information about the environment. Representations can be physical symbol structures, or distributed states of neural networks.

retrograde amnesia: the loss of memory of events before a brain injury.

robot reply (to the Chinese room argument): a response to John Searle's thought experiment that claims that the **Chinese room** is not intelligent because it is incapable of interacting with other Chinese speakers, rather than because of any gap between syntax and semantics.

saccadic eye movements: quick and unconscious eye movements scanning the visual field.

segregation, principle of: fundamental principle of neuroscience stating that the cerebral cortex is divided into separate areas with distinct neuronal populations.

selection processor: mechanism hypothesized by Leslie enabling people to inhibit the default setting of a true belief. It is not until the selection processor is fully in place that children can pass the **false belief task**, according to Leslie.

selective attention: the ability of individuals to orient themselves toward, or process information from, only one stimulus within the environment, to the exclusion of others.

semantic priming: a priming task in which the priming effect is due to information processing of the meaning of words, and not their phonology (how they are pronounced) or their orthography (how they are spelled).

semantic property: a property of a representation that holds in virtue of its content, i.e. how it represents the world (e.g. a semantic property of the word "apple" is the fact that it represents a crisp and juicy fruit).

simulation theory (radical): the theory that mindreading takes place when people think about the world from another person's perspective, rather than thinking about the other person's psychological states.

simulation theory (standard): the theory that people are able to reason about the mental states of others and their consequent potential behaviors by inputting "pretend" beliefs and desires into their own decision-making systems.

situated cognition: situated cognition theorists complain that traditional cognitive science has focused on disembodied systems that operate in highly simplified and prepackaged environments. They call instead for an approach to cognitive science that takes seriously the fact that cognitive agents are both embodied and situated within a complex environment.

spatial resolution: the degree of spatial detail provided by a particular technique for studying the brain.

state space: the state space of a system is a geometrical representation of all the possible states that the system can be in. It has as many dimensions as the system has independently varying quantities.

striate cortex: see **primary visual cortex.**

sub-cortex: the part of the brain, popularly called "white matter," that developed earlier in evolution than the cerebral cortex.

subsumption architecture: architectures in robotics that are built up incrementally from semi-autonomous layers. Subsumption architectures (originally proposed by Rodney Brooks) typically exploit direct links between perception and action.

surface structure: in Chomskyan linguistics, the surface structure of a sentence is given by the actual arrangement of written or spoken lexical items - as opposed to its **deep structure.**

symbol grounding problem: the problem of determining how syntactically manipulated symbols gain semantic meaning.

synapse: the site where the end of an axon branch comes close to a dendrite or the cell body of another neuron. This is where signals are transmitted from one neuron to another.

systems neuroscience: the investigation of the function of neural systems, such as the visual system or auditory system.

systems reply (to the Chinese room argument): a response to John Searle's thought experiment claiming that the Chinese room as a whole understands Chinese, even though the person inside the room does not.

temporal resolution: the degree of temporal detail provided by a particular technique for studying the brain.

theory of mind mechanism (TOMM): a hypothesized cognitive system specialized for attributing **propositional attitudes** and using those attributions to predict and explain behavior.

threshold: the minimum amount of activity necessary to initiate the firing of a unit in an **artificial neural network.**

TIT FOR TAT: a successful strategy used in social exchanges such as the **prisoner's dilemma** whereby a player co-operates with his/her opponent during the first round and in subsequent rounds copies the action taken by the opponent on the preceding round.

transformational grammar: a theoretical account of the rules governing how **surface structures** in natural languages are generated from **deep structures.**

truth condition: the state of affairs that makes a particular statement true.

truth rule: a rule that states the truth condition for a given statement.

Turing machine: a theoretical model of an abstract computation device that can (according to the **Church–Turing thesis**) compute any effectively calculable function.

unilateral spatial neglect: a neurological disorder typically due to damage to the posterior parietal cortex in one hemisphere in which patients describe themselves as unaware of stimuli in the contralateral half of their visual field.

ventral pathway: the neural pathway believed to be specialized for visual information relevant to recognizing and identifying objects. This pathway runs from the primary visual cortex to the temporal lobe.

Wason selection task: experiment developed to test people's understanding of conditional reasoning. Subjects are asked to identify the additional information they would need in order to tell if a given conditional statement is true or false.

well-formed formula: a string of symbols in a formal language that is legitimately constructed through the formation rules of that language.

BIBLIOGRAPHY

Abu-Akel, A., and Shamay-Tsoory, S. (2011). Neuroanatomical and neurochemical bases of theory of mind. *Neuropsychologia, 49*, 2971-84.

Adams, F., and Aizawa, A. (2010). *The Bounds of Cognition.* Oxford: Wiley-Blackwell.

Adolphs, R. (2009). The social brain: Neural basis of social knowledge. *Annual Review of Psychology, 60*, 693-716.

Adolphs, R., and Tranel, D. (2000). Emotion recognition and the human amygdala. In J. P. Aggleton (ed.), *The Amygdala: A Functional Analysis.* Oxford: Oxford University Press.

Adolphs, R., Tranel, D., Damasio, H., and Damasio, A. (1994). Impaired recognition of emotion in facial expressions following bilateral damage to the human amygdala. *Nature, 372*, 669-72.

Aglioti, S., DeSouza, J. F. X., and Goodale, M. A. (1995). Size-contrast illusions deceive the eye but not the hand. *Current Biology, 5*, 679-85.

Anderson, J. A. (2003). McCulloch-Pitts neurons. In L. Nadel (ed.), *Encyclopedia of Cognitive Science.* New York: Nature Publishing Group.

Anderson, J. R., Bothell, D., Byrne, M. D., Douglass, S., Lebiere, C., and Qin, Y. (2004). An integrated theory of the mind. *Psychological Review, 4*, 1036-1160.

Anderson, M. L., Richardson, M. J., and Chemero, A. (2012). Eroding the boundaries of cognition: Implications of Embodiment. *Topics in Cognitive Science, 4*, 717-30.

Apperly, I. A., Samson, D., Chiavarino, C., and Humphreys, G. W. (2004). Frontal and temporo-parietal lobe contributions to theory of mind: Neuropsychological evidence from a false-belief task with reduced language and executive demands. *Journal of Cognitive Neuroscience, 16*, 1773-84.

Apperly, I. A., Samson, D., and Humphreys, G. W. (2005). Domain-specificity and theory of mind: Evaluating neuropsychological evidence. *Trends in Cognitive Science, 9*, 572-7.

Arbib, M. A. (1987). *Brains, Machines, and Mathematics.* New York: Springer.

Arbib, M. A. (2003). *The Handbook of Brain Theory and Neural Networks.* Cambridge, MA; London: MIT Press.

Arkin, R. C. (1998). *Behavior-Based Robotics.* Cambridge, MA: MIT Press.

Ashby, F. G. (2011). *Statistical Analysis of fMRI Data.* Cambridge, MA: MIT Press.

Baars, B. J. (1988). *A Cognitive Theory of Consciousness.* Cambridge: Cambridge University Press.

Baars, B. J. (2002). The conscious access hypothesis: Origins and recent evidence. *Trends in Cognitive Science, 6*, 47-52.

Baars, B. J., and Gage, N. M. (eds.) (2010). *Cognition, Brain, and Consciousness: An Introduction to Cognitive Neuroscience* (2nd edn.). Burlington, MA: Elsevier.

Baars, B. J., and Gage, N. M. (2012). *Fundamentals of Cognitive Neuroscience: A Beginner's Guide.* Waltham, MA: Academic Press.

Baddeley, A. D. (2003). Working memory: Looking back and looking forward. *Nature Reviews Neuroscience, 4*, 829-39.

Baddeley, A. D. (2007). *Working Memory, Thought, and Action.* New York: Oxford University Press.

Baddeley, A. D., and Hitch, G. J. L. (1974). Working memory. In G. A. Bower (ed.), *The Psychology of Learning and Motivation: Advances and Research.* New York: Academic Press.

Baillargeon, R. (1986). Representing the existence and the location of hidden objects: Object permanence in 6- and 8-month-old infants. *Cognition, 23,* 21-41.

Baillargeon, R. (1987). Object permanence in 3- and 4-month-old infants. *Developmental Psychology, 23,* 655-64.

Baillargeon, R., and Carey, S. (2012). Core cognition and beyond: The acquisition of physical and numerical knowledge. In S. Pauen (ed.), *Early Childhood Development and Later Outcome.* Cambridge: Cambridge University Press.

Baillargeon, R., Li, J., Gertner, Y., and Wu, D. (2010). How do infants reason about physical events? In U. Goswami (ed.), *The Wiley-Blackwell Handbook of Childhood Cognitive Development* (2nd edn.). Oxford: Blackwell.

Baillargeon, R., Scott, R. M., and He, Z. (2010). False-belief understanding in infants. *Trends in Cognitive Science, 14,* 110-18.

Bandettini, P. A., and Ungerleider, L. G. (2001). From neuron to BOLD: New connections. *Nature Neuroscience, 4,* 864-6.

Baron-Cohen, S. (1995). *Mindblindness: An Essay on Autism and Theory of Mind.* Cambridge, MA: MIT Press.

Baron-Cohen, S. (2005). The empathizing system: A revision of the 1994 model of the mindreading system. In B. Ellis and D. Bjorklund (eds.), *Origins of the Social Mind.* New York: Guilford.

Baron-Cohen, S. (2009). The empathizing-systemizing (E-S) theory. *Annals of the New York Academy of Sciences, 1156,* 68-80.

Baron-Cohen, S., Leslie, A. M., and Frith, U. (1985). Does the autistic child have a "theory of mind"? *Cognition, 21,* 37-46.

Baron-Cohen, S., Tager-Flusberg, H., and Cohen, D. J. (eds.) (2000). *Understanding Other Minds: Perspectives from Developmental Cognitive Neuroscience.* New York: Oxford University Press.

Barrett, H. C., and Kurzban, R. (2006). Modularity in cognition: Framing the debate. *Psychological Review, 113,* 628-47.

Bassett, D. S., and Bullmore, E. (2006). Small-world brain networks. *Neuroscientist, 12,* 512-23.

Bayne, T. (2012). *The Unity of Consciousness.* New York: Oxford University Press.

Beate, S. (2011). Theory of mind in infancy. *Child Development Perspectives, 5,* 39-43.

Bechtel, W. (1999). Unity of science. In R. A. Wilson and F. Keil (eds.), *The MIT Encyclopedia Of Cognitive Science.* Cambridge, MA: MIT Press.

Bechtel, W., and Abrahamsen, A. A. (2002). *Connectionism and the Mind: Parallel Processing, Dynamics and Evolution in Networks.* Cambridge, MA: Blackwell.

Bechtel, W., Mandik, P., Mundale, J., and Stufflebeam, R. S. (eds.) (2001). *Philosophy and the Neurosciences: A Reader.* Malden, MA: Blackwell.

Bermúdez, J. L. (2005). *Philosophy of Psychology: A Contemporary Introduction.* New York: Routledge.

Bermúdez, J. L. (ed.) (2006). *Philosophy of Psychology: Contemporary Readings.* London: Routledge.

Bernstein, I. H., Bissonnette, V., Vyas, A., and Barclay, P. (1989). Semantic priming: Subliminal perception or context? *Perception and Psychophysics, 45,* 153-161.

Berti, A., and Rizzolatti, G. (1992). Visual processing without awareness: Evidence from unilateral neglect. *Journal of Cognitive Neuroscience, 4,* 345-51.

Bickle, J. (2006). Reducing mind to molecular pathways: Explicating the reductionism implicit in current cellular and molecular neuroscience. *Synthese, 151,* 411-434.

Bisiach, E., and Luzzatti, C. (1978). Unilateral neglect of representational space. *Cortex, 14,* 129-33.

Blank, A. (2010). On interpreting Leibniz's Mill. In P. K. Machamer and G. Wolters (eds.), *Interpretation: Ways of Thinking About the Sciences and the Arts*. Pittsburgh, PA: University of Pittsburgh Press.

Block, N. (ed.) (1981). *Imagery*. Cambridge, MA: MIT Press.

Block, N. (1995a). The mind as the software of the brain. In D. Osherson, L. Gleitman, S. M. Kosslyn, E. Smith, and R. J. Sternberg (eds.), *An Invitation to Cognitive Science*. Cambridge, MA: MIT Press.

Block, N. (1995b). On a confusion about the function of consciousness. *Behavioral and Brain Sciences*, **18**, 227-47.

Block, N. (2007). Consciousness, accessibility, and the mesh between psychology and neuroscience. *Behavioral and Brain Sciences*, **30**, 481-548.

Block, N. (2011). Perceptual consciousness overflows cognitive access. *Trends in Cognitive Science*, **15**, 567-75.

Block, N., Flanagan, O., and Güzeldere, G. (eds.) (1997). *The Nature of Consciousness: Philosophical Debates*. Cambridge, MA: MIT Press.

Bloom, P., and German, T. P. (2000). Two reasons to abandon the false belief task as a test of theory of mind. *Cognition*, **77**, B25-B31.

Boden, M. A. (1990a). Escaping from the Chinese room. In *The Philosophy of Artificial Intelligence*. Oxford: Oxford University Press.

Boden, M. A. (ed.). (1990b). *The Philosophy of Artificial Intelligence*. Oxford; New York: Oxford University Press.

Boden, M. A. (2006). *Mind as Machine: A History of Cognitive Science*. Oxford; New York: Oxford University Press.

Boucher, J. (1996). What could possibly cause autism? In P. Carruthers and P. K. Smith (eds.), *Theories of Theory of Mind*. Cambridge: Cambridge University Press.

Bowers, J. S. (2009). On the biological plausibility of grandmother cells: Implications for neural network theories in psychology and neuroscience. *Psychological Review*, **16**, 220-51.

Brachman, R. J., and Levesque, H. J. (eds.) (1985). *Readings in Knowledge Representation*. Los Altos, CA: M. Kaufmann.

Bremner, G. J. (1994). *Infancy*. Oxford: Wiley-Blackwell.

Bressler, S. L., Tang, W., Sylvester, C. M., Shulman, G. L., and Corbetta, M. (2008). Top-down control of human visual cortex by frontal and parietal cortex in anticipatory visual spatial attention. *Journal of Neuroscience*, **28**, 10056-61.

Broadbent, D. E. (1954). The role of auditory localization in attention and memory span. *Journal of Experimental Psychology*, **47**, 191-6.

Broadbent, D. E. (1958). *Perception and Communication*. London: Pergamon Press.

Brook, A. (2007). *The Prehistory of Cognitive Science*. Basingstoke; New York: Palgrave Macmillan.

Brooks, R. (1991). Intelligence without representation. *Artificial Intelligence*, **47**, 139-59. Reprinted in J. Haugeland (ed.) (1997), *Mind Design II: Philosophy, Psychology, Artificial Intelligence*. Cambridge, MA: MIT Press.

Brooks, R. (1999). *Cambrian Intelligence: The Early History of the New AI*. Cambridge, MA: MIT Press.

Bullmore, E., and Sporns, O. (2009). Complex brain networks: Graph theoretical analysis of structural and functional systems. *Nature Reviews Neuroscience*, **10**, 186-98.

Byrne, R. M. J., and Johnson-Laird, P. N. (2009). 'If' and the problems of conditional reasoning. *Trends in Cognitive Sciences*, **13**, 282-7.

Carey S. (2009). *The Origin of Concepts*. Oxford: Oxford University Press.

Carey, S., and Spelke, E. S. (1996). Science and core knowledge. *Philosophy of Science*, **63**, 515-33.

Carrasco, M. (2011). Visual attention: The past 25 years. *Vision Research*, **51**, 1484–1535.

Carrington, S. J., and Bailey, A. J. (2009). Are there theory of mind regions in the brain? A review of the neuroimaging literature. *Human Brain Mapping*, **30**, 2313–35.

Carruthers, P. (2000). *Phenomenal Consciousness*. Cambridge: Cambridge University Press.

Carruthers, P. (2006). *The Architecture of the Mind*. Cambridge: Cambridge University Press.

Carruthers, P. (2008a). On Fodor-fixation, flexibility, and human uniqueness: A reply to Cowie, Machery, and Wilson. *Mind and Language*, **23**, 293–303.

Carruthers, P. (2008b). Precis of *The Architecture of the Mind: Massive Modularity and the Flexibility of Thought*. *Mind and Language*, **23**, 257–62.

Carruthers, P. (2013). Mindreading in infancy. *Mind and Language*, **28**, 141–72.

Carruthers, P., and Smith, P. K. (eds.) (1996). *Theories of Theory of Mind*. Cambridge: Cambridge University Press.

Chalmers, D. (1995). Facing up to the problem of consciousness. *Journal of Consciousness Studies*, **2**, 200–19.

Chalmers, D. (1996). *The Conscious Mind*. Oxford: Oxford University Press.

Charpac, S., and Stefanovic, B. (2012). Shedding light on the BOLD fMRI response. *Nature Methods*, **9**, 547–9.

Chelazzi, L., and Corbetta, M. (2000). Cortical mechanisms of visuospatial attention in the primate brain. In M. S. Gazzaniga (ed.), *The New Cognitive Neurosciences* (2nd edn.). Cambridge, MA: MIT Press.

Chemero, A. (2009). *Radical Embodied Cognitive Science*. Cambridge, MA: MIT Press.

Cherry, E. C. (1953). Some experiments on the recognition of speech, with one and two ears. *Journal of the Acoustical Society of America*, **25**, 975–9.

Chomsky, N. (1957). *Syntactic Structures*. Gravenhage: Mouton.

Chomsky, N. (1959). A review of B. F. Skinner's *Verbal Behavior*. *Language*, **35**, 26–58.

Christiansen, M. H., and Chater, N. (2001). *Connectionist Psycholinguistics*. Westport, CT: Ablex.

Chun, M. M., Golomb, J. D., and Turk-Browne, N. B. (2011). A taxonomy of external and internal attention. *Annual Review of Psychology*, **62**, 73–101.

Churchland, P. M. (1990a). On the nature of theories: A neurocomputational perspective. In *A Neurocomputational Perspective: The Nature of Mind and the Structure of Science*. Cambridge, MA: MIT Press.

Churchland, P. M. (1990b). Cognitive activity in artificial neural networks. In N. Block and D. Osherson (eds.), *Invitation to Cognitive Science*. Cambridge, MA: MIT Press. Reprinted in R. Cummins and D. D. Cummins (2000), *Minds, Brains, and Computers: The Foundations of Cognitive Science: An Anthology*. Malden, MA: Blackwell.

Churchland, P. M. (2007). *Neurophilosophy at Work*. Cambridge: Cambridge University Press.

Churchland, P. S. (1986). *Neurophilosophy: Toward a Unified Science of the Mind/Brain*. Cambridge, MA: MIT Press.

Churchland, P. S., and Sejnowski, T. J. (1992). *The Computational Brain*. Cambridge, MA: MIT Press.

Clancey, W. J. (1997). *Situated Cognition: On Human Knowledge and Computer Representations*. Cambridge: Cambridge University Press.

Clark, A. (1989). *Microcognition: Philosophy, Cognitive Science, and Parallel Distributed Processing*. Cambridge, MA: MIT Press.

Clark, A. (1993). *Associative Engines: Connectionism, Concepts, and Representational Change*. Cambridge, MA: MIT Press.

Clark, A. (1997). *Being There: Putting Brain, Body, and World Together Again*. Cambridge, MA: MIT Press.

Clark, A. (1998). Time and mind. *Journal of Philosophy,* 95, 354-76.

Clark, A. (2001). *Mindware: An Introduction to the Philosophy of Cognitive Science.* New York: Oxford University Press.

Clark, A. (2008). *Supersizing the Mind: Embodiment, Action, and Cognitive Extension.* New York: Oxford University Press.

Clark, A. (2011). Précis of *Supersizing the Mind: Embodiment, Action, and Cognitive Extension. Philosophical Studies,* 152, 413-16.

Clearfield, M. W., Dineva, E., Smith, L. B., Diedrich, F. J., and Thelen, E. (2009). Cue salience and infant perseverative reaching: Tests of the dynamic field theory. *Developmental Science,* 12, 26-40.

Colby, C. L., and Goldberg, M. E. (1999). Space and attention in parietal cortex. *Annual Review of Neuroscience,* 22, 319-49.

Cook, V. J., and Newson, M. (2007). *Chomsky's Universal Grammar: An Introduction* (3rd edn.). Oxford: Blackwell.

Cooper, L. A., and Shepard, R. N. (1973). The time required to prepare for a rotated stimulus. *Memory and Cognition,* 1, 246-50.

Copeland, J. G. (1993). *Artificial Intelligence: A Philosophical Introduction.* Oxford; Cambridge, MA: Blackwell.

Corkin, S. (2002). What's new with the amnesic patient H.M.? *Nature Reviews Neuroscience,* 3, 153-60.

Cosmides, L. (1989). The logic of social exchange: Has natural selection shaped how humans reason? Studies with the Wason selection task. *Cognition,* 31, 187-276.

Cosmides, L., Barrett, H. C., and Tooby, J. (2010). Adaptive specializations, social exchange, and the evolution of human intelligence. *Proceedings of the National Academy of Sciences USA,* 107, 9007-14.

Cosmides, L., and Tooby, J. (1992). Cognitive adaptations for social exchange. In J. Berkow, L. Cosmides, and J. Tooby (eds.), *The Adapted Mind: Evolutionary Psychology and the Generation of Culture.* New York: Oxford University Press.

Cosmides, L., and Tooby, J. (1994). Origins of domain-specificity: The evolution of functional organization. In L. A. Hirschfeld and S. F. Gelman (eds.), *Mapping the Mind: Domain Specificity in Cognition and Culture.* Cambridge: Cambridge University Press. Reprinted in J. L. Bermúdez (ed.) (2006), *Philosophy of Psychology: Contemporary Readings.* London: Routledge.

Cosmides, L., and Tooby, J. (2013). Evolutionary psychology: New perspectives on cognition and motivation. *Annual Review of Psychology,* 64, 201-29.

Cowie, F. (2008). Us, them and it: Modules, genes, environments and evolution. *Mind and Language,* 23, 284-92.

Crane, T. (2003). *The Mechanical Mind: A Philosophical Introduction to Minds, Machines, and Mental Representation.* London; New York: Routledge.

Craver, C. (2007). *Explaining the Brain: Mechanisms and the Mosaic Unity of Neuroscience.* New York: Oxford University Press.

Crick, F., and Koch, C. (2003) A framework for consciousness. *Nature Neuroscience,* 6, 119-26.

Cummins, R. (2000). "How does it work?" versus "What are the laws?" In F. C. Keil and R. A. Wilson (eds.), *Explanation and Cognition.* Cambridge, MA: MIT Press.

Cummins, R., and Cummins, D. D. (2000). *Minds, Brains, and Computers: The Foundations of Cognitive Science: An Anthology.* Malden, MA: Blackwell.

Cutland, N. J. (1980). *Computability: An Introduction to Recursive Function Theory.* Cambridge: Cambridge University Press.

Davies, M., and Stone, T. (eds.) (1995a). *Folk Psychology.* Oxford: Blackwell.

Davies, M., and Stone, T. (eds.) (1995b). *Mental Simulation*. Oxford: Blackwell.

Davis, M. (2000). *The Universal Computer: The Road from Leibniz to Turing*. New York: Norton.

Davis, M. (2001). *Engines of Logic: Mathematicians and the Origin of the Computer*. New York: Norton.

Davis, S. (1993). *Connectionism: Theory and Practice*. New York: Oxford University Press.

Dawkins, R. (1979). Twelve misunderstandings of kin selection. *Zeitschrift für Tierpsychologie*, **51**, 184-200.

Dawson, M. R. W. (1998). *Understanding Cognitive Science*. Oxford: Blackwell.

Dawson, M. R. W. (2004). *Minds and Machines: Connectionism and Psychological Modeling*. Oxford: Blackwell.

Dawson, M. R. W. (2005). *Connectionism: A Hands-On Approach*. Oxford: Blackwell.

Dayan, P., and Abbott, L. F. (2005). *Theoretical Neuroscience: Computational and Mathematical Modeling of Neural Systems*. Cambridge, MA: MIT Press.

Dehaene, S., and Changeux, J. (2011). Experimental and theoretical approaches to conscious processing. *Neuron*, **70**, 200-27.

Dehaene, S., Changeux, J., Naccache, L., Sackur, J., and Sergent, C. (2006). Conscious, preconscious, and subliminal processing: A testable taxonomy. *Trends in Cognitive Science*, **10**, 204-11.

Dehaene, S., Kerszberg, M., and Changeux, J. P. (1998). A neuronal model of a global workspace in effortful cognitive tasks. *Proceedings of the National Academy of Sciences USA*, 95, 14529-34.

Dehaene, S. and Naccache, L. (2001). Towards a cognitive neuroscience of consciousness: Basic evidence and a workspace framework. *Cognition*, **79**, 1-37.

Dennett, D. C. (1969). *Content and Consciousness*. London: Routledge & Kegan Paul.

Dennett, D. (1984). Cognitive wheels: The frame problem in artificial intelligence. In C. Hookway (ed.), *Minds, Machines, and Evolution*. Cambridge: Cambridge University Press.

Dennett, D. C. (1991). *Consciousness Explained*. Boston: Little, Brown and Company.

Dreyfus, H. L. (1977). *Artificial Intelligence and Natural Man*. New York: Basic Books.

Driver, J., and Mattingly, J. B. (1998). Parietal neglect and visual awareness. *Nature Neuroscience*, **1**, 17-22.

Driver, J., and Vuilleumier, P. (2001). Perceptual awareness and its loss in unilateral neglect and extinction. *Cognition*, **79**, 39-88.

Duncan, S. (2011). Leibniz's Mill arguments against materialism. *Philosophical Quarterly*, **62**, 250-72.

Eliasmith, C. (1996). The third contender: A critical examination of the dynamicist theory of cognition. *Philosophical Psychology*, **9**, 441-63.

Elliott, M. H. (1928). The effect of change or reward on the maze performance of rats. *University of California Publications in Psychology*, **4**, 19-30.

Elman, J. L. (2005). Connectionist models of cognitive development: Where next? *Trends in Cognitive Sciences*, **9**, 111-17.

Elman, J. L., Bates, E. A., Johnson, M. H., and Karmiloff-Smith, A. (1996). *Rethinking Innateness: A Connectionist Perspective on Development*. Cambridge, MA: MIT Press.

Evans, J. S. B. T., and Over, D. (2004). *If*. Oxford: Oxford University Press.

Fang, F., and He, S. (2005) Cortical responses to invisible objects in the human dorsal and ventral pathways. *Nature Neuroscience*, **10**, 1380-5.

Felleman, D. J., and Van Essen, D. C. (1991). Distributed hierarchical processing in the primate cerebral cortex. *Cerebral Cortex*, **1**, 1-47.

Finkbeiner, M., and Forster, K. I. (2008). Attention, intention and domain-specific processing. *Trends in Cognitive Science*, **12**, 59-64.

Flanagan, O. J. (1991). *The Science of the Mind*. Cambridge, MA: MIT Press.

Fodor, J. (1975). *The Language of Thought*. Cambridge, MA: Harvard University Press.

Fodor, J. (1983). *The Modularity of Mind*. Cambridge, MA: MIT Press.

Fodor, J. (1985). Precis of *The Modularity of Mind*. *Behavioral and Brain Sciences*, **1**, 1-5.

Fodor, J. (1987). *Psychosemantics*. Cambridge, MA: MIT Press.

Fodor, J. (2000). *The Mind Doesn't Work That Way: The Scope and Limits of Computational Psychology*. Cambridge, MA: MIT Press.

Fodor, J. (2008). *LOT 2: The Language of Thought Revisited*. Oxford: Oxford University Press.

Fodor, J., and Pylyshyn, Z. (1988). Connectionism and cognitive architecture: A critical analysis. *Cognition*, **28**, 3-71.

Frankish, K., and Ramsey, W. (eds.) (2012). *The Cambridge Handbook of Cognitive Science*. Cambridge: Cambridge University Press.

Franklin, S. (1995). *Artificial Minds*. Cambridge, MA: MIT Press.

Franz, V. H., Gegenfurtner, K. R., Bülthoff, H. H., and Fahle, M. (2000). Grasping visual illusions: No evidence for a dissociation between perception and action. *Psychological Science*, **11**, 20-5.

Friedenberg, J., and Silverman, G. (2006). *Cognitive Science: An Introduction to the Study of Mind*. Thousand Oaks, CA: Sage.

Frith, C., and Frith, U. (2012). Mechanisms of social cognition. *Annual Review of Psychology*, **63**, 287-313.

Funt, B. V. (1980). Problem-solving with diagrammatic representations. *Artificial Intelligence*, **13**, 201-30. Reprinted in R. J. Brachman and H. J. Levesque (eds.) (1985), *Readings in Knowledge Representation*. Los Altos, CA: M. Kaufmann.

Gallistel, C. R. (1990). *The Organization of Learning*. Cambridge, MA: MIT Press.

Gardner, H. (1985). *The Mind's New Science: A History of the Cognitive Revolution*. New York: Basic Books.

Gazzaniga, M. S. (ed.) (1995). *The New Cognitive Neurosciences* (1st edn.). Cambridge, MA: MIT Press.

Gazzaniga, M. S. (ed.) (2000). *The New Cognitive Neurosciences* (2nd edn.). Cambridge, MA: MIT Press.

Gazzaniga, M. S. (ed.) (2004). *The New Cognitive Neurosciences* (3rd edn.). Cambridge, MA: MIT Press.

Gazzaniga, M S., Halpern, T., and Heatherton, D. (2011). *Psychological Science* (4th edn.). New York: Norton.

Gazzaniga, M. S., Ivry, R. B., and Mangun, G. R. (2008). *Cognitive Neuroscience: The Biology of the Mind*. New York: Norton.

Gleitman, H., Fridlund, J., and Reisberg, D. (2010). *Psychology* (8th edn.). New York: Norton.

Glover, S. R., and Dixon, P. (2001). Dynamic illusion effects in a reaching task: Evidence for separate visual representations in the planning and control of reaching. *Journal of Experimental Psychology: Human Perception and Performance*, **27**, 560-72.

Goense, J., Whittingstall, K., and Logothetis, N. K. (2012). Neural and BOLD responses across the brain. *WIREs Cognitive Science*, **3**, 75-86.

Goldman, A. (2006). *Simulating Minds*. New York: Oxford University Press.

Goodale, M. A., and Milner, A. D. (2013). *Sight Unseen* (2nd edn.). New York: Oxford University Press.

Gopnik, A., and Meltzoff, A. N. (1997). *Words, Thoughts, and Theories*. Cambridge, MA: MIT Press.

Gordon, R. (1986). Folk psychology as simulation. *Mind and Language*, **1**, 158-71.

Gorman, R. P., and Sejnowski, T. J. (1988). Analysis of hidden units in a layered network trained to identify sonar targets. *Neural Networks*, **1**, 75-89.

Grainger, J., and Jacobs, A. M. (1998). *Localist Connectionist Approaches to Human Cognition*. Mahwah, NJ: Lawrence Erlbaum.

Greenwald, A. G., Draine, S. C., and Abrams, R. L. (1996). Three cognitive markers of unconscious semantic activation. *Science*, **273**, 1699-1702.

Griggs, R. A., and Cox, J. R. (1982). The elusive thematic materials effect in the Wason selection task. *British Journal of Psychology,* **73**, 407-20.

Hadley, R. F. (2000). Cognition and the computational power of connectionist networks. *Connection Science,* **12**, 95-110.

Harnad, S. (1990). The symbol-grounding problem. *Physica D,* **42**, 335-46.

Haugeland, J. (1985). *Artificial Intelligence: The Very Idea.* Cambridge, MA: MIT Press.

Haugeland, J. (1997). *Mind Design II: Philosophy, Psychology, Artificial Intelligence.* Cambridge, MA: MIT Press.

Heal, J. (1986). Replication and functionalism. In J. Butterfield (ed.), *Language, Mind and Logic.* Cambridge: Cambridge University Press.

Hebb, D. O. (1949). *The Organization of Behavior: A Neuropsychological Theory.* New York: Wiley.

Heeger, D. J., and Ress, D. (2002). What does fMRI tell us about neuronal activity? *Nature Reviews Neuroscience,* **3**, 142-51.

Heil, J. (2004). *Philosophy of Mind: A Guide and Anthology.* New York: Oxford University Press.

Henson, R. (2006). Forward inference using functional neuroimaging: Dissociations versus associations. *Trends in Cognitive Sciences,* **10**, 64-9.

Hespos, S. J., and van Marle, K. (2012). Physics for infants: Characterizing the origins of knowledge about objects, substances, and number. *WIREs Cognitive Science,* **3**, 19-27.

Hinton, G. E., McClelland, J. L., and Rumelhart, D. E. (1986). Distributed representations. In D. E. Rumelhart and J. L. McClelland and the PDP Research Group (eds.), *Parallel Distributed Processing: Explorations in the Microstructures of Cognition,* vol. 1: *Foundations.* Cambridge, MA: MIT Press.

Hirschfeld, L. A., and Gelman, S. F. (eds.) (1994). *Mapping the Mind: Domain Specificity in Cognition and Culture.* Cambridge: Cambridge University Press.

Hohwy, J. (2009). The neural correlates of consciousness: new experimental approaches needed? *Consciousness and Cognition,* **18**, 428-438.

Hopfinger, J. B., Luck, S. J., and Hillyard, S. A. (2004). Selective attention: Electrophysiological and neuromagnetic studies. In M. Gazzaniga (ed.), *The Cognitive Neurosciences* (3rd edn.). Cambridge, MA: MIT Press.

Houghton, G. (2005). *Connectionist Models in Cognitive Psychology.* Oxford: Oxford University Press.

Humphreys, G. W., Duncan, J., and Treisman, A. (eds.) (1999). *Attention, Space, and Action: Studies in Cognitive Neuroscience.* Oxford; New York: Oxford University Press.

Husain, M., and Nachev, P. (2007). Space and the parietal cortex. *Trends in Cognitive Science,* **11**, 30-6.

Hutchins, E. (1995). *Cognition in the Wild.* Cambridge, MA: MIT Press.

Iacoboni, M., and Dapretto, M. (2006). The mirror neuron system and the consequences of its dysfunction. *Nature Reviews Neuroscience,* **7**, 942-51.

Isac, D., and Reiss, C. (2013). *I-Language: An Introduction to Linguistics as Cognitive Science* (2nd edn.). Oxford: Oxford University Press.

Jackson, F. (1982). Epiphenomenal qualia. *Philosophical Quarterly,* **32**, 127-36.

Jackson, F. (1986). What Mary didn't know. *Journal of Philosophy,* **83**, 291-5.

Jackson, F. (2003). Mind and illusion. In A. O'Hear (ed.), *Minds and Persons: Royal Institute of Philosophy Supplement.* Cambridge: Cambridge University Press.

Jackson, P. (1998). *Introduction to Expert Systems.* Harlow, UK: Addison-Wesley.

Jacob, P., and Jeannerod, M. (2003). *Ways of Seeing: The Scope and Limits of Visual Cognition.* New York: Oxford University Press.

Jirsa, V. K., and McIntosh, A. R. (eds.) (2007). *The Handbook of Brain Connectivity.* Berlin: Springer.

Johnson, K. (2004). Gold's theorem and cognitive science. *Philosophy of Science*, **71**, 571–92.

Johnson-Laird, P. N. (1988). *Computer and the Mind: An Introduction to Cognitive Science.* Cambridge, MA: Harvard University Press.

Jones, J., and Roth, D. (2003). *Robot Programming: A Practical Guide to Behavior-Based Robotics.* New York: McGraw-Hill.

Kalat, J. W. (2010). *Introduction to Psychology* (9th edn.). Belmont, CA; London: Wadsworth Thomson Learning.

Kandel, E. R., Schwarz, J. H., and Jessell, T. M. (2012). *Principles of Neural Science* (5th edn.). New York: McGraw-Hill Medical.

Kanwisher, N. (2000). Domain specificity in face perception. *Nature Neuroscience*, **3**, 759–63.

Kanwisher, N., McDermott, J., and Chun, M. (1997). The fusiform face area: A module in human extrastriate cortex specialized for the perception of faces. *Journal of Neuroscience*, **17**, 4302–11

Kelly, W. M., Macrae, C. N., Wyland, C. L., Caglar, S., Inati, S., and Heatherton, T. F. (2002). Finding the self? An event-related fMRI study. *Journal of Cognitive Neuroscience*, **14**, 785–94.

Kiran, S., and Lebel, K. (2007). Crosslinguistic semantic and translation priming in normal bilingual individuals and bilingual aphasia. *Clinical Linguistics and Phonetics*, **4**, 277–303.

Koch, C. (2004). *The Quest for Consciousness: A Neurobiological Approach.* Englewood, CO: Roberts.

Koch, C., and Tsuchiya, N. (2007). Attention and consciousness: Two distinct brain processes. *Trends in Cognitive Science*, **11**, 229–35.

Kosslyn, S. M. (1973). Scanning visual images: Some structural implications. *Perception and Psychophysics*, **14**, 341–70.

Kosslyn, S. M., Thompson, W. L., and Ganis, G. (2006). *The Case for Mental Imagery.* Oxford: Oxford University Press.

Kotz, S. A. (2001). Neurolinguistic evidence for bilingual language representation: A comparison of reaction times and event-related brain potentials. *Bilingualism: Language and Cognition*, **4**, 143–54.

Kouider, S., de Gardelle, V., Sackur, J., and Dupoux, E. (2010). How rich is consciousness? The partial awareness hypothesis. *Trends in Cognitive Sciences*, **14**, 301–7.

Kouider, S., and Dehaene, S. (2007). Levels of processing during non-conscious perception: A critical review of visual masking. *Philosophical Transactions of the Royal Society of London B*, **362** (1481), 857–75.

Kouider, S., Dehaene, S., Jobert, A., and Le Bihan, D. (2007). Cerebral bases of subliminal and supraliminal priming during reading. *Cerebral Cortex*, **17**, 2019–29.

Laird, J. E. (2012). *The Soar Cognitive Architecture.* Cambridge, MA: MIT Press.

Lamme, V. A. F. (2003). Why visual attention and awareness are different. *Trends in Cognitive Science*, **7**, 12–18.

Lamme, V. A. F. (2006). Towards a true neural stance on consciousness. *Trends in Cognitive Science*, **10**, 494–501.

Lashley, K. S. (1951). The problem of serial order in behavior. In A. L. Jeffress (ed.), *Cerebral Mechanisms in Behavior: The Hixon Symposium.* New York: Wiley.

Laureys, S. (2005). The neural correlate of (un)awareness: Lessons from the vegetative state. *Trends in Cognitive Sciences*, **9**, 556–9.

Lavie, N. (2005). Distracted and confused? Selective attention under load. *Trends in Cognitive Science*, **9**, 75–82.

Lebiere, C. (2003). ACT. In L. Nadel (ed.), *Encyclopedia of Cognitive Science.* New York: Nature Publishing Group.

Leslie, A. M. (1987). Pretense and representation: The origins of "theory of mind." *Psychological Review*, **94**, 412–26.

Leslie, A. M., Friedman, O., and German, T. P. (2004). Core mechanisms in "theory of mind." *Trends in Cognitive Sciences*, **8**, 529-33.

Leslie, A. M., German, T. P., and Polizzi, P. (2005). Belief-desire reasoning as a process of selection. *Cognitive Psychology*, **50**, 45-85.

Leslie, A. M., and Polizzi, P. (1998). Inhibitory processing in the false belief task: Two conjectures. *Developmental Science*, **1**, 247-53.

Levine, J. (1983). Materialism and qualia: The explanatory gap. *Pacific Philosophical Quarterly*, **64**, 354-61.

Logothetis, N. K. (2001). The underpinnings of the BOLD functional magnetic resonance imaging signal. *Journal of Neuroscience*, **23**, 3963-71.

Logothetis, N. K. (2008). What we can do and what we cannot do with fMRI. *Nature*, **453**, 869-78.

Logothetis, N. K., Pauls, J., Augath, M., Trinath, T., and Oeltermann, A. (2001). Neurophysiological investigation of the fMRI signal. *Nature*, **412**, 150-7.

Lovett, M. C., and Anderson, J. R. (2005). Thinking as a production system. In K. J. Holyoak and R. G. Morrison (eds.), *The Cambridge Handbook of Thinking and Reasoning*. Cambridge: Cambridge University Press.

Low, J., and Perner, J. (2012). Implicit and explicit theory of mind: State of the art. *British Journal of Developmental Psychology*, **30**, 1-30.

Luck, S. J. (2005). *An Introduction to the Event-Related Potential Technique*. Cambridge, MA: MIT Press.

Luck, S. J., and Ford, M. A. (1998). On the role of selective attention in visual perception. *Proceedings of the National Academy of Sciences, USA*, **95**, 825-30.

Luck, S. J., and Kappenman, E. S. (2011). *The Oxford Handbook of Event-Related Potential Components*. Oxford: Oxford University Press.

Ludlow, P., Nagasawa, Y., and Stoljar, D. (eds.) (2004). *There's Something About Mary*. Cambridge, MA: MIT Press.

Luo, Y., and Baillargeon, R. (2010). Toward a mentalistic account of early psychological reasoning. *Current Directions in Psychological Science*, **19**, 301-7.

Luria, A. R. (1970). The functional organization of the brain. *Scientific American*, **222**, 66-72.

Macdonald, C., and Macdonald, G. (1995). *Connectionism*. Oxford, UK; Cambridge, MA: Blackwell.

Machery, E. (2008). Massive modularity and the flexibility of human cognition. *Mind and Language*, **23**, 263-72.

Machery, E. (2012). Dissociations in neuropsychology and cognitive neuroscience. *Philosophy of Science*, **79**, 490-518.

Mack, A., and Rock, I. (1998). *Inattentional Blindness*. Cambridge, MA: MIT Press.

Marcus, G. (2003). *The Algebraic Mind: Integrating Connectionism and Cognitive Science*. Cambridge, MA: MIT Press.

Marcus, G., Ullman, M., Pinker, S., Hollander, M., Rosen, T. J., and Xu, F. (1992). *Overregularization in Language Acquisition*. Chicago: University of Chicago Press.

Mareschal, D., and Johnson, S. P. (2002). Learning to perceive object unity: A connectionist account. *Developmental Science*, **5**, 151-85.

Mareschal, D., Plunkett, K., and Harris, P. (1995). Developing object permanence: A connectionist model. In J. D. Moore and J. F. Lehman (eds.), *Proceedings of the Seventeenth Annual Conference of the Cognitive Science Society*. Mahwah, NJ: Lawrence Erlbaum.

Margolis, E., Samuels, R., and Stich, S. (eds.) (2012). *The Oxford Handbook of Philosophy of Cognitive Science*. Oxford: Oxford Universsity Press.

Marr, D. (1982). *Vision: A Computational Investigation into the Human Representation and Processing of Visual Information*. San Francisco: W. H. Freeman.

Marr, D. (2010). *Vision: A Computational Investigation into the Human Representation and Processing of Visual Information*. London, UK; Cambridge, MA: MIT Press. (Original work published 1982.)

Marr, D., and Hilldreth, E. (1980). Theory of edge detection. *Proceedings of the Royal Society of London*, **204**, 187-217.

Marshall, J. C., and Halligan, P. W. (1988). Blindsight and insight in visuospatial neglect. *Nature*, **366**, 766-7.

Martens, S., and Wyble, B. (2010). The attentional blink: Past, present, and future of a blind spot in perceptual awareness. *Neuroscience and Biobehavioral Reviews*, **34**, 947-57.

Matarić, M. (1997). Behavior-based control: Examples from navigation, learning, and group behavior. *Journal of Experimental and Theoretical Artificial Intelligence*, **9**, 323-36.

Matarić, M. (1998). Behavior-based robotics as a tool for synthesis of artificial behavior and analysis of natural behavior. *Trends in Cognitive Science*, **2**, 82-7.

Matarić, M. (2007). *The Robotics Primer*. Cambridge, MA: MIT Press.

McClelland, J. L., Botvinick, M. M., Noelle, D. C., *et al.* (2010). Letting structure emerge: Connectionist and dynamical systems approaches to cognition. *Trends in Cognitive Sciences*, **14**, 348-56.

McClelland, J. L., and Jenkins, E. (1991). Nature, nurture, and connectionism: Implications for connectionist models of development. In K. van Lehn (ed.), *Architectures for Intelligence: The 22nd (1988) Carnegie Symposium on Cognition*. Hillsdale, NJ: Lawrence Erlbaum.

McClelland, J. L., and Patterson, K. (2002). Rules or connections in past-tense inflections: What does the evidence rule out? *Trends in Cognitive Sciences*, **6**, 465-72.

McClelland, J. L, Rumelhart, D. E., and the PDP Research Group (1986). *Parallel Distributed Processing: Explorations in the Microstructures of Cognition*, vol. 2: *Psychological and Biological Models*. Cambridge, MA: MIT Press.

McCulloch, W. S., and Pitts, W. H. (1943). A logical calculus of the ideas immanent in nervous activity. *Bulletin of Mathematical Biophysics*, **5**, 115-33.

McDermott, J. H. (2009) The cocktail party problem. *Current Biology*, **19**, R1024-R1027.

McLeod, P., Plunkett, K., and Rolls, E. T. (1998). *Introduction to the Connectionist Modelling of Cognitive Processes*. Oxford; New York: Oxford University Press.

Medsker, L. R., and Schulte, T. W. (2003). Expert systems. In L. Nadel (ed.), *Encyclopedia of Cognitive Science* (vol. 2). New York: Nature Publishing Group.

Melcher, D., and Colby, C. L. (2008). Trans-saccadic perception. *Trends in Cognitive Sciences*, **12**, 466-73.

Merikle, P. M., Joordens, S., and Stolz, J. (1995). Measuring the relative magnitude of unconscious influences. *Consciousness and Cognition*, **4**, 422-39.

Metzinger, T. (ed.) (2000). *Neural Correlates of Consciousness: Empirical and Conceptual Issues*. Cambridge, MA: MIT Press.

Michalski, R. S., and Chilausky, R. L. (1980). Learning by being told and learning from examples: An experimental comparison of the two methods for knowledge acquisition in the context of developing an expert system for soybean disease diagnosis. *International Journal of Policy Analysis and Information Systems*, **4**, 125-61.

Miller, G. A. (1956). The magical number seven, plus or minus two: Some limits on our capacity for processing information. *Psychological Review*, **63**, 81-97.

Miller, G. A. (2003). The cognitive revolution: A historical perspective. *Trends in Cognitive Science*, **7**, 141-4.

Milner, A. D. (2012). Is visual processing in the dorsal stream accessible to consciousness? *Proceedings of the Royal Society B*, **279**, 2289-98.

Milner, A. D., and Goodale, M. A. (1998). *The Visual Brain in Action* (Precis). *Psyche*, **4**.

Milner, A. D., and Goodale, M. A. (2006). *The Visual Brain in Action* (2nd edn.). Oxford: Oxford University Press.

Milner, A. D., and Goodale, M. A. (2008). Two visual systems reviewed. *Neuropsychologia*, **46**, 774-85.

Milner, B. (1966). Amnesia following operation on the temporal lobes. In C. W. M. Whitty and O. L. Zangwill (eds.), *Amnesia*. London: Butterworth.

Minsky, M., and Papert, S. (1969). *Perceptrons*. Cambridge, MA: MIT Press.

Mishkin, M. L., Ungerleider, G., and Macko, K. A. (1983/2001). Object vision and spatial vision: Two cortical pathways. *Trends in NeuroSciences*, **6**, 414-17. Reprinted in W. Bechtel, P. Mandik, J. Mundale, and R. Stufflebeam (eds.) (2001), *Philosophy and the Neurosciences: A Reader*. Oxford: Blackwell.

Mitchell, J. P., Banaji, M. R., and Macrae, C. N. (2005). The link between social cognition and self-referential thought in the medial prefrontal cortex. *Journal of Cognitive Neuroscience*, **17**, 1306-15.

Mitchell, T. M. (1997). *Machine Learning*. Boston, MA: McGraw-Hill.

Molenberghs, P., Sale, M. V., and Mattingley, J. B. (2012). Is there a critical lesion site for unilateral spatial neglect? A meta-analysis using activation likelihood estimation. *Frontiers in Human Neuroscience*, **6**, 1-10.

Mukamel, R., Gelbard, H., Arieli, A., Hasson, U., Fried, I., and Malach, R. (2005). Coupling between neuronal firing, field potentials, and fMRI in human auditory cortex. *Science*, **309**, 951-4.

Munakata, Y. (2001). Graded representations in behavioral dissociations. *Trends in Cognitive Science*, **5**, 309-15.

Munakata, Y., and McClelland, J. L. (2003). Connectionist models of development. *Developmental Science*, **6**, 413-29.

Munakata, Y., McClelland, J. L., Johnson, M. H., and Siegler, R. S. (1997). Rethinking infant knowledge: Toward an adaptive process account of successes and failures in object permanence tasks. *Psychological Review*, **104**, 686-713.

Nadel, L. (ed.) (2005). *Encyclopedia of Cognitive Science*. Chichester: Wiley.

Needham, A., and Libertus, K. (2011). Embodiment in early development. *WIREs Cognitive Science*, **2**, 117-23.

Newmeyer, F. J. (1986). *Linguistic Theory in America*. London: Academic Press.

Nichols, S., Stich, S., Leslie, A., and Klein, D. (1996). Varieties of off-line simulation. In P. Carruthers and P. K. Smith (eds.), *Theories of Theory of Mind*. Cambridge: Cambridge University Press.

Nilsson, N. J. (1984). Shakey the robot. SRI International, Technical Note 323.

Norman, D. A., and Shallice, T. (1980). Attention to action: Willed and automatic control of behaviour. Reprinted in M. Gazzaniga (ed.), *Cognitive Neuroscience: A Reader*. Oxford: Blackwell (2000).

Oakes, L. M. (2010). Using habituation of looking time to assess mental processes in infancy. *Journal of Cognition and Development*, **11**, 255-68.

Oaksford, M., and Chater, N. (1994). A rational analysis of the selection task as optimal data selection. *Psychological Review*, **101**, 608-31.

Oberauer, K. (2006). Reasoning with conditionals: A test of formal models of four theories. *Cognitive Psychology*, **53**, 238-83.

O'Grady, W., Archibald, J., Aronoff, M., and Rees-Miller, J. (2010). *Contemporary Linguistics: An Introduction* (6th edn.). Boston: Bedford/St. Martin's.

Onishi, K. H., and Baillargeon, R. (2005). Do 15-month-old infants understand false beliefs? *Science*, **308**, 255-8.

Orban, G. A., Van Essen, D., and Vanduffel, W. (2004). Comparative mapping of higher visual areas in monkeys and humans. *Trends in Cognitive Science*, **8**, 315-24.

O'Reilly, R. C., and Munakata, Y. (2000). *Computational Explorations in Computational Neuroscience: Understanding the Mind by Simulating the Brain.* Cambridge, MA: MIT Press.

Owen, A. M., Coleman, M. R., Boly, M., Davis, M. H., Laureys, S., and Pickard, J. D. (2006). Detecting awareness in the vegetative state. *Science*, **313**, 1402.

Page, M. (2000). Connectionist modeling in psychology: A localist manifesto. *Behavioral and Brain Sciences*, **23**, 443-67.

Passingham, R. (2009). How good is the macaque monkey model of the human brain? *Current Opinion in Neurobiology*, **19**, 6-11.

Perner, J. (1991). *Understanding the Representational Mind* (new edn. 1993). Cambridge, MA: MIT Press.

Perner, J., and Leekam, S. (2008). The curious incident of the photo that was accused of being false: Issues of domain specificity in development, autism, and brain imaging. *Quarterly Journal of Experimental Psychology*, **61**, 76-89.

Perner, J., and Roessler, J. (2012). From infants' to children's appreciation of belief. *Trends in Cognitive Science*, **16**, 519-25.

Peru, A., Moro, V., Avesani, R., and Aglioti, S. (1996). Overt and covert processing of left-side information in unilateral neglect investigated with chimeric drawings. *Journal of Clinical and Experimental Neuropsychology*, **18**, 621-30.

Petersen, S. E., and Fiez, J. A. (2001). The processing of single words studied with positron emission tomography. In W. Bechtel, P. Mandik, J. Mundale, and R. S. Stufflebeam (eds.), *Philosophy and the Neurosciences: A Reader.* Malden, MA: Blackwell.

Petersen, S. E., Fox, P. T., Posner, M. I., and Mintun, M. (1988). Positron emission tomographic studies of the cortical anatomy of single-word processing. *Nature*, **331**, 585-9.

Pfeifer, R., Iida, F., and Gómez, G. (2006). Morphological computation for adaptive behavior and cognition. *International Congress Series*, **1291**, 22-9.

Phillips, M. L., Young, A. W., Senior, C., *et al.* (1997). A specific neural substrate for perceiving facial expressions of disgust. *Nature*, **389**, 495-8.

Piaget, J. (1954). *The Construction of Reality in the Child.* New York: Basic Books.

Piccinini, G. (2004). The first computational theory of mind and brain: A close look at McCulloch and Pitts' "Logical calculus of the ideas immanent in nervous activity." *Synthese*, **141**, 175-215.

Piccinini, G., and Craver, C. (2011). Integrating psychology and neuroscience: Functional analyses as mechanism sketches. *Synthese*, **183**, 283-311.

Pinker, S. (1997). *How the Mind Works.* New York: Norton.

Pinker, S. (2005). So how does the mind work? *Mind and Language*, **20**, 1-24.

Pinker, S., and Prince, A. (1988a). On language and connectionism: Analysis of a parallel distributed processing model of language acquisition. *Cognition*, **28**, 73-193.

Pinker, S., and Prince, A. (1988b). Rules and connections in human language. In R. Morris (ed.), *Parallel Distributed Processing.* Oxford: Oxford University Press.

Pinker, S., and Ullman, M. T. (2002). The past and future of the past tense. *Trends in Cognitive Sciences*, **6**, 456-63.

Plaut, D. C., Banich, M. T., and Mack, M. (2003). Connectionist modeling of language: Examples and implications. In M. T. Banich and M. Mack (eds.), *Mind, Brain, and Language: Multidisciplinary Perspectives.* Mahwah, NJ: Lawrence Erlbaum.

Plaut, D. C., and McClelland, J. L. (2010). Locating object knowledge in the brain: Comment on Bowers's (2009) attempt to revive the grandmother cell hypothesis. *Psychological Review,* **117**, 284-90.

Plotnik, R., and Kouyoumdjian, H. (2010). *Introduction to Psychology* (9th edn.). Belmont, CA: Wadsworth Thomson Learning.

Plunkett, K., and Elman, J. L. (1997). *Exercises in Rethinking Innateness: A Handbook for Connectionist Simulations.* Cambridge, MA: MIT Press.

Plunkett, K., and Marchman, V. (1993). From rote learning to system building: Acquiring verb morphology in children and connectionist nets. *Cognition,* **48**, 21-69.

Poldrack, R. A. (2006). Can cognitive processes be inferred from neuroimaging data? *Trends in Cognitive Sciences,* **10**, 59-63.

Poldrack, R. A., Mumford, J. A., and Nichols, T. E. (2011). *Handbook of Functional MRI Data Analysis.* Cambridge: Cambridge University Press.

Pollard, P., and Evans, J. St. B. T. (1987). Content and context effects in reasoning. *American Journal of Psychology,* **100**, 41-60.

Poole, D. L., and Mackworth, A. K. (2010). *Artificial Intelligence: Foundations of Computational Agents.* Cambridge: Cambridge University Press.

Pöppel, E., Frost, D., and Held, R. (1973). Residual visual function after brain wounds involving the central visual pathways in man. *Nature,* **243**, 295-6

Port, R. F., and Van Gelder, T. (1995). *Mind as Motion: Explorations in the Dynamics of Cognition.* Cambridge, MA: MIT Press.

Posner, M. I. (1980). Orienting of attention. *Quarterly Journal of Experimental Psychology,* **32**, 3-25.

Posner, M. I. (1989). *Foundations of Cognitive Science.* Cambridge, MA: MIT Press.

Posner M. I. (ed.) (2004). *The Cognitive Neuroscience of Attention.* New York: Guilford.

Posner, M. I., and Raichle, M. E. (1994). *Images of Mind.* New York: Scientific American Library.

Prince, A., and Pinker, S. (1988). Rules and connections in human language. *Trends in Neurosciences,* **11**, 195-202.

Prinz, J. (2012). *The Conscious Brain.* New York: Oxford University Press.

Purves, D., Augustine, G. J., Fitzpatrick, D., Hall, W. C., Anthony-Samuel, L., and White, L. E. (2011) *Neuroscience* (5th edn.). Sunderland, MA: Sinauer Associates.

Pylyshyn, Z. (1980). Computation and cognition: Issues in the foundations of cognitive science. *Behavioral and Brain Sciences,* **3**, 111-69.

Pylyshyn, Z. (1984). *Computation and Cognition: Toward a Foundation for Cognitive Science.* Cambridge, MA: MIT Press.

Pylyshyn, Z. (ed.) (1987). *The Robot's Dilemma: The Frame Problem in Artificial Intelligence.* Norwood, NJ: Ablex.

Quinlan, P. T., van der Maas, H. L. J., Jansen, B. R. J., Booij, O., and Rendell, M. (2007). Re-thinking stages of cognitive development: An appraisal of connectionist models of the balance scale task. *Cognition,* **103**, 413-59.

Raichle, M. E., and Mintun, M. A. (2006). Brain work and brain imaging. *Annual Review of Neuroscience,* **29**, 449-76.

Ramnani, N., Behrens, T. E. J., Penny, W., and Matthews, P. M. (2004). New approaches for exploring functional and anatomical connectivity in the human brain. *Biological Psychiatry,* **56**, 613-19.

Ramsey, W., Stich, S. P., and Rumelhart, D. E. (1991). *Philosophy and Connectionist Theory.* Hillsdale, NJ: Lawrence Erlbaum.

Rees, G., Friston, K., and Koch, C. (2000). A direct quantitative relationship between the functional properties of human and macaque V5. *Nature Neuroscience,* **3,** 716-23.

Riley, M. A., and Holden, J. G. (2012). Dynamics of cognition. *WIREs Cognitive Science,* **3,** 593-606.

Ritter, F. E. (2003). Soar. In L. Nadel (ed.), *Encyclopedia of Cognitive Science.* New York: Nature Publishing Group.

Rizzolatti, G., Fogassi, L., and Gallese, V. (2001). Neurophysiological mechanisms underlying the understanding and imitation of action. *Nature Reviews Neuroscience,* **2,** 661-70.

Rizzolatti, G., Fogassi, L., and Gallese, V. (2006). Mirrors of the mind. *Scientific American,* **295,** 54-61.

Rizzolatti, G., and Sinigaglia, C. (2008). *Mirrors in the Brain: How Our Minds Share Actions and Emotions.* Trans. F. Anderson. Oxford: Oxford University Press.

Rizzolatti, G., and Sinigaglia, C. (2010). The functional role of the parieto-frontal mirror circuit: Interpretations and misinterpretations. *Nature Reviews Neuroscience,* **11,** 264-74.

Robbins, R., and Aydede, M. (eds.) (2008). *The Cambridge Handbook of Situated Cognition.* Cambridge: Cambridge University Press.

Roediger, H. L., Dudai, Y., and Fitzpatrick, S. M. (2007). *Science of Memory: Concepts.* Oxford; New York: Oxford University Press.

Rogers, R. (1971). *Mathematical Logic and Formalized Theories.* Amsterdam: North-Holland.

Rogers, T. T., and McClelland, J. L. (2004). *Semantic Cognition: A Parallel Distributed Processing Approach.* Cambridge, MA: MIT Press.

Rohde, D., and Plaut, D. C. (1999). Language acquisition in the absence of explicit negative evidence: How important is starting small? *Cognition,* **72,** 67-109.

Rollins, M. (1989). *Mental Imagery: The Limits of Cognitive Science.* Cambridge, MA: MIT Press.

Rolls, E. T., and Milward., T. (2000). A model of invariant object recognition in the visual system: Learning rules, activation functions, lateral inhibition, and information-based performance measures. *Neural Computation,* **12,** 2547-72.

Rosenblatt, F. (1958). The perceptron: A probabilistic model for information storage and organization in the brain. *Psychological Review,* **65,** 386-408.

Rösler, F., Ranganath, C., Röder, B., and Kluwe, R. (2009). *Neuroimaging of Human Memory: Linking Cognitive Processes to Neural Systems.* New York: Oxford University Press.

Rowe, J. B., and Frackowiak, R. S. J. (2003). Neuroimaging. In L. Nadel (ed.), *Encyclopedia of Cognitive Science.* New York: Nature Publishing Group.

Rumelhart, D. E. (1989). The architecture of mind: A connectionist approach. In M. I. Posner (ed.), *Foundations of Cognitive Science.* Cambridge, MA: MIT Press. Reprinted in J. Haugeland (ed.) (1997), *Mind Design II: Philosophy, Psychology, Artificial Intelligence.* Cambridge, MA: MIT Press.

Rumelhart, D. E., and McClelland, J. L. (1986). On learning the past tenses of English verbs. In J. L. McClelland, D. E. Rumelhart, and The PDP Research Group (eds.), *Parallel Distributed Processing: Explorations in the Microstructures of Cognition,* vol. 2: *Psychological and Biological Models.* Cambridge, MA: MIT Press.

Rumelhart, D. E., McClelland, J. L., and The PDP Research Group (1986). *Parallel Distributed Processing: Explorations in the Microstructures of Cognition,* vol. 1: *Foundations.* Cambridge, MA: MIT Press. For vol. 2, see McClelland *et al.* (1986).

Russell, S. J., and Norvig, P. (2003). *Artificial Intelligence: A Modern Approach* (2nd edn.). Upper Saddle River: Prentice Hall.

Russell, S. J., and Norvig, P. (2009). *Artificial Intelligence: A Modern Approach* (3rd edn.). New Delhi: Prentice-Hall of India.

Samson, D., Apperly, I. A., Chiavarino, C., and Humphreys, G. W. (2004). Left temporoparietal junction is necessary for representing someone else's belief. *Nature Neuroscience*, **7**, 499-500.

Samson, D., Apperly, I. A., Kathirgamanathan, U., and Humphreys, G. W. (2005). Seeing it my way: A case of a selective deficit in inhibiting self-perspective. *Brain: A Journal of Neurology*, **128**, 1102-11.

Saxe, R. (2009). Theory of mind (neural basis). In W. Banks (ed.), *Encyclopedia of Consciousness*. Cambridge, MA: MIT Press.

Saxe, R., Carey, S., and Kanwisher, N. (2004). Understanding other minds: Linking developmental psychology and functional neuroimaging. *Annual Review of Psychology*, **55**, 87-124.

Saxe, R., and Kanwisher, N. (2005). People thinking about thinking people: The role of the temporo-parietal junction in "Theory of Mind." In J. T. Cacioppo and G. G. Berntson (eds.), *Social Neuroscience: Key Readings*. New York: Psychology Press.

Schenk, T., and McIntosh, R. D. (2010). Do we have independent visual streams for perception and action? *Cognitive Neuroscience*, **1**, 52-78.

Schlatter, M., and Aizawa, K. (2008). Walter Pitts and "A logical calculus." *Synthese*, **162**, 235-50.

Schneider, S. (2011). *The Language of Thought: A New Philosophical Direction*. Cambridge, MA: MIT Press.

Schneider, S., and Katz, M. (2012). Rethinking the language of thought. *WIREs Cognitive Science*, **3**, 153-62.

Schoonbaert, S., Duyck, W., Brysbaert, M., and Hartsuiker, R. J. (2009). Semantic and translation priming from a first language to a second and back: Making sense of the findings. *Memory & Cognition*, **37**, 569-86.

Schyns, P. G., Gosselin, F., and Smith, M. L. (2008). Information processing algorithms in the brain. *Trends in Cognitive Sciences*, **13**, 20-6.

Searle, J. (1980). Minds, brains, and programs. *Behavioral and Brain Sciences*, **3**, 417-57.

Searle, J. (2004). *Mind: A Brief Introduction*. New York: Oxford University Press.

Shadmehr, R., and Krakauer, J. W. (2008). A computational neuroanatomy for motor control. *Experimental Brain Research*, **185**, 359-81.

Shallice, T., and Warrington, E. K. (1970). Independent functioning of memory stores: A neuropsychological study. *Quarterly Journal of Experimental Psychology*, **22**, 261-73.

Shanahan, M. P. (2003). The frame problem. In L. Nadel (ed.), *Encyclopedia of Cognitive Science*. New York: Nature Publishing Group.

Shannon, C. E. (1948). A mathematical theory of communication. *Bell System Technical Journal*, **27**, 379-423 and 623-56.

Shapiro, L. (2007). The embodied cognition research programme. *Philosophy Compass*, **2**, 338-46.

Shapiro, L. (2011). *Embodied Cognition*. New York: Routledge.

Shepard, R. N., and Metzler, J. (1971). Mental rotation of three-dimensional objects. *Science*, **171**, 701-3.

Shepherd, G. (1994). *Neurobiology* (3rd edn.). New York: Oxford University Press.

Siegelmann, H., and Sontag, E. (1991). Turing computability with neural nets. *Applied Mathematics Letters*, **4**, 77-80.

Simons, D., and Chabris, C. (1999). Gorillas in our midst: Sustained inattentional blindness for dynamic events. *Perception*, **28**, 1059-74.

Simons, D., and Rensink, R. A. (2005). Change blindness: Past, present, and future. *Trends in Cognitive Sciences*, **9**, 16-20.

Singer, W. (1999). Neuronal synchrony: A versatile code for the definition of relations? *Neuron*, **24**, 49-65.

Sloman, A. (1999). Cognitive architecture. In R. A. Wilson and F. C. Keil (eds.), *The MIT Encyclopedia of Cognitive Science*. Cambridge, MA: MIT Press.

Smith, L., and Thelen, E. (2003). Development as a dynamical system. *Trends in Cognitive Science*, 7, 343–8.

Spelke, E. S. (1988). The origins of physical knowledge. In L. Weiskrantz (ed.), *Thought without Language*. Oxford: Oxford University Press.

Spelke, E. S., Gutheil, G., Van de Walle, G., Kosslyn, S. M., and Osherson, D. N. (1995). The development of object perception. In S. M. Kosslyn and D. N. Osherson (eds.), *An Invitation to Cognitive Science*, vol. 2: *Visual Cognition* (2nd edn.). Cambridge, MA: MIT Press.

Spelke, E. S., and Kinzler, K. D. (2007). Core knowledge. *Developmental Science*, 10, 89–96.

Spelke, E. S., and Van de Walle, G. (1993). Perceiving and reasoning about objects: Insights from infants. In N. Eilan, R. McCarthy, and B. Brewer (eds.), *Spatial Representation*. Oxford: Blackwell.

Spencer, J. P., Austin, A., and Schutte, A. R. (2012). Contributions of dynamic systems theory to cognitive development. *Cognitive Development*, 27, 401–18.

Spencer, J. P., Perone, S., and Buss, A. T. (2011). Twenty years and going strong: A dynamic systems revolution in motor and cognitive development. *Child Development Perspectives*, 5, 260–6.

Spencer, J. P., Thomas, M. S. C., and McClelland, J. L. (2009). *Toward A Unified Theory of Development: Connectionism and Dynamic Systems Theory Reconsidered*. New York: Oxford University Press.

Sperber, D., Cara, F., and Girotto, V. (1995). Relevance theory explains the selection task. *Cognition*, 57, 31.

Sperling, G. (1960). The information available in brief visual presentations. *Psychological Monographs*, 74, 1–29.

Spivey, M. (2007). *The Continuity of Mind*. New York: Oxford University Press.

Stein, J. F., and Stoodley, C. S. (2006). *Neuroscience: An Introduction*. Oxford: Oxford University Press.

Sterelny, K. (1990). *The Representational Theory of Mind*. Oxford: Blackwell.

Sullivan, J. A. (2009). The multiplicity of experimental protocols: A challenge to reductionist and non-reductionist models of the unity of neuroscience. *Synthese*, 167, 511–39.

Sun, R. (ed.) (2008). *The Cambridge Handbook of Computational Psychology*. Cambridge: Cambridge University Press.

Tamir, D. I., and Mitchell, J. P. (2010). Neural correlates of anchoring-and-adjustment during mentalizing. *Proceedings of the National Academy of Sciences, USA*, 107, 10827–32.

Thelen, E., Schöner, G., Scheier, C., and Smith, L. B. (2001). The dynamics of embodiment: A field theory of infant perseverative reaching. *Behavioral and Brain Sciences*, 24, 1–86.

Thelen, E., and Smith, L. (eds.) (1993). *A Dynamical Systems Approach to the Development of Cognition and Action*. Cambridge, MA: MIT Press.

Tolman, E. C. (1948). Cognitive maps in rats and men. *Psychological Review*, 55, 189–208.

Tolman, E. C., and Honzik, C. H. (1930). "Insight" in rats. *University of California Publications in Psychology*, 4, 215–32.

Tolman, E. C., Ritchie, B. F., and Kalish, D. (1946). Studies in spatial learning, II: Place learning versus response learning. *Journal of Experimental Psychology*, 36, 221–9.

Tononi, G., and Koch, C. (2008). The neural correlates of consciousness. *Annals of the New York Academy of Sciences*, 1124, 239–61.

Trappenberg, T. (2010). *Fundamentals of Computational Neuroscience* (2nd edn.). Oxford, UK; New York: Oxford University Press.

Trauble, B., Marinovic, V., and Pauen, S. (2010). Early theory of mind competencies: Do infants understand others' beliefs? *Infancy*, **15**(4), 434-44.

Trevethan, C. T., Sahraie, A., and Weiskrantz, L. (2007). Form discrimination in a case of blindsight. *Neuropsychologia*, **45**, 2092-2103.

Tsotsos, J. K. (2011). *A Computational Perspective on Visual Attention*. Cambridge, MA: MIT Press.

Tulving, E. (1972). Episodic and semantic memory. In E. Tulving and W. Donaldson (eds.), *Organization of Memory*. New York: Academic Press.

Turing, A. M. (1936-7). On computable numbers: With an application to the Entscheidungsproblem [Decision Problem]. *Proceedings of the London Mathematical Society*, **42**, 3-4.

Turing, A. M. (1950). Computing machinery and intelligence. *Mind*, **59**, 433-60.

Tye, M. (1991). *The Imagery Debate*. Cambridge, MA: MIT Press.

Umilta, M. A., Kohler, E., Gallese, V., *et al.* (2001). I know what you are doing: A neurophysiological study. *Neuron*, **31**, 155-65.

Ungerleider, L. G., and Mishkin, M. (1982). Two cortical visual systems. In D. J. Ingle, R. J. W. Mansfield, and M. A. Goodale (eds.), *Analysis of Visual Behavior*. Cambridge, MA: MIT Press.

Vaina, L. M. (ed.) (1991). *From the Retina to the Neocortex*. Boston, MA: Springer.

Van den Bussche, E., Hughes, G., Humbeeck, N. V., and Reynvoet, B. (2010). The relation between consciousness and attention: An empirical study using the priming paradigm. *Consciousness and Cognition*, **19**, 86-9.

Van Essen, D. C., and Gallant, J. L. (1994). Neural mechanisms of form and motion processing in the primate visual system. *Neuron*, **13**, 1-10. Reprinted (2001) in W. Bechtel, P. Mandik, J. Mundale, and R. S. Stufflebeam (eds.), *Philosophy and the Neurosciences: A Reader*. Malden, MA: Blackwell.

Van Gelder, T. (1995). What might cognition be, if not computation? *The Journal of Philosophy*, **92**, 345-81.

Van Gelder, T. (1998). The dynamical hypothesis in cognitive science. *Behavioral and Brain Sciences*, **21**, 615-28.

Voyer, D., Voyer, S., and Bryden, M. P. (1995). Magnitude of sex differences in spatial abilities: A meta-analysis and consideration of critical variables. *Psychological Bulletin*, **117**, 250-70.

Wang, S.-H., and Baillargeon, R. (2008). Detecting impossible changes in infancy: A three-system account. *Trends in Cognitive Sciences*, **12**, 17-23.

Warrington, E., and Taylor, A. M. (1973). The contribution of the right parietal lobe to object recognition. *Cortex*, **9**, 152-64.

Warrington, E., and Taylor, A. M. (1978). Two categorical stages of object recognition. *Perception*, **7**, 695-705.

Warwick, K. (2012). *Artificial Intelligence: The Basics*. London, UK; New York: Routledge.

Watson, J. B. (1913). Psychology as the behaviorist sees it. *Psychological Review*, **20**, 158-77.

Waytz, A., and Mitchell, J. (2011). Two mechanisms for simulating other minds: Dissociations between mirroring and self-projection. *Current Directions in Psychological Science*, **20**, 197-200.

Weiskopf, D. A. (2004). The place of time in cognition. *British Journal for the Philosophy of Science*, **55**, 87-105.

Westermann, G., and Ruh, N. (2012). A neuroconstructivist model of past tense development and processing. *Psychological Review*, **119**, 649-67.

White R. L., III, and Snyder, L. H. (2007). Subthreshold microstimulation in frontal eye fields updates spatial memories. *Experimental Brain Research*, **181**, 477-92.

Wicker, B., Keysers, C., Plailly, J., Royet, J. P., Gallese, V., and Rizzolatti, G. (2003). Both of us disgusted in my insula: The common neural basis of seeing and feeling disgust. *Neuron*, **40**, 655-64.

Wilson, R. A. (2008). The drink you have when you're not having a drink. *Mind and Language,* **23,** 273-83.

Wimmer, H., and Perner, J. (1983). Beliefs about beliefs: Representation and constraining function of wrong beliefs in young children's understanding of deception. *Cognition,* **13,** 103-28.

Winfield, A. F. T. (2012). *Robotics: A Very Short Introduction.* Oxford: Oxford University Press.

Winograd, T. (1972). *Understanding Natural Language.* New York: Academic Press.

Winograd, T. (1973). A procedural model of language understanding. In R. C. Schank and A. M. Colby (eds.), *Computer Models of Thought and Language.* San Francisco: W. H. Freeman.

Womelsdorf, T., Schoffelen, J. M., Oostenveld, R., *et al.* (2007). Modulation of neuronal interactions through neuronal synchronization. *Science,* **316,** 1609-12.

Woodward, A., and Needham, A. (2009). *Learning and the Infant Mind.* Oxford; New York: Oxford University Press.

Wu, X., Kumar, V., Quinlan, J. R., *et al.* (2008). Top 10 algorithms in data mining. *Knowledge and Information Systems,* **14,** 1-37.

Zacks, J. M. (2008). Neuroimaging studies of mental rotation: A meta-analysis and review. *Journal of Cognitive Neuroscience,* **20,** 1-19.

Zeki, S. M. (1978). Functional specialization in the visual cortex of the rhesus monkey. *Nature,* **274,** 423-8.

Zelazo, P. D., Moscovitch, M., and Thompson, E. (eds.) (2007). *The Cambridge Handbook of Consciousness.* Cambridge: Cambridge University Press.

Zylberberg, A., Dehaene, S., Roelfsema, P. R., and Sigman, M. (2011). The human Turing machine: A neural framework for mental programs. *Trends in Cognitive Sciences,* **15,** 293-300.

INDEX